Crossword
Companion

CROSSWORD COMPANION

Edited by

Anne Stibbs

Published by Parragon Book Service Limited
in arrangement with
Bloomsbury Publishing Plc
2 Soho Square, London W1V 6HB

Copyright © 1996 by Bloomsbury Publishing Plc

British Library Cataloguing in Publication Data

A CIP catalogue record for this book is available
from the British Library

ISBN 0 75252 041 5

10 9 8 7 6 5 4 3 2 1

Designed by Hugh Adams, AB3
Compiled and typeset by Market House Books, Aylesbury, Bucks.
Printed in Great Britain by Cox & Wyman Limited, Reading

INTRODUCTION

This book is a companion to the *Bloomsbury Crossword Solver*, which lists words in alphabetical order according to their number of letters, and *Crossword Lists*, which contains lists of categories of words.

The *Crossword Companion* is designed to help people searching for words or ideas to solve cryptic clues. It is divided into three parts. The first part, A Guide to Crosswords, contains a brief survey of common types of clues, with examples of how the wording of the clue may indicate certain types of solution (anagram, split word, etc.).

The second, and main, part of the book contains over 6000 entries, which are alphabetically arranged by headword. Each entry consists of a list of words that are in some way associated with the headword. These may be synonyms of the headword in its various senses, but also words that are otherwise connected – for example, shortened forms of the headword or words that are connotationally linked. Where appropriate, 'indicator words' are flagged at the end of the entry and other hints are given – for example, that 'flower' may be a river (something that flows) as well as a plant.

In using the book, the reader should be aware of the inflection of words. Thus, it is usually apparent from the wording of a clue whether the answer is a singular or a plural word. Another point is that this book uses -*ize* endings for verbs and -*ization* endings for nouns that may have the alternative endings -*ise* and -*isation* in the puzzle.

Two other features of the alphabetical part of the book should be mentioned. A short list of abbreviations commonly used in crossword clues is given at the start of each alphabetical section. In addition, useful lists are included at various places in the text, with many cross-references to these throughout the book.

The final part of the *Companion* is an Appendix containing a number of lists of common indicator words for such things as anagrams, split clues, hidden words, and palindromes.

A number of people have helped in the compilation of this book and I would like to thank John Daintith, Elizabeth Martin, Sandra McQueen, Brenda Tomkins and, especially, Fran Alexander for their contributions and support. We hope that the reader will find the book interesting and useful.

AS 1996

A GUIDE TO CROSSWORDS

There are basically two kinds of crossword puzzle, noncryptic and cryptic. Clues for noncryptic puzzles tend to be short and simple, often merely a synonym for the answer. Cryptic clues, on the other hand, are altogether more complex – but not necessarily longer – than noncryptic clues and are often deliberately ambiguous. Most cryptic clues can be broken down into distinct parts:

a) a definition – a word or phrase that gives the meaning of the answer (in noncryptic puzzles this is usually the only part of the clue).

b) one or more indicators – key words or phrases that provide instructions to the reader. For example, 'formerly' may indicate that the answer (or part of the answer) takes the form of an archaic word; 'cockney' might indicate that the answer is formed by removing the initial 'h' from another word in the clue. Comprehensive lists of indicators are given in the appendix.

c) the 'working material' of the clue – the word or words to which the indicators apply.

Often, however, the boundaries between these parts are by no means distinct – the entire clue could provide the definition, within which are embedded indicators and working material.

The following sections describe some of the most common types of cryptic clue.

Anagrams

An anagram is a word or phrase that can be rearranged to form a new word or phrase. For example:

cheap	peach
simple diet	speed limit
pure ice	epicure
dishonest	hedonists

Words or phrases indicating that the answer is an anagram include 'badly', 'cocktail', 'poor', and 'tipsy'.

For example, in the clue

My man left the taverns tipsy. (7)

the indicator is **tipsy**, **taverns** is the anagram, and the definition is **my man**. The answer is **servant**, another word for my man.

In the clue

Traps set for small fish. (5)

the indicator is **set**, **traps** is the anagram, and the definition is **small fish**. The answer is **sprat**, a type of small fish.

Hidden words

These are words that are found embedded within a phrase. For example:

ankle, rankle	can be found in	crank leaflet
rates, grates	can be found in	migrate South
alto	can be found in	musical to

Words or phrases such as 'in', 'some', 'a bit of', 'found in' act as indicators for hidden words.

For example, in the clue

Juice extracted from delicious apples. (3)

the indicator is **extracted from**, the definition is **juice**, and the answer, **sap** (another word for juice), is found in delicious **ap**ples.

In the clue

The place in which to find a good man is Aintree. (5)

the indicator is **in which to find**, the definition is **a good man**, and the answer, **saint** (a synonym for a good man), is embedded in the words is **Aint**ree.

Backwords

There are a number of words which, when reversed, form other words. For example:

peek	keep
time	emit
lever	revel
denier	reined

These words are often used by crossword setters to form clues; they may be indicated by such words or phrases as 'capsized', 'turned back', or 'sent up'.

For example, in the clue

Produced a revolutionary Dutch cheese. (4)

the definition is **produced** and the indicator is **revolutionary**, applying to **Dutch cheese**. The answer is **made**, another word for produced, from **Edam**, a type of Dutch cheese.

Clues using backwords are often deliberately ambiguous and have two possible definitions (i.e. answers). For example, in the clue

Have a quick look round part of the castle. (4)

the indicator is **round** and the two possible definitions are **Have a quick look** (for which the answer is **peek**), and **part of the castle** (for which the answer is **keep**); the indicator is positioned so that it could apply to either.

Guide

Split words

In this case one word is split and a second put inside it. For example:

age + pants	pageants
band + rig	brigand
ending + ear	endearing

These clues have such indicators as 'enveloped by', 'taken in', or 'wrapping'.

For example, in the clue

It's in the payment to the clergy. (5)

the indicator is **in, it** put in **the** gives **tithe** which is the definition of **payment to the clergy**.

A slightly more complicated example is found in the clue

A vicar has to tear around at all times. (8)

The definition is **vicar**, and **around** indicates that rend (another word for **tear**) goes around ever (i.e. **at all times**) to give the answer, **reverend** (a vicar).

Palindromes

These are words or phrases that read the same backwards and forwards, such as

ewe
gig
sees
peep
civic
rotavator

and the classic

Able was I ere I saw Elba.

The clues are indicated by such words as 'both ways', 'revolutionary', 'forwards and backwards'.

For example, in the clue

The action is to-and-fro. (4)

the indicator is **to-and-fro** and the definition is **the action**. The answer is **deed** (an action), reading the same forwards and backwards.

In the clue

Revolutionary arm of the distributor. (5)

the indicator is **revolutionary** and the **arm of the distributor** is a **rotor** (the answer).

Shortenings

There are many devices used by crossword setters to indicate that certain letters should be removed or that an abbreviation is to be used. Such words as

headless	remove the first letter
tailless	remove the last letter
heartless	remove the middle letter
in short	an abbreviation
originally	use the first letter
ultimately	use the last letter

are used as indicators.

For example, in the clue

Endlessly prepared to peruse. (4)

the indicator is **endlessly**, another word for **prepared** is ready and, with the final letter deleted, we have the answer, **read**, a synonym for **peruse** (the definition).

In the clue

In short, a good man finds drink overused. (5)

the indicator is **in short**, **a good man** is a saint, abbreviated to St., ale is a **drink**, and **stale** (the answer) is another word for **overused**.

Homophones

Homophones are words that are pronounced in the same way, but have different meanings and spellings. For example:

flee	flea
hall	haul
lays	laze

Clues based on homophones use such indicators as 'sounds like', 'we hear', and 'it's said'.

For example, in the clue

The menu is said to be quite good. (4)

the indicator is **said to be**, another word for menu is **fare** (the answer), which sounds like fair, meaning **quite good**.

In the clue

The grizzly was naked, we hear. (4)

we hear indicates that **bear** (the answer, another word for **grizzly**) sounds like bare meaning **naked**.

·A·

ABBREVIATIONS

A	ace • acre • adult • advanced • age • alto • America • annual • anonymous • ante • article • key • note • year
AA	Alcoholics Anonymous • Automobile Association • battery size
AB	able-bodied seaman • Alberta
ABE	Abraham Lincoln
ABR	abridged
AC	account • actinium • aircraftman • alternating current • new line (Italian: *a capo*)
AD	advertisement • age • year (Latin: *anno Domini*)
AF	across flats • air force
AG	silver
AI	first class • tiptop
AKA	also known as
AM	Albert Medal • morning
AOB	any other business
AP	before a meal (Latin: *ante prandium*)
AQ	water (Latin: *aqua*)
AR	monarch • queen (Latin: *Anna Regina*)
ASAP	as soon as possible
AU	gold • to the (French)
AV	the Bible (Authorized Version)
AVE	avenue
AWOL	absent without leave

abandon blackball, blacklist, deny, desert, disdain, ditch, freedom, refuse, reject, scorn, spurn, waive

abase abash, bring low, crush, debase, degrade, demean, diminish, dump (on), put down, reduce, set down, take down, trip up

abbreviate abridge, condense, shorten
may indicate a shortening

abducent centrifugal, diamagnetic, repelling

abduction kidnapping, slavery

aberrant
may indicate an anagram

ability aptitude, attribute, bent, capability, capacity, compass, competence, effectuality, efficacy, efficiency, endowment, facility, faculty, fitness, flair, genius, gift, grasp, knack, know-how, mastery, native wit, potentiality, proficiency, property, qualification, quality, range, reach, savvy, scope, skill, talent, tendency, virtue

ablutions bathing, dipping, hygiene, lathering, lavage, rinsing, shampoo, soaking, soaping, toilet, washing

abnegating relinquishing, self-denying, self-renunciatory, self-sacrificing

abnegation relinquishment, self-denial, self-renunciation, self-restraint, self-sacrifice

abnormal aberrant, anomalous, de-

1

viant, irregular, mutant, odd, perverted, queer, unnatural, variant
may indicate an anagram

abnormality aberrance, irregularity, oddness, perversion, queerness

about c, circa, re
may indicate an anagram or a split word

about-turn about-face, backtrack, swingaround, turnaround, U-turn, volte-face

abrogation abnegation, apostasy, cancellation, denial, disavowal, negation, recantation, repudiation

abrupt brusque, curt, gruff, irascible, rude, short-tempered
may indicate a shortening

abruptness brusqueness, curtness, gruffness, irascibility, rudeness

absence emptiness, lack, nihility, nobody, nonbeing, none, nonentity, nonexistence, nonoccurrence, nonpresence, no-one, nullity, unreality

absent inexistent, nonattendant, nonexistent, nonoccurrent, not present, null, unavailable, unreal, void

absentee AWOL, defector, deserter, missing person, runaway, truant

absenteeism defection, desertion, French leave, hooky, truancy

absent-minded daydreaming, stargazing, Walter Mitty, woolgathering

absolution acquittal, deliverance, discharge, exculpation, exoneration, justification, release, vindication

absolve acquit, cancel, deliver, discharge, exculpate, exonerate, free, let off, release, vindicate

absorb adsorb, assimilate, blot, incorporate, mop up, soak, sponge, take up
may indicate a split word

absorbent absorptive, adsorbent, assimilative, blotting, imbibitory, ingestive, sorbent, spongy

absorption absorbency, adsorption, assimilation, blotting, engrossment, incorporation, percolation, resorbence, resorption, sorption

abstain deny oneself, do without, forbear, forswear, hold back, pass up, refrain

absurd
may indicate an anagram

abundance plenty, profusion

abundant ample, copious, lavish, overflowing, plentiful, profuse, superabundant

abusive forceful, harmful, injurious, offensive, profane, violent

abut adjoin, amalgamate, attach, border, brush, bump, clash, collide, conjoin, connect, contact, converge, couple, crash, crunch, glance, graze, impact, impinge, interface, intersect, join, kiss, meet, overlap, reach, skim, splice, touch, verge on

academic authoritative, pedagogical, preachy, scholastic, schoolmarmish, teacher, theoretical, tutor

accelerate bolt, dart off, dash, gather momentum, lap, leave standing, outclass, outdistance, outrun, outstrip, overhaul, overtake, pass, quicken, romp home, scamper, speed up, spring, sprint, spurt, tear off

accent broagh, brogue, burr, drawl, emphasize, lisping, nasality, stridor, trill, twang

accept acquiesce, adopt, agree, assent, authorize, condone, consent, countenance, endorse, grant permission, license, nod, OK, pass, ratify, rubberstamp, sanction, wink

accession assumption, changeover, elevation, inauguration, inheritance, promotion, takeover, transfer

accidental calamitous, chance, disastrous, fatal, infelicitous, unfortunate, unintentional, unlucky

acclaim applause, big hand, cheering,

clap, curtain call, encore, hail, honour, ovation, plaudit, praise, stamping, whistling

acclamation applause, bravo, cheer, hallelujah, hip-hip hurrah, hosanna, huzzah, paean, whoop

accommodate
may indicate a split word

accompany belong with, coincide, come with, complement, concur, escort, go together, go with, synchronize

accomplish complete, succeed, win

accomplished completed, done, skilled, won

accord accedence, acceptance, accommodation, accordance, acquiescence, agreement, compliance, comply, compromise, concede, concession, concord, concurrence, consensus, empathize, identify with, like-mindedness, mutual understanding, one mind, one voice, solidarity, sympathy, unanimity, unity, vox populi

accounting audit, calculation, computation, enumeration, explaining, reckoning, score, tally

accuracy acuity, correctness, definition, detail, exactness, fastidiousness, fine tuning, high fidelity, meticulousness, pedantry, perfection, perfect pitch, preciseness, precision, refinement, rigidity, rigorousness, scrupulousness, strictness

accurate absolute, apt, bang-on, correct, dead-on, defined, definitive, delicate, detailed, documented, exact, faithful, faultless, fine, flawless, mathematical, meticulous, microscopic, nice, particularized, perfect, pinpoint, precise, punctilious, refined, right, rigorous, scientific, set, spot-on, squared, straight, subtle, trimmed, trued, word-perfect

accusation action, allegation, charge, citation, complaint, denunciation, imputation, lawsuit, litigation, plaint, reproach, suit, summons

accuse allegate, blame, charge, cite, complain, denounce, impute, insinuate, litigate, reproach, sue, summon

ace card, expert, I, one, pilot

acid acerbic, acidulous, acrid, biting, bitter, dry, green, immature, lemony, pungent, sharp, sour, tangy, tart, unripe, unsweetened, vinegary

acknowledge attribute, credit, recognize

acknowledgment answer, confirmation, official reply, receipt, rescript, return correspondence, RSVP, written reply

acquiescence amenability, compliance, docility, obedience, persuasability, pliancy, tractability

acquire accrete, accumulate, amass, assemble, bunch, catch, collect, glean, harvest, heap, hoard, pool, save, stack, stockpile

acquit absolve, discharge, dismiss, exculpate, excuse, exonerate, forgive, grant absolution, let go, let off, liberate, pardon, release, show mercy, spare

acquittal absolution, discharge, exculpation, excuse, exoneration, freedom, independence, liberation, liberty, pardon, release

acquitted absolved, cleared, exculpated, exonerated

acrimony aversion, bad blood, bitterness, grudge, ill feeling, ill will, peevishness, rancour, resentment, soreness, sourness

acrobat contortionist, trapeze artist, tumbler

act attempt, carry out, characterize, decree, do, dramatize, enact, execute, feign, get going, impersonate, implement, improvise, law, legislate, masquerade, mime, mimic, move, perform, perpetrate, play, playact, portray, pose as, present, pretend, proceed, sham, take steps, try, undertake
See also list at **theatre**.

activate actuate, boot, effectuate, kick-start, launch, plug in, prompt, provoke, rev up, set going, spark off, start up, switch on, trigger off, turn on, wind up

active able, agile, alive, animated, brisk, dashing, dynamic, eager, energetic, enterprising, expeditious, fast, forceful, frisky, going, in action, incessant, keen, lively, moving, nimble, operative, pushing, quick, running, smart, speedy, spirited, sprightly, spry, strenuous, strong, thrusting, unceasing, vigorous, vivacious, working

activist achiever, agent, campaigner, lobbyist, motivator

activity action, ado, agitation, business, bustle, career, commotion, dash, disturbance, drama, excitation, fidget, flap, flurry, flutter, fuss, hassle, hobby, hustle, interest, motion, movement, occupation, pastime, recreation, scramble, scurry, skedaddle, spurt, stimulation, stir, whirl, work

actor actress, comedian, darling, diva, extra, film star, improviser, lovie, luvvie, matinée idol, narrator, play-actor, player, prima donna, speaker, spear-carrier, stand-in, superstar, Thespian, tragedian, trouper, understudy *See also list at* **theatre**.

adapt adjust, fashion, fit, moderate, modify, qualify *may indicate an anagram*

adaptability adjustability, buoyancy, compliance, flexibility, resilience, responsiveness

add affix, annex, append, attach, augment, calculate, carry over, clip to, compute, conjoin, contribute to, count up, expand, extend, glue onto, infix, insert, interject, interpolate, interpose, introduce, join, pin to, preface, prefix, staple to, stick in, suffix, sum up, supplement, swell, tack on, tag, tie to, tot, total up, unite

addicted drug-dependent, hooked, obsessive

addictive besetting, clinging, habit-forming, haunting

addition accession, accessory, accrual, addendum, add-on, adjunct, afterword, aggregate, appendage, appendix, attachment, augmentation, calculation, chorus, coda, codicil, computation, conclusion, enlargement, extension, increase, increment, insert, insertion, interposition, postlude, postposition, postscript, PS, refrain, subjunction, subscript, suffixation, sum, summation, supplement, supplementation, tally, toll, total

address allocution, apostrophe, apostrophize, declaim, discourse, domicile, harangue, hold forth, home, lecture, location, orate, oration, perorate, presentation, rail, rant, reading, residence, sermonize, speech, speechify, talk, tub-thump

adequate able, appropriate, apt, capable, competent, enough, fit, sufficient, suitable, up to

adhere agglomerate, bunch together, cleave to, clinch, cling to, close with, coagulate, cohere, conglomerate, hang together, hold fast, stick, twine around

adhesive adherent, beeswax, birdlime, Blu-tack, cement, chicle, cohesive, connective, flypaper, glue, gluey, grout, gum, gummy, mastic, mortar, paste, plaster, putty, resin, sealing wax, size, solder, sticking plaster, sticky, sticky tape, superglue, tacky, tar, wax

adjacent abutting, adjoining, bordering, bumper-to-bumper, cheek-by-jowl, close, connecting, conterminous, contiguous, continuous, coterminous, elbow-to-elbow, end-to-end, eyeball-to-eyeball, face-to-face, interactive, intercommunicating, interfacial, joined, juxtaposed, liminal, meeting, near, next to, nose-to-nose, nose-to-tail, side-by-side, tangential, touching

adjust
may indicate an anagram

administer anoint, apply, govern, insert, organize, rule

administration board, bosses, cabinet, committee, council, directorate, employers, executive, management, paperwork, quango, staff

admirable creditable, deserving, laudable, meritorious, praiseworthy, worthwhile

admiration acknowledgment, adoration, adulation, awe, credit, esteem, idolization, recognition, regard, respect, reverence, veneration, worship

admired in demand, popular, respected

admirer fan, follower, groupie, hero-worshipper, rooter, supporter

admission access, avowal, confession, deposition, disclosure, immigration, importation, open-door policy, pass, passport, permission, permit, ticket, visa

admit acknowledge, affirm, allow, assent, avow, bring in, come clean, concede, confess, depose, disclose, grant, import, include, let in, own up, plead guilty, receive, take in

adornment decoration, embellishment, enhancement, enrichment, garnish, ornamentation, ornateness, richness

adrift
may indicate an anagram

adult elder, experienced, grown-up, mature, prepared, senior

adultery affair, amour, cheating, concubinage, cuckolding, infidelity, intrigue, liaison, two-timing, unfaithfulness

adulthood adultness, manhood, maturation, maturity, womanhood

advance achievement, ahead, ascent, elevation, enterprise, furtherance, gain, leg-up, lift, loan, preferment, progress, promotion, rise, success

advantage benefit, edge, favour, flying start, head start, lead, lion's share, pole position, seeded position, upper hand, vantage point, whip hand

adventurer entrepreneur, explorer, innovator, pioneer, speculator, workaholic

adventurous danger-loving, foolhardy, gambling, game, rash, venturesome

adverse bad, bleak, conflicting, contrary, difficult, dire, dreadful, hard, hostile, ominous, opposing

adversity accident, affliction, bad patch, bad spell, bad times, decline, difficulty, hardship, hard times, lean period, misadventure, misfortune, mishap, opposition, predicament, rough patch, setback, struggle, troubles

advice aside, caution, counselling, criticism, guidance, hint, indication, opinion, pointer, recommendation, suggestion, tip-off, view, warning, whisper, wisdom

advisable expedient, judicious, politic, practical, prudent, sensible, wise

advise advocate, brief, counsel, criticise, enjoin, guide, hint, inform, instruct, moralize, move, prescribe, prompt, propose, put to, recommend, submit, suggest, teach, tell

adviser advisor, advocate, arbitrator, consultant, counsellor, guide, mentor, minister, pastor, troubleshooter

advocate attorney, backer, champion, lawyer, patron, preach, recommender, sponsor, supporter, urge

aerate aerify, air, air-condition, beat, clean, deodorize, freshen, fumigate, oxygenate, ventilate, whip, whisk

affect accomplish, achieve, act, alter, change, end in, grieve, impact, issue, move, precipitate, produce, reach, result in, soften, touch

affectation extravagance, false front, grandiloquence, loftiness, magniloquence, ostentation, pomposity, pretension, showiness

affected artificial, changed, conceited, mannered, moved, precious, pretentious, self-conscious, stilted, touched, unnatural

affection amativeness, amorousness, attachment, fondness, kindness, love, tenderness

affectionate amorous, attached, caressing, clinging, coquettish, courting, coy, dating, demonstrative, engaged, familiar, flirtatious, fond, fondling, lovey-dovey, loving, philandering, sentimental, sloppy, spooning, toying, wooing

affirm allege, announce, assert, asseverate, attest, aver, certify, declare, predicate, proclaim, profess, pronounce, propose, put forward, state, submit, swear, utter, vouch

affirmation allegation, assertion, asseveration, attestation, averment, certification, declaration, swearing, vouching

afflict blast, blight, burden, curse, decay, harm, infest, mar, mildew, mould, plague, pressurize, rot, rust, shrivel, strain, strike down, torment, visit, wither, worry

afflicted damaged, depressed, distressed, grief-stricken, grievous, hurt, ill, injured, in pain, miserable, plagued, sad, sick, sore, sorrowful, troubled, unhealthy, woeful, wounded
may indicate an anagram

affliction adversity, bitter pill, disease, distress, dose, infestation, malady, pest, pestilence, plague, ruin, running sore, scourge, task, trial, trouble, visitation

afterlife Abraham's bosom, Dis, Elysian fields, future state, Hades, heaven, hell, hereafter, next world, paradise, Sheol, Stygian shore, Styx, underworld
See also list at **imaginary**.

aftermath aftereffect, afterglow, aftertaste, by-product, fallout, hangover, legacy, spin-off

afternoon pipemma, PM, postmeridian

afterthought epilogue, postscript, PS, second thoughts

age aeon, become obsolete, burn out, crumble, decay, decline, decompose, deteriorate, dodder, epoch, era, fade, lifespan, lifetime, moulder, rot, rust, spoil, timespan, wither

aged antique, elderly, geriatric, greyhaired, matriarchal, old, patriarchal, venerable, white-haired

ageing greying, senescent

agelessness datelessness, deathlessness, everlastingness, immortality

agelong aeonian, immemorial, millennial

agent ambassador, arbitrator, attaché, attorney, broker, cause, commissioner, delegate, deputy, diplomat, emissary, envoy, functionary, go-between, influence, instrument, intermediary, legate, mediator, middleman, minister, negotiator, officer, operator, practitioner, proxy, representative, spokesperson, stimulus, tool, trustee

aggravate deepen, enhance, exacerbate, heighten, increase, inflame, intensify, make worse, worsen

aggravating annoying, exasperating, irritating, provoking, vexatious, vexing

aggravation deepening, deterioration, enhancement, exacerbation, heightening, intensification, irritation, worsening

aggressive antagonistic, at loggerheads, bellicose, belligerent, clashing, contentious, disputatious, hostile, inimical, militant, opposing, provocative, pugnacious, quarrelsome, threatening, truculent, unfriendly

agitate beat, brandish, churn, discompose, disquiet, disturb, excite, flourish, fluster, flutter, mix, move, paddle, perturb, perturbate, rile, roil, ruffle, rumple, shake, stir up, swirl, trouble, untidy, upset, wave, whip, whisk, work up, worry

agitated confused, discomposed, disturbed, edgy, embarrassed, flurried, flustered, jittery, nervous, nervy, perturbed, ruffled, shaken up, shocked, stirred up, troubled, uneasy, unsteady, upset, worked up
may indicate an anagram

agitation discomposure, disquiet, disquietude, distress, edginess, jerkiness, jumpiness, nerviness, nervousness, panic, perturbation, unease

agitator protester, rabble-rouser, ringleader

agree accept, acquiesce, affirm, assent, bless, comply, concede, concur, confirm, consent, ditto, echo, jump at, subscribe to, support, unite, welcome

agreeable acceptable, concordant, harmonious, peaceful, unopposed, viable

agreed carried, countersigned, ratified, sealed, signed, underwritten, validated

agreement acceptance, accord, accordance, acquiescence, affirmation, affirmative, approbation, approval, assent, blessing, compliance, concord, concordance, concurrence, confirmation, consensus, consent, cooperation, permission, thumbs up, unanimity, unison, unity, willingness

agriculture farming, husbandry, sharecropping

aid assistance, deliverance, emancipation, help, liberation, release, rescue, salvage, salvation, succour, support

aim aspiration, aspire, design, drift, goal, head for, intend, intention, objective, overreach, plan, plot, point to, propose, purpose, reason, scheme, target

aimless futile, inconsequential, pointless, purposeless, vain, worthless

aimlessness arbitrariness, fortuity, haphazardness, indeterminacy, purposelessness, randomness

air airspace, atmosphere, broadcast, ether, gas, oxygen, ozone, rarity, thin air, ventilate

aircraft
See list at **aviator**.

airiness buoyancy, ethereality, lightness, weightlessness

airy aerial, aeriferous, aeriform, aery, airlike, ethereal, exposed, flimsy, insubstantial, light, lighter-than-air, rare, rarified, roomy, thin, weightless

alarm alarum, alert, beacon, bell, blast, flare, fright, honk, horn, klaxon, light, mayday, panic, ring, shout, siren, SOS, tattoo, tocsin, toot, trumpet-call, warning, war-whoop, whistle

alcohol beer, booze, cocktail, drink, grog, home brew, hooch, John Barleycorn, juice, liquor, moonshine, plonk, rotgut, spirits, vino, wine
See list at **drink**.

alcoholism delirium tremens, dipsomania, DT's, red nose, tremors

alive animate, breathing, conscious, existent, extant, incarnate, living, quick, surviving

all entire, everybody, everything, total, whole

allegiance dedication, devotion, fealty, homage, loyalty

alliance affiliation, amalgamation, association, cartel, coalition, collaboration, collusion, connection, consortium, conspiracy, entente (cordiale), federation, fellowship, guild, league, link, merger, partnership, synergy, trust, union

allied affiliated, associated, bonded, conjoint, connected, corporate, joint, linked, merged

allocated allotted, apportioned, assigned, distributed, dividable, divided, divisible, shared out

allocation allotment, appointment, apportionment, assignment, distribution, division, partition, sharing, subdivision

allot allocate, apportion, appropriate, bisect, carve up, cut, delimit, demarcate, dispense, distribute, divide, earmark, limit, measure, mete out, prorate, ration, share, split, subdivide, tag

allowed forgiven, gratified, indulged, pardoned, permitted, pitied, spoiled

allurement allure, appeal, charisma, charm, come-on, enticement, fascination, pull, seduction, seductiveness, sex appeal, temptation

almanac dictionary, encyclopedia, thesaurus

alone abandoned, aloof, apart, deserted, detached, forsaken, friendless, insular, isolated, isolationist, lonely, reclusive, separate, solitary, unilateralist, withdrawn

aloneness aloofness, apartness, detachment, friendlessness, insularity, isolation, isolationism, loneliness, privacy, seclusion, separateness, solitude, unilateralism

aloof antisocial, discrete, isolated, private, separate, solitary, unsociable

alter activate, adapt, adjust, affect, cause, change, commute, convert, detour, deviate, diversify, divert, ferment, fluctuate, influence, innovate, invent, modernize, modify, modulate, qualify, rearrange, redecorate, reform, relocate, remodel, remould, renew, reorder, reorganize, reshape, restructure, shift, turn, vary
may indicate an anagram

alternative backup, choice, different, double, either, locum (tenens), or, proxy, replacement, reserve, stand-in, sub, substitute, surrogate, understudy, unorthodox, unusual
may indicate an anagram

amaze astonish, astound, boggle, disconcert, dumbfound, electrify, flabbergast, floor, gobsmack, impress, shock, stagger, stun, stupefy

amazed admiring, astonished, astounded, awed, dumbfounded, flabbergasted, gobsmacked, impressed, marvelling, shocked, speechless, staggered, struck dumb, stunned, stupefied, thunderstruck

amazement astonishment, astoundment, incredulity, stupefaction, wonder

ambush capture, ensnare, pounce on, spring upon, trap

amenable acquiescent, biddable, compliant, docile, manageable, obedient, persuadable, pliable, pliant, tractable

American New Englander, New Yorker, Uncle Sam, US, Yank, Yankee

amiability affability, chivalry, civility, cordiality, courtesy, friendliness, kindliness, politeness

amicable accepting, accommodating, acquiescent, compatible, compliant, complying, compromising, conceding, conciliatory, congenial

amid
may indicate a hidden word

ammunition ack-ack, ammo, blank, buckshot, bullet, cannonball, cartouche, cartridge, dud, flak, grapeshot, missile, pellet, projectile, round, shell, shot, shrapnel, slug, wad
*See also list at **weapon**.*

amnesty absolution, forgiveness, pardon

amorous adoring, ardent, coquettish, coy, desirous, emotional, flirtatious, longing, lustful, melting, passionate, romantic, seductive, sentimental, soft, tender, yearning

ample abundant, bumper, copious, galore, plentiful, profuse, rife

amplified expanded, extended

amplifier loudhailer, loudspeaker, megaphone, PA, public-address system

amplify blether on, bore, detail, dilate, draw out, elaborate, enlarge upon, expand, expatiate, extend, flow, gush, harangue, lengthen, never end, orate, pad out, particularize, pour out, protract, ramble on, reiterate, repeat, spin out, tautologize, waffle, wax eloquent

amusement diversion, enjoyment, entertainment, fun, hilarity, laughter, merriment, mirth

amusing diverting, entertaining, funny, humorous, wacky, zany

anachronism metachronism, misdating, mistiming, parachronism, prochronism, untimeliness

anaesthetic analgesic, barbiturate, deadening, downers, drug, hypnotic, narcotic, nepenthes, numbing, painkiller, sleeping draught, sleeping pill, soporific, tranquillizer

anaesthetize benumb, blunt, brain, concuss, deaden, desensitize, etherize, freeze, hypnotize, knock out, mesmerize, narcotize, put under, render unconscious, stun, stupefy

analgesia anaesthesia, dullness, insensitiveness, paralysis

analgesic acupuncture, anaesthesia, analgesia, anodyne, balm, demulcent, hypnosis, nepenthe, painkiller, palliative, salve

analogous comparable, metaphoric, similar

analogy allegory, analogue, comparison, metaphor, simile

anarchic anarchical, chaotic, disobedient, disorderly, disorganized, insubordinate, lawless, mutinous, rampant, rebellious, revolutionary, riotous, seditious, ungoverned, unofficial, unruly, wild, wildcat
may indicate an anagram

anarchist assassin, fifth columnist, guerrilla, mutineer, rebel, revolutionary, seditionary, subversive, terrorist

anarchy chaos, disorder, disorganization, disruption, impotence, indiscipline, irresponsibility, lawlessness, lynch law, mob rule, powerlessness, turmoil, unrestraint, unruliness

ancestor aborigine, Adam, forefather, precursor, predecessor, primitive, prophet, sire

ancient archaic, hoary, old, primeval, Ur

android automaton, bionic man, cyborg, humanoid, robot

angel angelhood, angelic host, archangel, archangelship, celestial, cherub, guardian angel, heavenly being, heavenly host, putto, seraph

angelic angelical, archangelic, cherubic, saintly, seraphic

anger aggravate, aggression, bellicosity, belligerence, blow-up, choler, convulsion, crossness, enrage, explosion, ferment, flare-up, fret, fury, heat, huff, infuriate, ire, madden, outburst, paddy, passion, put out, rage, roaring, scene, shouting, snappishness, stew, storm, sullenness, tantrum, temper, tizzy, vehemence, violence, wax, wrath

angle acute, bend, bias, chevron, corner, dog-leg, fish, fly-fish, fork, hairpin bend, net, obtuse, perpendicular, seine, shrimp, slant, spin, trawl, viewpoint, zigzag
See also list at **geometry**.

angry aggressive, apoplectic, bad-tempered, bellicose, belligerent, berserk, beside oneself, boiling, burning, choleric, cross, cursing, dangerous, enraged, evil-speaking, fierce, foaming, foul-mouthed, frenzied, fuming, furious, gnashing, growling, hopping mad, huffed, implacable, incensed, indignant, infuriated, irate, ireful, livid, mad, profane, rabid, raging, rampaging, ratty, roaring, savage, sizzling, smouldering, snapping, spitting feathers, stuttering, sulphurous, swearing, violent, waxy, wrathful

animal amphibian, animalcule, arthropod, beast, biped, bird, bloodsucker, browser, brute, carnivore, chordate, commensal, creature, creeping thing, dumb animal, dumb friend, ectoparasite, endoparasite, filter-feeder, fish, flesh-eater, four-legged friend, furry friend, gastropod, grazer, herbivore, host, insect, insectivore, intermediate host, invertebrate, mammal, marsupial, meat-eater, mollusc, omnivore, parasite, predator, prey, protist, protozoan, quadruped, reptile, rodent, scavenger, symbiont, varmint, vector, vertebrate, worm, zooid
See list of animals.
See also lists at **insect**; **reptile**.

animosity bad feeling, bitterness, dislike, ill will, offence, resentment

annihilate abort, annul, cancel, destroy, end, eradicate, exterminate, extinguish, invalidate, kill, murder, negate, nuke, nullify, vaporize, veto, wipe out

annihilated destined, destroyed, dissolved, doomed, eliminated, exterminated, fated, liquidated, ruined

annihilation destruction, dissolution, elimination, extermination, extinction, liquidation, ruin

anniversary Armistice Day, Bastille Day, bicentenary, birthday, centenary, commemoration, D-Day, feast day, field day, flag day, great day, high day, Independence Day, jubilee, millennium, poppy day, Remembrance Sunday, Republic Day, saint's day, sesquicentennial, special day, Thanksgiving, tricentenary, VE Day, wedding anniversary
See list of wedding anniversaries.

annotate comment on, footnote, gloss, inscribe

annotation apparatus criticus, comment, commentary, footnote, gloss, marginalia, note, scholium, variorum

annoy anger, antagonize, exasperate, goad, hassle, irritate, peeve, provoke, tease, vex

annoyance anger, exasperation, irritation, provocation, vexation

annulment invalidation, negation, nullification

anoint baste, beeswax, butter, cream, daub, dress, embrocate, glycerolate, lard, oil, pomade, salve, slick, smear, spread, unguent, wax

answer acknowledge, backchat, back talk, comeback, confirm, insolence, rejoin, rejoinder, repartee, replication, reply, respond, response, responsion, retort, return, riposte

WEDDING ANNIVERSARIES					
1st	PAPER	9th	POTTERY/WILLOW	25th	SILVER
2nd	COTTON	10th	TIN/ALUMINIUM	30th	PEARL
3rd	LEATHER	11th	STEEL	35th	CORAL
4th	FRUIT/FLOWERS	12th	SILK/LINEN	40th	RUBY
5th	WOOD	13th	LACE	45th	SAPPHIRE
6th	IRON	14th	IVORY	50th	GOLD
7th	WOOL/COPPER	15th	CRYSTAL	55th	EMERALD
8th	BRONZE/POTTERY	20th	CHINA	60th	DIAMOND

ANIMALS

AARDVARK
AARDWOLF
ACOUCHI
ADDAX
AGOUTI
AI
ALPACA
ANGWAN-
  TIBO
ANOA
ANT BEAR
ANTEATER
ANTELOPE
ANTHROPOID
  APE
AOUDAD
APE
ARCTIC FOX
ARGALI
ARMADILLO
ASS
AUROCH
AXIS DEER
AYE-AYE
BABIRUSA
BABOON
BADGER
BANDICOOT
BANTENG
BARBARY APE
BARBASTELLE
BARKING DEER
BAT
BEAR
BEAVER
BIGHORN
BINTURONG
BISON
BLACK BEAR
BLACKBUCK
BLESBOK
BLUE FOX
BLUE WHALE
BOBCAT
BONGO
BONTEBOK
BOTTLENOSE
BROWN BEAR
BUFFALO
BUSHBABY
BUSHBUCK
CACHALOT
CACOMISTLE
CAMEL
CANE RAT
CAPUCHIN
  MONKEY
CAPYBARA
CARACAL
CARIBOU

CAT
CATTLE
CAVY
CHAMOIS
CHEETAH
CHEVROTAIN
CHIMPANZEE
CHINCHILLA
CHINESE
  WATER DEER
CHIPMUNK
CHIROPTERA
CHIRU
CHITAL
CIVET
CLOUDED
  LEOPARD
COATI
COLOBUS
COLUGO
CONY
COUGAR
COYOTE
COYPU
CRABEATER
  SEAL
CUSCUS
DASYURE
DEER
DEER MOUSE
DESERT RAT
DESMAN
DHOLE
DIK-DIK
DINGO
DOG
DOLPHIN
DONKEY
DORCAS
  GAZELLE
DORMOUSE
DOUROUCOULI
DRILL
DROMEDARY
DUCK-BILLED
  PLATYPUS
DUGONG
DUIKER
ECHIDNA
ELAND
ELEPHANT
ELEPHANT SEAL
ELK
ENTELLUS
ERMINE
FALLOW DEER
FELIDAE
FENNEC
FERRET
FIELDMOUSE

FISHER
FLYING FOX
FLYING LEMUR
FLYING
  PHALANGER
FLYING
  SQUIRREL
FOSSA
FOX
FRUIT BAT
GALAGO
GAUR
GAYAL
GAZELLE
GELADA
GEMSBOK
GENET
GERBIL
GERENUK
GIBBON
GIRAFFE
GLUTTON
GNU
GOAT
GOLDEN CAT
GOLDEN MOLE
GOPHER
GORAL
GORILLA
GRAMPUS
GRASS
  MONKEY
GRISON
GRIZZLY BEAR
GROUNDHOG
GROUND
  SQUIRREL
GUANACO
GUENON
GUINEA PIG
GYMNURE
HAMADRYAS
HAMSTER
HARBOUR SEAL
HARE
HARTEBEEST
HARVEST
  MOUSE
HEDGEHOG
HINNY
HIPPOPOTA-
  MUS
HONEY
  BADGER
HONEY
  MOUSE
HOODED SEAL
HORSE
HORSESHOE
  BAT

HOWLER
  MONKEY
HUMPBACK
  WHALE
HUTIA
HYAENA
HYENA
HYRAX
IBEX
IMPALA
INDRI
IRISH ELK
JACKAL
JAGUAR
JAGUARUNDI
JERBOA
JUMPING
  MOUSE
KANGAROO
KANGAROO
  RAT
KIANG
KILLER WHALE
KINKAJOU
KLIPSPRINGER
KOALA
KOB
KODIAK BEAR
KUDU
LANGUR
LEMMING
LEMUR
LEOPARD
LEOPARD SEAL
LIGER
LINSANG
LION
LLAMA
LORIS
LYNX
MACAQUE
MAMMOTH
MANATEE
MANDRILL
MANGABEY
MARGAY
MARKHOR
MARMOSET
MARMOT
MARSUPIAL
  MOLE
MARTEN
MEERKAT
MINK
MOLE
MOLE RAT
MONA
  MONKEY
MONGOOSE
MONKEY

MONOTREME
MOON RAT
MOOSE
MOUFLON
MOUNTAIN
  BEAVER
MOUNTAIN
  LION
MOUSE
MOUSE DEER
MULE
MUSK DEER
MUSK OX
MUSKRAT
MUSQUASH
NARWHAL
NEW WORLD
  MONKEY
NILGAI
NOCTULE
NUMBAT
NUTRIA
NYALA
OCELOT
OKAPI
OLD WORLD
  MONKEY
OLINGO
ONAGER
OPOSSUM
ORANG-UTAN
ORIBI
ORYX
OTTER
OTTER SHREW
OUNCE
PACA
PACHYDERM
PACK RAT
PALM CIVET
PAMPAS CAT
PANDA
PANGOLIN
PANTHER
PATAS
  MONKEY
PECCARY
PÈRE DAVID'S
  DEER
PHALANGER
PIG
PIKA
PILOT WHALE
PINE MARTEN
PIPISTRELLE
PLATYPUS
POCKET
  GOPHER
POLAR BEAR
POLECAT

11

ANIMALS continued

PORCUPINE	RHESUS	SIFAKA	TAMARIN	WATER
PORPOISE	MONKEY	SIKA	TAMAROU	BUFFALO
POSSUM	RHINOCEROS	SILVER FOX	TAPIR	WATER RAT
POTTO	RIGHT WHALE	SITATUNGA	TARSIER	WATER SHREW
POUCHED	ROAN	SKUNK	TASMANIAN	WATER VOLE
RAT	ANTELOPE	SLOTH	DEVIL	WEASEL
PRAIRIE DOG	ROE DEER	SLOTH BEAR	TASMANIAN	WHALE
PRAIRIE WOLF	RORQUAL	SNOW	WOLF	WHITE RHI-
PRIMATE	ROYAL	LEOPARD	TENREC	NOCEROS
PROBOSCIS	ANTELOPE	SNOWSHOE	THYLACINE	WHITE WHALE
MONKEY	RUMINANT	HARE	TIGER	WILD BOAR
PRONGHORN	SABLE	SOLENODON	TIGON	WILDCAT
PROSIMIAN	SABLE	SOUSLIK	TIMBER WOLF	WILDEBEEST
PUMA	ANTELOPE	SPECTACLED	TITI	WISENT
PYGMY HIPPO-	SAIGA	BEAR	TREE	WOLF
POTAMUS	SAKI	SPERM WHALE	KANGAROO	WOLVERINE
RABBIT	SCALY-TAILED	SPIDER	TREE SHREW	WOMBAT
RACCOON	SQUIRREL	MONKEY	URUS	WOODCHUCK
RACCOON	SEA COW	SPRINGBOK	VAMPIRE BAT	WOOLLY
DOG	SEAL	SPRINGHAAS	VERVET	MONKEY
RAT	SEALION	SQUIRREL	VICUNA	WOOLLY RHI-
RATEL	SEA OTTER	SQUIRREL	VISCACHA	NOCEROS
RAT	SEI WHALE	MONKEY	VOLE	WOOLLY
KANGAROO	SEROTINE BAT	STEINBOK	WALLABY	SPIDER
RED DEER	SEROW	STOAT	WALLAROO	MONKEY
RED FOX	SERVAL	SUN BEAR	WALRUS	YAK
RED SQUIRREL	SHEEP	TAHR	WAPITI	ZEBRA
REEDBUCK	SHREW	TALAPOIN	WARTHOG	ZEBU
REINDEER	SIAMANG	TAMANDUA	WATERBUCK	ZORILLA

answerability accountability, duty, liability, obligation, responsibility

answerable accountable, beholden, dutiful, duty bound, liable, obliged, responsible, under obligation

ant emmet, formic, pismire, termite, worker
See also list at **insect**.

antagonize aggravate, alienate, cause offence, disgust, disunite, divide, embitter, enrage, envenom, estrange, exacerbate, grate, incense, infuriate, irritate, jar, madden, nauseate, poison, provoke, repel, set against, sour

anthropology demography, ethnology, folklore, humanism, mythology, sociology

anticipate forestall, introduce, prearrange, precede, pre-empt, preface, preview

antifreeze de-icer, ethylene glycol

antiquarian ancestral, antecedent, archaeologist, archaist, classicist, foregoing, medievalist, preceding

anyhow
may indicate an anagram

anyway
may indicate an anagram

apart asunder, broken, cleft, cloven, dispersed, distant, divergent, fugitive, radiating, rent, riven, scattered, schizoid, separate, shattered, split, sundered

apathetic absent, aloof, distant, impassive, indifferent, noncommittal, phlegmatic, resigned, retired, uninterested, withdrawn

apathy half-heartedness, indifference, listlessness

ape copy, imitate, impersonate, mimic, monkey, simulate
See also list at **animal**.

apocalyptic cataclysmic, catastrophic, doom-laden, eschatological, ruinous

apologize apologise, appease, atone, beg forgiveness, beg pardon, conciliate, defend, explain, make amends, pacify, propitiate, say sorry

apology acknowledgment, breast-beating, confession, contrition, excuse, flagellation, hair shirt, mortification, oblation, offering, penance, penitence, piaculum, purgation, purification, regrets, remorse, repentance, sacrifice

apostasy betrayal, collaboration, conversion, defection, desertion, going over, perfidy, ratting, recreancy, treachery, turning traitor

apparent
may indicate a hidden word

appealing addictive, affecting, attractive, charismatic, charming, compelling, contagious, emotional, encouraging, fascinating, gripping, hypnotic, infectious, inspirational, irresistible, magnetic, mesmeric, motivating, moving, seductive, suggestive, tempting

appear appear like, attend, be, break forth, come out, crop up, dawn upon, emerge, imitate, leak out, look, loom, manifest, materialize, resemble, seem, show up, transpire

appearance advent, arrival, aspect, birth, coming, contour, debut, dimensions, embodiment, entrance, exterior, façade, face, features, form, format, front, guise, image, impression, incarnation, introduction, look, manifestation, materialization, mien, outline, outside, persona, presentation, profile, realization, relief, seemingness, semblance, shallowness, shape, silhouette, superficiality, superficies, surface, veneer

appetizer apéritif, dainty, delicacy, drop, hors d'oeuvre, morsel, mouthful, nibble, nip, sample, soupçon, starter, titbit

applaud cheer, clap, congratulate, cry, give thanks, praise, shout, yell

approach accost, advance, buttonhole, call to, collision course, confrontation, driveway, greet, hail, method, narrowing gap, run-up, salute, tackle

approaching advancing, coming, homeward-bound, imminent, impending, inbound, incoming, inwardbound, nearing, oncoming, terminal

approval acceptance, acquiescence, adoption, advocacy, agreement, approbation, assent, authorization, backing, blessing, championship, consent, countenance, endorsement, go-ahead, imprimatur, licence, mandate, nod, OK, patronage, permission, recommendation, rubber stamp, sanction, satisfaction, support, vote, wink

approve admire, agree, esteem, hold with, like, permit, prize, regard highly, respect, value

approved accepted, backed, endorsed, favoured, passed, recommended, supported, tested

aptitude ability, aptness, bent, endowment, faculty, fitness, flair, genius, gift, inclination, instinct, knack, know-how, propensity, qualification, talent, tendency

arboretum orangery, orchard, pinery, pinetum, tree nursery

arcade aisle, cloister, colonnade, esplanade, gallery, loggia, nave, parade, portico, promenade, triforium

archer Artemis, bowman, Cupid, Diana, (Robin) Hood, marksman, Orion, Sagittarius, (William) Tell, toxopholite

architecture building, design, planning
See lists of architectural terms and architectural styles.

area acre, belt, borough, community, constituency, county, district, division,

ARCHITECTURAL TERMS

ABACUS	CINQUEFOIL	FESTOON	MODILLION	STRIA
ACANTHUS	CONGÉ	FILLET	MOULDING	STRIGIL
ACCOLADE	COPESTONE	FINIAL	MULLION	STUCCO
ANNULET	CORDON	FLUTE	MUTULE	TAENIA
ANTHEMION	CORNICE	FOIL	NECKMOULD	TALON
APOPHYGE	CORONA	FOLIATION	OGEE	TELEMON
ARCHITRAVE	COVING	FRET	OVOLO	TERMINAL
ASTRAGAL	CROCHET	FRIEZE	PENDANT	THUMB
ATLAS	CROWNPIECE	FRONTISPIECE	POLYCHROMY	TOPPING
BAGUETTE	CUSP	GADROON	PUTTO	TORUS
BANDEROLE	CYMA	GORGERIN	QUADREGA	TRACERY
BAS RELIEF	DENTIL	GUILLOCHE	QUARTER	TRANSOME
BAY LEAF	DOGTOOTH	GUTTA	ROUND	TREFOIL
BEZANT	ECHINUS	HEAD MOULD	QUATREFOIL	TRIGLYPH
BILLET	ECTYPE	HEADPIECE	QUIRK	TYMPANUM
BOSS	EGG AND	HELIX	QUOIN	VAULTING
CALOTTE	ANCHOR	HERMS	REED	VIGNETTE
CANEPHORAE	EGG AND DART	HOOD MOULD	REGLET	VOLUTE
CAPSTONE	EGG AND	HYPOPHYGE	RESPOND	ZIGZAG
CARTOUCHE	TONGUE	LIERNE	RUSTICATION	
CARYATID	EPISTYLE	LISTEL	SCOTIA	
CAVETTO	FACET	MEDALLION	SCROLL	
CHEVRON	FASCIA	METOPE	SPLAY	

ARCHITECTURAL STYLES

ART DECO	EARLY RENAISSANCE	MORESQUE
ART NOUVEAU	EGYPTIAN	MOZARABIC
BAROQUE	EMPIRE	MUDÉJAR
BAUHAUS	FEDERATION	NEOCLASSICAL
BEAUX-ARTS	FLAMBOYANT	NORMAN
BRUTALIST	FUNCTIONAL	PALLADIAN
BYZANTINE	GOTHIC	PERPENDICULAR
CAROLINGIAN	GOTHIC REVIVAL	PERSIAN
CHURRIGUERESQUE	GRAECO-ROMAN	POSTMODERNIST
CINQUECENTO	GRECIAN	RENAISSANCE
CLASSICAL	GREEK REVIVAL	ROCOCO
COLOSSAL	IONIC	ROMAN
CORINTHIAN	ISLAMIC	ROMANESQUE
CYCLOPEAN	MANNERIST	ROMANTIC CLASSICAL
DECONSTRUCTIONISM	MEDIEVAL	SARACEN
DECORATED	MESOPOTAMIAN	TRANSITIONAL
DE STIJL	MODERNIST	TUSCAN
DORIC	MOORISH	VERNACULAR

enclave, extent, hectare, metropolitan county, neighbourhood, parish, province, region, room, space, speciality, state, township, vicinity

arguable challenging, contentious, controversial, debatable, disputable, doubtful, dubious, in question, misunderstood, moot, problematic, questionable, refutable, topical, undecided, unsettled

argue altercate, bicker, brawl, clash, conflict, contend, contest, contradict, debate, differ, disagree, dispute, dissent, feud, fight, fuss, gainsay, hassle, lock horns, oppose, polemicize, quarrel, quibble, remonstrate, row, scrap, scuffle, spar, squabble, tiff, tussle, wrangle

argument altercation, argy-bargy, barney, bickering, brawl, breach, clash, cleft, conflict, controversy, debate, difference, disagreement, discord, dispute, diversity, donnybrook, dust-up, falling-out, feud, fight, fisticuffs, fracas, fray, fuss, incompatibility, misunderstanding, polemic, quarrel, rift, row, ruckus, ruction, rumpus, run-in, rupture, schism, scrap, scrimmage, set-to, shindy, slanging match, spat, split, squabble, strife, struggle, tiff, tussle, wrangle

argumentative cantankerous, choleric, contrary, cross, disagreeable, disputatious, dissentious, factious, fractious, grouchy, irascible, irritable, litigious, peevish, petulant, quarrelsome, querulous, testy

aristocracy ancien régime, beau monde, élite, gentlefolk, gentry, high society, landed gentry, lordship, nobility, nobs, peerage, ruling class, toffs

aristocratic baronial, blue blooded, classy, ducal, ennobled, first-class, gentlemanly, high-born, high-caste, high-class, ladylike, lordly, noble, patrician, princely, thoroughbred, titled, top-drawer, U, upper-class, well-born, well-bred

armed force auxiliary fleet, battalion, battery, brigade, column, company, corps, detachment, detail, division, file, fleet, flight, flotilla, outfit, phalanx, platoon, rank, regiment, section, squad, squadron, task force, troop, wing
See also list at **military**.

arms archery, armaments, escutcheon, gunnery, heraldic, missilery, munitions, musketry, rocketry, weaponry
See list at **weapon**.

around
may indicate a split word or a backword

arouse excite, heat up, inflame, rouse, stir, wake, warm

arrange align, allocate, array, bargain, compose, compromise, contract, covenant, deal, display, dispose, distrib-

ute, group, line up, locate, make terms, marshal, negotiate, order, place, pledge, position, promise, settle, structure, transact
may indicate an anagram

arrangement alignment, arraying, bargain, bond, compact, composition, contract, convention, covenant, deal, disposition, grouping, line-up, location, marshalling, order, pact, placement, pledge, promise, settlement, structuring, transaction, treaty
may indicate an anagram

arrangements groundwork, plans, preparations

array arrangement, assemblage, composition, display, layout, pattern, structure, style

arrival advance, advent, appearance, approach, coming, emergence, entrance, onset

arrogance conceit, haughtiness, loftiness, pride, pushiness, shamelessness, tyranny, uppishness, uppitiness

arrogant bold, brazen, haughty, lofty, overconfident, overweening, proud, pushy, self-satisfied, smug, tyrannical, uppish, uppity

article a, an, apprentice, column, criticism, critique, editorial, leader, news item, notice, puff, review, the, write-up

articulate clear, eloquent, fluent, jointed, pronounce, utter, voice
may indicate a homophone

articulation diction, elocution, enunciation, utterance, vocalization

artillery ballistics, firing, gunnery, musketry, skeet, trapshooting
See also list at **weapon**.

artisan apprentice, architect, artificer, blacksmith, bricklayer, builder, carpenter, chippie, collier, cooper, craftsman, decorator, electrician, engineer, fitter, foundryman, glass-blower, goldsmith, gunsmith, jeweller, joiner, journeyman, learner, locksmith, ma-

chinist, mason, master, mechanic, metalworker, miner, painter, plasterer, plumber, potter, sawyer, shipwright, silversmith, steelworker, tailor, technician, thatcher, tradesman, turner, watchmaker, weaver, welder, wheelwright, woodworker
See also list at **occupation**.

artist animator, aquarellist, artisan, caricaturist, cartoonist, colourist, copyist, craftsman, dauber, delineator, designer, doodler, draughtsman, drawer, enameller, illuminator, illustrator, limner, miniaturist, old master, painter, pastellist, pavement artist, portraitist, RA, sign painter, sketcher

artistic aesthetic, arty, arty-crafty, arty-farty, decorative, painterly, picturesque

artistry art, artiness, artisanship, artsy-craftiness, artsy-fartsiness, artycraftiness, brushwork, composition, connoisseurship, craftsmanship, draughtsmanship, flair, foreshortening, invention, mastery, painterliness, perspective, skill, talent, taste, technique, virtu

ascend climb, curl upwards, go up, grow up, levitate, lift, mount, rise, soar, spiral, spire, swarm up, sweep up, upsurge

ascending ascent, climbing, mounting, retroussé, rising, soaring, turned-up, uphill, upward
may indicate a backward

aspect datum, detail, element, facet, fact, factor, feature, incidental, item, minutia, particular, point, thing

aspersion defamatory remark, innuendo, insinuation, slur, smear

aspiration aim, ambition, desire, dream, Erewhon, fantasy, fool's paradise, great expectations, high hopes, intention, longing, pipe dream, promised land, Utopia, vision, wish, yearning

aspire aim, anticipate, await, desire, dream, expect, long, wish, yearn

ass burro, donkey, fool, hinny, idiot, Jack, mule, Jenny, Ned, Neddy

assault attack, charge, onrush, sortie

assemblage accumulation, agglomeration, aggregation, batch, collection, congeries, conglomeration, group, hoard, set, stockpile, store

assemble accumulate, agglomerate, aggregate, amass, bank up, bring together, build up, collect, gather, group, heap, hoard, mass, mound, pile, stack, stockpile, store
may indicate an anagram

assembly agglomeration, aggregation, anthology, assemblage, bloc, collage, collection, coming together, company, compendium, confluence, conglomeration, congregation, connection, consortium, construction, convergence, corporation, erection, fitting together, forgathering, gathering, grouping, ingathering, manufacture, mobilization, montage, muster, rally, set, syndicate

assent accede, acceptance, acquiescence, affirmation, agreement, allow, approbation, approval, authorize, compliance, comply, concede, concur, confirmation, consent, corroboration, grant, nod, permit, sanction, say yes

assertive assertory, assured, blunt, confident, decided, decisive, dogmatic, driven, forceful, incisive, insistent, outspoken, plain, self-assertive, thrustful

assertiveness assurance, bluntness, decisiveness, drive, forcefulness, go, incisiveness, insistence, oomph, outspokenness, peremptoriness, plainness, positiveness, push, thrust, vigour, zip

assiduity application, attention, concentration, diligence, industriousness, intentness

assign allocate, allot, apportion, consume, deploy, enjoy, motivate, possess, requisition

assist aid, back, ease, help, reinforce, support

associate adhere, ally, befriend, clan, club together, cohabit, cohere, consort, contact, couple, entangle, escort, frequent, friend, gang up, hobnob, intercommunicate, interface, involve, kin, kinsman, kith, liaise, match, meet, network, pair up, partner, relate, relation, relative, socialize, team up, tribe

associated combined, coupled, hand-in-glove, inseparable, joined, married, paired, partnered, wedded

association affiliation, alignment, alliance, amalgamation, cartel, coadunation, coalescence, coalition, combination, commerce, consolidation, consortium, fusion, incorporation, integration, intercommunication, intercourse, liaison, merger, network, nexus, relationship, unification, union

assorted allotropic, chequered, dapple, divers, diverse, kaleidoscopic, miscellaneous, mixed, motley, multifarious, omnifarious, sundry, various
may indicate an anagram

assortment hotchpotch, medley, miscellany, mixture, motley

assurance affirmation, authority, composure, confidence, equanimity, guarantee, promise, self-confidence

assured authoritative, bold, composed, guaranteed, self-confident

astray
may indicate an anagram

astronaut cosmonaut, spaceman, spacewoman

astronomer astronomer royal, astrophysicist, cosmochemist, cosmogenist, cosmologist, observer, star gazer, uranographer
See list of the constellations.
See also list at **planet**.

at home
may indicate in

atmosphere air, ambience, aura, feeling, milieu, overtone, situation, stratosphere, tone, undertone, vibes, vibrations

atone answer, appease, compensate, conciliate, expiate, indemnify, make amends, make good, make right, pacify,

THE CONSTELLATIONS

ANDROMEDA	COLUMBA	LEO	PYXIS
ANTLIA	COMA BERENICES	LEO MINOR	RETICULUM
APUS	CORONA	LEPUS	SAGITTA
AQUARIUS	AUSTRALIS	LIBRA	SAGITTARIUS
AQUILA	CORONA BOREALIS	LUPUS	SCORPIUS
ARA	CORVUS	LYNX	SCULPTOR
ARIES	CRATER	LYRA	SCUTUM
AURIGA	CRUX	MENSA	SERPENS
BOÖTES	CYGNUS	MICROSCOPIUM	SEXTANS
CAELUM	DELPHINUS	MONOCEROS	TAURUS
CAMELOPARDALIS	DORADO	MUSCA	TELESCOPIUM
CANCER	DRACO	NORMA	TRIANGULUM
CANES VENATICI	EQUULEUS	OCTANS	TRIANGULUM
CANIS MAJOR	ERIDANUS	OPHIUCHUS	AUSTRALE
CANIS MINOR	FORNAX	ORION	TUCANA
CAPRICORNUS	GEMINI	PAVO	URSA MAJOR
CARINA	GRUS	PEGASUS	URSA MINOR
CASSIOPEIA	HERCULES	PERSEUS	VELA
CENTAURUS	HOROLOGIUM	PHOENIX	VIRGO
CEPHEUS	HYDRA	PICTOR	VOLANS
CETUS	HYDRUS	PISCES	VULPECULA
CHAMELEON	INDUS	PISCIS AUSTRINUS	
CIRCINUS	LACERTA	PUPPIS	

pay back, propitiate, reconcile, rectify, redeem, redress, reimburse, repair, repay, requite, satisfy, square it, suffer

atonement appeasement, blood money, compensation, conciliation, expiation, indemnity, making amends, making good, making right, pacification, payment, propitiation, quits, quittance, recompense, reconciliation, rectification, redemption, redress, reimbursement, reparation, requital, restitution, satisfaction, squaring, wergild

attack abuse, advance, aggression, aggressiveness, ambush, armed robbery, aspersion, assail, assault, barrage, beat up, bellicosity, belligerence, blitz, blitzkrieg, boarding, bombardment, calumny, camisado, cannonade, censure, charge, collide with, combativeness, criticism, dash at, decrial, defamation, denigration, denunciation, disparagement, drive against, enfilade, engage, fly against, foray, force, foul play, gallop at, go for, harassment, harry, hit, hostility, hunt, ill-treat, indecent assault, injustice, intimidation, libel, march against, mugging, offensive, onset, onslaught, physical violence, pincer, pound, pugnacity, push, raid, ram, rape, ravish, revilement, ride against, run at, rush, sail against, slander, slur, smear, strike, surprise, thrust, tilt at, torture, verbal attack, vilification, violate
See also list at **weapon**.

attempt aim, bid, dead set, effort, endeavour, essay, gambit, last try, move, offer, seek, step, strain, struggle, tackle, try

attend appear, follow, observe, participate, see, shadow, spectate, stand by, tag along, tail, take part, track, turn up, view, visit, wait on, watch, witness

attendant batman, butler, caddie, caretaker, concierge, hostess, janitor, maid, maitre d'hotel, page, porter, pot-boy, sommelier, steward, stewardess, usher, valet, waiter, waitress

attestant advocate, affirmant, affirmer, ally, announcer, asserter, assurer, backer, champion, confessor, corroborator, enunciator, fortifier, guarantor, helpmate, oath-taker, patron, proclaimer, promoter, seconder, sponsor, submitter, supporter, testifier, witness

attitude affinity, disposition, humour, mood, proclivity, susceptibility, vein

attract adduct, appeal, charm, drag, draw towards, induce, influence, magnetize, move, persuade, pull, spellbind, tug

attraction affinity, attractiveness, desire, drag, draw, itch, pull, sympathy, tug

attractive alluring, appealing, captivating, charismatic, charming, dishy, enticing, fascinating, fetching, good-looking, hunky, irresistable, seductive, sexy, tempting

audacious assured, blatant, bold, brazenfaced, flagrant

audit catalogue, inspect accounts, inventory, list, take stock

auditorium concert hall, listening post, music room, opera house

augment add, appreciate, broaden, develop, escalate, expand, flower, grow, increase, inflate, mushroom, proliferate, spread, widen

augmentation advance, appreciation, betterment, dilation, escalation, expansion, growth, improvement, increase, increment, inflation, rise

aural acoustic, audio, auditory
may indicate a homophone

auspicious encouraging, fair, favourable, fortunate, golden, hopeful, likely, optimistic, possible, potential, promising, propitious, rosy

authentic bona fide, echt, genuine,

hall-marked, legitimate, original, pukka, real, true, valid, verified

authenticate atttest, endorse, indenture, mark, ratify, seal, second, stamp

author allegorist, annalist, autobiographer, biographer, chronicler, diarist, dramatist, dramaturge, elegist, fabler, fabulist, historian, historiographer, modernist, mythologist, novelettist, novelist, penman, playwright, poet, poetess, romancer, satirist, screenwriter, scribe, sonneteer, storyteller, symbolist, wordsmith, writer

authoritative authoritarian, definitive, dominant, empowered, ex officio, leading, learned, noble, official, potent, powerful, predominant, regal, reigning, royal, ruling

authority ascendancy, authorization, charge, charter, clout, command, control, direction, dominance, domination, dominion, governance, government, hegemony, leadership, licence, magistrality, mandate, mastery, nobility, permission, permit, power, predominance, prerogative, regality, royalty, rule, seniority, sovereignty, superiority, supremacy, suzerainty, sway, trust, warrant, warranty, writ

autocratic arbitrary, authoritarian, dictatorial, tyrannical

autodidactic perceptive, receptive, self-schooled, self-taught

autonomy discretion, free will, independence, self-determination

autumn fall, harvest, harvest moon, hunter's moon

availability accessibility, immediacy, nearness, plenty, propinquity, proximity, sufficiency

available accessible, accounted for, at hand, close by, convenient, handy, here, immediate, in attendance, in view, near, nearby, on, on tap, plenty, ready, standing by, sufficient, there

avenge punish, requite, revenge

average bisect, characteristic, common, commonness, compromise, conformity, conventionality, criterion, divide, fifty-fifty, general, generality, halve, mean, measure, median, mediocre, middling, norm, normal, ordinariness, par, prevailing, regularity, representative, rule, standard, standardness, the ordinary, the usual, typical, usual, yardstick

avert foil, hinder, obstruct, prevent

avian anseriform, anserine, aquiline, birdlike, birdy, columbine, corvine, fringilline, gallinaceous, goosy, hawkish, hirundine, oscine, owlish, passerine, psittacine, rasorial, struthious, turdine, vulturine

aviation aerodynamics, aeronautics, flight, flying, gliding, pilotage, piloting

aviator aircraftsman, air hostess, air-traffic controller, copilot, flight attendant, flyer, groundcrew, ground engineer, groundling, navigator, ob-

AIRCRAFT			
AEROPLANE	DIRIGIBLE	JET	SAILPLANE
AEROSTAT	FIGHTER	JUMBO-JET	SEA-PLANE
AIR CAR	FIRE-BALLOON	JUMP-JET	SHUTTLE
AIRPLANE	FLYING BEDSTEAD	KITE	STRATOCRUISER
AIRSHIP	FLYING-BOAT	MAIL-PLANE	TRIPLANE
AUTOGIRO	FREIGHT-PLANE	MONOPLANE	TURBO-JET
BALLOON	GAS-BALLOON	MONTGOLFIER	TURBO-PROP
BIPLANE	GLIDER	BALLOON	WARPLANE
BOMBER	HELICOPTER	PASSENGER PLANE	ZEPPELIN
CLIPPER	HOVERCRAFT	PLANE	
CONCORDE	HYDROPLANE	ROTODYNE	

server, pathfinder, pilot, steward, stewardess
See list of aircraft.

avoid bypass, circumvent, cold-shoulder, cut, eschew, escape, evade, hang back, hesitate, ignore, retire, shun, snub, steer clear

avoidable avertable, escapable, preventable, unattempted, unsought

away absconded, dematerialized, departed, disappeared, distant, fled, flown, gone, lost, missing, off, out, vamoosed, vanished

awkwardness clumsiness, difficulty, embarrassment, ham-fistedness, precariousness, stubbornness, unhelpfulness, unwieldiness

awry amiss, askew, crooked, defective, malfunctioning, twisted, wrong
may indicate an anagram

axle axis, axlebar, pivot, rod, shaft, spindle

·B·

B	Bachelor • bass • black • British • key • note • secondary road
BA	Bachelor of Arts • barium • British Airways • British Association • degree • graduate • scholar
BACS	Bankers' Automated Clearing Service
BAFTA	British Academy of Film and Television Arts
BAR	baritone • barometer • barrister • Browning Automatic Rifle
BASIC	beginners' all-purpose symbolic instruction code
BBC	British Broadcasting Corporation
BC	before Christ • old times
BE	beryllium • British Empire
BEM	British Empire Medal
BFI	British Film Institute
BI	bismuth
BIT	binary digit
BK	berkelium
BLITT	Bachelor of Letters (Latin: *Baccalaureus Literarum*)
BMA	British Medical Association
BMJ	British Medical Journal
BOC	British Oxygen Corporation
BOF	beginning of file
BR	British Rail • trains
BSC	Bachelor of Science
BSI	British Standards Institution
BV	farewell (Latin: *bene vale*)
BW	black and white

baby carriage baby buggy, baby walker, carrycot, perambulator, pram, pushchair, stroller

back ally with, ebb, rear, regress, retrogress, reverse, side with, stand behind, stand by, subside, wane
may indicate a backword

backward retrocessive, retrograde, retrogressive

backwards and forwards
may indicate a palindrome

bad abominable, awful, base, beastly, criminal, crooked, depraved, disagreeable, dishonest, dreadful, evil, execrable, ghastly, gross, heinous, horrendous, horrible, horrid, horrific, incompetent, inferior, irredeemable, lamentable, nasty, objectionable, obnoxious, poor, sinful, terrible, unpleasant, unspeakable, villainous, wicked
may indicate an anagram

bad-mannered abusive, badly behaved, barbarian, boorish, caddish, churlish, coarse, crude, cursing, foulmouthed, gross, ill-bred, impertinent, impudent, injurious, insolent, loutish, obstreperous, offensive, rude, saucy, savage, truculent, unchivalrous, uncouth, uncultured, unrefined, vulgar

bag bundle, carryall, diplomatic pouch, grip, handbag, holdall, kitbag, nosebag, poke, pouch, purse, sack, saddlebag, satchel, swag

baggage attaché case, backpack, Boston bag, briefcase, carpet bag, carryall, Gladstone bag, grip, haversack, holdall, knapsack, luggage, portfolio, portmanteau, rucksack, suitcase, trunk, valise

bake apricate, bleach, burn, insolate, roast, scorch, sun, toast

baked bleached, burnt, parched, scorched, sun-baked, sun-dried

bald bare, hairless, plain, receding

ban abolish, brake, curb, no, outlaw, prohibit, taboo, veto

band bandoleer, belt, collar, cummerbund, fillet, girdle, gang, group, headband, neckband, orchestra, ribbon, sash, strap, stripe, waistband

bang backfire, blast, blowout, boom, burst, clash, crash, detonation, discharge, explosion, kaboom, kapow, kazam, peal, report, round, salvo, shot, slam, thud, thump, thunderclap, volley, whack, wham, zap

banging booming, bursting, crashing, deafening, ear-splitting, exploding, slamming, thundering

bank accumulation, building society, coast, damp, deposit, extinguish, friendly society, heap, invest, rim, save, swell, tilt

bankrupt broke, bust, insolvent, red

bar ban, court, inn, prevent, pub, save, slab, stripe

barbed notched, prickly, scratchy

bargain chaffer, deal, dicker, haggle, higgle, huckster, incentive, negotiate, sale, snip

barrier barbed wire, breakwater, buffer, bulwark, bunker, dam, dike, ditch, earthwork, embankment, fence, hindrance, jetty, levee, moat, mole, obstacle, parapet, portcullis, rampart, wall, weir

bashfulness chastity, coyness, demureness, prudishness, shamefacedness, skittishness, virtue

basket bassinet, creel, hamper, Moses basket, pannier, punnet, skep, trug

basted beaten, greased, oiled, stitched, thrashed

bat cut, drive, flutter, fruit bat, glance, hit, lift, loft, pipistrelle, pull, shank, slam, slice, slog, smash, strike, volley
See also list at **cricket**.

bath basin, bathtub, bidet, bowl, douche, eyebath, footbath, hipbath, Jacuzzi, sauna, shower, sink, trough, tub, vat, washbasin, washstand

bathe dip, douche, drench, dunk, lather, lave, rinse, shampoo, shower, sluice, soak, soap, steep, swill, wash

battle action, attack, blitz, brush, charge, clash, collision, combat, confront, contend, contest, defence, dispute, dogfight, engagement, fight, fire, offensive, rally, resist, scrap, shoot-out, skirmish, stand
See also list at **weapon**.

battleground beachhead, bridgehead, combat zone, front line, killing field, theatre of war

bauble bric-a-brac, frippery, gewgaw, knick-knack, novelty, trinket, trumpery

be exist, happen, live, remain, stand

bear abide, brook, carry, countenance, endure, stand, stick, stomach, suffer, tolerate, undergo
See also list at **animal**.

bearing air, bent, carriage, compass bearing (N,S,E,W), carriage, course, deportment, drift, heading, inclination, lay, lie, line, mien, path, route, run, set, short cut, tack, tendency, tenor, thrust, track, trend, vector, way

beat batter, cane, circuit, cut, defeat, flail, flog, hammer, lambaste, lash, leather, lick, pound, pulse, pulverize, pummel, rhythm, spank, stripe, tempo, thrash, trounce, vibrate, wallop, whip

beautician barber, beauty specialist, coiffeur, coiffeuse, cosmetician, crimper, hairdresser, hair-stylist, make-up artist, manicurist, pedicurist, plastic surgeon, trichologist
See also list at **occupation**.

beautified adorned, decorated, embellished, embroidered, improved, touched up, trimmed

beautiful attractive, bonny, bright, comely, cute, exquisite, fair, fine, glamorous, good looking, gorgeous, handsome, Junoesque, lovely, lush, pretty, shapely, statuesque, sweet, winsome

beautify adorn, bejewel, decorate, glamorize, prettify, primp, prink, smarten up, spruce up, titivate, transform

bed base, bedstead, berth, bunk, camp, canopied, chaise longue, Colonial, cot, cradle, crib, day, divan, Empire, feather, flower, foldaway, footboard, four-poster, futon, ground, hammock, headboard, panelled, plant, sofa, truckle, water, zed
See also list at **furniture**.

bee bumble, drone, honey, queen, spelling, worker
See also list at **insect**.

beef back rib, best end, blade, brawn, brisket, chuck, complain, entrecôte, filet (mignon), fillet steak, flank, fore rib, fore shank, grumble, hind shank, leg, muscle, neck, Porterhouse steak, rib, rolled ribs, round, round steak, rump, shin, short loin, short plate, silverside, sinew, sirloin, T-bone, tenderloin, thick rib, thin rib, topside, undercut steak

beggarly barefoot, dilapidated, dirty, homeless, hungry, in rags, mean, mendicant, scruffy, seedy, shabby, slummy, squalid, starving, tatty, threadbare

begging beseeching, cadging, freeloading, mendicant, mooching, pleading, scrounging, sponging

begin commence, dawn, debut, establish, generate, inaugurate, initiate, launch, open, originate, premiere, start, unveil

beginner greenhorn, L, learner, novice, rookie, starter

beginning auspication, birth, commencement, dawn, debut, first night, generating, grand opening, inauguration, inception, initiation, launching, maiden voyage, opening, premiere, start, unveiling

belief angle, attitude, certainty, conjecture, conviction, faith, feeling, hypothesis, idea, impression, intuition, judgment, notion, opinion, persuasion, position, premise, principle, proposition, sentiment, speculation, stance, standpoint, supposition, surmise, theory, thought, truth, viewpoint

believability credibility, plausibility, reliability, trustworthiness

believable commanding, convincing, credible, creditable, impressive, likely, persuasive, plausible, possible, probable, realistic, reasonable, reliable, tenable, trustworthy

believe accept, affirm, buy, credit, declare, hold, know, maintain, opine, profess, think, trust

believed accepted, accredited, alleged, authoritative, creedal, doctrinal, putative, received, supposed, undisputed

believing acceptance, assurance, blind faith, certain, confidence, conformist, convinced, credence, dependence, expectation, faith, faithful, gullibility, hope, orthodox, pledge, positive, reliance, sure, trust, trusting, undoubting, unhesitating, unquestioning, unsuspecting

bellicosity aggressiveness, combativeness, hawkishness, militancy, pugnacity, Ramboism, sabre-rattling

belonging appurtenant, essential, fundamental, inherent, integral, intrinsic, one of, part of

beloved admired, adored, cherished, chosen, darling, dear, esteemed, fancied, favourite, pet, preferred, regarded, respected, revered, sweetheart, well-liked

bemuse addle, baffle, bedazzle, bewilder, confound, confuse, flummox, muddle, mystify, perplex, stump, stun *may indicate an anagram*

bend arc, arch, camber, circle, circuit, coil, corner, crease, crescent, crumple, curl, detour, fold, hyperbola, loop, meniscus, oval, parabola, rondure, roundness, S-curve, semicircle, spiral, turn, undulation, U-turn, wave

benefactor backer, fairy godmother, guardian angel, patron, patron saint, philanthropist, promoter, sponsor, tutelary, well-wisher

beneficial advantageous, beatific, bettering, edifying, expedient, favourable, good, improving, profitable, propitious, salutary, useful, worthwhile

beneficiary assignee, claimant, co-heir, devisee, heir, heir apparent, heiress, inheritor, inheritress, legatee, owner, successor

benefit advantage, avail, behalf, benediction, betterment, blessing, boon, edification, gain, gift, happiness, improvement, interest, profit, profitability, prosperity, return, serve, usefulness, welfare, well-being, worthwhileness

benevolence affability, amiability, attentiveness, benignity, compassion, consideration, cordiality, courteousness, forgiveness, geniality, good-naturedness, goodness, goodwill, grace, helpfulness, humaneness, kind-heartedness, kindness, love, niceness, open-heartedness, tolerance

benevolent accommodating, affectionate, amiable, beneficent, benign, charitable, compassionate, considerate, decent, forgiving, friendly, generous, good, helpful, humane, indulgent, kind-hearted, lax, lenient, loving, maternal, neighbourly, nice, obliging, open-hearted, paternal, philanthropic, sociable, soft-hearted, thoughtful, warm-hearted, well-disposed, well-intentioned, well-meaning

benighted arcane, blind, cheerless, clouded, cryptic, dejected, depressed, dismal, enigmatic, esoteric, evil, forbidding, gloomy, grim, hidden, ignorant, inscrutable, menacing, mournful, murky, mysterious, mystic, obfuscated, oblivious, obscure, occult, ominous, secret, shadowy, shady, sinister, sombre, threatening, unenlightened, wicked

bequeath confer, give, hand down, leave, pass on, transfer, will

berate abuse, assail, attack, lambast(e), lay into, pitch into, rail, tongue-lash

berating abuse, attack, diatribe, execration, lambasting, laying into, onslaught, railing, revilement, tirade, tongue-lashing, vilification, vituperation

berserk
may indicate an anagram

besiege beleaguer, beset, blockade, encircle, enclose, encroach, hem in, infringe, invest, starve out, surround

best A1, ace, beat, best-ever, blue-ribbon, capital, cardinal, central, champion, chart-busting, chart-topping, chief, choice, class A, crack, crowning, dominant, elite, essential, first, first-class, first-rate, flawless, focal, foremost, gold-medal, greatest, hegemonic, highest, immortal, incomparable, inimitable, invincible, main, matchless, maximal, nonpareil, number-one, optimum, paramount, peerless, perfect, platinum, pre-eminent, preponderant, prevailing, prime, principal, record, record-breaking, record-holding, superlative, supernormal, supreme, tip-top, top, topmost, top-notch, top-ranking, tops, transcendent, triumphant, ultimate, unapproachable, unbeatable, unequalled, unique, unparalleled, unrivalled, unsurpassed, upmost, utmost, victorious, winning, world-beating

betray cheat, con, counterfeit, cozen, deceive, delude, double-cross, dupe, fake, falsify, flimflam, forge, forsake, fraud, hoax, misdirect, misguide, misinform, mislead, play false, sham, sting, swindle, trick

bewitch bedevil, charm, curse, demonize, diabolize, enchant, entrance, fascinate, hex, hypnotize, jinx, mesmerize, possess, shamanize, sorcerize, spellbind, thaumaturgize, theurgize

bias angle, bent, jaundice, predispose, prejudice, slant, twist, warp

bicycle bike, boneshaker, cycle, hobbyhorse, minibike, mountain bike, penny-farthing, push-bike, rat trap, roadster, sit-up-and-beg, tandem, trailbike, tricycle, trike, trishaw, unicycle, velocipede
See list of parts of a bicycle.

big almighty, ample, astronomical, baggy, broad, bulky, bumper, capacious, colossal, commodious, comprehensive, considerable, economy-size, enormous, epic, expansive, extensive, family-size, full-blown, full-grown, full-scale, Gargantuan, generous, giant-size, gigantic, ginormous, grand, great, healthy, huge, immense, imposing, infinite, jumbo, king-size, large, large-scale, limitless, macroscopic, mam-moth, man-size, massive, mega, megalithic, mighty, monster, monstrous, monumental, prodigious, record-size, roomy, spacious, spanking, stupendous, substantial, thumping, thundering, tidy, titanic, towering, tremendous, vast, voluminous, walloping, whacking, whopping

bigger amplified, augmented, bloated, blown-up, broadened, built-up, developed, dilated, dispersed, distended, drawn-out, dropsical, expanded, extended, fanned out, fatter, flared, full-blown, fully developed, fully fledged, heightened, hypertrophied, incrassate, increased, inflated, larger, lengthened, magnified, mature, oedematous, overgrown, overweight, padded, puffed-up, pumped-up, raised, splayed, spread-out, stretched, stuffed, swollen, tumid, turgid, widened, widespread

bill account, beak, books, daybook, docket, invoice, journal, ledger, manifest, overdraft, receivables, reckoning, score, statement, tally

billow break, foam, froth, ripple, roll, surge, swell, undulate

bind anchor, batten, bolt, chain, clamp, clasp, fetter, grip, handcuff, harness, lasso, latch, leash, lock, manacle, moor, padlock, secure, shackle, tether, tie, yoke

bird flier, fowl, songster, warbler, woman
See list of birds.

bird song bird call, caw, chattering, cheep, chirping, chirruping, cluck,

---

PARTS OF A BICYCLE

BRAKE	DIAMOND FRAME	HUB GEAR	SADDLE
BRAKE BLOCK	DRUM BRAKE	INNER TUBE	SPOKES
BRAKE CALIPER	DYNAMO	KICKSTAND	SPROCKET
CARRIER	FORK	LIGHTS	STABILIZERS
CHAIN	FRAME	MUDGUARD	TOE CLIP
COASTER BRAKE	GEAR	PANNIER	TYRE
CRANK	GEARWHEEL	PEDAL	
CROSSBAR	HANDLEBARS	REFLECTOR	
DERAILLEUR	HUB	ROLLER CHAIN	

BIRDS

ACCENTOR
ADJUTANT BIRD
ALBATROSS
AMERICAN EAGLE
ANTBIRD
ARCTIC TERN
AUK
AUKLET
AVADAVAT
AVOCET
BABBLER
BALD EAGLE
BALTIMORE ORIOLE
BARBET
BARNACLE GOOSE
BARN OWL
BATELEUR
BEE-EATER
BELLBIRD
BIRD OF PARADISE
BITTERN
BLACKBIRD
BLACKCAP
BLACK SWAN
BLUE-BILL
BLUEBIRD
BLUE TIT
BOAT-BILL
BOBOLINK
BOOBY
BOWERBIRD
BRAMBLING
BRENT-GOOSE
BROAD-BILL
BRUSH TURKEY
BUDGERIGAR
BULBUL
BULLFINCH
BUNTING
BURROWING OWL
BUSH TIT
BUSH WREN
BUSTARD
BUTCHER-BIRD
BUZZARD
CANADA GOOSE
CANARY
CANVAS-BACK
CARACARA
CARDINAL
CARRION CROW
CASSOWARY
CATBIRD
CHAFFINCH
CHAT
CHICKADEE
CHICKEN
CHIFFCHAFF
CHIPPING
  SPARROW

CHOUGH
COAL TIT
COCKATIEL
COCKATOO
COLY
CONDOR
COOT
CORMORANT
CORNCRAKE
COURSER
COWBIRD
CRAKE
CRANE
CRESTED TIT
CROCODILE BIRD
CROSSBILL
CROW
CUCKOO
CUCKOO SHRIKE
CURLEW
DABCHICK
DARTER
DEMOISELLE CRANE
DIAMOND-BIRD
DIPPER
DIVER
DOVE
DRONGO
DUCK
DUNLIN
DUNNOCK
EAGLE
EAGLE OWL
EGRET
EIDER DUCK
EMPEROR PENGUIN
EMU
EMU-WREN
ERNE
FAIRY PENGUIN
FALCON
FANTAIL
FIELDFARE
FINCH
FINFOOT
FIRECREST
FISH OWL
FLAMINGO
FLICKER
FLOWER-PECKER
FLYCATCHER
FRANCOLIN
FRIAR-BIRD
FRIGATE BIRD
FROGMOUTH
FULMAR
GADWALL
GALLINULE
GANNET
GARGANEY

GNAT-CATCHER
GODWIT
GOLDCREST
GOLDEN EAGLE
GOLDEN-EYE
GOLDFINCH
GOOSANDER
GOOSE
GOSHAWK
GRACKLE
GRASSFINCH
GREAT TIT
GREBE
GREENFINCH
GREENSHANK
GREYLAG GOOSE
GRIFFON VULTURE
GROSBEAK
GROUSE
GUILLEMOT
GULL
GYRFALCON
HAMMERHEAD
HARLEQUIN DUCK
HARPY EAGLE
HARRIER
HAWAIIAN GOOSE
HAWFINCH
HAWK
HAWK-OWL
HEDGE SPARROW
HEN
HERON
HERRING GULL
HOATZIN
HOBBY
HONEYCREEPER
HONEYEATER
HONEYGUIDE
HOODED CROW
HOOPOE
HOOT OWL
HORNBILL
HORNED OWL
HOUSE MARTIN
HOUSE SPARROW
HUIA
HUMMINGBIRD
IBIS
JABIRU
JACAMAR
JACANA
JACKDAW
JAY
JUNCO
KAGU
KAKAPO
KEA
KESTREL
KILLDEER

KINGBIRD
KINGFISHER
KINGLET
KITE
KITTIWAKE
KIWI
KNOT
KOOKABURRA
LAMMERGEIER
LANNER
LAPWING
LARK
LAUGHING
  JACKASS
LAUGHING OWL
LILY-TROTTER
LINNET
LITTLE OWL
LONG-TAILED TIT
LORIKEET
LORY
LOVEBIRD
LYRE-BIRD
MACAW
MAGPIE
MALLARD
MALLEE BIRD
MANAKIN
MANDARIN DUCK
MARABOU STORK
MARSH HARRIER
MARTIN
MEADOWLARK
MEGAPODE
MERGANSER
MERLIN
MINIVET
MISTLE THRUSH
MOCKINGBIRD
MOORHEN
MOTHER CAREY'S
  CHICKEN
MOTMOT
MOURNING DOVE
MOUSEBIRD
MURRE
MUSCOVY DUCK
MUTE SWAN
MUTTONBIRD
MYNAH BIRD
NENE
NIGHTHAWK
NIGHT HERON
NIGHTINGALE
NIGHTJAR
NODDY
NOTORNIS
NUTCRACKER
NUTHATCH
OIL-BIRD

BIRDS continued

ORIOLE	REEDLING	SMEW	TURKEY VULTURE
ORTOLAN	REED WARBLER	SNAKE BIRD	TURNSTONE
OSPREY	RHEA	SNIPE	TURTLE-DOVE
OSTRICH	RHINOCEROS BIRD	SNOW BUNTING	TWITE
OUZEL	RICE-BIRD	SNOW GOOSE	TYRANT
OVENBIRD	RIFLE BIRD	SNOWY OWL	FLYCATCHER
OWL	RING-DOVE	SONG THRUSH	UMBRELLA BIRD
OWLET-	RING-NECKED	SPARROW	VULTURE
FROGMOUTH	PHEASANT	SPARROWHAWK	WAGTAIL
OXPECKER	RING OUZEL	SPOONBILL	WALLCREEPER
OYSTERCATCHER	ROADRUNNER	STARLING	WARBLER
PARAKEET	ROBIN	STILT	WATTLEBIRD
PARROT	ROCK-DOVE	STONECHAT	WAXBILL
PARTRIDGE	ROLLER	STONE CURLEW	WAXWING
PEACOCK	ROOK	STORK	WEAVER-BIRD
PEAFOWL	ROSELLA	STORM PETREL	WEAVER FINCH
PEEWEE	RUDDY DUCK	SUNBIRD	WHEATEAR
PEEWIT	RUFF	SUN BITTERN	WHIMBREL
PELICAN	SACRED IBIS	SWALLOW	WHINCHAT
PENGUIN	SADDLEBACK	SWAN	WHIPBIRD
PEREGRINE FALCON	SANDERLING	SWIFTLET	WHIPPOORWILL
PETREL	SAND MARTIN	TAILOR-BIRD	WHISTLER
PHALAROPE	SANDPIPER	TAKAHE	WHITE-EYE
PHEASANT	SAPSUCKER	TANAGER	WHITETHROAT
PHOEBE	SCAUP	TAWNY OWL	WHOOPING
PIGEON	SCOPS OWL	TEAL	CRANE
PIGEON-HAWK	SCREAMER	TERN	WHYDAH
PINTAIL	SCREECH OWL	THICKHEAD	WIGEON
PIPIT	SCRUB TURKEY	THORNBILL	WILLET
PLAINS-WANDERER	SEAGULL	THRASHER	WILLOW WARBLER
PLOVER	SECRETARY BIRD	THRUSH	WOODCHAT
POCHARD	SERIEMA	TINAMOU	WOODCOCK
PTARMIGAN	SERIN	TITLARK	WOODCREEPER
PUFFIN	SHAG	TITMOUSE	WOOD-DUCK
QUETZAL	SHEARWATER	TOUCAN	WOODPECKER
RAIL	SHEATHBILL	TOWHEE	WOOD PIGEON
RAVEN	SHELDUCK	TRAGOPAN	WREN
RAZORBILL	SHOEBILL	TREECREEPER	WREN-BABBLER
REDHEAD	SHOVELER DUCK	TROGON	WRYBILL
REDPOLL	SHRIKE	TROPIC BIRD	WRYNECK
REDSHANK	SISKIN	TRUMPETER	YELLOWHAMMER
REDSTART	SKIMMER	TUI	YELLOWLEGS
REDWING	SKUA	TURACO	ZEBRA FINCH
REED-BIRD	SKYLARK	TURKEY	

cock-a-doodle-doo, coo, croak, cuckoo, gobble, hiss, hoot, note, quack, screech, squawk, squeak, trill, tu-whit tu-whoo, tweet-tweet, twitter, warble, whoop

birth control coil, coitus interruptus, condom, contraception, contraceptive, diaphragm, Dutch cap, family planning, femidom, johnny, loop, prophylactic, rhythm method, rubber, sheath, spermicide, the pill

bit of
may indicate a hidden word

bitterness acerbity, acidity, acrimony, asperity, beastliness, bile, bitchiness, cattiness, causticity, gall, grudge, mordacity, rancour, resentment, sharpness, snideness, sourness, spite, spleen, tartness, vengefulness, venom, vindictiveness, virulence, vitriol, waspishness

black blackish, blue-black, brown-black, coal-black, ebon, ebony, fuligi-

nous, grey-black, inky, jet, nigrescent, pitch-black, raven, sable, sloe-black, sooty
See also list at **colours**.

blacken black, blackball, blacklead, blacklist, blot, boycott, burn, char, darken, deepen, dirty, ink in, japan, niello, singe, smirch, smudge, sully, suntan, tan

black-hearted blackguardly, evil, heinous, nefarious, villainous, wicked

blackness blackening, chequer, chiaroscuro, colour, darkness, depth, duskiness, inkiness, melanism, Negroism, night, nigrescence, obscuration, pigmentation, swarthiness

blame accusation, accuse, admonishment, black mark, carpeting, castigation, censure, charge, chastisement, chiding, complaint, condemnation, denounce, denunciation, dressing-down, earful, home truths, impeachment, incriminate, lecture, lesson, rebuke, recrimination, reprehension, reprimand, reproach, reprobation, reproof, rocket, scolding, stricture, talking-to, telling-off, ticking-off, upbraiding, warning, wigging

blameworthy criminal, culpable, guilty, impeachable, objectionable, reprehensible, responsible

blank absent-minded, amnesic, clean, empty-headed, forgetful, Lethean, nirvanic, vacant, vacuous, white

blarney bunkum, charm, flannel, honeyed words, oil, salve, smarm, soft-soap, sugar, sweet-talk

blatant brazen, crude, extravagant, flagrant, lurid, obtrusive, sensational, shameless, vulgar

bleach blanch, blench, dye, fade, lighten, overexpose, pale, peroxide, whiten

blemish crack, deface, deform, disfigure, distort, flaw, impair, mar, misshape, mutilate, pimple, pustulate, scar, smear, smudge, soil, spoil, spot, stain

blemished cracked, damaged, defaced, defective, deformed, disfigured, flawed, imperfect, masked, polluted, shop-soiled, soiled, spoiled

blend infiltrate, integrate, mix, penetrate, permeate, pervade, stain
may indicate an anagram

blighting baneful, cursed, decaying, evil, harmful, malevolent, mildewed, mouldy, noisome, noxious, pestilent, poisonous, rotting, toxic, venomous, virulent

blind amaurotic, blindfold, blinker, blur, camouflage, darken, dazzle, deceive, eclipse, eyeless, glaucomatous, hoodwink, mask, obscure, screen, sightless, stone-blind, unseeing, visionless

blinkered benighted, blind, ignorant, imperceptive, inconsiderate, oblivious, thoughtless, unaware, unconcerned, unconscious, undiscerning, unenlightened, unmindful, unobservant

block bar, blockade, bottleneck, chunk, dam, deadlock, delay, deter, embargo, fence, filibuster, impede, inconvenience, intervene, lock out, lump, malfunction, picket, protract, sab, sabotage, snag, stall, strike, trip, wall

blood ancestry, antibody, antigen, bank, bloodstream, cell, circulation, claret, clot, count, dextran, erythrocyte, globulin, gore, group, haemoglobin, ichor, kin, leucocyte, lifeblood, lymphocyte, neutrophil, opsonin, phagocyte, plasma, platelet, pressure, race, Rhesus factor, serum, synthetic plasma, thrombosis, transfusion

bloody bleeding, bloodshot, blood-stained, gory, haemal, haemic, haemogenic, haemophilic, incarnadine, sanguineous

bloomer blossom, gaffe, knickers, loaf of bread, mistake, underwear
may indicate a flower

blow bang, bash, belt, biff, blast, bonk, brunt, brush, buffet, butt, chuck, clop, clout, clump, cuff, cut, dab, dash, dent, dig, dint, drub, exhale, fan, fillip, flick, flip, gust, heave, hit, huff, hustle, jab, jog, jolt, jostle, kick, knock, nudge, pat, peck, pelt, plunk, poke, pound, press, prod, puff, punch, punt, push, rap, shove, slam, slap, slog, slug, smack, spank, stamp, stomp, stress, strike, stroke, swat, swing, swipe, tap, thrust, thump, thwack, tip, touch, whisk, whop

bludgeon baseball bat, battering ram, bicycle chain, blunt weapon, club, cosh, cudgel, knuckle-duster, mace, sandbag, staff, truncheon, warhammer
See also list at **weapon**.

blue air-force, aquamarine, azure, Cambridge, cerulean, cobalt blue, cyan, duck-egg, eggshell, electric, French navy, green-blue, grey-blue, hyacinthine, indigo, kingfisher, midnight, navy, obscene, Oxford, pale, peacock, perse, powder, royal, sad, sapphire, saxe, sky, slate, turquoise, ultramarine, Wedgwood
See also list at **colours**.

bluish black-and-blue, bruised, caesious, cyanotic, freezing, livid

blunder balls-up, bloomer, boner, boob, boo-boo, botch-up, bungle, clanger, cock-up, faux pas, foul-up, gaffe, howler, louse-up, screw-up, stumble
may indicate an anagram

blunt bated, blunted, blunt-nosed, candid, curving, dull, edgeless, faired, flatten, frank, obtund, obvious, outspoken, plain, round, smooth, snub, square, stubby, turn, unpointed, unsharp, unwhetted, worn

blushing awkward, colouring, crimsoning, flushed, nervous, reddening, ruddy, shamefaced, sheepish

boast bombast, brag, flatter, huckster, hype, inflate, overpraise, overrate, oversell, rant, rave, self-glorify

boastful affected, arrogant, big-headed, blatant, bumptious, cocky, dogmatic, elated, exhibitionistic, inflated, know-it-all, opinionated, ostentatious, peacockish, pompous, pretentious, proud, puffed up, self-glorifying, self-opinionated, smart-alecky, smart-arsed, strutting, stuck-up, swaggering, swanky, ungracious

boat HMS, ship, vessel
See also list at **vessel**.

boatman bargee, canoeist, ferryman, galley slave, gondolier, oarsman, paddler, punter, rower, sculler, waterman, yachtsman

bogginness dewiness, marshiness, muddiness, swampiness

boldness arrogance, audacity, bottle, brassiness, bravery, brazenness, cheek, effrontery, front, nerve, sauce

bomb atom bomb, blitz, blockbuster, booby trap, carbomb, cluster bomb, depth charge, doodlebug, firebomb, fragmentation bomb, Greek Fire, grenade, hydrogen bomb, letter bomb, megaton bomb, mine, Molotov cocktail, nailbomb, napalm bomb, neutron bomb, nuclear bomb, nuke, pineapple, plaster, prang, shell, time bomb, tin fish, torpedo, V-1, V-2
See also list at **weapon**.

bombast boasting, bragging, flattery, grandiloquence, huckstering, hype, inflatedness, magniloquence, overpraise, overrating, pomposity, purple prose, ranting, raving, self-glorification

bombastic boasting, bragging, fustian, grandiloquent, hyping, inflating, magniloquent, pompous, raving, self-glorifying

bond authority, charter, contract, copyright, covenant, franchise, grant, guarantee, join, licence, link, patent, permit, qualification, security, title deed, unite, warranty

border abut, adjoin, bind, confine, edge, rim, skirt, verge

bore cloy, drill, drone on, dull, glut,

harp on, jade, nuisance, pall, ream, repeat, sate, satiate, tire, tunnel

bored disinterested, dissatisfied, dreary, drowsy, fatigued, fed-up, jaded, sated, satiated, sullen, tired, weary, world-weary

boredom aridity, banality, commonplaceness, devil's tattoo, dislike, dissatisfaction, drawing out, dreariness, dryness, dullness, ennui, fatigue, flatness, heaviness, humdrum, inactivity, indifference, insipidity, irksomeness, languor, longueur, long-windedness, melancholy, monotony, plainness, ponderousness, prolixity, prosaicness, prosiness, repetition, sameness, satiety, slowness, staleness, stodginess, stuffiness, sullenness, tastelessness, tedium, thumb-twiddling, tiresomeness, triteness, uniformity, weariness, Weltschmerz, world-weariness

boring arid, banal, blah, cloying, commonplace, deadly, disliked, drab, dragging, draggy, drawn out, dreary, dreich, drilling, dry, dry-as-dust, dull, flat, heavy, humdrum, humourless, inactive, indifferent, insipid, invariable, irksome, languorous, long-winded, monotonous, pedestrian, plain, prolix, prosaic, prosy, repeated, repetitious, satiating, sleep-inducing, slow, soporific, stale, stodgy, suburban, tasteless, tedious, thumb-twiddling, time-killing, tiresome, tiring, too much, unenjoyable, unfunny, uniform, uninteresting, unreadable, unvarying, wearing, wearisome, world-weary

born begotten, by, dammed, dropped, fathered, foaled, hatched, laid, littered, mothered, née, newborn, produced, sired, spawned

borrowed adopted, appropriated, copied, credit-card, ersatz, fake, imitated, infringed, instalment, loaned, money-raising, mortgaged, outstanding, pawned, pirated, plagiarized, plastic, repayable, secured, stolen

borrowing advance, begging, financing, fund-raising, loan application, money-raising, mortgaging, pawning, pledging, popping

botched
may indicate an anagram

bottle balthazar, bravery, calabash, carafe, courage, decanter, demijohn, flagon, flask, gourd, hip flask, jeroboam, magnum, methuselah, phial, rehoboam, thermos, vial, wineskin

bought bribable, bribed, charged, emptional, purchased, ransomed, redeemed

bound battened, bolted, chained, clamped, clasped, fettered, gripped, handcuffed, harnessed, lassoed, latched, leap, leashed, locked, manacled, obliged, padlocked, secured, shackled, tethered, tied, yoked

boundary border, curtain, fence, frontier, ha-ha, hedge, limit, screen, wall

bounty baksheesh, douceur, generosity, gift, gratuity, pourboire, premium, reward, tip, trinkgeld

bout contest, fight, fit, match, paroxysm, round, seizure, spasm, spell

bow accept, beak, bend, bob, cower, cringe, crossbow, curtsy, do reverence, duck, genuflect, grovel, kiss hands, kneel, knot, kowtow, longbow, make obeisance, nod, pay respects, prostrate oneself, prow, revere, salaam, wallow, welter, yield

box boxfile, caddy, can, canister, carton, case, casket, chest, coffer, coffin, confine, container, crate, Esky, eucalyptus, file, locker, matchbox, moneybox, pack, prizefight, punch, punnet, safe, sarcophagus, tea chest, tin, tinderbox

boyfriend Adonis, beau, beefcake, boy, bridegroom, date, dish, escort, fiancé, hunk, lover, lover boy, partner, sweetheart, toyboy

bra female supporter, undergarment, underwear

brag boast, swagger, swank, swell, talk big

braid arabesque, cat's cradle, crochet, espalier, filigree, fretwork, grid, knitting, knotting, lace, lattice, macramé, mesh, netting, network, pigtail, plait, skein, spider's web, tatting, tracery, trellis, twist, wattle, weave, webbing, wickerwork, wreath

brain cerebrum, grey matter, head, IQ, loaf, mind, noddle, nous

brain-teaser acrostic, anagram, brain-twister, charade, Chinese puzzle, cipher, code, coder, conundrum, crossword, cryptogram, decoder, hieroglyphics, labyrinth, maze, rebus, riddle, tangram
See also list at **game**.

branch fork, furcate, limb, offshoot, ramification, ramify, scion, shoot, spread-eagle, sprig, stem, step wide, straddle, sucker

bravado back-slapping, bluster, bonhomie, defiance, heroics, machismo, presumption

brave bold, dashing, gallant, heroic, intrepid, macho, valiant

bread banana-nut, beer, black, brown, chapat(t)i, cinnamon toast, crouton, crumb, crust, dough, food, French toast, fried, granary, malt, Melba toast, milk loaf, money, na(a)n, nut, pitta, poppadom, pumpernickel, puri, raisin, rusk, rye, sliced, soda, toast, white, wholemeal

breadth amplitude, bagginess, beam, bore, broadness, calibre, catholicity, diameter, dilation, expanse, extent, flare, fullness, gauge, handbreadth, latitude, openness, radius, range, roominess, scope, spaciousness, span, splay, wideness, width, wingspan

breakfast cereal bran, bran flakes, brewis, brose, cornflakes, gruel, muesli, oatmeal, polenta, porridge, skilly, wheat germ

breezy blowy, fresh, gusty, windy
See also list at **wind**.

brew
may indicate an anagram

bribe backhander, buy off, corrupt, grease, kickback, reward, slush fund, square, suborn, sweetener, tip, vail

bridal party attendant, best man, bride, bridegroom, bridesmaid, flower girl, groom, pageboy, usher

bridge aqueduct, cantilever, cards, catwalk, drawbridge, footbridge, link, overbridge, overcrossing, overpass, pontoon, span, steppingstones, suspension, viaduct

brief coach, concise, educate, inform, instruct, lawyer, short, teach, train

bright blazing, blinding, brilliant, clever, coruscating, dazzling, effulgent, fiery, flamboyant, flaming, flaring, flashy, fluorescent, garish, glaring, glinting, glittering, intelligent, kaleidoscopic, light, lurid, resplendent, scintillating, shining, sparking, sparkling, splendid, twinkling, vivid

brighten animate, cheer up, enliven, exhilarate, gladden, hearten, lighten, uplift

bring down bowl over, couch, deck, depress, floor, lay out, overthrow, overturn, scuttle, spreadeagle, subvert, topple, torpedo

British Brit, Briton, Englishman, John Bull, Limey, Pom

brittle breakable, bursting, chipping, crackable, crazy, crispy, crumbly, crushable, delicate, dilapidated, explosive, fissile, flaky, flimsy, fragile, frail, frangible, friable, gimcrack, inelastic, insubstantial, jerry-built, papery, powdery, rigid, scissile, shatterable, shoddy, short, splintery, splitting, tearable, tumbledown, unsteady, unsturdy, vulnerable, wafer-thin, weak

broad ample, baggy, beamy, broadcast, deep, expansive, extensive, flared, full, lake, open, patulous, river, roomy, splayed, spread-out, transverse, wide, widespread, woman

broadcast diffuse, disperse, disseminate, programme, sow, transmit

broaden expand, extend, spread, widen

broad-minded candid, direct, disinterested, explicit, frank, free, free-thinking, impartial, liberal, open, open-minded, unbiased, unbigoted, unprejudiced

brothel bagnio, bawdyhouse, bordello, honkytonk, massage parlour, red-light district, whorehouse

brought back
may indicate a backword

brown amber, auburn, bay, beige, biscuit, bronze, buff, burn, café-au-lait, char, chestnut, chocolate, coffee, copper, dun, ecru, embrown, fawn, ferruginous, foxy, fulvous, fuscous, grill, hazel, khaki, liver-coloured, mahogany, maroon, mocha, mushroom, nut-brown, oatmeal, peat-brown, puce, roan, rubiginous, russet, rust-coloured, singe, snuff-coloured, sorrel, sunburn, suntan, tan, tawny, toast, walnut
See also list at **colours**.

browned bronzed, brunette, charred, dark, grilled, singed, sunburnt, suntanned, tanned, toasted

bubble effervesce, ferment, fizz, fluff, foam, froth, gurgle, lather, simmer, sparkle, suds

bubbly aerated, effervescent, fizzy, foamy, frothy, yeasty

budgeting budget, budget estimates, cash budget
See also list at **economic**.

building material asphalt, breeze block, building block, cement, cobble, compo, composition, concrete, flagstone, gravel, hard core, macadam, marble, masonry, paving stone, shingle, slate, stone, Tarmac, thatch, tile

bullion gold bar, ingot, nugget

bumpy agitated, choppy, jolting, lumpy, tempestuous, turbulent, uneven

bunch bouquet, crowd, gang, group, huddle, nosegay, posy, spray

bundle bale, batch, bolt, bunch, clump, cluster, crop, hank, hassock, haystack, knot, package, parcel, quiver, roll, sheaf, skein, truss, tussock, wad

bungle botch, ruin, spoil

burden albatross, charge, debts, dependants, duty, encumbrance, handicap, imposition, inconvenience, last straw, overload, white elephant

burial catacomb, charnel house, cremation, crematorium, dead-house, embalming, entombment, funeral pile, grave, incineration, inhumation, interment, morgue, mortuary, mummification, mummy-case, pyre, sarcophagus, sepulture, tomb, vault

buried below ground, coffined, cremated, embalmed, entombed, hidden, inhumed, interred, mummified, urned

burn blaze, brand, burn up, calcine, carbonize, cauterize, char, crackle, cremate, fire, flame, flare, fume, ignite, incinerate, kindle, scorch, sear, set alight, singe, smoke, smoulder, torch, vaporize

burner barbecue, cooker, Dutch oven, gas ring, griddle, grill, haybox, hob, hotplate, kettle, kitchen range, microwave oven, oven, spit, stove, toaster

bury bemoan, coffin, cremate, embalm, encoffin, ensepulchre, entomb, eulogize, grieve, hide, incinerate, inhume, inter, keen, lament, lay out, mourn, mummify, plant, regret, urn

bus charabanc, coach, double decker, omnibus, single decker, trolleybus
See also list at **vehicle**.

busy active, astir, bustling, employed, engaged, eventful, hectic, humming, hustling, in harness, lively, occupied, overworked, pottering, slogging

butt Aunt Sally, barrel, dupe, easy mark, fair game, fall guy, fool, joke, laughing stock, monkey, mug, stooge, target, vat, victim

buying acquisitive, bargaining, bidding, bullish, cash-and-carry, cut-price, haggling, investing, marketing, pre-emptive, purchasing, redemptive, shopping, speculative, teleshopping

buy off bribe, corrupt, pay off, square, suborn

by beside, gone, near, past, via

by arrangement
may indicate an anagram

by the sound of it
may indicate a homophone

·C·

C	about • carbon • Celsius • centigrade • century • circa • clubs • note • one hundred
CA	calcium • current account
CAA	Civil Aviation Authority
CAB	Citizens' Advice Bureau
CAD	computer-aided design
CAL	calorie
CAMRA	Campaign for Real Ale
CAP	capital • Common Agricultural Policy
CB	citizens' band • columbium • Companion of the (Order of the) Bath
CBE	Commander of the Order of the British Empire
CBS	Columbia Broadcasting System
CC	carbon copy • County Council • cubic centimetre
CD	cadmium • compact disc
CE	cerium • church • let the buyer beware (Latin: *caveat emptor*)
CERT	certificate
CF	californium • carried forward • compare (Latin: *confer*)
CFI	cost, freight, and insurance
CGM	Conspicuous Gallantry Medal
CGT	capital-gains tax
CH	church • Companion of Honour
CHIPS	Clearing House Inter-Bank Payments System
CI	Chief Inspector
CIA	Central Intelligence Agency
CID	Criminal Investigation Department
CM	centimetre • curium
CMG	Companion of the Order of St Michael and St George
CO	care of • cobalt • Commanding Office • company • firm
COD	cash on delivery
CR	chromium • credit • king (Latin: *Carolus Rex*) • monarch • queen (Latin: *Carolina Regina*)
CRO	Criminal Records Office
CS	caesium
CU	Cambridge University • copper
CV	curriculum vitae • horsepower (French: *cheval-vapeur*)
CWT	hundredweight

cab hackney, hire car, minicab, taxi, taxicab
See also list *at* **vehicle**.

cabinet chest, council, cupboard, sideboard, unit, whatnot
See list *at* **furniture**.

cableway funicular, monorail, telpher, wireway

cacophony Babel, bedlam, caterwauling, cat's chorus, cat's concert, clamour, din, discord, dissonance, hubbub, hullabaloo, pandemonium, racket, row, tumult, turmoil, uproar, yowling

caesura diaeresis, ellipsis, fermata, hiatus, lacuna, pause, rest

cagebird budgerigar, canary, cockatoo, mynah bird, parakeet, parrot *See also list at* **birds**.

cajole blandish, coax, court, curry favour, inveigle, toady, wheedle

cajolery blandishments, ingratiation, inveiglement, wheedling

cake angel cake, apple fritter, apple pie, Bakewell tart, Bath bun, Battenburg, birthday cake, block, carrot cake, cheesecake, Chelsea bun, chocolate cake, chocolate gateau, Christmas cake, coat, coffee cake, cover, Danish pastry, doughnut, Dundee cake, Eccles cake, eclair, flan, fritter, fruitcake, fudge cake, gateau, gingerbread, jam tart, lardy cake, lump, macaroon, Madeira cake, madeleine, mince pie, parkin, seed cake, spice cake, sponge cake, Swiss roll, tart, torte, turnover, wedding cake, yule log

calculable computable, countable, estimable, measurable, mensurable, numerable, quantifiable, reckonable

calculate cipher, compute, count, determine, estimate, figure, reckon, score, solve, tally

calculation assessment, computation, determining, enumeration, estimation, figuring, numeration, reckoning

calculative computative, enumerative, estimative, numerative, numerical, quantifying

calculator abacist, computer, counter, enumerator, estimator, pollster, reckoner, teller

calculus differentiation, integration

callous austere, cold, dour, flinty, grim, gruff, hard, harsh, heartless, obdurate, rough, rugged, severe, steely, stern, stony, tough, unfeeling, unnatural

callousness coldness, grimness, hardheartedness, hardness, harshness, heartlessness, obduracy, roughness, ruthlessness, severity, sternness, unfeelingness, unnaturalness

calm composed, pacify, quieten, soothe, still, Stoic, tranquil

calmness composure, sangfroid, Stoicism

camera automatic camera, box Brownie, camcorder, camera obscura, cine camera, compact camera, disc camera, gamma camera, large-format camera, photo booth, pinhole camera, plate camera, security camera, TV camera, twin-lens reflex, videocamera

camouflage cosmetics, disguise, dissimulation, make-up, mimicry, simulation *may indicate an anagram*

campanology bell ringing, change ringing

can able, billy, capable, is able, may, pot, tin, vessel

cancelled annulled, deleted, erased, off, removed, scrapped

candid chatty, communicative, divulging, downright, forthcoming, frank, imprudent, indiscreet, informative, maieutic, open, outspoken, revealing, unreserved

canon bibliography, charter, code, constitution, rulebook

capital *may indicate the first letter of a word*

capless *may indicate a shortening (delete first letter)*

caprice arbitrariness, capriciousness, changeableness, crankiness, eccentricity, faddishness, fecklessness, fickleness, fitfulness, flightiness, fretfulness, frivolousness, giddiness, impulse, inconsistency, inconstancy, instability, irresponsibility, levity, mischief, motivelessness, pettishness, playfulness, purposelessness, uncertainty, unpredictability, unreliability, variability, waywardness, whim, whimsicality

capricious arbitrary, captious, changeable, crazy, erratic, faddy, fanciful, feckless, fickle, fitful, flighty, fluctuating, frivolous, giddy, idiosyncratic, inconsistent, inconstant, irresponsible, mercurial, mischievous, motiveless, particular, prankish, random, refractory, skittish, temperamental, uncertain, unexpected, unpredictable, unreasonable, unreliable, unstable, variable, volatile, wanton, wavering, wayward, whimsical, wilful
may indicate an anagram

capriciousness changeableness, fickleness, fitfulness, fluctuation, fluidity, inconstancy, mutability, randomness, variability, volatility, wavering, whimsicality

capsize careen, heel over, keel over, list, overturn, turn turtle
may indicate a backword

caption cameo, exposé, heading, indication, legend, outline, subtitle, summary, thumbnail sketch, vignette, word portrait

car auto, automobile, banger, buggy, carriage, convertible, couchette, coupé, dining car, estate, freight car, gondola, guard's van, hatchback, hoppercar, jalopy, limousine, low-loader, luggage van, mailcoach, motor, motorcar, Pullman, railcar, rattletrap, runabout, saloon, sleeper, sports car, tank wagon, vehicle, wheels
See also lists at **registration**; **vehicle**.

caravan camper, campervan, convoy, houseboat, mobile home, pavilion, tent, tepee, trailer, wigwam

carefree easygoing, happy-go-lucky, unworried

careful alert, anticipatory, assiduous, attentive, cagey, canny, chary, circumspect, conservative, diligent, discreet, doubtful, exact, faddy, fastidious, gingerly, guarding, heedful, judicious, meticulous, mindful, neat, observant, orderly, painstaking, particular, pedantic, perfectionist, pernickety, politic, precise, prepared, provident, prudent, ready, reticent, scrupulous, suspicious, tentative, thorough, tidy, unadventurous, vigilant, wary, watchful

careless devil-may care, disregarding, dizzy, flighty, heedless, hit-or-miss, inattentive, lax, neglectful, negligent, precipitous, rash, reckless, remiss, slack, slapdash, slipshod, sloppy
may indicate an anagram

carelessness disregard, heedlessness, inattention, inexactitude, laxity, looseness, negligence, rashness, recklessness, slackness

cargo baggage, consignment, container, contents, freight, goods, load, luggage, mail, pallet, payload, shipment

caricature cartoon, lampoon, misrepresent, satirize

carnality concupiscence, eroticism, fleshliness, lecherousness, libido, lickerishness, lust, sexiness

carnivorousness anthropophagy, cannibalism, creophagy, flesh-eating, ichthyophagy, insectivorousness, meateating, omophagy

carp bug, cavil, crab, derogate, hassle, henpeck, nag, niggle, nit-pick, pester, pick holes, quibble, split hairs
See also list at **fish**.

carpenter cabinet-maker, chippie, coachbuilder, cooper, joiner, sawyer, turner, wheelwright, woodcarver
See also list at **occupation**.

cart carry, dolly, handbarrow, handcart, lug, pushcar, pushcart, trolley, wheelbarrow

cash boodle, brass, bread, change, coin, coinage, coppers, dib, dosh, dough, filthy lucre, gelt, gold, gravy, lolly, loot, mammon, moolah, pelf, poppy, readies, rhino, shekels, silver, spondulix, sugar, swag

cast characters, chorus, company, ensemble, hurl, outfit, throw, troupe

castrate emasculate, fix, geld, neuter, spay, sterilize

cat gib, grimalkin, kit, kitten, mog, mouser, puss, queen, ratter, tom

catalogue compendium, digest, directory, file, gazetteer, index, inventory, list, listing, log, record, register

catcall boo, deride, derision, disapprove, disparage, hoot, jeer, raspberry, scorn, whistle

catchword adage, catchphrase, cliché, jingo, maxim, moral, motto, proverb, quotation, quote, saw, slogan

categorical classificatory, hierarchical, positive, taxonomic, unconditional

categorization alphabetization, analysis, cataloguing, classification, codification, compartmentalization, filing, grading, graduation, grouping, hierarchy, indexing, listing, pigeonholing, placement, ranking, rating, seeding, sorting, stratification, tabulation, taxonomy

categorize alphabetize, analyse, catalogue, classify, codify, compartmentalize, file, grade, group, index, inventory, list, pigeonhole, place, process, program, rank, rate, record, register, screen, seed, select, sieve, sift, sort, tabulate

category class, compartment, department, division, family, grade, group, heading, level, niche, order, pigeonhole, place, position, rank, section, set, slot, status, subcategory

caterer alewife, chef, confectioner, cook, host, hotelier, housekeeper, innkeeper, landlord, licensee, maître d'hôtel, pastrycook, publican, purveyor, restaurateur

causal agential, answerable, blameworthy, causative, central, compelling, crucial, decisive, determinant, effectual, embryonic, etiological, explanatory, formative, generative, genetic, germinal, impelling, inceptive, influential, initiatory, inspiring, instrumental, pivotal, productive, responsible, seminal, significant, suggestive

cause attribution, authorship, beget, causation, compulsion, create, cultivation, derivation, determinant, encouragement, etiology, evocation, father, fomentation, force, generation, impulsion, initiation, inspiration, instigation, invent, invention, make, motivation, occasion, originate, origination, produce, propagation, provocation, spark, stimulation, temptation

caused consequent upon, contingent upon, effected, ensuing, sequential, subject to, subsequent

causeless groundless, inadvertant, inexplicable, unaccountable, undesigned, unintended, unintentional, unmeant, unmotivated, unplanned, unpremeditated

caution advise, alertness, carefulness, cautiousness, chariness, circumspection, consideration, deliberation, discretion, foresight, forewarn, guardedness, heedfulness, judiciousness, protection, providence, prudence, reticence, scepticism, tentativeness, vigilance, wariness, warn, watchfulness, wisdom

cavity alcove, basin, bowl, cranny, cup, dent, dimple, honeycomb, niche, nook, pockmark, recess, socket, sump, trough

cease abort, abrogate, annul, brake, cancel, conclude, desist, die, discontinue, end, finish, fold, halt, jam, polish off, quit, relinquish, scotch, scrap, scratch, stall, stick, stop, terminate

celebrate adore, exalt, extol, felicitate, fête, give thanks, glorify, honour, junket, laud, maffick, magnify, merrymake, minister, officiate, party, praise, propitiate, rejoice, revel, revere, venerate

celebration banquet, beanfeast, beano, bender, binge, blow-out, carnival, carousal, do, feast, festival, festivities, fête, fiesta, function, gala, high jinks, holiday, jamboree, jubilation, jubilee, observance, occasion, party, performance, picnic, rage, rave, revel, saturnalia

celebrative celebratory, convivial, dithyrambic, festive, gay, jolly, merry, rejoicing

celibacy bachelorhood, independence, misogamy, spinsterhood

celibate bachelorly, fancy-free, mateless, misogamic, old-maidish, single, sole, spinsterly, spouseless, unattached, unmarried, unpartnered

cemetery boneyard, burial ground, catacomb, churchyard, cinerarium, columbarium, God's acre, Golgotha, graveyard, necropolis, plot

censor black out, blue-pencil, cancel, delete, kill, prohibit, proscribe, repress, restrain, restrict, stifle, stop, suppress

censored banned, blue-pencilled, classified, deleted, proscriptive, restricted, top-secret, unmentionable, unprintable, unsayable

censorship bowdlerization, deletion, expurgation, proscription

censure admonish, carpet, castigate, chastise, chide, lecture, rebuke, reprehend, reprimand, reproach, reprove, scold, upbraid, warn

censured abused, admonished, assailed, attacked, berated, castigated, chastised, lambasted, rebuked, reprimanded, reproached, scolded, upbraided

censuring admonitory, castigatory, chastising, chiding, rebuking, reprimanding, reproaching, scolding, upbraiding

centennial bicentennial, tricentennial

centre amid, balance, core, focus, interpolate, interpose, middle, pivot, sandwich
may indicate the middle *letters of a word*

ceramics agateware, basaltware, biscuit ware, bone china, china, chinaware, clayware, crackle, crockery, crouch ware porcelain, earthenware, enamelware, encoustic, faience, glazed ware, ironstone, lustreware, ovenware, pottery, redware, sgraffito, slipware, spongeware, stanniferous ware, stoneware, terracotta, tin-enamelled ware, whiteware

cereal barleycorn, bran, chaff, corncob, durum, emmer, grain, grass, husk, oats, rye, straw, stubble, wheat

ceremonial custom, customary, formal, formality, procession, ritual, sacramental, solemn, triumphal

ceremonious courtly, formal, liturgic, polite, pompous, stately

ceremony barmitzvah, celebration, Christening, convocation, coronation, drill, fête, field day, formalism, function, funeral, gala, graduation, inauguration, initiation, liturgy, march past, mummery, observance, office, ovation, pageant, parade, practice, procedure, red-letter day, review, rite, ritual, ritualism, routine, scene, service, show, spectacle, tableau, tattoo, tournament, triumph, turnout, wedding

certain absolute, actual, ascertained, certified, definite, demonstrable, demonstrated, documented, established, factual, given, historical, known, necessary, obvious, ostensible, proved, real, safe, secure, self-evident, sure, true, unmistakeable, veracious, verifiable

certainty absoluteness, actuality, authoritativeness, confidence, definiteness, evidence, factuality, historicity, indisputability, indubitability, knowledge, necessity, obviousness, proof, reality, surety, truth, validity, veracity, verity

certificate affidavit, authorization, charter, credential, daybook, deed, deposition, diploma, document, ID, muniments, passport, testimonial, ticket, title, warranty

certify authenticate, cover, insure, pledge, promise, verify

cessation abandonment, abrogation, annulment, breakoff, cancellation, ceasing, closing, death, desistance, discontinuance, end, expiry, finish, halt, relinquishment, stop, stopping, termination, withdrawal

chair armchair, bench, preside, professorship, recliner, settle, sofa, stall, stool
See list at **furniture**.

challenge backchat, contumely, dare, demonstration, dispute, dissent, insult, question, risk, strain, struggle, taunt, tax, test, threat, venture

chance accident, casualness, coincidence, contingency, destiny, fate, fortuitousness, fortune, gamble, hazard, indeterminacy, inexplicability, jeopardy, lot, luck, odds, randomness, risk, toss-up, unaccountability, uncertainty, unpredictability

change adaptation, adjustment, adulteration, alteration, amelioration, amendment, betterment, break, coup, degeneration, deterioration, detour, deviation, difference, dilution, distortion, diversification, diversion, diversity, emendation, eversion, fluctuate, improvement, inconsistency, innovation, interpretation, invention, inversion, modernization, modification, modulation, move, mutability, mutate, mutation, qualification, rearrangement, redecoration, reformation, relocation, remodeling, remoulding, renewal, reordering, reorganization, repairing, reshaping, restoration, restructuring, restyling, reversal, revision, revival, revolt, revolution, shift, transcription, transference, transition, translation, turn, variation, variegation, vary, vicissitude

changeable alterable, alternating, ameliorative, better, capricious, desultory, deviatory, different, diverse, ephemeral, ever-changing, fickle, fitful, flickering, flip-flop, fluctuating, fluid, imbalanced, impermanent, inconsistent, inconstant, indecisive, innovative, inventive, irregular, kaleidoscopic, mobile, mutable, oscillating, perverse, plastic, pliant, precarious, protean, reformative, reverse, revolutionary, shifting, shifty, spasmodic, subversive, tidal, transient, transitional, transitory, turning, uncertain, unpredictable, unreliable, unsettled, unstable, unsteady, vacillating, variable, varied, variegated, versatile, vibrating, wavering, whimsical
may indicate an anagram

changeableness alternation, disequilibrium, flexibility, fluctuation, fluidity, flux, imbalance, impermanence, inconsistency, inconstancy, instability, irregularity, metamorphosis, mobility, mutability, oscillation, plasticity, pliancy, softness, suppleness, transience, turning, uncertainty, unpredictability, unreliability, unsteadiness, variability, variety, veering, versatility, vicissitude

changed altered, amended, degenerated, deteriorated, diversified, emended, improved, modernized, modified, qualified, rearranged, redecorated, remodeled, renewed, reordered, reorganized, repaired, reshaped, restored, restructured, restyled, revised, revived, varied
may indicate an anagram

changeless immutable, imperishable, incorruptible, indestructible, permanent

channel aisle, alley, canal, conduit, culvert, delta, dike, direct, ditch, estuary, exit, focus, fountainhead, gulf, headstream, inlet, lane, lock, outlet,

river, riverhead, sewer, sound, strait, stream, watercourse, waterway
may indicate an anagram

characteristic defining, distinctive, distinguishing, idiosyncratic, particular, peculiar, specific, typical

characterize delineate, demarcate, depict, designate, differentiate, distinguish, identify, inform, mark, portray, represent, stamp

characterless automatic, bland, blank, faceless, featureless, normal, orderly, plain

charge accuse, attack, care, cost, electrify, exact, explosive, ion, levy, price, rush at, tax, tithe

charisma allurement, attraction, charm, fascination, it, lure, magnetism, sex appeal, winning ways

charitable altruistic, beneficent, bountiful, generous, hospitable, liberal, magnanimous, philanthropic, unselfish

charity aid, alms, altruism, benefaction, bountifulness, donation, fund, generosity, gift, good works, hand-out, hospitality, liberality, magnanimity, patronage, philanthropy, relief, unselfishness

charmer Casanova, Don Juan, enchanter, enchantress, hunk, ladies' man, man-eater, matinée idol, seducer, seductress, sex symbol, siren, stud, temptress, vamp

chart diagram, flow chart, graph, plan, programme, schedule, schema, scheme, spreadsheet, table, Venn diagram

chastity abstinence, celibacy, continence, Encratism, maidenhood, virginity

chat babble, blab, blabber, blah, causerie, chatter, chinwag, chit-chat, confab, confabulation, conflab, crack, gab, gabble, gas, gibber, gossip, heart-to-heart, jabber, jaw, natter, prate, prattle, ramble on, rattle on, small talk, tête-à-tête, waffle, witter

cheap affordable, bargain, bargain-basement, base, bearish, brummagem, budget, catchpenny, cheapo, cut-price, depreciated, devalued, dime-store, dirt-cheap, discount, down-market, economy-size, five-and-ten, giveaway, good-value, inexpensive, knockdown, manageable, markdown, mean, moderate, modest, nominal, off-peak, reasonable, reduced, sale-price, sensible, slashed, stingy, twopenny-halfpenny, uncostly, unexpensive, vulgar

cheapen cut, degrade, devalue, discount, mark down, sacrifice, slash, trim, undercut, undersell

cheapness affordability, inexpensiveness, reasonableness, tackiness, tawdriness

cheat bilker, cardsharp, charlatan, con(fidence) man, counterfeiter, cowboy, cozener, crook, deceive, defrauder, diddler, double cross, fake, fraud, gyp, horsetrader, humbug, hypocrite, impersonator, imposter, land-grabber, mealy-mouth, mountebank, pettifogger, phoney, poser, pretender, quack, rip off, sham, shark, short-changer, shyster, swindler, trickster, two-timer, whited sepulchre

check audit, constrain, stop, study, test, verify

cheek answer back, backchat, brass, brazenness, chutzpah, crust, face, gall, lip, mouth, nerve, provoke, retort, sass, shout down

cheeky brassy, brazen, crusty, gally, mouthy, nervy, sassy, saucy, smart-alecky, smart-arsed

cheer applaud, clap, encourage, happiness, hooray, hurrah, shout, spur on, whoop, yell

cheerful beaming, bouncy, buoyant, carefree, cheery, chirpy, convivial, exhilarated, funny, gay, genial, glad, good-humoured, grinning, happy, high, high-spirited, jolly, jovial, joyful, laughing, light-hearted, lively, merry, optimistic, radiant, smiling, sociable, sparkling, sunny, up, vivacious

cheerfulness animation, cheeriness, conviviality, exhilaration, gaiety, geniality, happiness, high spirits, jauntiness, jollity, joviality, joy, laughter, levity, light-heartedness, liveliness, merriment, mirth, optimism, sociability, sunniness, vivacity

cheering auspicious, bright, encouraging, favourable, golden, heartening, heart-warming, promising, propitious, reassuring, reviving, rose-coloured, rose-tinted, rosy, rousing, sunny, uplifting

cheers! bottoms up!, chug-a-lug!, cin cin!, here's health!, prosit!, skol!, slainte!, thanks!, to us!

chemical alchemical, analytic, astrochemical, biochemical, catalytic, crystallographic, inorganic, metallurgical, medicinal, organic, photochemical, physiochemical, radiochemical, synthetic, zymurgic
See list of chemical elements.

chess bishop, board, castle, castling, check, checkmate, chessman, end game, fork, king, knight, mate, opening, pawn, piece, pin, queen, rook, square
See also list at **game.**

chew bite, browse, chomp, crop, gnaw, graze, manducate, masticate, munch, nibble, pasture, peck, rend, ruminate, tear

chewing biting, champing, chomping, gnashing, manduction, mastication, munching

chic black-tie, clothes-conscious, dapper, dolled up, fashionable, glitzy, groomed, modish, natty, ritzy, smart, soignée, spiffed up, spruce, spruced up, stylish, tricked out, well-dressed, white-tie

---

THE CHEMICAL ELEMENTS

NAME	SYMBOL	NAME	SYMBOL	NAME	SYMBOL	NAME	SYMBOL
ACTINIUM	AC	ERBIUM	ER	MOLYBDENUM	MO	SELENIUM	SE
ALUMINIUM	AL	EUROPIUM	EU	NEODYMIUM	ND	SILICON	SI
AMERICIUM	AM	FERMIUM	FM	NEON	NE	SILVER	AG
ANTIMONY	SB	FLUORINE	F	NEPTUNIUM	NP	SODIUM	NA
ARGON	AR	FRANCIUM	FR	NICKEL	NI	STRONTIUM	SR
ARSENIC	AS	GADOLINIUM	GD	NIOBIUM	NB	SULPHUR	S
ASTATINE	AT	GALLIUM	GA	NITROGEN	N	TANTALUM	TA
BARIUM	BA	GERMANIUM	GE	NOBELIUM	NO	TECHNETIUM	TC
BERKELIUM	BK	GOLD	AU	OSMIUM	OS	TELLURIUM	TE
BERYLLIUM	BE	HAFNIUM	HF	OXYGEN	O	TERBIUM	TB
BISMUTH	BI	HELIUM	HE	PALLADIUM	PD	THALLIUM	TL
BORON	B	HOLMIUM	HO	PHOSPHORUS	P	THORIUM	TH
BROMINE	BR	HYDROGEN	H	PLATINUM	PT	THULIUM	TM
CADMIUM	CD	INDIUM	IN	PLUTONIUM	PU	TIN	SN
CAESIUM	CS	IODINE	I	POLONIUM	PO	TITANIUM	TI
CALCIUM	CA	IRIDIUM	IR	POTASSIUM	K	TUNGSTEN	W
CALIFORNIUM	CF	IRON	FE	PRASEODYMIUM	PR	URANIUM	U
CARBON	C	KRYPTON	KR	PROMETHIUM	PM	VANADIUM	V
CERIUM	CE	LANTHANUM	LA	PROTACTINIUM	PA	WOLFRAM	W
CHLORINE	CL	LAWRENCIUM	LR	RADIUM	RA	XENON	XE
CHROMIUM	CR	LEAD	PB	RADON	RN	YTTERBIUM	YB
COBALT	CO	LITHIUM	LI	RHENIUM	RE	YTTRIUM	Y
COLUMBIUM	CB	LUTETIUM	LU	RHODIUM	RH	ZINC	ZN
COPPER	CU	MAGNESIUM	MG	RUBIDIUM	RB	ZIRCONIUM	ZR
CURIUM	CM	MANGANESE	MN	RUTHENIUM	RU		
DYSPROSIUM	DY	MENDELEVIUM	MD	SAMARIUM	SM		
EINSTEINIUM	ES	MERCURY	HG	SCANDIUM	SC		

child ankle-biter, baby, bairn, brat, daughter, infant, issue, kid, kiddie, mite, nipper, offspring, rug-rat, son, sprog, toddler, tot, whippersnapper, youngster

childbirth accouchement, Caesarian, confinement, contractions, delivery, labour, travail

chill benumb, chilblain, cold, coryza, exposure, fan, freeze, frostbite, glaciate, hypothermia, pneumonia, refrigerate

chivalrous gallant, heroic, knightly

chivalry adventure, derring-do, gallantry, heroics, prowess

choice alternative, excellent, fine quality, inclination, option, predilection, preference, selection, sympathy, tendency

choose decide, favour, opt, prefer, select

chorus burden, canon, choir, refrain, round, sing

chosen advisable, assorted, better, designate, desirable, elect, elected, elite, fancy, favourite, hand-picked, pet, picked, preferable, preferred, recherché, seeded, selected, sorted, special

chronicle account, annals, archive, autobiography, biography, description, diary, documentary, dossier, file, folk tale, history, journal, legend, life story, log, memoirs, minutes, myth, narration, notes, recollection, record, report, track record, tradition

chronologize calendar, chronicle, date, diarize, record

chronometry clockmaking, horology, time-keeping, watchmaking
See also list at **clock**.

church abbey, aisle, altar, ambulatory, apse, basilica, blindstorey, cathedral, CE, CH, chancel, chapel, chevet, choir, clerestory, clergy, cloister, conch, confessional, crossing, crypt, denomination, dome, flèche, flying buttress, font, galilee porch, house of god, lectern, narthex, nave, pew, presbytery, pulpit, RC, religious movement, rood screen, sacristy, sanctuary, spirelet, stall, temple, transept, tribune gallery, triforium, vestibule, vestry, westwork
See also list at **religion**.

circle ambit, annulation, annulus, arc, circuit, circulate, circumambulate, circumference, circumnavigate, curve, cycle, encircle, epicycle, lap, loop, mandala, orb, orbit, oval, revolve, ring, rotate, roundabout, semicircle, sphere, surround, zodiac
See also list at **geometry**.

circuit ambit, beat, circle, circling, circulate, circumambulate, circumference, circummigrate, circumnavigate, circumvent, cycle, ellipse, gyre, lap, loop, orbit, oval, reeling, revolution, revolve, ring, round, roundabout, spinning, spiral, tour, turn, twirling, wheeling, whirling

circuitous ambagious, backhanded, circumlocutory, deviating, devious, diffuse, digressive, discursive, excursive, indirect, long-winded, meandering, oblique, periphrastic, roundabout

circuitousness ambages, circulation, circumbendibus, circumlocution, cornering, deviance, digression, excursion, meandering, roundaboutness, turning

circuitry accumulator, anode, battery, capacitor, cathode, cell, chip, choke, component, condenser, conductor, diode, earth, inductor, insulator, integrated circuit, resistor, rheostat, semiconductor, terminal, transistor, tube, valve, wires

circular annular, circulatory, circumambulatory, circumferential, circumfluent, circumnavigatory, coiled, curved, cyclic(al), discoid, egg-shaped, elliptic(al), gyratory, helical, looped, orbicular, orbital, oval, ovate, ovoid, rotary, rotund, rounded, semicircular, spherelike, spheric(al), spheroidal, spiral

circularity annularity, curvedness,

orbicularity, rotundity, roundness, sphericalness

circulate broadcast, distribute, entertain, host, interact, join in, mingle, mix, participate, revolve, spread
may indicate an anagram

circumlocution aimlessness, ambage, conundrum, departure, deviation, digression, discursion, double talk, equivocalness, equivoque, excursion, indirectness, irrelevance, periphrasis, pointlessness, rambling, sidetrack, wandering

circumlocutory aimless, ambagious, circuitous, excursive, indirect, oblique, periphrastic, rambling, roundabout, sidetracked, wandering

circumspection alertness, preparation, prudence, readiness, scrupulousness, vigilance, watchfulness

circumstances atmosphere, background, basis, case, climate, conditions, context, environment, footing, layout, means, milieu, outfit, picture, place, position, resources, scene, setting, setup, situation, standing, standpoint, state, status, surroundings

circumstantial atmospheric, background, based, climatic, conditional, contextual, contingent, environmental, grounded, incidental, indirect, inferential, placed, relative, situational, surrounding

circumstantiate adduce, anatomize, atomize, cite, detail, document, instance, itemize, particularize, specify, spell out, substantiate

city Athens, capital, Carthage, conurbation, EC, megalopolis, metropolis, municipality, Rome, town, Ur, urban spread

civil rights civil liberties, First Amendment, free speech, rights

clap applaud, bang, blast, boom, burst, clang, clash, clatter, crash, deafen, din, drill, explode, fulminate, hammer, rattle, resound, reverberate, slam, stamp, storm, thunder

clarify brighten, cleanse, crystallize, decipher, define, demist, demonstrate, disambiguate, elucidate, enlighten, explain, explicate, illuminate, interpret, open, purify, refine, uncloud

clarity accuracy, austerity, blatancy, brightness, brilliance, clearness, coherence, comprehensibility, definiteness, definition, directness, distinctness, exactness, explicitness, exposure, focus, intelligibility, limpidity, lucidity, obviousness, pellucidity, perspicuity, plainness, prominence, purity, sharpness, showiness, simplicity, starkness, straightforwardness, transparency, unambiguousness, vividness

class band, bracket, branch, caste, category, clique, compartment, coterie, department, division, grade, group, heading, league, level, list, niche, order, pigeonhole, pocket, section, set, slot, sphere, standing, station, status, stratum, subclass, tier

classification categorization, grading, grouping, hierarchy, ordering, ranking, taxonomy

classificatory categorical, hierarchical, indexical, tabular, taxonomic

classify assign, brand, catalogue, categorize, class, designate, dispose, distribute, fix, group, label, pigeonhole, place, type

clay adobe, argil, china clay, engobe, kaolin, marl, petuntse, potter's earth, slip

clean beat, blank, brush, carbolize, clear up, comb, decent, disinfect, dryclean, dust, freshen, groom, hoover, hygienic, iron, launder, mop, neaten, new, phenolate, polish, pure, scour, scrub, shave, shine, sponge, spotless, spruce, starch, swab, sweep, thorough, tidy, trim, vacuum, valet, wash, whisk, wipe

cleaned brushed, cleansed, decontaminated, disinfected, expurgated, filtered, freshened, laundered, pasteurized, polished, purged, purified, refined, scoured, scrubbed, sterilized, swept, washed

cleaning bleaching, dry cleaning, laundering, stain removal, washing

cleanness daintiness, fastidiousness, freshness, immaculateness, polish, purity, shine, spotlessness, whiteness

cleansing ablutionary, abstergent, antisepsis, aperient, balneal, clarification, cleaning, decontamination, defecation, delousing, desalination, detergent, disinfectant, disinfection, disinfestation, distillation, enema, filtration, freshening, hygienic, laxative, lustral, pasteurization, purgative, purgatory, purging, purification, purificatory, refining, sanitary, sterilization

clear acquit, authorize, certain, cloudless, distinct, limpid, lucid, obvious, pellucid, perspicuous, plain, pure, straightforward, transparent, unblemished, unblock, understandable, unobstructed

cleave adhere, breach, break, check, cling, crack, cut, ditch, fracture, furrow, gape, gash, groove, incise, nick, notch, open, rend, rive, rupture, slit, slot, split, tear, trench

cleverness acuity, alertness, aptitude, astuteness, braininess, brains, brightness, brilliance, canniness, erudition, flair, genius, incisiveness, knowledgeableness, quick-wittedness, sagacity, sapience, sharpness, shrewdness, slyness, subtlety, trickery, wisdom, wit

cliché assonance, buzzword, catchword, rhyme, slogan, truism

climate continental, macroclimate, maritime, microclimate, moderate, polar, subpolar, subtropical, temperate, tropical, tundra, weather system

climax close, culminate, end, finish, orgasm, peak, terminate

climb breast, clamber up, clear, escalade, hurdle, monkey up, mount, mountaineer, ramp, scale, scrabble up, scramble, shinny up, shin up, skylark, struggle up, surmount, top
may indicate a backword

cliquish clannish, closed, close-knit, exclusive, narrow, restrictive

clock horologe, strike, Tim, timekeeper, timepiece, timer, watch
See list of timepieces.

close bar, bolt, button, cease, collapse, conclude, confined, contain, cover, dense, discontinue, ending, fail, fasten, finish, foreclose, fulfill, imminent, intimate, latch, lock, near, padlock, resolve, road, seal, secretive, secure, shut, terminate, wind up, zip up

closed airtight, barred, bolted, buttoned, fastened, hermetically sealed,

TIMEPIECES		
ALARM CLOCK	CUCKOO CLOCK	QUARTZ-CRYSTAL CLOCK
ALARM WATCH	DIGITAL CLOCK	QUARTZ WATCH
ANALOG CLOCK	DIGITAL WATCH	REPEATER
ANALOG WATCH	ELECTRIC CLOCK	STEMWINDER WATCH
ASTRONOMICAL CLOCK	ELECTRONIC CLOCK	STOPWATCH
ATOMIC CLOCK	GRANDFATHER CLOCK	SUNDIAL
BRACKET CLOCK	GRANDMOTHER CLOCK	TALL-CASE CLOCK
CALENDAR CLOCK	HALF-HUNTER WATCH	LONG-CASE CLOCK
CHRONOMETER	HUNTER	TRAVELLING CLOCK
CHRONOSCOPE	HUNTING WATCH	TURNIP WATCH
CESIUM CLOCK	JOURNEYMAN WATCH	WALL CLOCK
CLEPSYDRA	PENDULUM CLOCK	WATCH
CLOCK RADIO	POCKET WATCH	WATER CLOCK
CLOCK WATCH	QUARTZ CLOCK	WRISTWATCH

impermeable, impervious, latched, lightproof, locked, nonporous, padlocked, private, sealed, secured, shut, unopened, vacuum-packed, waterproof, watertight, zipped

closeness contiguity, intimacy, nearness, proximity

closure bankruptcy, cessation, collapse, completion, conclusion, discontinuance, end, finish, foreclosure, fulfilment, resolution, shutdown, stop, termination

cloth
See list at **fabric**.

cloud altocumulus, altostratus, anvil, blur, cirrocumulus, cirrostratus, cirrus, cloud cover, cloudiness, confuse, cumulonimbus, cumulous, dark, dreich, dull, gloom, grey, haze, mackerel sky, nimbostratus, nimbus, noctilucent, obscure, overcast, rain, scud, storm, stratocumulus, stratus, swarm, throng, thundercloud

club assail, association, attack, blackjack, ·concuss, cosh, crown, cudgel, group, league, sandbag, society

clumsy awkward, bulky, cumbersome, hulking, lumbering, ponderous, ungainly, unwieldy
may indicate an anagram

coal anthracite, bituminous coal, black diamond, briquette, coke, lignite

coalition alliance, bloc, caucus, cell, commonweal, commonwealth, confederation, cooperative, federation, league, union

coarse basic, bawdy, blistered, bouclé, broken, chapped, corrugated, cracked, craggy, crude, deckle-edged, encrusted, furrowed, gnarled, grainy, granulated, grated, gravelly, hispid, indecent, jagged, knobbly, knobby, knotted, knurled, lumpy, nodose, nubby, obscene, pimply, pitted, pockmarked, potholed, ridged, rocky, rough, rude, rutty, scabby, scaly, scraggly, serrated, sharp, shattered, slubbed, snaggy, spiny, stony, studded, tweed, unrefined, villous, warty

coarsen gnarl, grain, granulate, knob, roughen

coast beach, coastland, coastline, continental shelf, cruise, freewheel, pebbles, sand, seaboard, seaside, shingle, shoreline, strand

coat blanket, carpet, cover, crombie, daub, dreadnought, duffel coat, duster, enamel, fearnought, frock coat, frost, gaberdine coat, gild, glaze, greatcoat, ice, layer, mac, mackintosh, oilskins, overcoat, overlay, paint, parquet, pea jacket, plaster, plate, polish, raglan, raincoat, southwester, spread, stain, surcoat, tile, top, topcoat, trench coat, ulster, upholster, varnish, veneer, waterproof, wax

coated faced, laminated, lined, overlaid, overlapped, overlaying, plated, sheathed, veneered

coating coat, enamel, film, frosting, furniture polish, glaze, icing, japan, lacquer, layer, paint, plate, stain, varnish, veneer, wax

coax beguile, blarney, cajole, flatter, temporize, wheedle

cockiness aggressiveness, bumptiousness, obtrusiveness, perkiness, pertness, pompousness, self-confidence, swank

cockney
may indicate a shortening (delete 'h')

cocky affected, aggressive, bumptious, cheeky, obtrusive, perky, pert, pompous, pretentious, saucy, self-confident, swanky

coded arcane, classified, closed, cryptographic, dark, impenetrable, murky, obscure, restricted, secret, undiscoverable, unintelligible

coercion browbeating, brute force, bullying, constraint, duress, enforcement, force, intimidation, mandate, pressure, restraint, threat, violence

coherent apod(e)ictic, comprehensible, consistent, intelligible, logical

coil corkscrew, corrugation, curl, curlicue, helix, intricacy, kink, loop, meandering, ringlet, screwthread, shimmy, spiral, spring, squiggle, squirm, turbination, turn, twirl, twist, whorl, wriggle

coincidence accident, casualty, chance, fluke, lucky break, misadventure, serendipity, synchronicity

cold algid, Arctic, biting, bitter, bleak, bracing, breezy, chill, cool, cough, dead, frappé, freezing, fresh, frigid, frosted, frosty, frozen, gelid, glacial, glazed, heartless, hoar, iced, icy, inclement, influenza, invigorating, nippy, parky, perishing, pinched, polar, raw, severe, sharp, shivery, Siberian, sleety, snow-bound, snowy, uncaring, unemotional, wintry

coldness chill, cold snap, coolness, freshness, inclemency, nippiness, pitilessness, ruthlessness, unresponsiveness, wind-chill factor, wintriness

collaborate affiliate, ally, associate with, collude, combine with, conspire, fraternize, join with, partner, pull together, side with, unite

collected accumulated, amassed, boarded, heaped, piled, stacked, stockpiled

collection accumulation, archive, bundle, diary, file, folder, gathering, inventory, portfolio, record, repository, set, yearbook

collide attack, bang, bash, brunt, bulldoze, bump, butt, cannon into, careen, charge, clash, confront, converge, crash, crunch, encounter, fence, hammer, hurtle, impact, jolt, meet, nudge, percuss, ram, shoulder, slam into, smash, tamp

collision bump, cannon, charge, concussion, convergence, crash, crunch, encounter, friction, impact, jolt, meeting, nudge, percussion, pile-up, scrape, shock, smash

colour
See list of colours.

column abutment, buttress, cap, capital, chapiter, colonnade, columniation, Composite order, Corinthian order, diastyle, Doric order, drum, entablature, entasis, fluting, hexastyle, impost, intercolumniation, Ionic order, pedestal, peristyle, pier, pilaster, pillar, post, shaft, stylobate, support, Tuscan order
*See also list at **architecture**.*

combatant adversary, aggressor, agonist, assailant, assassin, assaulter, attacker, battler, belligerent, besieger, blade, brave, bravo, bully, contender, dueller, escalader, fighter, gunman, hitman, hooligan, knight, man-at-arms, militarist, opponent, paladin, phansigar, rough, skinhead, soldier, stormer, storm trooper, strong-arm man, struggler, swashbuckler, swordsman, thug, tough, warrior

combative adversarial, aggressive, agonistic, antagonistic, bellicose, belligerent, bloodthirsty, buccaneering, chauvinistic, crusading, expansionistic, gung-ho, hardline, hostile, imperialistic, inimical, jingoistic, militant, militaristic, opposing, piratical, pugnacious, rough, rowdy, thuggish, tough, trigger-happy, warlike

combination absorption, alloy, amalgam, amalgamation, assimilation, association, blend, centralization, coalescence, cocktail, coincidence, composition, compound, concoction, concurrence, confection, conflation, conjunction, digestion, embodiment, fusion, incorporation, infusion, integration, joining together, marriage, mélange, merger, mingling, mixing, pastiche, potion, potpourri, solution, symbiosis, symphysis, synchronicity, syncretism, synthesis, unification

combine absorb, aggregate, amalgamate, assemble, assimilate, blend,

COLOURS

AAL
ABA
ABSINTHE
ACAJOU
ALESAN
ALICE BLUE
ALIZARIN
AMARANTH
AMBER
ANAMITE
APRICOT
AQUAMARINE
ARDOISE
ARGENT
AUBERGINE
AUBURN
AUREATE
AURICOMOUS
AURULENT
AZURE BLUE
BABY BLUE
BABY PINK
BALL PARK BLUE
BASANÉ
BEIGE
BISCUIT
BISHOP'S PURPLE
BISHOP'S VIOLET
BISTRE
BLACK
BLEU
BLONDE
BLUE
BLUE-GREEN
BOIS
BOIS DE ROSE
BORDEAUX
BOTTLE GREEN
BRONZE
BROWN
BURE
BURGUNDY
BURNET
BURNT ALMOND
CADET BLUE
CADET GREY
CAFÉ AU LAIT
CALDRON
CALEDONIAN
   BROWN
CAMBRIDGE BLUE
CAMEL
CANARY YELLOW
CAPRI
CAPUCINE
CARAMEL
CARDINAL RED
CARMINE
CARNATION
CARNELIAN

CARROT COLOUR
CASTILIAN RED
CASTOR
CASTOR GREY
CELADON GREEN
CENDRÉ
CERISE
CHAIR
CHALDERA
CHAMOIS
CHAMPAGNE
CHARTREUSE GREEN
CHARTREUSE
   YELLOW
CHÂTAINE
CHERRY
CHESTNUT
CHOCOLATE
CHROMA
CIEL BLUE
CINNAMON
CITRON
CLAIR DE LUNE
CLARET
COBALT BLUE
COCHINEAL
COCOA
CONGO BROWN
COPPER
CORAL
CORBEAU
CREAM
CREVETTE
CRIMSON
CUIR
CYCLAMEN
CYMAR
DELFT
DELPH BLUE
DORADO
DRAB
DUN
DUTCH BLUE
EAU DE NIL
EBON
ÉCARLATE
ÉCRU
EGGPLANT
EGGSHELL
EMERALD
ENSIGN BLUE
FILBERT
FLAXEN
FLESH
FLESH PINK
FOREST GREEN
FUCHSIA
GARNET
GOBELIN BLUE
GOLD

GOLDEN
GREEN
GREEN-BLUE
GRÈGE
GREY
GRIS
GRIZZLE
GRIZZLED
GUN METAL
HARLEQUIN
HAZEL
HAZEL NUT
HEATHER
HEATHER MIXTURE
HENNA
HOPI
HORIZON BLUE
HUNTER'S GREEN
HUNTER'S PINK
HYACINTH
HYACINTH BLUE
INDIGO
INGÉNUE
IRIS
IVORY
JACINTH
JADE
JASPÉ
JASPER
JAUNE
JET
JEWEL
JONQUIL
KHAKI
LACQUER
LAKE
LAPIS LAZULI
LARK
LARKSPUR
LAVANDE
LAVENDER
LEAF GREEN
LEMON YELLOW
LIME GREEN
LIPSTICK RED
LIVER BROWN
LODEN
LOGWOOD
   BROWN
MADDER
MAGENTA
MAHOGANY
MAIZE
MARINA BLUE
MARINE BLUE
MAROON
MATARA
MAUVE
MIDNIGHT BLUE
MOLE GREY

MOONSTONE
MOSS GREEN
MOTHER-OF-PEARL
MOTLEY
MOTTLED
MULBERRY
MULTICOLOURED
MUSTARD
NACARAT
NATURAL
NAVY
NAVY BLUE
NEUTRAL
NILE GREEN
NOIR
OCHRE
OLD ROSE
OLIVE
OLIVE DRAB
OMBRÉ
ONYX
OPAL
ORANGE
ORCHID
OVERSEAS BLUE
OXFORD BLUE
OYSTER
PARCHMENT
PARROT GREEN
PARTI-COLOURED
PASTEL
PEACH
PEACOCK BLUE
PEA GREEN
PEARL
PEARLED
PEARL GREY
PEARLY
PÊCHE
PEPPER-AND-SALT
PERIWINKLE BLUE
PETROL BLUE
PIED
PINK
PIRNED
PISTACHE
PISTACHIO GREEN
PLATINA
PLUM
POLYCHROME
POMEGRANATE
POPPY RED
POWDER BLUE
PRIMARY COLOUR
PRIMROSE
PRUNE
PUCE
PURPLE
RACHEL
RAISIN

COLOURS continued			
RASPBERRY	SECONDARY	TEA ROSE	VERDANT GREEN
RED	COLOUR	TERRACOTTA	VERDIGRIS
RESEDA	SEPIA	THISTLE	VERMILION
ROSE	SHADE	TILE RED	VERSICOLOUR
ROUGE	SHAGREEN	TILLEUL	VERT
ROYAL BLUE	SHOT	TITIAN	VIOLET
RUBY	SHRIMP	TOMATO RED	VIOLINE
RUSSET	SILVER	TOPAZ	VIRIDIAN
SAFFRON	SKY BLUE	TORTOISE SHELL	WALLY BLUE
SALMON	SMOKED PEARL	TURKEY RED	WALNUT BROWN
SAND	SOLFERINO RED	TURQUOISE BLUE	WHITE
SAPPHIRE	SOLID COLOUR	TURQUOISE GREEN	YELLOW
SAPPHIRE BLUE	SPECTRUM	TUSSORE	YELLOW OCHRE
SCARLET	TAN	TYRIAN PURPLE	ZENITH BLUE
SEA BLUE	TANGERINE	ULTRAMARINE	ZIRCON
SEA GREEN	TAUPE	UMBER	

centralize, coalesce, collect, compose, compound, congregate, conjoin, conjugate, connect, consolidate, converge, digest, dilute, embody, fuse, group, hydrate, imbue, impregnate, incorporate, inculcate, infuse, inoculate, instil, integrate, intertwine, interweave, join together, link, lump together, make up, merge, mingle, mix, network, pool, soak up, syncretize, synthesize, unify, unite, yoke

combustible explosive, flammable, incendiary, inflammable

comedy alternative comedy, burlesque, camp, caricature, cartoon, farce, humour, knockabout, lampoon, parody, satire, slapstick, stand-up

comfort alleviate, appease, assure, auspiciousness, cheer, coddle, convince, cosset, cuddle, ease, encourage, encouragement, featherbed, luck, lull, mother, pacify, pamper, persuade, pet, placate, promise, propitiousness, prosperity, reassurance, refresh, relieve, salve, security, slake, soften, soothe, spoil, success, support, sympathize with, warm, well-being

comfortable auspicious, comfy, cosy, dulcet, easy, emollient, favourable, lucky, mellow, opportune, prosperous, relaxing, restful, secure, snug, soothing, suitable, well⁻

command act, administer, advise, behest, boss, captain, captaincy, chair, charge, compel, conduct, control, countermand, counterorder, declaration, decree, dictate, dictum, direct, direction, directive, dominate, edict, embargo, enactment, encyclical, fiat, govern, government, guide, head, hold sway, impose, indicate, instruction, interdict, invitation, law, lead, legislation, manage, manifesto, manipulate, navigate, order, ordinance, oversee, pilot, police, pontificate, precept, predominate, prescribe, prescription, preside, proclaim, proclamation, prohibition, promulgate, pronounce, pronouncement, proscribe, proscription, regulation, reign, rule, run, shepherd, sign, signal, skipper, statement, steer, superintend, supervise, ukase, veto, word

commanding authoritative, banned, compelling, compulsory, countermanded, dictatorial, directive, embargoed, encyclical, governmental, imperative, injunctive, interdicted, legislative, mandatory, obligatory, ordering, papal, pontifical, prescriptive, prohibitive, proscriptive, regulatory, ruling, vetoed

commemorate celebrate, hallow, honour, jubilate, keep, mark, memorialize, observe, perform, remember, sanctify, solemnize, toast

commemoration anniversary, ceremonial, holiday, honouring, jubilee, memorialization, memorial service, observance, remembrance, solemnization *See also list at* **anniversary**.

commemorative ceremonial, honourable, memorial, solemn

commercial ad, advertisement, economic, financial, fiscal, monetary, profitable

commission accreditation, appointment, assignment, committee, coronation, decentralization, delegation, deputation, devolution, election, empowerment, enthronement, entrustment, federation, inauguration, induction, installation, instatement, investiture, nomination, ordination, patronage, power, representation, responsibility, voting

commitment application, assiduity, attention, concentration, duty, effort, exertion, indefatigability, industriousness, obligation, sedulity, single-mindedness, tirelessness

committee board, body, cabinet, commission, council, panel

common accustomed, average, conventional, customary, downmarket, everyday, familiar, habitual, heath, middlebrow, middle-of-the-road, normal, ordinary, pedestrian, plebeian, park, quotidian, rec(reation ground), regular, routine, run-of-the-mill, standard, unexceptional, usual, vernacular, vulgar

commonplace clichéd, hackneyed, jaded, overused, platitudinous, stereotyped, trite, unimaginative, uninspired

common sense discernment, horse sense, judgment, native wit, nous, prudence, savvy, sensibleness

commotion ado, bedlam, bother, brouhaha, clamour, din, disorder, disturbance, ferment, fracas, fray, furore, fuss, hubbub, hullabaloo, hurly-burly, noise, outburst, outcry, racket, riot, ruction, rumpus, scuffle, shemozzle, to-do, trouble, tumult, turmoil, uproar

communicate advertise, amplify, announce, bleep, broadcast, convey, describe, disseminate, document, fax, impart, inform, link, narrate, page, post, propagate, publicize, publish, radio, recount, relay, report, signal, speak, talk, telecast, telegraph, telephone, televise, telex, transmit, wire, write

communication announcement, briefing, broadcast, bulletin, cable, communiqué, diffusion, dispatch, dissemination, fax, instruction, message, narration, notice, notification, order, publication, report, review, statement, telegram, telex, transmission, wire

communicational advertised, amplified, announced, broadcast, demodulated, epistolary, modulated, oral, postal, propagated, radioed, recorded, relayed, taped, telecommunicational, telegraphic, telephonic, televised, transcribed, transmissional, transmitted, verbal, videoed

communications broadcasting, correspondence, media, radio, signalling, speech, talking, telecommunications, television, the press, writing

communism collective, collectivism, communalization, commune, community, kibbutz, kolkhoz, socialism

companion associate, buddy, classmate, colleague, comrade, co-worker, fellow, flatmate, friend, mate, partner

companionship association, cohabitation, community, company, consortship, fellowship, friendship, marriage, mateyness, partnership, society, togetherness

company assembly, business, co, companionship, concern, corporation, firm, group, plc, works

compartment alcove, bay, booth, box, cage, cell, cranny, cubbyhole, cubicle, inglenook, niche, nook, pew, recess, snuggery, stall

compass astrocompass, attain, bearings (N,S,E,W), binnacle, card, chart, chronometer, compass card, encircle, ephemeris, gyrocompass, needle, range

compatibility conformation, conformity, congruity, consistency, correspondence, equality, parallelism, similarity, synchronization, timeliness, uniformity

compatible coinciding, conforming, congruent, congruous, consistent, corresponding, equal, matching, parallel, similar, synchronized, uniform

compel bind, coerce, command, constrain, demand, dictate, discipline, drive, emphasize, enforce, force, hold back, impel, impose, insist on, make, mandate, necessitate, oblige, oppress, order, pin down, press, pressure, prevail, regiment, require, restrain, squeeze, strain, stress, urge

compelling attractive, coercive, cogent, commanding, compulsive, convincing, driving, hypnotic, imperative, inevitable, influential, inspiring, involuntary, irresistible, mesmeric, necessary, overriding, persuasive, pressing, unavoidable, urgent

compendium album, anthology, chrestomathy, collection, compilation, corpus, cuttings, ephemera, excerpts, extracts, miscellany, scrapbook, selection

compensable amendable, atonable, propitiable, reclaimable, recoupable, recoverable, rectifiable, redeemable, remittable, repleviable, requitable, restorable, satisfiable

compensate atone, distrain, expiate, guerdon, indemnify, make amends, mend, pay off, propitiate, recompense, rectify, redeem, redress, refund, reimburse, remedy, remit, remunerate, repay, replace, replevy, requite, resti-

tute, restore, reward, satisfy, settle, square

compensation amendment, amends, atonement, blood money, comeuppance, costs, damages, distraint, eric, expiation, golden handshake, golden parachute, guerdon, indemnification, indemnity, meed, money back, pay-off, penalty, penance, propitiation, ransom, recompense, recoupment, recovery, rectification, redeemability, redemption, redress, redundancy money, refund, reimbursement, remedy, remittance, remuneration, reparation, repayment, replacement, replevin, requital, restitution, restoration, retaliation, retrieval, reward, satisfaction, settlement, solatium, wergild

compensator amender, guerdoner, indemnifier, propitiator, redeemer, remitter, requiter, restorer, rewarder, satisfier

compensatory amendatory, expiatory, indemnificatory, penitential, piacular, propitiative, redemptory, remedial, reparatory, reparatory, restitutory, restorative, retaliatory, retributive

competitive aggressive, ambitious, cliffhanging, close-run, cutthroat, dingdong, dog-eat-dog, keen, well-fought

compilation anthology, collection, compendium, composition, corpus, roundup

compile anthologize, consolidate, excerpt, select

complacency nonchalance, pococurantism, self-satisfaction, smugness

complain bellyache, boo, catcall, gripe, groan, grouse, grumble, hiss, howl, jeer, moan, rant, squawk, tut-tut, whine, whinge, whistle

complaint ailment, boo, criticism, grievance, gripe, grouse, hiss, injury, injustice, rebuke, remonstration, reprimand, reproof, rocket, snub, tort, whistle

complete accomplish, achieve, bring about, cap, climax, compass, complement, compose, conclude, construct, consummate, crown, culminate, discharge, dispatch, effect, enact, end, entire, execute, finalize, finish, fulfil, implement, integrate, join, peak, perfect, perform, realize, round off, succeed, total, unite, whole

completed attained, blooming, compassed, comprehensive, consummate, discharged, effected, entire, executed, exhaustive, fulfilled, implemented, intact, matured, perfect, polished, realized, ripe, secured, thorough, thoroughgoing, total, unabridged, unbroken, utter, well done, whole

completeness accomplishment, balance, carrying through, close, completion, comprehensiveness, conclusion, concord, culmination, end, entirety, exhaustiveness, expiration, finalization, fullness, harmony, ideal, integrality, maturity, peak, perfection, readiness, realization, ripeness, solidity, success, sufficiency, summit, termination, thoroughness, totality, unity, universality, wholeness, zenith

compliance abidance, acquiescence, obedience, observance, respect, submission, subordination

compliant accommodating, acquiescent, agreeable, complaisant, docile, lemming-like, obedient, passive, sheeplike, submissive, tractable, willing, yielding

compliment accolade, citation, commendation, congratulation, encomium, eulogy, felicitation, panegyric, praise, tribute

compliments blandishments, flattery, praise, sweet-talk

comply accede, accommodate, acquiesce, adapt, adjust, agree, consent, copy, emulate, follow, imitate, obey, observe, respect, submit, yield

component aspect, constituent, content, detail, element, facet, factor, feature, ingredient, integrant, item, link, part, particular

components engine, guts, innards, insides, machinery, mechanism, workings, works

compose adapt, amalgamate, arrange, colligate, combine, compile, comprise, connect, constitute, construct, contribute, erect, fabricate, fit together, instrumentate, join, make up, orchestrate, score, transcribe, transpose
may indicate an anagram

composing comprising, constituting, containing, embodying, including, inclusive of, incorporating

compound alloy, amalgam, blend, cocktail, colony, composite, courtyard, enclosure, hybrid, make-up, mixture, portmanteau word, quadrangle, settlement, solution, suspension

comprehension apprehension, comprehensiveness, inclusiveness, perception, understanding

compress abbreviate, abridge, clip, compact, condense, contract, cut, epigrammatize, précis, shorten, squeeze, truncate

comprise consist of, contain, cover, embody, embrace, encompass, include, incorporate, involve, subsume

compromise accommodation, adaptation, adjustment, agree, arbitration, arrangement, average out, balance, bargain, cede, concede, concession, cooperate, deal, give-and-take, happy medium, meet halfway, middle way, negotiate, play politics, readjust, settlement, sharing, trade-off, understanding

compromising accommodating, adaptable, agreeing, balancing, conceding, give-and-take, halfway, negotiable, settled

compulsion coercion, compulsiveness, drive, irresistibility, necessity, need, obligation, obsessiveness, preoccupation, prerequisite, requirement, urge

compulsory ineluctable, mandatory, necessary, obligatory, prerequisite, required, requisite, unavoidable

computing calculating, computation, cybernetics, data entry, information processing, numbercrunching, programming, robotics, systems analysis

con against, conservative, study, trick

concatenate catenate, chain, connect, join, link, string, thread

concave abyss, borehole, burrow, canal, canyon, cave, cavern, cavernous, col, combe, cove, crater, crevasse, cutting, dell, den, dented, depressed, dimpled, dingle, dip, excavation, fosse, foxhole, gap, glen, gorge, grave, gulf, gully, hole, hollow, incurvate, indented, inlet, mine, moat, pass, pit, pitted, pockmarked, porous, pothole, quarry, ravine, sap, spongy, sunken, trench, trough, tube, tunnel, vale, valley, warren

concavity depression, hollowness, impression, incurvation, indentation, indention, sinking

conceal blanket, bottle up, bury, censor, cloak, confine, cover up, curtain, ensconce, gag, gloss over, hide, hush up, inter, keep mum, lock up, mask, muffle, overlay, paint over, paper over, restrict, screen, seal up, seclude, secrete, shroud, smother, stash, stifle, store, stow away, suppress, varnish, veil, wall up, whitewash, withhold, wrap up

concealed backroom, blotted out, censored, covered, covert, disguised, eclipsed, hidden, incommunicado, invisible, lurking, masked, muffled, obscured, out-of-touch, overprinted, private, reclusive, recondite, screened, secluded, sequestered, skulking, smothered, stealthy, stifled, suppressed, undercover, underground, under wraps, undetected, undisclosed, unexposed, unmanifested, unseen, unspied, veiled

concealment ambush, code, cryptography, disappearance, eclipse, hiding, imperceptibility, intrigue, invisibility, lurking, obscurity, occultation, plot, privacy, reconditeness, restriction, seclusion, secrecy, secretion, sequestration, skulking, stealth, submergence, undercurrent

conceit affectation, arrogance, egotism, haughtiness, hubris, insolence, overambitiousness, overconfidence, pretension, self-admiration, self-praise, snobbery, uppitiness, vainglory, vanity

conceited affected, arrogant, brazen, condescending, egotistic, haughty, insolent, nose-in-the-air, pompous, purse-proud, self-admiring, self-praising, smug, snobbish, snooty, strutting, toffee-nosed, unabashed, unblushing, uppity, vain, vainglorious

concentrate condense, contemplate, congregate, distillate, essence, home in, mull over, reflect, study

concentration ardour, coagulation, commitment, concretion, condensation, congealment, consolidation, constriction, dedication, devotion, drive, eagerness, earnestness, energy, gelatinization, haemostasis, seriousness, single-mindedness, solidification, vigour, zeal

conception babyhood, beginning, birth, delivery, nativity, notion, parturition, pregnancy, thought

concise abbreviated, abridged, aphoristic, brachylogous, brief, brisk, brusque, clipped, compact, compendious, compressed, condensed, contracted, crisp, curt, cut, elliptic, epigrammatic, epitomical, exact, incisive, laconic, monosyllabic, outlined, pithy, pointed, portmanteau, sententious, short, shortened, succinct, summarized, syncopal, taciturn, telegraphic, terse, tight-knit, trenchant, truncated

conciseness abbreviation, abridgment, apocope, brachylogy, brevity, briefness, briskness, brusqueness, compactness, compendiousness, compression, contraction, crispness, curtness, elision, ellipsis, exactness, incisiveness, laconism, monosyllabism, nutshell, pithiness, pointedness, sententiousness, shortening, shortness, succinctness, syncope, telegraphese, terseness, truncation, witticism

conclude arrive, climax, close, culminate, deduce, end, finish, settle, terminate

concluded crowned, done, ended, final, finalized, finished, inferred, last, terminal, terminated, ultimate, wound up

conclusion arrival, climax, close, completion, death, denouement, end, end product, epilogue, final chapter, finale, finality, final story, finis, finish, last act, last words, payoff, resolution, result, solution, swan song, termination, upshot, wind-up

concordant accordant, agreeing, at one, concurrent, consentient, consenting, in concert, in rapport, like-minded, sympathetic, unanimous, united

concur collude, concert, connive, conspire, harmonize

concurrent coexistent, cohabiting, coincident, contemporaneous, contemporary, correlative, parallel, simultaneous, symbiotic

condensed binding, caked, clotted, coagulated, concentrated, congealed, consolidated, constipated, costive, crystalline, curdled, frozen, indissoluble, infusible, jelled, knotted, matted, ropy, set, shortened, solidified, tangled

condescend deign, demean oneself, lower oneself, patronize, stoop, unbend

condition circumstances, grounds, obligation, parameter, prerequisite, provision, qualification, requisite, reservation, small print, state, stipulation, train

conditional bound, checked, circumscribed, confined, contingent, controlled, curbed, defined, delimited, demarcated, determined, limiting, mandatory, obligatory, parametric, prescribed, proscribed, provisional, provisory, qualificatory, requisitional, reserved, restricted, specified, stipulatory

condolence comfort, commiseration, consolation, sympathy

condone connive, disregard, ignore, justify, let pass, overlook, pass over, wink at

conduct action, affectation, air, aspect, attitude, bearing, behaviour, carriage, comportment, delivery, demeanour, deportment, fashion, feeling, gesture, guise, lead, manage, manner, mien, mood, motion, opinion, outlook, port, pose, posture, style, tone, transmit

confectionery bonbon, candyfloss, chocolate, fondant, fudge, liquorice, lollipop, peppermint, sweeties, sweets, toffee

confer analyse, bargain, canvass, consult, debate, deliberate over, discuss, exchange views, hold talks, negotiate, parley, pow-wow, refer to, talk over, thrash out

conference caucus, conclave, congregation, congress, convention, convocation, council, diet, legislature, parley, symposium, synod, talks

conferring collusion, complicity, conference, connivance, conspiracy, consultation, teleconferencing

confirm ascertain, assure, attest, authenticate, back, certify, corroborate, demonstrate, determine, endorse, establish, prove, ratify, reinforce, substantiate, support, validate, verify

confirmation affirmation, ascertainment, assurance, attestation, authentication, backing, certification, corroboration, demonstration, determination, endorsement, establishment, evidence, facts, grounds, proof, ratification, reinforcement, signs, substantiality, substantiation, support, validation, verification

confiscation deprivation, disinheritance, dispossession, distraint, divestment, expropriation, impounding, repossession

conflict argue, attack, bad blood, battle, clashing, collision, competition, confrontation, contention, crosscurrent, debate, defence, differ, disaccord, disagree, discord, dispute, dissension, dissent, emulation, enmity, fighting, friction, quarrel, rivalry, row, squabble, strife, vying, war

conform accommodate, accord, adjust, agree, align, automate, complement, comply, concur, copy, correlate, correspond, drill, fall in, fit, follow, form, grade, harmonize, homogenize, interrelate, line up, mass-produce, match, meet, mirror, mould, normalize, order, pattern, press, reflect, regiment, resemble, shape, size, square with, stamp, standardize, stereotype, straighten, suit, tally, trim, typecast

conforming accordant, agreeing, analogous, compatible, concordant, conformable, congruent, congruous, consistent, consonant, correlated, correspondent, corresponding, equal, equivalent, even, harmonious, homogenous, homologous, identical, interchangeable, like, matching, mechanical, monolithic, normalized, paired, regimented, resembling, same, similar, standard, stereotyped, synonymous, twinned, typecast, undifferentiated, uniform

conformist bourgeois, conservative, conventional, correct, formal, grey, kosher, law-abiding, old-fashioned, orthodox, pedantic, prim, proper, provincial, prudish, square, staid, stodgy, strait-laced, stuffy, traditional, uptight

conformity accord, agreement, automation, blankness, cliché, coherence, compatibility, concurrence, conformance, congruence, congruity, consistency, constancy, continuity, copy, correlation, correspondence, emulation, equality, equivalence, harmony, homogeneity, homology, identicalness, imitation, interchangeability, likeness, method, normalization, oneness, orderliness, parrotry, pattern, plainness, regimentation, sameness, similarity, standardization, stereotype, synonymity, uniformity

confound babble, baffle, bewilder, confuse, doodle, flummox, gibber, mystify, perplex, puzzle, ramble, scrawl, stump

confront breast, clash, conflict, contend, emulate, face, grapple, rival, stem, vie

confuse balls-up, boggle, botch, bungle, challenge, deceive, foul up, mix up, mystify, pose, puzzle, snarl up, stump, trick

confused astray, at a loss, baffled, bewildered, confounded, convoluted, cryptic, difficult, discomposed, disconcerted, disorganized, disoriented, embarrassed, enigmatic, featherbrained, floundering, flummoxed, incoherent, muddleheaded, mystified, nonplussed, perplexed, problematic, puzzled, scatterbrained, shy, stumped, timid, wondering, worried
may indicate an anagram

confusion bafflement, beargarden, bedlam, bewilderment, chaos, confoundment, discomposure, disconcertion, embarrassment, hell, hullabaloo, madhouse, pandemonium, perplexity, predicament, puzzlement, quandary, tumult, turbulence, turmoil

congratulate compliment, drink to, pat on the back, praise, toast

congruent coextensive, coincident, coordinate, equidistant, equilateral, homologous, sharing

conjecture construction, gamble, gambling, guess, guessing, guesstimate, intuition, reconstruction, shot, speculation, surmise, suspicion, try

conjure evoke, invoke, juggle, summon spirits

connect attach, bandage, bind, bolt, bond, bracket, braid, bridge, buckle, button, couple, entangle, entwine, fasten, glue, graft, hook, interconnect, interweave, join, knot, lace, lash, ligate, link, merge, nail, peg, pin, plait, rivet, screw, sew, skewer, staple, stick, stitch, tack, tape, tie, unite, zip

connection adhesion, arch, attachment, band, beam, bond, brace, bracket, branch, canal, chain, cohesion, col, conjunction, connective, copula, coupling, entanglement, fastening, fetter, girder, graft, hinge, hoop, hyphen, interconnection, intermedium, involvement, isthmus, joining, joint, junction, ladder, link, meeting, merger, neck, nexus, parenthesis, ridge, shackle, stairs, stay, stepping stone, stretcher, strut, tie, union, yoke, zeugma

connective adhesive, associated, coherent, cohesive, communicative, conjunctive, interconnective, joint, liaising, related, sticky

conquer beat, capture, checkmate, crush, defeat, overcome, prevail, quell, subdue, subject, subjugate, suppress, take over, vanquish, win

conscious awake, aware, insomniac, intentional, sleepless

conscription call-up, enlisting, mobilization, national service, recruitment

consecution catenation, chain, concatenation, course, file, ladder, line, nexus, order, queue, run, sequence, series, steps, string, thread, train, turn

consecutive catenary, chronological, following, linear, ongoing, ordinal, progressive, running, sequential, serial, seriate, successive

consecutiveness line-up, procession, progression, queue, successiveness

consent accredit, affirm, agree, agreement, approval, assent, attest, authenticate, authorization, back, certify, confirm, endorsement, go-ahead, leave, ratification, ratify, recognition, recognize, support, underwrite, validate, vouchsafe

consenting accredited, affirming, agreed, approving, assentient, authorized, backed, confirming, consentient, endorsed, ratified, recognized

consequence effect, outcome, payoff, product, result, sequel, upshot

consequent caused, ensuing, following, resulting, subsequent

conservation ecology, environmentalism, preservation, protection, reservation, safekeeping, storing

conservationist ecologist, environmentalist, green

conservatism conformism, obstinacy, rightism, stubbornness, traditionalism

conservative cautious, conformist, old-fashioned, reactionary, right-wing, unprogressive

consider believe, deduce, infer, observe, reason, regard, study, think about

consideration allowance, care, compassion, factor, issue, mindfulness, solicitude, thought, thoughtfulness

conspicuous clear-cut, distinct, eye-catching, obvious, outstanding, unblurred, well defined

conspicuousness clarity, clearness, distinctness, fame, obviousness, obtrusiveness, prominence

conspire betray, infiltrate, plot, spy

constancy ceaselessness, continuance, diligence, fidelity, iteration, maintenance, permanence, repetition, staunchness, steadfastness

construct build, concoct, devise, erect, put up
may indicate an anagram

construction building, complex, construct, edifice, elevation, erection, establishment, foundations, infrastructure, pile, prefabrication, structure, superstructure, works

consult call in, confide in, deliberate, discuss, negotiate, parley, refer to, seek advice, seek opinion

consultation conference, council, discussion, negotiations, parley, pow-wow, tête-à-tête

consume burn, deplete, devour, drown, eat, engulf, envelop, exhaust, gobble, incinerate, overwhelm, squander, swamp, use, waste

consumer clientele, customer, spender, user

contagious aguish, catching, communicable, endemic, epidemic, germ-carrying, infectious, infective, malarious, morbific, pandemic, pathogenic, pestiferous, plague-stricken, zymotic

contain box, conceal, containerize, enclose, freight, hold, include, lade, load, package, parcel
may indicate a split word

container depository, frame, holder, receptacle, repository, reservoir, store, vessel

containing bagged, binned, bottling, boxed, bundled, caged, canning, cocooning, covering, enclosing, entombed, enveloping, garaged, holding, ladled, locked up, packing, potting, reserved, scooped, sheathed, sheltering, shelved, shovelled, spooned, stabling, storage, storing, surrounded, tinning, wrapping
may indicate a hidden word

contemplative absorbed, meditative, pensive, reflective, thoughtful

contemporary brother, classmate, coeval, compeer, current, friend, modern, peer, sister

contempt contumely, despite, disdain, disparagement, loftiness, scorn, sneer, superciliousness, superiority

contemptuous arrogant, contumelious, disdainful, disparaging, haughty, lofty, pejorative, scornful, sneering, snobbish, snooty, snotty, supercilious

contend argue for, attempt, battle, bet, challenge, combat, compete, contest, emulate, enter, essay, insist, joust with, oppose, play against, race, resist, rival, stake, strive, struggle, tackle, take on, tilt with, try, tussle, venture, vie with, wager, withstand, wrestle

contending agonistic, athletic, battling, challenging, competing, contesting, fighting, grappling, outdoing, racing, rival, running, sporting, starting, struggling, surpassing, vying

contention altercation, argument, battle, clash, combat, competition, conflict, debate, dispute, dissent, emulation, encounter, engagement, fight, ink-slinging, jealousy, mud-slinging, polemics, provocation, quarrel, rivalry, skirmish, spat, squabble, strife, struggle, tussle, war, wrangle

contentious aggressive, argumentative, at loggerheads, bellicose, belligerent, close, combative, controversial, debatable, fight-hungry, gladiatorial, hawkish, head-to-head, irascible, irritable, moot, pugilistic, pugnacious, quarrelsome, warlike, warmongering, warring

contents components, composition, constituents, constitution, elements, embodiment, essence, factors, features, gist, ingredients, makeup, material, matter, meat, nub, parts, quintessence, spirit, structure, stuff, substance
may indicate a hidden word

contiguity confluence, conjunction, connection, convergence, interface, intersection, joining, joint, junction, meeting, nexus, node, overlap, seam

continent chaste, land, land mass, mainland, restrained, subcontinent

continual additional, cohesive, constant, continuous, incessant, interconnected, interrelated, ongoing, progressive, recurrent, repetitive, sequent, steady, sustained, unbroken, uninterrupted

continue add, advance, cohere, connect, extend, flow, interrelate, maintain, preserve, proceed, progress, recur, remain, repeat, run, succeed, supplement, support, sustain, uphold

continuity ceaselessness, constancy, continuation, endlessness, extension, incessancy, maintenance, monotony, progression, prolongation, protraction, recurrence, repetition, sameness, sequence, succession, unbrokenness, uniformity

continuous ceaseless, constant, endless, featureless, incessant, interminable, monotonous, never-ending, nonstop, perpetual, seamless, serried, solid, unbroken, undifferentiated, unending, uniform, uninterrupted, unrelieved, unremitting

continuum circle, cycle, Klein bottle, Möbius strip, periodicity, recurrence, rotation, round, treadmill

contract authentication, bargain, bond, compact, concordat, covenant, deal, decrease, endorsement, obligation, pact, pledge, promise, ratification, sanction, seal, settlement, shorten, shrink, transaction, treaty, undertaking
may indicate a shortening

contraction abbreviation, abridgement, astringency, atrophy, clamping, clenching, coarctation, collapse, compaction, compression, concentration, condensation, congestion, constriction, constringency, cramping, crush, curtailment, decrease, deflation, diminu-

endo, elision, emaciation, flattening, gathering, hindrance, implosion, lessening, limitation, marasmus, minaturization, narrowing, pinching, précis, pressure, pruning, puckering, pursing, reduction, shortening, shrinking, shrivelling, slimming, squeeze, stenosis, strangulation, syneresis, synizesis, synopsis, systole, tabescence, thinning, tightening, trimming, waning

contractor architect, astringent, builder, clamp, compacter, compressor, condenser, constrictor, corset, crusher, foller, grinder, jobber, journeyman, mangle, press, squeezer, straitjacket, styptic, tourniquet, trimmer, vice

contractual agreed, allied, arranged, assenting, assigned, consensual, conspiratorial, covenanted, leveraged, matrimonial, negotiated, promised, ratified, sworn, tendered, united

contradiction antinomy, contrariety, denial, false note, grating, jarring, mésalliance, misalliance, misjoinder, mismatch, negation, oppositeness, oxymoron, paradox, rebuttal, refutation

contradictory absurd, anomalous, antinomic, contrary, grating, jarring, maladjusted, misallied, mismatched, odd, opposite, oxymoronic, paradoxical

contrariety antithesis, contradistinction, contraposition, contrast, difference, disagreement, discrepancy, disparity, inconsistency, opposition, polarity

contrariness disobedience, fractiousness, obstinacy, oppugnancy, perverseness, reaction, recalcitrance, refractoriness, stubbornness

contrary adversative, antithetical, con, contradictory, diametric, incompatible, inconsistent, irreconcilable, opposite, polarized, repugnant, reverse
may indicate a backward

convene convoke, marshal, mobilize, muster, rally, summon

convenience accommodation, adaptation, advantage, advisability, aid, amenity, appliance, application, auspiciousness, benefit, contrivance, expedience, expedient, facilities, facility, fitness, handiness, helpfulness, means, opportunism, opportunity, practicality, pragmatism, profit, propriety, prudence, qualification, suitability, timeliness, timeserving, tool, usability, usefulness, utilitarianism, utility, workability

convenient acceptable, adapted to, advantageous, applicable, appropriate, auspicious, beneficial, commendable, commodious, desirable, effective, expedient, fit, handy, helpful, opportune, practicable, practical, pragmatic, proper, seemly, suitable, timely, usable, useful, well-timed, workable, worthwhile

convention custom, fashion, form, party line, policy, practice, received idea, rule, style, tradition, trend, vogue

conventionalism Babbittry, bourgeois ethic, conformism, conservatism, etiquette, formality, old school, orthodoxy, primness, prudery, severity, strictness, traditionalism

converge approach, close in, draw near, funnel, intersect, taper

convergence collision, concentration, concourse, concurrence, confluence, conflux, meeting, mutual approach

convergent asymptotic, centring, centripetal, centrolineal, concurrent, confluent, confocal, conical, focal, focusing, knock-kneed, meeting, narrowing, pointed, pyramidal, radial, radiating, tangential, tapering, uniting

conversation bandy words, chat, colloquy, communicate, communication, communion, confabulate, converse, dialogue, discourse, duologue, exchange, pleasantries, intercourse, interlocution, parley, speak, talk, two-hander

conversational chatting, chatty, colloquial, communicative, confabulatory, forthcoming, gossipy, informal, informative, interlocutory, loquacious, newsy, talkative, unreserved

conversion alchemy, alteration, bewitchment, change, converting, crystallization, dehydration, fermentation, interpretation, leaven, magic, melting, metamorphosis, misinterpretation, modification, movement, mutation, processing, reduction, reorganization, resolution, shift, transference, transfiguration, transformation, transition, translation, transmutation, transposition
may indicate an anagram

convert apostate, backslider, brainwash, catechumen, change, evangelize, indoctrinate, influence, modify, neophyte, persuade, propagandize, proselyte, proselytize, renegade, tergiversator, traitor, turncoat, win over

converted assimilated, bewitched, brainwashed, changed, degenerated, enchanted, improved, metamorphosed, mutated, naturalized, proselytized, regenerated, transfigured, transformed, translated, transmuted, transposed

converting altering, becoming, changing, crystallizing, deteriorating, developing, evolving, fermenting, growing, improving, leavening, maturing, melting, mutating, processing, progressing, regenerating, transfiguring, transforming, transmuting

convex arched, arcuated, billowing, bowed, bulbous, bulging, distended, excrescent, gibbous, humped, lenticular, meniscoid, prominent, protruding, swelling, swollen, tumescent, vaulted

convexity billowing, bulbousness, bulginess, camber, distention, excrescence, gibbousness, meniscus, prominence, protrusion, protuberance, swelling, tumescence

conviction acceptance, assertiveness, assurance, belief, bias, bigotry, certainty, cocksureness, confidence, credence, dogmatism, faith, fanaticism, fideism, narrow-mindedness, obstinacy, orthodoxy, overconfidence, partisanship, positiveness, positivism, self-assurance, self-confidence, stubbornness, sureness, trust

convinced accepting, assertive, assured, believing, biased, bigoted, certain, cocksure, confident, doctrinaire, dogmatic, fanatical, narrow-minded, obstinate, opinionated, orthodox, overconfident, partisan, persuaded, positive, satisfied, self-assured, self-confident, stubborn, sure, trusting, undeviating, undoubting, unhesitating, unquestioning, unswerving

convolute braid, coil, corkscrew, corrugate, curl, distort, enlace, loop, meander, roll, scallop, shimmy, snake, spiral, squiggle, squirm, turn, twine, twirl, twist, undulate, wave, weave, wind, wriggle, writhe

convolution anfractuosity, circumvolution, intricacy, involution, sinuousness, twistedness, undulation

convolutional braided, circumlocutory, cochleate, coiled, corrugated, entwined, helical, intricate, involutional, labyrinthine, meandering, serpentine, sinuous, spiral, squiggly, squirming, tortuous, turbinate, twirled, twisted, undulatory, vermiform, wavy, whorled, winding, wriggling

convulsive cataleptic, choreal, choreic, eclamptic, epileptic, fitful, jarring, jerky, jolting, jolty, jumping, jumpy, orgasmic, palsied, paroxysmic, saltatory, spasmodic, spastic, twitchety, twitchy, vellicative

cook bake, baker, barbecue, bard, baste, beat, blanch, blend, boil, bone, braise, brown, casserole, caterer, charcoal-grill, chef, chop, coddle, commis chef, cuisinier, curry, cut, deep-fry, devil, dice, double-fry, draw, dress, fillet, flavour, flip, fold in, fry, garnish, grate, griddle, grill, grind, gut, knead, lard, liquidize, microwave, mince, mix, parboil, poach, pot-roast, pressure-cook, reheat, roast, sauce, sauté, scald, scramble, season, seethe, shallow-fry, shred, simmer, sous chef, spatchcock, spice, spit-roast, steam, stew, stir, stir-fry, stuff, toast, whip, whisk
may indicate an anagram

cooker Aga, barbecue, Dutch oven, fan oven, gas ring, griddle, grill, hob, hotplate, kettle, kitchen range, microwave, oven, sandwich-maker, spit, stove, toaster

cookery catering, cooking, cuisine, domestic science, food processing, gastronomy, haute cuisine, home economics, lean cuisine, nouvelle cuisine, provisioning

cool aloof, arctic, chilly, composed, frosty, icy, nippy, parky, perishing, sleety, slushy, snowy, stand-offish, unperturbed

cooperate aid, assist, blend, coact, collaborate, concur, dovetail, help, interpenetrate, permeate, support, work together

cooperation agreement, alliance, assistance, association, backup, cabal, chord, coaction, coagency, collaboration, collage, concord, concurrence, confederation, conjunction, conspiracy, counterpoint, federation, harmony, helpfulness, jigsaw, league, marriage, mosaic, orchestration, patchwork, plot, support, synchronization, synergy, tessellation, union, unity

cooperative accommodating, allied, associated, cabbalistic, coactive, coadjutant, coadjuvant, coagent, coincident, collaborative, concurrent, confederate, conjunctive, conspiratorial, contributory, federated, in league, leagued, orchestrated, participatory, supportive, symbiotic, synchronized, synergetic

copier duplicator, mimic, photocopier, press, printer, stenciller

copy bootleg, borrow, camouflage, clone, counterfeit, crib, disguise, doppelgänger, dummy, duplicate, duplication, facsimile, fake, forge, forgery, image, imitation, likeness, Mimeograph, mock-up, model, pastiche, phoney, photocopy, picture, pirate, plagiarism, plagiarize, portrait, replica, replicate, reproduce, reproduction, rip-off, sham, simulation, stencil, twin, Xerox

copycat ape, automaton, impersonator, mimic, parrot, robot

core basics, bedrock, centre, cornerstone, elite, essence, fulcrum, fundamentals, gist, grass roots, heart, hub, kernel, keynote, kingpin, linchpin, mainstay, nexus, nitty-gritty, nub, nucleus, pivot, priority, substance

corporate limited, merged, nationalized, private, privatized, public

corpse body, cadaver, carcass, carrion, casualty, fatality, fossil, mummy, remains, skeleton, stiff, stillbirth

correct accurate, amend, authentic, dead-right, exact, factual, faithful, genuine, legitimate, lifelike, literal, precise, proper, realistic, rectify, right, true, true-to-life, true-to-the-letter, truthful, unerring, valid, veracious, verbatim, word-perfect
may indicate an anagram

correctness accurateness, authenticity, genuineness, legitimacy, literalness, precision, truth, validity, veracity

correlate align, answer, balance, compare, correspond, equal, equalize, harmonize, match, parallel, proportion, resemble, tally

correlation allegory, analogue, analogy, comparability, correspondence, equivalence, identity, match, parallelism, pattern, proportionality, similarity, symmetry, tally

correlative allegorical, analogous, comparable, correspondent, equivalent,

identical, matching, parallel, patterned, proportional, similar, symmetric

correspond acknowledge, agree, answer, cable, coalesce, coincide, dispatch, e-mail, exchange letters, fax, forward, harmonize, imitate, interchange, mail, match, merge, post, reciprocate, reflect, reply, shadow, tally, telegraph, telex, wire, write

corrupt amoral, bribe, crooked, debase, debauch, decadent, defile, demoralize, deprave, disgrace, dishonest, dishonour, immoral, impure, lead astray, pervert, rotten, ruin, shame, sinful, smirch, soil, spoiled, sully, tainted, vitiate, wreck
may indicate an anagram

cosmetics blusher, eye-liner, eye-shadow, greasepaint, kohl, lipstick, make-up, mascara, nail polish, nail varnish, paint, powder, rouge, slap

cost damage, expenditure, expenses, inflation, outlay, price

costly dear, exorbitant, expensive, high-priced, inflationary, overpriced, prohibitive, sky-high, unaffordable

could be
may indicate an anagram

council agency, assembly, audience, board, board room, bureaucracy, cabinet, civil service, comitia, commission, committee, conclave, conference, congregation, congress, consistory, conventicle, convention, convocation, court, crew, delegation, deputation, diet, durbar, ecclesia, embassy, envoy, establishment, executorship, folkmoot, genro, governorship, group, hearing, legation, meeting, mission, moot, panel, party, presidium, public service, regency, regentship, round table, session, sitting, soviet, summit, synod, tribunal, trusteeship, vestry, zemstvo

count accounting, adding, calculating, census, ciphering, compute, counting, earl, inventory, make a difference, matter, nobleman, numbering, onetwo-three, poll, reckoning, signify, stocktaking, sum, tally, telling, totalling

counter annul, answer, apologize, appeal, calculator, computer, confute, contradict, contraindicate, counterblast, countercharge, counterclaim, countermand, counterorder, demur, deny, enumerator, invalidate, marker, negate, nullify, oppose, opposite, piece, protest, rebut, refute, rejoin, resist, retaliate, retort, token, worktop

counteract act against, annul, backfire, boomerang, cancel out, compensate for, contravene, counter, counterattack, counterbalance, countercheck, countermine, counterpoise, countervail, cure, deactivate, invalidate, kick back, match, moderate, negate, neutralize, obviate, offset, oppose, polarize, react, recoil, undo

counteracting antagonistic, antidotal, antipathetic, balancing, clashing, compensatory, conflicting, contraceptive, contrary, contravening, corrective, frictional, frustrating, hostile, inimical, interfering, intolerant, intractable, invalidating, moderating, neutralizing, nullifying, obstructive, offsetting, opposing, polarized, preventive, reactionary, reactive, recalcitrant, remedial, repressive, resistant, restraining, retroactive, suppressive

counteraction backlash, compensation, contravention, countermove, counterpressure, defence, deregulation, deterrent, hostility, inhibitor, invalidation, kick, kickback, moderation, negation, neutralizer, offset, opposition, polarization, reaction, recalcitrance, recoil, remedy, repercussion, resistance, retroaction, veto

counterbalance antidote, atonement, avenge, balance, ballast, cancellation, compensate, contraposition, correct, counteract, counterblast, countermeasure, counterpoise, countervail, counterweigh, counterweight, deactivation, equalization, equilibrate, equilibrium,

equiponderance, equiponderate, level, neutralization, nullification, offset, reprisal, retaliate, retaliation, revenge, setoff, square, vengeance

countercharge answer, comeback, counteraccusation, counteraction, counter-argument, counterblast, counterclaim, counterstatement, defence, demur, demurral, objection, parry, rebuttal, rejoinder, reply, respond, response, retaliate, retort, riposte

counterclaimant denier, devil's advocate, rebutter, refuter

counterevidence answer, apology, appeal, comeback, confutation, contradiction, contraindication, counteraccusation, counterblast, countercharge, counterclaim, countermand, defence, demurrer, denial, equivocation, rebuttal, refutation, rejoinder, retaliation, retort

countering answering, apologetic, apostatic, confutative, contradictory, contrary, counteractive, defensive, denying, oppositional, rebutting, refutative, retaliatory

countermeasure counteraction, counterargument, counterattack, countercheck, countermove, counterproposal, counterwork

counterpart clone, companion, coordinate, copy, correspondent, doppelgänger, double, equivalent, fellow, image, ka, lookalike, mate, other, pendant, reciprocal, reflection, shadow, spit, twin, understudy

counterstatement answer, argument, contradiction, counterblast, countercharge, defence, objection, plea, rebuttal, refutation, retaliation

country agrarian, body politic, farmland, greenbelt, homeland, land, nation, provinces, rural, rustic, state

countryman apple-knocker, backwoodsman, bumpkin, bushman, clod, cottager, crofter, farmer, frontiersman, hick, highlander, hillbilly, parishioner, peasant, provincial, redneck, ruralist, rustic, smallholder, villager, yokel

courage audacity, backbone, boldness, bottle, braveness, bravery, courageousness, daring, dauntlessness, derring-do, doughtiness, fearlessness, fighting spirit, grit, guts, hardiness, lion-heartedness, mettle, nerve, pluck, spirit, spunk, stout-heartedness, toughness, valour, vim

courageous audacious, ballsy, bold, brave, daring, dauntless, doughty, fearless, gallant, gutsy, hardy, heroic, lion-hearted, mettlesome, plucky, spirited, spunky, stout-hearted, tough, unbowed, undaunted, unflinching, unshakeable, unshrinking, valiant

course career, current, flow, march, ongoing, passage, progression, route, series, studies, tide, track, way

court arena, assizes, chase, circuit, civil, coquet, coroner, courtyard, criminal, crown, dally, date, escort, flirt, High, kangaroo, law, lure, make eyes, petty sessions, philander, playing field, propose, proposition, pursue, quadrangle, quarter sessions, Queen's Bench, royal household, serenade, spoon, squire, Star Chamber, sue, sweet-talk, tempt, the bench, the Woolsack, toy, tribunal, trifle, vamp, woo

courteous affable, agreeable, amenable, amiable, chivalrous, civil, considerate, courtly, decent, discreet, fair, friendly, gallant, genial, graceful, gracious, humble, obliging, polite, sociable, solicitous, tactful, thoughtful, urbane, welcoming

courtesies amenities, ceremonies, civilities, compliments, dignities, elegances, formalities, gentilities, graces, pleasantries, regards, respect, rites, urbanities

courtesy affability, agreeableness, amenity, amiability, chivalry, civility, comity, consideration, courtliness, decency, deference, discretion, friendliness, gallantry, gracefulness, gra-

ciousness, kindness, mansuetude, noblesse oblige, obligingness, politeness, respect, sociability, suavity, tact, thoughtfulness

courtship addresses, advances, amourette, coquetry, dalliance, dating, engagement, familiarity, favours, flirtation, gallantry, going out, lovemaking, love-play, love suit, necking, pass, petting, philandering, poodle-faking, proposal, sheep's eyes, smooching, spooning, wooing

courtyard patio, plaza, quadrangle, square

couturier clothier, costume designer, costumier, draper, dressmaker, fashion designer, furrier, garmentmaker, glover, haberdasher, hatter, hosier, milliner, modiste, outfitter, sartor, tailor

cover bung, bury, cap, coat, cork, crown, defence, disguise, incorporate, lid, plug, report, shield, stop, stopper, substitute, suffice, superimpose, top

covered bricked, capped, copperplated, corked, faced, glazed, painted, panelled, papered, roofed, stained, thatched, tiled, topped, varnished, wallpapered, whitewashed

covering bark, blanket, bloom, blotting out, casing, cloaking, coat, coating, cuticular, dross, eclipsing, enclosement, enfoldment, envelopment, epidermal, facing, fascia, film, flooding over, foil, hiding, imbrication, including, incorporating, integumental, lamella, lamina, leaf, membrane, obscuring, overarching, overlapping, overlay, overlaying, overlying, overshadowing, paving, patina, peel, pellicle, plate, screening, scum, sheathe, sheet, shielding, skin, spanning, stratification, superimposed, superimposition, topping, veneer, walling in, wrapping

coward baby, chicken, craven, dastard, deserter, funk, jellyfish, milksop, mouse, poltroon, rabbit, rat, scaredy-cat, sissy, weed, wimp, yellow-belly

cowardice cowering, cravenness, dastardliness, defeatism, desertion, faint-heartedness, fearfulness, funk, overcaution, poltroonery, pusillanimity, timidity, timorousness, weakness

cowardly afraid, chicken, chicken-hearted, cowed, cowering, craven, dastardly, daunted, defeatist, faint-hearted, fearful, frightened, gutless, lily-livered, namby-pamby, panicky, pusillanimous, rattled, recreant, scared, shy, sissy, soft, spineless, timid, timorous, unheroic, weak-kneed, wet, yellow, yellow-bellied

cower cringe, desert, flee, funk, quail, recoil, retreat, run away, scuttle, shrink, skulk, sneak, turn tail

crack aperture, bang, breach, break, cavity, check, chink, cleft, cranny, crevice, cut, ditch, dyke, fault, fissure, flaw, fracture, furrow, gash, groove, ha-ha, hit, hole, incision, interstice, moat, nick, notch, opening, orifice, rent, rift, rupture, scissure, slit, slot, split, strike, tear, trench

cracked broken, cleft, cloven, crazy, cut, dehiscent, fissured, fractured, furrowed, gaping, gappy, grooved, open, rent, rimose, riven, ruptured, slit, split, torn
may indicate an anagram

cram compact, compress, concentrate, crowd, mass, pack, ram down, squeeze, study, swot, tamp

crapulence dizziness, drunkenness, giddiness, hangover, intemperance, sickness, thick head

crapulous dizzy, drunk, giddy, hung over, sick

create actualize, cause, compose, devise, factualize, form, invent, make, realize, reify

created actualized, evolved, formed, invented, made, materialized, moulded, shaped

creation actualization, appearance, arrival, beginning, birth, emergence, evolution, genesis, materialization, origin
may indicate an anagram

credit acclaim, balances, believe, buying, charge card, credit card, creditworthiness, glory, instalment, plastic, praise, prestige, receipts, right-hand entry, the black, tick

crepitation clap, clatter, click, clunk, crack, effervesce, knock, plonk, plop, plunk, pop, rap, rat-tat-tat, rattle, sizzling, slap, smack, snap, snap, spitting, staccato, tap

cricket
See list of cricketing terms and expressions.

crime bribery, civil disturbance, confidence trick, criminality, crookedness, delinquency, dirty dealings, disorder, embezzlement, extortion, felony, fiddle, foul play, fraudulency, graft, guilt, illegality, infraction, infringement, law-breaking, lawlessness, misdemeanour, murder, racket, racketeering, riot, robbery, scam, shadiness, sharp practice, skulduggery, swindle, tax evasion, thieving, transgression, trespass, turmoil, vandalism

criminal accusable, bent, blameworthy, bribing, crook, crooked, culpable, delinquent, embezzling, felon, felonious, fishy, foul, fraudulent, guilty, illegal, lawbreaker, light-fingered, offensive, robber, shady, swindling, thief, thieving, underhanded, unlawful, wicked

criminalize ban, censor, forbid, illegalize, outlaw, prohibit, proscribe, veto

criminology penology, prison management

crimp clop, coif, curl, frizz, furrow, pleat, rumple

crisis catastrophe, crux, eleventh hour, emergency, nexus, pinch, rub

critic fault-finder, knocker, nit-picker, pettifogger, quibbler, reviewer

critical abusive, analytical, censorious, crucial, damaging, dangerous, decrying, defamatory, denigrating, denunciatory, deprecatory, disparaging, dispraising, execratory, libellous, important, maligning, poor, precarious, significant, slanderous, uncomplimentary, unfavourable, vituperative

criticism brickbat, dispraise, flak, knock, panning, rap, slam, slating

criticize abuse, belittle, berate, carp, censure, condemn, decry, defame, denigrate, denounce, deplore, deprecate, depreciate, disparage, dispraise, fault, inveigh against, knock, libel, malign, nit-pick, pan, rap, revile, slam, slander, slate, slur, smear, snipe, vilify, vituperate

critique analysis, criticism, evaluation, notice, puff, review

crockery china, dinner service, dishware, glassware, pottery, teaset, Tupperware, utensils

cross angry, annoyed, bestride, bridge, convey, crucifix, ford, hybrid, interchange, intersect, irritable, mix, negotiate, oppose, overfly, peevish, span, straddle, thwart, traject, transfer, transit, transmit, transport, traverse, trick

crossing excursion, extravagation, ford, jump, leap-frog, opposing, thwarting, transcendence, transcursion, transilience

crossroads match point, point of no return, Rubicon, turning point

crouch bend, bow, crawl, creep, grovel, slouch, squat, stoop

crowd brim, bristle, burst, buzz, congregate, cram, crawl, crush, flock, flood, flow, horde, host, hum, jam, mass, mill, mob, multitude, overflow, pack, pour, press, pullulate, rabble, ruck, rush, seethe, stream, surge, swarm, sweep, teem, the masses, throng, troop

crowded bristling, chock-a-block, close, cluttered, congested, crammed, crawling, crushed, dense, jam-packed, massed, milling, mobbed, overpopulated, overrun, packed, seething, serried, swarming, teeming, thronged

crucial critical, decisive, key, momentous, pivotal

crude basic, coarse, crass, gauche, gaudy, gross, indecent, inelegant, in-

CRICKETING TERMS AND EXPRESSIONS

ALL ROUNDER	DONKEY DROPPER	LEG SLIP	SILLY POINT
BAIL	DUCK	LEG TRAP	SNICK
BAT	FIELDER	LONGSTOP	SPIN BOWLER
BATS(WO)MAN	FLIPPER	MAIDEN OVER	SQUARE CUT
BATTING CREASE	GLANCE	NELSON	SQUARE LEG
BEAMER	GLIDE	NO BALL	STICKY WICKET
BODYLINE	GOOGLY	OFF-SIDE FIELDER	STONEWALLING
BOWLING	GREENTOP	ON-SIDE FIELDER	STRIKER
BOSIE	GULLY	OUTSWINGER	STUMP
BOUNCER	HAT TRICK	OVER	TEST MATCH
BOUNDARY	HIT WICKET	OVERTHROW	THE COVERS
BOWLER	HOOK	POPPING CREASE	THE SLIPS
BYE	HOW'S THAT!	RAISED SEAM	THIRD MAN
CENTURY	HOWZAT!	REVERSE SWEEP	UMPIRE
COVER	INNINGS	RUN	WICKET
CREASE	INSWINGER	RUN OUT	WICKET KEEPER
CUTTER	KING PAIR	SEAMER	WICKET MAIDEN
DAISYCUTTER	LBW	SHOOTER	WIDE
DEEP SQUARE	LEG BEFORE WICKET	SIGHT SCREEN	WILLOW
DISMISSAL	LEG BYE	SILLY MID ON	YORKER

sensitive, obscene, racy, raw, rough, sick, tacky, tasteless, tawdry, undiscriminating, unrefined, vulgar

crudeness approximateness, bawdiness, cursoriness, incompleteness, indecency, rudeness, rudiment, shapelessness, sketchiness, vagueness

cruel atrocious, barbaric, bestial, bloodthirsty, brutal, cannibalistic, dehumanized, demoniac, devilish, diabolical, ferocious, fiendish, heinous, hellish, infernal, inhumane, monstrous, murderous, outrageous, sadistic, satanic, savage, subhuman, terrorful, vicious, violent

cruelty animality, atrocity, barbarism, bestiality, bloodlust, bloodthirstiness, brutality, cannibalism, ferocity, fiendishness, heinousness, inhumanity, monstrousness, sadism, savagery, terrorism, vandalism, viciousness, violence

crumble chip, collapse, decay, flake, pulverize

crumbliness brittleness, flakiness, friability, looseness, pulverableness

crumbly crisp, flaky, friable, scaly, scurfy

cry battle cry, bawl, bellow, call, caterwaul, clamour, gasp, groan, holler, howl, hubbub, hullabaloo, moan, outburst, outcry, roar, scream, screech, shout, shriek, sob, squall, squawk, squeal, uproar, vociferate, vociferation, wail, whimper, yawl, yell, yelp, yowl

crying blubbering, blubbing, groaning, howling, moaning, sighing, sobbing, ululant, wailing, weeping, whimpering

cryogenics cryonics, cryostat, cryosurgery

crystalline amorphous, crystallite, crystallized, crystalloid, microcrystalline, noncrystalline, supernatant

cul-de-sac blind alley, dead end, no through road

culinary epicurean, gastronomic

cultivate bale, broadcast, civilize, crop, cut, delve, dig, direct, drill, dung, encourage, enlighten, farm, fertilize, form, gather, glean, grow, harrow, harvest, hoe, improve, irrigate, manure, mould, mow, muck, mulch, plant, plough, rake, reap, refine, rotavate, scatter seed, shape, sharecrop, sow, spade, spray, swathe, till, topdress, turn, weed

cultivation acculturation, agriculture, edification, enlightenment, farming, illumination

cumulate agglomerate, aggregate, collective, combined, confluent, conglomerate, convergent, glomerate

cunning acuity, artfulness, beguilement, cageyness, caution, chicanery, circumvention, cleverness, conspiracy, craftiness, deception, diplomacy, duplicity, evasion, finesse, foxiness, gamesmanship, gerrymandering, imagination, ingenuity, intelligence, intrigue, inventiveness, jobbery, knavery, know-how, Machiavellianism, manoeuvring, plot, realpolitik, resourcefulness, sharpness, shiftiness, shrewdness, slipperiness, slyness, smartness, sophistication, sophistry, stealthiness, subtlety, tactics, temporizing, trickery, wariness, wiliness

cup beaker, coffeecup, eggcup, mug, stoup, teacup, trophy

cure antidote, detoxify, doctor, heal, medicate, nurse, physic, preserve, remedy, restore, revive, smoke, treat

cured better, convalescent, healed, healthy, kippered, smoked

curiosity inquiry, inquisition, inquisitiveness, interest, probing, prying, questioning, soul-searching, wonder

curious adventurous, inquisitive, inquisitorial, interested, keen, nosey, puzzlement, questioning
may indicate an anagram

currency
See list at **money**.

current backflow, backwash, capacitance, capacity, charge, contemporary, counterflow, course, crosscurrent, drift, ebb, eddy, flux, impedance, inductance, ion, maelstrom, millrace, millstream, modern, present, reactance, reflux, resistance, ripple, river, torrent, undercurrent, undertow, up-to-date, voltage, vortex, wake, wash, whirlpool

curse billingsgate, blasphemy, cursing, cuss, dysphemism, dysphemize, expletive, filth, foul mouth, four-letter word, hoodoo, imprecation, invective, jinx, malediction, oath, obscenity, profanity, ribaldry, sacrilege, scatologize, scatology, scurrility, swearing, swearword, talking dirty, voodoo, vulgarity

curtain blind, cloak, drape, partition, screen, shade, shield, shutter, veil

curvature arching, bending, circularity, concavity, convexity, curliness, curvilinearity, sinuousity

curve arc, arch, bend, bow, circle, coil, curl, detour, entwine, loop, spiral, swerve, turn, twine
See also list at **geometry**.

curved arched, arciform, bent, bowed, cambered, circular, coiled, concave, convex, crescentic, curled, curviform, curvilinear, domical, hyperbolic, looped, lunar, meniscal, oval, parabolic, round, semicircular, sinusoidal, sloping, spiraled, stooped, turning, vaulted

custom behaviour patterns, ceremony, convention, craze, cult, drill, fashion, folklore, form, groove, habit, institution, lore, method, mores, observance, policy, practice, praxis, procedure, religion, rite, ritual, routine, rut, system, tradition, trend, usage, way, wont

customary accustomed, conventional, copybook, habitual, methodical, normal, orderly, regulated, regulation, routine, standard, systematic, traditional, typical, usual, wonted

cycle beat, bicycle, biological clock, biorhythm, circadian rhythm, circuit, go, iteration, lap, menstrual cycle, orbit, photoperiodism, relay, return, revolution, rota, rotation, round, season, series, shift, turn

cyclic circular, cyclical, orbital, periodic, recurrent, repetitive, revolving, rhythmic, rotational

cylinder column, pipe, rod, roller, tube

cynosure centre, focus, guide, limelight, spotlight, star

·D·

ABBREVIATIONS

D	daughter • deuterium • diamonds • died • doh • five hundred • God (Latin: *Deus*) • key • note • penny
DA	American lawyer • District Attorney
DAR	Daughters of the American Revolution
DB	decibel
DBE	Dame Commander of the Order of the British Empire
DC	current • Detective Constable • from the beginning (Italian: *da capo*)
DCI	Detective Chief Inspector
DD	clergyman • direct debit
DFC	Distinguished Flying Cross
DFM	Distinguished Flying Medal
DG	thanks be to God (Latin: *Deo gratias*)
DI	Detective Inspector • Diana • didynium • Princess
DIM	diminuendo
DIP	diploma
DJ	dinner jacket • disc jockey
DOA	dead on arrival
DOB	date of birth
DOS	disk operating system
DR	doctor • Drive
DS	Detective Sergeant • repeat from the sign (Italian: *dal segno*)
DSC	Distinguished Service Cross
DSM	Distinguished Service Medal
DSO	(Companion of the) Distinguished Service Order
DV	God willing (Latin: *Deo volente*)
DWT	pennyweight
DY	dysprosium

damn anathematize, ban, curse, excommunicate, imprecate, proscribe

damned accursed, blankety-blank, blasted, bothersome, confounded, devilish, diabolic, dratted, execrable, hellish, infernal

dance ball, barn dance, bop, caper, ceilidh, choreograph, disco, hop, jiggle, knees-up, masquerade, rave, shindig, tea dance
See list of dances.

dancer ballerina, bebopper, belly dancer, cancan dancer, clog dancer, coryphée, disco dancer, entertainer, erotic dancer, figurant, foxtrotter, go-go dancer, high-kicker, hoofer, jitterbug, jiver, jumper, shuffler, tap dancer, Terpsichorean, waltzer

dancing bodypop, bop, breakdance, caper, cavort, disco-dance, frolic, gambol, hop, jig, jive, leap, pogo, prance, rock, rollick, rotate, shuffle, skip, slam, stomp, trip, twist, vogue, whirl

danger ambush, black spot, crisis, dire straits, dragon's lair, emergency, hazard, hazardousness, jeopardy, lion's mouth, menace, near miss, peril, perilousness, pitfall, predicament, razor's

DANCES

ABRASAX
ABRAXAS
ABUANG
AHIDOUS
AHIR
ALEGRIAS
AMENER
Ã MOLESON
APARIMA
ARNAOUT
ATINGA
ATNUMOKITA
AURRESKU
BABBITY BOWSTER
BABORÁK
BABORASCHKA
BAGUETTES
BAILECITO
BALL PLA
BALZTANZ
BAMBUCO
BANDLTANTZ
BANJARA
BARIS
BARN DANCE
BATON DANCE
BATUQUE
BATUTA
BERGERETTA
BHARANG
BLACKBOTTOM
BOLERO
BOOGIE
BOULANGER
BOURRÉE
BREAKDANCING
BULBA
BULL-FOOT
BUMP
CACHUCHA
CAKEWALK
CALATA
CANA
CANACUAS
CANARIE
CANARIO
CANARY
CAN-CAN
CANDIOTE
CARDADORA
CAROL
CAROLE
CEBELL
CHA CHA
CHANIOTIKO
CHARLESTON
CHARRADA
CINQ PAS
CLOG DANCE
CONGA

COTILLION
COUNTRY
   BUMPKIN
COURANTE
CREUX DE VERVI
CSARDAS
CUECA
DAMHSA NAM BOC
DANSA
DANSE MACABRE
DANSURINGUR
DEBKA
DITHYRAMBOS
DJOGED
DOG
ECOSSAISE
EIGHTSOME REEL
EIXIDA
ESPRINGALE
FACKELTANZ
FANDANGO
FARANDOLE
FARANDOULO
FLORAL DANCE
FORLANA
FOX-TROT
FUNKY CHICKEN
FURIANT
FURLANA
FURRY DANCE
GALLEGADA
GALLIARD
GANGAR
GAVOT
GAVOTTE
GAY GORDONS
GERANOS
GHARBA DANCE
GHILLIE CALLUM
GIENYS
GIG
GIGUE
GLOCSEN
GOMBEYS
GONDHAL
GOPAK
GOSHIKI
GREEN GARTERS
GYMNASKA
HABANERA
HAJDUTÂNC
HAKA
HALOA
HAND JIVE
HASTE TO THE
   WEDDING
HIGHLAND FLING
HIMINAU
HOKEY-COKEY
HOPAK

HORA
HORN DANCE
HORNPIPE
HUAPANGO
HUSTLE
JABADAO
JACARA
JARABE
JARANA
JIG
JITTERBUG
JIVE
JOTA
KAGURA
KALELA
KOLOMEJKA
KUMMI
KYNDELDANS
L'AG-YA
LAMBETH WALK
LAMENTO
LANCERS
LANDLER
LAUTERBACH
LIMBO
LLORONA
LOCOMOTION
LOURE
MADISON
MAILEHEN
MAMBO
MAYPOLE
MAZURKA
MEASURE
MILITARY TWO-STEP
MILKMAIDS'
   DANCE
MILONGA
MINUET
MISTLETOE
MOHOBELO
MOKOROTLO
MOONWALK
MORRIS DANCE
MUNEIRA
MUTCHICO
NAZUN
NUMBA
OKINA
OLE
OXDANSEN
PALAIS GLIDE
PAMPERRUQUE
PASILLO
PASO DOBLE
PASSEPIED
PAVANE
PERICON
PERICOTE
PESSAH

PLANXTY
POGO
POLKA
POLONAISE
POLSKA
PURPURI
QUADRILLE
QUICKSTEP
REEL O'TULLOCH
RENNINGEN
RIGAUDON
ROCK AND ROLL
ROCK 'N' ROLL
RUEDA
RUMBA
RUNNING SET
RUTUBURI
SAMBA
SARABANDE
SARBA
SARDANA
SATACEK
SATECKOVA
SCHOTTISCHE
SELLINGER'S ROUND
SHAG
SHAKE
SHIMMY
SIBEL
SIBYL
SIKINIK
SIR ROGER DE
   COVERLEY
SQUARE DANCE
STOMP
STRATHSPEY
STRIP TEASE
STRIP THE WILLOW
SURUVAKARY
TAMBORITO
TANDAVA
TANGO
TANTARA
TARANTELLA
TEWRDANNCKH
TIRANA
TRAIPSE
TRATA
TRENCHMORE
TROYANATS
TSAMIKOS
TURKEY TROT
TWIST
VALETA
VELAL
VELETA
VIRA
WAKAMBA
WALTZ
YUMARI

edge, risk, riskiness, slippery slope, snag, threat, trap, treacherousness, urgency

dangerous alarming, at stake, chancy, critical, deadly, dicey, difficult, dodgy, foreboding, frightening, hairy, harmful, hazardous, iffy, infectious, in question, life-threatening, menacing, nasty, ominous, perilous, risky, serious, sticky, threatening, toxic, treacherous, tricky, ugly, uncertain, unhealthy, unknown, unlit, venturous

Danish bacon, Dane, pastry

dare brave, courageous, gamble, lord it, outface, presume, queen it, risk, venture

daredevil adventurer, eccentric, hothead, madcap

dark achromatic, black, brunette, Cimmerian, darkling, deep, dim, dingy, dusky, ebony, gloomy, ill-lit, inky, jet-black, leaden, lightless, louring, melanic, melanistic, moonless, murky, nocturnal, overcast, pigmented, pitch-black, pitch-dark, sable, shady, smoky, smudgy, starless, Stygian, sunless, swart, swarthy, tenebrous, thundery, umbrageous, underexposed, unilluminated, unlit

darken adumbrate, black out, blindfold, cloud, cover, dim, eclipse, fog, hood, obfuscate, obscure, occult, shade, shadow, shroud, shutter, underexpose, veil

darkening blackening, blackout, dimming, eclipse, extinguishment, fadeout, lights out, obfuscation, obscuration, occultation, power cut, screening, shading, shadowing, underexposure

darkness blackness, blackout, blindness, darkest hour, dimness, drabness, eclipse, gloom, leadenness, murk, night-blindness, obscurity, pitch-darkness, shade, shadow, sombreness, Stygian gloom, sunlessness

dart arrow, dash, harpoon, javelin, scurry, spear

date anniversary, appointment, date palm, day, occasion, red-letter day

dawn beginning, cockcrow, crack of dawn, daybreak, lighten, origin, sunrise, unearthly hour

daydream abstractedness, autosuggestion, brown study, deep thought, delirium, desire, escapism, fancy, fantasia, fantasizing, frenzy, insensibility, muse, pensiveness, pipe dream, reverie, romanticism, sleepwalking, somnambulism, sophistry, subjectivism, trance, window-shopping, wish, wishful thinking, woolgathering

de of France, of the French

dead breathless, cold, deceased, defunct, demised, departed, erstwhile, ex, exanimate, extinct, finished, former, gone, inanimate, kaput, killed, lamented, late, lifeless, murdered, no more, old, passed away, past, posthumous, previous, released, sometime, stiff, still, stillborn

deadline immediacy, importance, lateness, pressure, time limit, urgency, zero hour

deadly deathly, fatal, incurable, inoperable, insalubrious, killing, lethal, life-threatening, malignant, miasmic, mortal, murderous, poisonous, terminal, toxic, unhealthy

deaf deaf-mute, hearing-impaired, stone deaf, tone deaf, unhearing

deafening ear-shattering, ear-splitting, piercing

dear beloved, bullish, costly, excessive, exorbitant, expensive, extortionate, extravagant, fancy, high-priced, inflationary, luxury, overcharging, precious, pricey, profiteering, prohibitive, ritzy, sky-high, steep, stiff, treasured, unreasonable, up-market, usurious

death annihilation, curtains, death's-head, decease, demise, departure, dying, end, exit, expiration, expiry, extinction, fate, grave, Grim Reaper, martyrdom, memento mori, mortality, passing, quietus, stillbirth, tomb

deathbed death throes, extreme unction, last rites, moribundity, obsequies

deathly ashen, cadaverous, fatal, ghastly, ghostly, haggard, livid, pale, pallid, skeletal, wan

debase abase, adulterate, cashier, debunk, deflate, degrade, demote, dilute, downgrade, humble, humiliate, snub, water down

debasement degradation, demotion, deterioration, downgrading, grovelling, humiliation

debate answer, antithesis, apologetics, argue, argument, argumentation, challenge, colloquy, consideration, contend, contest, contradict, conversation, criticize, deduction, deliberation, deny, dialectics, dialogue, discourse, discussion, disputation, dispute, dissent, doubt, elenchus, eristic, hermeneutic, heuristic, induction, inquiry, interlocution, litigation, logic, logomachize, logomachy, maieutic, negate, oratory, polemicize, polemics, questioning, ratiocination, reasoning, reflection, refute, respond, rhetoric, sophistry, syllogism, symposium, synthesis, thesis, thought

debt accountability, commitment, encumbrance, indebtedness, liability, obligation, owing, responsibility

debts bills, charge, debit, overdraft, the red

decapitate
may indicate a shortening (delete first letter)

decay corrode, corrupt, decompose, fester, go bad, go off, go septic, moulder, putrefy, rankle, rot, rust, spoil, suppurate

deceitful artful, artificial, calculating, collusive, conning, crafty, cunning, devious, dishonest, dodgy, duplicitous, fabricating, fake, false-hearted, fibbing, flimflam, forswearing, fraudulent, furtive, guileful, indirect, libelling, lying, malingering, manipulative, perfidious, perjuring, prevaricating, sharp, shifty, slandering, slippery, smooth, sneaky, surreptitious, treacherous, treasonous, tricky, wily

deceitfulness artfulness, artifice, cunning, duplicity, falseheartedness, fraudulence, guile, improbity, Judas kiss, lying, malingering, sneakiness, treachery, treason, wile

deceive bamboozle, betray, bilk, blag, blindfold, bluff, charm, cheat, chisel, circumvent, con, confuse, connive, contrive, defraud, design, diddle, dissemble, dissimulate, dodge, double-cross, double-deal, dupe, elude, embezzle, ensnare, entrap, evade, fake, feign, feint, fleece, fool, hoax, hoodwink, lie, manipulate, masquerade, misdirect, misguide, misinform, mislead, outmanoeuvre, outsmart, outwit, pretend, scheme, sneak, spoof, sweet-talk, swindle, swizzle, trick, two-time

deceiver beguiler, charlatan, cheat, deluder, duper, fake, fraud, guiser, hoaxer, hypochondriac, hypocrite, impersonator, imposter, liar, malingerer, masquerader, misleader, mountebank, phoney, poser, pretender, quack, sham, spoofer

deceleration brake, curb, flagging, friction, restraint, retardation, slackening

decentralization assigning, consigning, deconcentration, deputizing, devolution, federalization, localization, regionalization, subsidiarity

deception artfulness, circumvention, craftiness, cunning, deceitfulness, deviousness, dishonesty, disinformation, dissimulation, double-dealing, duplicity, falsehood, fraudulence, furtiveness, guile, indirection, insidiousness, lying, misinformation, perjury, shiftiness, sneakiness, subterfuge, surreptitiousness, trickery, underhandedness

deceptive conspiratorial, contrived,

deceiving, dishonest, duplicitous, fallacious, false, fixed, fraudulent, gerrymandered, gimmicky, illicit, insidious, misleading, sorcerous, tongue-in-cheek, underhand, untrustworthy

decided established, fixed, incontrovertible, indubitable, irrefutable, settled, unambiguous, unchallengeable, uncontestable, undeniable, undisputed, unequivocal, unimpeachable, unrefuted

decipher decode, demystify, disentangle, enucleate, read, resolve, solve, spell out, unravel, unriddle, unscramble, work out

decline bottoming out, collapse, deflation, depression, deterioration, downturn, downward trend, drop, ebb, fall, levelling out, plunge, sinking, slump, tailspin

decomposed
may indicate an anagram

deconstruct analyse, catalyse, compartmentalize, decentralize, delegate, demerge, demolish, destroy, devolve, disband, dismantle, dismember, disorder, disperse, dissect, dissolve, divide, electrolyse, hydrolyse, liquefy, melt, parse, partition, regionalize, scatter, separate, simplify, smash, split, syllabify, wreck

deconstruction analysis, anatomization, breakdown, catabolism, compartmentation, decentralization, delegation, deliquescence, demolition, destruction, devolution, dismantling, dismemberment, dispersal, dissection, dissolution, division, separation, simplification, syllabification

decorate abut, adorn, arch, array, articulate, award a medal, bedeck, bedizen, bejewel, boss, buttress, chase, coffer, colour, crown, dome, embellish, emblazon, emboss, embroider, engrave, enhance, etch, festoon, flute, fret, garland, illuminate, illustrate, mould, ornament, paint, rib, smock, tool, trace, vault, wreathe
See also list at **jewellery**.

decorating housepainting, interior design, ornamenting, wallpapering

decorative baroque, bejewelled, embellished, embroidered, enamelled, enhanced, enriched, fancy, garnished, gilded, gilt, inlaid, non-functional, ornamental, ornamented, ornate, patterned, picturesque, pretty-pretty, rococo, scenic, trimmed, worked

decoy false scent, fool's errand, red herring, wild-goose chase

decrease abatement, abbreviation, abridgment, atrophy, attrition, belittlement, compression, consumption, contraction, corrosion, curtailment, cutback, damage, decay, deceleration, decrement, decrescendo, deduction, de-escalation, degeneration, depreciation, detumescence, dilapidation, diminishing, diminuendo, dimming, disappearance, drain, dwindling, easing, ebb, economization, enfeeblement, erosion, evanescence, extinction, fading, failure, impoverishment, leakage, lessening, limitation, loss, moderation, precis, rationalization, reduction, regression, restriction, retardation, retrenchment, shortage, shortening, shrinking, shrivelling, slackening, slowdown, squeeze, subsidence, subtraction, undervaluation, waning, wastage, weakening, wear, withering

decrescent declining, decreasing, deliquescent, loss-making, shrinking, waning

dedicate consecrate, contribute, devote, donate, subscribe

deed accomplishment, achievement, act, action, blow, coup, deal, drama, exploit, feat, gesture, handicraft, job, masterpiece, move, overthrow, posture, skill, step, stroke, tactics, task, transaction, undertaking, work

deep abysmal, abyssal, ankle-deep,

booming, bottomless, cavernous, deep-down, deep-set, fathomless, full, gaping, knee-deep, low, mellow, plangent, plunging, rich, sepulchral, sonorous, sunken, thundering, unfathomable, unplumbed, unsounded, vibrant, yawning

deepen bury, descend, dig, dive, drill, drop, excavate, fall, fathom, founder, gape, immerse, inter, lower, mine, plunge, probe, sink, submerge, take soundings, touch bottom, tunnel, yawn

deepness baritone, bass, basso profondo, booming, contralto, lowness, plangency, profundity, sonorousness, thundering

deep-seated earnest, extreme, heartfelt, intense, profound, serious, sincere

defamation backbiting, calumny, character assassination, gossip, libel, muckraking, mudslinging, obloquy, scandal, slander, smear campaign, traducement

defamatory abusive, aspersive, backbiting, besmirching, bitchy, bitter, blackening, calumnious, catty, caustic, damaging, destructive, gossiping, injurious, insinuating, insulting, libellous, mud-slinging, scandalous, scurrilous, slanderous, smearing, snide, tarnishing, venomous, whispering

defame backbite, calumniate, discredit, dishonour, libel, malign, muckrake, slander, sling mud, traduce

default absence, bilk, failure, lapse, levant, welsh

defeat beat, beating, best, climax, collapse, culminate, deathblow, drubbing, eclipse, hiding, licking, loss, outdistance, overcome, overleap, overlook, override, overshadow, overstep, overtop, pass, peak, retreat, reversal, rout, subjugation, submission, thrashing, top, tower above, trashing, trouncing, trump, Waterloo

defeated beaten, bested, depressed, down, knocked out, KO'd, licked,

lost, outclassed, outgunned, outmanoeuvred, outmatched, outplayed, outshone, outvoted, outwitted, overthrown, pipped, routed, thrashed

defecate evacuate, foul, pass, purge, shit, soil, void

defect Achilles' heel, blemish, blind spot, blot, catch, change sides, chink, chip, crack, deficiency, desert, difficulty, disability, disadvantage, drawback, error, failing, fault, flaw, handicap, hang-up, hindrance, kink, lack, lacuna, leak, limitation, loophole, mark, obstacle, quirk, rift, scratch, shortcoming, shortfall, smudge, snag, soft spot, spot, stain, taint, weakness

defective blemished, broken, catalectic, cursory, deficient, disappointing, failed, failing, faulty, imperfect, inadequate, inferior, marred, perfunctory, poor, shopsoiled, spoilt, substandard, unsound
may indicate an anagram

defence alibi, cause, counterargument, excuse, explanation, grounds, justification, mitigation, palliation, plea, reason, rebuttal, recrimination, refutation, rejoinder, retort, truth

defend guard, oppose, picket, police, protect, protest, resist

defensive dismissive, hostile, protective, resistant, watchful

deference bowing, complaisance, compliance, condescension, currying favour, fawning, fulsomeness, glibness, ingratiation, kowtowing, nodding, obeisance, oiliness, salaaming, sycophancy, toadying, unctuousness

deferential bowing, buttery, complaisant, compliant, condescending, fulsome, glib, ingratiating, kowtowing, nodding, obeisant, oily, slimy, smug, soapy, sycophantic, unctuous

defiance arrogance, assurance, audacity, belligerence, bluster, boldness, bottle, brashness, brassiness, bravado, bravura, brazenness, bumptiousness, cheekiness, cockiness, contrariness, courage, cussedness, daringness, effrontery, impertinence, impudence, insolence, lip, nerve, pertness, presumption, provocativeness, rashness, sauce, self-assertion, shamelessness, temerity

defiant arrogant, assertive, assured, audacious, bold, brash, brassy, brazen, bumptious, cheeky, cocky, contemptuous, courageous, daring, derisive, disdainful, emphatic, impertinent, impudent, insolent, insulting, obstinate, offensive, outspoken, pert, presumptuous, reckless, saucy, shameless, stiff-necked, stubborn, unabashed

deficiency blemish, decline, defect, deterioration, disadvantage, failure, fault, handicap, impairment, imperfection, insufficiency, poverty, reversion, shortfall, stain, worsening

defile desecrate, gorge, mountain pass, pollute, profane, single file, violate

define detail, explain, interpret, inventorize, itemize, mention, name, particularize, specify

definite absolute, categorical, certain, indisputable, indubitable, sure, undisputed, unequivocal, unquestionable

definiteness absoluteness, categoricalness, indubitability, indubitableness, undisputedness, unequivocalness, unquestionability

deflated cut-back, cut-down, depreciated, depressed, punctured

deflation collapse, depreciation, devaluation, puncturing, shrinking

deflect bend, diffract, diffuse, disperse, diverge, refract, scatter

deflection counterattack, counterstroke, defence, diversion, foil, parry, resistance

deform bend, blemish, cicatrize, damage, deface, disfigure, distort, impair, malform, mark, misshape, pit, pock-

mark, spot, stain, twist, warp, weal, welt

deformed blemished, defaced, disfigured, distorted, grotesque, hideous, ill-made, imperfect, malformed, marked, pitted, pockmarked, scarred, spotty, twisted, ugly, warped, zitty
may indicate an anagram

deformity defacement, disfigurement, grotesquerie, hideousness, imperfection, malformation, misshapenness, mutation, ugliness

defraud adulterate, bilk, burn, cheat, con, copy, counterfeit, deal underhandedly, dodge, embezzle, fake, falsify, fence, fiddle, fix, fleece, flimflam, forge, gull, gyp, hoax, juggle, load, nobble, pilfer, racketeer, rob, salt, scam, screw, sell, shoplift, short-change, stack, steal, sting, swindle, swizzle, thieve, trick, wangle, whitewash

defray contribute, donate, finance, fund, give, stand, treat

defy affront, brave, challenge, dare, flout, oppose, outstare, presume, protest, withstand

defying antagonistic, challenging, disagreeing, disobedient, obstinate, rebellious, recalcitrant, refractory

degeneration alienation, decadence, decay, denaturalization, perversion

degraded debased, deferential, demoted, depressed, downcast, downgraded, grovelling, humiliated, kneeling, kowtowing

degree altitude, amount, amplitude, BA, BEd, breadth, BSc, calibre, compass, depth, duration, extent, frequency, gradualism, height, intensity, key, latitude, limitation, MA, magnitude, measure, MSc, Phd, pitch, quantity, range, rate, reach, register, scale, scope, size, slowness, speed, stint, tenor, value

dehydrate air-dry, anhydrate, dehumidify, desiccate, drain, dry, evaporate, exsiccate, freeze-dry, vaporize

deification adulation, angelization, apotheosis, assumption, beatification, canonization, consecration, dedication, dignification, divinization, elevation, ennoblement, enshrinement, exaltation, fetishization, glorification, idolization, immortalization, lionization, magnification, sainting, santification

deify adulate, angelize, apotheosize, ascend, beatify, bless, canonize, consecrate, dedicate, dignify, divinize, elevate, enlighten, ennoble, enshrine, exalt, glorify, hallow, idolize, immortalize, magnify, sanctify, sublimate, transcend

deity deva, devi, divinity, god, goddess, immortal
See also list at **God**.

delay adjourn, afterthought, blockage, cease-fire, defer, detain, detention, dilatoriness, dilly-dally, esprit d'escalier, extend, file, filibuster, halt, hang on, hinder, hindrance, hold-up, jam, last-ditch stand, lull, moratorium, mothball, obstruct, obstruction, pause, pigeonhole, postpone, prevent, procrastinate, procrastination, prolong, prorogue, protract, red tape, remand, reprieve, reserve, respite, restrain, retard, shelve, spin out, stall, stand by, stay, stonewall, suspend, suspension, table, temporize, truce, wait, withhold

delaying blocking, dawdling, detaining, dilatory, dilly-dallying, following, hindering, lagging, late-running, lingering, loitering, obstructive, procrastinating, restraining, retarding, shillyshallying, slowing

delegate accredit, agent, ambassador, anoint, appoint, appointee, assign, authorize, cabinet member, chargé d'affaires, clerk, commission, commissioner, consign, consul, councillor, crown, decentralize, delegate, depute, deputize, deputy, devolve, diplomat, elect, emissary, empower, enthrone, entrust, envoy, inaugurate, induct, install, instate, intermediary, invest, job-share, legate, messenger, middleman, minister, name, negotiator, nominate, nominee, ordain, Parliamentarian, patronize, representative, transfer, vote

delegated ambassadorial, appointed, consular, deputy, diplomatic, elected, intermediary, legatine, legationary, ministerial, nominated, representative

delegation appointment, assignment, authorization, consignation, decentralization, deputation, devolution, devolvement, election, nomination

deliberate advised, calculated, consider, contrived, controlled, designed, devised, fixed, framed, intentional, loaded, measured, muse, planned, prearranged, pre-established, premeditated, prepense, preplanned, preset, primed, put-up, set-up, stacked, study, weighed, willed

deliberation abstractedness, debate, pondering, profundity

delicate dainty, filmy, fine-drawn, finespun, gossamery, subtle, thin-spun, wire-drawn

delightful captivating, charming, Elysian, enchanting, enthralling, entrancing, gorgeous, heavenly, lovely, marvellous, wonderful

deliver acquit, bail out, bring, buy off, disencumber, emancipate, excuse, exempt, extract, extricate, free, liberate, purchase, ransom, recover, redeem, release, relieve, reprieve, rescue, restore, retrieve, salvage, save, spare, transport to, unbind, unburden, unfetter, unlock, unravel, untie

deliverable extricable, free, liberated, redeemable, rescuable, rescued, salvable, salvageable, saveable

deliverance acquittal, amnesty, bail, buying off, cessation, delay, discharge, disencumberment, dispensation, emancipation, escape, excuse, exemption, extraction, extrication, freedom, let-off, let-out, liberation, purchase, ransom, recovery, redemption, release, relief, reprieve, rescue, respite, restoration, retrieval, riddance, salvage, salvation, saving, standstill, truce, unravelling, untangling, way out

delude belie, deceive, distort, embellish, mislead, misrepresent, pervert, twist, waffle, whitewash

delusion fallacy, hallucination, illusion, magic, self-deception, trompe l'oeil

demand bidding, bill, blackmail, call, charge, citation, claim, command, dun, exact, exaction, extort, extortion, habeas corpus, impose, indent, injunction, insist, interdict, invoice, levy, mittimus, need, notice, order, process, require, requisition, subpoena, summons, tax, threat, threaten, ultimatum, want, warrant, wish, writ

demanding blackmailing, calling for, claiming, difficult, exacting, exigent, extortive, forcible, imperative, injunctive, insistent, nagging, pressing, requisitionary, threatening, urgent

dematerialize disembody, disincarnate, insubstantialize, vanish

demented
may indicate an anagram

demolish atomize, batter, blast, blitz, bomb, bombard, bulldoze, crush, dismantle, dynamite, explode, fell, flatten, mine, overthrow, pulp, pulverize, rend asunder, shatter, smash, steamroller, topple, wreck

demonetize clip, debase, depreciate, devalue

demonstrable apparent, attestable, certain, clear-cut, conclusive, confirmable, distinct, evident, indisputable, obvious, perspicuous, positive, provable, self-evident, undeniable, unquestionable, verifiable

demonstrate brandish, disclose, display, exhibit, expose, flaunt, flourish, manifest, perform, point out, publish, put forward, reveal, show

demonstrated apod(e)ictic, clear, disclosed, displayed, exhibited, exhibitional, explicit, exposed, expository, express, manifest, obvious, plain, publicized, published, revealed, revelatory

demonstrating agitating, boycotting, dissenting, marching, objecting, opposing, parading, picketing, protesting, proving, rallying, showing, striking

demonstration boycott, demo, disclosure, display, exhibition, expo, exposition, manifestation, march, occupation, performance, picket, presentation, presentment, protest, publication, rally, revelation, showing, sit-in, sleep-in, strike, takeover, work-in

demonstrative affectionate, candid, dramatic, effusive, emotional, exhibitionist(ic), expansive, flamboyant, flashy, frank, histrionic, open, ostentatious, showy, stagy, theatrical, unrestrained, warm

demonstrativeness affection, candour, dramatics, effusiveness, emotionalism, emotionality, exhibitionism, expansiveness, flamboyance, flashiness, frankness, histrionics, openness, ostentation, showiness, staginess, theatrics

den haunt, lair, retreat, study

denial abnegation, apostasy, confutation, contention, contradiction, contravention, disaffirmation, disavowal, disclaimer, disownment, negation, rebuttal, recantation, recusance, rejection, renunciation, repudiation, reversal, withdrawal

dense abundant, assembled, chock-a-block, close-packed, clotted, coagulated, cohesive, compact, condensed, congealed, crowded, firm, full, full-bodied, heavy, impenetrable, impermeable, impervious, incompressible, intensified, jammed, massed, monolithic, packed, serried, solid, strong, swarming, teeming, thick, thickened, thickset, viscous, weighty

denseness abundance, coagulation, condensation, congealment, impenetrability, intensity, thickening, viscosity

density bulk, closeness, coalescence, coherence, cohesion, compactness, concreteness, consistency, hardness, impenetrability, impermeability, imperviousness, incompressibility, mass, solidity, thickness, toughness

dent cavity, concavity, depress, depression, dip, hollow, impress, imprint, indent, indentation, sinkhole, stamp, well

dental endodontic, exodontic, oral, orthodontic, periodontal, periodontic, prosthodontic

dentist endodontist, exodontist, oral pathologist, orthodontist, periodontist, periodontologist, prosthodontist

deny abnegate, argue, contradict, contravene, controvert, disaffirm, disavow, disclaim, disown, dispute, gainsay, naysay, oppose, recant, reject, renounce, repudiate, repugn, reverse, withdraw

depart absent oneself, bow out, decamp, escape, exit, flee, fling off, flounce off, fly, go, go AWOL, leave, make tracks, melt away, play truant, retire, retreat, run, scarper, slink off, slip away, slope off, stamp off, stay away, storm out, take leave, toddle along, trot along, vacate, vamoose, withdraw

departing farewell, final, last, leave-taking, leaving, parting, valedictory

departure abandonment, decampment, egress, elopement, emigration, escape, evacuation, exit, exodus, flight, flit, getaway, going, Hegira, leaving, migration, retirement, retreat, withdrawal

dependent charge, conditional, follower, hanger-on, parasite, protege, reliant, satellite, subject, ward

depilation alopecia, haircut, hair loss, plucking, shearing, tonsure

depositor hoarder, investor, saver

depot entrepot, quay, warehouse, wharf

depreciate belittle, deflate, puncture, underpraise

depress dampen, dishearten, dispirit, push down, squash

depressed atrabilious, blue, dejected, despondent, dismal, dispirited, downcast, dreary, droopy, flattened, gloomy, glum, grey, joyless, lacklustre, listless, long-faced, low, lugubrious, melancholy, moody, moping, morose, pushed, reduced, sad, suicidal, sunk, unhappy

depression cheerlessness, dejection, dent, despair, despondency, dispiritedness, dreariness, droopiness, gloom, glumness, hollow, joylessness, lowness, malaise, melancholy, the doldrums

deprivation expropriation, poverty, removal

depth bottomlessness, cavernousness, deepness, drop, fall, fathomlessness, profundity

deputize appoint, authorize, charge, commission, delegate, designate, empower, entrust, nominate

deputizing acting, ambassadorial, consular, deputy, diplomatic, ersatz, imitative, intermediary, ministerial, plenipotentiary, proconsular, provisional, representing, second-best, standing in, substituting, temporary

deputy aide, assistant, backup, lieutenant, locum, number two, nuncio, proconsul, propraetor, replacement, reserve, right-hand man, second-in-command, stand-in, stop-gap, substitute, supporter, twelfth man, understudy, vicar-general, vice chairman, vice president, viceregent, viceroy

derange drive insane, drive mad, enrage, unbalance, unhinge

deranged demented, disordered, disturbed, gaga, hung-up, insane, mad,

maladjusted, neurotic, psychotic, un-balanced, unhinged, unstable
may indicate an anagram

derangement insanity, instability, madness

deride caricature, debunk, deflate, de-nounce, guy, jeer at, lampoon, laugh at, mock, pillary, put down, satirize, scoff at, send up, snigger about

derider caricaturist, cartoonist, joker, lampooner, mimic, satirist

derisive quizzical, ridiculing, sarcas-tic, sardonic, satirical

descend abate, decline, decrease, drop off, ebb, fall off, gravitate, lower, plunge, seep, settle, sink, soak in, sub-merge, subside

descendants heirs, inheritors, pos-terity, successors

descending bearish, collapsing, crashing, deciduous, declining, de-clivitous, decreasing, decurrent, down, downflowing, downrushing, down-turning, downward, drowning, foun-dering, lowering, plunging, pouring, sinking, slumping, subsiding, totter-ing, tumbling

descent comedown, contraction, de-clension, decline, demotion, down, downdraught, downthrow, downturn, lowering

describe adumbrate, characterize, de-lineate, depict, design, doodle, draft, draw, fashion, form, illustrate, limn, outline, paint, picture, portray, repre-sent, rough out, scribble, shape, sketch out

description account, case history, characterization, character sketch, de-lineation, depiction, details, explana-tion, particulars, picture, portrayal, profile, record, report, specification, statement, version

descriptive detailed, elucidatory, ex-planatory, explicatory, expository, full, graphic, illuminating, illustrative, in-formative, interpretive, representa-tional, vivid

desensitization anaesthesia, analge-sia, catalepsy, catatonia, coma, groggi-ness, hypnosis, narcosis, narcotization, numbness, paralysis, sluggishness, stu-pefaction, stupor, torpor, trance, un-consciousness

desensitize anaesthetize, blunt, brain, concuss, deaden, dope, drug, freeze, hypnotize, knock out, narcotize, numb, paralyse, stupefy

desensitized anaesthetized, co-matose, dead, dopey, drugged, frozen, groggy, inert, numb, paralysed, quies-cent, sluggish, stupefied, torpid, un-conscious, unfeeling

desert abandon, arid, bare, barren, brown, dust bowl, dusty, grassless, karoo, leave, powdery, Saharan, salt flat, sandy, walk out, wasteland

desertion absence, departure, elope-ment, flight, flit, French leave, truancy

deserved due, earned, fitting, mer-ited, warranted

design adjust, appearance, arrange, aspect, balance, compose, convention, draft, draw up, foreshorten, form, frame, improve, lay out, light, mode, mould, protocol, recast, redo, revise, schedule, set, shape, sketch, structure, style, tendency, timetable, work out
may indicate an anagram

desirability acceptability, advisabil-ity, expedience, meritoriousness, suit-ability

desirable acceptable, appealing, ap-petizing, attractive, inviting, likeable, mouth-watering, pleasant, pleasurable, tempting, welcome

desire aim for, ambition, amorous-ness, aphrodisia, appetancy, appetite, ardour, ask for, aspiration, avidity, call, caprice, carnal knowledge, cohabita-tion, coition, consummation, copula-tion, coupling, covetousness, crave, cupidity, curiosity, demand, dream of, eagerness, ecstasy, envy, eroticism, fancy, fascination, favour, fondness, fornication, greed, hanker after, hope, horniness, hunger for, impulse, inclination, intimacy, itch, lasciviousness, libertinage, libido, licentiousness, like, longing, love, lovemaking, lust, mating, need, pant for, partiality, passion, penchant, pining, pray for, predilection, preference, prurience, randiness, request, requirement, sex, summon, taste, urge, venery, voracity, want, wantonness, welcome, will, willingness, wish for, wistfulness, yearning, yen, zeal

desired coveted, envied, in demand, longed for, necessary, popular, requested, required, sought after, yearned for

desirous acquisitive, ardent, avid, covetous, craving, dying for, eager, envious, fond, gluttonous, greedy, homesick, insatiable, keen, nostalgic, partial to, passionate, possessive, voracious, wishful, wistful

desist abstain from, forbear, refrain from, restrain from

desisting abstaining, abstemious, denial, doing without, forbearance, refraining, refusal, self-restraint

despair brood, despond, droop, flag, hopelessness, lose heart, mope, sulk, wilt

dessert afters, banana split, blancmange, bread-and-butter pudding, cake, charlotte russe, cheese board, Christmas pudding, compote, crème caramel, crumble, custard, fool, fresh fruit, fruit flan, fruit salad, gateau, granita, ice cream, icing, jelly, knickerbocker glory, marquise, mousse, pastry, patisserie, pavlova, peach melba, pie, plum pudding, pudding, rice pudding, roly-poly, semolina, sorbet, soufflé, spotted dick, steamed pudding, stewed fruit, suet pudding, summer pudding, sundae, sweet, tapioca, trifle, water ice, yoghurt

destination bourn, end, finish, goal, harbour, haven, home, journey's end, last stop, objective, port, stop, terminal point, terminus, terra firma

destroy ablate, annihilate, annul, bankrupt, blot out, counteract, damage, decimate, denude, despoil, dispatch, dispel, disperse, dispose of, drown, efface, end, eradicate, erase, expunge, exterminate, extinguish, extirpate, harm, impair, injure, invalidate, kill, liquidate, massacre, misuse, murder, muzzle, negate, nullify, obliterate, overthrow, put down, quash, rub out, ruin, sabotage, sacrifice, scatter, silence, slaughter, smother, snuff out, spoliate, stifle, strangle, strike out, suffocate, suppress, tear up, terminate, undo, unmake, vaporize, wipe out, zap

destroyed broken up, buggered, crumbling, crushed, devastated, dished, disintegrated, done for, doomed, falling apart, ground, in ruins, in tatters, kaput, pulped, pulverized, ruined, shattered, shredded, sunk, torpedoed, wiped out, wrecked

destroyer defacer, demolisher, eraser, exterminator, iconoclast, leveller, liquidator, looter, Luddite, nihilist, pillager, raider, ravager, saboteur, spoiler, vandal, wrecker

destroying annihilating, breaking up, crushing, decimation, decomposition, defoliation, demolition, deracination, disintegration, disruption, dissolution, eradication, extirpation, flattening, grinding, incineration, knocking down, pulverization, razing, shattering, shredding, uprooting

destruction ablation, abolition, annihilation, arson, damage, deletion, denudation, despoilment, devastation, elimination, erasure, extermination, extinction, harm, havoc, impairment, injury, insidiousness, liquidation, looting, nullification, obliteration, overthrow, overturning, pillage, repression, ruin, sabotage, silencing, smothering, spoiling, stifling, subversion, suffocation, suppression, threatening, undoing, vandalism, wreck

destructive anarchistic, annihilating, apocalyptic, baneful, cataclysmic, catastrophic, consuming, cut-throat, deadly, devastating, disastrous, fatal, harmful, incendiary, injurious, insidious, internecine, lethal, noxious, overwhelming, pernicious, raging, rampaging, revolutionary, ruinous, subversive, suicidal

destructiveness arson, fire-raising, iconoclasm, sabotage, vandalism

detached calm, collected, composed, cool, disconnected, dispassionate, distinct, equanimous, imperturbable, level-headed, philosophical, separate, serene, stoical, tolerant, unconcerned, unemotional, unruffled

detachment aloofness, balance, calmness, commonsense, coolness, dispassion, isolation, objectivity, rationality, resignation, separation, serenity, stoicism, tolerance

detailed elaborate, exact, finicky, full, fussy, incidental, meticulous, minute, nit-picking, particular, pernickety, precise, special, specific
may indicate a shortening (delete final letter)

detain apprehend, arrest, besiege, blockade, bottle up, catch, clog, collar, confine, cork, enclose, envelop, fence in, guard, hold in, impound, imprison, incarcerate, intern, keep in, kidnap, lag, lock in, maintain, quarantine, refuse bail, remand, repress, restrain, retain, save, seize, starve out, steady, stop, store, support, suppress, wall in, withhold

detained arrested, besieged, captive, confined, delayed, enslaved, fogbound, housebound, impeded, imprisoned, incarcerated, in custody, kidnapped, obstructed, on remand, quarantined, restrained, retarded, sentenced, shut-in, snowbound

detect disclose, disinter, divulge, expose, ferret out, hunt, identify, lay bare, reveal, seek, show up, sniff out, track down, uncover, unearth, unmask, unveil

detection acquisition, betrayal, catching, disclosure, divulgence, excavation, exposure, eye-opener, hunt, leak, manifestation, pursuit, revelation, search, showdown, uncovering, unmasking, unveiling

detention arrest, bird, blockade, bondage, bottling up, captivity, cherishing, confinement, containment, cork, curfew, custodianship, custody, durance, enclosing, envelopment, guarding, immurement, impoundment, imprisonment, incarceration, internment, kidnapping, lag, locking in, maintenance, plug, porridge, preservation, quarantine, remand, repression, saving, sentence, servitude, siege, slavery, stretch, suppression, time

deter cow, daunt, frighten off, intimidate, rattle, shake, stagger, terrorize, threaten, unnerve

deteriorate age, break down, collapse, crumble, decline, degenerate, depreciate, descend, diminish, droop, ebb, fade, fail, flop, fray, lack, lapse, plunge, regress, relapse, retrograde, revert, self-destruct, shrivel, sicken, sink, slide, slip, slip back, slump, stoop, tergiversate, totter, wane, weaken, wear out, wilt, wither, worsen, wrinkle

deteriorated aggravated, corrupt, damaged, degenerate, depraved, drained, effete, exacerbated, exhausted, faded, failing, impaired, off, outdated, recidivist, regressive, retrograde, retrogressive, rotten, run-down, sapped, tergiversating, undermined, useless, weakened, withered, worn out, worse

deterioration backsliding, decline, depreciation, descent, downturn, ebb, fading, impoverishment, lapse, Malthusianism, misfortune, recidivism, regression, relapse, retrogradation, setback, slipping back, slowing down, slump, tergiversation, wane, worsening

determination aplomb, coolness, decision, doggedness, fixity, grimness, hardness, immovability, imperturbability, inelasticity, inflexibility, intransigence, iron will, irreversibility, nerve, obduracy, obstinacy, perseverance, resolution, resolve, single-mindedness, steeliness, stubbornness, tenacity, toughness, will, woodenness

determine advance, aid, contribute to, control, decide, foster, promote, settle

determined adamant, certain, cool, decided, fixed, hard, imperturbable, inflexible, iron-willed, obdurate, obstinate, purposeful, resolute, resolved, self-controlled, single-minded, steadfast, steely, stubborn, sure, tenacious, tough, unwavering, unyielding

deterrence deflection, disincentive, intimidation, restraint, terrorism

detour ambage, avoid, bypass, circumbendibus, circumlocution, deviate, digress, divagation, diverge, diversion, excursion, loop line, meander, periphrasis, ring road, roundaboutness, short-circuit, zigzag

detraction belittlement, deflection, discredit, disparagement, distraction

detrimental baleful, baneful, damaging, deleterious, destructive, distressing, harmful, hurtful, injurious, noxious, pernicious, toxic, troublous

devaluation bear market, belittlement, buyers' market, deflation, depreciation, depression, Dutch auction, plunge, recession, slump

devastate damage, defoliate, deforest, demolish, denude, depopulate, desolate, despoil, destroy, gut, kill, lay waste, loot, murder, nuke, obliterate, pillage, plunder, raid, ransack, rape, ravage, raze, ruin, run amok, sabotage, sack, strip, trash, vandalize, violate, wreak havoc

develop concoct, cultivate, elaborate, enlarge, evolve, force, grow, hatch, mature, mellow, metamorphose, nurse, nurture, print, process, produce, project, prosper, pupate, raise, ripen, show promise

developed adult, blooming, completed, elaborate, expanded, fledged, fruiting, full-grown, hardened, laboured, matured, mellow, perfected, ripened, seasoned, veteran, weathered, well-done, wrought

developing afoot, brewing, brooding, cooking, forthcoming, hatching, impending, incubating, marinating, maturing, stewing

development acclimatization, brewing, cultivation, evolution, furtherance, gestation, growth, hardening, hatching, incubation, inurement, maturation, next step, nursing, nurture, ripening, seasoning

deviant aberrant, eccentric, exorbitant, misdirected, nonconformist, off-centre

deviate bear off, bend, branch, circumlocute, crook, curve, deceive, deflect, detour, digress, dissemble, distort, divaricate, diverge, divert, equivocate, evade, filter, hedge, heel, meander, misalign, mismatch, mistime, prevaricate, sheer, skew, swerve, tack, tralineate, trend, turn, twist, vary, veer, yaw, zigzag

deviation aberration, abnormality, anomaly, bias, branching off, declension, declination, deflection, departure, deviance, digression, disorientation, divagation, divarication, divergence, diversion, eccentricity, exception, excursion, exorbitation, indirection, misdirection, mutation, nonconformism, obliqueness, perversion, skew, slant, tangent, unnaturalness, vagary, variant, variation
may indicate an anagram

device artifice, bomb, fiddle, gimmick, gizmo, pattern, ploy, ruse, shift, sting, stratagem, swindle, trick, wangle, wheeze

devil afreet, Antichrist, Archfiend, beast, Beelzebub, Belial, demon, demonkind, evil spirit, fallen angel, fiend, imp, incubus, Lucifer, Mephisto, Mephistopheles, rebel angel, Satan, spice, succubus, the Devil, the Enemy, the Tempter, villain, wretch

devilish abysmal, Avernal, chthonic, damned, demoni(a)c, demon-like, devil-like, diabolic(al), evil, fiendish, hell-born, hellish, infernal, Mephistophelean, pandemonic, Plutonian, purgatorial, satanic, subterranean, sulphurous, Tartarean

devilize bedevil, demonize, diabolize, possess

devious backhand, circuitous, circumlocutory, deceptive, dissembling, distorted, equivocal, euphemistic, evasive, fishy, fraudulent, furtive, hedging, indirect, periphrastic, roundabout, shady, sidelong, spurious

deviousness backhandedness, circuitousness, circumlocution, cunning, deception, dissemblance, distortion, equivocation, evasion, fraudulence, furtiveness, hedging, indirection, periphrasis, prevarication, spuriousness

devoted committed, constant, dedicated, faithful, fast, firm, loyal, staunch, steadfast, supportive, tested, tried-and-true, trustful

devour binge, bolt, cram, glut, gobble, gorge, gulp, guzzle, snap up, stuff, wolf

devout congregational, devotional, dutiful, observant, parochial, pious, prayerful, religious, reverent, solemn, worshipping

dew dewdrops, evening damp, false dew, fog drip, guttation

diagnosis analysis, biopsy, diagnostics, prognosis, sample, screening, test

diagnostic indicative, prognostic, symptomatic, symptomatological

diagrammatic analytic, graphic, schematic, tabular

dialect argot, idiom, isogloss, isolex, isophone, localism, patois, provincialism, regionism, vernacularism

dialogue conversation, exchange, interaction, interchange, interlocution, interview

diary agenda, calendar, compendium, curriculum, Filofax, itinerary, programme, prospectus, schedule, syllabus, synopsis, timetable

dice cube, die, double, snake eyes, spots, throw

dictatorship absolutism, atrocity, authoritarianism, autocracy, despotism, dictatorship, Fascism, iron hand, jackboot, militarism, Nazism, totalitarianism, tyranny

dictionary address book, almanac, atlas, concordance, directory, encyclopedia, gazetteer, gloss, glossary, gradus, guidebook, lexicography, lexicon, nomenclature, reference book, telephone directory, terminology, thesaurus, vocabulary, wordbook, yearbook

die become extinct, be taken, croak, decease, decompose, dice, drop off, expire, fall asleep, kick the bucket, pass away, perish, predecease, shuffle off this mortal coil, snuff it, succumb

diet assembly, calorie-counting, crash-dieting, nutrition, slimming, weight-watching

difference ambiguity, ambivalence, credibility gap, deviation, discord, discrepancy, disparity, dissimilarity, divergence, incompatibility, incongruity, inconsistency, inequality, nonconformity, variance

different alien, ambiguous, ambivalent, deviating, discordant, discrepant, dissimilar, divergent, incompatible, in-

congruous, inconsistent, odd, unequal, unsuitable, variant
may indicate an anagram

differentiate discriminate, distinguish, nit-pick, split hairs

difficult abstruse, ambiguous, amorphous, arduous, awkward, backbreaking, baffling, burdensome, challenging, complex, complicated, confusing, critical, crucial, decisive, demanding, effortful, elusive, enigmatic, equivocal, exacting, exhausting, exigent, fatiguing, formidable, gruelling, hard, heavy, herculean, inscrutable, laborious, mysterious, nebulous, obscure, onerous, oppressive, paradoxical, perplexing, pivotal, punishing, puzzling, recondite, steep, stiff, strenuous, superhuman, toilsome, tough, troublesome, unclear, uphill, vague, wearisome

difficulty abstruseness, arduousness, complexity, complication, convolution, effort, hardness, intricacy, knottiness, laboriousness, obscurity, reconditeness, ruggedness, severity, strain, strenuousness, technicality, toughness, unintelligibility

diffraction diaspora, diffusion, dispersion, fanning out, reflection, refraction, scattering

diffractive diffuse, dispersed, reflected, refractive, refrangible, scattered

diffuse bombastic, drawn out, effuse, empty, epic, excessive, flatulent, fluent, gushing, incoherent, inspired, lengthy, long-winded, loose-knit, loquacious, magniloquent, never-ending, nonstop, ornate, padded, pleonastic, polysyllabic, pretentious, prolix, prosy, protracted, reiterative, repetitive, rhetorical, sesquipedalian, superfluous, talkative, tautologous, turgid, verbose, voluminous, waffling, wordy

diffuseness blah, disquisition, dissertation, effusiveness, empty talk, enlargement, excess, expansion, expatiation, extension, extra, filler, gush, logorrhoea, long-windedness, loqua-

city, oration, padding, pleonasm, prolixity, protraction, reiteration, repetitiveness, rhetoric, richness, rigmarole, superfluity, talkativeness, tautology, tirade, verbiage, verboseness, waffle

digress deviate, diverge, get sidetracked, maunder, ramble, wander

digressive nonlinear, nonsequential, nonserial, parenthetic, wandering

dilapidated battered, broken, cracked, decrepit, derelict, dingy, dog-eared, down-and-out, down-at-heel, exhausted, falling apart, flea-bitten, frayed, holey, in disrepair, in rags, in ruins, in shreds, in tatters, kaput, leaking, moth-eaten, mouldering, ramshackle, rickety, ruined, run-down, rusty, seedy, shabby, shaky, shop-soiled, slummy, tatty, tottery, tumble-down, unkempt, unsteady, weakened, weather-beaten, wonky, worm-eaten, worn

dilapidation atrophy, blight, breakdown, collapse, corrosion, corruption, decay, decomposition, decrepitude, destruction, discoloration, disintegration, disrepair, marasmus, mouldiness, neglect, patina, putrefaction, rot, ruination, rust, senility, shabbiness, verdigris, weathering

dilemma crisis, Hobson's choice, predicament, puzzle, zero option

diligence fixation, obsession, pedantry, preoccupation, purism, single-mindedness, studiousness

diligent assiduous, engrossed, fastidious, fixated, hung-up, meticulous, obsessed, painstaking, pedantic, preoccupied, purist, rapt, sedulous, single-minded, studious, undistracted

dilute adulterate, attenuate, dissolve, liquefy, saturate, thin, water down, weaken

dilution attenuation, deliquescence, liquefaction, watering down

dim blurred, cloud, cloudy, crepuscular, dark, darken, darkish, dull, dusky, fade, film over, glaze over, grey, gutter, half-lit, ill-lit, leaden, livid, louring, mist over, obscure, overcast, pale, semi-dark, shadowy, shady, sombre, steam up, stupid, sunless, tenebrous, twilit, wane

dimmed clouded, dingy, dirty, drab, dull, dusty, faded, gloomy, lack-lustre, matt, rusty, tarnished, unpolished

dimness bad light, dusk, faintness, first light, gloaming, paleness, partial eclipse, penumbra, semi-darkness, shadiness, shadow, stupidity, twilight

diner bistro, brasserie, café, cafeteria, canteen, carvery, chippy, chophouse, crêperie, dinette, dining room, mess room, Naafi, pizzeria, refectory, restaurant, rotisserie, steakhouse, trattoria

dinosaur brontosaurus, diplodocus, ichthyosaurus, monster, old fogey, prehistoric, pterodactyl, tyrannosaurus

direct conduct, downright, guide, honest, honourable, lead, manage, simplistic, sincere, single-minded, unaffected, undisguised, unmitigated, unpretentious, unqualified, unsophisticated, wholehearted

direction bearing (N,S,E,W), instruction, location, management, position, quarter, set, situation

directness candour, clarity, fairness, honesty, plainness, scrupulousness, simplicity, straightforwardness, truth, truthfulness

directorship captaincy, chairmanship, command, control, dictatorship, guidance, helmsmanship, leadership, pilotage, premiership, responsibility, steering, steersmanship, superiority

dirt ash, blot, bog, castoff, cinder, clinker, crud, dandruff, deposit, dregs, droppings, dross, dung, dust, exuviae, feculence, filth, froth, fur, goo, grime, grounds, guano, gunge, gunk, lees, litter, manure, mark, matter, mildew, mire, mote, mould, muck, mucus, mud, mullock, night soil, ooze, patch,

plaque, pus, refuse, rot, rubbish, rust, scandal, scoria, scum, scurf, sediment, shavings, slag, slime, slough, sludge, smear, smoke, smudge, smut, snot, soil, soot, spot, stain, sweepings, tartar

dirtiness blackness, cloudiness, contagiousness, defilement, dinginess, duskness, encrustation, filth, foulness, griminess, grubbiness, infectiousness, infestation, insalubrity, insanitariness, messiness, miriness, mouldiness, muckiness, muddiness, mustiness, pollution, purulence, sepsis, sleaziness, sliminess, slovenliness, slumminess, sluttishness, soiling, squalidity, squalor, suppuration, turbidity, uncleanliness, uncleanness, unhealthiness, untidiness, unwholesomeness, verminousness

dirty bedraggled, besmirched, blacken, blot, blur, cake, clog, cobwebby, contaminate, corrupt, daub, defiled, desecrate, dingy, drabble, draggle, dusty, encrusted, filthy, foul, frowzy, furred up, fusty, greasy, grimy, grubby, infect, littered, maculate, matted, messy, miry, mouldy, mucky, muddy, murky, musty, obscene, oily, patch, poison, pollute, pornographic, profane, rile, roil, rude, scummy, slatternly, slaver, sleazy, slimy, slobber, slovenly, slummy, sluttish, smear, smirch, smoky, smudge, soiled, sooty, spatter, splash, spotted, squalid, stain, streak, sully, taint, tarnish, unburnished, unclean, unfair, unjust, unkempt, unpolished, unswept, untidy, unwashed

disability ataxia, atrophy, hemiplegia, invalidity, paraplegia, quadriplegia, tetraplegia, weakness

disable cripple, disarm, handicap, lame

disagree altercate, antagonize, argue, bicker, breach, challenge, clash, complain, conflict, confront, contend, contradict, counter, criticize, cross swords, defy, demur, differ, dispute, dissent, divide, fight, misunderstand, object, oppose, polarize, provoke, quarrel, remonstrate, rupture, show hostility, squabble, wrangle

disagreeable adverse, antipathetic, dissenting, hostile, inimical, opposite, unharmonious

disagreeing against, aggressive, agin, antagonistic, antipathetic, argumentative, at cross-purposes, at loggerheads, at odds, at variance, belligerent, bickering, brawling, cantankerous, challenging, clashing, conflicting, confrontational, contentious, contradicting, contrary, controversial, criticizing, defiant, differing, discordant, disharmonious, disparaging, disputing, dissenting, dissident, dissonant, divisive, fighting, hating, hostile, incompatible, inimical, irascible, irreconcilable, moot, noncooperative, objecting, opposite, polarizing, polemic, prickly, protesting, provocative, quarrelsome, schismatic, squabbling, uncongenial, unpleasant, unresolved, warring, wrangling

disagreement aggressiveness, altercation, antagonism, argument, bellicosity, bickering, cavil, challenge, clash, complaint, conflict, confrontation, contention, contradiction, controversy, criticism, defiance, difference, difficulty, disaccord, discordance, disharmony, dissent, dissidence, dissonance, disunity, division, enmity, estrangement, exception, fighting, friction, hatred, hostility, incompatibility, irascibility, irreconcilability, misunderstanding, noncooperation, objection, opposition, polarization, provocativeness, quarrel, samizdat, sore point, squabbling, strife, ticklish issue, uncongeniality, unpleasantness, uptightness, wrangling

disappear become extinct, blur, cease, darken, dematerialize, die out, dim, dissolve, dwindle, ebb, end, evanesce, evaporate, expire, fade, hide, melt, pass, perish, peter out, recede, retreat, vanish, wane

disappearance absence, cessation, death, dematerialization, departure, disembodiment, dispersal, dissipation, dissolution, dwindling, ebb, end, erosion, escape, evanescence, evaporation, exit, extinction, fading, going, invisibility, loss, melting, nonexistence, passing, scattering, vanishment, vaporization, wane, wearing away

disappeared absent, buried, camouflaged, concealed, dead, disguised, dispersed, dissipated, eclipsed, extinct, gone, hidden, invisible, lost, missing, nonexistent, obsolete, occulted, past, vanished

disappearing departing, evanescent, evaporating, fading, fleeting, fugitive, obsolescent, transient, vanishing, waning

disappoint amaze, crush, disenchant, dishearten, disillusion, dissatisfy, dumbfound, fail, let down, sadden, surprise, tantalize, tease, turn sour, upset

disappointed baffled, balked, bilked, chagrined, confounded, confused, crestfallen, crushed, defeated, dejected, denied, depressed, devastated, disconcerted, discontented, discouraged, disenchanted, disgruntled, disheartened, disillusioned, dissatisfied, foiled, frustrated, hampered, heartbroken, hindered, humbled, humiliated, jilted, let down, mortified, refused, rejected, soured, stonewalled, thwarted

disappointing abortive, falling short, frustrating, inadequate, inferior, insufficient, poor, second-best, second-rate, unfulfilling, unsatisfying, unsuccessful

disappointment chagrin, despair, discouragement, frustration, hopelessness, mortification, noncompletion, nonfulfilment, regret, tantalization

disapproval complaint, demur, denial, disapprobation, discontent, disfavour, dislike, displeasure, dissatisfaction, distaste, indignation, negation, objection, protest, refusal, rejection, thumbs down, unhappiness, unpopularity

disapprove boo, catcall, deride, discountenance, disfavour, dislike, frown on, heckle, hiss, jeer, lynch, mob, reject, ridicule, scorn, scowl, shout down, throw stones, tut-tut

disapproved banned, barred, blacklisted, boycotted, excluded, opposed, ostracized, refused, rejected, vetoed

disapproving disappointed, disapprobatory, discontented, disgruntled, displeased, disrespectful, dissatisfied, indignant, unhappy

disarrange confuse, derange, disorder, disorganize, muddle, roil
may indicate an anagram

disbanded deactivated, demobilized, dismissed, dissolved

disbar cashier, demote, deplume, depose, dethrone, disqualify, downgrade, drum out, excommunicate, expel, relegate, rusticate, send down, strike off, strip, suspend, unfrock

disbelief demur, disagreement, dissent, distrust, doubt, dubiousness, hesitancy, misgiving, mistrust, qualm, reservation, scepticism, scorn, scruple, suspiciousness, uncertainty

disbelieve apostatize, challenge, deny, disagree, discredit, dispute, dissent, distrust, doubt, hesitate, lapse, mistrust, mock, negate, question, ridicule, scoff at, scorn, suspect, waver

disbelieved discredited, disputable, exploded, far-fetched, implausible, impossible, improbable, incredible, questionable, suspect, suspicious, unbelievable, unreliable, untenable

disbelieving agnostic, atheistic, dissenting, distrustful, doubtful, dubious, faithless, heathen, heretical, hesitant, incredulous, mistrustful, pagan, sceptical, scornful, suspicious, uncertain, unfaithful

discard abandon, depose, dismiss, ditch, eject, eliminate, expel, jettison, junk, oust, renounce, scrap, set aside, supersede, throw away

discarding abandonment, dismissal, disuse, ejection, elimination, expulsion

discipline control, punish, restriction, severity, stability, strictness

disciplined controlled, law-abiding, punished, restrained

disclose bare, denude, diagnose, dig up, discover, disinter, expose, go public, let slip, make known, manifest, open up, reveal, show, uncover, unfold, unfurl, unpack, unroll, unveil, unwrap

disclosed acknowledged, admitted, avowed, confessed, exposed, leaked, open, revealed, shown, uncovered, unearthed, unmasked

disclosure anagnorisis, epiphany, explanation, exposure, manifestation, revelation, showdown, uncovering, unveiling

discompose addle, befuddle, confuse, convulse, derange, discomfit, disconcert, disorient, disturb, hassle, perturb, pester, unsettle, upset

disconnect break, cut, detach, disarticulate, disengage, disjoin, disjoint, dislocate, dismember, disunite, luxate, separate, sever, unhinge

discontinue break off, cease, cut off, drop, end, finish, give up, halt, leave off, quit, refrain from, stop, suspend, terminate

discontinuity brokenness, confusion, disconnectedness, disjointedness, disjunction, disorder, fitfulness, incoherence, intermittence, irregularity, nonuniformity, spasmodicalness, sporadicalness

discontinuous alternate, broken, ceased, desultory, disconnected, discrete, disjointed, disunited, ended, episodic, erratic, finished, fitful, fragmented, halted, intermittent, irregular, nonrecurrent, nonuniform, on-off, periodic, random, spasmodic, sporadic, stop-go, stopped, terminated, unconnected, unjoined, unrepeated, unsuccessive

discordant adversarial, anti, at issue, at odds, clashing, conflicting, contentious, different, disagreeing, dissentient, dissident

discount allowance, backwardation, cheapen, commission, concession, contango, cut, decrease, decrement, deduction, deferment, depreciate, drawback, dump, knock off, lower, margin, mark down, percentage, poundage, rebate, reduction, refund, slash, subtract, take off, tare

discounted bargain, cheap, cut-price, cut-rate, marked down, rebated

discourage depress, disenchant, dishearten, disillusion, dispirit

discourteous abrupt, abusive, acerbic, acrimonious, aggressive, awkward, backchatting, bantering, barbarian, bearish, beastly, blunt, boorish, brusque, brutal, cavalier, crusty, curt, defiant, discontented, disorderly, disrespectful, familiar, gauche, gruff, harsh, impatient, impolite, inattentive, inconsiderate, insensitive, inurbane, nasty, offhand, peevish, petulant, severe, sharp, short, snappy, sullen, surly, tactless, tart, tasteless, testy, thoughtless, uncivil, uncomplimentary, uncourtly, uncouth, uncultured, unflattering, ungallant, ungentlemanly, ungracious, unkind, unladylike, unpleasant, unpolished, unrefined, unseemly, unsolicitous, vituperative

discourtesy acerbity, asperity, backchat, banter, beastliness, bluffness, bluntness, brusqueness, crustiness, defiance, derision, disagreeableness, disrespectfulness, gruffness, harshness, impoliteness, inattention, incivility, inconsiderateness, insensitivity, inurbanity, mockery, nastiness, petulance, raillery, rejoinder, roughness, severity,

sharpness, shortness, sullenness, surliness, tactlessness, tartness, thoughtlessness, uncourtliness, ungallantness, ungraciousness, unpleasantness, unsolicitousness

discover come across, descry, encounter, find, glimpse, happen upon, identify, locate, meet with, notice, observe, perceive, place, recognize, see, sight, spot, spy, watch

discoverable detectable, findable, heuristic, identifiable, perceptible, recognizable

discovered exposed, found, located, revealed, seen, spotted, uncovered, unearthed, unmasked
may indicate a hidden word

discoverer archaeologist, colonist, detective, dowser, explorer, finder, forerunner, herald, inventor, mole, motivator, observer, originator, pathfinder, pioneer, prospector, scout, settler, spotter, spy

discovering experimental, exploratory, inventive, revelatory

discovery encounter, finding, glimpse, identification, location, meeting, observation, perception, recognition, serendipity, sight, spotting

discriminate analyse, choose, demarcate, differentiate, discern, distinguish, divide, favour, grade, graduate, judge, pick out, prefer, segregate, select, separate, sort

discriminating critical, diagnostic, differential, discerning, divisional, interpretational, judicious, selective, separating

discrimination appraisal, demarcation, diagnosis, differentiation, discernment, distinction, division, graduation, interpretation, segregation, selection, separation, sorting

discriminatory ageist, anti-semitic, biased, bigoted, chauvinist, classist, elitist, ethnocentric, fascist, homophobic, inequitable, jaundiced, jingoistic, misandrous, misogynous, nepotistic, one-sided, partial, partisan, preferential, prejudicial, racist, sexist, unfair, xenophobic

discuss cavil, challenge, chop logic, consider, debate, deduce, deliberate, doubt, induce, inquire, logicize, logomachize, moot, question, ratiocinate, reason, reflect, weigh up

discussing advisory, conferring, consultatory

discussion argy-bargy, bargaining session, cabinet meeting, conference, debate, high-level talks, moot, powwow, summit, teleconference

disdain condescend, despise, independence, obstinacy, overween, patronize, pull rank, self-sufficiency, stiff-neckedness, touchiness

diseased aguish, allergic, anaemic, arthritic, asthmatic, bronchial, cancerous, carcinomatous, consumptive, contagious, contaminated, croupy, degenerative, delirious, diabetic, distempered, epileptic, erysipelatous, febrile, feverish, gangrenous, gouty, haemophilic, hydrocephalic, iatrogenic, infected, infectious, inflamed, insalubrious, leprous, leukaemic, mangy, morbid, morbific, oedematous, painful, palsied, paralytic, pathogenic, pathological, peccant, phthistic, poisonous, psychosomatic, purulent, pyretic, rashy, rheumaticky, rickety, shivering, sniffly, snuffly, sore, spastic, spavined, spotty, stricken, syphilitic, tainted, tender, toxic, tuberculous, ulcerous, unhygienic

disentangle disengage, extricate, free, liberate, unravel, unscramble, unsnarl, untie

disentanglement clearing, disburdenment, disencumberment, disengagement, extrication, freeing, uncluttering, unscrambling, unsnarling

disentitle denaturalize, deport, depose, dethrone, disestablish, disfranchise, dispossess, disqualify, expel, expropriate, uncrown, unfrock

disentitled denaturalized, deposed, deprived, dethroned, disestablished, disfranchised, dispossessed, disqualified, unfrocked

disentitlement denaturalization, deportation, deposal, deprivation, dethronement, disestablishment, disfranchisement, dispossession, disqualification, expropriation, expulsion, forfeiture, unfrocking

disgorgement disemboguement, effusion, ejaculation, eruption, excretion, extravasation, extrusion, jet, obtrusion, outburst, outpour, secretion, spout, spurt, squirt

disguise burial, camouflage, cloak, cloud, conceal, concealment, darken, dim, eclipse, encode, erasure, fog, gloss, hiding, mask, masquerade, muddle, obfuscate, obliteration, obscure, occultation, paint, varnish, veil, whitewash

disguised anonymous, camouflaged, cloaked, coded, concealed, covert, cryptic, cryptographic, distorted, hidden, incognito, latent, masked, masquerading, occult, secret, unrecognized, veiled
may indicate an anagram

disgust abhorrence, appal, embitter, hatred, nauseate, offend, repel, revolt, sicken, upset

dish afters, beau, bowl, course, dessert, entrée, entremets, fish course, hors d'oeuvres, main course, plat du jour, plate, pud(ding), recipe, remove, salad, savouries, serve up, side-dish, soup, special(ity), starter, sweet

dishabille bathrobe, décolletage, informality, kimono, miniskirt, nightwear, pyjamas, rags, shorts, swimwear, tatters, underwear

dishonest cheating, deceitful, defrauding, disingenuous, duplicitous, fake, false, fraudulent, humbug, impersonating, insincere, mendacious, pretending, shamming, swindling, treacherous

dishonesty blackmail, cheat, con, counterfeiting, cozenage, deceitfulness, deception, dodge, duplicity, embezzlement, extortion, faithlessness, falseness, fiddle, flimflam, forgery, fraud, graft, improbity, mendaciousness, put-up job, racket, rip-off, scam, sting, swindle, treachery

dishonour blot, disgrace, scandal, shame, slur, stain, stigma

dishonourable bad, base, contemptible, corrupt, debased, depraved, devious, disgraceful, dishonest, disreputable, evil, good-for-nothing, ignoble, immoral, indecent, nefarious, rotten, shameful, unethical, unfair, ungentlemanly, unprincipled, unscrupulous, unsportsmanlike, venal, villainous, wicked, worthless

disingenuous crooked, foxy, lowdown, lying, shady, slippery, tricky, uncandid, untruthful, vulpine, wrangling

disintegrate blow up, break up, collapse, corrode, corrupt, crumble, decay, decompose, effloresce, explode, fall apart, granulate, mortify, moulder, perish, putrefy, rot, rust, shatter, splinter

disintegrated broken down, corroded, corrupted, decayed, decomposed, deconstructed, demolished, destroyed, dilapidated, dissolved, liquefied, melted, putrid, rotted, ruined, rusty, separated, shattered, smashed

disintegration breakup, chaos, collapse, corrosion, corruption, death, decay, decomposition, derangement, disorder, disturbance, erosion, explosion, mortification, mould, necrosis, putrefaction, rot, rust, wear

disinterest apathy, boredom, impassivity, imperturbability, indifference, insouciance, unconcern, uninvolvement

disinterested cool, detached, dispassionate, equitable, fair, impartial, impersonal, indifferent, neutral, nonaligned, non-partisan, objective, stoical, unbiased, uninvolved, unprejudiced

disinterestedness ataraxy, detachment, dispassion, equitableness, fairness, impartiality, indifference, justice, neutrality, nonalignment, noninvolvement, objectivity, stoicism

dislike abhor, abhorrence, abomination, animosity, antagonism, antipathy, aversion, bias, bitterness, despise, detest, disaffection, disagree, disapprove, discontent, disfavour, disgust, disinclination, displeasure, dissatisfaction, dissent, distaste, enmity, fear, hate, horror, hostility, ill will, loathe, mind, object to, phobia, prejudice, reject, reluctance, repugnance, repulsion, resent, sourness

disliked abhorrent, despised, disfavoured, insufferable, intolerable, rejected, repugnant, repulsive, revolting, spurned, unappreciated, unloved, unpopular, unwanted, unwelcome, yucky

disliking abhorring, antagonistic, antipathetic, averse, bitter, despising, detesting, disaffected, disapproving, discontented, disenchanted, disgusted, disillusioned, disinclined, displeased, dissatisfied, dissenting, fearful, hating, hostile, inimical, loath, loveless, queasy, reluctant, repelled, resentful, sickened, squeamish, undesirous, unwilling

dislodged deracinated, disengaged, displaced, eliminated, extracted, extricated, liberated, uprooted

dismantle deactivate, decommission, disassemble, sabotage, undo

dismiss axe, deactivate, demobilize, disband, discharge, disemploy, dissolve, drop, edge out, elbow out, expel, fire, lay off, make redundant, pension off, release, retire, rout, sack, send packing, superannuate, suspend

dismissal axing, cashiering, congé, degradation, demotion, depluming, discharge, disqualification, drumming out, exclusion, excommunication, externment, firing, laying off, redundancy, relegation, striking off, stripping, suspension, unfrocking

disobedience challenge, confrontation, defection, defiance, dereliction, desertion, disagreement, disloyalty, disregard, dissension, dissent, fractiousness, hindrance, immorality, indiscipline, indocility, insubordination, misbehaviour, mutiny, naughtiness, noncompliance, nonconformity, noncooperation, nonobservance, obstinacy, obstreperousness, obstruction, opposition, perfidiousness, perfunctoriness, rebelliousness, recalcitrance, refractoriness, refusal, resistance, sin, strike, stroppiness, sullenness, tergiversation, undependability, undutifulness, unfaithfulness, unreliability, unruliness, unwillingness, wickedness

disobedient bloody-minded, criminal, defiant, delinquent, disloyal, disorderly, dissenting, immoral, insubordinate, intractable, misbehaved, naughty, noncompliant, noncooperative, nonobservant, obstinate, obstreperous, obstructive, opposing, perfidious, recalcitrant, recusant, restless, riotous, sinning, stubborn, tergiversatory, transgressing, tumultuous, undisciplined, undutiful, unmanageable, unruly, unwilling, wicked, wild

disorder affray, aggro, agitation, anarchy, argy-bargy, bother, break up, chaos, commotion, confusion, coup d'état, derange, disarrange, disorganize, disperse, disrupt, disturbance, donnybrook, dust-up, entropy, fight, free-for-all, fuss, hurly-burly, insurgency, insurrection, jumble, lawlessness, mêlée, mix up, muddle, mutiny, pother, punch-up, putsch, rebellion, revolt, riot, roughhouse, row, rumpus, scatter, scramble, sedition, set-to, shindig, shuffle, stir, terrorism, to-do, treason, trouble, uprising, war

disordered deranged, disarranged, disjointed, dislocated, disorganized, displaced, disrupted, in disarray, jumbled, misplaced, muddled, shuffled *may indicate an anagram*

disorderliness confusion, derangement, disarrangement, disarray, discomfiture, discomposure, disconcertedness, discord, disharmony, disintegration, disjunction, disorganization, disruption, disturbance, incoherence, unintelligibility, upset

disorderly anarchic, boisterous, chaotic, contumacious, disobedient, disruptive, harum-scarum, hell-raising, insubordinate, laddish, lawless, mutinous, nihilistic, obstreperous, rampageous, rebellious, riotous, rowdy, stroppy, turbulent, uncontrolled, undisciplined, unmanageable, unruly, wild

disparage belittle, decry, denigrate, deprecate, depreciate, derogate, detract, minimize, play down, slight, underrate, understate

disparagement belittlement, decrial, denigration, deprecation, depreciation, derogation, detraction, faint praise, fault-finding, nit-picking, slighting, underestimation, understatement

disparaging critical, denigratory, deprecatory, depreciatory, derogatory, detractory, pejorative

disparate alien, ambiguous, ambivalent, asymmetric, contrasting, different, discrepant, disproportionate, dissimilar, diverse, equivocal, exotic, foreign, heterogeneous, immiscible, incommensurate, incongruent, inconsistent, inconsonant, irregular, nonuniform, odd, strange, unequal, unlikely, unrelated, unusual, variant

disparity ambiguity, ambivalence, asymmetry, contrast, difference, discrepancy, disproportionateness, dissimilarity, divergence, diversity, equivocality, gap, heterogeneity, incommensurability, incongruence, inconsistency, inconsonance, inequality, irregularity, nonuniformity, unrelatedness, variance

disperse break up, derail, detach, diffract, diffuse, dislocate, dislodge, disorient, dispel, displace, divide, drift apart, hive off, part, scatter, separate, split up, sunder

dispersed diffuse, dotted about, infrequent, sparse, sporadic, widespread

dispersion broadcast, casting, circulation, deployment, derailment, diffusion, dislocation, dislodgment, disorientation, dispensation, dispersal, displacement, dissemination, distribution, issuance, propagation, publication, scattering, seeding, sowing, spread, strewing

dispersive diffractive, diffusive, disseminative, dissipative, distributive

displace deflect, derail, disarrange, dislocate, dislodge, disorder, disorganize, disrupt, disturb, expel, express, lever out, move, prune, relocate, shift, shunt, smoke out, squeeze out, swerve, transfer, transport, unseat, upset, veer, weed out, wring out

displacement aberration, deflection, derailment, derangement, disarrangement, dislocation, dislodgment, disturbance, expression, expulsion, perturbation, pruning, relocation, removal, shift, shunt, squeezing out, swerve, switch, thinning, transference, translocation, transshipment, veer, weeding

display act, air, array, brandish, collection, dangle, demonstration, disclose, dramatize, emphasize, exhibition, explain, expo, exposition, fair, feature, flash, flaunt, flourish, headline, illuminate, indicate, instruct, manifest, market, model, parade, perform, point out, present, presentation, publish, release, retrospective, set out, show off, spectacle, sport, spotlight, stage, teach, vaunt, viewing, wave

displayed advertised, apodictic, apparent, brandished, cited, confronted, flaunted, flourished, made public, on view, paraded, produced, promoted, publicized, published, quoted, sported, visible, worn

displease appal, discomfort, disgust, embarrass, enrage, horrify, nauseate, offend, repel, revolt, sicken

disposal discarding, dismissal, dispensation, dissolution, dumping, ejection, firing, nonretention, releasing, riddance, sacking, scrapping

dispose of abandon, abjure, abrogate, cancel, cast away, cede, derestrict, destroy, discard, disclaim, disown, dispense with, dissolve, ditch, divorce, dump, eject, emit, forgo, forswear, give up, jettison, leak, maroon, marry off, open, recant, release, relinquish, renounce, replace, revoke, scrap, spare, supersede, surrender, waive, yield

disregard disgrace, dishonour, ignore, neglect, overlook, pejorate, shame, slight, underestimate, underrate

disreputable degrading, devious, dishonourable, dodgy, fraudulent, iffy, ignominious, immoral, infamous, nefarious, notorious, questionable, scandalous, shady, shameless, suspicious, underhand

disrepute disgrace, mortification, shame, shamefacedness, shamefastness

disrespect bad name, blasphemy, contempt, defamation, degradation, despite, dim view, discourtesy, discredit, disesteem, disfavour, disgrace, dishonour, disreputability, disrepute, ignominy, ill-repute, impertinence, impoliteness, impudence, incivility, infamy, insolence, irreverence, low esteem, misprize, notoriety, obloquy, opprobrium, rudeness, scandal, scurrility, shame, slur, underestimate, underrate, undervalue, unmannerliness

disrespectful audacious, blasphemous, bold, brazen, cheeky, discourteous, familiar, forward, fresh, impertinent, impolite, impudent, insolent, insubordinate, irreverent, pert, rude, saucy, scurrilous, uncivil, unmannered

disrupt distract, hinder, inconvenience, interfere, interrupt, intervene, intrude, molest, obstruct, pervert, put off, sabotage, tamper with

disruption distraction, disturbance, hindrance, inconvenience, interference, interruption, intervention, intrusion, molestation, obstruction, perversion, sabotage, untimeliness
may indicate an anagram

dissatisfaction censure, consternation, contempt, deprecation, derision, disappointment, disapprobation, disapproval, discontent, disgruntlement, disgust, disillusionment, dislike, displeasure, rejection, reprobation, scorn

dissatisfied brooding, complaining, contemptuous, critical of, derisive, disaffected, disappointed, disapproving, disgusted, disillusioned, malcontented, pejorative, scornful, sulking, unimpressed, whingeing

dissatisfy disappoint, disgust, disillusion, displease, revolt, sicken

dissemble camouflage, conceal, deceive, disguise

dissension aggravation, antagonism, controversy, disagreement, discord, disharmony, disunity, friction, squabbling

dissent abstain, altercation, argue with, ban, brawl, civil disobedience, clash, conflict, confrontation, confutation, contradict, contrariety, controversy, contumely, counterorder, demonstration, difference, disagree, disallow, discordance, disobedience, dispute, dissidence, dissociate oneself, divide, embargo, feud, fisticuffs, forbid, fracas, friction, gainsay, infraction, infringement, interdiction, make waves, noncompliance, nonconcurrence, nonobservance, nullify, object, obstruct, oppose, opt out, prohibit, protest, quarrel, rebel, rebellion, rebuff, rebuttal, recalcitrance, recusance, refutation, reject, renunciation, repudiation, revolt, schismatize, scrap, secede, separate, set-to, snub, spat, spurn, squabble, stonewall, strife, strike, take issue, tiff, variance, veto, vote against, walk out, war, withstand

dissenter agitator, anarchist, apostate, caviller, critic, detractor, disputer, dissentient, dissident, factionalist, fanatic, heckler, heretic, iconoclast, malcontent, nonconformist, objector, opponent, outlaw, partisan, protestant, protester, quarreller, radical, rebel, recusant, renegade, revolutionary, schismatic, sectarian, separatist, tergiversator, troublemaker, young Turk, zealot

dissentience counterculture, disaffection, discordance, disharmony, disobedience, dissidence, disunion, factionalism, intolerance, nonconformity, noncooperation, opposition, quarrelsomeness, rebellion, recrimination, secession, sectarianism, sedition, separatism, strike, unorthodoxy, unpleasantness, withdrawal

dissenting adversarial, arguing, at odds, bellicose, breakaway, cantankerous, clannish, conflicting, confrontational, confutative, contentious, contradictory, contrary, contravening, controversial, demurring, denying, differing, disallowed, discordant, disputatious, dissatisfied, dissident, divisive, heretical, heterodox, intolerant, irascible, nonconformist, objecting to, opposing, partisan, partyminded, protestant, protesting, quarrelling, rebellious, rebuffed, recusant, refuting, rejecting, renunciative, repudiating, resistant, revoking, sceptical, schismatic(al), secessionist, sectarian, seditious, separatist, unconvinced, unorthodox, unwilling, warlike

dissertation annotation, argument, commentary, composition, descant, discourse, discussion, disquisition, essay, examination, exegesis, explanation, exposition, gloss, harangue, homily, inquiry, interpretation, lecture, lesson, lucubration, memoir, monograph, oration, paper, peroration, prolegomenon, screed, sermon, study, summary, survey, symposium, theme, thesis, tirade, tract, tractate, treatise

dissident critic, dissenter, sectarian, separatist

dissimilar asymmetrical, contrasting, different, discrepant, disparate, distinctive, divergent, diverse, incommensurate, incomparable, incompatible, incongruous, matchless, multiform, new, nonpareil, nonuniform, original, peculiar, peerless, poles apart, singular, unequal, unique, unlike, unprecedented, unrelated, unresembling, untypical, various

dissimilarity contrast, difference, differentiation, discrepancy, discrimination, disparity, distinction, divergence, diversity, extraneousness, heterogeneity, multiformity, nonuniformity, variance, variation

dissipated debauched, dispersed, dissolute, fast-living, free-living, high-living, licentious, profligate, riotous, scattered

dissipation carousal, debauchery, dissoluteness, licentiousness, orgy, profligacy, saturnalia, scattering

dissociation abstention, aversion, detach, distance, divorce, recoil, repugnance, separation, wariness

dissolve decoagulate, decoct, infuse, leach, lixiviate, percolate, resolve, solubilize, solve, thin, unclot

dissonance clashing, discord, disharmony, flatness, harshness, hoarseness, sharpness, stridency, tunelessness, unmelodiousness

dissonant cacophonous, clashing, discordant, grating, harsh, inharmonious, jangling, jarring, rasping, raucous, scraping, shrill, strident
may indicate an anagram

dissuade advise against, argue against, castigate, caution, confute, discourage, expostulate, persuade against, protest against, put off, remonstrate, reprove, warn

dissuaded dampened, discouraged, disenchanted, disheartened, disillusioned, reluctant, unwilling

dissuasion admonition, caution, contrary advice, discouragement, expostulation, hindrance, objection, opposition, protest, remonstrance, reproof, resistance, setback, warning

dissuasive cautionary, chilling, contradictory, contrary, damping, deterrent, discouraging, disheartening, expostulatory, monitory, warning

distance aloofness, deviation, dispersion, divergence, farness, inaccessibility, long range, perspective, remoteness, removal, unapproachability, unavailability
See also list at **measure**.

distant antipodean, distal, exotic, far away, far-flung, farther, farthermost, further, furthermost, godforsaken, hyperborean, inaccessible, long-distance, long-range, offshore, outlying, out-of-the-way, overseas, peripheral, remote, transcontinental, transpolar, ulterior, ultimate, unapproachable, unavailable, unget-at-able, yon, yonder

distinct accurate, clear, exact, obvious, separate, uninvolved

distinction bearing, breeding, characteristic, chic, contrast, credit, differentiation, eminence, excellence, mark, merit, presence, prestige, style

distort bias, blemish, contort, deface, deform, disfigure, disproportion, imbalance, impair, mask, misshape, mutilate, scar, screw, skew, spoil, strain, stress, twist, warp

distorted askew, asymmetric(al), cockeyed, crooked, discordant, disproportionate, dissimilar, imbalanced, incongruent, irregular, lopsided, misshapen, off-centre, off-target, skewwhiff, unbalanced, unequal, unsymmetrical *may indicate an anagram*

distortion asymmetry, bias, contortion, crookedness, difference, disparity, disproportion, dissimilarity, imbalance, inequality, irregularity, lopsidedness, skewness, strain, stress, torsion, twist, warp

distressing depressing, dispiriting, grievous, harrowing, heartbreaking, lamentable, painful, sorry, tragic

distribute broadcast, circulate, deal, deploy, dispense, disseminate, dole out, issue, propagate, publish, spread

distributed broadcast, circulated, dispensed, issued, propagated, published, sown, spread, strewn

district arondissement, barony, block, canton, city centre, commune, department, eparchy, fylker, guberniya, high street, inner city, Län, Land, precinct, prefecture, region, quarter, square, vicinity, ward

distrust anxiousness, apprehensiveness, doubt, mistrust, possessiveness, solicitousness, suspicion, vigilance, watchfulness

distrustful anxious, apprehensive, Argus-eyed, doubtful, mistrustful, solicitous, suspicious, vigilant, watchful

disturb agitate, alarm, annoy, bother, bug, carp, concern, convulse, criticize, discomfit, discompose, disconcert, disquiet, disrupt, distress, fluster, harass, hassle, irk, irritate, perturb, pester, put out, rattle, ruffle, shake, spook, stir, trouble, unsettle, upset, vex, worry

disturbance agitation, annoyance, anxiety, bloodbath, bother, brouhaha, clash, commotion, convulsion, discomfiture, discomposure, disconcertedness, disquiet, fracas, nuisance, outburst, perturbation, punch-up, riot, roughhouse, rumpus, tumult, upheaval, uproar, upset, worry *may indicate an anagram*

disturbed agitated, alarmed, annoyed, anxious, bothered, bugged, concerned, confused, convulsed, discomfited, discomposed, disconcerted, disconnected, disquieted, dissociated, distressed, emotional, flustered, hypochondriacal, irritated, nervous, neurotic, paranoid, perturbed, psychopathic, psychotic, rattled, ruffled, schizoid, shaken, sociopathic, traumatized, troubled, uncomfortable, uneasy, unsettled, upset, vexed, worried

disturbing alarming, annoying, bothersome, disconcerting, disruptive, distracting, distressing, muddling, offputting, troubling, unsettling, upsetting, vexatious, worrying

disunity disagreement, dissension, hostility, opposition

disuse abandonment, dereliction, desuetude, disposal, idleness, inactivity, limbo, obsolescence, rejection, retirement, scrapping

disused abandoned, cast-off, decommissioned, derelict, discarded, discontinued, discredited, frozen, in limbo, jettisoned, junked, laid up, mothballed, neglected, obsolete, retired, rusting, scrapped, superannuated, superseded, supplanted

dithering hesitant, indecisive, vacillating, wavering

dive belly-flop, chute, crash-landing, dip, drop, duck, dump, fall, header, landing, nose-dive, plunge, pounce, power-dive, stoop, swoop, touchdown

diver frogman, submariner

diverge abandon, aberrate, bifurcate, branch out, depart, deviate, disperse, divaricate, escape, fan out, fork, leave, part, quit, radiate, ramify, relinquish, scatter, splay

divergence aberration, branching out, contradiction, contrariety, declination, decomposition, deflection, deviation, difference, diffraction, disintegration, divarication, fanning out, fragmentation, radiation, ramification, separation, splaying, split-up

divergent aberrant, centrifugal, contradictory, dendriform, deviating, different, divaricate, ramiform, separated

diverse abnormal, changeable, chequered, contrasting, deviant, different, dissimilar, diverging, erratic, fitful, freakish, haphazard, heterogeneous, incongruous, inconsistent, inconstant, manifold, nonuniform, spasmodic, sporadic, unique, unstable, varied, variegated

diversity abnormality, alterability, changeability, contrast, deviation, difference, discontinuity, dissimilarity, divergence, exception, freak, haphazardness, heterogeneity, incongruity, inconsistency, inequality, irregularity, miscellany, modifiability, multiplicity, nonconformity, nonuniformity, unevenness, variegation, variety, variousness, versatility .

divide alienate, analyse, anatomize, apportion, bisect, chasm, circumscribe, compartmentalize, dismember, dissect, divorce, estrange, factorize, fractionalize, fragment, halve, interpose, maroon, partition, quarantine, quarter, seclude, sectionalize, segment, segregate, sequester, split, sunder

dividing
may indicate a split word

divination arithmomancy, astrodiagnosis, astrology, astromancy, augury, bibliomancy, capromancy, cartomancy, casting lots, chirognomy, chiromancy, clairvoyance, crystal-gazing, dowsing, dream interpretation, fortune-telling, geomancy, haruspicy, hieromancy, horoscopy, hydromancy, I Ching,

ichthyomancy, logomancy, mantology, metereomancy, necromancy, numerology, oneiromancy, ophiomancy, palmistry, precognition, prediction, premonition, prophecy, psephomancy, psychomancy, pyromancy, pythonism, radiaesthesia, sideromancy, soothsaying, sortilege, Tarot-reading, tea-leaf reading, theomancy, vaticination, water-divining

divinatory astrological, augural, clairaudient, clairsentient, clairvoyant, haruspical, oracular, precognitive, premonitory, prophetic, sibylline

divine Christlike, Christly, deistic, dowse, Elohistic, epiphanic, excellent, extramundane, godlike, godly, guess, hallowed, holy, incarnate, intuit, messianic, numinous, perceive, priest, religious, sacred, sacrosanct, supernatural, supramundane, theistic, theomorphic, unearthly, wonderful, Yahwistic

diving-bell bathysphere, diving bird

divinity deity, divineness, godhead, godhood, godliness, godship, numinousness, religious studies, theology *See also list at* **God**.

division apartheid, border, breach, compartment, discrimination, distribution, schism, segregation, severance, zoning

divorce annulment, break-up, broken home, broken marriage, decree absolute, decree nisi, part, put asunder, separate, split-up

divorced dissolved, estranged, separated, split

divulge air, announce, breathe, broadcast, communicate, confide, declare, educate, hint, inform, leak, let drop, publicize, publish, speak, speak out, talk, tell all, utter, vent

divulgence acknowledgment, admission, affirmation, announcement, avowal, betrayal, broadcast, communication, confession, declaration, exposé, giveaway, hint, leak, publication, queen's evidence, telltale sign

do act, agitate, as before, cheat, con, ditto, execute, move, party, perform, rise, stir, wake up, work

doctor administer, consultant, cure, doc, DR, GP, heal, health officer, houseman, inject, intern, leech, locum, MB, MD, medic, medical practitioner, medicate, minister to, MO, physician, prescribe, psychiatrist, quack, registrar, rehabilitate, resident, sawbones

doctored
may indicate an anagram

document bumph, certificate, dossier, estimate, file, green paper, paper, record, report, review, specification, statement, tax return, white paper

documentation authority, case history, chit, credential, CV, ID, identity card, papers, passport, permit, receipt, recommendation, record, reference, résumé, security pass, testimonial, ticket, visa, voucher, warrant, warranty

doddle breeze, child's play, cinch, piece of cake, pushover

dog bitch, bow-wow, cur, Fido, follow, guide, gundog, harass, hound, lurcher, mongrel, mutt, pariah, pi-dog, pup, puppy, sheepdog, show, sniffer, tail, toy, tracker, trail, tyke, watchdog, whelp

dogmatic bigoted, blimpish, blind, blinkered, conservative, deaf, dry, fanatical, habituated, hard-line, hard-shelled, hidebound, impervious, obscurantist, obsessed, opinionated, pedantic, reactionary, unteachable

dome arc, arch, barrow, beehive, cupola, hillock, hummock, hump, mound, vault
See also list at **architecture**.

dominant all-pervading, authoritative, dictatorial, governing, imperial, international, magisterial, monopolistic, multinational, ordering, overrid-

ing, prevailing, royal, ruling, sovereign, ubiquitous, wide-ranging

dominate bestride, boss, bulldoze, bully, command, condescend, decree, demand, dictate to, discipline, domineer, drill, force, oppress, ordain, order, overarch, overshadow, play god, subjugate, trample over, tyrannize

dominating colonial, conquering, controlling, intimidating, oppressive, overcoming, overpowering, repressive, suppressive, tyrannical

domination colonialism, conquering, conquest, control, discipline, intimidation, mastery, oppression, overcoming, overpowering, repression, restraint, suppression, tyranny

dominion archduchy, archdukedom, chieftaincy, colony, domain, duchy, dukedom, earldom, empire, grand duchy, kingdom, mandate, mandatory, palatinate, principality, principate, protectorate, province, puppet regime, realm, satellite nation, settlement, sultanate, territory, toparchy

don assume, fellow, lecturer, nobleman, put on, Spaniard, tutor

donate back, commit oneself, contribute, defray, finance, give (alms), help, participate, pay for, stand, support, tithe, treat, volunteer

donation backing, contribution, finance, generosity, gift, giving, liberality, support

double biathlon, binoculars, biped, bipod, bivalve, cloned, copy, couplet, diptych, distich, doppelgänger, double-decker, doublet, duet, duplex, duplicate, echo, fold, geminate, increase twofold, mirror, repeated, second, square, tandem, trick, twin, twofold, two-hander, two-piece, two-seater, two-wheeler

double-edged ambiguous, ambivalent, double-barrelled, double-crossing, duplicitous, hypocritical, ironic, Januslike, two-faced, two-timing

doubt chance, confute, conjecture, contest, controvert, debate, disagree, disbelieve, discuss, dispute, dissent, distrust, guess, hesitate, impugn, mistrust, moot, object, propose, question, refute, risk, speculate, suspect

dovetail cog, frame, interlock, mitre, mortise, tenon, trim

downflow avalanche, cascade, cataract, chute, defluxion, downpour, downrush, landslide, nappe, precipice, rain, rapids, shower, snowslide, subsidence, waterfall

downplayed constrained, curtailed, de-emphasized, diminished, disregarded, moderated, reduced, restrained, shrugged-off, toned-down, watered-down

down-playing constraint, curtailment, deprecation, dilution, diminishment, disregard, moderation, restraint, underplaying

downthrow defenestration, downcast, flattening, grounding, levelling, overset, overthrow, overturn, precipitation, revolution, subversion, toppling, upset

drag brake, crawl, dawdle, draggle, dredge, elevate, lift, linger, nuisance, rake, smoke, snake, trail, trawl, troll, tug, winch

drag queen cross-dresser, female impersonator, transvestite

drama alternative theatre, amateur dramatics, crisis, dramaticism, experimental theatre, fringe theatre, greasepaint, histrionics, rep, repertory, street theatre, theatricals, Thespian art, the stage, the theatre
See also list at **theatre**.

dramatic antagonistic, balletic, choral, choreographic, cosmetic, daring, dramaturgic, histrionic, melodramatic, mimetic, musical, operatic, protagonistic, sensational, spectacular, stagey, stagy, Terpsichorean, theatrical, Thespian

dramatics camp, hamming, histrionics, sensationalism, theatre

dramatist choreographer, dramaturge, jokesmith, librettist, mimographer, playwright, scenarist, screen writer, script writer

dramaturgy choreography, sensationalism, showmanship, spectacle, stagecraft, theatrical

draw attract, caricature, cartoon, chalk, choose, copy, cross-hatch, dead heat, depict, doodle, draft, drag, enticement, extract, hatch, limn, outline, pencil, pull, select, silhouette, sketch, stalemate, stencil, tie, trace

dread be petrified, blench, draw back, fear, flinch, panic, quail, quiver, recoil, shake, shiver, shrink, shudder, take fright, tremble, turn pale

dream ambition, aspiration, fantasy, hope, imagine, vision

dreamland Arcadia, cloud-cuckoo land, El Dorado, Erewhon, fairyland, never-never land, promised land, Shangri-la, Utopia, wonderland
See also list at **imagine**.

dress accoutre, accoutrement, apparel, array, attire, cap, caparison, clad, cloak, clothe, clothes, clothing, costume, cover, creation, decorate, drape, duds, enfold, enrobe, envelop, finery, frippery, frock, garb, garment, garnish, gear, get-up, glove, gown, habiliments, hood, invest, kit, linen, mantle, menswear, number, outfit, panoply, rags, regalia, rig(out), robe, sheathe, shoe, shroud, swaddle, swathe, toggery, togs, trousseau, uniform, vest, vesture, wardrobe, wear, womenswear, wrap

dressed arrayed, bedecked, bewigged, bonneted, booted, costumed, decked out, embellished, frocked, habilimented, habited, hatted, invested, kitted out, liveried, rigged, shod, turned out, uniformed, vested

dressing casualness, couture, covering, fashion, foppishness, high fashion, investiture, investment, sauce, Savile Row, toilet, toilette, turnout, vestiture, vinaigrette, wardrobe

dress up array, beautify, bedeck, comparison, deck out, primp, prink, rig out, spruce up, titivate, turn out

dried bone-dry, corky, dehydrated, desiccated, drained, evaporated, exsiccated, faded, mummified, parched, parchment-like, scorched, sere, shrivelled, withered, wizened

drink beverage, bevvy, booze, bumper, carouse, chug, cocktail, compotation, concoction, decoction, down, drain, dram, drop, finger, fuddle, get drunk, gulp, guzzle, health, imbibe, indulge, infusion, knock back, lap up, libation, lush, mixed drink, nip, oblation, ocean, potate, potation, potion, pub-crawl, put away, quaff, round, sea, short drink, sip, snifter, snort, soak up, souse, sponge up, suck, sup, swallow, swig, swill, taste, tipple, toast, tope, wash down, wassail
See list of drinks.

drinker alehead, alkie, bibber, boozer, drunkard, guzzler, lush, quaffer, sipper, swiller, toper, wine-taster, wino

drinking alcoholism, beeriness, bibulous, boozing, dipsomania, drunkenness, fluid intake, gulping, imbibition, intemperance, lapping, nipping, potation, pulling, quaffing, sipping, soaking, sottishness, sucking, supping, swallowing, swigging, swilling, tasting, toping, vinous, wine-bibbing, wine-tasting

drip cascade, drizzle, droplet, patter, precipitate, shower, wimp

drip-dry air, evaporate, mangle, peg out, spin-dry, tumble-dry, wring

drive out chase out, drum out, force out, freeze out, hunt out, push out, rout out, smoke out

droop flop, hang down, plop, plump, sag, sit down, slouch, slump, swag

drooping demoted, depressed, downcast, sagging, wilting

drop bead, bellyflop, bow down, crash, crashland, decline, descend on, dip, discontinue, dive, drip, droplet, fall, flutter down, land, let go, light upon, nosedive, parachute, plummet, plunge, powerdive, prang, precipice, skydive, spiral down, splash, swoop, titubate, touch down

dropout beatnik, hippie, new age traveller, nonconformist

drops beads, droplets, globules, guttae

drown dive, flood, founder, overwhelm, submerge, swamp

drug acid, amphetamine, anaesthetize, bang, barb, barbiturate, candy, cannabis, catholicon, cocaine, coke, crack, cure-all, deaden, dex, dexie, dexo, dope, dose, draught, E, Ecstasy, elixir, excitant, fix, ganja, grass, gumball, H, hallucinogen, hash, hashish, healing agent, hemp, heroin, hit, horse, hypnotize, joint, junk, kef, knock out, marijuana, medication, medicine, mescaline, methadone, mooter, morphine, narcotic, opium, panacea, peyote, placebo, pot, potion, preparation, reefer, roach, rope, scag, sedate, shot, sleeping pill, smack, snort, snow, speed, speedball, spliff, stick, stimulant, tea, tranquillizer, upper, weed

drugged doped, floating, high, incapacitated, insensible, medicated, sedated, stoned, zonkers, zonko

drug-taking banging, blowing, buzz, drug abuse, drug addiction, drug dependence, freebasing, glue-sniffing, habit, injecting, mainlining, pill-popping, skin-popping, smoking, sniffing, snorting, trip

drum beat, bongo, boom, cylinder, echo, grumble, pound, pulse, resonate, resound, reverberate, roll, rumble, snare drum, tattoo, throb, thrum, tympanum, vibrate
See also list at **orchestra.**

DRINKS

ABSINTHE
ADVOCAAT
AGUARDIENTE
AKVAVIT
ALCAMAS
ALE
ALEXANDER
ALIGOTÉ
ALLASCH
ALOXE-CORTON
ALSACE
AMARETTO DI
  SARANNO
AMONTILLADO
ANGEL'S KISS
ANISE(TTE)
ANRAM
APPLE CAR
APPLEJACK
AQUAVIT
ARAK
ARCHBISHOP
ARMAGNAC
ARQUEBUSE
BACARDI
BAILEYS
BANDOL
BARBARESCO
BARLEY BEER
BARLEY WINE
BAROLO
BARSAC
BEACHCOMBER
BEADLE
BEAUJOLAIS
BEAUNE
BEEF TEA
BEE'S KNEES
BENEDICTINE
BETWEEN THE
  SHEETS
BISHOP
BITTER
BLACK MARIA
BLACK VELVET
BLANQUETTE DE
  LIMOUX
BLOODY MARY
BORDEAUX
BOUKH(R)A
BOURBON
BOURGUEIL
BRANDY
BROU DE NOIX
BROUILLY
BUCK JONES
BUCKS FIZZ
BULL'S BLOOD
BYRRH
CAHORS

CALVADOS
CAMPARI
CASSIS
CHABLIS
CHAMBOLLE-
  MUSIGNY
CHAMPAGNE
CHAMPAGNE BUCK
CHA(R)
CHARTREUSE
CHASSAGNE-
  MONTRACHET
CHÂTEAU D'YQUEM
CHÂTEAU HAUT-
  BRION
CHÂTEAU LAFITE
CHÂTEAU LATOUR
CHÂTEAU MARGAUX
CHÂTEAU MOUTON-
  ROTHSCHILD
CHERRY BRANDY
CHIANTI
CHICHA
CHINON
CHOUM
CHURCHWARDEN
CIDER
CLAIRET(TE)
CLARET
COFFEE
COGNAC
COINTREAU
COLA
COMMODORE
CORPSE REVIVER
CORTON-
  CHARLEMAGNE
CÔTE-RÔTIE
CÔTES-DE-
  PROVENCE
CÔTES-DU-RHÔNE
CÔTES-DU-
  ROUSSILLON
CÔTES-DU-VENTOUX
CÔTES-DU-VIVARAIS
CRÉMANT
CRÈME DE CACAO
CRÈME DE MENTHE
CRÉPY
CROZES-HERMITAGE
CURAÇAO
DAIQUIRI
DIABOLO
DRAMBUIE
DUBONNET
ELEPHANT'S EAR
ENTRE-DEUX-MERS
ESCUBAC
FALERNO
FALERNUM

FALLEN ANGEL
FINE AND DANDY
FINO
FITOU
FIX
FIZZ
FLIP
FRAMBOISE
FRANGY
GAILLAC
GEVREY-
  CHAMBERTIN
GEWÜRZTRAMINER
GIGONDAS
GIMLET
GIN
GIN AND IT
GINGER BEER
GIN SLING
GRAND MARNIER
GRAPPA
GRAVES
GRENADINE
GROG
GUIGNOLET
GUINNESS
HARVEY
  WALLBANGER
HAUT POITOU
  WINES
HERMITAGE
HIGHBALL
HOCK
HORSE'S NECK
HYDROMEL
JOHN COLLINS
JULEP
KIR
KIRSCH
KNICKERBOCKER
KÜMMEL
KVASS
LACRIMA CHRISTI
LAGER
LAMBIC
LAMBRUSCO
LASSI
LEMONADE
MADEIRA
MAIDEN'S PRAYER
MÁLAGA
MANHATTAN
MANZANILLA
MARASCHINO
MARC
MARGAUX
MARSALA
MARTINI
MATÉ
MEAD

MÉDOC
MÊLISS
MERCUREY
MERRY WIDOW
MESCAL
METAXA
MEURSAULT
MILD
MILKSHAKE
MINT JULEP
MIRABELLE
MONBAZILLAC
MONTAGNY
MONTILLA
MONTLOUIS
MONTRACHET
MOONLIGHT
MOONSHINE
MOREY-SAINT-DENIS
MOSEL(LE)
MULLED ALE
MULLED WINE
MUSCADET
NEGUS
NIGHTCAP
NOG
NUITS-SAINT-
  GEORGES
OLD-FASHIONED
ORANGEADE
ORGEAT
ORVIETO
OUZO
PASTIS
PAUILLAC
PERNOD
PERRY
PERSICOT
PINA COLADA
PINK LADY
PLANTER'S PUNCH
POMMARD
PORT
POSSET
POUILLY-FUISSÉ
POUILLY-FUMÉ
PRAIRIE OYSTER
PRUNELLE
PULQUE
PUNCH
QETSCH
RAKI
RATAFIA
RETSINA
RICHEBOURG
RIESLING
RIOJA
RIVESALTES
ROMANÉE-CONTI
ROSÉ WINE

DRINKS continued			
RUM	SAVIGNY-LÈS-	STREGA	VIN DE PAILLE
RUM COLLINS	BEAUNE	TAVEL	VINHO VERDE
RYE WHISKEY	SCHNAP(P)S	TEA	VIN JAUNE
SAINT-EMILION	SCUBAC	TEQUILA	VODKA
SAINT ESTEPHE	SELTZER	TISANE	VOLNAY
SAINT JULIEN	SHANDY	TODDY	VOSNE-ROMANÉE
SAKÉ	SHERRY	TOKAY	VOUVRAY
SAKI	SIDECAR	TOM COLLINS	WALDORF
SAMBUCA	SLIVOVITZ	TONIC WATER	WASSAIL BOWL
SANCERRE	SODA	TRAPPISTINE	WATER
SANGRIA	SOUR	TRIPLE SEC	WHISK(E)Y
SANTENAY	SOUTHERN	VALENÇAY	WHITE GIN SOUR
SAUMUR	COMFORT	VALPOLICELLA	WHITE LADY
SAUTERNES	STOUT	VERMOUTH	WHIZ BANG

drumming beating, booming, echo, grumbling, incessant, insistent, loud, palpitation, persistent, pounding, pulsation, pulse, repeated, resonant, reverberant, reverberation, roll, rumbling, tattoo, throbbing, thrumming, tomtom, vibration

drunk alcoholic, blitzed, blotto, boozer, ebriate, fuddled, glassy-eyed, glazed, gulped, half-cut, half seas over, happy, hiccuping, high, inebriated, intoxicated, legless, lurch, maudlin, merry, muzzy, off one's head, out of it, paralytic, pickled, pie-eyed, pissed, pixilated, plastered, rat-arsed, reel, see double, sloshed, sozzled, squiffy, stagger, stammer, stoned, stuko, stupified, stutter, succumb, swallowed, tearful, three sheets in the wind, tiddly, tight, tipsy, tired and emotional, well-lubricated, well-oiled, wino, woozy
may indicate an anagram

drunkard alcoholic, alehead, bacchant, bibber, boozer, carouser, dipsomaniac, drunk, froth-blower, inebriate, maenad, piss-artist, pisshead, pubcrawler, reveller, Silenus, sot, souse, sponge, swiller, tippler, wineskin

drunken alcoholic, beery, bibulous, bloodshot, boozy, carousing, dipsomaniac, gin-sodden, gouty, guzzling, hard-drinking, inebriate, intemperate, liverish, red-nosed, sodden, sottish, swigging, swilling, tippling, toping, vinous, wassailing

drunkenness befuddlement, blackout, dizziness, Dutch courage, ebriety, inebriation, insobriety, intoxication, reeling, staggering, tipsiness, wooziness

dry anhydrous, arid, droughty, moistureless, plain, preserve, sober, thirsty, undamped, unemotional, unirrigated, unmoistened, waterless

drying airing, anhydration, bleaching, dehumidification, dehydration, desiccation, desiccative, exsiccation, fading, insolation, mummification, searing, siccative, withering

dryness aloofness, aridness, drought, laconicism, parchedness, siccity

duality ambidexterity, ambiguity, bilingualism, bisexuality, doubleness, double-sidedness, duplexity, duplicity

due acknowledgment, appropriate, cognizance, comeuppance, compensation, credit, deserts, deservings, directly, just deserts, merits, owing, punishment, recognition, reward, scheduled, sufficient, thanks, tribute

duel fencing, gladiatorial combat, hand-to-hand fight, head-to-head contest, joust, kendo, nose-to-nose confrontation, one-on-one, quarterstaff, single combat, singlestick, swordplay, tilt, tournament, tourney

dues contribution, fees, levy, payment

dull blunt, bore, deaden, dense, desensitize, dim, dreary, gloomy, hebetudinous, insensitive, numb, obtuse, overcast, slow, stupid, tedious, unfeeling, unperceptive

dullness gloom, hebetude, impercipience, insensitivity, monotony, murkiness, numbness, obtuseness, slow-wittedness

dumbfound cut short, deaden, gag, gobsmack, hush, muffle, mute, shout down, silence, suppress

dupe beginner, cat's paw, cinch, deceive, double-cross, fool, greenhorn, gull, innocent, instrument, mug, patsy, pawn, puppet, pushover, stooge, toy, trick, victim

duplicate ape, carbon copy, copy, ditto, enlargement, facsimile, fax, graph, hologram, imitation, impression, microcopy, Mimeograph, model, mould, negative, offprint, pantograph, photocopy, photograph, Photostat, print, replica, replicate, representation, reproduce, reproduction, rubbing, seal, shoot, stamp, stencil, tape recording, tracing, transcript, transfer, triplicate, video recording, Xerox

duplicitous ambidextrous, backhanded, deceiving, dissembling, double-dealing, equivocal, false, Janus-faced, tongue-in-cheek, two-faced

duplicity ambidexterity, betrayal, double-dealing, doubleness, equivocalness, false-heartedness, falseness, forked tongue, hypocrisy, irony, Judas kiss, machination, perfidy, treachery, treason, two-facedness

duration continuation, course, extent, lifespan, office, period, reign, shift, space, span, spell, stint, stretch, tenancy, tenure, term

dutiful conscientious, decent, duteous, ethical, honourable, moral, principled, punctilious, scrupulous, upright, virtuous

duty accountability, answerability, assignment, burden, charge, duteousness, dutifulness, imposition, inner voice, liability, moral imperative, obligation, onus, responsibility, willingness

dwell abide, inhabit, live at, lodge, reside at, stay

dye bleach, chromophore, chromotrope, colourant, crocein, dyestuff, eosin, fuchsine, garance, lake, lake naphthol, madder, mauveine, mordant, pincoffin, Tyrian purple, woad

dyed bleached, coated, coloured, dyed-in-the-wool, dyed-in-the-yarn, tie-dyed

dyeing batik, colouring, patterning, printing, screen printing, staining, tie dyeing

dying cadaverous, deathlike, deathly, expiring, fading, final, last, moribund, skeletal

dynamic animated, attractive, automated, drawing, driven, impelling, kinetic, live, lively, locomotive, moving, on line, on stream, pro-active, propulsive, pulling, spirited, vigorous, vivacious

·E·

ABBREVIATIONS

E	eastern • Ecstasy • key • note • oriental • Spain
EC	European Community • London district
ECU	European Currency Unit
ED	editor • Edward • Ted
E'ER	always • ever
EFTA	European Free Trade Association
EG	for example (Latin: *exempli gratia*)
ELF	extremely low frequency
EMI	Electric and Musical Industries
EOB	end of block
EOF	end of file
EP	record
EPOS	electronic point of sale
ER	erbium • hesitation • king (Latin: *Edwardus Rex*) • monarch • queen (Latin: *Elizabeth Regina*)
ESP	extrasensory perception
ETA	estimated time of arrival
ET AL	and elsewhere (Latin: *et alibi*) • and others (Latin: *et alii*)
EW	each way

eager alacritous, enthusiastic, keen, overenthusiastic, prompt, zealous

eagerness alacrity, ardour, enthusiasm, fervour, keenness, promptness, zeal

ear attention, heed, listener, lug, organ *may indicate a homophone*

earliness immediacy, promptness, punctuality, readiness, timeliness

early advanced, first, immediate, prompt, punctual

earnest committed, dedicated, determined, genuine, intent, purposeful, resolute, sincere

earnestness commitment, dedication, determination, resolution, sincerity

earnings advance, annuity, fee, income, makings, pay, pension, pickings, proceeds, receipts, remuneration, return, revenue, royalty, salary, stipend, takings, tontine, turnover, wages, winnings

earth Gaia, ground, mother earth, mud, planet earth, soil, the globe, the world

earthquake aftershock, earth tremor, epicentre, focus, foreshock, main shock, microseism, quake, shock

earthy bawdy, loamy, muddy, sandy, silty

ease abatement, advance, aid, alleviate, alleviation, assist, assuage, breather, clarify, clear, comfort, consolation, content, contentment, demulce, eudemonia, facilitate, free time, give scope, grease, hasten, help, holiday, idleness, inactivity, interim, interpret, interval, iron out, leave, leisure, lessen, loosen, lubricate, lull, massage, mellow, mitigate, moderate, mollification, mollify,

101

oil, palliation, promote, reassurance, recess, refreshment, relax, relaxation, relieve, remission, repose, respite, rest, restfulness, serenity, shuteye, simplify, slacken, smooth, snooze, soothe, speed, stillness, subdue, temper, tranquillity, unclog, unwind, vacation, well-being

easing clarifying, expediting, facilitation, simplifying, smoothing

easy clear, elementary, facile, glib, intelligible, plain, simple, smooth, straightforward, superficial, uncomplicated, undemanding, uninvolved

easygoing acquiescent, biddable, compliant, docile, indulgent, lenient, permissive, tolerant, tractable, undemanding

eat absorb, banquet, board, break bread, breakfast, consume, devour, digest, dine out, engulf, feast, feed, graze, gulp, ingest, ingurgitate, lunch, mess, partake, regale, slurp, snack, suck, sup, swallow

eating absorption, consumption, deglutition, digestion, dining, feeding, grazing, gulping, ingestion, ingurgitation

eccentric crackpot, deviant, freak, idiosyncratic, oddball, oddity, offbeat, quirky, wacko, weirdo
may indicate an anagram

ecology conservation, environmentalism, green movement

economic budgetary, cheap, commercial, deflationary, financial, fiscal, frugal, inflationary, mercantile, monetary, pecuniary, profitable, thrifty
See list of economic terms and theories.

ecosystem food chain, habitat, microhabitat

ECONOMIC TERMS AND THEORIES

ADDED VALUE	ECONOMIC	INVESTMENT	PRIVATE SECTOR
AGGREGATE	EQUILIBRIUM	KEYNESIANISM	PRODUCTIVITY
DEMAND	ECONOMIC	LAISSEZ-FAIRE	PROPERTY
BALANCED BUDGET	GROWTH	ECONOMICS	PROTECTION
BEAR MARKET	ECONOMIC	LENINISM	PUBLIC SECTOR
BOOM CYCLE	POLICY	LIQUIDITY	PUT OPTION
BROAD MONEY	ECONOMIC RENT	MACROECONOMICS	RECESSION
BULL MARKET	ECONOMIES OF	MARGINALISM	RETAIL PRICE INDEX
BUST CYCLE	SCALE	MARKET FORCES	REVISIONISM
CAPITALISM	ELASTICITY OF	MARXISM	SLAVERY
COLONIALISM	DEMAND	MATERIALISM	SLUMP
COMMAND	EXCHANGE VALUE	MEANS OF	STAGFLATION
ECONOMY	FIFO	PRODUCTION	STATICS
COMPETITION	FISCAL DRAG	MERCANTILISM	SUPPLY AND
CONSUMERISM	FISCAL POLICY	MICROECONOMICS	DEMAND
CORPORATE STATE	FIVE-YEAR PLAN	MIXED ECONOMY	SUPPLY-SIDE
COST OF	FREE MARKET	MONETARISM	ECONOMICS
PRODUCTION	FREE TRADE	MONETARY POLICY	SURPLUS
DEFICIT FINANCING	FUNGIBLE	MONOPOLY	SURPLUS VALUE
DEMAND CURVE	FUTURES MARKET	NARROW MONEY	SYNDICALISM
DEMAND	GDP	NATIONAL INCOME	TOTALITARIANISM
ECONOMY	GNP	NEO-CLASSICISM	TRADE BARRIER
DEPRESSION	GOLD STANDARD	NEW DEAL	TRADE CYCLE
DIALECTICAL	GROSS DOMESTIC	NEW ECONOMICS	TROTSKYISM
MATERIALISM	PRODUCT	OLIGOPOLY	VALUE ADDED
DIMINISHING	GROSS NATIONAL	OPTIONS MARKET	VELOCITY OF
RETURNS	PRODUCT	PERFECT	MONEY
DIVISION OF LABOUR	IMPERIALISM	COMPETITION	WAGE-PRICE
DUOPOLY	INELASTIC	PHYSIOCRACY	SPIRAL
ECONOMETRICS	INFLATIONARY	POSITIONAL GOODS	WELFARE
ECONOMIC	GAP	PRICES AND	ECONOMICS
CLASSICISM	INSTITUTIONALISM	INCOMES POLICY	WINDFALL PROFIT

edge advantage, border, boundary, brim, brink, circumference, creep, extremity, face, flank, fringe, frontier, hem, limit, lip, margin, marginal, marginalize, perimeter, peripheral, periphery, rim, sideline, sidle, skirt, verge

edible alimental, alimentary, comestible, consumable, digestible, esculent, nutritious

edit
may indicate an anagram

educatable teachable, trainable

educate coach, drill, instruct, school, teach, train, tutor

education advice, catechization, coaching, drilling, guidance, indoctrination, instruction, pedagogy, schooling, teaching, training, tuition, tutelage, tutoring

educational edifying, enlightening, helpful, illuminating, informative, instructive

educator academic, adviser, chancellor, coach, dean, doctor, dominie, don, duenna, expert, fellow, governess, guru, headmaster, headmistress, instructor, intern, lecturer, mentor, mullah, pedagogue, preacher, preceptor, preceptress, principal, professor, reader, teacher, trainer, tutor

effect achieve, consequence, denouement, end, impression, issue, outcome, payoff, product, repercussion, result, spin-off, upshot

effective forceful, functional, powerful, productive, useful

efficiency competence, effectiveness, profitability, readiness, speed

effluent effusive, expended, extravasated, outflowing, outpouring, sewage, spent, waste

effusive blabbing, chatty, communicative, conversational, expansive, flip, gossipy, gushing, lippy, mouthy, prating, prattling, sociable, tattling, yakking

effusiveness communicativeness, gushiness, sociability

egalitarian democratic, equitable, fair, impartial, just

egalitarianism democracy, evenness, fairness, impartiality, justice

egoism conceit, ego, egocentricity, narcissism, self-centredness, self-love, vanity

egoistic conceited, egocentric, narcissistic, self-absorbed, self-centred, self-loving, vain

eight eighter, eightfold, eighth, octad, octadic, octagon, octagonal, octahedral, octahedron, octangular, octarchy, Octateuch, octatonic, octave, octavo, octennial, octet, octonary, octopus, octuple, octuplet

eighty fourscore, octogenarian

eject banish, cast out, defenestrate, deport, evict, exile, expatriate, expel, extradite, oust, outlaw, throw out

ejection banishment, defenestration, deportation, dismissal, eviction, exile, expatriation, expulsion, extradition, removal, riddance

elaborate artistic, classical, complicate, embellish, finished, manicured, ornamented, polished, soigné, well-groomed, well-turned

elaboration finish, flourish, ornament, polish

elastic bouncy, distend, distensible, ductile, expand, extend, extensible, flex, flexible, give, plastic, pliant, resilient, rubbery, spring, springy, stretch, stretchable, supple, tensile

elasticity bounciness, distension, ductility, extensibility, flex, flexibility, plasticity, pliancy, resilience, rubberiness, springiness, stretchability, suppleness, tensibility

elected appointed, chosen, delegated, selected

electioneering campaigning, canvassing, doorstepping, vote-catching

elective electoral, enfranchised, psephological, voting

electrician sparks
See also list at **occupation**.

electronics electrotechnics, electrotechnology, microelectronics, telecommunications

elegance beauty, culture, delicacy, dignity, distinction, euphony, finish, gentility, grace, harmony, polish, propriety, purity, quality, refinement, seemliness, sophistication, style, suavity, taste

elegant beautiful, euphonious, exquisite, fine, graceful, harmonious, majestic, smart, stately, stylish, tasteful

element
See list at **chemical**.

elemental atmospheric, basic, fundamental, inert, metallic, metalloid, meteorological, primordial, superheavy, transuranic

elevate
may indicate a backword

eleven hendecagon, hendecahedron, undecagon

eleventh hendecagonal, undecennial

elicit call up, educe, evoke, glean, induce, procure, summon up, worm out

eliminate annihilate, cancel, delete, destroy, dispense, eradicate, expurgate, obliterate, remove

elimination deletion, eradication, expurgation, obliteration

elite chosen few, crème de la crème, gentry, jet set, nobility

ell length, measure

eloquent bombastic, declamatory, grandiloquent, magniloquent, rhetorical, silver-tongued, smooth-talking

elude avoid, dodge, evade, hide, lie low

emaciated anorexic, cadaverous, drawn, frail, gaunt, haggard, malnourished, marasmic, peaked, pinched, skeletal, starved, tabescent, underfed, undernourished, wasted, wraithlike

emaciation atrophy, boniness, cadaverousness, gauntness, haggardness, malnutrition, marasmus, starvation, tabes, tabescence, wasting

embellished dressed-up, embroidered, gilded, glossed, overdone, touched-up, varnished

embrace assimilate, compose, comprise, constitute, embody, encompass, epitomize, hug, incarnate, include, incorporate, personify, subsume
may indicate a hidden word

embryonic budding, dawning, developing, emergent, fetal, germinal, inchoate, nascent

emerge appear, arise, arrive, begin, come forth, come out, dawn, debouch, effuse, emanate, erupt, issue, materialize, sally forth, show, spring, sprout, surface, turn up

emerging arising, coming out, egressive, issuing, surfacing
may indicate an anagram or *a hidden word*

emigration expatriation, migration, moving, outmigration, relocation

eminent distinctive, esteemed, exalted, glorious, important, impressive, prominent, salient

emission discharge, emanation, emissivity, radiation, radioactivity

emit exhale, fume, give off, reek, smoke, steam

emotion ardour, attitude, fervour, mood, obsession, passion

emotionalism bathos, emotiveness, mawkishness, romanticism, sentimentality

emotive affecting, controversial, impassioned, moving, poignant, sensitive, touching

empathize bleed for, commiserate, grieve for, pity, relate to, sympathize, understand

emphasis accent, insistence, iteration, priority, reiteration, repetition, stress, urgency

emphasize accentuate, dwell on, enhance, feature, hammer home, highlight, italicize, plug, point out, press home, reaffirm, reassert, reiterate, repeat, rub in, spotlight, stress, underline, underscore

emphasized accentuated, accusé, enhanced, highlighted, marked, pointed, pronounced, stressed, underlined

emphatic dogmatic, earnest, firm, insistent, iterative, reiterative, repetitive, uncompromising, urgent, vehement

employ conscript, engage, enlist, enrol, hire, occupy, post, recruit, use

employed busy, engaged, mercenary, paid, working

employment job, livelihood, occupation, office, place, position, post, service, station
See also list at **occupation**.

emporium arcade, mall, precinct, shopping centre

empower accredit, allow, animate, anoint, appoint, approve, arm, authorize, charge, charter, consecrate, coronate, declare, delegate, deputize, drive, elect, electrify, enable, endow, energize, grant, legalize, legitimatize, license, magnetize, permit, plug in, sanction, select, strengthen, switch on, transistorize, turn on

emptiness bareness, barrenness, blankness, hollowness, nothingness, vacancy, vacuity, vacuum, voidness

emulate ape, compete with, copy, follow, imitate, rival

emulsion collodion, colloid, mixture

enable allow, contrive, empower, equip, facilitate, finance, find, float, fund, furnish, permit, plan, prepare, promote, provide, sponsor, staff, subsidize, supply

enamoured besotted, bewitched, captivated, charmed, devoted, enchanted, enraptured, enslaved, ensnared, fascinated, infatuated, lovelorn, lovesick, smitten

enchant allure, attract, becharm, beguile, bewitch, captivate, enamour, enrapture, enthral, fascinate

encircle embrace, encompass, flank, girdle, skirt, surround
may indicate a hidden word

encirclement circumambience, encompassment, enfoldment, envelopment

enclose cloister, confine, corral, dyke, impound, moat, paddock, pale, pen, pen, reserve, surround
may indicate a hidden word

enclosed built-in, cloistered, closed in, confined, fenced-in, hemmed-in, imprisoned, indoor, jailed, penned, pent-up, shut-in, walled-in

enclosure close, confine, pen, precinct

encourage animate, assure, embolden, exhort, hearten, incite, inspire, inspirit, reassure

encouragement advocacy, animation, approval, assistance, assurance, backing, empathy, endorsement, exhortation, favour, furtherance, incitement, intercession, moral support, reassurance, sympathy

end cap, close, complete, completion, conclude, conclusion, consummate, crown, culminate, death, decide, destroy, doom, edge, extremity, finale, finalize, finis, finish, goal, object, remnant, resolve, round off, scrap, settle, wind-up

endanger compromise, gamble, hazard, imperil, jeopardize, risk, stake, venture

endearment angel, baby, cherub,

chick, chickabiddy, darling, dear, deary, doll, duck, lamb, lambkins, love, lovey, pet, petal, poppet, precious, sweetheart, sweetie

endearments blandishments, compliments, flattery, sweet nothings, sweet talk

ended complete, concluded, decided, done, finalized, finished, over, settled, terminated, through

endless
may indicate a shortening (delete final letter)

endurance constancy, continuance, durableness, duration, fixity, perdurability, permanence, perpetuity, persistence, stability, survival

endure continue, hold, last, live on, persist, prevail, remain, stand, stay, survive

enemy adversary, aggressor, antagonist, archenemy, combatant, competitor, foe, invader, opponent, rival

energetic brisk, peppy, punchy, zingy

energy animation, dynamism, force, heat, high spirits, horsepower, impetus, liveliness, manpower, momentum, pep, pressure, thrust, traction, vigour, vitality, vivacity, work

enfold clasp, embrace, enclose, entwine, envelop, hug, intertwine, swathe, wrap

enfoldment clasp, embrace, enclosure, entwining, envelopment, hug, swathing, wrapping

engaged affianced, battle, betrothed, occupied, plighted, promised, spoken for

engineer architect, CE, contractor, designer, RE, sapper, surveyor, technician
See also list at **occupation**.

engrave aquatint, bite, chase, emboss, etch, grave, impress, incise, print, scrape

engulf
may indicate a hidden word

enigma brainteaser, catch, catch-22, controversy, conundrum, crisis, crux, dilemma, Hobson's choice, knotty problem, mind boggler, moot point, mystery, poser, riddle, stumper

enjoy bask, celebrate, delight in, gormandize, have fun, indulge oneself, luxuriate, make merry, purr, relish, revel in, splurge, wallow

enlarge accelerate, add to, aggrandize, aggravate, amplify, augment, bloat, blow up, boost, breed, broaden, build up, cube, deepen, develop, dilate, disperse, distend, double, draw out, duplicate, elevate, enhance, escalate, exacerbate, expand, extend, fan, fatten, fill up, flare, heighten, hike up, increase, inflate, intensify, lengthen, magnify, multiply, open, pad out, plump up, prolong, puff up, pump up, quadruple, raise, ramify, splay, sprawl, spread out, square, stoke, stretch, stuff, supplement, swell, thicken, triple, up, widen

enlargeable amplifiable, augmentative, dilatable, dispersive, distensible, elastic, expandable, expansile, expansionary, extendable, extensile, inflatable, magnifiable, multipliable, spreadable, stretchable

enlarged aggrandized, amplified, blown-up, dilated, expanded, heightened, inflated, magnified, maximized, puffed-up

enlargement aggrandizement, amplification, dilation, expansion, heightening, inflation, magnification, maximization

enlightened civilized, clarified, educated, elucidated, illuminated, informed, open-minded

enlightenment awareness, broadmindedness, clarification, comprehension, elucidation, illumination, insight, knowledge, revelation, understanding

enlist enrol, matriculate, procure, register, sign up

enlisted conscripted, drafted, enrolled, joined-up, recruited

enliven activate, agitate, animate, arouse, disturb, excite, galvanize, invigorate, quicken, stimulate, stir, thrill, titillate, wake, whet

enmity abhorrence, aggression, animosity, antagonism, antipathy, bellicosity, belligerence, clash, collision, conflict, contention, dislike, dissension, friction, hate, hostility, incompatibility, inimicality, loathing, malevolence, malice, opposition, quarrelling, repugnance, spite, unfriendliness, venom, virulence, vitriol

enrol admit, contend, crown, enlist, enter, induct, initiate, inscribe, install, institute, introduce, invest, join, ordain, sign on

enrolment enlistment, induction, initiation, installation, introduction, investiture, ordination

ensure affirm, ascertain, authenticate, certify, check, clear up, confirm, convince, decide, demonstrate, determine, endorse, establish, evince, find out, fix, ground, guarantee, pin down, pledge, promise, prove, secure, settle, solidify, stabilize, steady, substantiate, verify, warrant

enter arrive, board, burst upon, call in, check in, clock in, embark, go in, infiltrate, look in, mount, penetrate, percolate, permeate, pop in, punch in, ring in, sign in, visit

entering homing, immigrant, imported, inbound, incoming, ingoing, ingressive, inward

enterprise ambition, business, drive, get-up-and-go, go, initiative, push, venture

enterprising adventurous, ambitious, innovative, opportunist, pioneering, resourceful, speculative

entertain amuse, banter, clown, divert, jest, joke, josh, pun, quip, regale, wisecrack

entertainer artiste, busker, comic, conjuror, drag artiste, escapologist, host, hypnotist, impersonator, impressionist, jongleur, magician, memory artist, mimic, mindreader, minstrel, mountebank, performer, presenter, stand-up comic, stooge, troubadour, ventriloquist

enticement bait, decoy, lure, trap

entire absolute, accomplished, achieved, adequate, closed, compleat, complete, comprehensive, concluded, consummate, detailed, done, exhaustive, faultless, finalized, finished, intact, integral, mature, over, perfect, plenary, pure, quorate, sufficient, terminated, thorough, total, unabbreviated, unabridged, unbroken, uncut, undivided, unexpurgated, unimpaired, united, unqualified, utter, whole, wholesale

entitle allow, authorize, empower, enable, enfranchise, license, permit, qualify, warrant

entitled admitted, allowed, lawful, legal, legitimate, licit, permitted, qualified, sanctioned, warranted

entitlement due, duty, expectation, obligation

entrance access, adit, approach, archway, channel, conduit, door, doorway, entry, foyer, gate, hatch, infiltration, ingress, inlet, intervention, lobby, lychgate, mouth, opening, orifice, osmosis, passage, penetration, percolation, permeation, porch, portal, porte-cochere, portico, postern, propylaeum, scuttle, stile, threshold, tollgate, transudation, trapdoor, turnpike, turnstile, vestibule, way in

entrepreneur director, go-getter, manager, operative, whiz-kid, worker

entry access, admission, entrance, entrée, import, incoming, ingress, input, intergression, reception

envelop
may indicate a hidden word

envious covetous, desirous, green-eyed, jaundiced, jealous, longing

environment bailiwick, base, domain, element, habitat, hangout, haunt, home ground, locality, neighbourhood, niche, range, surroundings, territory

environmental conservationist, green

environmentalism conservationism, ecofeminism, ecology, Green Party, Greenpeace, green politics, Greens, preservationism

envy begrudge, covet, covetousness, crave, desire, grudge, hanker after, jealousy, long for, lust after, resent

epicurism connoisseurship, epicureanism, gastronomy, gourmandism

epitomize exemplify, indicate, mean, model, pattern, represent, signify

equal coequal, companion, compeer, comrade, convertible, corresponding, counterpart, ding-dong, drawn, equivalent, even, evenly matched, fellow, fifty-fifty, half-and-half, identical, level, match, mate, neck-and-neck, nip-and-tuck, one-to-one, parallel, peer, same, similar, tied, twin

equality coequality, correspondence, equiponderance, equivalence, likeness, parallelism, sameness, sharing

equalization adjustment, balancing, barter, compensation, counteraction, equation, equilibration, equipollence, exchange, interchange, isotropy, offset, reciprocation, synonymity, trade-off, weighing

equalize accommodate, adjust, balance, cancel out, compensate, coordinate, counterpoise, countervail, equate, even up, integrate, level up, offset, proportion, round up, square, stabilize, synchronize, tally

equilibrium balance, counterpoise, equipoise, evenness, homeostasis, poise, proportion, stability, status quo, steadiness, symmetry

equine equestrian, hors(e)y

equip fit, furnish, provide, rig out, supply

equipment chattels, gear, impedimenta, kit, paraphernalia, tackle, tools, trappings, utensils

equivalence accordance, agreement, concordance, congruence, correspondence, equipollence, harmony, interchangeability, reciprocation

equivalent accordant, agreeing, concordant, congruent, corresponding, equipollent, harmonious, interchangeable, reciprocal, tit-for-tat, two-way

equivocal ambiguous, ambivalent, epicene, two-edged

equivocalness ambiguity, ambivalence, indefiniteness, uncertainty, vagueness

equivocate delay, evade, fence, fudge, hedge, postpone, prevaricate, procrastinate, shuffle, sidestep, skirt round, stonewall, vacillate

equivocating apostate, disloyal, false, hypocritical, perfidious, recanting, recidivist, renegade, tergiversating, traitorous, treacherous, two-faced, unfaithful

equivocation ambivalence, dodging, double-talk, evasion, fencing, mystification, obfuscation, obscurity, prevarication, procrastination, pussyfooting, shiftiness, shuffling, side-stepping, vagueness, waffling

equivocator apostate, betrayer, collaborator, defector, fifth columnist, Judas, quisling, quitter, recreant, reneger, runaway, tergiversator, traitor, turncoat

era aeon, age, eon, epoch, period, time

erase cancel, eliminate, obliterate, remove, rub, scrub, steal, wipe

erect build, construct, elevate, raise, upend, upright

erode corrode, erase, fray, frazzle, skin, wear

erotica blue movie, facetiae, porn, pornography

err backslide, blunder, boob, bungle, caricature, cheat, degenerate, disgrace oneself, distort, fall, falsify, infringe, lapse, misbehave, miscalculate, misconstrue, mishit, misinterpret, misjudge, misprint, mispronounce, misquote, misrepresent, misspell, misstate, muff, offend, omit, overlook, parody, shock, sin, sink, slip up, stray, stumble, transgress, trespass, violate, wander

errancy aberrancy, culpability, deviancy, guiltiness, perversion, wrongdoing

errant aberrant, culpable, deviant, erring, guilty, perverse, perverted, roaming, sinful, wandering
may indicate an anagram

erroneous fallacious, false, falsified, faulty, flawed, incorrect, untrue, wrong

erroneousness fallaciousness, falsity, incorrectness, untruth, wrongness

error ambiguity, blunder, bull, erratum, Goldwynism, lapse, literal, malapropism, mishap, misprint, mispronunciation, misspelling, mistake, misusage, omission, oversight, slip, solecism, spoonerism, typo
may indicate an anagram

eructative belching, erupting, flatulent, gassy

erupting bursting, explosive, expulsive, volcanic

eruption blast, dissilience, explosion, flare-up

escape abscond, bolt, break out, decamp, decampment, depart, departure, flee, flight, fly, getaway, jailbreak, run away

escort accompany, chaperone, guard, guide, protector, squire

essence backbone, basis, centre, concentrate, core, cornerstone, crux, extract, fabric, focus, gist, gravamen, heart, highlight, kernel, keystone, lifeblood, marrow, material, matter, meat, nub, nucleus, pith, pivot, quid, quiddity, sap, structure, stuff, subject, substance

essential basic, crucial, extracted, indispensable, necessary, paramount, requisite, vital

established accepted, accredited, acknowledged, admitted, approved, created, de rigueur, done, founded, instituted, institutionalized, official, practised, received, recognized, understood

estate acquest, assets, bequest, capital, circumstances, collateral, contents, effects, funds, goods, heirloom, hereditament, income, inheritance, intangibles, legacy, means, merchandise, patrimony, plant, portfolio, resources, revenue, securities, state, status, stock, substance, tangibles, valuables, wares, wealth

estimate appraise, assess, calculate, conjecture, deem, esteem, evaluate, gauge, guess, judge, rate, reckon, regard, surmise, value

estimation opinion, reference, regard, report, reputation

estranged alienated, at variance, disaffected, disloyal, distant, disunited, divided, irreconcilable, separated, unfaithful

eternal endless, everlasting, forever, infinite, neverending, perpetual, timeless, unending

eternity continuity, endlessness, everlastingness, immortality, imperishability, infinity, permanence, perpetuity, sempiternity, timelessness

ethical honorable, moral, principled, righteous

ethics code of conduct, morality, morals, mores, principles

etiquette civilities, comity, convention, custom, decencies, decorum, elegancies, form, formalities, manners, mores, politeness, politesse, proprieties, protocol, punctilio, social graces

evade cower, dodge, duck, elude, escape, hide, skulk

evaporate boil away, dissipate, vaporize, volatilize

evaporation vaporization, volatilization

evasion avoidance, concealment, cowering, deflection, dodge, duck, elusion, parry, prevarication, quibble, skulking, untruth

evasive ambivalent, amphibolous, anagrammatic, circumlocutory, elusive, equivocal, homonymous, misleading, oracular, prevaricating, roundabout, shifty, vague

even beautiful, consistent, equal, eurrhythmic, evening, level, regular, shapely, smooth, stabilize, uniform, yet

evening afternoon, darkfall, dusk, eve, eventide, gloaming, moonrise, moonset, nightfall, postmeridian, sundown, sunset, twilight, vespers

evening star Hesperus, Lucifer, morning star, Phosphorus, Venus
See also list at **astronomer**.

evenness balance, beauty, conformity, consistency, eurhythmy, flatness, harmony, regularity, shapeliness, uniformity

events affair, business, goings-on, gossip, happenings, news, proceedings, rumour, story

everyday common, commonplace, familiar, general, household, identikit, normal, ordinary, quotidian, standard, stereotyped, stock, typical, unexceptional, usual

everyman everywoman, Joe Bloggs, Joe Public, John Doe, Mr Average

everyone all, everybody, everything

evict dislodge, dispossess, extirpate, oust, remove, repossess, unhouse, unkennel, uproot

eviction dislodgment, dispossession, ousting, removal

evidence admission, affidavit, confession, confirmation, counterevidence, credential, data, declaration, deposition, exhibit, facts, gen, grounds, information, intelligence, premises, proof, reasons, recommendation, record, reference, report, seal, signature, statement, testimonial, testimony

evident apparent, manifest, obvious, ostensible, prominent, self-evident, visible

evidential authentic, certain, demonstrative, direct, documented, empirical, factual, prima facie, recorded, relevant, reported, significant, tell-tale

evidentness appearance, manifestation, obviousness, prominence, self-evidence, visibility

evil atrocious, awful, bad, badness, beastly, blighted, contemptible, corrupt, deadly, defiled, demonic, deplorable, depraved, despicable, detestable, diabolic, dreadful, foul, hateful, horrible, immoral, iniquitous, lousy,-maleficent, malevolent, malicious, malignant, mean, mischievous, nasty, nefarious, obnoxious, odious, offensive, reprehensible, revengeful, rotten, sinful, sinister, terrible, ungodly, unkind, vicious, vile, vindictive, wicked, wickedness, worthless, wretched, wrong

evisceration disembowelment, gutting, shelling

evocative exciting, forceful, highly coloured, moving, poignant, striking, thrilling

evolution assimilation, catastrophism, Darwinism, development, growth, improvement, Lamarckism, Lysenkoism, naturalization, phylogeny, progress, regeneration, speciation, uniformitarianism, Weismannism

ex earlier, former, old flame, one-time

exaggerate caricature, embellish, embroider, hype, hyperbolize, overact, overcompensate, overdo, overemphasize, overenthuse, overestimate, overexpose, overplay, overrate, overstate, overstress, overvalue, overwrite, sensationalize, strain, stretch

exaggerated aggravated, embellished, embroidered, excessive, exorbitant, extreme, grandiose, hyped, hyperbolic, inflated, inordinate, intensified, laboured, overambitious, overcompensated, overdone, overemphasized, overestimated, overpraised, overrated, oversold, overstated, overstressed, overvalued, prodigious, puffed, sensationalized, strained, stretched, superlative, varnished

exaggeration aggravation, embellishment, embroidery, excessiveness, exorbitance, extremism, hype, hyperbolism, intensification, labouring, overcolouring, overcompensation, overemphasis, overenthusiasm, overestimation, overexposure, overkill, overreaction, overselling, overstatement, overstress, overvaluation, prodigality, sensationalism, straining, stretching, touching up, varnish

exalted elevated, eminent, highflown, lofty, prominent, sublime, superlative, supreme

examine criticize, inspect, investigate, review, scan, survey, test, vet

excavate archaeologize, bore, burrow, dig, exhume, gouge, hollow, honeycomb, mine, pockmark, scoop, spade, tunnel, uncover, unearth

excavation burial, digging, drilling, interment, mining, potholing, spelunking, tunnelling

excavator digger, miner, quarrier

exceed excel, lap, outbid, outclass, outdistance, outdo, outflank, outmanoeuvre, outride, outrival, outrun, outstrip, overtake, surmount, surpass, transcend

excel better, exceed, overtop, predominate, prevail, surpass, transcend, triumph, win

excellent A1, ace, adept, blue-chip, classic, competent, consummate, distinguished, eminent, expert, first-class, first-rate, important, major, master, masterly, outstanding, prestigious, professional, proficient, prominent, qualified, singular, skilful, specialist, star, superb, supreme, top-flight

excess abundance, avalanche, exaggeration, excessiveness, exorbitance, exuberance, flood, glut, nimiety, overflow, overpopulation, overspill, plenitude, saturation

excessive abundant, brimming over, crawling, disproportionate, exorbitant, extreme, exuberant, inordinate, overflowing, overfull, overpopulated, overwhelming, plentiful, plethoric, profuse, redundant, saturated, supersaturated, swarming, teeming

excessiveness arrogation, exaggeration, excess, greed, hyperbole, immoderateness, intemperance, overacting, overestimation, overfulfilment, overindulgence, overplaying, overrating, redundance, surplus

exchange alternate, alternation, barter, castle, commutability, commutation, commute, compensate, conversion, convert, displace, displacement, interchange, pawn, permutation, permute, reciprocate, recompense, replace, replacement, shuffle, shuttle, substitution, swap, switch, trade, traffic, transact, transpose, transposition, truck

exchangeable commutable, interchangeable, permutable, replaceable, substitutable, tradeable, transpositional

exchanged bartered, compensated, converted, interchanged, pawned, ransomed, reciprocated, requited, substituted, swapped, switched, traded, transposed

excision cutting off, deletion, excavation, exsection, extirpation

excite
may indicate an anagram

exciting breath-taking, emotive, impressive, keen, poignant, sensational, stimulating, stirring, striking, thrilling, titillating

exclamation ejaculation, expletive, hoot, interjection

exclude ban, banish, bar, blacklist, boycott, disregard, except, excuse, exempt, ignore, insulate, isolate, omit, ostracize, relegate

excluded banned, barred, deleted, dismissed, disregarded, embargoed, evicted, excepted, excused, exempt, expelled, forbidden, forestalled, omitted, outclassed, prevented, rejected, taboo

exclusion denial, dispensation, exception, exemption, omission, refusal, rejection, relegation, suppression

exclusiveness elitism, exclusivity, monopoly, restrictiveness

excrement crap, dejection, effluent, egesta, ejecta, excreta, extravasation, exudation, piss, sewage, shit, transudation, waste

excrete discharge, egest, ejaculate, eject, eliminate, emit, expectorate, expel, extravasate, extrude, exude, pass, secrete, transude, weep

excretion discharge, ecchymosis, effusion, egestion, ejaculation, ejection, elimination, emanation, emission, expectoration, expulsion, extravasation, extrusion, exudation, secretion, transudation

execute behead, bow-string, burn, carry out, complete, crucify, decapitate, decollate, dismember, electrocute, flay, garrotte, gas, gibbet, guillotine, hang, impale, kill, lapidate, lynch, shoot, stone, strangle, undertake

execution axe, block, bowstring, bullet, completion, cross, deathblow, electric chair, electrocution, final stroke, firing squad, gallows, garrotte, gas chamber, gibbet, guillotine, halter, hemlock, lethal injection, maiden, noose, performance, poison, quietus, scaffold, stake

exempt excepted, excluded, immune, nonliable, protected, shielded, unaccountable, unanswerable, unpunishable

exemption dispensation, exception, exclusion, immunity, impunity, nonliability, nonresponsibility, privilege

exercise aerobics, callisthenics, drill, employ, eurhythmics, jogging, keep fit, practise, prepare, train, warm up, work out, yoga
See also list at **sport**.

exertion ado, assiduity, drive, effort, elbow grease, energy, ergonomics, force, fray, hassle, heave, horsepower, lift, manpower, muscle power, overwork, pains, power, pressure, pull, push, rub, scrub, squeeze, strain, stress, stretch, struggle, throw, trouble, tug

exert oneself attempt, battle, campaign, endeavour, persevere, slog at, strain, strive, struggle, travail, try

exhalation breath, effluvium, emanation, emission, expiration

exhibitionism boasting, egotism, flaunting, peacockry, showing-off, strutting, swaggering, swashbuckling, vanity

exhortation clarion call, encouragement, rallying cry

exhume dig up, disentomb, disinter, exhume, unbury, unearth

exist be, breathe, coexist, corporealize, embody, externalize, incarnate, live, objectify, personify, reify, subsist, substantialize

existence being, coexistence, ens, entity, esse, life, occurrence, presence, subsistence

existing actual, being, coexistent, current, extant, living, manifest, occurring, present, prevalent, real, subsistent, substantial, tangible

exit breakout, departure, door, egress, emergence, eruption, evacuation, exodus, go, issue, leave, outburst, proruption, walk-out, withdraw

expansionism colonialism, colonization, emigration, imperialism

expect anticipate, apprehend, await, bet on, count on, daresay, dread, envisage, face, fear, forecast, foresee, forestall, forewarn, hope for, intend, look for, plan, predict, prepare for, presume, prognosticate, reckon, risk, suppose, wait for

expectation anticipation, apprehension, assumption, foreboding, presumption, prospect, suspense, waiting

expectations ambition, aspiration, demands, desires, dream, hopes, prediction, prognosis, prospects

expected anticipated, contemplated, desired, dreaded, feared, foreseen, hoped for, long-awaited, predicted

expel banish, cast out, discharge, eject, evict, exile

expend buy, disburse, invest, pay out, purchase, shop, spend, use up

expended blown, consumed, contributed, disbursed, invested, paid, spent

expenditure buying, disbursement, payment, shopping, spending

expense charge, cost, extras, fee, investment, outgoings, outlay, overheads, price, rate

experienced businesslike, competent, efficient, expert, practised, professional, proficient, qualified, seasoned, specialized, trained, tried, versed in, veteran

experiment analyse, analysis, assay, check, diagnosis, essay, examine, explore, feeler, inquire, inquiry, investigate, investigation, probation, probe, research, sample, tentation, test, trial

experimental analytic, avant-garde, empirical, exploratory, innovative, instrumental, investigative, pragmatic, probational, scientific

experimentation empiricism, examination, exploration, instrumentalism, investigation, pragmatism, research, testing, trying

expert accomplished, intellectual, knowledgeable, masterly, professional, skilled, specialist, virtuoso

expire die, pass away, perish, run out, terminate

explain clarify, delineate, depict, describe, elucidate, exemplify, expound, express, illuminate, illustrate, indicate, unfold

explained clarified, cleared up, delineated, depicted, described, elucidated, exemplified, expounded, illuminated, illustrated

explanation assumption, basis, cause, clarification, defence, excuse, grounds, justification, motive, premise, pretext, theory

explanatory descriptive, exegetic, exemplificatory, explicatory, illuminating, illustrative, indicative, representative

explode burst, decompose, disintegrate, dissipate, evaporate, fragment, shatter, splinter
may indicate an anagram

exploit abuse, drain, extract, maximize, milk, misuse

explosive cap, charge, cordite, detonator, dynamite, fiery, fireworks, fuse, gelignite, gun cotton, gunpowder, lyddite, melinite, nitroglycerine, plastic explosive, priming, propellant, saltpetre, semtex, TNT, volatile, warhead
See also list at **weapon**.

exposed bare, denuded, discalced, divested, revealed, stripped, topless, uncovered, unearthed, unveiled

exposition clarification, delineation, demonstration, depiction, description, elucidation, exegesis, exemplification, explanation, expounding, illumination, illustration, indication

expulsion ejection, eviction, propulsion, rejection

expulsive ejaculative, ejective, eliminant, eruptive, expellent, explosive

extend outreach, prolong, spreadeagle, stretch

extensive far-flung, global, intergalactic, interstellar, universal, wideranging, widespread, worldwide

exterior coating, covering, crust, envelope, façade, face, facet, integument, outside, pod, rind, shell, superstratum

exterminate annihilate, deracinate, destroy, dispel, eliminate, eradicate, erase, exorcise, liquidate, massacre, obliterate, purge, slaughter

external distant, exterior, extraterrestrial, extrinsic, outer, outside, outward, ulterior

externality exteriority, exteriorization, externalization, extrinsicality, extroversion, openness, projection

externalize exteriorize, project, reveal

extinct defunct, expired, lapsed, obsolete, passé

extinction annihilation, death, obliteration, oblivion, obsolescence

extort claim, demand, exact, extorsion, wrench, wrest, wring

extortion blackmail, deception, embezzlement, loan-sharking, manipulation, profiteering, rack-rent, rip-off, swindle, usury

extra by-product, peripheral, spare, superfluous, surplus

extract avulse, concentrate, condense, cream off, cutting, decoct, decoction, disengage, distil, distillate, dredge, eliminate, elixir, eradicate, essence, essentialize, evulse, excerpt, extricate, infuse, infusion, juice, marinate, melt down, press, purify, refine, remove, render, separate, soak, spirit, squeeze, steep, sublimate, vaporize, withdraw *may indicate an anagram* or *a hidden word*

extraction avulsion, deracination, dredging, elimination, eradication, evulsion, extrication, removal, withdrawal

extractor aspirator, mangle, pipette, press, pump, separator, siphon, squeezer, syringe, wringer

extraneous alien, exotic, foreign, otherworldly, strange

extraneousness foreignness, otherworldliness, strangeness

extras auxiliaries, provisions, reinforcements, spares, sundries

extravagance improvidence, lavishness, prodigality, profligacy, spending spree, splurge, squandering, unthriftiness, wastefulness

extravagant improvident, lavish, overspending, pound-foolish, prodigal, profligate, spendthrift, thriftless, uneconomic, unthrifty, wasteful

extreme *may indicate the* first *or last* letter of a word

eye aqueous humour, blind spot, cone, conjunctiva, cornea, eyeball, gaze, glance, iris, lens, ogle, optic nerve, orb, peepers, perception, pupil, retina, rod, sclera, sparklers, vitreous humour, watch

eyesore blemish, carbuncle, eyeful, eye-opener, fright

·F·

F   fah • Fahrenheit • Fellow • female • forte • key • musical term • note
FA   fanny adams • Football Association
FAO   for the attention of
FBI   Federal Bureau of Investigation
FD   Defender of the Faith (Latin: *Fidei Defensor*) • Henry VIII
FDR   Franklin Delano Roosevelt
FE   Far East • further education • iron
FF   folios • musical term• very loud (Italian: *fortissimo*)
FL   flourished (Latin: *floruit*) • flute
FM   fermium • frequency modulation • radio
FO   Foreign Office
FOC   father of the chapel • free of charge
FR   Brother (Latin: *Frater*) • Father • francium • Frau
FT   foot • measurement

fabric brickwork, broadcloth, broadloom, build, carpeting, cloth, content, drapery, material, print, rag, screen print, substance, synthetic, textile, texture, tissue, warp, weave, weft, work *See also list at* **materials**.

fabricate concoct, hatch, imitate, invent, manufacture, simulate *may indicate an anagram*

facade act, appearance, bluff, disguise, dissemblance, dressing-up, embellishment, embroidery, face, fake, fanfaronade, front, gild, gloss, mask, masquerade, ostentation, seeming, semblance, sham, show, simulacrum, simulation, touch-up, varnish, whitewash, window-dressing

face beard, brazen out, brick, chronogram, clad, clock, clockface, confront, countenance, curtain, defy, dial, drape, encrust, facade, fight, front, gnomon, grout, hands, kisser, mortar, mould, mug, outface, paint, pan, panel, parget, pebble-dash, phiz, physiognomy, plank, plaster, profile, puss, render, revet, size, stucco, visage, wallpaper, watchface

fact the case, the essentials, the fundamentals, the realities, the specifics

faction breach, division, rift, rupture, schism, separation, split

fade abate, decrease, die away, diminish, dissolve, evolve, lower, shade off, taper off, wane

fail ail, blunder, bungle, collapse, decline, disappoint, discontinue, disillusion, flag, flop, fold, go bankrupt, plough, reject, sink, tire

failed bankrupt, bootless, dud, fruitless, futile, hopeless, ineffective, insolvent, insufficient, kaput, ploughed, profitless, unproductive, unsuccessful, useless

failure ailing, bankruptcy, blunder, botch, breakdown, bungle, collapse, comedown, crash, debacle, decline, default, defect, dereliction, deterioration, downfall, error, failing, fall, fallibility, fiasco, halt, inability, insufficiency, mess, miss, mistake, noncompletion, nonfeasance, nonfulfilment, nonperformance, nonpractice, omission, ruin, setback, shortage, shortcoming, stalling, unproductiveness, uselessness

faint bated, damped, dead, distant, dull, feeble, gentle, hushed, inaudible, indistinct, low, muffled, muted, nonresonant, piano, quiet, soft, softpedalled, stifled, subdued, unaccented, unemphatic, unstressed, voiceless, weak, whispered

faintness drone, fizz, hiss, hoarseness, hum, inaudibility, indistinctness, moan, murmur, muteness, nonresonance, pad, pitter-patter, roll, sigh, sizzle, softness, sough, squash, susurration, voicelessness, whisper

fair balanced, equitable, exhibition, exposition, favourable, fête, honourable, just, moderate, pale, pretty, show, sunny

fairness equality, equity, even handedness, impartiality, justice, paleness, prettiness, square deal

faithful accurate, loyal, true, true-blue

faithfulness faith, fidelity, loyalty, trueness

faithless betraying, deceitful, deserting, disloyal, disobedient, doublecrossing, duplicitous, false, perfidious, questionable, rebellious, seditious, shaky, treacherous, treasonous, twofaced, undependable, unfaithful, unreliable, untrustworthy

faithlessness betrayal, broken promise, deceit, defection, desertion, disloyalty, disobedience, double-crossing, double-dealing, duplicity, falseness, infidelity, Judas kiss, perfidy, rebellion, sedition, sellout, tergiversation, treachery, treason, unreliability, untrustworthiness, U-turn, volte-face

fake artificial, bogus, bootleg, copy, counterfeit, dummy, fabricate, falsify, forge, imitation, imitative, invent, junk, mock, mythologize, paste, phoney, pseud, rubbish, sham, tinsel
may indicate an anagram

fall autumn, collapse, comedown, crash, curtains, debacle, demotion, dipping, downfall, dropping, end, failure, flop, header, humiliation, nightfall, overturning, plummeting, plunging, ruin, spill, sprawl, stumble, sunset, swooping, titubation, trip, tumble

fallen defenestrated, downcast, downthrown, soused, submerged, sunk

falling coasting, dipping, diving, dropping, ducking, falling, flopping, gliding, lurching, nose-diving, plummeting, plunging, precipitous, scattering, showering, skidding, sliding, slipping, slithering, spilling, sprawling, sprinkling, stooping, stumbling, swooping, titubant, toppling, tripping, tumbling
may indicate a backword

false deceptive, delusive, dishonest, dissembling, erroneous, fake, fallacious, imitation, inveracious, Machiavellian, mendacious, seeming, sham, simulated, spurious, ungenuine, untrue

falsehood bad faith, deception, delusion, dishonesty, erroneousness, error, fallaciousness, fib, inveracity, lie, Machiavellianism, mendaciousness, spuriousness, truthlessness, ungenuineness, untruth, unverity

falseness deceit, fallaciousness, hallucination, illusion, imposture, insubstantiality, mirage, misconception, misdirection, misguidance, misinformation, misleading, mockery, phantasm, trickiness, will-o'-the-wisp

falsification canard, collusion, concoction, confabulation, counterfeiting, distortion, doctoring, fable, fabrication, faking, fiction, fiddle, figment, fix, forgery, frame, frame-up, garbling, imagination, invention, juggling, legend, manipulation, misciting, misinterpretation, misquote, misreporting, misrepresentation, misstatement, myth, perversion, plant, retouching, rigging, slanting, straining, tampering, trumping up, twisting, wangle, warping

falsified cock-and-bull, concocted, confabulated, contrary-to-fact, counterfeit, distorted, exaggerated, fabled, fabricated, faked, fictional, half-true, imaginative, invented, legendary, libellous, made-up, manipulated, misrepresented, mythologized, perjurious, slanderous, stretched, trumped-up, twisted

falsify collude, concoct, confabulate, counterfeit, cry wolf, distort, doctor, fable, fabricate, fake, fiddle, fix, forge, frame, garble, imagine, invent, manipulate, miscite, misinterpret, misquote, misreport, misrepresent, misstate, mythologize, pervert, plant, retouch, rig, slant, strain, tamper with, trump up, twist, wangle, warp

falter back, pitch, reel, rock, roll, shake, shuttle, stagger, sway, swing, tack, teeter, totter, tremble, turn, veer, vibrate, wobble, yaw

familiar banal, beaten, clichéd, close, common, commonplace, current, everyday, favourite, folksy, hackneyed, hail-fellow-well-met, haymish, homely, household, inseparable, intimate, known, natural, near, obtaining, ordinary, plain, prevalent, simple, stock, thick, trite, trodden, unaffected, unexceptional, universal, unoriginal, well-worn, widespread

familiarity affinity, closeness, commitment, constancy, dedication, devotion, firmness, folksiness, homeliness, inseparability, intimacy, naturalness, nearness, plainness, simplicity, staunchness, steadfastness, triedness, trueness, unaffectedness

fancy caprice, choice, craving, craze, crush, desire, elaborate, fad, hobby, infatuation, mania, ornate, phase, pleasure, relish, selection, shine, taste, trend, whim, wish

fanfare applause, cheer, congratulations, cry, glory, hallelujah, hosanna, hurrah, huzzah, hymn, ovation, praise, salute, shout, thanksgiving, yell

fanlike deltoid, palmate, splayed, spread-eagled

fantasize daydream, exaggerate, fictionalize, idealize, muse, poeticize, rhapsodize, romanticize

fantastical absurd, airy-fairy, bizarre, extravagant, fanciful, grotesque, Heath Robinson, impractical, Laputan, otherworldly, outlandish, preposterous, quixotic, starry-eyed, unreal, visionary, whimsical

fantasy apparition, bogey, chimera, delusion, dream, error, fabrication, fancy, ghost, hallucination, illusion, improvisation, make-believe, mirage, nightmare, phantom, shadow, spectre, trompe l'oeil, vapour, vision

farm croft, cultivate, demesne, estate, farmstead, holding, homestead, kibbutz, kolkhov, plantation, ranch, smallholding, steading, toft

farmable arable, cropped, cultivable, fallow, farmed, fertile, fruitful, ploughable, productive, tillable, undersown

fashion craze, designer label, elegance, haute couture, high fashion, look, mode, mould, new look, rage, set, shape, style, the latest, trend, vogue *may indicate an anagram*

fashionable à la mode, chic, classy, clothes conscious, cool, crucial, dressy, glamorous, groovy, hip, posh, smart, snazzy, stylish, tasteful, well-dressed, well-groomed, with-it

fast abstain, diet, famish, firmly, hunger, Lent, quick, Ramadan, rapidly, secure, short, slim, speedy, starve, swift, tight

fastening attaching, bolt, brace, bracelets, braces, brad, brooch, buckle, button, buttonhole, catch, clasp, cleat, clip, cotter pin, cufflink, dowel, eyelet, fastener, fixing, hairgrip, hairpin, handcuffs, hasp, hatpin, hinge, holdfast, kingpin, latch, linchpin, lock, loop, manacles, nail, nut, peg, popper, ring, rivet, safety pin, screw, skewer, slide, staple, stitch, stud, suspender, tiepin, toggle, Velcro, zip

fastidiousness exactitude, faddiness, neatness, niceness, orderliness, particularity, pedantry, perfectionism, pernicketiness, tidiness

fasting abstemious, abstinence, anorexia, ascetic, atrophy, austerity, dieting, empty, famished, half-starved, hungry, lean cuisine, Lenten, Quadragesimal, ravenous, reducing, slimming, Spartan, starving, thin, underfed, unfed, wasting away, weight loss, Weightwatchers

fat adeps, adipocere, adipose, bloated, blubber, bonny, butter, buttermilk, buxom, cellulite, ceresin, chubby, corpulent, cream, distended, dumpy, endomorphic, ester, flab, flabby, fleshy, full, gross, hippy, lanolin, lard, margarine, obese, overfed, overweight, paunchy, plump, podgy, portly, pot-bellied, puffy, roly-poly, rotund, round, sebum, soap, soapflakes, soap powder, squab, steatopygic, stout, suet, swollen, tallow, tubby, wax, well-fed, well-upholstered

fate apocalypse, destiny, doomsday, eschatology, Götterdämmerung

fatigue annoy, blackout, boredom, bother, burn out, collapse, debilitation, distress, double up, drain, drowsiness, dullness, enervate, exertion, exhaust, faintness, gasping, harass, insensibility, irritate, jadedness, languishment, languor, lassitude, lethargy, listlessness, overburden, overdoing it, overdrive, overexertion, overload, overtask, overtax, overtiredness, overwork, palpitations, panting, prostration, sleepiness, staleness, strain, tax, tire, tiredness, trouble, weaken, weariness, whack, wind, work

fatigued beat, burned out, bushed, dog-tired, dopey, dozy, drained, drooping, drowsy, dull, enervated, exhausted, fainting, flagging, footsore, footweary, haggard, half-asleep, half-dead, hollow-eyed, jet-lagged, knackered, languid, lethargic, listless, nodding, overfatigued, overstrained, overtired, overworked, overwrought, sleepy, spent, stale, stiff, strained, swooning, tired, travel-weary, weak, weary, whacked, worn out, yawning

fatiguing annoying, boring, demanding, exacting, exhausting, gruelling, irksome, laborious, monotonous, punishing, tedious, tiresome, tiring, tough, trying, vexatious, wearing, wearying

fatness adiposity, bloatedness, bustiness, buxomness, chubbiness, corpulence, curvaceousness, endomorphy, flabbiness, fleshiness, fullness, greasiness, grossness, obesity, overweight, paunchiness, plumpishness, plumpness, podginess, portliness, pot-belly, puffiness, rotundity, roundness, stoutness, tubbiness

fatten coarsen, fill out, pad, thicken, upholster

fault criticize, defect, disloyalty, error, failing, flaw, foible, fracture, mortal sin, peccadillo, vice, weakness

fault-finding captiousness, carping, cavilling, censoriousness, crabbing, fastidiousness, fussing, hairsplitting, henpecking, hypercriticism, nagging, niggling, nit-picking, overcriticalness, pedantry, pestering, pettifoggery, quibbling

favour approbation, approval, boon, cachet, esteem, gift, indulgence, oblige, prefer, support

favourable advantageous, auspicious, beneficial, helpful, profitable, promising, propitious, useful

favouritism nepotism, partisanship, positive discrimination, preferential treatment

fawn beige, bootlick, brown-nose, buff, crawl, creep, curry favour, deer, flatter, grovel, lickspittle, soft-soap, spaniel, suck up, tawny, toady, truckle

fear affright, aversion, awe, dread, fright, funk, horror, panic, phobia, terror

fearful agitated, alarmed, anxious, apprehensive, disquieted, distressed, highly strung, jittery, jumpy, nervous, nervy, on edge, on tenterhooks, panicky, quaking, shaky, strained, tense, timid, timorous, trembling, tremulous, twitchy, uneasy, uptight

fearfulness agitation, alarm, anxiety, apprehension, consternation, dismay, disquiet, foreboding, misgivings, nerves, nervousness, palpitations, perturbation, qualms, tension, timorousness, trepidation, uneasiness

feasible possible, practicable, workable

feast bacchanalia, banquet, barbecue, beanfeast, beano, blowout, do, entertain, festival, gorge, harvest home, junket, nosh-up, orgy, party, picnic, reception, regale, spread, tea party, thrash, treat, wedding breakfast

feasting banqueting, celebrating, devouring, hospitality, regalement

feat achievement, act, deed, exploit, performance

fee ceiling, charge, commission, corkage, cut, demand, dues, extra, fare, floor, hire, quitrent, rate, refresher, rental, subscription, supplement, surcharge

feebleness enervation, frailty, meagreness, weakness

feel atmosphere, experience, handle, live through, perceive, realize, sense, surface, texture, touch, undergo, understand

feeling aesthesia, awareness, consciousness, experience, groping, impressionable, knowledge, perception, perceptive, reaction, realization, responsive, sensation, sense, sensible, sensing, sensitive, sentient, stroking, susceptible, touching, understanding

feelings affections, attitudes, beliefs, emotions, opinion, sensibilities, sentiments, susceptibilities, sympathies, view, viewpoint

fellowship accord, agreement, bipartisanship, clanship, comradeship, concord, concurrence, consensus, esprit de corps, fraternalism, freemasonry, friendship, harmony, morale, sodality, solidarity, sorority, sympathy, togetherness

female Amazon, Amazonian, childbearing, colleen, damsel, dowager, Eve, feminine, feminist, gal, girl, girlish, grisette, her, herself, lady, ladylike, lass, maiden, maidenly, matron, matronly, midinette, she, virago, woman, womanish, womanly

female title of address Dame, Donna, Frau, Fraulein, goodwife, goody, her ladyship, lady, Lady, ma'am, Madam, madame, mademoiselle, marm, memsahib, milady, Miss, missus, mistress, Mrs, Ms, señora, señorita, signora, signorina

femininity feminism, girlishness, muliebrity, womanliness

fend off deflect, head off, parry, ward off

fermentation aeration, commotion, leavening, raising agent, yeast
may indicate an anagram

fertile fecund, fructiferous, fruitful, generative, high-yielding, lucrative, multiparous, parturient, paying, philoprogenitive, pregnant, procreant, productive, profitable, prolific, propagatory, regenerative, remunerative

fertility abundance, cornucopia, exuberance, fecundity, fruitfulness, lushness, luxuriance, plenitude, plenty, profusion, rich harvest, richness

fertilizer ammonium salts, bonemeal, compost, dressing, dung, fishmeal, guano, lime, manure, marl, mulch, nitrates, phosphates, potash, slurry, sulphates, top-dressing

fester matter, rankle, run, suppurate, weep

festive carnival-like, entertaining, fun, joyous

fête bazaar, fair, honour, lionize, praise, salute

few couple, dash, handful, hint, little, scattering, smidgen, some, soupçon, sprinkling, suspicion, trickle

fewer diminished, least, less, minimal, minimum, reduced

fewness dearth, deficiency, exiguity, lack, meagreness, paucity, scantiness, scarcity, shortage, skimpiness, sparsity, underpopulation, undersupply

fibre denier, filament, monofilament, string, thread, tow, yarn

fickle adulterous, capricious, changeable, feather-brained, flighty, giddy, inconstant, irresponsible, mercurial, restless, superficial, temperamental, unfaithful, unstable, variable, whimsical

fiction adventure story, antinovel, autobiographical novel, Bildungsroman, blockbuster, bogus, cliff-hanger, conte, crime story, detective story, dystopia, epistolary novel, erotic novel, fable, fabrication, fairy tale, fictional biography, folk tale, geste, ghost story, gothic horror, historical novel, legend, lie, love story, metafiction, myth, novel, novelette, novella, parable, pornographic novel, romance, science-fiction novel, sci-fi, short-story, sketch, social novel, spy story, story, stream-of-consciousness novel, thriller, utopia, vignette, western, whodunit

fifteenth quindecagonal, quindecennial

fifth fivefold, pentadic, pentagonal, pentahedral, pentangular, pentatonic, quinary, quinquennial, quinquepartite, quintic, quintuple, quintuplicate

fifty half century, jubilee, quinquagenarian

fight affray, Armageddon, assail, attack, belligerency, blast, blows, bomb, box, brawl, broil, brouhaha, brush, campaign, charge, collision, dogfight, duel, dust-up, encounter, fence, fire, firefight, fisticuffs, fracas, fray, gang warfare, gigantomachy, grapple, hit, horseplay, hostilities, infighting, joust, lance, measure swords, meet, melee, open fire, oppose, pitched battle, psychomachia, punch-up, resist, riot, roughhouse, row, ruction, rumpus, scramble, scrap, scrimmage, scrum, scrummage, scuffle, set-to, shindig, shindy, shoot-out, showdown, skirmish, spar, spear, strike, theomachy, tilt, war, warfare, wrestle
See also list at **weapon**.

file dossier, emery board, line, nailfile, rasp, smooth, sort

fill bloat, cover, cram, extend to, jam, load, occupy, overrun, package, pack in, pad, quilt, ram in, refill, replenish, sate, satisfy, saturate, squeeze in, stock, stuff, supply, top up, wad

filled bloated, chock-a-block, contented, crawling, flush, full, glutted, multitudinous, overflowing, replete, sated, satisfied, stuffed, teeming, well-furnished, well-provided, well-provisioned, well-stocked

filling down, feathers, filler, foam, kapok, packaging, packing, padding, polystyrene, quilting, stuffing, wadding

film bromide paper, cine film, coating, infrared film, motion picture, movie, panchromatic film, photographic paper, photographic plate, roll film, scum, shoot, veil, veneer, video, X-ray film

final capping, closing, completing, concluding, conclusive, consummative, crowning, culminating, definitive, finishing, last, terminal, ultimate

finale appendix, catastrophe, climax,

coda, crowning glory, culmination, denouement, ending, envoy, epilogue, final curtain, finish, last act, postscript, suffix

finance advance, back, bale out, bestow, commerce, contribute to, donate, endow, fund, grant, guarantee, help out, keep, lend, loan, maintain, money, patronize, pay for, pension, pitch in, settle, sponsor, subsidize, subventionize, support, underwrite

financial support alimony, allowance, backing, contribution, grant, maintenance, patronage, pension, provision, sponsorship, stipend, subsidy, subsistence, sustenance, upkeep

find chance upon, come across, detect, discover, discovery, navigate, pinpoint, strike, survey, track down, treasure-trove, trouvaille, turn up

fine bracing, bright, brisk, calm, clear, cloudless, crisp, delicate, diaphanous, dry, end, excellent, exiguous, fair, filamentous, filiform, finale, finespun, flimsy, fragile, fresh, gauzy, gossamer, hairlike, insubstantial, invigorating, lacy, light, mild, papery, penalty, refine, scanty, settled, sheer, spidery, spindle-shaped, splendid, sunny, tenuous, threadlike, wafer-thin, well, wispy

fineness delicacy, diaphanousness, exiguity, flimsiness, fragility, gauziness, insubstantiality, laciness, lightness, paperiness, sheerness, spideriness, tenuity, wispiness

finished adjourned, bankrupt, closed, complete, ended, failed, in recess, interrupted, on hold, on ice, over, pending, resolved, shut down, stopped, wound up

fire aim, blast, blaze, bonfire, brazier, bring down, campfire, cannonade, combustion, conflagration, dismiss, enfilade, fireball, firebomb, firestorm, flame, forge, furnace, fusillade, glow, Greek fire, holocaust, incinerator, kiln, let fly, level, oasthouse, pepper, pick off, pop at, pyre, rake, rattle, sack, shell,

shoot, snipe at, straddle, strafe, torch, torpedo, towering inferno, volley, wildfire

firearm automatic, breechloader, calibre, carbine, Colt, elephant gun, gun, piece, pistol, repeater, revolver, rifle, rifled bore, semiautomatic, shotgun, smoothbore
See also list at **weapon**.

firing broadside, burst, fusillade, gunfire, gunnery, musketry, salvo, sharpshooting, shooting, sniping, spray, strafe, volley

fish angle, aquarium, bony, cartilaginous, cast, Chondrichthyes, crossopterygian, cyclostome, dipnoan, elasmobranch, flatfish, flying, holocephalan, jawless, lobe-finned, mouthbrooder, ray-finned, selachian, solicit, teleost, tropical
See list of types of fish.

fish anatomy air bladder, fin, gill, gill cover, gill slit, lateral line, operculum, roe, scale, spiracle, swim bladder

fish dish Arbroath smokey, Beluga caviar, bloater, Bombay duck, caviar, cured fish, finnan haddock, fish ball, fishcake, fish finger, fish pie, fish stick, gefilte fish, gravadlax, hard roe, jellied eel, kedgeree, kipper, kippered herring, lox, lumpfish caviar, pickled herring, quenelle, rollmop, scampi, smoked haddock, smoked mackerel, smoked salmon, smoked trout, smoky, soft roe, taramasalata

fisherman angler, fisher, fishman, fishmonger, fishwife, piscator, pisciculturalist, trawlerman, whaler

fishing angling, big-game fishing, catch, coarse fishing, deep-sea fishing, drift net, eel basket, fishery, fish farming, fish-finder, fishgig, fish-hold, fishhook, fishing bank, fishing fleet, fishing ground, fishing line, fish ladder, fishnet, fishtrap, fish weir, fly fishing, game fishing, gill net, piscary, piscatology, pisciculture, sea fishing, searching, seeking, seine, shark fishing, shark net, shrimper, soliciting, tonnara, trawl, whaling

fishy anguilliform, clupeoid, cyprinoid, dodgy, dubious, gadoid, ichthyic, ichthyoid, ichthyomorphic, percoid, piscatorial, pisciform, piscine, selachian, sharkish, sharklike, suspicious

fission atomization, atom smashing, chain reaction, fusion, nuclear fission, shattering, splitting

fit able, accord, appropriate, belong, capable, condign, dovetail, fashion, hale, healthy, hearty, modify, outburst, pertain, proper, qualify for, right, salu-

TYPES OF FISH

ALBACORE	COD	GUPPY	PADDLEFISH	SMELT
ALEWIFE	COELACANTH	GURNARD	PEARLFISH	SNAPPER
AMBERJACK	CONGER EEL	HADDOCK	PERCH	SNOOK
ANCHOVY	CORNETFISH	HAGFISH	PICKEREL	SOLE
ANEMONE FISH	CRAPPIE	HAKE	PIKE	SPRAT
ANGELFISH	CROAKER	HALFBEAK	PIKEPERCH	STARGAZER
ANGLERFISH	CUTLASS FISH	HALIBUT	PILCHARD	STICKLEBACK
ARCHER FISH	DAB	HAMMERHEAD	PILOT FISH	STINGRAY
BARBEL	DACE	SHARK	PIPEFISH	STONE BASS
BARRACUDA	DAMSELFISH	HATCHETFISH	PIRANHA	STONEFISH
BARRAMUNDA	DANIO	HERRING	PLAICE	STURGEON
BASKING	DARTER	HOGFISH	POLLACK	SUCKER
SHARK	DEALFISH	ICEFISH	POMPANO	SUNFISH
BASS	DOGFISH	IDE	PORBEAGLE	SURGEONFISH
BATFISH	DORADO	JEWFISH	PORCUPINE	SWORDFISH
BELUGA	DORY	JOHN DORY	FISH	SWORDTAIL
BLACKFISH	DRAGONET	KILLIFISH	PORGY	TARPON
BLEAK	DRAGONFISH	KINGFISH	POWAN	TAUTOG
BLENNY	DRUMFISH	LABYRINTH FISH	PUFFER	TENCH
BLINDFISH	EEL	LAMPREY	RABBITFISH	TETRA
BLOWFISH	EELPOUT	LANCET FISH	RATFISH	THORNBACK
BLUEFISH	ELECTRIC EEL	LANTERN FISH	RAY	THREADFIN
BLUE SHARK	ELECTRIC RAY	LEMON SOLE	REDFIN	TIGERFISH
BOMBAY DUCK	FIGHTING FISH	LING	REDFISH	TIGER SHARK
BONE FISH	FILEFISH	LIZARD FISH	REMORA	TOADFISH
BONITO	FLATFISH	LOACH	REQUIEM SHARK	TOPE
BOWFIN	FLATHEAD	LUMPSUCKER	RIBBONFISH	TORPEDO
BOXFISH	FLOUNDER	LUNGFISH	ROACH	FISH
BREAM	FLUKE	MACKEREL	RUDD	TRIGGERFISH
BRILL	FLYING FISH	MANTA RAY	SAILFISH	TROUT
BRISLING	FLYING	MARLIN	SAITHE	TRUNKFISH
BUFFALO FISH	GURNARD	MENHADEN	SALMON	TUNA
BULLHEAD	FOUR-EYED FISH	MIDSHIPMAN	SARDINE	TURBOT
BURBOT	FROGFISH	MILLER'S THUMB	SAURY	WAHOO
BUTTERFISH	GARFISH	MINNOW	SAWFISH	WEAKFISH
BUTTERFLY FISH	GLASSFISH	MOLLY	SCORPION FISH	WEEVER
CANDLEFISH	GLOBEFISH	MONKFISH	SCULPIN	WELS
CAPELIN	GOBY	MOONFISH	SCUP	WHITEBAIT
CARP	GOLDFISH	MOORISH IDOL	SEA HORSE	WHITEFISH
CATFISH	GOOSEFISH	MORAY EEL	SEA ROBIN	WHITE SHARK
CAVE FISH	GOURAMI	MUDFISH	SERGEANT FISH	WHITING
CHAR	GRAYLING	MUDSKIPPER	SHAD	WOLF FISH
CHARACIN	GRENADIER	MULLET	SHARK	WRASSE
CHIMAERA	GROUPER	MURRAY COD	SHOVELHEAD	WRECKFISH
CHUB	GRUNION	MUSKELLUNGE	SHOVELNOSE	YELLOWTAIL
CICHLID	GRUNT	NEEDLEFISH	SILVERSIDE	ZEBRA FISH
CISCO	GUDGEON	OARFISH	SKATE	
CLINGFISH	GUITAR FISH	OPAH	SKIPJACK	
COBIA	GUNNEL	ORFE	TUNA	

brious, seizure, serve, shape, spasm, suit
may indicate an anagram

fitting apposite, befitting, belonging, expedient, pertaining, pertinent, suitable

five cinque, cinquefoil, fifth, five-a-side, five-by-five, five-finger, five-pound note, fiver, fivesome, five stones, pentachord, pentacle, pentagon, pentagram, pentahedron, pentameter, pentarchy, pentastich, Pentateuch, pentathlon, quin, quincunx, quinquennium, quinquereme, quint, quintet, quintuplet, quintuplicate

fixed agreed, decided, deep-rooted, deep-seated, dyed-in-the-wool, fast, imbued, immovable, implanted, ingrained, irremovable, permeated, soaked, sound, stable, staunch, steadfast, steady, true-blue

flag banderole, banner, bannerette, bunting, burgee, canton, clip, colours, droop, ensign, fail, faint, flagpole, flagstaff, fly, gonfalon, grommet, guidon, halyard, heading, hoist, labarum, label, languish, mark, note, oriflamme, pennant, pennon, sink, sleeve, stagger, standard, streamer, swallowtail, swoon, truck, vexillum, wave

flamboyance excessiveness, exorbitance, extravagance, inordinacy, intemperance, lavishness, ostentation, outrageousness, profuseness

flamboyant excessive, exorbitant, extravagant, grandiose, inordinate, intemperate, lavish, meretricious, ostentatious, outrageous, overdone, overindulgent, overshot, overstepped, piled-on, profuse

flaming ablaze, alight, burning, flaring, intense, vehement

flashiness bombast, colourfulness, dash, dazzle, extravagance, flamboyance, garishness, gaudiness, glitter, loudness, meretriciousness, panache,

razamatazz, splash, splurge, tawdriness, tinsel

flashy bombastic, colourful, dazzling, exhibitionist, extravagant, flamboyant, foppish, frilly, garish, gaudy, glittering, jaunty, loud, meretricious, painted, rakish, snappy, snazzy, tawdry, tinselly

flatten chop, crush, demolish, dent, fell, ground, hew, level, lumber, mow down, rase, raze, tear down

flattened beaten flat, consolidated, ironed, levelled, pressed, rolled, smoothed, spread, squashed flat, trampled down, well-trodden

flatter adulate, compliment, creep, hype, overcommend, overesteem, overestimate, overlaud, overpraise, puff, toady

flattering adulatory, complimentary, hypocritical, insincere, laudatory, praising, tongue-in-cheek

flattery adulation, advocacy, blandishment, cajolery, coaxing, compliments, encouragement, enticement, eyewash, hagiography, honeyed words, hype, hypocrisy, incitement, insincerity, overcommendation, overlaudation, overpraise, panegyric, pleading, praise, solicitation, teasing, urging, wheedling

flatulent belching, eructative, gassy, windy

flavour bitterness, dress, enhance, feel, flavouring, garnish, gusto, relish, richness, saltiness, sauce, savour, seasoning, sourness, spice, sweetness, tone

flaw defect, deficiency, demerit, failing, fault, foible, frailty, imperfection, infirmity, laxity, shortcoming, weakness

flee absquatulate, bolt, cut away, dash off, hightail, nip off, rush off, scamper away, scarper, scram, skedaddle, skip off, split, take flight, vamoose, whip off

fleshy carnal, plump, ripe, succulent

flicker bicker, dance, flash, flick, flit,

flutter, gutter, quiver, spatter, spit, splutter, sputter, twinkle, wave, waver

flickering flickery, guttering, spluttering, sputtering, sputtery, wavery

flight path airlane, blastoff, orbit, runway, skyway, taxiway, trajectory

flock army, colony, drive, drove, gather, herd, host, kennel, pack, school, set, shoal, stable, string, swarm, troop, tuft

flood deluge, downpour, inundation, outflow

flooded awash, deluged, inundated, swamped

flood in congregate, cram in, crowd in, flow in, jam in, pack in, pour in, press in, rush in, squeeze in, swarm in, throng in, wedge in

floral bloomy, floreate, floriate, florid, floristic, flowered, flowery, ornate

floriculture floriculturist, florist, floristics

flourish bloom, brandish, decoration, embellishment, emblazon, flash, proclaim, prosper, succeed, trumpet, vaunt, wave

flow babble, bleed, braid, bubble, cascade, channel, course, ebb, eddy, fall, flood, fluency, flux, gurgle, gush, haemorrhage, meander, ooze, overflow, pour, race, ripple, run, secretion, seep, spew out, spout, stream, suppuration, sweat, trickle, trill, vomit forth, weep, well up

flower anther, bloom, blossom, blow, bouquet, boutonniere, bract, bud, buttonhole, catkin, daisy chain, effloresce, floret, flourish, floweret, garland, inflorescence, nosegay, petal, pollen, posy, spikelet, spray, whorl, wreath
may indicate a river
See list of flowers.

flowering anthesis, blooming, blossoming, blow, efflorescence, florescence, flourishing, flowerage, full bloom, inflorescent, unfolding

flowing fluent, fluxive, juicy, moist, runny, sappy, squashy, succulent, watery

flowmeter fluidmeter, hydrometer

fluffy downy, fuzzy, velutinous, velvety

fluid beverage, condensation, drink, flawless, fluent, fluidic, liquid, liquid extract, liquiform, liquor, mellifluous, smooth, unclotted, uncongealed, water
may indicate an anagram

fluidification colliquefaction, decoagulation, deliquation, deliquescence, dissolving, fluxibility, fusing, leaching, liquefaction, liquescency, lixiviation, melting, percolation, running, solubility, solubilization, solution, thawing, unfreezing

fluidity bloodiness, colliquation, fluxure, goriness, haemophilia, juiciness, liquefaction, liquidescence, liquidity, noncoagulation, nonviscosity, pulpiness, rheuminess, runniness, sappiness, semiliquidity, solubleness, wateriness

fluvial affluent, confluent, convergent, coursing, ebbing, effluent, falling, fluent, fluviomarine, inundant, meandering, profluent, racing, refluent, ripply, running, serpentine, streaming, torrential, vortical

flying aeropause, airspeed, approach, banking, barrel roll, ceiling, chandelle, climb, crab, descent, dive, glide path, groundspeed, headwind, hedgehopping, hunting, nose dive, pitching, rolling, rushing, sideslip, skidding, soaring, spin, spiral, stalling, tailwind, takeoff, touchdown, turn, vectoring, whipstall, wingover, yawing, zooming
See also list at **aviator**.

focus asymptote, centralize, centre, centrepiece, centring, clarify, concentralization, concentrate, converge, corradiate, focalization, home in, hub, pivot, radius, taper, target, zero in

focused angled, based, basic, central, clear, defined, founded, pointed, programmed, proposed, supposed, thematic

focus on argue, centre on, concentrate on, contain, include, propose, state, suppose

fog befog, bemist, brume, fogginess, freezing fog, fret, har, haze, haziness, mist, mistiness, peasouper, smog

foggy fogbound, hazy, misty, nebulous, opaque, smoggy

fold anticline, bend, buckle, buckling, coil, collapse, dog-ear, double over, flection, flexure, furl, lap, layer, overlap, plica, plication, roll, syncline, turn

folded bankrupt, bent, corrugated, creased, dog-eared, doubled over, flexed, flexuous, pleated, plicate, rolled, rucked up, turned over

folk music bluegrass, border ballad, country music, folk rock, folksong, hillbilly music, skiffle
See also list at **orchestra**.

follow discover, dog, prowl after, replace, scent out, segue, shadow, sleuth, sneak after, sniff out, spoor, stalk, succeed, supplant, tail, take over, track, trail

follower adherent, apostle, camp follower, dependant, disciple, fan, groupie, hanger-on, parasite, satellite,

shadow, sponger, suitor, supporter, sycophant, tail

folly absurdity, asininity, childishness, conceit, craziness, daftness, dotage, eccentricity, empty-headedness, extravagance, fatuousness, feeble-mindedness, flippancy, foolishness, frivolity, giddiness, heedlessness, idiocy, ignorance, imbecility, imprudence, inanity, indiscretion, ineptitude, insanity, irresponsibility, ludicrousness, lunacy, madness, pointlessness, puerility, rashness, recklessness, ridiculousness, senility, senselessness, silliness, stupidity, thoughtlessness, unintelligence

fondness amicability, cordiality, devotion, empathy, friendliness, identification, involvement, liking, love, responsiveness, sympathy, warmth

fool ass, birdbrain, blockhead, clown, cretin, deceive, dimbo, dimwit, dolt, dope, dotard, dumbo, dunce, fool around, halfwit, horse about, idiot, imbecile, jackass, jerk, lark about, meathead, monkey around, moron, nincompoop, ninny, nitwit, noodle, pillock, pinhead, prat, simpleton, skylark, sucker, trick, twit, wally

foolish absurd, asinine, barmy, birdbrained, brainless, childish, crazy, daft, devil-may-care, dim-witted, doltish, dull, eccentric, empty-headed, fatuous,

FLOWERS			
AMARYLLIS	CROCUS	IRIS	PIMPERNEL
ANEMONE	CYCLAMEN	JAPONICA	PLANTAIN
ASTER	DAFFODIL	JONQUIL	POPPY
BEGONIA	DAHLIA	LAVENDER	PRIMROSE
BELLADONNA	DAISY	LILAC	ROSE
BLUEBELL	DANDELION	LILY	SNAPDRAGON
BRYONY	ERICA	LING	SNOWDROP
BUTTERCUP	EUPHORBIA	LOTUS	SPEEDWELL
CAMPION	FORGET-ME-NOT	MAGNOLIA	STOCK
CARNATION	FOXGLOVE	MALLOW	SUNFLOWER
CELANDINE	FRANGIPANI	MARIGOLD	SWEET PEA
CAMOMILE	FRITILLARY	MIMOSA	TANSY
CHRYSANTHEMUM	FUCHSIA	NARCISSUS	TEASEL
CLEMATIS	GERANIUM	OLEANDER	THISTLE
CLOVER	HEATHER	ORCHID	TULIP
COLUMBINE	HELLEBORE	PANSY	VIOLA
COWSLIP	HYACINTH	PEONY	VIOLET

feeble-minded, flippant, foolhardy, frivolous, gaga, gormless, harebrained, headstrong, heedless, hellbent, hotheaded, idiotic, ignorant, ill-advised, ill-considered, imbecilic, imprudent, inane, inattentive, incautious, inept, injudicious, insane, ludicrous, lunatic, mad, moronic, nonsensical, nutty, pointless, potty, preposterous, prodigal, puerile, rash, reckless, ridiculous, senile, senseless, silly, simple, slow, spaced-out, stupid, uncircumspect, unintelligent, unwise
may indicate an anagram

footwear beetle-crushers, boots, brogues, bumpers, buskins, casuals, chappals, clodhoppers, clogs, court shoes, daps, flatties, flip-flops, footgear, galoshes, gumshoes, hobnail boots, jackboots, lace-ups, moccasins, mules, overshoes, Oxfords, plimsolls, pumps, sabots, sandals, shoes, slip-ons, slippers, sneakers, trainers, waders, wellies, Wellington boots, winkle-pickers

forbid ban, bar, disallow, embargo, interdict, prohibit, proscribe, stifle, suppress, taboo, veto

forbidden banned, barred, blocked, cancelled, denied, disallowed, prohibited, ruled out, stopped

force army, blackmail, bludgeon, browbeat, bulldoze, bully, call up, commandeer, conscript, constrain, corps, drag from, dragoon, exact, extort, foist on, force-feed, impress, inflict, influence, intimidate, kidnap, power, pressgang, railroad, requisition, squad, stampede, steamroller, strength, strong-arm, take, threaten, use violence, waterfall, wring from

forceful compelling, dynamic, powerful, strenuous

forceps pincers, pliers, tweezers

forecast foretell, herald, introduce, predict, presage, prognosis, prophecy, ring in, usher in, warn

forecaster astrologer, augur, auspex, consultant, crystal-gazer, diviner, dowser, fortune-teller, futurologist, haruspex, meteorologist, palmist, speculator, tipster

foreign alien, barbaric, continental, deviating, different, exotic, other, outlandish, overseas, strange, tramontane, transatlantic, unknown, unrelated
may indicate an anagram

foreignness alienism, difference, exoticness, otherness, strangeness, unconnectedness, unrelatedness

foresee anticipate, augur, divine, envisage, expect, forebode, forecast, forejudge, foreknow, foreshadow, forestall, foretell, forewarn, portend, predestine, predetermine, predict, presage, presume, promise, prophesy, scent, suppose, surmise

foreseeable forecast, imminent, near, predictable, probable

foreseen anticipated, awaited, expected, foretold, hoped for, looked for, predicted, promised

foresight anticipation, caution, certainty, clairvoyancy, expectation, forecast, foreknowledge, foretaste, precognition, prediction, prescience, prevision, prognosis, prophecy, second sight, telepathy

forest coniferous forest, jungle, rainforest, taiga, virgin forest, wood

forester arboriculturist, arborist, dendrologist, forest manager, logger, lumberjack, ranger, silviculturist, tapper, timberman, tree surgeon, verderer, woodcutter, woodlander, woodsman

forestry afforestation, agroforestry, arboriculture, conservation, deforestation, dendrology, reforestation, silviculture, tree farming

foretaste forerunner, foreword, herald, introduction, precursor, prediction, preface, prelude, prequel, prerelease, presage, presentiment, preview, prologue, trailer

forgather agree, ally, assemble, associate, bond, bunch, cluster, collaborate, concentrate, concur, confederate, congregate, conspire, cooperate, copulate, couple, federate, fraternize, gather, group, harmonize, huddle, join, marry, mate, meet, partner, plot, rally round, rendezvous, synchronize, unite

forget block out, miss, neglect, overlook, repress, suppress

forgetfulness absentmindedness, amnesia, mental block, repression, suppression

forgivable easily excused, excusable, pardonable, venial

forgive absolve, concede, conciliate, excuse, exempt, favour, forget, grant absolution, grant amnesty, humour, indemnify, make peace, pardon, reconcile, redeem, reprieve, shake hands, shrive, spare

forgiven absolved, acquitted, atoned, cancelled, condoned, delivered, discharged, exculpated, excused, exonerated, freed, granted amnesty, indulged, justified, let off, pacified, pardoned, reconciled, redeemed, rehabilitated, reinstated, released, remitted, reprieved, restored, shriven, spared, taken back, vindicated

forgiveness absolution, amnesty, dispensation, excuse, exemption, grace, immunity, indemnity, indulgence, pardon, remission, reprieve, shrift, sparing

forgotten beyond recall, lost, overlooked, past, unmemorable

fork branch, delta, diverge, fan, furcula, groin, inguen, offshoot, prong, trident

form anatomy, architecture, arrange, blow, body, build, carve, cast, chisel, class, coin, composition, composure, configuration, conformation, constitution, construction, contour, create, cut out, design, draft, draw, essence, express, fabrication, fashion, figure, forge, formality, formalize, format, formation, formulate, found, frame, gestalt, getup, hammer out, hew, idea, isomorphism, knead, lay out, lines, make, make-up, mint, model, morphology, mould, nominalism, order, outline, pattern, physique, Platonism, produce, profile, punch out, relief, round, sculpt, setup, shape, silhouette, sketch, smith, square, stamp, structure, substance, system, systematize, throw, turn, verbalize, whittle, work
may indicate an anagram

formal behavioural, ceremonial, ceremonious, conventional, correct, customary, decorous, dignified, elegant, exact, fashionable, fastidious, formalistic, formulary, grave, habitual, legalistic, litigious, methodical, meticulous, official, orderly, pedantic, pompous, precious, precise, prim, procedural, protocol, proud, punctilious, puristic, refined, rigid, ritual, ritualistic, routine, royal, scrupulous, sedate, smart, solemn, staid, starchy, stately, stiff, stilted, stylish, stylized, traditional, trendy, weighty

formalism ceremonialism, conventionalism, over-preciseness, over-refinement, pedantry, preciousness, preciseness, punctiliousness, purism, ritualism, scrupulousness

formality behaviour, ceremoniousness, ceremony, circumstance, conduct, convention, conventionality, correctness, custom, decorum, dignity, etiquette, fashion, fastidiousness, gravity, habit, hideboundness, litigation, pomp, practice, preciseness, pride, primness, procedure, propriety, protocol, rigidness, ritual, routine, sedateness, smartness, solemnity, staidness, starchiness, state, stiff-neckedness, stiffness, straitlacedness, stuffiness, style, stylization, tradition, trend, weightiness

formalize conventionalize, ritualize, solemnize, stylize

former deceased, emeritus, erstwhile,

ex, late, obsolescent, one-time, previous, prior, quondam, retired, sometime, superannuated

forming composition, construction, creation, expression, fashioning, formulation, knitting, makeup, modelling, morphogenesis, moulding, production, setup, shaping, tailoring, weaving

fortitude aplomb, backbone, bottle, bulldog breed, cast iron, clenched teeth, courage, daring, dash, dauntlessness, élan, grit, guts, mettle, moral fibre, pluck, spirit, spunk

fortune billions, century, crores, destiny, fate, grand, lakhs, loadsamoney, luck, megabucks, millions, riches, ton, wealth, zillions

forward advanced, brazen, cheeky, enterprising, forward-looking, go-ahead, pass on, go-getting, progressive, promote, reformist, up-to-date

fossil amber, ammonite, cast, coal, coprolite, dinosaur, fossil footprint, fossilization, fossil record, fossil track, graptolite, mammoth, mineralization, mould, oil, out-of-date, peat, petrification, petrified wood, petroleum, trilobite

found build, cast, detected, discovered, establish, forge, pinned down, pinpointed, tracked down, unearthed

found in
may indicate an anagram or *a hidden word*

four fourfold, four-in-hand, four-leaf clover, four-letter word, four-poster, four seasons, foursome, fourth, four winds, quad, quadratic, quadrennium, quadrille, quadruped, quadruple, quadruplet, quadruplex, quartet, quaternary, quaternity, quatrain, quatre, quatrefoil, square dance, tetrad, tetradactyl, tetragram, tetragrammation, tetralogy, tetrameter, tetrapod

four-legged four-footed, quadruped, tetramerous

fraction billionth, common, compound, decimal, division, eighteenth, eighth, eightieth, eleventh, fifteenth, fifth, fiftieth, fourteenth, fourth, fourtieth, half, hundredth, improper, mil, millionth, nineteenth, ninetieth, ninth, part, percentage, piece, portion, proper, proportion, quarter, ration, section, segment, seventeenth, seventh, seventieth, share, simple, sixteenth, sixth, sixtieth, subdivision, tenth, third, thirteenth, thirtieth, thou, thousandth, twelfth, twentieth, vulgar

fractional aliquot, decimal, differential, divisional, exponential, finite, fragmentary, half, incomplete, infinite, integral, logarithmic, logometric, partial, proportional, quarter, radical, sectional, segmental, subdivisional, surd

fragment atom, bit, crumb, disintegrate, drop, filing, fleck, iota, jot, minim, minutia, morsel, mote, particle, scrap, shatter, shaving, shred, sliver, snippet, speck, tittle, whit

fragrance aroma, aromatherapy, balminess, bouquet, muskiness, parfum, perfume, scent, spiciness

fragrant ambrosial, aromatherapeutic, aromatic, balmy, camphorated, floral, flowery, fruity, heady, musky, perfumed, pungent, scented, spicy, sweet-smelling

framework bodywork, cadre, cantilever, casement, chassis, doorframe, latticework, outline, plan, rack, scaffold, shell, skeleton
may indicate a split word

frangibility atomization, brittleness, crumbliness, fragileness, friability

frank aboveboard, blunt, candid, down-to-earth, honest, honourable, matter-of-fact, open, outspoken, sincere, stamp, straightforward, transparent, true, truthful, undesigning, veracious

fraternize date, hobnob, introduce oneself, network

fraud adulteration, ballot rigging,

canard, cardsharping, cheating, con, confidence trick, counterfeiting, crookedness, diddle, dishonesty, dodge, fakery, falsity, fiddle, fix, flim-flam, forgery, frame-up, gerrymandering, gyp, hoax, imposture, insider dealing, loaded dice, put-up job, racket, ramp, rip-off, scam, sell, sharp practice, stacked deck, sting, swindle, swiz, trickery, wangle

fraudulent blackmailed, cheating, copied, counterfeit, crooked, deceptive, dishonest, fake, false, fiddling, forged, illicit, imposturous, infringed, joyriding, misappropriated, pirated, plagiarized, put-up, rip-off, scrounging, swindling, tricky, unauthorized, underhanded, whitewashed

free acquitted, at large, autarchic, autarkic, authorized, autonomous, buckshee, charity, complimentary, constitutional, courtesy, discharged, discretionary, easygoing, eleemosynary, emancipated, excepted, exempt, franchised, giveaway, grace-and-favour, gratis, gratuitous, honorary, immune, inalienable, independent, indulgent, irregular, lax, liberal, liberate, loose, national, neutral, nonaligned, noninvolved, nonliable, nonpartisan, optional, permissive, post-paid, privileged, release, rent-free, scot-free, secluded, self-determining, self-governing, tax-free, unbound, unbridled, unchecked, unconfined, unconstrained, uncurbed, unfettered, ungoverned, unhindered, unilateral, unimpeded, unpaid, unregulated, unrestrained, unsalaried, unshackled, voluntary, zero-rated

freedom bohemianism, broad-mindedness, choice, deliverance, discharge, discretion, easygoingness, emancipation, exception, exemption, forbearance, free-and-easiness, free speech, freethinking, free will, high seas, immunity, independence, indulgence, initiative, irregularity, isolationism, latitude, latitudinarianism, laxity, leave,

leeway, liberalism, liberation, libertarianism, liberty, licence, looseness, margin, neutrality, nonalignment, noncoercion, nonconformity, noninterference, nonintervention, nonintimidation, noninvolvement, nonliability, open-mindedness, option, permissiveness, prerogative, privilege, relaxation, release, say-so, seclusion, toleration, toleration, unconstraint, unrestraint

free market capitalism, Common Market, open-door policy, open market, self-regulating market, single market
See also list at **economic**.

freezing absolute zero, algidity, freezing cold, frigidity, frost, gelidity, glacial, halting, iciness, sub-zero temperature, suspending, wintry

frenzy
may indicate an anagram

frequent haunt, often, recurrent, regular, visit

fresh blooming, cheeky, evergreen, flourishing, new, sappy, springlike, vernal, vigorous, young, youthful

friction adhesion, affriction, animosity, confrication, drag, force, frication, frottage, grip, perfrication, purchase, resistance, roughness, rub, rubbing, tension, viscosity

frictional ablative, abrasive, anatriptic, attritive, erosive, gnawing, irritant, rubbing

friend acquaintance, amigo, buddy, chum, classmate, colleague, companion, comrade, crony, fellow, mate, messmate, pal, playmate, roommate, schoolfellow, schoolmate, shipmate, sidekick

friendly affectionate, agreeable, amiable, amicable, ardent, back-slapping, benevolent, buddy-buddy, chummy, companionable, compatible, comradely, confraternal, congenial, cooperative, cordial, courteous, demonstrative, effusive, favourable, fraternal, generous, genial, gracious, harmonious, hearty, hospitable, kindly, matey, neighbourly, pally, palsy-walsy, peaceable, philanthropic, pleasant, receptive, simpatico, sociable, sympathetic, understanding, unhostile, warm, welcoming, well-meaning

friendship acquaintanceship, amiableness, amicableness, amity, ardency, benevolence, bonhomie, brotherhood, camaraderie, chumminess, colleagueship, companionship, compatibility, comradeship, concord, confraternity, cooperation, cordiality, courtesy, entente cordiale, favouritism, fellow feeling, fellowship, fraternalism, fraternization, freemasonry, geniality, good terms, good will, harmony, heartiness, hospitality, kindness, love, mateyness, mutual respect, mutual support, neighbourliness, palliness, partiality, partisanship, philanthropy, prejudice, rapport, regard, sisterhood, sociability, sodality, solidarity, sorority, support, sympathy, togetherness, understanding, warmth

frighten affright, alarm, appal, browbeat, bulldoze, bully, cow, daunt, dismay, distress, enervate, horrify, intimidate, menace, panic, petrify, scare, shake, shock, stagger, startle, terrify, terrorize, unnerve

frightened affright, afraid, aghast, ashen-faced, cowed, demoralized, fearing, fear-stricken, frit, horrified, horror-struck, intimidated, panic-stricken, petrified, scared, terrified, terrorized, terror-struck

frightening alarming, appalling, awesome, awful, daunting, dire, dismaying, dreadful, enervating, fearful, fearsome, formidable, frightful, ghastly, grim, hair-raising, hideous, horrendous, horrible, horrific, horrifying, intimidating, menacing, petrifying, scaring, scary, shocking, spooky, startling, terrible, terrifying, unnerving

frock backless dress, ballgown, cheongsam, cocktail dress, dinner dress, dinner gown, dress, evening gown, gown, gymslip, mantua, maternity dress, maxidress, minidress, Mother Hubbard, muu-muu, ordain, overdress, pinafore dress, sack, sheath dress, shirtdress, shirtwaister, strapless dress, sundress, tea gown, topless dress, tube dress, wedding dress

from
may indicate a hidden word

front antechamber, anterior, anteroom, appearance, avant-garde, beginning, brazenness, cheek, cover, entrance, facade, first, fore, forecourt, forefront, foreground, foremost, forward, foyer, frontage, frontal, full-faced, full-frontal, head, head-and-shoulders, introduction, leading, lobby, mask, overlook, physiognomic, preceding, preliminaries, proscenium, vanguard, vestibule

frost hoar frost, permafrost, rime

frown glare, glower lour, grimace, growl, pout, scowl, snap, snarl

frugivore frugivorousness, fruitarian, fruitarianism

fruit apple, bear fruit, be fruitful, benefit, berry, crop, dehisce, fructify, haw, hip, orange, pear, release seeds, result, reward, ripen, yield

fruiting fertile, fructiferous, fructuous, fruitful, leguminous, pomiferous, productive

fruits citrus fruit, crop, dried fruit, grain, green vegetables, kernels, legumes, nuts, produce, pulses, results, roots, salad vegetables, seeds, soft fruit, stone fruit, tubers, vegetables, yield

fruity citric, citrine, citrous, citrus, indecent, mellow, ripe, risque, rude

frustrate annoy, cross, discourage, foil, prevent, thwart

fuel ammunition, charcoal, charge, coal, detonate, electricity, electrify, explode, fill up, fire, fossil fuel, gas, kindle, nuclear power, oil, peat, peat bog, peat moss, plug in, power, recharge, refuel, set off, solid fuel, stoke, strike, switch on, wood

fugitive deserter, escaped, fleeting, refugee, runaway, transient, truant

fulfilled completed, contented, sated, satisfied

fulfilment completion, contentment, enjoyment, satisfaction

full chock-a-block, crammed, crowded, flush, gorged, jam-packed, level with, loaded, overrun, replenished, replete, sated, satisfied, saturated, stuffed, well-stocked

fullness bellyful, brimming, bumper, capacity, complement, filling, full house, maximum, plenitude, pregnancy, quorum, quota, replenishment, repletion, satiety, saturation, skinful

fun buzz, celebration, entertainment, halcyon days, heaven, high, holiday, honeymoon period, joy, kick, lark, merrymaking, paradise, party, revelry, thrill, treat, whizz

funds backing, balances, capital, cash, cash flow, cash supplies, credits, creditworthiness, exchequer, finances, income, investments, liquid assets, liquidity, means, money, monies, overdraft, payment, premises, property, purse, readies, ready money, receipts, remittance, reserves, revenue, sponsorship, subsidy, substance, support, treasure, wealth, wherewithal

funeral black, burial service, cinerary, crematorium, crematory, dark, dirge-like, elegiac, end, epitaphic, eulogistic, exequies, fate, funebrial, funerary, funereal, Irish wake, keen, lamentation, lamenting, lapidary, memorial service, mortuary, mournful, necrological, obituary, obsequial, obsequies, requiem, sad, sepulchral, sombre, wake

funny amusing, diverting, entertaining, hilarious, hysterical, laughable, odd, peculiar, risible, side-splitting, uproarious, weird
may indicate an anagram

furious angry, enraged, fuming, livid

furniture built-in furniture, cabinet-making, chinoiserie, fittings, furnishings, japanning, lacquering, marquetry, painting, parquetry, property, soft furnishings, trompe l'œil, unit furniture, upholstery, veneering
See list of furniture.

furrow canal, channel, chink, conduit, corrugate, corrugation, cut, ditch, engrave, etch, fissure, flute, groove, gutter, plough, rut, score, scratch, seam, slit, slot, track, trench, trough, wheel-track

furrowed chinky, grooved, rimose, rutty, scratched, wheel-tracked

further accelerate, advance, advantage, aid, augment, better, boost, bounce up, bring on, conduce, contribute to, develop, elevate, expedite, extra, facilitate, favour, force, forward, foster, grow, hasten, help along, improve, lift, make for, modernize, more, prefer, promote, propose, push, quicken, raise, speed, step up, subserve, subvene, supplementary, upgrade

furtherance advancement, expediting, facilitation, forwarding, preferment, promotion, special treatment

furthest border, boundary, brink, edge, extreme, extremity, far, farness, frontier, latitudinal, longitudinal, margin, outpost, verge, verging

fuss bluster, bother, bustle, dither, flap, flurry, fluster, flutter, flutteration, hop about, jerk, jump, mill around, rush, tiz-woz, tizz, tizzy, to-do, twitter

futile abortive, barren, fruitless, hopeless, idle, impossible, in vain, pointless, profitless, purposeless, Sisyphean, squandered, thankless, time-wasting, unavailing, uneconomic, unproductive, unrewarding, unsuccessful, useless, vain, wasted, worthless

futility bootlessness, failure, hopelessness, idleness, pointlessness, profitlessness, purposelessness, thanklessness, unproductiveness, vanity

future after ages, ahead, anticipated, approaching, by-and-by, coming events, destined, destiny, doomsday, due, eventual, fate, foreseeable, forthcoming, imminent, impending, Judgment Day, later, latter days, mañana, next week, next year, nigh, oncoming, overhanging, pending, possible, postexistence, potential, predicted, probable, prospective, the millennium, threatening, tomorrow

fuzzy bleared, blurred, dim, filmy, foggy, furry, hazy, ill-defined, indefinite, indistinct, low-definition, misty, obscured, shadowy, unclear, undefined, unfocused
may indicate an anagram

FURNITURE

ARMCHAIR	DECK CHAIR	PEMBROKE TABLE
BARREL CHAIR	DESK	PIER TABLE
BAR STOOL	DINING CHAIR	QUEEN-ANNE CHAIR
BEDSIDE TABLE	DINING TABLE	QUEEN-SIZE BED
BENCH	DIVAN	READING DESK
BENTWOOD CHAIR	DOUBLE BED	RECLINER
BERTH	DOUBLE DRESSER	RECLINING CHAIR
BOOKCASE	DRESSER	ROCKING CHAIR
BOOKSHELF	DRESSING TABLE	ROLL-TOP DESK
BOSTON ROCKER	DRINKS CABINET	SECRETAIRE
BOTTOM DRAWER	DROP-LEAF TABLE	SETTEE
BOX CHAIR	EASY CHAIR	SETTLE
BUCKET SEAT	EMPIRE BED	SHAKER CHAIR
BUNK BED	END TABLE	SHELVES
BUREAU	ESCRITOIRE	SHERATON CHAIR
CABINET	FEATHER BED	SIDEBOARD
CAMP BED	FOLDAWAY BED	SIDE CHAIR
CAMP CHAIR	FOLDING CHAIR	SIDE TABLE
CANE CHAIR	FOUR-POSTER BED	SINGLE BED
CANOPIED BED	FUTON	SLANT-TOP DESK
CANTERBURY	GAMING TABLE	SLOPE-TOP DESK
CAPTAIN'S CHAIR	GATE-LEG TABLE	SOFA
CARD TABLE	GRECIAN COUCH	SOFA BED
CARVER CHAIR	HAMMOCK	STALL
CASSONE	HIGHBOY *AMER*	STOOL
CHAISE LONGUE	HIGH CHAIR	STRAIGHT CHAIR
CHEST	HOPE CHEST *AMER*	STUDIO COUCH
CHESTERFIELD	KING-SIZE BED	SWIVEL CHAIR
CHEST OF DRAWERS	KITCHEN TABLE	TALLBOY
CHINA CABINET	KNEE-HOLE DESK	TEA TABLE
CHOIR STALL	LADDER-BACK CHAIR	TRUCKLE BED
CLUB CHAIR	LEATHER CHAIR	TWIN BED
COCKTAIL CABINET	LECTERN	UPHOLSTERED CHAIR
COFFEE TABLE	LIBRARY TABLE	WARDROBE
COLONIAL BED	LIQUOR CABINET *AMER*	WATER BED
COMMODE	LOUNGE CHAIR	WELSH DRESSER
CONSOLE TABLE	LOVE SEAT	WHATNOT
CONVERTIBLE SOFA	LOWBOY	WHEEL-BACK CHAIR
CORNER CUPBOARD	MILKING STOOL	WINDSOR CHAIR
COT	MIRROR CABINET	WING CHAIR
COUCH	MORRIS CHAIR	WOODEN CHAIR
CRADLE	NURSING CHAIR	WORK TABLE
CRIB	PANEL-BACK CHAIR	WRITING DESK
DAVENPORT	PANELLED BED	WRITING TABLE
DAY BED	PEDESTAL TABLE	Z-BED

·G·

ABBREVIATIONS

G	good • gram • grand • gravity • key • note • thousand
GA	gallium
GB	Great Britain
GBE	Grand Cross of the Order of the British Empire
GBS	George Bernard Shaw
GC	George Cross
GCB	Grand Cross of the Order of the Bath
GD	gadolinium
GE	germanium
GG	child's horse • Girl Guide
GI	American soldier
GP	doctor
GR	king (Latin: *Georgius Rex; Gulielmus Rex*) • monarch
GS	General Secretary • grammar school
GT	sports car (Italian: *Gran Turismo*)

gaffe bloomer, error, faux pas, mistake
may indicate an anagram

gag bind, chain, collar, fetter, girdle, handcuff, harness, hobble, interdict, joke, leash, manacle, muzzle, rein in, retch, shackle, silence, straitjacket, tether, tie up, yoke

gain acquire, acquisition, annex, appropriate, attain, benefit, breadwinning, bring in, come by, earn, fund-raising, gather in, get, greed, make, money-grubbing, moneymaking, obtain, procure, profit, profitableness, profiteer, raise funds, realize, reap, receiving, secure, taking, usury, win, winning

gainful acquiring, attainable, available, beneficial, beneficiary, capitalistic, compensatory, fund-raising, gratuitous, gross, inheriting, lucrative, moneymaking, money-spinning, net, obtainable, paid, procurable, profitable, remunerative, rewarding, useful, windfall

gait amble, bearing, canter, carriage, clip, creep, dance step, gallop, goosestep, hop, jog, jump, leap, lick, lope, march, pace, run, saunter, scamper, scramble, shuffle, skip, stalk, stamp, step, stride, stroll, strut, swagger, tramp, tread, trot, waddle, walk

gal girl

galaxy active, anagalactic nebula, arm, cluster, constellation, disc, dwarf elliptical, elliptical, filament, galactic centre, galactic nebula, giant elliptical, giant spiral, gravitational redshift, halo, Hubble classification, Hubble constant, irregular, island universe, lenticular, Local Group, Milky Way, nebula, nucleus, quasar, radio, Seyfert, spiral, starburst, star system, supercluster, supergiant elliptical, void
See also lists at **astronomer; planet**.

gamble bet, bingo, chance, lottery, raffle, risk, sweepstake, tombola, toss up

gambling bingo, draw, gaming, lot-

133

tery, lucky dip, raffle, sweepstake, tombola

game amusement, ball, board, cards, competition, computer, dauntless, dice, gamble, keen, lame, match, partridge, pheasant, sport, video, willing, word
See list of games.
See also list at **sport**.

gamebird capon, chicken, duck, game fowl, grouse, guinea fowl, partridge, pheasant, pigeon, ptarmigan, quail, snipe, turkey, woodcock
See also list at **birds**.

garble
may indicate an anagram

garden allotment, arboretum, arbour, bonsai, botanic, bottle, bower, cabbage patch, cultivate, flower, flowerbed, fruit farm, garden city, grotto, hanging, hedge, herb, hop, indoor, Japanese, Kew Gardens, kitchen, landscape, lawn, market garden, orchard, parterre, patio, rock, rockery, roof, rose, rosery, shrubbery, sunken, terrace, topiary, vegetable, vineyard, water, window box, winter, zoological

gas air, asphyxiate, atmosphere, butane, Calor gas, chat, coal gas, elastic fluid, ether, lighter fuel, methane, natural gas, producer gas, propane, rare gas, town gas, vapour, volatile

gaseous airy, frothy, gassy, vaporous

gaseousness effervescence, fermentation, fizziness, gassiness, pressure, vaporousness, vapour

gasify atomize, distil, etherify, evaporate, fractionate, sublimate, vaporize, volatilize

gassy aerated, bubbly, carbonated, effervescent, fizzy, sparkling

gather up collect, drag up, dredge up, haul up, pick up, pluck up, take up, trip, weigh

gelatin honey, jam, jelly, syrup, treacle

gelatinize gel, gelatinify, jellify

gelatinous jammy, jelly-like, syrupy, treacly, tremelloid

genealogy family history, family tree, lineage, pedigree

general across-the-board, all-comprehending, all-covering, all-embracing, all-encompassing, all-pervading, approximate, bird's-eye, blanket, broad, catholic, commander, comprehensive, cosmopolitan, diversified, eclectic, ecumenical, encyclopedic, extensive, heterogenous, inclusive, liberal, miscellaneous, officer, overall, panoramic, sweeping, synoptic, typical, universal, usual, vague, whole, wide

---

GAMES

AUNT SALLY	CONTRACT BRIDGE	MATADOR	SKITTLES
BACCARAT	CRAPS	MONOPOLY	SNAKE-EYES
BACKGAMMON	CRIBBAGE	OLD MAID	SNAKES AND
BAR BILLIARDS	DADDLUMS	PACHISI	LADDERS
BAT AND TRAP	DARTS	PAC-MAN	SNAP
BEZIQUE	DEVIL AMONG THE	PATIENCE	SNOOKER
BILLIARDS	TAILORS	POKER	SPACE INVADERS
BINGO	DOBBERS	POKER DICE	SPOOF
BIRD CAGE	DOMINOES	PONTOON	TIDDLYWINKS
BLACKJACK	DRAUGHTS	POOL	TIPCAT
BRAG	FIVES	QUOITS	TRIVIAL PURSUIT
CANASTA	GO	ROULETTE	VINGT-ET-UN
CASABLANCA	HAPPY FAMILIES	RUMMY	WHIST
CAVES	KNUR AND SPELL	RUNNING OUT	YAHTZEE
CHEMIN DE FER	LIAR DICE	SCRABBLE	
CHESS	MAHJONG	SHOGI	
CLUEDO	MARBLES	SHOVE HA'PENNY	

generality comprehensiveness, cosmopolitanism, globality, inclusiveness, internationalism, platitude, truism, universality, vagueness

generalization abstract, cliché, platitude, stereotype, sweeping statement, trite expression

generalize approximate, catholicize, ecumenicize, globalize, universalize

generalized abstract, approximate, broad, generic, ill-defined, imprecise, indefinite, indeterminate, inexact, loose, nebulous, nonspecific, sweeping, undetermined, unspecified, vague

generating
may indicate an anagram

generosity beneficence, bounteousness, bounty, charity, hospitality, liberality, munificence, open-handedness

generous beneficent, bountiful, giving, handsome, hospitable, lavish, liberal, munificent, open-handed, princely, ungrudging, unstinting

genetic chromosomal, diploid, dominant, factorial, genomic, genotypic, haploid, hereditary, meiotic, Mendelian, mitotic, mutant, polyploid, recessive

genetics biotype, chromosome, cytogenetics, dominance, eugenics, factor, gene, genecology, genetic engineering, genotype, heredity, inheritance, Mendel's laws, phenotype, recessiveness

gentleness adaptability, appeasement, compliance, delicacy, easiness, kindness, laxity, leniency, mellowness, mildness, mollification, mollifying, obedience, sensitiveness, tenderness

geological geochemical, geochronological, geodetic, geomorphological, geopolitical, glaciological, hydrological, mineralogical, palaeontological, pedological, petrological, stratigraphical
See list of geological time intervals.

geologist geochemist, geochronologist, geodesist, geomorphologist, glaciologist, hydrologist, mineralogist, palaeoclimatologist, palaeogeographer, palaeontologist, pedologist, petrologist, physiographer, planetologist, stratigrapher

geometry Euclid, shape
See list of geometric figures and curves.

geophysicist climatologist, geomagnetist, meteorologist, oceanographer, seismologist, volcanologist

geophysics climatology, geomagnetics, geophysics, gravimetry, meteorology, oceanography, plate tectonics, seismography, seismology, volcanology

germ bacterium, bug, cause, contagion, contagium, embryo, infection, lergy, microbe, microorganism, origin, root, seed, virus

germinate bloom, blossom, breed, bud, burgeon, flourish, flower, multiply, procreate, pullulate, reproduce, sprout, thrive

gestural clapping, dactylographic, gesticulative, glancing, grimacing, laughing, looking, moaning, patting, pushing, sighing, signing, slapping,

GEOLOGICAL TIME INTERVALS			
ARCHAEOZOIC	HOLOCENE	PALEOZOIC	RECENT
CAMBRIAN	JURASSIC	PERMIAN	SILURIAN
CARBONIFEROUS	MESOZOIC	PLEISTOCENE	TERTIARY
CENOZOIC	MIOCENE	PLIOCENE	TRIASSIC
CRETACEOUS	OLIGOCENE	PRECAMBRIAN	
DEVONIAN	ORDOVICIAN	PROTEROZOIC	
EOCENE	PALEOCENE	QUATERNARY	

smiling, stamping, thumbing, whistling, winking

gesture applause, beckon, bite, blush, boo, caress, catcall, cheer, clap, clenched fist, dactylology, demeanour, footsie, frown, gaze, gesticulate, glance, greet, grimace, grip, handshake, hiss, hoot, hug, imitate, jog, kick, kinesics, laugh, leer, look, mime, mimic, moan, motion, moue, nudge, ogle, pat, point, poke, pout, prod, push, raspberry, salute, scowl, shove, shuffle, sigh, sign, slap, smile, snap, stamp, stomp, stroke, tic, ticktack, token, touch, twinkle, twitch, V-sign, wave, whistle, wink

ghetto inner city area, quarter, slum

ghost apparition, demon, fetch, genius, ghoul, jinni, kobold, lemures, manes, manifestation, materialization, phantasm, phantom, poltergeist, presence, shade, spectre, spirit, spook, undead, vampire, wraith, zombie
See also list at **legend**.

giant behemoth, colossus, dinosaur, elephant, Gargantua, gigantic, Goliath, hippopotamus, huge, humdinger, jumbo, King Kong, leviathan, mammoth, mastodon, monster, redwood tree, spanker, whale, whopper

giddy
may indicate an anagram

GEOMETRIC FIGURES AND CURVES

ACUTE ANGLE	EXCIRCLE	NAPPE	RHOMBUS
ANCHOR RING	FOLIUM	NORMAL	RHUMB LINE
ANNULUS	FRACTAL	OBTUSE ANGLE	RIGHT ANGLE
ANTIPRISM	FRUSTRUM	OCTAGON	ROSE
ARC	GEODESIC	OCTAHEDRON	ROULETTE
BRACHISTO-	HELIX	OCTANT	SCALENE TRIANGLE
CHRONE	HEMISPHERE	OGIVE	SECTOR
CARDIOID	HEPTAGON	OVAL	SEGMENT
CATENARY	HEPTAHEDRON	PARABOLA	SEMICIRCLE
CATENOID	HEXAGON	PARABOLOID	SERPENTINE
CHORD	HEXAHEDRON	PARALLELOGRAM	SHEET
CIRCLE	HYPERBOLA	PARALLELOTOPE	SIGMOID CURVE
CIRCUMFERENCE	HYPERBOLOID	PEANO CURVE	SINE CURVE
CISSOID	HYPOCYCLOID	PEDAL TRIANGLE	SNOWFLAKE
CONCHOID	HYPOTROCHOID	PENCIL	CURVE
CONE	ICOSAHEDRON	PENTAGON	SOLID
CONIC	ICOSIDODECA-	PENTAGRAM	SPHERE
CONICOID	HEDRON	PENTAHEDRON	SPHEROID
CONOID	INCIRCLE	PENTANGLE	SPIRAL
CORNU SPIRAL	INVOLUTE	PERIGON	SPLINE
CRUCIFORM	ISOCHRONE	PERPENDICULAR	SQUARE
CUBE	ISOSCELES	PLANE	STROPHOID
CUBOCTAHEDRON	TRIANGLE	POLYGON	SURFACE
CYCLOID	KAPPA CURVE	POLYHEDRON	TANGENT
CYLINDER	KITE	PRISM	TAUTOCHRONE
CYLINDROID	KLEIN BOTTLE	PRISMATOID	TETRAHEDRON
DECAGON	KOCH CURVE	PRISMOID	TORUS
DIRECTRIX	LAMINA	PSEUDOSPHERE	TRACTRIX
DODECAGON	LATUS RECTUM	PYRAMID	TRAPEZIUM
ELLIPSE	LEMNISCATE	QUADRANGLE	TRAPEZOID
ELLIPSOID	LIMAÇON	QUADRANT	TREFOIL
ENVELOPE	LINE	QUADREFOIL	TRIANGLE
EPICYCLE	LOCUS	QUADRILATERAL	TRIDENT
EPICYCLOID	LOOP	RADIUS	TRISECTRIX
EPITROCHOID	LOXODROME	REFLEX ANGLE	TROCHOID
EQUILATERAL	LUNE	RHOMB	WEDGE
TRIANGLE	MÖBIUS STRIP	RHOMBOHEDRON	WITCH
EVOLUTE	MULTIFOIL	RHOMBOID	ZONE

gift aid, allotment, allowance, alms, award, backhander, baksheesh, benefit, bequest, blessing, bonanza, bonus, boon, box, bribe, consideration, contribution, covenant, donation, eckies, favour, fee, fellowship, grace, grant, gratuity, gravy, grease, hand-out, help, honorarium, incentive pay, inducement, inheritance, keepsake, kickback, legacy, memento, perk, perquisite, pocket money, present, presentation, prize, rake-off, reward, scholarship, souvenir, stipend, subscription, subsidy, subvention, support, sweetener, tip, token, tribute, trophy, whip-round, windfall

gifted endowed, talented

gigantism acromegaly, elephantiasis, giantism, hyperplasia, hypertrophy

give accord, aid, allot, award, bequeath, bestow upon, bribe, cede, commission, consecrate, consign, contribute, convey, covenant, dedicate, delegate, deliver, devote, dispatch, dispense, donate, endow, enrich, entertain, entrust, finance, fund, grant, honour with, impart, lavish upon, leave, lend, mete out, offer, pay, pour out, present, provide, render, reward, sacrifice, share, stand, subscribe, subsidize, supply, support, tender, tip, transfer, transmit, treat, vest, vouchsafe, vow, will, yield

given accorded, assumed, assumption, bequeathed, bestowed, bonus, complimentary, courtesy, donative, dowered, endowed, granted, gratis, gratuitous, impartable, inclined to, insurable, oblatory, pensionary, sacrificial, stipendiary, subsidized, tending, testate, tributary, voluntary, votive, willed

giving almsgiving, awarding, benefaction, benevolence, benevolent, bequeathal, bestowal, bountiful, bounty, bribing, charitable, charity, commitment, concession, conferral, consignment, contributing, conveyance, delivery, donation, dowry, endowing, enfeoffment, generosity, generous, gifting, granting, imparting, investment, largess, leaving, liberal, liberality, offering, open-handed, philanthropic, philanthropy, presentation, prizegiving, provision, service, settlement, subscription, subsidization, subvention, supplying, surrender, testament, tithing, transfer, voluntary work, will

giving rise to
may indicate a backword

glaciation freezing, ice age, interglaciation, postglaciation

gladden captivate, charm, cheer, delight, enchant, enrapture, enthral, intoxicate, please, thrill

glandular eccrine, endocrine, exocrine, hormonal

glare brightness, dazzle, frown, gaudiness, glower, grimace, lightness, lour, scowl, smoulder, stand out

glass brandy balloon, brandy snifter, bullet-proof, cannikin, chalice, champagne flute, crystal, drinking horn, fibreglass, goblet, jigger, loving cup, noggin, pannikin, reinforced, rummer, schooner, stained, Stein, tankard, Toby-jug, tumbler, window pane, windscreen, windshield, wineglass

glassware bottle glass, lead crystal, photochromic glass, Tiffany glass

glassy blank, crystalline, petrifactive, shiny, transparent, vitreous

glaze burnish, crackle, crazing, decalcomania, eggshell glaze, matt glaze, overglaze, polish, reflect, refract, slip, smear glaze, soft glaze, underglaze

gleam beam, blaze, blink, brightness, brilliance, burn, coruscate, dazzle, effulgence, flame, flare, flash, flicker, fluoresce, glance, glare, glassiness, glimmer, glint, glisten, glister, glitter, gloss, glow, incandesce, iridescence, lustre, opalescence, patina, phosphoresce, polish, radiate, scintillate, sheen, shimmer, shine, spangle, sparkle, tinsel, twinkle, wink

glide bowl along, coast, float, free-wheel, roll, skate, ski, skid, slide, slip

gloating Schadenfreude, self-satisfaction, smugness, unholy joy

global warming climatic change, desertification, greenhouse effect

glutton bacchanal, binger, cormorant, epicurean, foodie, gannet, gastronome, gobbler, gorger, gourmand, gourmet, guzzler, hog, hyena, locust, Lucullus, omnivore, pig, porker, trencherman, trencherwoman, wolf

gluttonous bingeing, bolting, cramming, devouring, edacious, epicurean, esurient, gastronomic, glutting, gobbling, gorging, greedy, gulping, guzzling, hedonistic, hoggish, insatiable, intemperate, omnivorous, overeating, overindulgent, piggish, polyphagous, rapacious, ravenous, self-indulgent, stuffing, voracious, well-nourished, wolfing

gluttony bingeing, concupiscence, edaciousness, greed, greediness, hedonism, hoggishness, insatiability, intemperance, overeating, overindulgence, piggishness, polyphagia, rapacity, ravenousness, self-indulgence, voraciousness, wolfishness

goal attraction, catch, desideratum, draw, ideal, lure, objective, prize, request, requirement, trophy

go around
may indicate a split word

go back
may indicate a backword

gobble binge, bolt, gluttonize, gorge, gormandize, guzzle, overeat, overindulge, scoff, wolf

goblin brownie, changeling, cluricaune, dwarf, elf, fairy, fay, gnome, gremlin, hobgoblin, imp, leprechaun, orc, piski, pixie, sprite, sylph, troll, trow

God Allah, Almighty God, Bodhisattva, Buddha, Everlasting Father, First Cause, Holy Trinity, Jehovah, Lord, Prime Mover, Providence, the Almighty, the Creator, the Eternal, the Father, the Lord, the Maker, the Trinity, Trimurti, Yahweh *See list of Greek and Roman gods.*

godly all-knowing, all-powerful, all-seeing, almighty, divine, eternal, holy, immeasurable, immortal, ineffable, infinite, mystical, omnipotent, omnipresent, omniscient, oracular, prescient, providential, theocratic, ubiquitous

going to
may indicate an anagram

good admirable, appropriateness, apt, auspiciousness, bad, better, boon, brill, corking, crack, crackerjack, dandy, deadly, excellent, exquisite, fab(ulous), famous, favourable, fine, first class, first-rate, goodness, greatness, healthy, heaven-sent, high-class, impressive, lucky, magnificent, meritorious, moral, praiseworthy, profitable, propitious, quality, rad(ical), right, salubrious, salutary, smashing, sound, spiffy, splendid, suitable, super, superb, superiority, swell, terrific, topnotch, valuable, wicked, wizard, wonderful, worthy

goodwill benevolence, collaboration, cooperation, cordiality, graciousness, helpfulness

gorgeousness agreeableness, appeal, attractiveness, beauteousness, beauty, brightness, brilliance, charm, chic, comeliness, delicacy, elegance, exquisiteness, fairness, glamour, grace, gracefulness, handsomeness, harmony, loveliness, magnificence, nobility, prettiness, pulchritude, radiance, refinement, shapeliness, splendour, symmetry

govern command, control, dictate, direct, dominate, exert authority, hold office, hold sway, lead, legislate, manage, oppress, police, reign, rule, tyrannize, wield power

governance apparat, clutches, colonialism, command, condominium, control, direction, directorship, dirigisme, domination, empery, grip, heteronomy, hold, imperialism, mastery, neocolonialism, overlordship, paternalism, presidency, raj, regency, regime, reign, rule, sovereignty, statism, subjection, superiority, supremacy, suzerainty, sway, whip hand

governing controlling, dictating, imperial, in charge, in power, magisterial, majestic, monarchical, regal, regnal, regnant, royal, ruling

government administration, anarchy, aristocracy, autarchy, autocracy, autonomy, Bolshevism, clericalism, collectivism, communism, constitutionalism, control, demagoguery, democracy, despotism, direction, duumvirate, ecclesiasticism, egalitarianism, elitism, executive, Fabianism, Fascism, federalism, feudalism, gerontocracy, gynocracy, hierarchy, hierocracy, home rule, isocracy, kingship, leadership, Leninism, majority rule, management, Maoism, Marxism-Leninism, matriarchy, meritocracy, mobocracy, mob rule, monarchy, National Socialism, Nazism, ochlocracy, oligarchy, pantisocracy, parliament, party system, paternalism, patriarchy, physiocracy, pluralism, plutocracy, politicking, polity, Poujadism, PR, proletarianism, proportional representation, republicanism, self-rule, socialism, sovietism, squirearchy, statism, stratocracy, syndicalism, tech-

GREEK AND ROMAN GODS	
GREEK GOD	ROMAN GOD
APHRODITE – goddess of beauty and love	VENUS
APOLLO – god of poetry, music, and prophecy	APOLLO
ARES – god of war	MARS
ARTEMIS – goddess of the moon	DIANA
ASCLEPIUS – god of medical art	AESCULAPIUS
ATHENE – goddess of wisdom	MINERVA
CHARITES – 3 daughters of Zeus: Euphrosyne, Aglaia, and Thalia; personified grace, beauty, and charm	GRACES
CRONOS – god of agriculture	SATURN
DEMETER – goddess of agriculture	CERES
DIONYSUS – god of wine and fertility	BACCHUS
EOS – goddess of dawn	AURORA
EROS – god of love	CUPID
FATES – 3 goddesses who determine man's destiny: Clotho, Lachesis, and Atropos	
HEBE – goddess of youth	JUVENTAS
HECATE – goddess of witchcraft	HECATE
HELIOS – god of the sun	SOL
HEPHAESTUS – god of destructive fire	VULCAN
HERA – queen of heaven, goddess of women and marriage	JUNO
HERMES – messenger of gods	MERCURY
HESTIA – goddess of the hearth	VESTA
HYPNOS – god of sleep	SOMNUS
NEMESIS – goddess of retribution	
PAN – god of woods and fields	FAUNUS
PERSEPHONE – goddess of the Underworld	PROSERPINE
PLUTO – god of the Underworld	PLUTO
PLUTUS – god of wealth	
POSEIDON – god of the sea	NEPTUNE
RHEA – goddess of nature	CYBELE
SELENE – goddess of the moon	LUNA
THANATOS – god of death	MORS
ZEUS – supreme god; god of sky and weather	JUPITER

nocracy, thearchy, theocracy, Titoism, totalitarianism, tribalism, triumvirate

governmental administrative, bureaucratic, centralized, civic, dictatorial, executive, federal, feudal, ministerial, official, parliamentary, political, presidential, republican, senatorial

governor controller, lawmaker, legislator, premier, president, prime minister, statesman, stateswoman, vice president

grab
may indicate a split word

graceless awkward, cack-handed, clownish, clumsy, cumbersome, dumpy, gauche, gawky, ham-fisted, heavy-handed, ill-proportioned, inelegant, undignified, ungainly

gradation bar, calibration, classification, comparison, differential, differentiation, grading, line, mark, measurement, notation, notch, peg, proportion, ranking, rating, ratio, ration, relativeness, remove, score, shading, standard, valuation

gradational calibrated, classified, comparative, differential, differentiated, diminishing, graded, gradual, proportional, relative, scaled, sized, slow-changing, slow-ranging

grain cereal, corn, daintiness, delicacy, denier, downiness, filminess, fineness, fluffiness, fuzziness, gossameriness, graininess, granulation, granule, grittiness, hardness, mote, particle, pattern, peachiness, refinement, roughness, satininess, silkiness, smoothness, softness, speck

graininess branniness, granularity, gravelliness, grittiness, mealiness, sabulosity, sandiness

grainy arenaceous, brecciated, detrital, granular, gravelly, gritty, pebbly, sabulous, sandy, shingly

graminivorous browsing, grazing, herbivorous

grammar accentuation, agreement, case, conjugation, construing, declension, gender, inflection, mood, number, paradigm, parsing, punctuation, syntax, tense, voice, word order

grammatical adjectival, adverbial, attributive, augmentative, comparative, conjunctive, coordinate, copular, definite, diminutive, direct, feminine, formative, indefinite, indirect, inflected, inflectional, intensive, interjectional, intransitive, masculine, modifying, morphemeic, neuter, objective, participial, plural, prepositional, pronominal, reflexive, singular, subjective, superlative, transitive, verbal

grand awe-inspiring, brilliant, chief, elaborate, elegant, expensive, glitzy, glorious, gorgeous, imposing, impressive, lavish, luxuriant, luxurious, magnificent, plush, posh, resplendent, ritzy, scenic, spectacular, splendid, sumptuous, supreme, swanky

grandeur brilliance, elaborateness, elegance, glory, gorgeousness, lavishness, luxuriousness, luxury, magnificence, plushness, poshness, resplendence, ritziness, splendour, sumptuousness, swankiness

grandiloquence bombast, magniloquence, orotundity, verbosity

grant acknowledge, aid, allowance, assistance, bribe, bursary, concede, contribution, damages, donation, exhibition, fellowship, grant-in-aid, indemnity, payoff, penalty, ransom, scholarship, stipend, subscription, subsidy, subvention, sweetener, tax, tribute

graph bar graph, chart, histogram, pie chart, plot, scatter diagram, scattergram

grass betray, cereal, fodder, graminaceous plant, inform on, lawn, ley, marijuana, meadow, mowing, ornamental, pasture, rush, sedge, shoot, true

grassland common, downs, field, grazing, green, greensward, hassock, heath, herbage, lawn, lea, ley, mead, meadow, moor, park, pasturage, pasture, plain, prairie, savanna, sod, steppe, sward, tuft, turf, tussock, veld, verdure

grassy farinaceous, graminaceous, gramineous, graminiferous, meadowy, oaten, poaceous, reedy, rushy, sedgy, swardy, turfy, verdant, verdured, wheaten

grate abrade, belch, caw, choke, cough, croak, crunch, file, fireplace, gasp, grind, grunt, gutteralize, hawk, hem, rasp, rub down, saw, scrape, scratch, scrunch, shred, snore, snort

grateful appreciative, beholden, gratified, indebted, obliged, pleased, thankful

gratitude appreciation, awareness, cognizance, gratefulness, mindfulness, obligation, thankfulness

grave barrow, burial chamber, cairn, cemetery, cenotaph, cromlech, crypt, dakhma, dangerous, dolmen, earthwork, fogou, graveyard, important, long home, mastaba, mausoleum, memorial, menhir, mound, mummy chamber, narrow house, pantheon, plague pit, pyramid, sepulchre, serious, shrine, solemn, sombre, tomb, tumulus, vault

gravity G, G force, gravitation, gravitational pull, importance, seriousness, solemnity, specific gravity

graze browse, crop, fodder, forage, pasture, ruminate, scrape, scratch

greedy acquisitive, avaricious, gluttonous, gold-digging, grasping, money-grubbing, plundering, voracious

green aquamarine, avocado, callow, celadon, celadonite, chartreuse, chlorophyll, eau-de-nil, emerald, envious, glaucous, greenish, inexpert, jade, lawn, mignonette, pallid, Paris green, reseda, terre verte, unripe, verdant, verditer, vert, virescent, viridian, Windsor green
See also list at **colours**.

greenness evergreen, freshness, grass, grassland, greenery, immaturity, jealousy, moss, sward, turf, verdancy, verdure, viridity, woodland

greet acquaint, embrace, introduce, present, shake hands

greeting celebrate, crown, embrace, fete, garland, hail, hello, honour, hug, kiss, obeisance, obsequy, parade, present arms, salutation, salute, say hello, shake hands, smile, squeeze, turn out, wave, welcome, wreathe

grieve cry, howl, lament, languish, moan, mourn, pine, sigh, sob, ululate, wail, weep

grimace contortion, frown, leer, moue, pout, rictus, scowl, snarl, sneer, squint, tic

grind catch, chafe, drudgery, file, flour, fret, gall, grain, granulate, grate, irritate, mill, mince, plane, pulverize, rasp, stick

grinding chafe, chafing, filing, fretting, galling, levigation, limation, rasping

grossness bad manners, boorishness, commonness, discourtesy, fatness, ill-breeding, impropriety, incivility, incorrectness, obviousness, tastelessness, unseemliness

ground arena, basis, earth, elevation, field, fix, floor, gardens, inform, keep down, landscape, powdered, pulverized, relief, soil, terrain, topography

group bale, band, batch, bevy, bind, body, brotherhood, bunch, bundle, categorize, circle, clan, class, clique, clump, cluster, collect, community, company, crowd, family, folk, gang, gather, ghetto, grouping, neighbourhood, pack, package, parcel, party, people, posse, race, ring, set, society, sort, tribe, truss, wrap

grouping cataloguing, categorization, classification, codification, indexing, listing, pigeonholing, specification, taxonomy

grow accrue, amplify, augment, balloon, bear fruit, belly, bloat, blossom, broaden, bud, build up, bulge, crescendo, develop, dilate, distend, draw out, enlarge, expand, extend, fatten, fill out, flare, flower, gain, germinate, harvest, hypertrophy, increase, inflate, lengthen, magnify, mushroom, open up, overdevelop, plump out, produce, profit, puff up, snowball, spread, sprout, stretch, swell, tumify, unfold, wax, widen

growing blooming, blossoming, branching, broadening, budding, bulbous, bulging, burgeoning, crescent, deltoid, developing, dilating, expanding, extending, fanning, flabellate, flaring, flourishing, flowering, fruit-bearing, germinating, increasing, lengthening, multiplying, mushrooming, opening, patulous, pullulating, rising, shooting, snowballing, splaying, sprawling, spreading, sprouting, stretching, swelling, thriving, tumescent, turgescent, unfolding, waxing, widening

growl beef, bellyache, bitch, carp, complain, crab, grouch, grouse, grumble, mutter, snap, snarl, spit

growth addition, aggrandizement, amplification, augmentation, bloating, blooming, blossom, blowing up, branching, broadening, bud, build-up, bulbousness, bulging, burgeoning, cancer, carcinoma, crescendo, development, diastole, dilation, dispersion, distension, drawing out, dropsy, enlargement, expansion, extension, fanning out, fattening, flaring, flourishing, flower, fruit, gain, germination, harvest, heightening, hypertrophy, increase, inflation, lengthening, lump, magnification, maturation, multiplication, oedema, opening, outgrowth, pro-

creation, produce, profit, puffiness, pullulation, raising, ramification, reproduction, rising, splaying, sprawling, spreading, sprouting, stretching, stuffing, swelling, thriving, tumefaction, tumescence, tumidness, turgidity, unfolding, waxing, widening

grudge animosity, begrudge, malevolence, resent, sulk

grumbler agitator, bellyacher, complainer, malcontent, moaner, objector, rabble-rouser, troublemaker

guarantee assurance, insurance, pledge, promise, warrant, warranty

guaranteed assured, attested, authenticated, bound, certain, certified, committed, contracted, covenanted, covered, gilt-edged, insured, mortgaged, obligated, pawned, pledged, promised, promissory, reliant, signed, underwritten, unshaken, warranted

guardian Argus, baby-sitter, benefactor, bodyguard, Cerberus, champion, chaperon, child-minder, coastguard, companion, conservator, curator, custodian, defender, detective, doorman, duenna, fireman, firewatcher, forester, gamekeeper, garrison, governess, guard, keeper, lifeguard, life-saver, lookout, mentor, militia, minder, nanny, nurse, patrolman, patron, picket, police, preserver, sentinel, sentry, shepherd, sheriff, surveillant, tutor, vanguard, vigilante, warden, warder, watchdog, watcher, watchman

guide adviser, automatic pilot, axiom, beam, binnacle, buoy, canon, catalogue, cicerone, compass, condition, controls, criterion, direction, escort, foghorn, helm, instruction, joystick, keynote, lighthouse, lodestar, manage, manual, maxim, needle, norm, pole star, precept, prescription, principle, radar, reins, rudder, standard, steer, supervise, teach, teacher, tenet, tiller, usher, wheel

guilt accusation, blame, blameworthiness, censure, complicity, conviction, culpability, delinquency, impeachability, implication, inculpation, indictability, liability, peccancy, red-handedness, reprehensibility, reproach, responsibility

guilty abominable, abusive, accusable, at fault, bad, blameworthy, censurable, censured, chargeable, condemned, convicted, criminal, crooked, culpable, delinquent, evil, impeachable, implicated, inexcusable, injurious, mischievous, offensive, peccant, reprehensible, reproachable, reprovable, responsible, sinful, transgressive, unforgivable, unjustifiable, unlawful, unpardonable, vicious, wicked

gulf abyss, bay, bight, canyon, chasm, chimney, clough, col, couloir, crevasse, cwm, defile, dell, draw, flume, gape, ghat, gorge, gulch, gully, inlet, pass, ravine, rift, separation, valley, void

gullible credulous, green, innocent, naive

gun
See list at **weapon**.

gush bore, drone on, hold forth, spout

gynaecology gyniatrics, obstetrics

·H·

ABBREVIATIONS

H	aspirate • hearts • hydrogen
HE	helium • His/Her Excellency
HF	hafnium
HG	mercury
HM	headmaster • headmistress • hectometre • monarch (Her/His Majesty)
HMS	boat • ship (Her/His Majesty's Ship)
HO	head office • holmium • Home Office • house
HP	hardy perennial • hire purchase • horsepower • sauce (Houses of Parliament)
HRH	monarch (Her/His Royal Highness)

habit addiction, custom, dress, familiarity, garment, inveteracy, pattern, praxis, regularity, second nature, use, wont

habitat abode, accommodation, billet, crib, domicile, habitation, home, house, living quarters, lodgings, pad, rooms, squat

habitual accustomed, annual, customary, everyday, invariable, occupational, predictable, professional, quotidian, regular, routine, usual, wonted

habituate acclimatize, adapt, brainwash, break in, condition, domesticate, harden, imbue, implant, indoctrinate, ingraft, inure, naturalize, orient, practise, season, tame, teach, train

habituated addicted, conversant, familiar, inveterate, used

habituation association, brainwashing, conditioning, drilling, hardening, indoctrination, institutionalization, maturing, memorization, naturalization, orientation, reflex, rote

hail freezing rain, greeting, hailstorm, salutation, sleet

hairdressing barbering, cutting, dyeing, styling, trichology

hairless bald, clean-shaven, depilatory, glabrous, smooth, thin, tonsured

hairstyle Afro, beehive, bob, braids, chignon, coiffure, crop, curls, dreadlocks, Eton crop, feathered cut, fringe, frizz, haircut, hair-do, layered cut, perm, plait, ponytail, quiff, rats' tails, short-back-and-sides, style, trim, wedge cut, wet-look

hairy bushy, curly, flocculent, frizzy, furry, fuzzy, hirsute, lanate, matted, risky, scary, shaggy, shockheaded, unshorn, woolly

half bifurcated, bisected, bisector, cleft, cloven, diameter, dichotomous, fifty percent, halfway, halved, hemisphere, moiety, partial, semicircle
may indicate a split word

half-measure makeshift, secondbest, stopgap, temporary

half-truth deception, economical with the truth, equivocation, misinterpretation, misleading, propaganda

halve bifurcate, bisect, cleave, dichotomize, sunder, transect
may indicate a split word

ham actor, amateur, gammon, over-act, radio

handicapped blind, crippled, deaf, disabled, dumb, halt, hindered, lame, maimed, mute, mutilated

handshake embrace, holding hands, hug, kiss, open arms, rubbing noses

hanger braces, clotheshorse, clothes-line, crane, gallows, gibbet, hook, knob, nail, peg, suspender

haphazard
may indicate an anagram

happen arise, befall, betide, blunder into, chance, crop up, end up, fall out, light upon, occur, pop up, run across, take place, transpire, turn up, work out

happiness bliss, cheerfulness, con-tentment, delectation, delight, delir-ium, ebullience, ecstasy, enchantment, enjoyment, euphoria, exaltation, ex-hilaration, exuberance, felicity, gaiety, gladness, glee, gusto, high spirits, in-toxication, joy, lightheartedness, mer-riment, pleasure, rapture, zest

happy blissful, blithe, captivated, cel-ebratory, cheerful, contented, de-lighted, delirious, ebullient, ecstatic, elated, enchanted, enraptured, eu-phoric, exuberant, felicitous, fortunate, gay, glad, joyful, jubilant, merry, over-joyed, pleased, prosperous, starry-eyed, thrilled, transported

hard cartilaginous, chewy, clinging, cohesive, coriaceous, difficult, fibrous, firm, forcefully, gristly, hardboiled, harsh, indigestible, inedible, intensely, leathery, ligneous, nonelastic, over-done, painful, rigid, rubbery, steely, stern, stiff, tough, uncompromising, unsprung, violent, viscid, woody

harden anneal, back, bake, brace, but-tress, case-harden, crisp, fortify, freeze, hard-boil, heat-treat, prove, reinforce, shore, starch, steel, stiffen, strengthen, tauten, temper, tense, tighten, toughen, vulcanize, wax

hardened armoured, calcified, cal-loused, crusted, crystallized, fossilized, frozen, granulated, hornified, icy, in-durate, ossified, petrified, set, solidi-fied, steeled, sun-baked, vitrified

hardness backing, cragginess, den-sity, difficulty, firmness, grittiness, impenetrability, inelasticity, inextensi-bility, inflexibility, lumpiness, nodos-ity, nodularity, resistance, rigidity, rigour, rockiness, solidity, starchiness, steeliness, stiffness, stoniness, strength, tautness, temper, tension, tightness, toughness

harmful accursed, adverse, blood-thirsty, calamitous, cruel, damaging, dangerous, deadly, degenerative, dele-terious, destructive, detrimental, dis-advantageous, disastrous, dreadful, harsh, hurtful, infectious, injurious, intolerant, malevolent, malicious, ma-lignant, mischief-making, noxious, ominous, outrageous, pernicious, poi-sonous, polluting, prejudicial, sinister, spiteful, vindictive, violent, virulent, wasting

harmfulness abuse, adversity, anxi-ety, bitterness, cruelty, damage, dan-ger, destruction, detriment, disaster, harassment, harm, hurt, ill, inhuman-ity, injury, intolerance, libel, malevo-lence, malice, malignancy, mischief, noxiousness, pain, poisonousness, pol-lution, slander, spell, spitefulness, suf-fering, violence, witchcraft

harmonic catchy, dulcet, euphonic, harmonious, homophonic, in tune, mellifluous, melodious, singable, sym-phonious, synchronous, tonal, tuneful

harmonics cadence, cantus firmus, continuo, counterpoint, faburden, fauxbourdon, heterophony, homopho-ny, melodics, monody, monophony, musicography, musicology, polyphony, resolution, rhythmics, tonality, unison

harmonious agreeing, assonant, at-tuned, balanced, blended, calm, choral, coincident, coinciding, concomitant, concordant, conjoint, consonant, coordinated, corresponding, echoing, harmonic, homophonic, in concert, in equilibrium, matching, melodic, merged, modulated, monodic, monophonic, peaceful, polyphonic, quiet, regulated, resonant, resounding, rhyming, stable, steady, symmetrical, symphonic, symphonious, synchronized, synchronous, tranquil, unanimous, unisonous

harmonize accord, adjust, agree, assonate, attune, balance, blend, chime, coincide, conform, conjoin, coordinate, correspond, counterpoise, echo, equilibrate, match, melodize, merge, modulate, regularize, regulate, resolve, resonate, rhyme, stabilize, symmetrize, symphonize, synchronize, tune

harmony balance, calm, coincidence, concomitance, concord, conjunction, consonance, coordination, detachment, echo, equilibrium, harmonization, peace, quiet, regularity, resonance, stability, stillness, symmetry, synchronism, synchronization, tranquillity

hash
may indicate an anagram

haste acceleration, alacrity, briskness, celerity, expeditiousness, hurry, promptness, quickness, rapidity, rush, speed, swiftness, velocity

hasten accelerate, bundle out, dispatch, drive, expedite, flog, goad, hurry, hustle, impel, incite, lash, precipitate, press, propel, push, quicken, railroad, rush, speed up, spur, stampede, urge, whip

hastiness impatience, impetuosity, impulsiveness, precipitance, rashness, recklessness, swiftness

hasty allegro, ardent, boisterous, breakneck, breathless, brisk, careless, cursory, driven, elbowing, expeditious, fast, fervent, feverish, fleet, forced, furious, haphazard, hard-pressed, headlong, heedless, hotfoot, hotheaded, hurried, ill-considered, immediate, impatient, impetuous, impulsive,

last-minute, negligent, perfunctory, precipitant, presto, prompt, pushed through, quick, racing, railroaded, rapid, rash, reckless, rough-and-tumble, running, rushed, scampering, shoving, slapdash, speeding, speedy, stampeded, superficial, swift, thoughtless, unprepared, unthinking, urgent, violent

hate abhorrence, abomination, acrimony, animosity, antagonism, antipathy, aversion, avoid, bad blood, bitterness, condemn, curse, denounce, despise, despitefulness, detest, disaffection, disapprobation, disapproval, disfavour, disgust, dislike, displeasure, disrelish, enmity, envy, execrate, gall, grudge, hatred, hostility, ill feeling, ill will, jealousy, loathing, malediction, malevolence, malice, malignity, odium, rancour, recoil at, refuse, reject, repugnance, repulsion, resent, resentment, revulsion, scorn, shrink from, shudder at, spite, spleen, spurn, sullenness, venom, virulence

hated abhorrent, abominable, accursed, baneful, beastly, condemned, contemptible, despicable, detestable, detested, discredited, disgusting, disliked, execrable, horrid, invidious, jilted, loathed, nasty, nauseous, obnoxious, odious, repelling, repugnant, repulsive, revolting, scorned, spurned, strange, unchosen, unlamented, unlovable, unloved, unmissed, unmourned, unpopular, unvalued, unwanted, unwelcome, vile

hatefulness alienation, beastliness, contemptibility, despicability, discredit, disrepute, estrangement, loathesomeness, obnoxiousness, unpopularity

hater Anglophobe, anti-Semite, bigot, Francophobe, misandrist, misanthrope, misanthropist, misogamist, misogynist, racist, xenophobe

hating acrimonious, antagonistic, antipathetic, averse, bitter, contemptuous, envious, execrative, green-eyed, grudging, hostile, ill-natured, jealous, maledictive, malevolent, malicious, malignant, poisonous, rancorous, resentful, sour, spiteful, spleenful, sullen, venomous, vicious, vindictive, virulent

havoc chaos, confusion, destruction, devastation, disaster area, mayhem, shambles, turmoil
may indicate an anagram

haywire
may indicate an anagram

hazard bet, chance it, danger, gamble, obstacle, risk, speculate, take a chance, venture, wager

haze cloud, film, fog, mist, peasouper, smoke, steam

head aim at, cap, commander, crown, crownpiece, heading, headpiece, intelligence, lead, leader, leadership, masthead, pinhead, promontary, source, spire, steer, top, topgallant, topknot, topmast, topsail, treetop
may indicate the first letter of a word

headache megrim, migraine, nuisance, trouble

head for aim, aim at, bear, collimate, dash for, dispose, fix on, go, incline, lead, make for, navigate, point, run for, sail for, set, sight on, tend, train upon, trend, turn, verge

headgear balaclava helmet, balmoral, baseball cap, beaver, beaverskin, beret, biretta, boater, bobble hat, bonnet, bowler, busby, cap, chapeau, clerical hat, cloche, cloth cap, cocked hat, coonskin hat, coronet, cowboy hat, cowl, crown, deerstalker, Easter bonnet, fedora, felt hat, fez, fillet, glengarry, hat, headband, headdress, headscarf, helmet, high hat, homburg, hood, kepi, lid, millinery, mortarboard, net, panama, picture hat, pillbox, pith helmet, poke bonnet, pork-pie hat, rain hat, ribbon, shako, shovel hat, silk hat, slouch hat, snood, sombrero, southwester, stetson, stovepipe hat, straw hat, sunbonnet, sunhat, sweatband, tam-o'shanter, ten-gallon hat, tiara, tile, titfer, topee, top hat, topper, toque, tricorn, trilby, turban, Tyrolean hat, veil, wimple, woolly hat, yashmak

headless
may indicate a shortening (delete first letter)

headline banner head, by-line, flag, head, masthead

healer acupuncturist, aromatherapist, bonesetter, chiropractor, doctor, faith healer, hakim, herbalist, homeopath, naturopath, nurse, osteopath, reflexologist, therapist

health bloom, condition, constitution, energy, eupepsia, fettle, fitness, form, haleness, heartiness, Hygeia, robustness, shape, soundness, state, strength, tone, trim, vigour, vitality, well-being

healthiness acuity, compulsion, dedication, energy, enthusiasm, fitness, goodness, healthfulness, hygiene, keenness, liveliness, nutritiousness, salubriousness, soundness, vehemence, vigour, vim, vitality, wholesomeness, youth, zeal

healthy beneficial, blooming, bonny, bouncing, bracing, convalescent, cured, energetic, eupeptic, fine, fit, flourishing, fresh, glowing, great, hardy, healed, healthful, hygienic, invigorating, lusty, nourishing, nutritious, robust, rosy-cheeked, ruddy, salubrious, salutary, sanitary, sound, stalwart, strapping, sturdy, thriving, tonic, vigorous, well, wholesome

hear attend, auscultate, bug, catch, concentrate, eavesdrop, gather, hark, hearken, heed, intercept, learn, listen, mind, monitor, perceive, pick up, sound, tap, tape, tune in
may indicate a homophone

heard audible, distinct, heeded, overheard
may indicate a homophone

hearer audience, audiophile, auditor,

eavesdropper, hearkener, listener, monitor, telephone tapper

hearing attention, audibility, audition, auscultation, good ear, heed, musicality, perfect pitch, sharp ear

hearsay
may indicate a homophone

heart anima, animus, character, core, guts, marrow, nitty-gritty, pith, pity, soul, spirit
may indicate the middle letter(s) of a word

heat calescence, cook, fervour, fug, hotness, inflame, passion, stuffiness, temperature, tepidity, warmness

heated baked, boiled, burnt, defrosted, double-glazed, molten, preheated, roasted, scorched, singed, toasted, warmed up

heater boiler, central heating, copper, fan heater, geyser, heating element, hot-water tank, hypocaust, immersion heater, radiator, solar heating, warmer

heather erica, heath, ling

heaven Avalon, bliss, Elysian fields, Elysium, empyrean, firmament, Kingdom come, nirvana, Olympus, paradise, sky, Valhalla, welkin
See also list at **imaginary**.

heavenly celestial, Elysian, empyreal, empyrean, ethereal, lovely, Olympian, on high, paradisial, paradisic(al), supernal, wonderful

heaviness beefiness, brawn, bulkiness, corpulence, fatness, heftiness, lumpiness, mass, massiveness, obesity, poundage, solid body, tonnage, weight, weightiness
See also list at **measurement**.

heavy beefy, bulky, considerable, corpulent, dense, depressing, fat, featherweight, great, heavyweight, hefty, large, leaden, lightweight, lumpish, massive, middleweight, obese, overweight, serious, solid, stout, weighty

heedlessness callousness, hard-heart-edness, hardness, heartlessness, impassivity, rashness, recklessness, thick skin

height altitude, elevation, eminence, exaltation, highness, lankiness, lift, loftiness, pitch, prominence, ranginess, rise, stature, sublimity, tallness
See also list at **measurement**.

held by or **in**
may indicate a hidden word

hell abyss, Acheron, bottomless pit, damnation, Dis, fire and brimstone, Hades, inferno, lake of fire, limbo, lower world, misery, nether world, perdition, purgatory, Styx, Tartarus, torment, underworld
See also list at **imaginary**.

hello bonjour, ciao, greetings, hail, hi, introduction, salutation

helm command, control, rudder, tiller, wheel
See also list at **vessel**.

help abet, advance, advantage, aid, assist, assistance, avail, benefit, better, bless, deliver, edify, favour, function, hand, improve, improvement, instrument, leg-up, mayday, profit, promote, rescue, save, serve, sos, springboard, use

helper abettor, adjutant, adjuvant, aid(e), ally, angel, assistant, attendant, auxiliary, backer, backing, backroom boys, collaborator, colleague, enabler, facilitator, fairy godmother, girl Friday, gofer, good Samaritan, hands, helpmate, helpmeet, henchman, man Friday, mate, partner, patron, reinforcements, reserves, right-hand man, saviour, sidekick, staff, support(er)

helpful benevolent, collaborative, conducive, constructive, contributory, convenient, cooperative, cordial, furthering, gracious, handy, informative, philanthropic, positive, practical, promoting, useful, utilitarian

helpfulness advantageousness, benevolence, collaboration, cooperation, goodwill, kindness, profitability, usefulness, utility, willingness

helping adjuvant, facilitative, instrumental

helplessness defencelessness, harmlessness, innocence, meekness, softness, vulnerability, weakness

helter-skelter
may indicate an anagram

heraldic blazoned, emblazoned, emblematic
See list of heraldic terms.

herd call in, corral, drive, flock, marshal, mass, mob, round up, shepherd, shoal, swarm, whip in

hereafter damnation, future, heaven, hell, hellfire, kingdom come, nirvana, paradise, the underworld

heresy dissidence, heterodoxy, iconoclasm, nonconformism, revisionism, unorthodoxy

heretical dissident, heterodox, iconoclastic, unconventional, unorthodox

hermit anchorite, ascetic, eremite, isolationist, loner, lone wolf, marabout, recluse, seclusionist, solitaire, solitary, solitudinarian, stylite

heroism chivalry, gallantry, knightliness, manliness, prowess, virility

herpetologist ophiologist, snake charmer

hesitant cautious, dawdling, drawling, foot-dragging, lagging, procrastinating, reluctant, softly-softly, tentative

hesitate avoid, back away, balk, dawdle, delay, dilly-dally, dither, drawl, equivocate, er, evade, falter, flag, hover, jib, lag, linger, loiter, pause, prevaricate, shillyshally, shirk, shy, tarry, trail, um, vacillate, waver

hesitation arrest, caution, check, delay, detention, drawling, er, foot-dragging, hold-up, hysteresis, obstruc-

---

HERALDIC TERMS

ACHIEVEMENT	COAT OF ARMS	GRIFFIN	POMME
ANIMAL CHARGE	COCKATRICE	GULES	PORTCULLIS
ANNULET	CORONET	GYRON	POTENT
ANTELOPE	COUCHANT	FLEURY	PURPORE
ARGENT	CRESCENT	HATCHMENT	QUARTERING
ARMORIAL	CREST	HELMET	RAMPANT
BEARINGS	CROSS	HERALDIC TINCTURE	REBUS
ARMORY	CROWN	HONOR POINT	REGARDANT
ARMS	DEVICE	IMPALEMENT	RUSTRE
AZURE	DEXTER	IMPALING	SABLE
BADGE	DIFFERENCE	LABEL	SALTIRE
BANDEAU	DIFFERENCING	LAMBREQUIN	SCUTCHEON
BAR	DIMIDIATION	LION	SEJANT
BAR SINISTER	EAGLE	LOZENGE	SEME
BASE	ERMINE	MANTLING	SHIELD
BATON	ERMINOIS	MARSHALING	SINISTER
BEARING	ESCUTCHEON	MARTLET	SPREAD EAGLE
BEND	FALCON	METAL	STATANT
BEND SINISTER	FESSE POINT	MOTTO	SUPPORTERS
BLAZON	FIELD	MULLET	TENNE
BLAZONRY	FLANCH	MURREY	TORSE
BORDURE	FLEUR-DE-LIS	NOMBRIL POINT	TREFOIL
CANTON	FLORAL CHARGE	OR	TRESURE
CHAPLET	FRET	ORDINARY	UNICORN
CHARGE	FUR	PALE	VAIR
CHEVRON	FUSIL	PASSANT	VERT
CHIEF	GARDANT	PEAN	WREATH
CINQUEFOIL	GARLAND	PILE	

tion, procrastination, reluctance, set-back, tardiness, tentativeness, um, un-willingness, work-to-rule

hex curse, evil eye, pishogue, spell, whammy

hidden camouflaged, dark, indistinct, invisible, obscure, unseen

hidden in
may indicate a hidden word

hide black out, blank out, blot out, blur, burrow, bury, camouflage, cloak, cloud, conceal, cover up, cowl, creep, darken, delete, dim, disguise, eclipse, erase, hood, lurk, mask, masquerade, obscure, screen, shroud, skulk, slink, submerge, tiptoe, veil

hideousness contortedness, deface-ment, deformity, disfigurement, grace-lessness, homeliness, mutilation, plainness, repulsiveness, unsightliness

hierarchical alphabetical, grada-tional, graded, numerical, progressive, ranked, sequential, serial, taxonomic

hierarchy gradation, pecking order, progression, sequence, series

higgledy piggledy
may indicate an anagram

high aerial, airy, altitudinal, ascend-ing, aspiring, beetling, cloud-topped, dizzy, dominating, elevated, ethereal, ecstatic, flying, giddy, happy, high-rise, high-up, hovering, lofty, mounting, multistorey, overhanging, overlooking, overshadowing, rising, sky-high, sky-scraping, soaring, supernal, tall, top-ping, towering, uplifted, upraised, upreared, uprising, vertiginous

higher superior, taller, topmost, up-most, upper, uppermost

highland acclivity, climb, down, es-carpment, fell, foothills, heights, in-cline, mesa, moorland, mountains, plateau, tableland, upland, wold

hill heap, hillock, hummock, knoll, mound, mount, mountain, pile, scarp, tor

hinder barrack, block, check, cir-cumscribe, control, counteract, crip-ple, curb, detain, deter, disable, dissuade, drag, encumber, forestall, frustrate, hamper, hold back, impede, inhibit, intercept, interfere with, inter-rupt, intervene, limit, meddle, obstruct, obviate, oppose, persecute, posterior, preclude, prevent, prohibit, rear, refuse, repress, resist, restrain, restrict, retard, scotch, snooker, spike, stall, sti-fle, stop, stymie, suppress, thwart, un-dermine, upset, withstand

hindering circumscriptive, contrary, counteractive, defensive, deterrent, dis-suasive, interventional, intrusive, ob-structive, off-putting, preclusive, preventive, prohibitive, prophylactic, repressive, restrictive, uncooperative, unhelpful, unwilling

hindmost back, end, last, rear, tail

hindrance circumscription, contrari-ness, control, counteraction, counter-measure, curb, detainment, detention, determent, discouragement, dissuasion, encumbrance, foiling, forestalling, fric-tion, frustration, hampering, impe-diment, injunction, interception, interdiction, interference, interposition, interruption, intervention, limitation, meddling, obstruction, obviation, op-position, preclusion, prevention, pro-hibition, refusal, repression, resistance, restraint, restriction, retardation, stop-ping, unwillingness

hint advice, clue, deduction, evidence, hunch, imply, induction, inference, inkling, insinuate, intimation, sugges-tion, suspicion, tip, trace

hire purchase credit, deferred pay-ment, instalments, the HP, the never-never, tick

hiss assibilation, boo, effervescence, fizz, froufrou, hush, jeer, lisp, plash, rale, rasp, rhonchus, rustle, shush, sibi-late, sizzle, sneeze, snuffle, splash, splutter, sputter, squash, squelch, squish, susurration, swish, swoosh, wheeze, whisper, whistle, white noise, whiz

hissing asthmatic, effervescent, fizzy, rustling, sibilant, sizzling, sneezing, wheezy, whispering

historian archaeologist, archivist, Assyriologist, biographer, Egyptologist, epigrapher, historiographer, palaeographer, palaeologist, palaeontologist, recorder, Sumerologist
See also list at **occupation**.

historic aboriginal, ancestral, ancient, antediluvian, antiquated, archaic, atavistic, classical, dated, diachronic, former, heroic, momentous, monumental, old, prehistoric, primal, primordial, prior, protohistoric, remaining, significant, vestigial

historical archaeological, epigraphical, historiographical, palaeographical, palaeological, prehistorical, protohistorical

history annals, antiquity, bygone days, chronicle, diary, historiography, life story, olden days, past, record, the past, yesteryear

hit affect, bang, bash, bastinado, bat, bayonetting, belabour, belt, biff, birch, blockbuster, blow, bonk, bop, box, buffet, cane, clobber, clout, coldcock, collide, cudgel, cuff, cut, dash, deck, dent, dint, drub, flagellate, flail, flay, flog, foin, fustigate, goring, horsewhip, impalement, jab, kick, knifing, knock, lambaste, lapidation, larrup, lash, lather, leather, lunge, paddle, pass, passado, paste, pelt, plunk, poke, pound, punch, rap, scourge, slam, slap, slipper, slog, slug, smack, sock, stab, stoning, strap, strike, stroke, swat, swing, success, swipe, switch, thrash, thrust, thump, thwack, trounce, wallop, welt, whack, whip, whop

hitting beating, bulldozing, bulling, butting, drumming, hammering, hiding, licking, pummelling, ramming, sledgehammering, smashing, spanking, tapping

hive antheap, anthill, apiary, beehive, hoard, store, termitarium, termite colony, vespiary, wasps' nest

hoard accumulate, cache, collect, save, scrimp, skimp, starve, stock, stint, treasure-trove

hoarse cawing, clanking, clinking, cracked, croaky, droning, dry, gravelly, gruff, gutteral, husky, low, nasal, nonresonant, rasping, rough, rusty, scraping, scratchy, stertorous, throaty, twanging

hoax bluff, deceive, deception, game, joke, leg-pull, rag, rag, sham, spoof, sport

holding
may indicate a hidden word or *a split word*

hole airhole, bayonet, blowhole, bore, borehole, burrow, buttonhole, cave, cavern, drill, excavate, excavation, eyehole, eyelet, fissure, gash, hollow, honeycomb, inject, keyhole, knife, knothole, lance, mine, peephole, penetrate, perforate, permeate, pierce, porthole, prick, probe, puncture, shaft, shoot, slash, slot, stab, trepan, trephine, tunnel, volcano, well

holed bored, cavernous, cribriform, excavated, hollowed, lanced, leaky, perforated, porous, punctured, sievelike, spongy, sunk

holiday break, breather, celebration, day off, fast day, feast, feast day, festival, festivity, fiesta, furlough, holy day, leave, peace, quiet, recess, recreation, relief, respite, sabbatical, time-out, vacation

home base, birthplace, cradle, domestic, domicile, fireside, habitat, hearth, homeland, homestead, in, inglenook, local, target, zoom in

homicide ethnic cleansing, fratricide, genocide, infanticide, manslaughter, matricide, murder, parricide, patricide, regicide, sororicide, tyrannicide, uxoricide

homing
may indicate a backword

honour accolade, award, badge, blue, decoration, esteem, exalt, favour, garter, glorify, gong, knight, lionize, medal, order, pips, prize, regard, respect, ribbon, spurs, star, stripes, title, value, wreathe

honourable above board, bona fide, candid, careful, chivalrous, conscientious, constant, decent, dependable, devoted, direct, dutiful, equitable, ethical, fair, faithful, fastidious, frank, gentlemanly, good, high-minded, honest, impartial, incorruptible, just, law-abiding, loyal, manifest, meticulous, moral, noble, open, overt, plain, principled, reliable, reputable, respectable, responsible, scrupulous, sincere, sound, sporting, steadfast, straight, straightforward, straight-up, sure, true, true-blue, trustworthy, truthful, unambiguous, undeceitful, upfront, upright, upstanding, veracious

hope assume, bank on, believe, bright side, buoyancy, cheerfulness, count on, feel confident, optimism, positive thinking, presume, rely on, rest assured, rose-coloured glasses, silver lining, wishful thinking

hopeful anticipating, bullish, buoyant, certain, cheerful, confident, desiring, optimistic, positive, sanguine, starry-eyed, sure, up, wanting

hopeless broken, cheerless, comfortless, cynical, defeated, dejected, depressed, desolate, despairing, desperate, despondent, disconsolate, discouraged, down, downcast, forlorn, gloomy, impenetrable, impervious, impractical, inaccessible, inoperable, insuperable, insurmountable, irrecoverable, irreparable, irrevocable, melancholic, negative, out, over, pessimistic, sceptical, suicidal, unachievable, unapproachable, unattainable, unavailable, unfeasible, unobtainable, unreachable, untenable, unviable, unworkable

hopelessness cynicism, defeatism, dejection, depression, despair, despondency, discouragement, doubt, impenetrability, imperviousness, impracticability, inaccessibility, inoperability, insuperability, insurmountability, melancholy, negativism, pessimism, scepticism, unattainability, unavailability, unfeasibility, unobtainability, unworkability

horizontal even, flat, flush, homaloidal, level, plain, planar, plane, smooth, tabular, two-dimensional, unwrinkled

horizontality evenness, flatness, flushness, levelness, lying, plainness, planeness, proneness, prostration, reclining, recumbency, smoothness, sprawling, supineness

horn alarm, antler, bugle, bullroarer, butt, hooter, klaxon, rattle, siren, trumpet, whistle
See also list at **orchestra**.

horny callous, corneous, leathery, lustful

horology clockmaking, watchmaking
See also list at **clock**.

horrible
may indicate an anagram

hors d'oeuvre antipasto, appetizer, blini, canapé, hummus, mezze, pakora, pâté, prawn cocktail, raita, samosa, smorgasbord, starter, taramasalata, vol-au-vent

horse ambler, bangtail, bay, bayo coyote, black, Black Beauty, Black Bess, bronco, brood mare, brumby, cayuse, Champion, charger, chestnut, cob, colt, courser, dam, dapplegrey, dobbin, dun, filly, foal, garron, garroway, gee-gee, gelding, GG, hack, hackney, horseflesh, hunter, jade, jennet, mare, montura, mount, mustang, nag, owlhead, packhorse, pad, pad-nag, palfrey, palomino, Pegasus, piebald, pinto, pony, quadruped, roadster, screw, sheltie, Silver, sire, skate, skewbald, sorrel, stallion, steed, stockhorse, strawberry roan, stud, Trigger, Velvet, warhorse, yearling

horseman black saddler, blacksmith, bookmaker, breaker, bronco-buster, buckaroo, cavalier, Cossack, cowboy, cowgirl, dragoon, drover, equestrian, equestrienne, eventer, farrier, gaucho, groom, horse doctor, huntsman, hussar, jockette, jockey, kennel man, knight errant, lancer, loriner, Mountie, ostler, postboy, postilion, racing steward, roughrider, saddler, show jumper, sowar, stable boy, steeplechaser, trainer, vet

horsemanship bareback riding, dressage, equestrianism, equitation, eventing, gymkhana, horseracing, manège, point-to-point racing, polo, pony trekking, riding, show jumping, steeplechasing

horticulture arboriculture, citriculture, floriculture, fruitage, gardening, market gardening, pomiculture, silviculture, viniculture, viticulture

horticulturist arboriculturist, floriculturist, fruiter, gardener, landscapist, market gardener, nurseryman, orchardist, plantsman, pomologist, rosarian, seedsman, topiarist, undergardener, viniculturist

hose bathe, douche, inject, lave, pipe, rinse, socks, sponge, squirt, stockings, syringe, wash

hospital asylum, clinic, dispensary, hospice, infirmary, lazaretto, sanatorium, surgery

host compère, entertain, fete, horde, introduce, invite, landlady, landlord, master of ceremonies, MC, multitude, regale, throng, swarm

hostile acrimonious, aloof, antagonistic, antipathetic, antisocial, baneful, beastly, bellicose, belligerent, bitter, brawling, cold, conflicting, cool, envious, eristic, feuding, fighting, icy, ill-disposed, inhospitable, inimical, jealous, malevolent, malicious, mean, nasty, poisonous, polemical, provocative, pugnacious, rancorous, resentful, snide, sore, sour, spiteful, splenetic, strained, tense, truculent, unamiable, uncordial, unfriendly, unharmonious, unsympathetic, venomous, vindictive, viperish, virulent, vitriolic, warlike, waspish

hot blistering, boiling, calefacient, calorific, candent, cauterizing, equatorial, fiery, fresh, fuggy, glowing, incandescent, lukewarm, mild, molten, new, red-hot, roasting, scalding, scorching, searing, simmering, sizzling, smoking, snug, steaming, stifling, stuffy, subtropical, suffocating, sultry, sweltering, tepid, thermal, tropical, warm

hotch potch *may indicate an anagram*

hotel boarding house, boozer, guest house, hostel, hostelry, inn, local, motel, pension, tavern

hourglass chronograph, chronoscope, egg timer, sandglass, sundial

house accommodate, apartment, bedsit, bingo, bungalow, cabin, chalet, cottage, detached house, dynasty, farmhouse, flat, House of Commons, House of Lords, love nest, maisonette, penthouse, pied-à-terre, semi, snuggery, store, studio, terraced house, town house, two-up-two-down, villa

householder addressee, boarder, flatmate, freeholder, guest, leaseholder, lessee, lodger, (owner-)occupier, paying guest, renter, roomer, roommate, tenant

housework clearing up, dry-cleaning, dusting, hoovering, laundry, mopping up, polishing, scrubbing, spring-cleaning, sweeping, tidying, vacuuming, washing, washing-up, wiping up

hum bombinate, buzz, drone, murmur, mutter, purr, stink, whirr, witter

human anthropocentric, anthropoid,

153

anthropological, anthropomorphic, bionic, civilized, creaturely, earthborn, fleshly, hominoid, humanistic, humanlike, humanoid, individual, mortal, personal, subhuman, tellurian

humankind earthlings, hominid, Homo sapiens, humanity, man, mankind, people, womankind

humble harmless, inoffensive, meek, modest, mouselike, unassuming, undistinguished, unimportant, unpretentious

humbled abashed, abject, broken-spirited, brought down, chagrined, crestfallen, crushed, dashed, debunked, defeated, deflated, degraded, dejected, diminished, disapproved, discomfited, disconcerted, embarrassed, hangdog, humiliated, laid low, lowered, mortified, rebuked, reduced, scorned, shamed, shamefaced, sheepish, squashed, wounded

humidity clamminess, closeness, dankness, dew point, humidification, moisture, mugginess, saturation, stickiness

humiliate abash, chasten, crush, degrade, disconcert, embarrass, humble, mortify, sit on, slight, snub, squash

humiliation come-down, deflation, descent, embarrassment, mortification

humility humbleness, meekness, modesty, simplicity, undistinguished, unimportance, unpretentiousness

humming bombination, buzzing, droning, monotonous, murmur, mutter, purr, repetitive, stench, stridulous, unvaried, whirring

humorist buffoon, caricaturist, cartoonist, clown, comedian, comic, gagster, ironist, jester, joker, jokesmith, lampooner, satirist, stand-up comic, tease(r), wag, wisecracker, wit

humorous amusing, comic, corny, droll, facetious, farcical, flippant, funny, ironic, jocose, jocular, jokey, joking, merry, pawky, quirky, sarcastic, satirical, slapstick, teasing, waggish, whimsical, witty, zany

humour bootlick, cajole, comedy, condescend, cosset, cultivate, flatter, gratify, indulge, pamper, patronize, placate, please, smarm, soft-soap, spoil, toady to

humouring ingratiating, oily, servile, slimy, smarmy, sycophantic, toadying, unctuous

humours choleric, melancholic, phlegmatic, sanguine

hundred C, centenarian, centenary, centennial, centennium, centesimal, centigrade, centimetre, centipede, centuple, centuplicate, centurion, century, ct, cwt, gross, hundredfold, hundredweight, monkey, percent, ton

hunger appetite, binge, bolting, craving, desire, devouring, engorgement, famine, feasting, gluttony, gobbling, gorging, gourmandism, greed, guzzling, overeating, overindulgence, starvation, thirst, voraciousness, wolfishness, yearning

hungry dehydrated, dry, eager, empty, famished, half-starved, parched, peckish, ravenous, starving, thirsty

hunt angle, bag, beat, catch, chase, course, ensnare, fish, flush, fowl, guddle, hawk, hook, lay traps, net, poach, set snares, shoot, shrimp, stalk, start game, start up, trap, trawl, whale

hunter angler, Artemis, beater, big-game hunter, cannibal, Diana, falcon, falconer, fisherman, fowler, guddler, gun, gun dog, hawk, hawker, headhunter, hounds, huntress, huntsman, marksman, mouser, Nimrod, Orion, oysterman, pack, piscator, poacher, rat-catcher, shot, shrimper, stalker, tracker, trailer, trapper, trawlerman, whaler, whipper-in

hurt ache, agonize, batter, beat, bite, blast, bore, bruise, bump, burn, castrate, chafe, claw, contuse, cramp, cripple, crucify, curtail, cut, damage, damnify, decay, demoralization, depletion, disable, disfigure, dislocation, dock, draining, eviscerate, excruciate, flinch, flog, fracture, fret, gash, gnaw, graze, grind, grip, hamper, hamstring, harm, harrow, hinder, hit, hobbling, impair, impale, injure, invade, jab, knife, lame, lameness, maim, mangle, martyr, maul, mischief, mutilation, nip, nobbling, pain, pinch, plague, pound, prick, puncture, punish, rack, sap, savage, scald, scar, scathe, scotch, scrape, scratch, sear, shake, shoot, slash, smart, smash, sprain, squirm, stab, sting, strain, suffer, tear, thrash, throb, tingle, torment, torture, traumatize, tweak, twitch, undermine, weaken, wince, wound, wring, writhe

husband benedick, bigamist, consort, cuckold, househusband, hubby, monogamist, monogynist, old man, polygamist, polygynist

hydraulics hydrodynamics, hydrogeology, hydrokinetics, hydrology, hydrometry, hydrostatics

hygiene antisepsis, asepsis, chlorination, cleanliness, decontamination, disinfection, fumigation, immunity, inoculation, isolation, pasteurization, prophylaxis, protection, purification, quarantine, sanitation, sterilization, vaccination

hygienic antiseptic, aseptic, chlorinated, clean, disinfected, germ-free, healthy, innocuous, pasteurized, pure, refreshing, remedial, restorative, salubrious, salutary, sanative, sanitary, sterilized, uninfectious, wholesome

hymn anthem, antiphon, carol, chant, cherubicon, doxology, exultet, gospel song, kanon, kontakion, mantra, paean, plainsong, psalm, response

hypocrisy artifice, blandishments, blarney, bubble, camouflage, cant, charlatanism, chicanery, concealment, crocodile tears, cupboard love, deception, delusion, disguise, disingenuousness, dissembling, double-dealing, duplicity, empty gesture, evasion, fakery, falseness, flattery, guile, hollowness, humbug, insincerity, lip service, mealy-mouthedness, mendacity, meretriciousness, mockery, mountebankery, mouthing, mummery, oiliness, ostentatiousness, Pecksniffery, Pharisaism, play-acting, pretence, quackery, religiosity, sanctimony, sham, sweet-talk, Tartuffery, tokenism, uncandidness, unctuousness, unfrankness, varnish, veneer, window-dressing

hypocrite apostate, canter, fairweather friend, mealy-mouth, phoney, sham, snuffler, spy, turncoat, whited sepulchre

hypocritical deceptive, delusive, dishonest, disingenuous, fake, false, feigning, fraudulent, insincere, lying, mealy-mouthed, mendacious, meretricious, oily, Pecksniffian, Pharisaic, phoney, pretending, pseudo, religiose, sham, so-called, soft-soaping, sweet-talking, tongue-in-cheek, two-timing

·I·

I	iodine • island • myself • one (Roman numeral)
IBID	in the same place (Latin: *ibidem*)
IC	identity card • in charge
ICU	intensive care unit
ID	identity • I had • Intelligence Department • I would
IE	that is (Latin: *id est*)
II	eleven • team
IM	I am
IQ	intelligence quotient • the same as (Latin: *idem quod*)
IV	intravenous

ice berg, diamonds, floe, freeze-up, frost, glacier, icicle, Jack Frost, rime, sleet

ichthyological fishy, piscatorial, piscicultural, scaly, squamous

ichthyologist aquarist, ichthyophile, pisciculturist

idea abstraction, apprehension, assumption, attitude, awareness, belief, brainchild, brainwave, comprehension, concept, conclusion, conjecture, construct, essence, estimation, fancy, feeling, fiction, hypothesis, ideatum, imago, inkling, intuition, memory, notion, noumenon, observation, perception, precept, premise, presumption, principle, quantum leap, reaction, reflection, sentiment, supposition, surmise, theory, thinking, thought, understanding

ideal archetype, archetypical, dream(y), epitome, exemplary, fancy, fantastic, fantasy, idealistic, ideological, impractical, model, optimistic, paradigm, paradigmatic, paragon, pattern, prototype, prototypical, quintessential, romantic, sentimental, standard, utopian, vision, visionary, wishful thinking

idealism daydreaming, fable, Hegelianism, ideality, idealization, impracticality, Kantianism, millennium, myth, Neo-Platonism, optimism, Platonism, romanticism, transcendentalism, utopianism, visionariness, wishful thinking

idealistic Hegelian, impractical, Kantian, Neo-Platonic, optimistic, Platonic, romantic

ideality absurdity, appearance, brainchild, caprice, conceit, concept, crinkum-crankum, daydream, exaggeration, extravaganza, fairy tale, falsehood, fantasy, fiction, figment, idea, idealization, image, impression, maggot, notion, picture, poetic licence, projection, quixotry, rhapsody, romance, sciamachy, shadow-boxing, thought, unreality, vagary, whim, whimsy

idealize deify, exalt, put on a pedestal, romanticize

ideational aware, cerebral, conceived, conceptualized, creative, fanciful, imagined, ingenious, inspired, intellectual, inventive, mental, original, reflective, visualized

identification analysis, authentication, autograph, badge, bookplate, cachet, card, cataloguing, categorization, certificate, characteristic, characterization, chit, classification, colophon, colour, corroboration, credentials, denomination, designation, detection, diagnosis, differentiation, docket, emblem, endorsement, establishing, fingerprint, form, hallmark, ID, impress, imprint, indication, initials, label, letterhead, logo, mannerism, mark, monogram, name, nameplate, outline, passport, password, permit, pinpointing, recognition, seal, shape, shibboleth, sigil, signature, signet, size, sticker, substantiation, superscription, tag, tally, tessera, ticket, title, token, trademark, trait, verification, visa, watermark

identified branded, categorized, characterized, classified, corroborated, denoted, designated, earmarked, fingerprinted, hallmarked, known, labelled, marked, photographed, recognized, referenced, substantiated, tagged, tattooed, trademarked

identify analyse, annotate, blaze, brand, catalogue, categorize, chalk, classify, corroborate, designate, detect, diagnose, differentiate, disfigure, distinguish, docket, earmark, emblazon, emboss, engrave, establish, etch, exhibit, hallmark, impress, imprint, indicate, label, limit, mark off, name, notch, overprint, photograph, pierce, pinpoint, point out, punch, recognize, record, reference, register, scar, seal, show, specify, stamp, substantiate, tab, tag, tattoo, tick, ticket, underline, underscore

identity distinctiveness, individuality, name, particularity, personality, self, uniqueness

ideology beliefs, credo, creed, ethos, ideals, manifesto, morals, opinion, philosophy, position, prejudices, principles, stance, stand, standards, teachings, tenets, view

idiosyncrasy kink, mannerism, peculiarity, quirk

idiot buffoon, clown, eccentric, fool, nut, twit

idiotic
may indicate an anagram

idleness dawdling, delay, dullness, indolence, languor, laziness, lethargy, listlessness, procrastination, sloth, slowness, sluggishness, torpor

idol deity, effigy, fetish, god, icon, image, joss, lingam, symbol, yoni

idolatrize admire, apotheosize, deify, fetishize, heathenize, hero-worship, idealize, idolize, lionize, paganize, totemize

idolatry allotheism, ancestor-worship, animism, anthropolatry, bibliolatry, cult, demonism, dendrolatry, devilry, devil worship, diabolism, ecclesiolatry, fetishism, heathenism, heliolatry, iconolatry, Mammonism, necrolatry, obi, ophiolatry, paganism, pagano-Christianism, phallicism, priestcraft, pyrolatry, Sabaism, Satanism, superstition, theriolatry, totemism, zoolatry *See also list at* **God**.

ignorance artlessness, awkwardness, backwardness, blankness, empty-headedness, folly, gaucherie, illiteracy, incognizance, incomprehension, innocence, insensibility, naivety, nescience, nonrecognition, stupidity, unawareness, uncertainty, unconsciousness, unenlightenment, unfamiliarity, unintelligence, unskilfulness

ignorant awkward, backward, blank, clueless, dim-witted, dull, dumb, empty-headed, gauche, green, illiterate, incognizant, innocent, low-brow, misled, naive, nerdy, nescient, oblivious, Philistine, simple, slow-witted, stupid, thick, unaware, unconscious, uneducated, unenlightened, uninformed, uninitiated, unknowing, unskilled, unwitting

ignore avoid, ban, banish, blackball, blacklist, blink at, boycott, cold-shoulder, conceal, confine, deport, disbar, displace, disregard, exclude, exile, expel, imprison, isolate, jail, ostracize, outlaw, overlook, prohibit, quarantine, rebuff, reject, repel, seclude, segregate, sequester, shun, snub, wink at

ill anaemic, anorexic, asthenic, badly, bloodless, crippled, decrepit, dimwitted, emaciated, faint, feeble, feebleminded, frail, gammy, groggy, hobbling, infirm, lame, languid, pale, pallid, poorly, shaky, sickly, skin-and-bone, skinny, slow, thin, unwell, wasted, weakly
may indicate an anagram

illness addiction, affliction, ailment, apoplexy, attack, bug, complaint, complication, condition, contagion, disease, disorder, distemper, epidemic, fever, fit, indisposition, infection, malady, malaise, malnutrition, nausea, pestilence, plague, poisoning, seizure, shock, sickness, spasm, visitation

illogical arbitrary, distant, forced, impractical, incoherent, irrational, laboured, out-of-the-way, random, self-contradictory, silly, strained

ill-treat abuse, burden, crush, distress, harass, mishandle, misuse, molest, oppress, persecute, torment, violate, wrong
may indicate an anagram

illusion chimera, daydream, doppelgänger, fancy, fantasy, Fata Morgana, figment, ghost, hallucination, ignis fatuus, jack-o'-lantern, mirage, nightmare, phantasmagoria, pipe dream, shade, spectre, spirit, spook, will-o'-the-wisp, wraith

illusory chimerical, delusory, dreamlike, fanciful, fantastic, figmental, hallucinatory, imaginary, phantasmagorical, subjective, visional

image after-image, appearance, bust, duplicate, effigy, figure, figurine, gargoyle, hologram, icon, idea, idol, likeness, model, photograph, projection, reflection, sculpture, silhouette, statue, statuette, symbol, thought, visual, waxwork

imaginable conceivable, fanciable, plausible, possible, thinkable

imaginary abstract, chimerical, conceptual, contrived, created, devised, dreamy, ethereal, fabricated, fabulous, fanciful, fictional, fictitious, hypothetical, ideal, illusory, invented, legendary, make-believe, mythical, nonexistent, notional, pretend, shadowy, simulated, storybook, subjective, suppositional, unreal, untrue, visionary
See list of imaginary places.

imagination apparition, artistry, chimera, clairvoyance, conceptualization, creativity, crystal-gazing, daydreaming, enterprise, fancifulness, fantasy, figment, hallucination, illusion, imagery, ingenuity, inspiration, invention, inventiveness, mirage, objectification, originality, perception, phantom, pipedream, resourcefulness, scrying, semblance, skill, stargazing, vision, visualization, word-painting

imaginative clever, creative, dreamy,

IMAGINARY PLACES

ASGARD	EMERALD CITY	LAPUTA	PERN
ATLANTIS	EREWHON	LILLIPUT	RURITANIA
AVALON	FLATLAND	LOOKING-GLASS	SHANGRI-LA
BROBDINGNAG	FORTUNATE ISLES	LAND	TREASURE ISLAND
CAMELOT	FOUNTAIN OF	LYONNESSE	UTOPIA
CLOUDCUCKOO-	YOUTH	MIDDLE-EARTH	VALHALLA
LAND	GARDEN OF EDEN	NARNIA	WONDERLAND
COCKAIGNE	HOUYHNHNM	NEVER-NEVER LAND	ZANTH
DRACULA'S CASTLE	LAND	OLYMPUS	
EL DORADO	ISLANDIA	OZ	

eidetic, enterprising, enthusiastic, exaggerated, fancy-led, fictional, highflown, idealistic, ingenious, innovative, inspired, inventive, lively, original, perceptive, poetic, resourceful, rhapsodic, romancing, skilful, utopian, visualizing, vivid

imagine coin, conceive, conceptualize, concoct, conjure up, create, crystalgaze, daydream, deliberate, devise, dream, envisage, envision, exaggerate, excogitate, fabricate, fancy, fantasize, feel, foresee, formulate, hallucinate, hatch, idealize, ideate, improvise, invent, make believe, make up, originate, perceive, picture, pipedream, pretend, produce, reflect, romanticize, scry, stargaze, summon up, suppose, think, visualize

imitate alliterate, ape, burlesque, camouflage, caricature, clone, copy, counterfeit, duplicate, echo, emulate, fax, flatter, follow, impersonate, mime, mimic, mirror, mock, parody, parrot, portray, reflect, repeat, replicate, reproduce, rhyme, satirize, simulate, spoof, travesty, Xerox

imitation artifact, artificiality, canon, conformity, copied, copycat, counterfeit, cultured, echo, emulation, ersatz, fake, following, forged, fugue, image, impersonation, imposture, literalism, man-made, mimesis, mirroring, mock, onomatopoeia, parody, phoney, plagiarized, pseudo, reflection, repetition, representation, shadow, sham, simulation, slavishness, so-called, synthetic

imitative apish, artificial, bogus, copied, counterfeit, cultured, derivative, echoic, emulating, fake, following, forged, man-made, mimetic, mock, onomatopoeic, parodied, parrot-like, phoney, plastic, posing, quack, rubbishy, sham, shoddy, simulated, substituted, synthetic, transcribed, unnatural, unoriginal

immaterial airy, celestial, dematerializing, disembodied, disincarnated, eternal, ethereal, extramundane, ghostly, heavenly, higher, illusory, imaginary, impalpable, imponderable, incorporeal, insubstantial, intangible, irrelevant, metaphysical, nonmaterial, nonphysical, otherworldly, perpetual, psychic, religious, shadowy, spiritual, supernal, transcendent, unearthly, unreal, unworldly

immature adolescent, amateurish, apprentice, aspiring, backward, budding, callow, childish, clean, crude, dewy, elementary, embryonic, forced, forward, fresh, green, imperfect, inchoate, inexperienced, ingenuous, innocent, juvenile, larval, naive, newborn, nonadult, novice, parvenu, precocious, premature, puerile, pupal, raw, retarded, rough-hewn, rudimentary, unblown, unborn, uncut, undeveloped, unfashioned, unfinished, unfledged, unformed, ungrown, unhatched, unhewn, unmellowed, unpolished, unripe, unseasoned, unworked, unwrought, upstart, virginal, young, youthful
may indicate a shortening

immaturity awkwardness, callowness, childishness, cleanness, coarseness, crudeness, dewiness, freshness, greenness, imperfection, incompleteness, inexperience, ingenuousness, innocence, naivety, newness, precocity, prematurity, rawness, undevelopment, unripeness, virginity, youth

immeasurability countlessness, incalculability, incomprehensibility, indeterminableness, innumerability, numberlessness

immeasurable astronomical, enormous, immense, incalculable, incomprehensible, indeterminate, inestimable, innumerable, mind-boggling, myriad, numberless, transcendent, uncountable, unfathomable, untold, vast

immediacy directness, emergency,

exigency, instantaneousness, promptness, urgency

immediate direct, fast, instantaneous, on-the-spot, prompt, quick, rapid, speedy, split-second, swift, urgent

immerse absorb, baptize, bury, dip, drench, duck, dunk, flood, immerge, inter, occupy, plunge, souse, steep, submerge, submersed

immersion baptism, bath, burial, dip, ducking, interment, plunge, submersion

imminent expected, forthcoming, impending, looming, soon

immobilize catch, jam, lock, lodge, stalemate, stick, suspend

immoral amoral, bad, carnal, corrupt, criminal, debauched, degenerate, degraded, depraved, disgraceful, dishonest, dishonourable, evil, gross, illegal, impure, indecent, infamous, lustful, obscene, outrageous, perverse, profligate, ruined, sacrilegious, scandalous, scarlet, shameful, shocking, unchaste, unethical, unprincipled, unscrupulous, unvirtuous, vicious, vulgar, wicked, wrong

immorality amorality, badness, criminality, dishonesty, evil, moral turpitude, unethicalness, unscrupulousness, vice, viciousness, wickedness, wrong

immune exempt, inoculated, invulnerable, protected

immunization inoculation, safeguarding, vaccination

immutability continuance, continuity, inevitability, permanence, perpetuity

imp elf, hobgoblin, limb, little devil, rascal

impair botch, bungle, damage, deactivate, destroy, dismantle, mar, maul, meddle, mess up, ruin, spoil, tamper, tinker, trifle with
may indicate an anagram

impairment adulteration, contagion, contamination, damage, debasement, demolition, derangement, destruction, detriment, devastation, havoc, infection, loss, ruination, spoiling, waste

impartial broad-minded, disinterested, equanimous, fair, indiscriminate, just, liberal, moderate, mugwumpish, neutral, nonaligned, nonjudgmental, nonpartisan, objective, open-minded, tolerant, unbiased, uncriticizing, unprejudiced

impartiality broad-mindedness, disinterest, equanimity, fairness, indiscrimination, justice, moderation, mugwumpism, neutrality, nonalignment, objectivity, tolerance

impel accelerate, actuate, animate, butt, compel, dig, drive, eject, elbow, expel, frogmarch, galvanize, goad, heave, hustle, incite, jerk, jog, joggle, jolt, jostle, motivate, move, poke, power, press, prod, project, propel, push, run, shoulder, shove, spur, start, stress, thrust, thwack, traject, tug, urge, wrench

impelling driving, dynamic, flogging, impellent, impulsive, motive, moving, pulsive, ramming, smashing, thrashing, thrustful, thrusting

impending approaching, forthcoming, hanging, imminent, looming, on the horizon

impenitence callousness, cold-heartedness, hardness, incorrigibility, induration, nonrepentance, obduracy, obstinacy, pitilessness, remorselessness, shamelessness, stubbornness

impenitent brazen, callous, cold-hearted, dyed-in-the-wool, hardened, hard-hearted, heartless, incorrigible, inveterate, irredeemable, obdurate, obstinate, remorseless, shameless, unapologetic, unashamed, unblushing, unmoved, unrecanting, unreformed, unregretting, unrepentant, unshriven

imperceptible faint, inconspicuous,

indistinct, inaudible, intangible, invisible, shadowy, unimpressive, vague

imperfect bad, below par, blemished, botched, broken, bungled, chipped, corked, cracked, damaged, defective, dodgy, fallible, faulty, flawed, inferior, irregular, leaky, marked, off, off-colour, off form, overripe, patchy, peccable, poor, scratched, second-best, second-rate, soiled, spotted, stained, stale, tainted, unacceptable, uneven, unfit, unhealthy, unimpressive, unsatisfactory, unsound, unsteady, vulnerable, weak, worthless
may indicate an anagram

imperfection adulteration, botch, bungle, carelessness, crudeness, curate's egg, cursoriness, damage, defectiveness, deficiency, deformity, distortion, erroneousness, failure, fallibility, faultiness, frailty, immaturity, inadequacy, incompleteness, inferiority, infirmity, insufficiency, irregularity, lack, need, overripeness, patchiness, peccability, peccadillo, perfectibility, perfunctoriness, rawness, requirement, second rate, shortfall, staleness, underachievement, undevelopment, unevenness, unfitness, unripeness, unsoundness, vulnerability, want, weakness, worthlessness

impermanent mortal, nondurable, one-off, temporary, throwaway

imperviousness impassability, impenetrability, impercipience, impermeability, obstruction, obtuseness, occlusion, unawareness

impetuosity flightiness, foolhardiness, impulsiveness, precipitance, rashness, recklessness

impious accursed, blasphemous, damned, devilish, diabolical, fiendish, infernal, irreligious, Mephistophelian, profane, reprobate, sacrilegious, satanic, ungodly

imply allude, connote, hint, implicate, indicate, insinuate, intimate, involve, mean, spell, suggest, symbolize

importance affirmation, concern, consequence, degree, distinction, eminence, emphasis, essentiality, excellence, gravity, import, influence, insistence, interest, irreplaceability, mark, materiality, memorability, merit, moment, momentousness, note, noteworthiness, paramountcy, power, precedence, pre-eminence, prestige, primacy, priority, prominence, rank, rating, reputation, seriousness, severity, significance, solemnity, standing, status, stress, substance, superiority, supremacy, urgency, use, value, weight, weightiness, worth

important basic, bedrock, big, capital, cardinal, central, chief, consequential, considerable, critical, crucial, distinct, earth-shaking, eminent, essential, fateful, foremost, fundamental, grand, grave, great, helpful, high, high-level, high-priority, imperative, indispensable, irreplaceable, key, leading, life-and-death, main, major, material, meaningful, momentous, necessary, noble, overriding, overruling, paramount, pivotal, pre-eminent, primary, prime, prominent, radical, relevant, required, serious, significant, solemn, staple, summit, superior, supreme, telling, top, top-level, top-secret, trenchant, uppermost, urgent, useful, valuable, vital, weighty, world-shattering, worthwhile

impose awe, enforce, impress, inflict, overwhelm, rank high

impossibility absurdity, illogicality, inconceivability, nonexistence, paradox, self-contradiction, unimaginability, unreality, unthinkability

impossible absurd, illogical, inconceivable, irrational, paradoxical, preposterous, ridiculous, self-contradictory, self-defeating, unimaginable, unquestionable, unreasonable, unthinkable

impotent debilitated, disabled, drifting, etiolated, exhausted, fatigued, feeble, frail, helpless, incapacitated, paralysed, tired, unconscious, weak

impoverish bankrupt, beggar, deprive, disendow, disinherit, dispossess, fleece, pauperize, rob, ruin, strip

impression belief, clairvoyance, dent, divination, edition, effect, face value, fancy, hint, hunch, idea, image, impact, impersonation, imprint, impulse, inkling, insight, instinct, intimation, intuition, notion, nuance, parody, presentiment, reflection, reflex, representation, similarity, suggestion, undercurrent, vibes

impressionable adapting, appeasing, complying, easing, formable, mollifying, nonresistive, sensitive, susceptible

imprison confine, detain, impound, incarcerate, intern, jail, jug, lock up, put away, send down

imprisoned behind bars, captive, confined, doing time, in, incarcerated, in detention, inside, in stir, interned, on remand, restricted
may indicate a split word

imprisonment captivity, confinement, durance, forced labour, immurement, internment, porridge, solitary

improbability doubt, long odds, long shot, outside chance, uncertainty, unlikeliness

improbable doubtful, dubious, far-fetched, inauspicious, remote, uncertain, unexpected, unlikely, unpromising, unrealistic

improbity badness, baseness, bias, chicanery, contrivance, corruption, crookedness, debasement, depravity, deviousness, disgrace, dishonesty, dishonour, disingenuousness, disrepute, disrespect, evilness, falsehood, foul play, hypocrisy, immorality, indecency, injustice, insincerity, knavery, lie, opportunism, partiality, prejudice, shame, trickery, turpitude, unfairness, unscrupulousness, untruthfulness, venality, villainy, wickedness, worthlessness

improper inappropriate, inapt, incongruous, incorrect, indecorous, unbecoming, unfit, unseemly, unsuitable, vulgar

impropriety boorishness, churlishness, coarseness, crudeness, discourtesy, grossness, indecorousness, indelicacy, roughness, rudeness, tastelessness, uncouthness, unrefinement, unseemliness, vulgarity

improvable ameliorable, corrigible, curable, perfectible, reformable

improve advance, ameliorate, beautify, better, convalesce, cure, develop, do up, elaborate, elevate, encourage, enhance, enrich, evolve, forward, foster, further, graduate, increase, learn, make headway, make progress, mature, mellow, mend, modernize, perfect, pick up, polish, progress, promote, prosper, purify, raise, rally, recondition, recover, recruit, rectify, recuperate, redeem, refine, reform, refresh, refurbish, regenerate, rehabilitate, renew, renovate, repair, restore, revive, ripen, shape up, study, sublimate, succeed, upgrade, uplift, vamp up

improved beautified, better, edited, enhanced, modernized, recovering, recuperating, reformed, renovated, repaired, restored, revised, rewritten, rising, superior, transformed, wiser

improvement amelioration, betterment, cure, decoration, elaboration, enhancement, face-lift, furtherance, headway, modernization, ornamentation, perfection, polish, progress, promotion, reconditioning, recovery, refinement, reform, refreshment, refurbishment, regeneration, rehabilitation, remedy, renewal, renovation, repair, restoration, revival, rise, sea change, sublimation, upgrading, uplift, upswing, upturn

improving ameliorative, chiliastic, cultural, extreme, idealistic, millenarian, perfectionist, progressive, radical, reformative, remedial, restorative, utopian

improvise ad-lib, blurt, contrive, devise, extemporize, invent, jam, think up, vamp

improvised ad hoc, ad-lib, catch-as-catch-can, extemporaneous, impromptu, inventive, jury-rigged, makeshift, offhand, off-the-cuff, spontaneous, uncalculated, unpremeditated, unprepared, unrehearsed

impudent bold, brassy, brazen, cheeky, cocky, flippant, fresh, impertinent, pert, shameless, unblushing

impulsion compulsion, force, impellent, impetus, incentive, incitement, momentum, power, propulsion

in amid, at home, batting, fashionable, not out, trendy, wearing
may indicate a hidden word

inaccuracy approximation, carelessness, generalization, guesswork, imprecision, inexactness, laxity, looseness, negligence, randomness, sloppiness, speculation

inaccurate distorted, illogical, inconsistent, inexact, loose, self-contradictory, vague
may indicate an anagram

inaction abeyance, abstention, apathy, avoidance, calm, cowardice, deadlock, defeatism, delay, doldrums, do-nothingism, dormancy, Fabianism, idleness, immobility, impassivity, impotence, inactivity, indifference, indolence, inertia, insensibility, laziness, leisure, loafing, motionlessness, neglect, negligence, noninterference, nonintervention, nonuse, paralysis, passivity, procrastination, quiescence, quiet, redundancy, refraining, relaxation, repose, rest, sinecure, stagnation, stalemate, standstill, stillness, stop, suspension, tranquillity, unemployment, vegetation

inactive abstaining, apathetic, be-numbed, blind, calm, cunctative, dead, deadlocked, deaf, dormant, dull, extinct, Fabian, fallow, frozen, half-dead, hands-off, idle, immobile, impassive, impotent, inanimate, indifferent, indolent, inert, inoperative, insensible, jobless, laid off, lazy, leisured, lifeless, loafing, lounging, mooching, motionless, negligent, neutral, ostrich-like, paralysed, passive, phlegmatic, powerless, procrastinating, quiescent, quiet, redundant, refraining, relaxed, sedentary, skiving, slouching, sluggish, stagnant, stalemated, static, stationary, still, suspended, tranquil, unemployed, unoccupied

inactivity cessation, extinction, immobility, inertia, inertness, lifelessness, lull, passivity, quiescence, quietness, silence, stillness, suspension

inadequacy dearth, deficiency, fault, flaw, insufficiency, lack, meagreness, paucity, scantness, scarcity, shortage, skimpiness

inadequate deficient, insufficient, lacking, meagre, not up to scratch, scant, scarce, skimpy, substandard

inadmissible extra, foreign, peripheral, unacceptable, unusable

inalienable inviolable, sacrosanct, uninfringeable, unquestionable

inanimate dead, inert, inorganic, insentient, lifeless, mineral

inappropriateness impropriety, inadmissibility, inapplicability, inappositeness, inaptitude, incapacity, incompetence, inelegance, inexpedience, infelicity, intrusiveness, irrelevance, undecorousness, unfitness, unskilfulness, unsuitability, untimeliness, wrongness

inarticulate aphasic, babbling, dysphasic, dysphemic, hissing, incoherent, jumbled, lisping, paraphasic, sibilant, sighing, stammering, stuttering, unintelligible

inattention aberration, apathy, carelessness, cold shoulder, desultoriness, detachment, disregard, distraction, forgetfulness, heedlessness, indifference, nonobservance, obliviousness, rashness, superficiality, thoughtlessness, unmindfulness

inattentive apathetic, detached, disregarding, distracted, forgetful, heedless, listless, oblivious, thoughtless, unconcerned, unmindful, unobservant, unthinking

inaugural establishing, foundational, inauguratory, inchoative, incipient, instigatory, institutionary

inaugurate auspicate, broach, cause, commission, erect, establish, float, found, induct, initiate, install, instigate, institute, launch, open, premiere, present, set up, start up, unveil

inauguration embarkation, establishment, foundation, inception, inchoation, incipience, installation, instigation, institution, launch, setting up

inauspicious accursed, adverse, doomed, ill-omened, ill-starred, jinxed, ominous, unfavourable, unfortunate, unlucky, unpropitious

incapacitate cripple, disable, immobilize, paralyse, stun

incense ambergris, anger, aroma, camphor, chypre, civet, enrage, eucalyptus, frangipani, frankincense, infuriate, joss stick, musk, myrrh, olibanum, otto, patchouli, perfume, resin, sandalwood, spikenard, vetiver

incentive fillip, goad, inducement, nudge, prod, slap, spur, stimulus, threat

incisive keen, meaty, penetrating, pithy, pointed, sententious, thought-provoking, trenchant

incite aggravate, anger, enrage, exacerbate, exasperate, foment, goad, inflame, infuriate, irritate, jolt, madden, sharpen, whet, whip up

inclination aptitude, bent, bias, choice, eagerness, favour, intention, leaning, mind, partiality, penchant, predilection, predisposition, preference, prejudice, proclivity, propensity, readiness, selection, slope, tendency, turn, willingness

include accommodate, admit, allow, boast, compose, comprehend, comprise, consist of, constitute, contain, count, cover, embody, embrace, encapsulate, encircle, enclose, encompass, envelop, have, hold, implicate, incorporate, integrate, involve, mean, number, receive, recognize
may indicate a split word

included added, admissible, appurtenant, built-in, combined, component, constituent, entered, inherent, integrated, intrinsic, joined, linked, listed, merged, noted, pertinent, recorded

including across-the-board, all-in, blanket, broad-based, comprehensive, encyclopedic, expansive, extensive, general, global, nondiscriminatory, nonexclusive, overall, umbrella, wall-to-wall, wholesale, widespread

inclusion accommodation, admission, comprehension, comprisal, containment, elegibility, embodiment, encapsulation, encirclement, enclosure, implication, incorporation, integration, involvement, membership, participation, presence, reception

inclusive comprehensive, embodied, encompassing, incorporated

income aliment, alimony, allowance, annuity, bursary, earnings, emolument, fees, fellowship, grant, maintenance, palimony, pay, pension, privy purse, remuneration, salary, scholarship, tontine, wages

incomplete abbreviated, abridged, bitty, blemished, broken, cropped, crude, cursory, curtailed, defective, deficient, docked, exaggerated, flawed, fragmentary, garbled, half-filled, half-finished, half-hearted, immature, impaired, imperfect, inadequate, ineffective, ineffectual, insufficient, interrupted, jerry-built, lacking, lopped, maimed, makeshift, missing, needing, omitting, overwrought, partial, perfunctory, provisional, raw, requiring, scant, scrappy, scratch, short, shortened, short of, shy of, sketchy, skimpy, stained, truncated, under-developed, underdone, undermanned, undeveloped, unequipped, unfilled, unfinished, unpolished, unprepared, unready, unrefined, unripe, unsatisfactory, untrained, wanting

incompleteness bittiness, defectiveness, half-heartedness, hollowness, immaturity, impairment, imperfection, inadequacy, ineffectiveness, insubstantiality, insufficiency, lack, need, nonfulfilment, nonsatisfaction, partialness, perfunctoriness, poverty, rawness, roughness, scantness, scrappiness, sketchiness, superficiality, underdevelopment, unpreparedness, unreadiness, unripeness, want

inconsiderate bothering, discourteous, heedless, inattentive, inhospitable, insensitive, neglectful, oblivious to, pestering, selfish, sullen, tactless, thoughtless, unaccommodating, uncaring, uncharitable, unchristian, unconcerned, unfeeling, unfriendly, ungenerous, ungracious, unheedful, unhelpful, unkind, unmindful, unobliging, unresponsive, unsympathetic

inconstancy capriciousness, changeableness, fickleness, fluctuation, irresponsibility, levity, variability, whimsicality

inconvenience annoyance, awkwardness, bother, box in, burden, corner, cumbersomeness, detriment, difficulty, disability, disadvantage, discomfort, discommode, disruption, disturbance, drawback, embarrass, hamper, handicap, harm, hinder, hindrance, impediment, incommodiousness, inexpedience, irritation, nuisance, obstacle, obstruct, pain, snooker, stump, trap, trouble, troublesomeness, undueness, unfitness, unsuitability, untimeliness, unwieldiness, upset, vexation, wrongness

inconvenient adverse, aggravating, annoying, awkward, boring, bothersome, burdensome, clumsy, cumbersome, detrimental, disadvantageous, discommodious, disruptive, disturbing, exasperating, hindering, hulking, ill-contrived, ill-planned, inept, inexpedient, infelicitous, inopportune, irksome, irritating, lumbering, objectionable, onerous, tedious, tiresome, troublesome, trying, unapt, undue, unfit, unfortunate, unhelpful, unprofessional, unprofitable, unseasonable, unsettling, unsuitable, untimely, untoward, unwieldy, useless, vexatious, worrying

incorrect erroneous, fallacious, false, imprecise, inaccurate, inappropriate, invalid, misinformed, mistaken, unsound, untrue, wrong
may indicate an anagram

incorrectness error, faux pas, gaffe, impropriety, inaccuracy, mistake

increase acceleration, accretion, accrual, accumulation, addition, advance, aggrandizement, aggravation, amplification, appreciate, augment, blossom, boom, breed, broaden, bud, build-up, bulge, burgeon, climb, crescendo, culmination, deepening, develop, dilation, distend, duplication, elevation, enhancement, enlargement, escalate, exacerbation, exaggeration, exaltation, exceed, expand, expansion, extension, fatten, fill out, flourish, flower, gain, grow, growth, heightening, improve, increment, inflate, intensification, intumesce, magnification, mount, multiplication, mushroom, profit, progress, proliferation, prolongation, propagation, prosper, protraction, reproduction, rise, rocket, skyrocket, snowball, soar, spawn, speeding, spiral, spread, sprout, stepping up, supplement, surge, swarm, swell, thicken, thrive, unfold, wax, widening

increased augmented, bloated, enhanced, enlarged, expanded, extended, heightened, intensified, magnified, stretched, supplemented, swollen

increasing additional, augmentative, crescent, cumulative, progressive, prolific, supplementary

incredulity amazement, bafflement, bewilderment, denial, discredit, nonbelief, perplexity, rejection, scepticism

incurable beyond recall, gone, incorrigible, inoperable, irredeemable, irremediable, irreparable, irretrievable, irreversible, irrevocable, lost, terminal

incurious credulous, gullible, trusting, uninquisitive, unquestioning

indecency bad taste, bawdiness, bawdry, coarseness, corruption, defilement, depravity, dirt, double entendre, filth, grossness, indelicacy, lewdness, loose talk, obscenity, prurience, ribaldry, salaciousness, smut, uncleanness, vulgarity

indecent arousing, bawdy, blue, coarse, crude, dirty, erotic, filthy, fruity, improper, indelicate, insalubrious, lewd, louche, lubricious, naughty, obscene, offensive, pornographic, provocative, prurient, Rabelaisian, racy, ribald, risqué, salacious, scabrous, scatalogical, scrofulous, shocking, smutty, strong, suggestive, titillating, uncensored, unexpurgated, unwholesome, vulgar

indecision doubt, dubiety, equivocation, hesitation, irresolution, tergiversation, uncertainty, vacillation, wavering

indecisiveness cowardliness, doubtfulness, gutlessness, hesitance, ineffectuality, irresolution, nervelessness, nervousness, pusillanimity, sheepishness, slowness, spinelessness, timorousness

indecorous barbaric, boorish, churlish, coarse, crude, discourteous, gross, impolite, improper, indelicate, infra

dig(nitatem), rude, tasteless, uncouth, unpolished, unrefined, unseemly, vulgar

indecorum impoliteness, impropriety, indiscretion, rudeness, unseemliness

indemonstrable improbable, unconfirmable, unlikely, unpredictable, unprovable, unverifiable

independence autarky, authority, autonomy, bachelorhood, citizenship, disinterestedness, franchisement, individualism, maidenhood, objectivity, self-determination, self-expression, self-government, self-reliance, self-sufficiency, statehood, unilaterality, wealth

independent autonomous, free, freelance, free-minded, freewheeling, indifferent, individual, individualistic, inner-directed, maverick, neutral, non-aligned, self-contained, self-employed, self-motivated, self-reliant, self-sufficient, self-supporting, unattached, unbound, uncompelled, unconstrained, uncontrolled, ungoverned, uninfluenced, unrestricted, unsubjected, wildcat

indeterminacy ambiguity, amorphousness, broadness, equivocalness, generality, imprecision, inaccuracy, indefiniteness, indistinctness, inexactness, obscurity, unclearness, vagueness

indeterminate ambiguous, amorphous, borderline, broad, equivocal, general, imprecise, inaccurate, indefinite, indistinct, inexact, obscure, unclear, undefined, vague

index bibliography, catalogue, contents, database, discography, file, filing system, filmography, forefinger, indication, list, menu, sign, spreadsheet, syllabus, window

indicate aim, conduct, determine, direct, fix, guide, lead, point to, present, put right, set, set straight, signpost, steer

indication clue, footprint, mark, pointer, remains, scent, sign, spoor, symptom, token, track, (vapour) trail, wake

indifference aloofness, apathy, ataraxia, calmness, casualness, coldness, coolness, detachment, disinterestedness, dispassion, dispiritedness, dullness, half-heartedness, inactivity, inappetance, incuriosity, inertia, inexactitude, inexcitability, informality, insensibility, insensitivity, insouciance, lackadaisicalness, laissez-faire, laziness, lethargy, listlessness, lukewarmness, messiness, nonchalance, noninvolvement, numbness, off-handedness, oscitation, passiveness, perfunctoriness, phlegmaticalness, procrastination, shallowness, shoddiness, slackness, sloppiness, slovenliness, sluggishness, sluttishness, superficiality, unconcern, unscrupulousness, untidiness

indifferent aloof, apathetic, ataractic, benumbed, blasé, calm, carefree, casual, cold, cold-blooded, coldhearted, cool, deadpan, detached, dirty, disinterested, dispassionate, dispirited, dull, easy-going, fancy-free, frigid, frosty, grotty, half-done, half-hearted, impassive, impersonal, inactive, inappetant, incomplete, incurious, inert, inexcitable, informal, insensible, insensitive, insouciant, lackadaisical, laid-back, lax, lazy, lethargic, listless, lukewarm, matter-of-fact, messy, nonchalant, noncommittal, numb, passionless, perfunctory, phlegmatic, pococurante, shoddy, slack, slapdash, slipshod, sloppy, slovenly, sluggish, sluttish, thick-skinned, unaffected, unaffectionate, uncaring, unconcerned, undesirous, unemotional, unfeeling, unimpressed, uninquisitive, uninvolved, unmoved, unresponsive, unruffled, unsurprised, untidy, withdrawn

indignity chagrin, degradation, embarrassment, humiliation, mortification

indirect astray, bending, crooked, curving, deflected, labyrinthine, lost, mazy, meandering, off-course, off target, out-of-the-way, roundabout, serpentine, shifting, snaking, swerving, turning, twisting, veering, wide, winding, zigzag

indiscriminate assorted, chaotic, confused, disordered, haphazard, higgledy-piggledy, intermingled, jumbled, miscellaneous, mixed, motley, muddled, random, scrambled, unorganized, unselected, unsorted, unsystematic

indiscriminateness confusion, generality, heap, inexactitude, jumble, mixture, muddle, randomness, universality, vagueness

indispensable essential, necessary, needed, vital

individualist anchorite, ascetic, bohemian, dissenter, eccentric, free spirit, hermit, independent, isolationist, loner, lone wolf, maverick, monk, nonconformist, nun, separatist

indoctrinate advise, brainwash, brief, guide, illuminate, inculcate, inform, instill, prime, tell

indomitable game, gutsy, plucky, unbeaten, unconquerable, undaunted, undefeated, undeterred, undiscouraged

inducement attraction, bewitchment, blandishment, cajolery, charm, coaxing, encouragement, enticement, fascination, incentive, influence, invitation, lure, magnetism, persuasion, provocation, seductiveness, solicitation

industrial ceramics adobe, brick, cement, chemical porcelain, concrete, crystallized glass, devitrified glass, electrical porcelain, firebrick, floor tile, foam glass, glass fibre, laminated glass, optical glass, photosensitive glass, plate glass, porcelain insulation, quarry tile, roofing tile, safety glass, terracotta

industrious assiduous, businesslike, diligent, efficient, energetic, hardworking, indefatigable, laborious, persevering, plodding, professional, sedulous, slogging, studious, tireless, unflagging, workaholic, workmanlike

inelegance affectation, awkwardness, cack-handedness, clumsiness, commonness, gaucheness, gawkiness, gracelessness, heavy-handedness, lumpishness, overelaboration, plainness, uncouthness

inelegant affected, artificial, artless, cacological, cacophonous, clumsy, dowdy, dumpy, dysphemistic, formal, frumpy, grandiloquent, grating, grotesque, heavy-handed, ill-sounding, incorrect, jarring, laboured, ludicrous, overelaborate, plain, pompous, solecistic, stiff, stilted, tortuous, turgid, uneuphonious, unfluent, unnatural, wooden

inequality asymmetry, difference, disadvantage, discrepancy, disequilibrium, disparity, disproportion, dissimilarity, distortion, diversity, dizziness, handicap, heterogeneity, imbalance, imparity, irregularity, lopsidedness, nonuniformity, obliquity, oddness, patchiness, roughness, skewness, unevenness, variability

inert apathetic, dead, doltish, dormant, dull, fallow, flaccid, heavy, hibernating, idle, immobile, inactive, indecisive, indifferent, indolent, insensible, irresolute, languid, latent, lax, lazy, lifeless, limp, lumpish, motionless, numb, pacific, paralysed, passive, peaceful, quiescent, quiet, slack, sleepy, slothful, slow, sluggish, slumbrous, smouldering, stagnant, static, still, stolid, torpid, unaggressive, unexcitable, unmoving, unreactive, unresponsive, unwarlike, vegetating

inertness apathy, deathliness, dormancy, dullness, fallowness, gutlessness, hibernation, idleness, immobility, impassivity, inaction, inactivity, indecision, indecisiveness, indifference, indolence, inexcitability, insensibility,

irresolution, languor, latency, laxity, laziness, lifelessness, motionlessness, numbness, paralysis, passivity, peacefulness, quiescence, slackness, sleepiness, sloth, slowness, sluggishness, stagnation, stillness, stolidity, torpidity, torpor, vegetation

inevitability certainty, destiny, determination, doom, fate, fatefulness, force majeure, ineluctability, inescapableness, inevasibleness, inexorability, irrevocability, karma, necessity, nemesis, predestination, predetermination, relentlessness, unavoidability, unpreventability

inevitable certain, destined, determined, directed, doomed, fated, fixed, ineluctable, inescapable, inevasible, inexorable, inflexible, karmic, necessary, ordained, predestined, predetermined, preordained, relentless, set, unavoidable, unpreventable, unstoppable, unyielding

inexperience amateurism, bluff, charlatanism, dabbling, dilettantism, inexpertness, quackery, sciolism, semi-literacy, superficiality

infallibility dependability, fidelity, firmness, loyalty, predictability, regularity, reliability, security, solidity, soundness, stability, staunchness, steadfastness, steadiness, stoicism, trustworthiness

infallible dependable, faithful, firm, loyal, predictable, regular, reliable, secure, solid, sound, stable, staunch, steadfast, steady, stoical, trustworthy, unchanging, undeviating, unshakeable, unwavering

infect canker, contaminate, dirty, envenom, foul, poison, pollute, taint, ulcerate

infer deduce, derive, presume, understand

inferior assistant, bad, cheap, crappy, crummy, defective, dependant, deputy, dupe, failure, faulty, flawed, flunky, follower, groupie, henchman, imperfect, junior, lesser, loser, lower, low-grade, low-quality, menial, minor, naff, no-hoper, nonentity, pathetic, pawn, private, punk, reject, ropy, rubbishy, satellite, secondary, second-best, second-class, second-rate, servant, shoddy, sidekick, slave, subaltern, subject, subordinate, subsidiary, substandard, tacky, tawdry, tool, trashy, underling, unsatisfactory, unworthy, vassal, younger

inferiority abasement, baseness, botch, bungle, cheapness, clumsiness, crap, crumminess, defect, dependence, faultiness, flaw, humbleness, humility, imperfection, incompetence, inefficiency, insignificance, junk, lowliness, rubbish, secondariness, shoddiness, subordination, subservience, tackiness, tawdriness, trashiness, unimportance

infertile arid, barren, blasted, bleak, celibate, childless, dead, desert, desolate, drought-stricken, dry, fallow, fruitless, gaunt, impotent, infecund, low-yield, recessionary, shrivelled, stagnant, sterile, stony, uncultivated, unproductive, unprolific, waste, wild, withered

infertility aridity, barrenness, celibacy, childlessness, defoliation, deforestation, desert, desertification, desolation, dustbowl, fallowness, fruitlessness, impotence, infecundity, sterility, unproductiveness, wasteland, wilderness

infest bite, buzz, contaminate, crawl with, drone, flyblow, invade, parasitize, plague, sting, swarm, teem with

infiltrate bite into, bore in, break through, creep in, drip, filter in, insert, insinuate, leak in, penetrate, percolate, permeate, pierce, puncture, seep, slink in, slip in, sneak in, soak in

infinite bottomless, boundless, endless, interminable, limitless, recurring

infinity bottomless pit, boundless-ness, endlessness, infinite supply, interminability, limitlessness

inflammable combustible, flammable, igneous, incendiary

inflexibility implacability, inexorableness, intractability, relentlessness, unyieldingness

inflexible immovable, obstinate, resolute, rigid, stubborn, unbending, unrelenting

influence ability, activate, actuate, advantage, affect, atmosphere, authority, bear upon, bias, brainwash, capability, carry weight, clout, colour, destiny, direct, drive, encourage, fate, force, gravity, greatness, guide, impact, importance, impress, inspiration, lead, leverage, lobby, lure, magnetism, magnitude, might, motivate, persuasion, potency, potentiality, power, predispose, predominance, prejudice, pressure, pressurize, prevalence, promote, push, significance, strength, suggest, tempt, weight, whip hand

influential authoritative, causal, commanding, contributing, decisive, directing, educative, effectual, forceful, guiding, important, impressive, instructive, interfering, leading, mighty, momentous, persuasive, potent, powerful, prestigious, reigning, ruling, significant, superior, telling, world-shattering

influx affluence, afflux, indraught, indrawing, inflooding, inflow, inhalation, inrun, inrush, intake, stream

inform accuse, acquaint, advise, apprise, betray, blab, brief, correct, delate, denounce, disabuse, educate, enlighten, grass, instruct, nark, notify, peach, point out, rat, shop, sing, snitch, split, squeal, teach, tell tales, tergiversate, testify, turn Queen's evidence

informal casual, degage, easy-going, familiar, indifferent, nonconformist, offhand, relaxed, spontaneous, unaffected, unassuming, unbuttoned, unceremonious, unconventional, unofficial, unstuffy, willing

informality candidness, candour, casualness, ease, familiarity, frankness, friendliness, indifference, nonconformity, offhandedness, openness, relaxation, unceremoniousness, unconstraint

informant advertiser, broadcaster, correspondent, eyewitness, grass, hack, herald, informer, journalist, messenger, nark, newscaster, newshound, publicizer, publisher, rat, reporter, spokesperson, squealer, tell-tale

information accomplishment, acquaintance, aptitude, data, dirt, dope, expertise, facts, forte, gen, info, inkling, intelligence, intimation, know-how, knowledge, low-down, métier, news, skill, smattering, suspicion, technique, tidings, touch, word

informative advisory, big-mouthed, candid, cautionary, clear, communicative, definite, educational, enlightening, explicit, expository, expressive, gossipy, illuminating, indicating, indiscreet, insinuating, instructive, monitory, plain-spoken, revealing, suggesting

informed advised, alert, au fait, aware, briefed, enlightened, in touch, posted

informer blabber, blackleg, contact, delator, gossip, grass, informant, messenger, mole, nark, newsmonger, rat, scab, snitch, source, squealer, stool pigeon, strike-breaker, supergrass, tattler, telltale, tipster, whistle-blower

ingest drink, eat, engorge, engulf, gulp, ingurgitate, swallow

ingratitude discourteousness, forgetfulness, inconsiderateness, rudeness, selfishness, thanklessness, thoughtlessness, unappreciation, ungraciousness, ungratefulness

ingredient additive, appurtenance, bit, component, constituent, contents, element, enclosure, factor, feature, item, part, piece

ingredients
may indicate an anagram

inhabit abide in, board, colonize, dwell, lease, live, lodge, occupy, populate, rent, reside, settle, sojourn, squat, stay, visit

inhabitant aborigine, autochthon, denizen, dweller, incumbent, indian, indigene, inmate, local, native, occupant, resident

inhabitants citizenry, clan, colony, commune, community, dwellers, family, household, ménage, neighbourhood, people, populace, population, public, residents, tribe

inhabited indwelt, leased, let, occupied, rented, residential, tenanted

inhabiting at home, billeted, domiciled, dwelling, housed, lodged, residential, roofed, sheltered

inhalant aerosol, atomizer, nebulizer, spray

inhibition conservativeness, embarrassment, hang-up, hindrance, introversion, negativism, obstacle, shyness

inhibitive conservative, forbidding, hindering, introversive, obstructive

inject decant, enter, imbue, implant, impregnate, infuse, inoculate, instil, introduce, penetrate, perfuse, pierce, poke in, pop in, pour in, shoot, squirt in, transfuse, vaccinate

injection drip, entry, epidural, implantation, impregnation, infusion, ingress, inoculation, intubation, penetration, perfusion, shot, transfusion, vaccination, venoclysis

injured broken, bruised, cut, fractured, grazed, lacerated, punctured, scraped, sprained, torn, wounded
may indicate an anagram

injury abrasion, bite, black eye, bruise, bump, burn, contusion, cut, fracture, gash, graze, hit, jab, laceration, lesion, puncture, scald, scrape, scratch, shiner, slash, sprain, stab, tear, trauma, wound

injustice bias, bigotry, chauvinism, discrimination, fanaticism, favouritism, inequality, inequity, insularity, intolerance, mistrial, narrow-mindedness, nepotism, one-sidedness, parochialism, partiality, partisanship, predilection, predisposition, prejudice, provincialism, sectarianism, tunnel vision, unfairness, unlawfulness

inlaid boulle, inset, marquetried, parquetried

inland central, continental, heartland, hinterland, interior, landlocked, midland, upcountry, upstate

inlet backwater, bay, bight, channel, cove, delta, estuary, fiord, firth, fleet, gulf, gut, harbour, mouth, outlet, port, sound, straits

innocence absolution, acquittal, blamelessness, chastity, exculpation, exoneration, faultlessness, goodness, guiltlessness, ignorance, immaculacy, impeccability, incorruption, inculpability, irreproachability, morality, naivety, perfection, probity, purity, saintliness, sinlessness, spotlessness, stainlessness, uprightness, virginity, virtue, whiteness

innocent acquitted, angelic, blameless, chaste, clean, cleared, discharged, dismissed, faultless, gentle, good, guiltless, harmless, ignorant, immaculate, impeccable, inculpable, innocuous, inoffensive, irreprehensible, naive, pardoned, perfect, prelapsarian, pure, rehabilitated, released, saintly, spotless, stainless, unblemished, undefiled, unerring, unknowing, unsullied, untainted, upright, virginal, virtuous

in order
may indicate an anagram

inquest autopsy, disentombment, disinterment, inquiry, necropsy, PM, postmortem

insane abnormal, alienated, anile, bananas, barmy, bats, batty, bonkers, certifiable, crack-brained, cracked, crackers, cranky, crazy, cuckoo, daft, demented, deranged, dippy, disturbed, doited, dolally, dotty, kinky, loopy, mad, mental, nuts, nutty, odd, peculiar, rambling, raving, running amok, screwy, touched, unbalanced, unhinged, wacky, weird

insanity aberration, abnormality, battiness, crankiness, craziness, derangement, diminished responsibility, eccentricity, freakishness, idiocy, incoherence, irrationality, kinkiness, lunacy, madness, nuttiness, oddness
may indicate an anagram

inscribe carve, cut, engrave, etch, incise, jot, minute, note, transcribe, write

inscription autograph, corollary, epitaph, graffiti, initials, legend, obsequies, signature

inscrutable ambiguous, arcane, baffling, cryptic, enigmatic, indecipherable, indefinite, mystifying, recondite, unclear, unfathomable, unintelligible, unknowable

insect creepy-crawly, drone, emmet, king, pismire, worker
See list of insects.

insensitive apathetic, blind, blunt, callous, cold-blooded, cold-hearted, deaf, dull, frigid, hard, heartless, immune, impassive, imperceptive, impervious, indifferent, insensate, insensible, obtuse, tactless, thick(-skinned), tough, unaffected, unaware, uncaring, unconscious, unemotional, unfeeling, unimaginative, unimpressionable, unresponsive, unsusceptible

insensitiveness apathy, bluntness, callousness, cold-heartedness, coldness, dullness, hardness, heartlessness, impassivity, indifference, insensibility, Philistinism, tactlessness, unawareness, unresponsiveness, unsusceptibility

insensitivity anaesthesia, brutality, cruelty, indelicacy, mercilessness, numbness, unawareness, vulgarity

insert add, drop in, hole, import, in-

INSECTS

ALDERFLY
AMAZON ANT
AMBROSIA BEETLE
ANOPHELES
ANT
ANTLION
APHID
ARMY ANT
ARMY WORM
ASSASSIN BUG
BACKSWIMMER
BAGWORM MOTH
BARK BEETLE
BEDBUG
BEE
BEETLE
BLACK BEETLE
BLACKFLY
BLISTER BEETLE
BLOODWORM
BLOWFLY
BLUEBOTTLE
BOLL WEEVIL
BOMBARDIER BEETLE
BOOKLOUSE
BOOKWORM
BOT FLY
BRIMSTONE
BRISTLETAIL
BUFFALO GNAT
BUG
BUMBLEBEE
BURYING BEETLE
BUSH CRICKET
CABBAGE ROOT FLY
CABBAGE WHITE
  (BUTTERFLY)
CACTOBLASTIS
CACTUS MOTH
CADDIS FLY
CAMBERWELL
  BEAUTY
  (BUTTERFLY)
CANTHARIDIN
CAPSID
CARPENTER BEE
CARPET BEETLE
CATERPILLAR
CECROPIA MOTH
CHAFER
CHIGOE
CHINCH BUG
CICADA
CINNABAR
CLEARWING MOTH
CLICK BEETLE
CLOTHES MOTH
COCKCHAFER
COCKROACH
CODLING MOTH

COLEOPTERA
COLORADO BEETLE
CORN BORER
COTTON STAINER
CRANEFLY
CRICKET
CUCKOO-SPIT
  INSECT
CUTWORM
DADDY LONGLEGS
DAMSELFLY
DARKLING BEETLE
DEATH'S-HEAD
  MOTH
DEATHWATCH
  BEETLE
DEVIL'S COACH
  HORSE
DIGGER WASP
DIPTERA
DIVING BEETLE
DOBSONFLY
DOR BEETLE
DRAGONFLY
DRIVER ANT
DRONE
DROSOPHILA
DUNG BEETLE
EARWIG
ELM BARK BEETLE
EMPEROR MOTH
FIRE ANT
FIREBRAT
FIREFLY
FLEA
FLY
FRITILLARY
FROGHOPPER
FRUIT FLY
GAD FLY
GALL MIDGE
GALL WASP
GEOMETRID MOTH
GIANT WATER BUG
GLOWWORM
GNAT
GOAT MOTH
GOLIATH BEETLE
GRASSHOPPER
GREENFLY
GROUND BEETLE
GROUND BUG
GYPSY MOTH
HAIRSTREAK
HAWK MOTH
HERCULES BEETLE
HERCULES MOTH
HONEY ANT
HONEYBEE
HORNET

HORNTAIL
HORSE FLY
HOUSEFLY
HOVERFLY
ICHNEUMON
IO MOTH
JUNE BEETLE
KATYDID
LACEWING
LAC INSECT
LADYBIRD
LEAF BEETLE
LEAFCUTTER ANT
LEAFCUTTER BEE
LEAF HOPPER
LEAF INSECT
LOCUST
LOOPER
LOUSE
LUNA MOTH
MAGGOT
MANTIS
MASON BEE
MAYFLY
MEALWORM
MEALYBUG
MIDGE
MILKWEED
  (BUTTERFLY)
MOLE CRICKET
MONARCH
  (BUTTERFLY)
MOSQUITO
NOCTUID MOTH
NYMPHALID
  (BUTTERFLY)
OIL BEETLE
OWLET MOTH
PAINTED LADY
  (BUTTERFLY)
PAPILIONID
  (BUTTERFLY)
PEACOCK
  (BUTTERFLY)
PEPPERED MOTH
PHASMIDA
PHYLLOXERA
PLANT BUG
PLANT HOPPER
POND SKATER
POTTER WASP
PROTURA
PUSS MOTH
PYRALID MOTH
RED ADMIRAL
  (BUTTERFLY)
RINGLET
ROBBER FLY
ROVE BEETLE
SANDFLY

SATURNIID MOTH
SATYRID (BUTTERFLY)
SAWFLY
SCALE INSECT
SCARAB BEETLE
SCORPION FLY
SCREWWORM
SEXTON BEETLE
SHEEP KED
SHIELD BUG
SILKWORM
SILVERFISH
SKIPPER (BUTTERFLY)
SLAVE-MAKING ANT
SNAKEFLY
SOLDIER BEETLE
SPANISH FLY
SPIDER WASP
SPITTLEBUG
SPRINGTAIL
STAG BEETLE
STICK INSECT
STINK BUG
STONEFLY
STYLOPS
SWALLOWTAIL
  (BUTTERFLY)
SWIFT MOTH
TERMITE
THRIPS
TIGER BEETLE
TIGER MOTH
TINEID MOTH
TORTOISE BEETLE
TORTOISESHELL
  (BUTTERFLY)
TREEHOPPER
TSETSE FLY
TUSSOCK MOTH
UNDERWING
  MOTH
WARBLE FLY
WASP
WATER BEETLE
WATER BOATMAN
WATER BUG
WATER SCORPION
WATER STRIDER
WAX MOTH
WEBSPINNER
WEEVIL
WHIRLIGIG
WHITE FLY
WIREWORM
WOODWASP
WOODWORM
WOOLLY BEAR

clude, insinuate, intercalate, interject, interpolate, introduce, introject, intromit, pot, put in, stick in

inserted added, by-the-by, embedded, imported, included, inlaid, intercalated, interpolated, introduced, introjected, parenthetical

insertion addition, embedment, embolism, graft, impaction, implantation, import, infiltration, infixion, insinuation, intercalation, interjection, interpenetration, interpolation, introduction, introjection, intromission, intrusion, leakage, parenthesis, penetration, percolation, planting, seepage, tessellation, transplantation

inset box, circumscribe, cover, dovetail, embed, encapsulate, encase, ensheathe, frame, inlay, mount

inside cell, centre, confinement, core, depths, heart, home, indoors, jail, middle, prison, recesses, retreat, room, sanctuary, seclusion

insides belly, bowels, contents, core, entrails, guts, heart, innards, intestines, kernel, marrow, offal, pith, viscera

insight empathy, feeling, flash, foreboding, hunch, impression, impulse, moral sensibility, sensitivity, sympathy, understanding

insignia badge, decoration, garland, laurels, markings, medal, regalia, ribbon, trophy, wreath

insignificance immateriality, inconsequence, irrelevance, triviality, unimportance

insignificant blah, boring, diminished, immaterial, inconsequential, irrelevant, lightweight, minimal, onehorse, small, small-time, small-town, trivial, unimportant

insipid bland, diluted, half-hearted, pallid, tasteless, vapid, watered-down, wersh, wishy-washy

insipidness blandness, dullness, flatness, half-heartedness, insipidity, pallidness, tastelessness, thinness, vapidity, wanness, wateriness, wishy-washiness

insist adhere, demand, press, require, urge

insolence bad behaviour, bad manners, boorishness, bumptiousness, caddishness, cheek, churlishness, coarseness, contumely, crudeness, effrontery, grossness, ill-breeding, impertinence, impudence, incivility, lip, loutishness, misconduct, offensiveness, procacity, rudeness, sauce, truculence, vulgarity

insolent bumptious, contumelious, flip, impertinent, impudent, malapert

insolvency bankruptcy, debt, dependence, depression, disinheritance, dispossession, indebtedness, recession, ruin, slump, unsoundness

insolvent bankrupt, broken, bust, dispossessed, fleeced, impoverished, in debt, owing, pauperized, ruined, skint, stony-broke, strapped, stripped

inspect examine, eyeball, peruse, read, reconnoitre, scan, scrutinize, study, survey, view

in speech *may indicate a homophone*

inspiration afflatus, creativity, ecstasy, frenzy, genius, idea, muse, stimulus

inspire animate, enliven, exhilarate, inspirit

install admit, auspicate, crown, enlist, enrol, enthrone, inaugurate, induct, initiate, instate, invest, launch, ordain, present, sign up

instant at once, flash, immediate, jiffy, mo, moment, second, split second, straightaway, tick

instinct drive, gut feeling, hunch, intuition, knee-jerk reaction, Pavlovian response, proclivity, reflex

instinctive automatic, impulsive, innate, intuitive, involuntary, knee-jerk,

Pavlovian, reflex, spontaneous, subconscious, unconscious

instructions briefing, discourse, guidebook, lecture, manual

instrument agency, apparatus, appliance, catalyst, compromise, contraption, contrivance, device, equipment, expedient, factor, force, gadget, implement, influence, machine, means, mechanism, medium, organ, tool, vehicle
See also list at **orchestra**.

instrumental advancing, aiding, applicable, assisting, conducive, cooperative, effective, effectual, efficacious, efficient, employable, handy, helping, hymnal, liturgical, operatic, orchestral, powerful, promoting, subordinate, subservient, subsidiary, supportive, useful, utilizable

instrumentality ability, achievement, agency, application, automation, cause, clout, competence, computerization, effectiveness, efficacy, employment, functionality, handiness, influence, instrumentation, means, mechanization, medium, occasion, operation, performance, potency, power, practicality, responsibility, result, serviceability, significance, subordination, subservience, usefulness, utility, weight

insubstantial airy, bubbly, buoyant, cobwebby, dainty, delicate, downy, effervescent, ethereal, feathery, flimsy, floaty, fluffy, foamy, frothy, gaseous, gentle, gossamery, illusory, imaginary, irrelevant, levitative, rare, soft, sparkling, sublime, substandard, tender, unreal, unsinkable, unsupported, volatile, whipped, whisked

insufficiency defect, deficiency, deficit, disappointment, discontent, failure, imperfection, inadequacy, incompetence, incompleteness, inferiority, insolvency, meagreness, noncompletion, nonfulfilment, scantiness, shortfall, skimpiness, slippage, weakness

insufficient below par, cramped, deficient, disappointing, inadequate, incapable, incompetent, incomplete, inconclusive, inferior, insubstantial, invalid, jejune, lacking, limited, meagre, mean, miserly, niggardly, pathetic, poor, scanty, sketchy, skimpy, slender, substandard, thin, unacceptable, unconvincing, underfed, undernourished, unsatisfactory, wanting, watery, weak, wersh

insulation double glazing, lagging, protection

insult affront, aspersion, backhanded compliment, cold shoulder, cutting remark, gesture, offend, put-down, rebuff, repulse, slight, snub, spurn, taunt

insulting abusive, contumacious, cutting, defamatory, offensive, opprobrious, outrageous, pejorative, rebuffing, repulsing, slighting, snubbing, spurning, taunting

insurance assurance, cover, precaution, safeguard, security

intake breathing in, consumption, drinking, eating, engorgement, engulfment, gulp, ingestion, inhalation, inspiration, sniffing, sucking, swallow

integral built-in, component, constituent, indivisible, ineradicable, inseparable, integrated

intellect brain(s), faculty, intelligence, mind, suss, wit

intelligence aptitude, brain, brainwave, brightness, brilliance, cleverness, common sense, comprehension, gen, genius, gumption, information, inspiration, intellect, intellectualism, judgment, KGB, low-down, mentality, MI, mind, motivation, nous, quick-wittedness, reason, receptivity, sense, smartness, spying, talent, understanding, wit

intelligent able, acute, alert, astute, brainy, bright, brilliant, calculating, canny, clear-headed, clever, crafty, cunning, farsighted, gifted, keen-witted, quick-witted, sagacious, sage, sharp, shrewd, skilful, smart, smartarse, understanding, wise

intelligibility certainty, coherence, comprehensibility, meaningfulness, precision, sense, unambiguity, unambivalence

intelligible apprehensible, audible, certain, clear-cut, coherent, comprehensible, explicable, fathomable, focused, interpretable, knowable, luminous, meaningful, penetrable, precise, realizable, sane, scrutable, teachable, unambiguous, understandable, unequivocal, univocal, visible

intend aim, bring about, calculate, cause, contemplate, design, destine, determine, effect, entail, expect, foresee, involve, mean to, meditate, plan to, ponder, portend, predestine, prepare for, propose, purpose, reckon on, result in, shall, think of, will

intended aforethought, calculated, deliberate, designed, eschatological, fiancé(e), intentional, meant, planned, predetermined, premeditated, purposeful, studied, volitional, voluntary, wilful

intending ambitious, aspiring, disposed, hellbent, hopeful, inclined, prospective, purposive, resolute, seeking, serious, teleological, would-be

intensity cogency, concentration, depth, emphasis, extent, incisiveness, keenness, pressure, rashness, severity, strength, stress, trenchancy, urgency, weight

intention aim, meaning, motive, plan, purpose

intentionality calculation, deliberateness, determination, predetermination, premeditation, resolve

interaction blend, communication, cooperation, dovetail, interpenetration, reciprocation

interchange alternation, balance, bartering, comeback, compensation, compromise, counteraction, exchange, interaction, interplay, justice, reaction, reciprocation, recoil, requital, retaliation, retort, return, swap, trade-off

interconnected bilateral, complementary, cooperative, interdependent, interlinked, interlocking, interrelated, mutual, opposite, symbiotic, two-way

interconnection cooperation, interdependence, interrelationship, mutuality, partnership, sharing, symbiosis, synergy

interest advantage, arouse, curiosity, excite, fascination, hobby, investment, premium, relevance, stake

interface abut, abutment, adjacency, adjoin, battlefront, border on, boundary, confront, contact, contiguity, divide, interact, meet, meeting point, share, threshold, touch

interior cave, central, centrality, deep, depth, domestic, enclosed, endemic, endodermal, endodermis, homelike, indoor, inner, inside, internal, internality, intravenous, inward, inwardness, local, mental, nonexternal, personal, pothole, solipsist, subconscious, subcortex, subcortical, subcutaneous, subjective, subsoil, substrative, substratum, undersurface, undersurfaced

intern bury, cage, entomb, immure, imprison, incarcerate, jail, junior doctor, prisoner

internal ear anvil, auditory ossicle, cochlea, eardrum, Eustachian tube, hammer, incus, inner ear, labyrinth, malleus, middle ear, semicircular canals, stapes, stirrup bone, tympanic membrane

internalization egocentrism, engrossment, id, intellect, introversion, inwardness, mind, nonexternality, privacy, psyche, secretiveness, self-absorption, selfhood, solipsism, soul, spirit, subconscious, subjectivity, superego, the unconscious

internalize absorb, bottle up, conceal, confine, contain, hide, hold within

internationalism cosmopolitanism, globalism, universalism

interpret analyse, clarify, conflate, construe, deduce, define, demonstrate, describe, disambiguate, edit, elucidate, emend, estimate, exemplify, explain, explicate, expound, facilitate, illuminate, illustrate, infer, judge, popularize, reason, render, show, simplify, spell out, understand

interpretation amendment, analysis, answer, application, clarification, clue, conflation, construction, decipherment, deconstruction, definition, demonstration, description, editing, edition, eisegesis, elucidation, emendation, enlightenment, estimate, example, exegesis, exemplification, explanation, explication, exposition, illumination, illustration, insight, isogesis, judgment, key, lection, reading, rendering, rendition, resolution, simplification, solution, understanding, version

interpretive clarifying, constructive, definitional, demonstrative, demythologizing, descriptive, elucidative, euhemeristic, exegetic, exemplary, explanatory, explicatory, expositive, hermeneutic, illuminating, illustrative, insightful, semiological

interrelate complement, cooperate, pair, participate, partner, share, twin

interrelated analogous, associated, commensurate, comparable, complementary, correlated, corresponding, cross-referred, engaged, equal, homologous, interacting, interallied, interassociated, interchanged, interconnected, interdependent, interlinked, interlocked, intermeshed, intertwined, interworking, interwoven, mutual, opposite, parallel, proportional, reciprocal, relational, relative, similar

interrelatedness alternation, association, comparability, complementarity, correlation, covariation, cross-reference, engagement, equality, homology, interaction, interalliance, interassociation, interchanging, intercommunication, interconnection, intercourse, interdependence, interlacing, interlinkage, interlocking, intermeshing, interpenetration, interplaying, intertwining, interweaving, interworking, mutuality, proportionality, reciprocity, relativeness, relativity, similarity

interrogate cross-examine, cross-question, examine, grill, pump, question, torture, witch-hunt

interrupt adjourn, arrest, defer, delay, discontinue, disrupt, disturb, interject, interpolate, interpose, intervene, pause, postpone, procrastinate, shelve, stay, stop, suspend, table, withhold

interrupted abeyant, adjourned, broken off, deferred, delayed, discontinued, disrupted, disturbed, dormant, pending, postponed, shelved, stayed, stopped, suspended, tabled, withheld
may indicate a split word

interruption abeyance, adjournment, breach, break, crack, crevasse, cut, deferment, delay, discontinuance, dormancy, fault, fissure, fracture, gap, moratorium, pause, postponement, procrastination, split, stay, stopping, suspension, withholding, wound

intersection clover leaf, crossing, crossroads, flyover, interchange, junction, roundabout

interval acciaccatura, appoggiatura, arpeggio, blank, break, breather, cadenza, caesura, chord, clearance, crisis, daylight, diapason, diatessaron, discontinuity, distance, duration, firebreak, freeboard, gamut, gap, headroom, hiatus, interim, interlude, intermission, interregnum, interruption, interspace, jump, juncture, lacuna, lapse, leap, leeway, let-up, lull, margin, meantime, nuance, part, passage, pause, period, place, plane, plateau, point, portion, remove, respite, rest, room, rung, separation, shade, shadow, shift, space, span, spell, stage,

invent

stair, step, steppingstone, stint, stretch, time, timeout, turning point

intervention disruption, disturbance, intercession, interfering, interjection, interpolation, interruption, mediation

interweave braid, crisscross, crochet, entangle, espalier, filigree, intercrop, interdigitate, interfile, interfuse, interlace, interlay, interline, interlock, intermingle, interpenetrate, intertwine, knit, knot, lace, macramé, mesh, net, plait, pleach, reticulate, sew, shuttle, spin, tat, twist, warp, web

interweaving crisscross, entanglement, intercommunication, interdigitation, interfusion, interlineation, interpenetration, intertexture, interwork, reticulation

interwoven crisscross, reticulate

intimate confidante, egocentric, engrossed, friend, hidden, hint, inmost, introverted, inward, personal, private, secret, secretive, self-absorbed, suggest, veiled

intimidation bullying, cowing, demoralization, frightening, hassling, hectoring, terrorism, threatening

intolerance apartheid, bigotry, bullying, harassment, impatience, intimidation, persecution, prejudice, racism, tyrannization, victimization

intolerant bigoted, impatient, irritable, narrow-minded, oppressive, persecuting, prejudiced, unforgiving

intoxicant dope, drug, narcotic, sedative, tranquillizer

intoxicating addictive, alcoholic, beery, exhilarating, habit-forming, hard, heady, inebriating, neat, potent, proof, spiritous, stimulant, strong, temulent, vinous, winy

intransigence bloody-mindedness, doggedness, mulishness, obduracy, obstinacy, pigheadedness, self-will, stubbornness, waywardness, wilfulness

intrinsic basic, bred-in-the-bone, con-

crete, constitutional, deep-rooted, deep-seated, essential, fundamental, immanent, inborn, inbred, ingrained, inherent, innate, innermost, material, natural, ontological, primary, radical, substantial, substantive

introduce baptize, bring in, enlist, enrol, inaugurate, initiate, install, invest, ordain, take on

introduction baptism, enlistment, enrolment, exordium, foreword, frontispiece, inauguration, induction, initiation, installation, investiture, lead-in, opening, ordination, preamble, preface, preliminaries, prelims, prelude, registration
may indicate the first letter of a word

intuit feel, guess at, perceive, sense

intuition feeling, hunch, inkling, insight, inspiration, perception, sixth sense

intuitive clairvoyant, fey, impulsive, insightful, inspirational, inspired, instinctive, perceptive, sensing, sensitive

invade ambush, attack, barge in, beleaguer, besiege, break in, burst in, butt in, encroach, escalade, gatecrash, horn in, interrupt, irrupt, manoeuvre, march, muscle in, raid, rush in, storm, trespass

invalid case, faulty, not binding, patient, shut-in, spurious, sufferer, unfounded, valetudinarian
may indicate an anagram

invasion attack, bloodbath, burglary, devastation, dragonnade, havoc, housebreaking, incursion, incursion, ingress, irruption, laying waste, occupation, overrunning, overstepping, pillage, raid, rape, slaughter, subjection, trespassing

invasive incursive, intrusive, irruptive

invent attempt, chance, coin, conceive, concoct, contrive, create, dare, design, devise, discover, dream up, endeavour, engineer, explore, form, for-

177

mulate, gamble, generate, hatch, herald, hit upon, innovate, originate, pioneer, rediscover, risk, think up, undertake, venture

invention coinage, conception, contrivance, creation, design, device, discovery, experiment, exploration, formation, idea, innovation, inspiration, origination
may indicate an anagram

inventive conceptional, creative, innovative, original

inventiveness imagination, inspiration, originality

inventory cadaster, cadastre, catalogue, glossary, list, log

inversion antithesis, capsizing, contrary, converse, evagination, introversion, invagination, opposite, overturning, retroversion, reversal, reversion, transposition, upset

invert capsize, evaginate, introvert, invaginate, overturn, retrovert, reverse, somersault, transpose, turn turtle, upend, upset
may indicate a backword

invertebrate arachnid, insectiform, spineless, worm-like

inverted arsy-versy, bottom-up, capsized, head-over-heels, reversed, topsy-turvy, transpositional, upside-down

investigation analysis, calculation, challenge, computation, deliberation, elenchus, examination, introspection, questioning, speculation

invigorate reanimate, rejuvenate, restore, resurrect, revitalize

invisibility absence, concealment, disappearance, hiding, imperceptibility, indiscernibility, indistinctness, indistinguishability, insubstantiality, latency, non-appearance, obscurity, secrecy, transparency, undetectability, vanishing

invisible buried, eclipsed, immaterial, imperceptible, inappreciable, indiscernible, indistinguishable, insubstantial, latent, lurking, submerged, transparent, unapparent, undetectable, unidentifiable, unidentified, unmarked, unnoticeable, unobserved, unperceivable, unrecognizable, unseeable, unseen, unsighted, unwitnessed

invitation acknowledgment, enticement, introduction, presentation, reception, request, welcome

involuntary automatic, autonomic, compulsory, impulsive, instinctive, intuitive, knee-jerk, mechanical, Pavlovian, reflex

invulnerable defensible, immune, impregnable, inexpugnable, sacrosanct, unassailable, unattackable, unbreakable, unchallengeable, ungettable

irascibility acerbity, acidity, asperity, belligerence, bile, bitchiness, churlishness, contentiousness, crabbiness, cussedness, fractiousness, fretfulness, gall, grouchiness, gruffness, grumpiness, impatience, irritability, meanness, peevishness, petulance, prickliness, querulousness, resentfulness, sharpness, shrewishness, sourness, sullenness, tartness, testiness, tetchiness, touchiness, vinegar

irascible acerbic, acid, angry, annoyed, argumentative, bearish, bellicose, belligerent, bilious, cantankerous, churlish, contentious, crabby, cross, crotchety, crusty, disputatious, dyspeptic, fractious, fretful, grouchy, gruff, grumpy, highly-strung, hot-blooded, hot-tempered, huffy, ill-humoured, impatient, irritable, jumpy, mean, nervous, nettled, ornery, oversensitive, peevish, peppery, petulant, prickly, quarrelsome, querulous, quick-tempered, resentful, riled, sharp-tongued, short, short-tempered, shrewish, snappish, sore, sour, strained, sullen, tart, temperamental, testy, tetchy, thin-skinned, touchy, uptight, vixenish, waspish

iridescent chatoyant, moiré, nacreous, opalescent, pavonine, pearly, semi-transparent, shot, watered

irk aggravate, annoy, bedevil, exasperate, raise Cain

irregular asymmetric, broken, bumpy, capricious, careening, changeable, choppy, desultory, disconnected, discontinuous, disorderly, diverse, erratic, fitful, flickering, fluctuating, formless, halting, haphazard, hit-or-miss, inconsistent, inconstant, infrequent, intermittent, jerky, lurching, nonstandard, nonuniform, oscillatory, patchy, random, restless, rough, shaky, shapeless, spasmodic, sporadic, spotty, staggering, unequal, uneven, unmethodically, unpredictable, unrhythmic, unstable, unsteady, unsystematic, variable, veering, wavering, wobbly
may indicate an anagram

irregularity asymmetry, brokenness, bumping, capriciousness, careening, changeability, choppiness, desultoriness, disconnection, discontinuation, disorder, disproportion, diversity, fitfulness, flickering, fluctuation, haphazardness, inconsistency, inequality, infrequency, instability, intermittence, jerkiness, lurching, misshapenness, nonsymmetry, nonuniformity, oscillation, patchiness, randomness, restlessness, roughness, shakiness, shapelessness, spottiness, staggering, unevenness, unpredictability, unsteadiness, variability, variety, veering, wavering, wobbliness
may indicate an anagram

irrelevance extraneousness, immateriality, inapplicability, incidentalness, inessentiality, insignificance, pleonasm, pointlessness, redundancy, secondariness, superficiality, superfluity, triviality

irrelevant adventitious, extra, extraneous, immaterial, inapplicable, incidental, inessential, insignificant, irrelative, pleonastic, pointless, redun-

dant, secondary, superficial, superfluous, trivial, unconnected, unrelated

irresolute ambivalent, capricious, cop-out, desultory, discredited, dishonourable, disloyal, dizzy, equivocating, evasive, faltering, fencing, fickle, fidgety, flighty, giddy, hedging, hesitant, impressionable, indecisive, lightheaded, light-minded, lukewarm, malleable, mercurial, moody, neutral, noncommital, restless, scatterbrained, scatty, seesawing, shifty, traitorous, undecided, unfaithful, unsettled, vacillating, volatile, wavering, wayward, whimsical, yielding

irresolution agitation, caprice, darting, disloyalty, disquiet, equivocation, erraticism, fickleness, fitfulness, hesitation, infidelity, inquietude, moodiness, procrastination, restlessness, tergiversation, treacherousness, uncertainty, vacillation, volatility, whimsicality

irritable abrupt, acid, bad-tempered, beefing, bellyaching, bilious, bitchy, bitter, brusque, cantankerous, churlish, cross, curmudgeonly, disagreeable, discontented, dissatisfied, dyspeptic, frowning, glowering, grouchy, grousing, gruff, grumbling, grumpy, irascible, louring, mumpish, peevish, petulant, quarrelsome, resentful, scowling, shirty, shrewish, smouldering, snapping, snarling, surly, tart, temperamental, testy, tetchy, touchy, unsmiling, vinegary, vixenish

irritableness bile, biliousness, bitchiness, crankiness, crossness, cussedness, discontent, dissatisfaction, grouchiness, gruffness, grumpiness, irascibility, liver, peevishness, petulance, spitefulness, spleen, temperament, touchiness

irritate annoy, bother, chafe, discontent, dissatisfy, embitter, envenom, nettle, peeve, rile, rouse, vex

irritated
may indicate an anagram

irritation annoyance, grating, irascibility, itch, prickliness, sore, tension

island ait, archipelago, atoll, cay, holm, inch, isle, islet, key, reef, sandbank, sandbar, skerry

isolation detachment, loneliness, quarantine, seclusion, separation, solitude

issue agenda, case, child, concern, daughter, edition, emerge, focus, item, moot point, motion, offspring, point, problem, publication, publish, question, son, spring, topic

itchy desirous, electric, hair-raising, prickly, tickly, tingly

item article, bit, detail, instance, piece

itemize catalogue, classify, divide, enumerate, file, index, list, programme, register, schedule, schematize, section, subdivide, tabulate, tally

itemized charted, coded, divided, schematic, sectioned, tabled, tabular, thematic, topical

iterate cite, perorate, quote, recap, recapitulate, recite, recount, reemphasize, reiterate, relate, repeat, restate, resume, retell, review, summarize

iterated emphasized, repeated, retold, twice-told

iteration peroration, quotation, recap, recapitulation, reiteration, restatement, résumé, review, summary, tautology

it's said
may indicate a homophone

·J·

ABBREVIATIONS

J   jack
JC   Jesus Christ • Julius Caesar
JFK airport • president (John Fitzgerald Kennedy)
JP   Justice of the Peace • magistrate
JR   junior • king (Latin: *Jacobus Rex*) • monarch

jacket anorak, blazer, bolero, bomber, bumfreezer, cagoule, cover, donkey, Eton, hunting, jerkin, kagool, lumber, matinee, midicoat, morning coat, Norfolk, parka, reefer, shooting, spencer, sports, tabard, tails, tunic, waistcoat, windcheater

jailer custodian, guard, keeper, prison officer, screw, turnkey, warder

jar clash, crash, drone, grate, jangle, pot, preserve, rasp, saw, scrape, thrum, vessel, whine
may indicate an anagram

jargon argot, cant, journalese, legalese, newspeak, officialese, patter, psychobabble, technobabble, technospeak, telegraphese

jazz acid jazz, Afro-Cuban, avant-garde, bebop, blue note, blues, boogie-woogie, bop, cool, cool jazz, Dixieland, doowop, enliven, folksy, fusion, jive, mainstream, modern, paraphernalia, punk, ragtime, spice, swing, swinging, syncopated, syncopation, third-stream, trad, traditional
may indicate an anagram

jealous competitive, covetous, emulative, envious, green(-eyed), hostile, invidious, jaundiced, jaundice-eyed, lynx-eyed, possessive, resentful, rival, sour, yellow(-eyed)

jealousy competition, covetousness, enviousness, envy, green-eyed monster, heartburn, hostility, jaundice, possessiveness, resentment, rivalry, sour grapes

jeer bawl out, boo, catcall, curse, deride, exclaim, hiss, hoot, howl. raspberry, ridicule, shout down, sneer, squawk, taunt, tell off, V-sign, whistle

jerk bob, flick, flip, hitch, idiot, jiggle, jog, jolt, pluck, snatch, start, tweak, twitch, wrench, yank, yerk

Jesus Christ, Emmanuel, God the son, Jesus Christ, Lord Jesus, Messiah, the Redeemer, the Saviour, the Way

jewellery anklet, badge, bangle, baubles, bracelet, brooch, chain, ear ring, hat-pin, medallion, necklace, nose-ring, pin, ring, stud, tiara, tie-pin, torque
See list of gemstones used in jewellery.

jittery
may indicate an anagram

job business, calling, career, craft, employment, game, métier, mission, occupation, profession, racket, task, trade, vocation
See also list at **occupation**.

join ally, amalgamate, associate, belong to, coalesce, combine, confederate, consolidate, enlist, enrol, federate, fuse, initiate, merge, sign up, subscribe to affiliate, unite

joined affiliated, dovetailed, herringbone, jointed, joisted, linked, mitred, mortised, united

joint accessory, ankle, associate, bar, bevel, birdsmouth, bond, bracket, catch, clasp, collective, collectivist, combined, common, communal, communalist, communist(ic), concerted, conjunction, cooperative, copula, corporate, correlational, dovetail, ecumenic, elbow, fastening, fish, general, ginglymus, hasp, hinge, hitch, hook, hyphen, interactive, interrelating, involved, join, junction, knee, knot, knuckle, lap, link, mitre, mortise and tenon, mutual, nightclub, node, partaking, participating, pooled, profit-sharing, reciprocal, scarf, seam, shared, socialist(ic), splice, suture, timber, together, united, weld, wrist

joist beam, strut, truss

joke caper, clowning, drollery, gag, howler, jape, jest, lark, leg-pull, malapropism, old chestnut, one-liner, pleasantry, prank, pun, quip, spoonerism, tall story, trick, wisecrack, witticism, yarn

jolt bob, bounce, bump, dig, hustle, jar, jerk, jig, jigget, jog, joggle, jostle, jounce, judder, jump, knock, nudge, shock, shudder, start, throb, tremor, twitch
may indicate an anagram

jostled
may indicate an anagram

jot iota, memo, note, tittle, whit

journal annual, comic, daily, diary, gazette, magazine, monthly, newsletter, newsmagazine, news-sheet, organ, pamphlet, periodical, quarterly, review, seasonal, serial, series, trade paper, weekly

journalism broadsheets, Fleet Street, fourth estate, gutter press, rapportage, reporting, tabloids, the press

journalist agony aunt, anchorman, columnist, correspondent, critic, ed, editor, freelancer, hack, muckraker, newscaster, news hound, newsman, newsreader, reporter, scandalmonger, sportscaster, stringer, subeditor

journalistic editorial, informative, newsworthy, newsy, reportable, reported, reportorial

judge acquit, adjudge, adjudicate, adjudicator, adviser, appraiser, arbiter, arbitrate, arbitrator, assessor, award, beak, bench, censor, censure, conclude, condemn, coroner, counsellor, critic, criticize, decide, decree, determine, estimator, examiner, find, hear, hold court, inspector, judiciary, jurist, justice, justiceship, justiciary, magistracy, magistrate, mediator, ombudsman, preside, pronounce sentence, recorder, Recording Angel, referee, reviewer, Rhadamanthus, rule, settle, Solomon, sum up, surveyor, tester, try, umpire, valuer, verderer

judging criticizing, discerning, discriminating, inquisitional, judgmental, selecting

judgment adjudication, appraisal, arbitration, assessment, belief, calculation, choice, comment, conjecture,

GEMSTONES USED IN JEWELLERY			
AGATE	CARBUNCLE	HYACINTH	ONYX
ALMANDINE	CARNELIAN	JASPER	OPAL
AMBER	CHALCEDONY	LAPIS LAZULI	PLASMA
AMETHYST	CORUNDUM	MADAGASCAR	RUBY
AQUAMARINE	DIAMOND	AQUAMARINE	SAPPHIRE
BALAS RUBY	EMERALD	MORION	SARDONYX
BLOODSTONE	FIRE OPAL	MOSS AGATE	TOPAZ
BONE TURQUOISE	GARNET	NEW ZEALAND	TURQUOISE
CAIRNGORM	HAWK'S-EYE	GREENSTONE	ZIRCON

consideration, critique, differentiation, discernment, discretion, discrimination, distinction, evaluation, inspection, notice, opinion, rating, remark, report, review, selection, sense, speculation, surmise, survey, taste, umpirage, valuation, view, wisdom

judicious discerning, discriminating, dispassionate, fair, judicial, just, sensitive, shrewd, unbiased, wise

judiciousness acumen, appreciation, connoisseurship, criticism, delicacy, dilettantism, discernment, discretion, discrimination, fastidiousness, feel, finesse, flair, insight, judgment, meticulousness, palate, perception, refinement, sensibility, sensitivity, taste

juggle
may indicate an anagram

juice buttermilk, extract, ghee, gippo, gravy, latex, milk, sap, sauce, soup, stock, water, whey

juiciness chylifaction, lactescence, moisture, serosity, succulence

juicy fleshy, lactiferous, milky, overripe, runny, sappy, succulent, watery

jumble
may indicate an anagram

jump bounce, bound, flinch, gap, high jump, hop, hurdle, leap, omit, overlook, pole-vault, recoil, saltation, ski-jump, skip, spring, steeplechase, vault

junction alliance, crossroads, decussation, focus, intersection, rendezvous

junk bric-a-brac, castoff, flotsam, jetsam, jumble, refuse, rubbish, tatt, white elephant

junkie acid-head, coke-head, DA, drug addict, druggie, freak, head, hophead, mainliner

jurisdiction bailiwick, bumbledom, cognizance, function, judicature, magistracy, mandate, mayoralty, municipality, portfolio, shrievalty

jurisprudence legal advice, nomology

jury assize, jurist, juror, panel

justice coroner, district attorney, equity, fairness, judge, magistrate, recorder, right, the bench, the judiciary, the magistracy

justify alibi, argue, attest to, champion, corroborate, defend, demonstrate, explain, extenuate, mitigate, palliate, plead, prove, rebut, recriminate, refute, rejoin, retort, substantiate, uphold, warrant

juxtapose abut, adjoin, appose, border, connect, join, neighbour, touch

juxtaposition abuttal, adjacency, apposition, bordering, closeness, connection, contact, contiguity, continuity, frontier, junction, nearness, tangency, touching

·K·

ABBREVIATIONS

K	kilo • king • knit • one thousand • potassium
KBE	Knight Commander of the Order of the British Empire
KCB	Knight Commander of the Order of the Bath
KG	kilogram • Knight of the Order of the Garter
KM	kilometre
KO	boxing • kick off • knock out
KW	kilowatt

keen dedicated, eager, energetic, enthusiastic, howl, lament, mourn, wail, zealous

keyboard ivories, keys
See also list at **orchestra**.

kick boot, clop, clump, dribble, drub, knee, pass, punt, quit, stamp, stomp, thrill, trample, tread on, zest
may indicate an anagram

kidnapping abduction, crimping, dognapping, impressment, shanghaiing

kill annihilate, cull, destroy, dispatch, dissolve, eliminate, exterminate, extinguish, kayo, KO, knock out, liquidate, massacre, murder, poison, put down, savage, shoot down, slaughter, slay, snuff, stab, wipe out, zap

killer assassin, barbarian, executioner, Hun, murderer, Vandal, Viking

killing blood-letting, blood-shedding, destruction, euthanasia, execution, manslaughter, murder, slaying

kin family, kith, like, nearest, relation, sibling

kind benevolent, branch, character, class, family, generous, genre, genus, goodly, gracious, helpful, inscape, nice, order, phylum, sort, species, thoughtful, type, variety

kindness benevolence, fairness, generosity, goodliness, grace, graciousness, helpfulness, kindliness, niceness, thoughtfulness

kiss buss, caress, cosset, cuddle, drool, embrace, enfold, fondle, neck, nestle, nuzzle, osculate, pet, slobber, smack, smooch, snog, snuggle, spoon, stroke

kitchen bakehouse, bakery, cookhouse, galley

knighted decorated, honoured

knock bang, bump, criticize, disparage, drip, drip-drop, knock-knock, patter, pitter-patter, rat-a-tat, rub-a-dub, setback, tap, ticktock

knotted
may indicate an anagram

know accept, appreciate, apprehend, believe, comprehend, conceive, convinced, credit, depend on, discern, distinguish, feel sure, identify, ken, master, perceive, realize, recognize, rely on, retain, savvy, see, twig, understand

knowledge acquaintance, apprehension, awareness, cognition, cognizance, comprehension, consciousness, enlightenment, familiarity, foreknowledge, foresight, gnosis, grasp, illumination, intuition, ken, mastery, perception, realization, savoir faire, savvy, understanding

knowledgeable acquainted, astute,

attentive, au fait, brainy, briefed, cognizant, competent, conscious, conversant with, efficient, encyclopedic, enlightened, experienced, expert, informed, instructed, mindful, omniscient, perceptive, polymathic, practised, primed, proficient, qualified, sagacious, shrewd, skilled, smart, streetwise, sussed, trained, versed, well-informed, wise

known celebrated, certain, discovered, explored, famous, heard of, infamous, notorious, perceived, proved, recognized, renowned, seen, true, verified

·L·

ABBREVIATIONS

L   fifty • lake • learner • left • litre • live • loch • money • pound (Latin: *libra*)
LA   Los Angeles • note • the (Frenchwoman)
LBJ president (Lyndon Baines Johnson)
LE   the (Frenchman)
LF   low frequency
LH   left hand
LI   lithium
LP   disc • Labour Party • long-playing • record
LPG liquefied petroleum gas
LR   lawrencium
LSD drug (lysergic acid diethyamide) • pounds, shillings, pence (Latin: *librae, solidi, denarii*)
LSE London School of Economics and Political Science
LT   Lieutenant • light
LTA Lawn Tennis Association
LTD limited
LU   lutetium

laboratory field station, lab, proving ground, research establishment, studio, think tank, workshop

laborious arduous, backbreaking, burdensome, crushing, detailed, difficult, elaborate, exhausting, fussy, gruelling, hard, hard-fought, hard-won, heavy, Herculean, heroic, killing, laboured, nit-picking, painful, painstaking, punishing, strenuous, thorough, tiring, toilsome, troublesome, unremitting, uphill, weary

labour backbreaker, bastard, bitch, bugger, childbirth, handful, hard graft, overdo, roll, sod, struggle, tall order, task, toil, trial, tribulation, uphill struggle, workforce

lack fault, inadequacy, lag, lose, miss, need, regress, require, shortcoming, want

lactate breast-feed, milk, nurse, suckle

ladder hierarchy, Jacob's ladder, ratlin(e), rope ladder, staircase, stepladder

ladder-like climbable, scalable, scalar, scalariform, stepped

lair anthill, beehive, burrow, cave, covert, den, drey, earth, eyrie, hideout, hole, holt, nest, perch, roost, sett, study, tunnel, warren

lake broad, fishpond, flash, lagoon, lakelet, linn, llyn, loch, lough, mere, millpond, oxbow lake, pond, pool, reservoir, salina, tarn

lakelike lacustral, lacustrine, limnologic, limnophilous, marshy, pondlike

lamb baby, breast, chump (chop), dupe, fool, fore shank, hind shank, innocent, lambkin, leg, loin (chop), middle neck, neck slice, rib, riblets, scrag end, shoulder, yearling

lament bemoan, bewail, complain, complaint, coronach, cry, deplore, dirge, elegy, funeral oration, grieve, groan, howl, keen, knell, lamentation, last post, moan, mourn, obsequies, plangency, regret, requiem, rue, sigh, sob story, sorrow, swansong, thanatopsis, threnody, ululation, wail

lamentable deplorable, depressing, distressing, pitiful, regrettable, tearjerking

lamenting depressed, dirgelike, disconsolate, doleful, down, elegiac, lachrymose, miserable, plaintive, plangent, red-eyed, sad, sorrowful, tearful, threnodic, unhappy, weeping, woebegone, wretched

laminate inlay, lacquer, paint, veneer

landing beach, berth, debark, debarkation, disembark, disembarkation, dismount, dock, landfall, moor, pier, quay, touchdown, wharf

landslide avalanche, creep, debris flow, earthflow, glide, lahar, mudflow, overwhelming, plastic flow, rock fall, slide, slump

larva antlion, caterpillar, chrysalis, cocoon, glowworm, grub, imago, leatherjacket, maggot, mealworm, nymph, pupa, silkworm, spiderling
See also list at **insect**.

last abide, anvil, bottom, endure, extreme, final, hold out, outlast, outlive, remain, stand, stay, survive, Z

lasting abiding, chronic, constant, continual, continuous, durable, enduring, eternal, evergreen, everlasting, immemorial, lifelong, long-lasting, long-lived, longstanding, long-term, perpetual, persistent, surviving, time-honoured

late behindhand, dead, delayed, dilatory, former, overdue, parachronistic, postdated, recent, slow, sluggish, tardy, unprepared, unpunctual, unready

latency abeyance, aestivation, anonymity, clandestineness, delitescence, dormancy, hibernation, inactivity, inertness, passivity, possibility, potentiality, quiescence, sleep, subconsciousness, sublimity, virtuality

lateness belatedness, delay, lag, retardation, slowness, tardiness, unpreparedness, unpunctuality, unreadiness

latent aestivating, archetypal, delitescent, dormant, hibernating, inactive, inert, passive, possible, potential, quiescent, sleeping, subconscious, subliminal, submerged, unacknowledged, underlying, undeveloped, virtual

later distant, future, subsequent, upcoming

laugh cachinnate, chortle, chuckle, giggle, guffaw, hoot, howl, roar, snicker, snigger, titter, whoop

laughable absurd, comic, hilarious, humorous, ridiculous, side-splitting

lavatory bathroom, bog, crapper, earth closet, gents, head, john, khazi, ladies, latrine, loo, outhouse, powder room, privy, public convenience, rest room, toilet, urinal, washroom

law act, bylaw, canon, charter, civil, common, criminal, decree, edict, institution, legislation, litigation, Murphy's, natural, order, ordinance, Parkinson's, penal code, police, precept, Procrustean, rescript, rule, sod's, standing order, statute

law-breaker assassin, bandit, bolshie, brawler, burglar, criminal, extortionist, gangster, handful, hooligan, killer, Mafioso, mugger, murderer, rapist, robber, rowdy, ruffian, thief

lawcourt assizes, court-martial, sessions

lawless anarchic, chaotic, random, undisciplined, wild
may indicate an anagram

lawlessness amorality, anarchy, boisterousness, chaos, disobedience, disorder, nihilism, rebelliousness, revolution, unruliness, upheaval, uprising

lawmaker Draco, lawgiver, Law Lord, legislator, Moses, MP, Solomon, Solon

lawyer advocate, attorney, barrister, brief, counsel, DA, judge, jurist, jury, magistrate, silk, solicitor

lax abandoned, careless, droopy, excess, free-for-all, immoderate, impure, incontinent, intemperate, licentious, loose, permissive, sloppy, unbridled, uninhibited, unruly, wanton

layer band, bed, bedding, belt, coat, course, cover, deck, face, flap, fold, interlining, laminate, lap, lay, line, lining, lode, overlap, overlay, overlayer, plate, pleat, ply, sandwich, seam, shingle, spread, stratify, stratum, strip, substratum, superstratum, table, thickness, tier, topcoat, topsoil, undercoat, underlayer, vein, veneer, zone

layered foliated, laminate, multistage, straticulate, stratified

layering foliation, lamellation, lamination, stratification

lazy bone idle, dawdling, dilatory, dull, idle, indolent, laggard, languid, lax, lethargic, listless, loafing, lolling, parasitic, procrastinating, slack, slothful, slow, sluggish, tardy, torpid, workshy

lead captain, direct, front, head, manage, run, spearhead, star

leader agitator, authority, autocrat, ayatollah, captain, chancellor, chief, chieftain, commissioner, compere, condottiere, conductor, constable, consul, demagogue, despot, dictator, director, emperor, empress, executive, governor, guru, head, headline, headman, king, maharajah, Mahdi, manager, mandarin, marshal, mayor, mayoress, Messiah, minister, monarch, official, pacemaker, pasha, patrician, potentate, precentor, premier, president, priest, prime minister, proconsul, protector, queen, rabble-rouser, rajah, ringleader, ringmaster, ruler, sheik, shepherd, sheriff, sovereign, spearhead, superior, suzerain, top man, tyrant, viceroy

leadership authority, authorization, captaincy, command, control, directorship, dominion, generalship, headship, hegemony, imperium, jurisdiction, kingship, lordship, management, mastership, power, premiership, presidency, rule, sovereignty, sway

leak discharge, divulge, dribbling, drip, drivel, drool, effusion, emanate, emerge, emission, emit, excrete, exfiltrate, extravasation, exudate, exude, gush, issue, leach, leakage, lixiviation, loss, ooze, outflow, percolate, perspire, reveal, salivate, secrete, seep, seepage, slaver, slobber, spurt, sweat, trickle, weep

leaky excretory, exudative, oozy, permeable, porous, runny, transudative, weeping

lean bend, desolate, incline, meagre, scrawny, skinny, thin, tilt, tip

leaping bouncing, bounding, hopping, jumping, prancing, saltant, saltatorial, saltatory, skipping, skyrocketing, spiralling, springing, vaulting *may indicate an anagram*

learn acquire, apprehend, ascertain, comprehend, con, contemplate, cram, determine, discover, find out, grasp, peruse, read, realize, remember, research, rub up, study, swot, train, understand

learned academic, brainy, enlightened, erudite, intellectual, profound, sagacious, scholarly, wise

learner abecedarian, apprentice, beginner, bluestocking, bookworm, egghead, initiate, L, neophyte, novice, postgraduate, pupil, recruit, researcher, rookie, scholar, student, swot, tiro, trainee, undergrad(uate)

learning accomplishments, attainments, bookishness, brainwork, civilization, cleverness, conning, contemplation, craftsmanship, cramming, cultivation, culture, education, erudition, instruction, intelligence, letters, literacy, lore, mastery, numeracy, omniscience, perusal, polymathy, proficiency, reading, sagacity, scholarship, schooling, study, swotting, teaching, wisdom

least last, less, minimum, minority, smallest

leave abandon, bequeath, cast off, deposit, discard, except, exclude, holiday, omit, permission, reject, time off

leavening barm, diastasic, enlivening, enzyme, fermentation, raising, seasoning, yeast, zymotic

lecherous carnal, concupiscent, debauched, depraved, dissipated, dissolute, fleshly, goatish, hot, incontinent, lascivious, lewd, libertine, libidinous, licentious, lickerish, lustful, Paphian, priapic, profligate, rakish, randy, sex-mad, sexy, turned-on, vicious, voluptuous, whoremongering, wild

left abandoned, discarded, larboard, leftwing, liberal, port, sinister, socialist, verso

left-handed dextrosinistral, sinistral, southpaw

legacy bequest, birthright, dower, heritage, inheritance, patrimony

legal allowable, authorized, decriminalized, judicial, just, lawful, legalized, legit, legitimate, legitimatized, legitimized, licensed, licit, official, permissible, permitted, proper, right, sanctioned, valid, warranted

legalistic contentious, disputatious, litigious, quibbling

legalize allow, authorize, decriminalize, legitimize, license, permit, sanction, validate, warrant

legend caption, code, corollary, epic, fable, myth, old wives' tale, saga, story, tale, tradition, yarn
See list of legendary creatures.
See also list at **imagine**.

legislate affirm, codify, confirm, decree, enact, endorse, establish, formalize, ordain, order, pass, ratify, vest, vote

legislation affirmation, codification, confirmation, constitutionalism, enactment, lawgiving, lawmaking, legislature, ratification, regulation, validation

legislative decretal, jurisprudential, legislational, legislatorial, nomological, nomothetic

legwear argyles, bobby socks, fleshings, galligaskins, half-hose, hold-ups, hose, hosiery, leggings, legwarmers, nylons, socks, stockings, tights

leisure convenience, ease, freedom, free time, idleness, inactivity, liberty, opportunity, recreational, relaxation, repose, rest, sinecure, spare time, unoccupied

leisurely deliberate, easy, laboursaving, relaxed, reposeful, resting, slow, unhurried

lend accommodate, advance, credit, dun, grant, loan, seek payment

lender debt collector, dun, extortionist, loan-maker, mortgagee, pawnbroker, pledgee, usurer

length distance, duration, elongation, endlessness, extension, extent, foot, footage, inch, infinity, interminability, knot, lengthiness, light-year, longitude, measure, metre, mile, mileage, parsec, prolongation, protraction, reach, sesquipedalianism, span, stretch, yard, yardage
See list at **measurement**.

lengthen continue, drag out, draw out, drop, elongate, extend, increase, produce, prolong, protract, spin out, stretch, string out, uncoil, unfold, unfurl, unroll

lenient accepting, accommodating, benevolent, charitable, clement, compassionate, considerate, easy, easygoing, forbearing, forgiving, generous, gentle, gracious, humane, indulgent, kid-glove, kind, lax, live-and-let-live, long-suffering, magnanimous, merciful, mild, moderate, patient, permissive, pitying, reasonable, soft, spoiling, tender, tolerant

lessen deplete, depreciate, deteriorate, dim, diminish, drain, dwindle, evaporate, fade, haemorrhage, leak, seep away, shrink, wane, wear away

lessening depletion, depreciation, deterioration, diminution, erosion, evaporation, impoverishment, leakage, outflow, shrinkage

letter character, cuneiform, digraph, epistle, grapheme, hieroglyph, ideogram, initial, inscribe, leaser, monogram, note, pictogram, postcard, print, rune, sign, symbol, type, wen

level deck, equalize, even, fell, flatten, floor, flush, grade, iron, landing, ledge, plane, press, raze, roll, row, shelf, smooth, spread, stage, step, storey, terrace, tier

lever corkscrew, crowbar, hoist, lift, prise, screwdriver, wrench

levy aid, benevolence, blackmail, charge, collect, customs, duty, exaction, excise, fine, imposition, impost, penalty, ransom, tariff, toll, tribute

liable accountable, accusable, actionable, answerable, cognizable, responsible, triable

liar equivocator, fabricator, fabulist, false witness, falsifier, fibber, mythomaniac, perjurer, phoney, pseudologist, pseudologue, storyteller, yarnspinner

liberality charity, excess, free-for-all, generosity, immoderation, intemperance, laxity, laxness, libertinism, licence, permissiveness, tolerance, uninhibitedness, unruliness, wantonness

liberate absolve, acquit, bail, decontrol, deliver, demob(ilize), deregulate, disband, discharge, disencumber, disengage, dismiss, emancipate, enfranchise, escape, except, excuse, exempt, extricate, free, grant immunity, let go, loose, manumit, pardon, parole, redeem, release, relieve, reprieve, rescue, save, unbind, unburden, unchain, unfetter, unknot, unleash, unlock, unshackle, untie

liberated acquitted, deregulated, emancipated, free, independent, liberalized, loose, released, relieved, reprieved, rescued, saved, scot-free,

---

LEGENDARY CREATURES

ABOMINABLE SNOWMAN	GARUDA	KELPIE	SASQUATCH
AMPHISBAENA	GHOUL	KING KONG	SATYR
BANSHEE	GIANT	KOBOLD	SCYLLA
BASILISK	GODZILLA	KRAKEN	SEA SERPENT
BEHEMOTH	GOLEM	LAMIA	SENMURV
BIGFOOT	GORGON	LEPRECHAUN	SIMURG
BOGEYMAN	GREMLIN	LEVIATHAN	SIREN
BUNYIP	GRIFFIN	LOCH NESS MONSTER	SNARK
CENTAUR	GRIFFON	MANTICORE	SPHINX
CERBERUS	GRYPHON	MEDUSA	THUNDERBIRD
CHIMERA	HARPY	MERMAID	TROLL
COCKATRICE	HIPPOGRIFF	MERMAN	UNICORN
CYCLOPS	HIPPOGRYPH	MIDGARD SERPENT	VAMPIRE
DRACULA	HOBBIT	MINOTAUR	WENDIGO
DRAGON	HOUYNHNHNM	ONI	WEREWOLF
FIREDRAKE	HUMANOID	ORC	WYVERN
FOMORIAN	HYDRA	PEGASUS	YAHOO
FRANKENSTEIN'S MONSTER	IBLIS	PHOENIX	YETI
	ICEMAN	ROC	ZOMBI
	JINN		

unbound, unchained, untied

liberation absolution, acquittal, decontrol, deliverance, deregulation, discharge, disencumberment, disengagement, dismissal, emancipation, escape, exemption, extrication, forgiveness, freedom, immunity, impunity, loosing, manumission, pardoning, quitclaim, quittance, redemption, relaxation, release, relief, reprieve, rescue, riddance, salvation, unbinding, unburdening, unchaining, unfettering, unknotting, unleashing

libertine bounder, buck, cad, Casanova, Don Juan, gigolo, heartbreaker, ladies' man, philanderer, rake, slag, stallion, stud

licence authorize, charter, franchise, intemperance, liberty, leave, patent, permission, permit, privilege, profligacy

lid bung, cap, cork, cover, crust, flap, hat, limit, plug, shutter, stopper, top

lie bull, burlesque, concoct, deceive, delude, dissemble, distort, fable, fabricate, falsehood, falsify, fantasy, fib, fictionalize, flimflam, implausibility, incredibility, parody, perjure, porky, propaganda, questionableness, recline, rest, romanticize, tall story, tall tale, taradiddle, terminological inexactitude, travesty, unbelievability, whopper, yarn

life animation, being, biography, energy, entity, existing, liveliness, nature, sensation, sensibility, sentience, soul, spirit, sprightliness, subsistence, vital force, vitality, vivacity, vivification, wildlife

lifelike eidetic, exact, faithful, graphic, natural, naturalistic, photographic, realistic, representative, unmistaken, veracious, verisimilar, vivid

life story autobiography, biography, history, memoirs

lift aid, assumption, boost, buoyancy, cable car, elevator, escalator, exaltation, funicular, leg-up, lionization, pla-

giarize, promotion, raise, steal, upgrading, upswinging

light albino, amusing, aurora australis, aurora borealis, bantamweight, beam, bleached, blond, brighten, brightness, brilliance, candle, colourless, daylight, dazzle, disembark, earthshine, faded, fair, featherweight, fire, flaxen, floodlight, fluorescence, handy, highlight, ignite, illuminate, illumination, incandescence, irradiate, ivory, kindle, lamp, lightened, lightning, lightweight, lucency, luminescence, luminosity, lustre, moonlight, moonshine, northern lights, overexposed, pale, pallid, pastel, pasty, phosphorescence, photon, portable, radiance, radiation, ray, refulgence, resplendence, splendour, spotlight, starlight, sunbeam, sunlight, sunshine, switch on, trivial, vividness, weightless, white

lighten alleviate, buoy, disburden, disencumber, ease, jettison, raise, relieve, unballast, unlade, unload, unsaddle, untax, uplift

lightening aeration, alleviation, bleaching, brightening, disburdening, disencumbering, easement, easing, illumination, overexposure, relief, unburdening, unlading, unloading

lighter brand, brighter, brushwood, burning glass, cap, detonator, explosive, faggot, firebrand, firelighter, firewood, flint, fuse, kindling, log, lucifer, match, paler, punk, scintilla, spark, sparking plug, spill, spunk, taper, tinder, torch, touchpaper, vesta, wick

lightness airiness, blondness, bubbliness, buoyancy, colourlessness, daintiness, delicacy, downiness, effervescence, ethereality, fairness, flimsiness, fluffiness, foaminess, frothiness, gaseousness, gentleness, imponderableness, joviality, levity, paleness, pallor, pastiness, portability, rarity, softness, sparkling, tenderness, thinness, triviality, unheaviness, unimportance, unweighableness, vaporization, volatileness, weightlessness, yeastiness

lightning ball lightning, fork lightning, sheet lightning, thunderbolt

likable admired, adorable, affable, affectionate, alluring, amiable, amicable, amusing, appealing, appreciated, attractive, bright, captivating, chivalrous, civilized, compatible, congenial, cordial, courteous, easygoing, endearing, engaging, fascinating, favoured, friendly, good, good-natured, infatuating, kindly, lovable, lovely, pleasing, polite, popular, sunny, well-mannered

like admire, adore, appreciate, care for, chase, cherish, court, delight in, desire, enjoy, esteem, fancy, hanker after, hold dear, long, love, lust after, prize, pursue, relish, run after, savour, sympathize with, take to, treasure, want, wish, woo, yearn

liking admiration, adoration, affection, affinity, appetite, approval, attachment, attraction, bending, biased, desirous, devotion, empathetic, empathy, fascination, favouring, fondness, friendship, infatuation, intimacy, leaning, love, passion, predisposed, preferring, prejudiced, sympathetic, sympathy, tenderness, tending, turning, zest

limit border, boundary, check, circumscribe, confine, constrain, contain, control, curb, curtail, cusp, define, demarcate, edge, enclose, exclude, extent, extreme, fringe, frontier, hamper, hinder, inhibit, mitigate, moderate, peak, point, pole, prohibit, proscribe, ration, repress, restrain, restrict, specify, summit, tip, top, verge, zenith

limitation circumscription, constraint, containment, control, definition, demarcation, exclusion, inhibition, mitigation, moderation, proscription, restraint, restriction

limited confined, cramped, curtailed, exclusive, finite, frozen, hidebound, inhibiting, narrow, no-go, off-limits, prohibitive, proscripted, repressive, restricted

linctus douche, eyebath, gargle, mouthwash, undine, wash

line back, band, bandage, binding, bloodline, braid, cable, coat, cord, cravat, descent, drawstring, dynasty, face, family tree, genealogy, guy, hawser, insulate, interface, interline, knot, lashing, lifeline, ligament, ligature, lineage, panel, pedigree, plait, queue, raffia, ribband, ripcord, rope, shoelace, soundproof, stitch, stock, string, tag, tape, tendon, thong, thread, tie, tourniquet, towrope, twine, umbilical cord, undercoat, wallpaper, wire

lineage descent, family tree, race, tribe

lingering dawdling, dilly-dallying, lagging, loitering, persistent, shilly-shallying

linguist classicist, dialectician, epigrammatist, epigraphist, etymologist, glossologist, grammarian, interpreter, lexicographer, logophile, philologist, phonetist, phrasemonger, poet, polyglot, semanticist, semasiologist, translator, writer

linguistic bilingual, colloquial, common, conversational, dialectal, etymological, formal, glossological, grammatical, idiomatic, informal, jargonish, jingoistic, journalistic, lexicographic, lexicological, literary, multilingual, philological, phonetic, politically correct, polyglot, scatological, semantic, slangy, standard, syntactic, vernacular

linguistics bilingualism, etymology, glossology, lexicography, multilingualism, philology, phonetics, phonology, polyglottism, pronunciation, semantics, semasiology, syntactics

lining backing, coating, facing, insulation, interfacing, interlining, undercoating

link affix, annex, attach, bind, bolt, braid, bridge, buckle, cement, clamp, clasp, clinch, clip, communicate, concatenate, connection, contact, dovetail, engage, entwine, fasten, fetter, fit, fuse, gird, glue, grip, handcuff, harness, hitch, interconnect, interlace, join, knot, lash, leash, lock, nail, network, pin, prefix, rivet, screw, sew, shackle, solder, span, splice, staple, stick, stitch, straddle, suffix, suture, swaddle, swathe, tape, tether, thread, tie, truss, twist, weave, wed, weld, wrap, yoke

liquefiable dissoluble, dissolvable, fusible, meltable, soluble, thawable

liquefied decoagulated, deliquescent, dissolved, liquefacient, liquescent, melted, molten, solvent, thawed

liquefy blend, emulsify, fluidify, fluidize, liquidize, melt, run, thaw

list border, catalogue, chart, chronicle, classify, diarize, edge, enumerate, enumeration, file, index, inventory, itemization, itemize, items, note, pigeonhole, record, register, registry, repertory, schedule, series, slant, stock, table, tabulate, tally, tilt, timetable

listed catalogued, charted, classificatory, filed, indexed, inventoried, itemized, noted, programmed, recorded, registered, scheduled, tabulated, taxonomic, timetabled

listen attend, ear, hark, hear, heed *may indicate a homophone*

lit alight, bright, brightened, candlelit, drunk, firelit, floodlit, highlighted, illuminated, lamplit, landed, moonlit, spotlit, starlit, sunlit, torchlit

literal chapter-and-verse, denotative, misprint, textual, true, verbatim, word-for-word

literate academic, cultivated, cultured, donnish, educated, erudite, highbrow, intellectual, numerate, scholarly, schooled, sophisticated

literature belles-lettres, brochure, bumph, letters, the arts, the classics, the humanities, writing

lithify cement, consolidate, crystallize, fossilize, mineralize, petrify, recrystallize

litigant accused, accuser, appellant, claimant, defendant, informer, intervener, libellant, libellee, litigator, objector, petitioner, plaintiff, prosecutor, pursuer, respondent, suitor

litigate accuse, advocate, arraign, charge, cite, claim, impeach, implead, indict, petition, plead, prosecute, request, sue, summon, try

litigated on trial, sub judice

litigating accusing, argumentative, claiming, contesting, disputing, litigant, litigious, objecting, quarrelsome, suing

litigation accusation, affidavit, assertion, case, claim, contest, dispute, lawsuit, legal action, objection, petition, plea, request, suit, summons, trial, writ

litter bier, brood, clutter, disarrange, dump, garbage, hash, heap, higgledy-piggledy, hodgepodge, jumble, lumber, mess, midden, mishmash, muddle, pallet, pickle, pigsty, rat's nest, rubbish, scatter, sedan, shambles, slum, stretcher, tip, topsy-turviness, trash, young

little baby, bantam, bijou, contracted, cramped, dainty, diminutive, dinky, dumpy, dwarfish, elfin, exiguous, fine, infinitesimal, insignificant, itsy-bitsy, itty-bitty, Lilliputian, limited, meagre, microcosmic, microscopic, mini, miniature, miniaturized, minimal, minuscule, minute, paltry, petite, petty, piddling, pint-size, pocket-size, poky, puny, scant, short, shrunk, skimpy, slight, small(-scale), squat, stunted, teeny-weeny, tenuous, thin, tiddly, tiny, titchy, trifling, wee

littleness compactness, diminutiveness, dinkiness, dumpiness, dwarfishness, exiguity, fineness, handiness, meagreness, miniaturization, minuteness, paltriness, petiteness, pettiness, portability, puniness, runtiness, scantness, scragginess, scrawniness, scrubbiness, shortness, shrunkenness, skimpiness, slightness, smallness, squatness, stuntedness, tenuousness, thinness

live alive, be, breathe, carry on, continue, endure, exist, last, persist, quicken, respire, revive, subsist, survive

lively active, animated, dynamic, energetic, gingery, spirited, sprightly, vigorous, vivacious

livid black and blue, blue, bruised, enraged, furious, pale, purple, white

living alive, animate, biotic, current, inhabiting, livelihood, organic, viable, vital

load ballast, burden, cargo, charge, encumber, freight, hamper, hinder, lade, lading, overburden, overload, payload, saddle, shipment, stowage, tonnage

loaded burdened, burdensome, charged, containing, crammed, full, holding, laden, lined, packed, padded, squeezed, stuffed, topped up .

loaf bagel, baguette, bannock, bap, barm cake, biscuit, bloomer, brain, bread stick, breakfast roll, bridge roll, brioche, bun, cob, cottage loaf, (cream)cracker, crêpe, crispbread, croissant, crumpet, currant bun, digestive biscuit, drop scone, farmhouse, flapjack, French bread, French stick, head, idle, laze, lounge, muffin, oatcake, pancake, pan (loaf), pikelet, plait, roll, scone, shortbread, split tin, teacake, tin, wafer, waffle, water biscuit

loan debt, IOU, lend, leverage, mortgage, overdraft

local diocesan, domestic, familiar, inhabitant, inn, native, nearby, neighbour, neighbouring, next-door, parochial, provincial, pub, tavern

locality approaches, area, beat, circuit, confines, environs, foreground, front, haunt, manor, neighbourhood, orbit, patch, precinct, purlieus, round, surroundings, turf, vicinage, vicinity, walk

locate base, billet, emplace, ensconce, establish, fix, install, place, plant, position, post, quarter, site, situate, spot, station, stick

locating chancing upon, coming across, detecting, discovering, finding, hitting on, pinning down, pinpointing, tracking down, turning up, unearthing

location beat, environment, environs, habitat, haunt, hole, locality, manor, patch, pitch, place, position, post, seat, setting, site, situation, spot, station, surroundings, territory, turf, whereabouts

locational cartographical, geographical, navigational, topographical

locomotive chuffer, engine, iron horse, jigger, loco, puffer, shunter, tank engine, train
See list at **vehicle**.

logic acumen, argumentation, deduction, dialectics, induction, insight, inspiration, instinct, intuition, rationale, reasoning, (sixth) sense

logical compatible, consistent, deductive, elenctic, equivalent, heuristic, hypothetical, inductive, inferential, necessary, propositional, sophistic

lonely deserted, desolate, forlorn, friendless, isolated, secluded, solitary

loner anchorite, ascetic, eremite, hermit, isolationist, lone wolf, marabout, recluse, seclusionist, solitary, stylite

long dragged out, drawn out, endless, extended, extensive, far-reaching, full-length, interminable, lengthy, long-winded, overlong, polysyllabic, prolonged, protracted, sesquipedalian, spun out, straggling, stretched, strung out, sustained, unabridged, verbose

longitudinal endways, lengthways, linear, longways

long-sighted far-sighted, hypermetropic, presbyopic

long-windedness bombast, cumbrousness, grandiloquence, pomposity, ponderousness, sesquipedalianism, stiffness, stiltedness, turgidity

look air, aspect, butcher's, dekko, eye, focus, gander, gape, gawk, gawp, gaze, glance, glare, glimpse, glower, goggle, leer, ogle, peek, peep, regard, scowl, shufty, squint, stare

lookalike alter ego, ba, clone, cloned, doppelgänger, double, homophyllic, homophyly, ka, like, match, pair, portrait, reflection, suit, twin

loom bode ill, forebode, intimidate, menace, soar, threaten, tower

looseness bagginess, floppiness, fluidity, liquid, runniness, slipperiness, wateriness

lose consume, decrease, deprive, dispossess, divest, evict, expropriate, face defeat, fail, forfeit, forget, mislay, misplace, miss, relinquish, rob, sacrifice, strip, subtract

loser also-ran, bungler, dud, failure, flop, has-been, no-hoper, nonstarter, reject, second-rater, underachiever, washout

loss bankruptcy, bereavement, cost, cut price, debit, decrease, defeat, deficit, deprivation, dispossession, divestment, eviction, expenditure, expense, expropriation, failure, insolvency, mislaying, misplacing, overdraft, overspending, perdition, poor return, robbery, sacrifice, shortfall, stripping, subtraction

lost astray, bereft, depleted, forgotten, hopeless, incorrigible, irrecoverable, irredeemable, irretrievable, lacking, mislaid, misplaced, missing, ruined, shorn, spent, squandered, stripped

loud bellowing, blaring, boisterous, booming, brassy, braying, cacophonous, carrying, clamorous, clangorous, crashing, deafening, dinning, ear-splitting, echoing, gaudy, lusty, noisy, ostentatious, pealing, piercing, plangent, powerful, rackety, rambunctious, rattling, resonant, ringing, rowdy, rumbustious, shouting, shrill, sonorous, stentorian, strident, thundering, vociferous, whooping, yelling

loudness blare, boom, brassiness, bray, cachinnation, cacophony, clang, extravagance, fanfare, ostentation, resonance, reverberation, shrillness, sonority, stertorousness, stridency, volume

love admiration, adoration, affection, Agape, Amor, Aphrodite, appreciate, ardour, Astarte, attachment, attraction, bewitchment, charity, cherish, compatibility, crush, Cupid, desire, devotion, ecstasy, enchantment, Eros, esteem, fancy, fascination, fervour, fondness, Freya, friendship, idolize, Kama, like, loyalty, lust, mush, nil, O, pash, popularity, prize, regard, relish, respect, revere, sentiment, shine, transport, treasure, uxoriousness, value, Venus, worship

loveability adorability, agreeability, allurement, amiability, attractiveness, charm, desirability, enchantment, endearment, likeability, sexiness, winsomeness

loveable adorable, alluring, angelic, appealing, beguiling, captivating, congenial, cuddly, desirable, divine, enchanting, endearing, engaging, interesting, intriguing, kissable, pleasing, popular, tempting, winning

lover admirer, adorer, aficionado, beau, boyfriend, bride-to-be, Casanova, conquest, date, escort, fan, fiancé(e), gigolo, girlfriend, jo, mistress, paramour, Romeo, seducer, suitor, sweetheart, wooer

loving affectionate, agapistic, amicable, amorous, attached, charitable, demonstrative, devoted, faithful, fond, fraternal, friendly, kind, loyal, motherly, paternal, platonic, sentimental, sympathetic, uxorious

low base, crouched, depressed, flattened, humble, inferior, knee-high, low-slung, mean(-spirited), moo, quiet, shallow, short, smutty, squat, stooped, stumpy, stunted

lower bottom, darken, decrease, deflate, depress, deteriorate, devalue, flatten, frown, gloom, hypodermic, inferior, nether, reduce, subcartilaginous, subcranial, subcutaneous, subjacent, subscript, underlaid, underlying, undermost, worsen
may indicate cattle

lowering debasing, decrease, de-escalation, deflation, demeaning, demolition, depressing, depression, descendent, descent, deterioration, diminution, downfall, drop, frowning, humiliating, immersion, looming, reduction, sinking, submersion

lowland campo, depression, field, flats, foothills, grassland, heath, hillock, hollow, hummock, inch, lea, level, llano, low-lying, mead, meadow, pampas, piedmont, plain, polder, prairie, range, savanna, steppe, strath, subalpine, submerged, submontane, sunken, vale, valley, veld, weald

lowliness meanness, modesty, poorness, smallness

lowly humble, low, mean, plebeian, poor, small

lowness baseness, coarseness, flattening, quietness, shallowness, shortness, squatness, stumpiness, stuntedness

loyal amenable, compliant, constant, dedicated, deferential, devoted, docile, faithful, leal, obedient, respectful, reverential, staunch, steadfast, submissive, sycophantic, tractable, true(-blue), willing

loyalty allegiance, comity, constancy, devotion, faithfulness, fealty, fidelity, service, staunchness, steadfastness

lubricant antifriction, emollient, glycerine, graphite, grease, lather, lenitive, mucilage, mucus, oil, plumbago, saliva, silicone, soap, soothing, spit, synovia, tallow, wax

lubricate beeswax, butter, glycerolate, grease, lard, lather, oil, soap, wax

lubricated greasy, slippery, smooth-running, well-greased, well-oiled

lubrication greasing, lube, nonfriction, oiling, sleekness, slickness, slipperiness, smoothness

lucent aglow, beaming, burning, candescent, fluorescent, glimmering, glowing, illuminating, incandescent, lambent, luminous, phosphorescent, radiant, refulgent, shining

luck auspiciousness, blessings, bonanza, destiny, fate, favour, fluke, fortune, golden age, good fortune, halcyon days, lot, Midas touch, potluck, providence, serendipity, winning streak

ludicrousness absurdity, bathos, bizarreness, buffoonery, clowning, comicality, daftness, drollery, eccentricity, fatuity, folly, foolishness, laughableness, senselessness, whimsicality, zaniness
may indicate an anagram

lump aggregate, block, cake, chunk, clod, clot, clump, coagulum, concretion, conglomerate, curd, endure, mass, nugget, protuberance, rock, stone, tolerate

lure allure, bait, captivate, charm, coax, decoy, ensnare, enthral, entice, fascinate, hypnotize, mesmerize, seduce, siren, snare, tantalize, tempt

lush abundant, alcoholic, booming, bountiful, drunk, exuberant, fat, fecund, fertile, flourishing, fresh, luxuriant, plenteous, plentiful, productive, prolific, prosperous, rich, rife, sot, thriving, verdant

lust ardour, carnality, concupiscence, lechery, libidinousness, libido, nymphomania, passion, randiness, satyriasis, sexuality

lustful concupiscent, horny, hot,

lascivious, lecherous, libidinous, randy, sexy

lustrous burnished, glassy, gleaming, glistening, glossy, iridescent, opalescent, pearly, polished, shimmering, shiny

luxury compliment, delicacy, flattery, holiday, honeymoon, honour, pleasantry, praise, treat, tribute

lying accumbent, ambiguous, couchant, decumbent, defamation, doggo, equivocating, evasive, fabrication, face down, false witness, falsification, fibbing, flimflamming, forswearing, frame-up, libel, mendacious, mendaciousness, mythomania, perfidious, perfidy, perjury, procumbent, prone, propagandizing, prostrate, pseudology, reclining, recumbent, romancing, shifty, slander, sprawling, spread-eagled, storytelling, supine, untruthful

·M·

ABBREVIATIONS

M	Majesty • male • mass • Master • me • mega- • Member • metre • Metropolitan Police • Military Medal • mile • million • minute • Monsieur • motorway
MA	Master of Arts • mother
MAG	magazine
MASH	mobile army surgical hospital
MB	Bachelor of Medicine • doctor • millibar
MBE	Member of the Order of the British Empire
MC	machine • Master of Ceremonies • Military Cross
MD	doctor • managing director • mendelevium • right hand (French: *main droite*)
ME	mechanical engineer • Middle East • myalgic encephalomyelitis
MED	medical • Mediterranean • medium
MET	meteorology • Metropolitan Police
MF	millifarad • moderately loudly (Italian: *mezzo forte*)
MI	Military Intelligence • motorway
MIN	minimum • minute
MJ	megajoule
ML	millilitre
MM	millimetre • thousand • with the necessary changes (Latin: *mutatis mutandis*),
MN	manganese
MO	Medical Officer • modus operandi • money order
MP	melting point • Member of Parliament • Military Police • moderately softly (Italian: *mezzo piano*)
MPG	miles per gallon
MPH	miles per hour
MS	manuscript • millisecond • multiple sclerosis
MT	Mountain

machination demagoguery, intrigue, manipulation, mystification, obfuscation

machine automaton, axle, bearing, belt, boring machine, broaching machine, bush, cam, clockwork, clutch, component, computer, contraption, coupling, crank, differential, drill, dynamo, engine, gear, gearwheel, generator, grinder, hub, journal, lathe, machinery, mechanism, milling machine, motor, part, planer, pulley, robot, rod, saw, servomotor, shaft, shaper, spring, synchromesh, turbine, wheel, wheelwork, works

macho man caveman, he-man, muscleman

maculation blotchiness, brindling, dappling, freckling, mottling, patchiness, pointillism, speckling, spottiness, stippling

madden anger, confuse, dement, derange, enrage, unbalance, unhinge

made blown, carved, composed, constructed, expressive, fashioned, modelled, moulded, produced, rounded, sculptured, set-up, shaped, squared, styled, stylish, tailored, thrown, turned
may indicate an anagram

madly
may indicate an anagram

magnanimous benevolent, charitable, humanitarian, philanthropic

magnet allure, electromagnet, focus, lodestar, lodestone, magnetite, magnetizer, paramagnet, polestar, siderite, solenoid

magnetic attractive, charismatic, dynamic, exciting

magnetism attraction, charisma, drawing power, electromagnetism, traction

magniloquence bombast, fanfaronade, flourish, grandiloquence, pomposity

maintain continue, insist, nurture, preserve, support, sustain

majestic ceremonious, dignified, fine, formal, grand, palatial, proud, regal, royal, solemn, starchy, stately, stiff

majesty dominion, grandeur, gravity, HM, HRH, lordliness, princeliness, sedateness, solemnity, sovereignty, venerability

majority adulthood, bulk, greater, lion's share, many, mass, more, most, preponderance

make assemble, build, compile, compose, compound, construct, erect, fabricate, fashion, fit together, form, put together, set up, structure

make-up blusher, composition, constitution, cosmetics, eyeliner, facepaint, foundation, greasepaint, lipstick, mascara, paint, perfume, powder, rouge
may indicate an anagram

male Adam, blade, bloke, boy, butch, card, chap(pie), cove, fellow, gent, gentleman, guy, he, him, himself, lad, lad-dish, macho, man, manly, mannish, masculine, swain, virile, yob, youth

malediction anathema, ban, charm, commination, curse, damnation, excommunication, imprecation, jinx, malison, proscription, spell, whammy

malevolence animosity, antagonism, bad blood, bloody-mindedness, cussedness, devilry, enmity, evilness, hate, hostility, ill will, loathing, maleficence, malice, malignity, meanness, nastiness, truculence, wickedness

malevolent baleful, evil, harassing, hateful, ill-disposed, ill-natured, ill-willed, intimidatory, intolerant, malefic, malicious, malignant, menacing, oppressive, pernicious, persecuting, tyrannical, wicked

malfunction break, crash, error, fail, glitch, go wrong, jam, misfire, seize, stall
may indicate an anagram

mammalian homoiothermic, marsupialian, warm-blooded

man Adam, bloke, boy, brother, chap, counter, crew, dad, daddy, don, father, fellow, godfather, godson, grandfather, grandson, guy, he, him, homo(sexual), househusband, husband, nephew, pater, paterfamilias, patriarch, pawn, people, pop, servant, son, staff, the human race, uncle, widower

manage administer, conduct, control, cope, direct, govern, handle, lead, manipulate, manoeuvre, mastermind, minister, motivate, orchestrate, organize, oversee, regulate, rule, run, superintend, supervise

management administration, authority, care, charge, conduct, control, direction, effectiveness, efficiency, government, handling, maintenance, managership, manipulation, manoeuvring, motivation, orchestration, organization, patronage, proctorship, regimen, responsibility, running, service, statesmanship, stewardship, superintendence, supervision, support

manager administrator, agent, bailiff, caretaker, curator, custodian, executive, executor, foreman, gaffer, ganger, inspector, overseer, protector, steward, superintendent, supervisor, warden

managerial administrative, authoritative, bureaucratic, directional, directorial, executive, governmental, gubernatorial, hegemonic, judicial, legislative, navigational, nomothetic, official, officious, organizational, presidential, supervisory

mangled
may indicate an anagram

mania agromania, cacoethes, complex, compulsion, craze, dipsomania, erotomania, fad, fetishism, fixation, kleptomania, megalomania, necromania, nymphomania, obsession, onomatomania, pyromania, satyriasis, theomania

manic berserk, delirious, demented, frantic, frenetic, frenzied, hysterical, rabid, ranting, raving, wild
may indicate an anagram

manifest apparent, appear, blatant, conspicuous, definite, disclose, divulge, evident, flagrant, inventory, marked, notable, obtrusive, obvious, ostensible, overt, patent, prominent, pronounced, public, recognizable, reveal, salient, show, striking, uncover, unmistakable, visible

manifestation appearance, avatar, conspicuousness, demonstration, disclosure, discovery, display, epiphany, exhibition, exposition, exposure, incarnation, indication, materialization, omen, ostentation, performance, personification, proclamation, projection, publication, representation, revelation, show, sign, signal, symbolization, theophany, token, typification
may indicate an anagram

manikin automaton, doll, dwarf, fantoccini, gingerbread man, golliwog, guy, marionette, model, puppet, robot, scarecrow, snowman, soft toy, tailor's dummy

manipulate bias, browbeat, bully, entice, goad, handle, hypnotize, incite, inveigle, lobby, lure, mislead, play on, prejudice, prod, push, seduce, tempt
may indicate an anagram

manners breeding, convention, correctness, culture, custom, diplomacy, elegance, etiquette, formality, gentility, gentlemanliness, ladylikeness, mannerliness, polish, protocol, refinement, savoir-faire, savoir-vivre, sophistication, urbanity

manual guidebook, hand-operated, instructions, touch-operated

manufacture assembly, automation, building, concoct, construction, create, engineering, fabrication, machining, making, mass production, processing, treatment

manufactured architect-designed, artificial, created, custom-built, engineered, handmade, homemade, homespun, machine-made, man-made, mass-produced, processed, ready-made, synthetic, tailor-made

Manx
may indicate a shortening (tailless – delete the last letter)

many considerable, hundreds, lots, majority, some, umpteen

map atlas, blueprint, cartogram, chart, describe, diagram, elevation, explore, globe, layout, plan, scale drawing, survey

marked conspicuous, doomed, labelled, noted, pitted, pock-marked, scabrid, scabrous, scarred, spotted, striking

market agora, auction, bazaar, exchange, fair, forum, marketplace, mart, peddle, promote, saleroom, sell, shop, trade, traffic

marketplace agora, forum, piazza, plaza, shopping centre, shopping mall

marquetry boulle, Certosina work, intarsia, parquetry, wood inlay

marriage alliance, bigamy, cohabitation, concubinage, conjugality, coverture, deuterogamy, endogamy, exogamy, intermarriage, levirate, love match, match, matrimony, mesalliance, misalliance, miscegenation, mixed marriage, monogamy, morganatic marriage, nuptial bond, polyandry, polygamy, polygyny, remarriage, trial marriage, trigamy, union, wedlock

marriageable adult, eligible, nubile, suitable

married coupled, espoused, hitched, hooked, joined, matched, mated, newlywed, one, paired, partnered, spliced, united, wedded

marry betroth, cohabit, elope, espouse, honeymoon, unite, wed, wive

marsh bog, carr, delta, fen(land), flat, marshland, mire, moor, morass, moss, mud, mudhole, ooze, playa, quagmire, quicksand, salina, saltpan, slime, slough, sludge, sudd, swamp(land), the Everglades, wallow, wetlands

marshy boggy, fenny, flooded, muddy, oozy, sludgy, slushy, sodden, soggy, splashy, squashy, squelchy, swampy, waterlogged

martial armed, auxiliary, belligerent, gladiatorial, mercenary, naval, pugilistic, soldierly, war-like

masculinity laddishness, machismo, manliness, patriarchy, virility

mask act, appear, bluff, colour, deodorize, disguise, dissemble, dress up, embellish, embroider, face, fake, gilt, gloss, hide, impersonate, masquerade, overdo, seem, show, simulate, touch up, varnish, vizor, whitewash, window-dress

mass assemble, block, cake, chunk, clod, clump, cluster, dollop, glob, gobs, group, heap, hunk, lump, majority, mound, mountain, pile, size, stack, wad, weight, wodge

massacre butcher, carnage, decimate, genocide, murder, slaughter

massage caress, iron out, knead, pet, pulverize, pummel, reflexology, rub down, shampoo, Shiatsu, smooth, stroke
may indicate an anagram

master aristocrat, beat, become skilled in, boss, bwana, cardinal, command, conquer, control, crush, dame, defeat, dictate, direct, dominate, dowager, elder, expert, govern, governor, guvnor, head, housemother, husband, instruct, lady, laird, landlady, landlord, landowner, lead, learn, liege, lord, madam, manage, matriarch, matron, mistress, nobleman, oppress, overcome, overlord, overpower, patriarch, proprietor, quell, rule, sahib, seigneur, sir, squire, subdue, subjugate, teacher, vanquish, wife

masterful aristocratic, authoritarian, autocratic, coercive, commanding, despotic, dictatorial, divine, dominating, domineering, executive, great, imperious, lordly, magisterial, magistral, main, majestic, major, managerial, matriarchal, matronly, noble, oppressive, parliamentary, patriarchal, principal, royal

masterpiece act, best-seller, bravura, brilliance, classic, coup, creation, deed, exploit, feat, hit, jewel, magnum opus, masterwork, trump

masterstroke brainwave, bright idea, coup, improvisation, inspiration, invention, notion, tour de force

matchmaker broker, go-between, mediator, middleman, Pandarus

material bodily, carnal, concrete, corporal, earthly, embodied, empirical, fabric, fleshly, incarnate, massive, massy, materialized, natural, palpable, physical, ponderable, real, realized, reincarnated, sensible, sensual, solid, somatic, spatiotemporal, substance, tangible, unspiritual, weighty, worldly *See also list at* **materials**.

materialization corporation, embodiment, epiphany, incarnation, manifestation, realization

materialize actualize, arise, be born, become, come about, develop, evolve, factualize, grow, realize, reify, take shape, unfold, visualize

materials acrylic, basics, beam, board, carbon fibre, cellulose, clay, cloth, components, constituents, elements, essentials, fabric, fibre, fibreglass, fuel, glass, grain, grist, hide, latex, lath, matter, meat, metal, mineral, nylon, parchment, plank, plastic, polyester, polystyrene, polythene, polyurethane, resources, rope, sand, soil, staple, stave, stock, stuff, substance, textile, timber, vellum, wood, yarn *See list of materials*.

mathematical algebraic, algorithmic, analytical, arithmetical, differential, geometric, integral, logarithmic, statistical, topological, trigonometrical

mathematician algebraist, arithmetician, geometrician, numerical analyst, statistician, systems analyst

mathematics addition, algebra, algorithm, analysis, approximation, arithmetic, calculation, calculus, computation, convolution, counting, differentiation, division, enumeration, equation, evolution, extrapolation, figures, figuring, geometry, integration, interpolation, inversion, involution, logarithm, measurement, multiplication, numbering, numbers, numeracy, numeration, permutation, quantification, quantifying, reckoning, reduction, statistics, subtraction, sums, transformation, trigonometry *See also list at* **geometry**.

matriarchy gynarchy, gynocracy

matrimonial bridal, concubinal, conjugal, connubial, husbandly, hymeneal, marital, matronly, nuptial, premarital, spousal, wifely

matter atom, body, business, cells, component, constituent, corpus, element, fabric, factor, frame, isotope, issue, make a difference, mass, material, materiality, mineral, molecule, monad, organism, origin, plasma, principle, protoplasm, pus, situation, structure, stuff, substance

maturing blooming, budding, burgeoning, developing, flowering, growing, pullulating

maturity adulthood, experience, matureness, ripeness

maxim adage, aphorism, apophthegm, axiom, banality, bromide, byword, catchphrase, catchword, cliché, commonplace, dictum, epigram, epigraph, epithet, formula, gnome, law, mantra, moral, mot, motto, observation, oracle, order, platitude, precept, principle, proverb, rule, saw, saying, slogan, tag, theorem, truism, truth, watchword, witticism

mayhem
may indicate an anagram

meal breakfast, brunch, buffet, collation, corn, cream tea, dinner, elevenses, fare, grain, high tea, lunch, luncheon, potluck, provisions, refection, refreshment, repast, snack, supper, tiffin

mealy branny, crumbly, farinaceous, floury, furfuraceous

mean affirm, assert, average, betoken, cheeseparing, communicate, connote, convey, declare, denote, designate, evidence, express, grudging, imply, import, indicate, inform, intend, midpoint, mingy, miserly, money-grubbing, niggardly, parsimonious, penny-pinching, penurious, point to, purport, represent, scrimping, signify, spell, stingy, symbolize, tell, tight, tight-arsed, tightfisted, ungenerous

MATERIALS

ABACA
ABB
ABBOT CLOTH
ABRADED YARN
ABSORBENT
  COTTON
ACCA
ACELE
ACETA
ACETATE
  RAYON
ACRILON
ACRYLIC
ADA CANVAS
ADMIRALITY
  CLOTH
AERATED YARN
AGA BANEE
AGRA GAUZE
AIDA CANVAS
AIRPLANE
  CLOTH
ALACHA
ALAMODE
ALASKA
ALBERT CREPE
ALGERIAN
  STRIPE
ALMA
ALOE LACE
AMERICAN
  CLOTH
AMERICAN
  COTTON
ANGOLA YARN
ANGORA
ARABIAN LACE
ARALAC
ARDIL
ARGENTINE
  CLOTH
ARIDEX
ARMOZEEN
ARMOZINE
ARMURE
ARMURE-LAINE
ARMURE-
  SATINÉE
ART LINEN
ART SILK
ASBESTALL
ASBESTOS
ASTRAKHAN
AUSTINIZED
BABY FLANNEL
BAGGING
BAGHEERA
BAG SHEETING
BAIZE
BAKU

BALBRIGGAN
BALINE
BALLOON
  CLOTH
BAN
BANDLE LINEN
BANDOLIER
  CLOTH
BARATHEA
BARÉGE
BARK CLOTH
BARK CREPE
BARLEYCORN
BARONETTE
  SATIN
BARRACAN
BASCO
BASKET CLOTH
BATH COATING
BATISTE
BATSWING
BATTING
BAUDEKIN
BAUM MARTEN
BEAVER(ETTE)
BEAVERTEEN
BEDFORD CORD
BEMBERG
BENGAL(INE)
BERBER
BERLIN CANVAS
BEUTANOL
BIRETZ
BLANCARD
BLATTA
BOBBINET
BOLIVIA CLOTH
BOLTING
  CLOTH
BOMBAZET
BOMBAZINE
BOMBER
  CLOTH
BOMBYCINE
BOOK CLOTH
BOOK LINEN
BOOK MUSLIN
BOTANY
BOUCLÉ YARN
BOX CLOTH
BRABANT
BRILLIANTINE
BRIN
BRITTANY
  CLOTH
BROADCLOTH
BROAD GOODS
BROADTAIL
  CLOTH
BROCATELL

BROWN
  HOLLAND
BRUNETE
BRUSHED
  RAYON
BRUSHED
  WOOL
BUCKSKIN
BUFFSKIN
BUNTING
BURE
BUREAU
BURLAP
BURNET
BURRAH
BUSTIAN
BUTCHER LINEN
BYRD CLOTH
BYSSUS
CACHEMIRE DE
  SOIE
CADET CLOTH
CADIS
CAFFA
CAFFOY
CALAMANCO
CALF(SKIN)
CALICO
CAMACA
CAMBAYE
CAMBRESINE
CAMBRIC
CAMEL'S HAIR
  CLOTH
CAMLET
CANDLEWICK
  FABRIC
CANGAN
CANNEQUIN
CANTON CREPE
CANTON
  FLANNEL
CANTON
  LINEN
CANTOON
CANVAS
CAPENET
CAPESKIN
CARACAL
CARACUL
CARDINAL
  CLOTH
CASEMENT
  CLOTH
CASHA
CASHMERE
CASTOR
CATALIN
CATALOWNE
CATGUT

CAVALRY TWILL
CELANESE
CELENESE
CHALLIS
CHAMBRAY
CHAMOIS(ETTE)
CHARMEEN
CHARMEUSE
CHARVET
CHEESECLOTH
CHEKMAK
CHENILLE
CHESS CANVAS
CHEVIOT
CHEYNEY
CHIFFON
CHILLO
CHINA
  COTTON
CHINA SILK
CHINO CLOTH
CHINTZ
CHIRIMEN
CHIVERET
CHROME
CHUNAN
CIRCASSIAN
CLAY WORSTED
CLOISTER
  CLOTH
COBURG
CONGO
  CLOTH
CONSTITUTION
CORD
CONTRO
CONVENT
  CLOTH
COOTHAY
CORD
CORDUROY
CORKSCREW
  TWILL
COSSAS
COSTUME
  VELVET
CÔTELÉ
COTELINE
COTTONADE
COTTON CREPE
COTTON
  FLANNEL
COTTON REP
COTTON
  SUITING
COTTON
  VELVET
COTTON
  WORSTED

COWHIDE
CRAPE
CRASH
CREA
CREPELINE
CREPE LISSE
CRETON(NE)
CRINKLE CLOTH
CRINOLINE
CRISP
CROISE
CROISÉ VELVET
CROSS FOX
CROSS-STITCH
  CANVAS
CROWN
CRUSHED
  VELVET
CUBICA
CUT VELVET
DACCA
  MUSLIN
DACCA SILK
DAMASK
DAMMASÉ
DELAINE
DENIM
DENMARK
  SATIN
DIAGONAL
  CLOTH
DIAPER (CLOTH)
DIAPER
  FLANNEL
DIAPHANE
DIMITY
DJERSA
DOESKIN
DOMETT
DORIA
DORNICK
DOTTED SWISS
DOUBLE
  DAMASK
DOWLAS
DRABBET
DRAP DE BERRY
DRAP D'ÉTÉ
DREADNOUGHT
DRESS FLANNEL
DRESS LINEN
DRUGGET
DRUID'S CLOTH
DUCAPE
DUCHESS(E)
DU PONT
  RAYON
DURANCE
DUVETYN
EARL GLO

ÉCRU CLOTH
ÉCRU SILK
EGYPTIAN
  CLOTH
EGYPTIAN
  COTTON
ÉLASTIQUIF
ELECTORAL
  CLOTH
ELEMENT
  CLOTH
EMBROIDERY
  LINEN
EMPRESS CLOTH
END-TO-END
  CLOTH
EOLIENNE
ÉPINGLÉ
ÉPONGE
ERMINE
ESKIMO CLOTH
ESPARTO
ESTAMENE
ETAMINE
EVERFAST
EVERLASTING
FABRIC
FAILLE
FAKE FUR
FARADINE
FELT
FISHER
FISHNET
FITCH
FITCHEW
FLANNEL
FLANNELET(TE)
FLORENCE
FORFAR
FOULARD
FRIEZE
FRUIT OF THE
  LOOM
FUJI
FUR
FUR FABRIC
FUR FELT
FUSTIAN
GABARDINE
GALATEA
GALYAC
GALYAK
GAUZE
GENET
GEORGETTE
GINGHAM
GLAZED CHINTZ
GOATSKIN
GOBELIN
GOSSAMER

GRASS CLOTH
GRENADINE
GRENAI
GROGRAM
GROS(GRAIN)
GUANACO
GUIPURE
GUNNY
GURRAH
HAIRCLOTH
HARRIS TWEED
HEMP
HESSIAN
HIDE
HOLLAND
HOMESPUN
HONAN
HONEYCOMB
  CLOTH
HOP SACKING
HORSECLOTH
HORSEHAIR
HUCKABACK
INDIAN LAMB
INDIENNE
IRISH LINEN
IRISH POPLIN
JACONET
JACQUARD
  FABRIC
JAP SILK
JEAN
JUPON
KAPOK
KASHMIR
KERSEY
KIDSKIN
KOLINSKY
LACE
LAINE
LAMBSKIN
LAMÉ
LAMPAS
LAPIN
LASTEX
LAWN
LEATHER
LEATHERETTE
LEGHORN
LEOPARD
LIBERTY
LINEN
LINENE
LINON
LINSEY-
  WOOLSEY
LISLE
LONGCLOTH
LUREX
LUSTRINE

LUSTRING
MADRAS
MARABOU
MARCELINE
MARCELLA
MAROCAIN
MARQUISETTE
MARSEILLES
MATERIAL
MELTON
MERCERIZED
  COTTON
MERINO WOOL
MESSALINE
MILANESE
MILIUM
MINIVER
MOGADORE
MOHAIR
MOIRE
MOLESKIN
MOQUETTE
MOROCCO
MOSS CREPE
MOUSSELINE
MOUTON
MULL
MULMUL
MUSLIN(ET)
MUSQUASH
MUTATION
  MINK
NAINSOOK
NANKEEN
NAPA LEATHER
NAPERY
NET(TING)
NINON
NUN'S VEILING
NUTRIA
NYLON
OCELOT
OILCLOTH
OILSKIN
ORGANDIE
ORGANDY
ORGANZA
ORGANZINE
ORLON
OSTRICH
  FEATHERS
OTTOMAN
OVERCOATING
OXFORD
PAILLE
PAISLEY
PANNE VELVET
PARACHUTE
  FABRIC
PARAGON

PATCHWORK
PATENT LEATHER
PEAU DE SOIE
PEKIN
PELT
PERCALE
PERSIAN LAMB
PETERSHAM
PIECE GOODS
PIGSKIN
PILOT CLOTH
PIQUÉ
PLUSH
PONGEE
POODLE CLOTH
POPLIN
POULT-DE-SOIE
PRINT
PURE SILK
PYTHON
RABBIT
RACCOON
RANCH MINK
RAWHIDE
RAW SILK
RAYON
REP
RIBBON
ROAN
ROMAINE
RUBBER
RUSSIA LEATHER
SACKCLOTH
SACKING
SAFFIAN
SAIL CLOTH
SAMITE
SARCENET
SARSENET
SATEEN
SATIN
SATINET(TE)
SAXONY
SCOTCH PLAID
SCRIM
SEA-ISLAND
  COTTON
SEALSKIN
SEERSUCKER
SENNIT
SERGE
SHAGREEN
SHANTUNG
SHARKSKIN
SHEEPSKIN
SHEPHERD'S
  PLAID
SHETLAND
  WOOL
SHIRTING

SHODDY
SHOT SILK
SILK
SILVER FOX
SISAL
SIS(S)OL
SKIN
SKIVER
SLIPPER SATIN
SNAKESKIN
SOUPLE
SPONGE
  CLOTH
STOCKINET
STRAW
STUFF
SUEDE (CLOTH)
SUITING
SUMMER
  ERMINE
SURAH
SWANSDOWN
TAFFETA
TAMMY
TAPESTRY
TARLATAN
TARLETAN
TARPAULIN
TARTAN
TATTERSALL
  CHECK
TATTERSALL
  PLAID
TERRY CLOTH
TEXTILE
TICKING
TIE SILK
TIFFANY
TINSEL
TISSU(E)
TOILE (DE JOUY)
TOILINET(TE)
TOWELLING
TRICOT
TRICOTINE
TROPICAL
  SUITING
TULLE
TURKISH
  TOWELLING
TUSSAH
TUSSEH
TUSSORE
TWEED
TWILL
UNION
VAIR
VALENCE
VALENCIA
VELOURS

MATERIALS continued				
VELURE	VOILE	WELSH	WILD SILK	WORCESTER
VELVET(EEN)	WAFFLE	FLANNEL	WINCEY(ETTE)	WORSTED
VISCOSE	CLOTH	WHIPCORD	WITNEY	ZIBELINE
(RAYON)	WAX CLOTH	WHITE FOX	WOOL	
VIYELLA	WEBBING	WILD MINK	WOOLLEN	

meandering
may indicate an anagram

meaning antonym, application, bearing, colouring, connotation, construction, contents, context, core, definition, denotation, derivation, drift, effect, equivalence, essence, etymology, explanation, expression, force, gist, idea, identity, idiom, implication, import, intelligibility, intention, interpretation, jargon, latency, literality, matter, meaningfulness, message, metaphor, nonsense, opposite, pith, plainness, practice, purport, reference, relevance, scope, sense, shift, signification, spirit, substance, sum, synonym, tenor, text, topic, trope, usage, value

meaningful affirmative, allegorical, comprehensible, declaratory, eloquent, evocative, explicit, express, expressive, figurative, idiomatic, important, importing, indicative, intelligible, interpretative, literal, lucid, metaphorical, perspicuous, pointed, purporting, significant, significative, special, symbolic, telling

meaningless absurd, amphigoric, banal, clichéd, commonplace, empty, fatuous, foolish, futile, hackneyed, hollow, illegible, illogical, inane, incoherent, ineffective, ineffectual, invalid, irrelevant, mystifying, nonsense, nonsignificant, null, piffling, platitudinous, pointless, rubbishy, senseless, sophistic, trashy, trifling, trite, trivial, unapt, unexpressive, unidiomatic, unimportant, unintelligible, unmeaning, vacuous

meaninglessness absurdity, amphigory, emptiness, illegibility, illogicality, inanity, incoherence, ineffectuality, insignificance, invalidity, irrelevance, nonsense, nullity, scribble, sophistry, triteness, truism, unimportance, unintelligibility, vacuity

means ability, ace, agency, alternative, appliances, approach, capability, capacity, choice, contrivance, conveniences, course, cure, device, expedient, facilities, instrument, knack, know-how, knowledge, last resort, makeshift, manner, measure, medium, method, mode, power, process, recourse, remedy, resort, skill, steps, substitute, technique, technology, the basics, the wherewithal, tool, tools, trump card, vehicle, way

meant deliberate, designed, destined, expected, implied, intended, obliged, planned, predestined, purposeful, required

measurable appraisable, assessable, calculable, computable, determinable, estimable, gaugeable, mensurable, meterable, quantifiable

measure appraise, assay, assess, bar, calculate, calibrate, class, classify, compare, cost, criterion, determine, differentiate, estimate, evaluate, fathom, gauge, grade, graduate, lead, mark, meter, order, peg, place, plumb, position, precede, probe, quantify, rank, rate, rhythm, scale, score, shade, size, sort, sound, survey, time, triangulate, value, weigh

measurement assessment, calculation, calibration, computation, determination, evaluation, gauging, measure, mensuration, metage, metrology, quantification, rating, survey, triangulation, valuation
See list of weights and measures.

measuring instrument astrolabe, callipers, chain, dipstick, dividers, echo sounder, feeler gauge, foot rule, log, measuring rod, milestone, octant, Plimsoll line, plumb line, protractor, quadrant, ruler, scale, set square, sextant, tape measure, vernier, waterline, yardstick

WEIGHTS AND MEASURES

ACRE	DR	LB	PINT
AMP	DRACHM	LEAGUE	PIPE
AMPERE	DRAM	LIGHT-YEAR	POINT
ÅNGSTROM	DWT	LINE	POISE
ARE	DYNE	LINK	POLE
BALE	ELL	LITRE	POUND
BAR	ERG	LUMEN	POUNDAL
BARLEYCORN	FARAD	LUX	QUADRANT
BARN	FARADAY	MAXWELL	QUART
BARREL	FATHOM	MEGACYCLE	QUARTER
BEL	FERMI	MEGAFARAD	QUINTAL
BIT	FIRKIN	MEGAHERTZ	QUIRE
BOARD-FOOT	FLUID OUNCE	MEGATON	RAD
BOLT	FOOT	MEGAWATT	RADIAN
BUSHEL	FOOT-POUND	MEGOHM	REAM
BYTE	FT	METRE	RÉAMUR
CABLE	FURLONG	METRIC TON	REM
CALORIE	GALLON	MG	ROD
CANDELA	GAUGE	MHO	RÖNTGEN
CANDLE	GAUSS	MICROFARAD	ROOD
CARAT	GILBERT	MICROGRAM	RUTHERFORD
CASK	GILL	MICRON	SCANTLING
CENTAL	GR	MICROOHM	SCRUPLE
CENTIGRAM	GRAIN	MICROWATT	SECOND
CENTILITRE	GRAM(ME)	MIL	SIEMENS
CENTIMETRE	HAND	MILE	SLUG
CENTNER	HECTARE	MILLIGRAM	SPAN
CHAIN	HECTOGRAM	MILLILITRE	SQUARE
CHALDRON	HECTOLITRE	MILLIMETRE	SQUARE
CM	HENRY	MILLISTERES	CENTIMETRE
CORD	HERTZ	MIM	SQUARE INCH
COULOMB	HIDE	MINIM	SQUARE KILOMETRE
CRAN	HL	MINUTE	SQUARE MILE
CRITH	HOGSHEAD	ML	SQUARE YARD
CUBIC FOOT	HORSEPOWER	MM	STADE
CUBIC INCH	HOUR	MOLE	STERADIAN
CUBIC METRE	HUNDREDWEIGHT	NAIL	STERE
CUBIC YARD	IN	NANOMETRE	STILB
CUBIT	INCH	NANOSECOND	STOKE
CURIE	JOULE	NEPER	STOKES
CUSEC	KELVIN	NEWTON	STONE
CWT	KG	NIT	TESLA
CYCLE	KILO	OERSTED	THERM
DEBYE	KILOBAR	OHM	TOISE
DECAGRAMME	KILOCYCLE	OUNCE	TON
DECALITRE	KILOGRAM(ME)	OZ	TONNE
DECAMETRE	KILOHERTZ	PARSEC	TORR
DECIBEL	KILOLITRE	PASCAL	TROY
DECIGRAMME	KILOMETRE	PECK	TUN
DECILITRE	KILOTON	PENNYWEIGHT	VOLT
DECIMETRE	KILOWATT	PERCH	WATT
DEGREE	KM	PHON	WATT-HOUR
DENIER	KNOT	PHOT	WEBER
DIOPTER	LAMBERT	PICA	YARD
			YD

measuring system apothecaries' measure, avoirdupois weight, imperial system, metric system, troy weight

meat beef, beefburger, chicken, duck, essence, faggots, flesh, game, gist, goat, goose, ground meat, grouse, hamburger, hare, lamb, meatballs, mince, minced meat, mutton, partridge, pheasant, pigeon, plover, pork, poultry, quail, rabbit, rissoles, snipe, squab, substance, turkey, veal, venison, woodcock

meat-eating cannibalistic, carnivorous, creophagous, flesh-eating, omophagic

mechanical automated, automatic, computerized, electronic, habitual, hydraulic, instinctive, instrumental, labour-saving, motorized, power-driven, powered, robotic, technological

mechanics automation, computerization, cybernetics, electronics, engineering, hydraulics, procedures, robotics, technology, workings

meddle boss, butt in, dun, fiddle, harass, hassle, interfere, interrupt, intervene, pester, pry, spy, tinker

meddler big-ears, busybody, dabbler, eavesdropper, fusspot, gossipmonger, interferer, mole, rubbernecker, scandalmonger, snoop, spy, stirrer, tittle-tattler

meddling intrusive, meddlesome, nosy, officious

media advertisement, broadcasting, broadsheet, cablecasting, cable-vision, circular, colour supplement, communication, electronic media, extra, gutter press, hatches, heavy, journalism, journals, junk mail, magazines, mailshot, matches, mediums, narrowcasting, news, newscast, newsmagazine, press, publicity, radio, scoop, tabloid, telecommunication, television, yellow press

median average, balance, golden mean, happy medium, intermediate, mean, medial, mesial, par

mediate arbitrate, bargain, compromise, conciliate, intercede, interfere, interpose, intervene, judge, meddle, moderate, negotiate, officiate, pacify, pander, propitiate, reconcile, referee, umpire

mediation arbitration, coming-together, conciliation, diplomacy, give-and-take, intercession, interposition, intervention, moderation, negotiation, pacification, propitiation, reconciliation, statesmanship, stepping-in, troubleshooting, umpirage

mediator appeaser, arbiter, conciliator, diplomat, dove, go-between, intercessor, intermediary, judge, liaison, matchmaker, middleman, moderator, negotiator, pacifier, pander, peacemaker, propitiator, referee, statesman, troubleshooter, umpire

medical Aesculapian, allopathic, clinical, dermatological, epidemiological, Galenic, gynaecological, Hippocratic, homeopathic, iatric, neurological, obstetric, ophthalmological, osteopathic, pathological, radiological, surgical, urological

medicine acupressure, acupuncture, alternative, aromatherapy, Ayurvedic, balm, balsam, bolus, capsule, chiropractic, complementary, decoction, dose, draught, drench, drip, drug, electuary, elixir, faith healing, folk, fringe, herb, herbalism, holistic, homeopathy, infusion, injection, jab, linctus, lozenge, medication, mixture, naturopathy, osteopathy, pastille, pharmaceutical, pharmacopoeia, physic, pill, placebo, plaster, potion, powder, preparation, prescription, reflexology, remedy, shiatsu, shot, simple, supplementary, tablet, tabloid

mediocre adequate, alright, average, banal, commonplace, così-così, downmarket, dull, fair, grey, indifferent, inferior, lukewarm, middling, moderate, ordinary, passable, pedestrian, prosaic, run-of-the-mill, small-time, so-so, tolerable, unexceptional, unremarkable

mediocrity adequacy, half-measure, indifference, inferiority, mixed blessing, second best

medium average, balanced, central, clairvoyant, fifty-fifty, halfway, instrument, intermediary, intermediate, mean, median, method, middle(-of-the-road), midpoint, midsection, midway, moderate, procedures, regular, spiritualist, standard

medley
may indicate an anagram

meet appropriate, assemble, concur, confront, contest, encounter, face, greet, intercommunicate, interface, meeting, suitable, tackle

meeting appointment, assembly, assignation, calling, concourse, confrontation, date, encounter, engagement, frequentation, gathering, get-together, impingement, interface, interview, meet, reception, rendezvous, reunion, social, soirée, stay, tête-à-tête, tryst, visiting

melodious canorous, catchy, chiming, dulcet, euphonious, fine-toned, full-toned, golden-toned, harmonious, lilting, lyrical, mellifluous, musical, Orphean, resonant, singable, tuneful, well-pitched

melodiousness attunement, chime, concord, consonance, euphony, harmoniousness, musicality

melody air, aria, canto, cantus, chorus, descant, euphony, leitmotif, line, measure, motif, refrain, reprise, solo, song, strain, subject, theme, tune

melt clarify, defrost, deliquesce, dwindle, flux, fuse, mollify, render, run, smelt, thaw, unfreeze

member affiliate, arm, associate, belonger, cardholder, component, element, fellow, initiate, insider, leg, limb, MP, wing

memento commemoration, keepsake, memorabilia, memorial, monument, plaque, relic, souvenir, statue, token, tribute, trophy

memorable evocative, haunting, indelible, mnemonic, nostalgic, notable, noteworthy, remembered, reminding, reminiscent, unforgettable, unforgotten

memorial celebratory, commemoration, commemorative, funeral, gravestone, mausoleum, monument, remembrance, tombstone

memorize learn, remember, retain

memory anamnesis, evocation, hindsight, identification, memorization, nostalgia, RAM, recall, recognition, recollection, reflection, remembrance, reminiscence, reputation, retention, retrospection, ROM, souvenir, storage, store

menstruation catamenia, courses, menses, monthlies, period, the curse

mental cephalic, cerebral, conceptual, crazy, deductive, instinctive, intellectual, intuitive, logical, noetic, phrenic, psychological, psychotic, rational, reasoning, thinking

mental block amnesia, blank spot, blind spot, brainstorm

mercantile capitalist, commercialistic, exchangeable, marketable, merchantable, retail, saleable, trading, wholesale

merchandise article, cargo, commodity, durables, freight, goods, line, load, perishables, product, range, repertoire, staple, stock, store, sundries, supplies, vendible, wares

merchant businessman, dealer, entrepreneur, exporter, importer, marketer, merchandiser, middleman, monopolist, oligopolist, operator, speculator, wholesaler
See also list at **occupation**.

merciful benevolent, clement, compassionate, forbearing, forgiving, indulgent, kind, lenient, long-suffering, magnanimous, patient, placable, stoic, tolerant, unreproachful, unresentful, unrevengeful

mercifulness benevolence, clemency, compassion, kindness, lenity, long-suffering, magnanimity, placability, unresentfulness, unrevengefulness

merciless cruel, heartless, pitiless, revengeful, ruthless

mercy acquittal, clemency, compassion, favour, forbearance, forgiveness, grace, leniency, long-suffering, mercifulness, mitigation, pardon, quarter, relief, reprieve, second chance

merge ally, amalgamate, associate, blend, connect, consolidate, link, unite

merit deserve, earn, excellence, qualify, rate, value, worth

meritorious commendable, deserving, meriting, worthy

messy
may indicate an anagram

metamorphose alter, change into, melt, move, mutate, shift, transfer, transfigure, transform, translate, transmute, transpose
may indicate an anagram

meteor bolide, comet, falling star, fireball, meteorite, meteoroid, micrometeorite, radiant, shooting star
See also lists at **astronomer**; **planet**.

meteorologist aerographer, climatologist, weather forecaster

meteorology aerography, anemology, climatology, weather forecasting

meter ammeter, count, electrometer, galvanometer, measure, oscilloscope, potentiometer, voltmeter, wattmeter

method coherence, coordination, custom, discipline, habit, manner, mode, organization, pattern, plan, proportion, regularity, routine, rule, scheme, structure, symmetry, system, technique, uniformity

methodicalness accuracy, meticulousness, punctiliousness, straightness, systematics, systematization

metre accentuation, Alexandrine, amphibrach, amphimacer, anacrusis, anap(a)est, beat, caesura, catalexis, choriamb, counterpoint, cretic, dactyl, dactylic hexameter, diaeresis, dimeter, dipody, distich, elegiac couplet, elegiac distich, elegiac pentameter, emphasis, foot, heptameter, heroic couplet, hexameter, iamb, iambic pentameter, ionic, measure, metrics, numbers, octameter, paeon, pentameter, prosody, pyrrhic, quantity, rhythm, scansion, spondee, sprung rhythm, stress, tetrameter, tribrach, trimeter, trochee
See also list at **measurement**.

metrical barometric, cartographic, cubic, geodetic, linear, mensural, mensurational, metric, metrological, optometric, photometric, psychometric, quantitative, rhythmic, tachometric, topographic, volumetric

miasma damp, firedamp, fume, malaria, mephitis, reek, smog, smoke

miasmic effluvial, foetid, fumy, mephitic, reeking

microbe amoeba, animalcule, bacillus, bacterium, germ, microorganism, protozoan, virus

microscopically impalpably, imperceptibly, imponderably, indiscernibly, infinitesimally, microcosmically, subatomically

middle central, centre, epicentre, equidistant, even, fifty-fifty, grey, half-and-half, halfway, impartial, intermediate, irresolute, medial, mid, middlemost, middle-of-the-road, midmost, midpoint, midst, midway, moderate, neutral, nonaligned, nonpartisan, unextreme, waist
may indicate the middle *letter(s) of a* word

middle age maturity, middle life, middle years

middle-aged climacteric, fatherly, fortysomething, matronly, mature, menopausal, motherly, overblown, thirtysomething

middle class Babbittry, bourgeoisie, burgherdom, merchant class, professional class, suburban, suburbia, white-collar class

middleman agent, arbitrator, broker, counsellor, distributor, go-between, intercessor, intermediary, interventionist, linkman, mediator, medium, messenger, moderator, mouthpiece, negotiator, ombudsman, panderer, pig-in-the-middle, pimp, referee, spokesperson, third party, umpire

middling average, fair, indifferent, mediocre, ordinary, run-of-the-mill, so-so, undistinguished

midline bisection, diameter, equator, midriff, mid-section, waistline

militant aggressive, bellicose, belligerent, combative, hawkish, martial, militaristic, offensive, sabre-rattling, warlike

militarist buccaneer, chauvinist, condottiere, conqueror, conquistador, crusader, expansionist, freebooter, hardliner, imperialist, jingoist, marauder, mercenary, militant, pirate, plunderer, privateer, raider, robber, samurai, warmonger

militarize arm, commission, conscript, enlist, enrol, fight, mobilize, overthrow, rally, rebel, recruit, revolt, rise, volunteer

military aggressive, air force, army, battle-scarred, bellicose, belligerent, chivalrous, citizen's army, combative, defensive, gladiatorial, Home Guard, irregulars, knightly, marines, martial, mercenary forces, militant, militia, national defence, naval, navy, offensive, operational, pre-emptive, pugnacious, RE, regular forces, reserves, RN, TA, Royal Engineers, SAS, Senior Service, shell-shocked, soldierly, special forces,

SS, strategic(al), tactical, Territorial Army, the services, veteran, volunteer army, warlike
See list of British and American military ranks.

milky cloudy, lacteal, lacteous, lactescent, lactic, lactiferous, opaque

millinery hatmaking, hatting

millions billion, centrillion, crore, decillion, duodecillion, googol, googolplex, lots, milliard, myriad, nonillion, novemdecillion, octillion, octodecillion, quadrillion, quattuordecillion, quindecillion, quintillion, septendecillion, septillion, sexdecillion, sextillion, tredecillion, trillion, undecillion, vigintillion

mind awareness, brains, care, cautious, cognition, consciousness, guard, heed, intellect, mentality, object, perception, prepare, protest, psyche, rationality, tread carefully, tread warily, vigilant, watch

mindlessness absent-mindedness, blankness, calm, empty-headedness, fatuity, folly, inanity, oblivion, tranquility, vacancy, vacuity

mineral amphibole, chromite, chrysolite, clay mineral, feldspar, magmatite, mica, oligoclase, olivine, orthoclase, pegmatite, plagioclase, pyroxene, silicate, spinel

minority childhood, fewness, inadequacy, littleness, meagreness, meanness, smallness

mirage delusion, false dawn, fool's gold, fool's paradise, hallucination, illusion, phantasm

misanthrope antifeminist, hermit, homophobe, loner, male chauvinist, misandrist, misogynist, racist, sexist, solitary, xenophobe

misanthropic antisocial, baleful, hateful, malevolent, mean, unsociable

miscellanea kaleidoscope, lucky dip,

BRITISH MILITARY RANKS

ARMY	ROYAL NAVY	ROYAL AIR FORCE
FIELD MARSHAL	ADMIRAL OF THE FLEET	MARSHAL OF THE ROYAL AIR
GENERAL	ADMIRAL	FORCE
LIEUTENANT-GENERAL	VICE-ADMIRAL	AIR CHIEF MARSHAL
MAJOR-GENERAL	REAR-ADMIRAL	AIR MARSHAL
BRIGADIER	COMMODORE	AIR VICE-MARSHAL
COLONEL	CAPTAIN	AIR COMMODORE
LIEUTENANT-COLONEL	COMMANDER	GROUP CAPTAIN
MAJOR	LIEUTENANT-	WING COMMANDER
CAPTAIN	COMMANDER	SQUADRON LEADER
LIEUTENANT	LIEUTENANT	FLIGHT LIEUTENANT
SECOND	SUBLIEUTENANT	FLYING OFFICER
LIEUTENANT	MIDSHIPMAN	PILOT OFFICER

AMERICAN MILITARY RANKS

ARMY AND AIR FORCE	NAVY
CHIEF OF STAFF	CHIEF OF NAVAL OPERATIONS
GENERAL OF ARMY (ARMY ONLY)	FLEET ADMIRAL
GENERAL	ADMIRAL
LIEUTENANT GENERAL	VICE ADMIRAL
MAJOR GENERAL	REAR ADMIRAL
BRIGADIER GENERAL	CAPTAIN
COLONEL	COMMANDER
LIEUTENANT COLONEL	LIEUTENANT COMMANDER
MAJOR	LIEUTENANT
CAPTAIN	LIEUTENANT (JUNIOR GRADE OR J.G.)
FIRST LIEUTENANT	ENSIGN
SECOND LIEUTENANT	MIDSHIPMAN

mosaic, patchwork quilt, ragbag, rainbow, stained-glass window

miscellany anthology, assortment, babel, chrestomathy, circus, clamour, clatter, collection, confusion, conglomeration, dappling, farrago, gallimaufry, hash, hotchpotch, imbroglio, job lot, jumble, kaleidoscope, linseywoolsey, medley, menagerie, mess, miscellanea, mishmash, mixture, mosaic, motley, muddle, oddments, pandemonium, paraphernalia, patchwork, phantasmagoria, potpourri, ragbag, smorgasbord, snippets, speckling, sundries, tangle, thesaurus, variegation, variety, zoo

misconnection mesalliance, misalliance, misapplication, misreference, misrelation

misdirect avert, divert, misinform, mislead

miser hoarder, meanie, misanthrope, money-grubber, niggard, penny-pincher, Scrooge, skinflint, tight-arse

misfit alien, anarchist, beatnik, bohemian, dissenter, dissident, eccentric, freak, heretic, hypocrite, individualist, loner, maverick, nonconformist, oddball, outsider, pretender, rebel, stranger, Tartuffe, weirdo

misfortune adversity, bad luck, evil star, inauspiciousness, missed chance

misgovern mismanage, misrule, mistreat, misuse

mishap accident, calamity, contretemps, disaster, misadventure

misinform camouflage, cheat, contrive, deceive, disguise, disinform, distort, dupe, embroider, falsify, fool, fudge, garble, gloss, juggle, machinate, manipulate, mask, misevaluate, misinterpret, mislead, misquote, misrepresent, misstate, misteach, mystify, obfuscate, outsmart, propagandize, rig, scheme, slant, strain, trick, twist, warp, whitewash

misinformation disinformation, distortion, misevaluation, misinterpretation, misquotation, misstatement, propaganda

misinterpret add, blunder, caricature, distort, equivocate, err, exaggerate, falsify, garble, inflate, misapprehend, misconceive, misconstrue, misdiagnose, misjudge, misquote, misread, misrepresent, misspell, mistake, mistranslate, misunderstand, omit, overestimate, parody, pervert, subtract, suppress, traduce, travesty, twist, underestimate, wrench

misinterpretation blunder, caricature, error, exaggeration, falsification, garbling, inflation, misapplication, miscomputation, misconception, misjudgment, misquotation, misrepresentation, misspelling, mistake, overestimation, parody, solecism, traducement, travesty, underestimation

misjudge blunder, bungle, distort, miscalculate, misconceive, misconstrue, misinterpret, misread, misreckon, miss, mistake, mistime, misunderstand, overestimate, prejudge, slip, stumble, trip, twist, underestimate

misjudged foolish, ill-advised, ill-timed, misconstrued, misinterpreted, mistaken, misunderstood, out, wrong

misjudgment cross purposes, deception, distortion, fallacy, fallibility, false reading, fool's paradise, gullibility, inexactness, miscalculation, misconception, misconstruction, misinterpretation, misunderstanding, overestimation, overvaluation, underestimation, undervaluation

misplaced gone missing, lost, mislaid, mislocated, missing

misrepresent botch, burlesque, caricature, colour, daub, defame, deform, distort, exaggerate, falsify, flatter, frame, guy, libel, lie, overdramatize, overembellish, overemphasize, parody, pervert, plant evidence, slander, slant, travesty, twist

misrepresentation caricature, colouring, deformation, distortion, exaggeration, falsehood, falsification, fib, grotesquerie, lie, misquotation, misstatement, overdramatization, overemphasis, parody, perversion, travesty
may indicate an anagram

misrepresented biased, caricatured, deformed, dissimilar, distorted, exaggerated, false, grotesque, inaccurate, incorrect, parodied, perverted, slanted, twisted, unfair, unjust, unlike, unrepresentative, untrue, wrong

miss claim, clamour for, crave, desire, err, fail, go astray, lack, long for, maiden, miscarry, misfire, pine, want

missile antimissile missile, antitank weapon, arrow, ball, ballistic missile, bazooka, bolt, brickbat, bullet, cannonball, Cruise missile, dart, ejectamenta, ejector, Exocet, flare, grapeshot, guided missile, mortar, Patriot, pellet, Polaris, projectile, rocket, rocket-launcher, Scud, shaft, shell, shot, shrapnel, slingstone, slug, stone, torpedo, trajectile, Trident, V-1, V-2, weapon, whiz-bang
See also list at **weapon**.

missing absent, deficient, deleted, excluded, lacking, left out, minus, mislaid, omitted, short, subtracted, taken away, wanted, wanting

mission crusade, duty, embassy, errand, function, job, office, quest, task, vocation

misspelling cacography, error, literal (error), typo(graphical) error

mist becloud, blur, drizzle, fog, haze, peasouper, smoke

mistake bloomer, blooper, blunder, boob, bungling, clanger, error, fault, howler, misapprehension, miscalculation, misconception, misconstruction, misinterpretation, misjudgment, misunderstanding

mistaken biased, blundering, bungling, deluded, erring, erroneous, misjudging, prejudiced, self-contradicting, wrong

mistime antedate, anticipate, butt in, disrupt, disturb, interrupt, intrude, lag, misjudge, postdate, pre-empt

mistimed anachronistic, inappropriate, inopportune, metachronistic, misdated, premature

mistiness cloud, drizzle, fogginess, mizzle, pluviosity, rain, scotch mist, showeriness

mistreat abuse, befoul, blight, condemn, corrupt, damage, defile, despoil, destroy, harm, hurt, impair, injure, maltreat, molest, pervert, poison, pollute, torment, violate, wound

misty cloudy, dewy, drizzling, foggy, frosted, milky, mizzly, opalescent, pearly, rainy, roric, semiopaque, showery, smoky, stained, tinted, translucent, watery

misuse abuse, assault, attack, barbarism, batter, beat, bungle, damage, defile, defraud, desecrate, distort, diversion, divert, embezzle, evil, exploit, expropriate, extravagance, fatigue, force, fraud, fritter, harm, ill-treat, illuse, impair, injure, injury, maladminister, malapropism, malpractice, manhandle, manipulation, misapply, misappropriate, misdirect, misemploy, misgovern, mishandle, misjudge, mismanage, misrule, mistreat, molest, oppress, oppression, outrage, overreact, overtax, overuse, overwork, peculation, pervert, pollute, profane, prostitute, solecism, spoil, strain, violate, violation, violence, waste

mitigate leaven, moderate, mollify, temper

mix admix, adulterate, alloy, amalgamate, blend, brew, colour, combine, compound, confound, contaminate, crossbreed, cross-fertilize, dapple, dilute, doctor, dye, fortify, fuse, generalize, harmonize, heap, hybridize, imbue, impregnate, infuse, instil, integrate, interlace, interlard, interlay, interleave, intersperse, intertwine, interweave, jumble, knead, lace, lump together, mash, meddle, merge, mingle, mixture, mongrelize, muddle up, pound, pulverize, season, shake, speckle, spice, spike, sprinkle, stir, suffuse, tamper, temper, tinge, variegate

mixed adulterated, alloyed, amalgamated, blended, chaotic, combined, confused, cross-bred, crossed, diluted, disordered, eclectic, fifty-fifty, fused, half-and-half, half-caste, heterogeneous, higgledy-piggledy, hybrid, integrated, interbred, intermarried, intertwined, interwoven, jumbled, kaleidoscopic, merged, mingled, miscegenetic, miscellaneous, mongrel, motley, multicultural, multiracial, patchy, phantasmagoric, random, stirred, syncretic, tangled, topsy-turvy, unsorted, variegated
may indicate an anagram

mixed race half-breed, half-caste, mulatto, octaroon, quadroon

mixed-up bewildered, confounded, confused, jumbled, mistaken, muddled, puzzled, scrambled

mixture adulteration, amalgamation, association, chaos, combination, composition, confusion, conglomeration, disorder, eclecticism, entanglement, fusion, hybridization, integration, involvement, jumble, merger, mongrelism, muddle, scramble, syncretism, union, variety

mix up bewilder, cock-up, confound, confuse, entangle, foul-up, hash, jumble, mess, muddle, puzzle, scramble, shuffle, snarl-up
may indicate an anagram

moan bawl, boohoo, complaint, howl,

keening, lamentation, sigh, sob, ululation, wail, whinge

mockery apery, badinage, banter, burlesque, caricature, cartoon, denunciation, derisiveness, impersonation, joke, lampoon, mime, mimicry, pantomime, parody, parrotry, piss-take, put-down, sarcasm, satire, scoffing, send-up, spoof, takeoff, travesty, wind-up

model archetype, carve, clothes horse, coathanger, epitome, example, fashion plate, ideal, mannequin, mould, original, paradigm, prototype, sculpt, shape, T, test design

moderate abate, allay, alleviate, appease, arbitrate, assuage, average, balanced, calm, centre, chair, circumscribe, composed, confine, control, cool, curb, cushion, dampen, ease, equable, extenuate, fair, gentle, harmless, indifferent, judicious, just, liberal, low-key, lull, mediate, mediocre, medium, middling, mild, mitigate, modest, modulate, mollify, neutral, neutralize, non-committal, non-extreme, non-radical, non-reactionary, nonviolent, pacify, palliate, peaceful, poor, prudent, quiet, quieten, rational, reasonable, referee, regulate, relieve, restrained, sensible, sober, soften, soothe, so-so, steady, still, subdue, tame, temper, temperate, tolerant, tone down, tranquil, umpire, unexceptional, untroubled, weak, weaken

moderation abatement, adjustment, alleviation, assuagement, average, calmness, check, composure, compromise, control, coolness, decrease, diminution, equanimity, fairness, golden mean, happy medium, impartiality, justness, mitigation, modulation, mollification, neutrality, nonviolence, prudence, quietness, reasonableness, reduction, regulation, relaxation, remission, restraint, sang-froid, sedateness, self-possession, sobriety, steadiness, temperance, tranquillization

moderator anaesthetic, analgesic, arbitrator, balm, brake, buffer, chairperson, controller, cushion, judge, lenitive, mediator, opiate, palliative, peacemaker, referee, restraint, sedative, soporific, umpire

modest humble, meek, unaspiring, unassuming, unboastful, unimposing, unimpressive, unobtrusive, unostentatious, unpretending, unpretentious

modesty humility, meekness, unassumingness, unobtrusiveness, unostentatious, unpretentiousness

modification adaptation, adjustment, alteration, attunement, change, improvement, modulation, qualification, regulation, variation
may indicate an anagram

modify adapt, adjust, allow, alter, attune, change, colour, condition, coordinate, extenuate, improve, mitigate, moderate, modulate, palliate, qualify, reconcile, regulate, soften, temper, tone down, vary

modular atomic, cellular, molecular

moist clammy, close, damp, dank, humectant, humid, muggy, sodden, soggy, sticky, tacky, wet

moisten dampen, humectate, humidify, wet

moisture dampness, dew, humectation, humour, rain, soddenness, sogginess, soppiness, water, wateriness, wetness

momentum action, activity, actuation, agitation, bustle, course, current, flight, flow, flux, impetus, impulsion, mobilization, motivation, propulsion, restlessness, run, rush, stir, stream

monastic Encratite, friar, monachal, monkish, nunnish, priestly, religious, sister

monetary budgetary, chrysological, coined, demonetized, fiduciary, financial, fiscal, minted, numismatic, nummary, nummular, pecuniary, stamped
See also list at **economic**.

monetize circulate, coin, counterfeit, forge, issue, mint, print, stamp

money assignat, banknote, bond, brass, bread, bullion, bundle, cash, certificate, cheque, coin, coinage, coupon, cowrie, currency, debenture, dosh, dough, draft, Eurocheque, filthy lucre, gold, greenbacks, IOU, legal tender, lolly, mammon, money order, note, packet, paper money, pelf, postal order, premium bond, promissory note, readies, riches, scrip, siller, silver, specie, spondulicks, sterling, traveller's cheque, wad, wampum, zillions *See list of money.*

monk abbess, abbot, anchorite, ascetic, bhikku, bhikkunis, bonze, bo-

MONEY

AMANIA	DUCAT(OON)	MILREIS	SEQUIN
AMBROSIN	DUPONDIUS	MITE	SESTERCE
ANGEL	EAGLE	MNA	SESTERTII
ANGELOT	EASTERLING	MOHAR	SESTERTIUM
ANNA	ECU	MOHUR	SEXTANS
AS	ESCUDO	MOIDORE	SHILLING
ASPER	FAR	MONKEY	SHO
AUREUS	FARTHING	NAPOLEON	SILVERLING
BAUBEE	FIRST BRASS	NGUSANG	SILVER PENNY
BAWBEE	FLORENCE	NICKEL	SILVER-STATER
BEKA	FLORIN	NOBLE	SIXPENCE
BELGA	FRANC	OBANG	SOL
BETSO	FUORTE	OBOL	SOLDO
BEZART	GOLD BROAD	P	SOU
BIGA	GOLD NOBLE	PAGODE	SOVEREIGN
BIT	GOLD PENNY	PAOLO	SPADE GUINEA
BOB	GOLD STATER	PFAG	SPUR ROYAL
BOLIVIANO	GROAT	PENCE	STATER
BROAD	GUILDER	PENGO	STICA
BUCK	GUINEA	PENNY	STIVER
CAROLUS	GULDEN	PESETA	STOOTER
CASH	HALFPENNY	PESO	STOUR-ROYAL
CENT	HONG KONG	PICAYUNE	STYCA
CENTAVA	DOLLAR	PICE	SYCEE
COB	JACOBUS	PIE	TAEL
CONDOR	JOEY	PISTAREEN	TALARI
CONTO	JOHANNES	PISTOLE	TALENT
COPANG	KIP	PLACK	TANNER
COPEC	KOPECK	PONY	TESTER
COPPER	KRAN	POUND	TESTO(O)N
CROWN	KREUTZER	QUADRUSSIS	TETRADRACHMA
CUARTILLO	L	QUARTER	THALER
D	LAT	QUETZALE	THREEPENCE
DAM	LIARD	QUID	THREEPENNY BIT
DARIC	LIBRA	QURSH	TICAL
DAUM	LIRA	REAL	TICCY
DÉCIME	LITAS	REE	TOMA(U)N
DENARII	LIVRE	REI	TRIBUTE PENNY
DENARIUS	LOCHO	RIXDOLLAR	TRIPONDIUS
DIDRACHM(A)	LOUIS (D'OR)	ROSE-NOBLE	UNCIA
DIME	MAIL	R(O)UBLE	UNICORN
DINAR	MARAVEDI	RYAL	UNIK
DOBLON	MARK	S	UNITE
DOIT	MEDIO	SCEAT(T)	VENEZOLANO
DOLLAR	MERK	SCUDI	YELLOW BOY
DOUBLOON	MIL	SCUDO	YEN
DRACHMA	MILL SIXPENCE	SEMIS	ZECHIN

san, brother, caloyer, cenobite, dervish, fakir, friar, hermit, kalogeros, monastic, nun, pilgrim, pillarist, prior, prioress, shonin, sister, stylite, talapoin, trapa

monopolize dominate, hang onto, hog, possess

monotonous boring, changeless, clichéd, drab, droning, dull, familiar, grey, habitual, hackneyed, humdrum, identical, invariable, methodical, monotone, mundane, repetitious, routine, same, singsong, stale, tedious, trite, uniform, yawn-making

monotony boredom, ding-dong, drabness, drill, droning, dullness, greyness, groove, humdrumness, identicalness, invariability, repetition, routine, rut, sameness, singsong, staleness, tediousness, tedium, treadmill

monument barrow, bust, cairn, column, cromlech, cup, decoration, dolmen, earthwork, gravestone, mausoleum, medal, megalith, memento, memorial, menhir, monolith, mound, obelisk, pillar, plaque, prize, pyramid, ribbon, shrine, slab, souvenir, statue, tablet, testimonial, tomb, tombstone, trophy

mood attitude, disposition, fettle, humour, morale, spirits, temper, temperament, vein

moon Artemis, crescent, Cynthia, daydream, Diana, first quarter, full, gibbous, half, harvest, horned, hunter's, last quarter, Luna, mope, new, satellite, Selene, waning, waxing

moor disembark, dock, downs, heath, land, North African, Othello, plateau, tie up

moral adage, apophthegm, decent, epigram, ethical, fair, high-minded, homily, honourable, just, lesson, maxim, message, motto, point, precept, principled, proper, proverb, righteous, saintly, saw, saying, scrupulous, teaching, upright, upstanding, virtuous

moralist censor, prig, prohibitionist, prude, puritan, teetotaller, Victorian, watchdog

moralistic censorious, grave, holier-than-thou, mealy-mouthed, narrow-minded, old-maidish, pietistic, pious, priggish, prim, prudish, puritan, sanctimonious, self-righteous, serious, severe, smug, stern, strait-laced

morality attitudes, behaviour, beliefs, conduct, customs, ethics, ethos, habits, ideals, manners, morals, mores, principles, scruples, standards

moralize harangue, hold forth, lecture, pontificate, preach, sermonize

morals conscience, decency, fairness, goodness, honesty, honour, integrity, justice, nobility, piousness, probity, propriety, rectitude, right, righteousness, saintliness, spirituality, uprightness, virtue

morning ack emma, AM, antemeridian, Aurora, cockcrow, dawn, daybreak, daylight, Eos, first light, forenoon, matins, morn, prime, sunrise, sunup, terce

motion actuation, dynamics, gesture, going, kinetics, locomotion, marching, migration, mobility, motility, motivity, movement, pedestrianism, perambulation, proposal, running, rushing, signal, walking

motionless becalmed, fixed, frozen, immobile, immotive, immovable, inactive, paralysed, petrified, spellbound, stagnant, standing, static, stationary, stiff, still, stock-still, stuck, transfixed, unmoving

motionlessness abeyance, cessation, deadliness, deadlock, deathliness, dormancy, fixity, halt, immobility, inactivity, inertness, latency, lock, lull, numbness, pause, rigidity, stagnancy, stagnation, stalemate, standstill, stasis, stiffness, stillness, stop, stoppage, suspense, suspension, trance, vegetation

motivate actuate, arouse, begin, bring on, cause, challenge, dispose, electrify, encourage, energize, enlist, excite, exhort, galvanize, hustle, incline, induce, influence, initiate, inspire, instigate, interest, move, prompt, provoke, recruit, spur on, start, stimulate, sweet-talk, talk into

motivated committed, devoted, eager, egged on, energized, galvanized, goaded, influenced, inspired, keen, lobbied, moved, persuaded, pressured, prodded, provoked, spurred on, stimulated, urged

motivational attractive, directional, energizing, galvanizing, hortatory, incentive, incitive, inflaming, inflammatory, influential, instigative, inviting, kinetic, magnetic, persuasive, provocative, rousing, tempting

motive aim, ambition, aspiration, calling, causation, cause, compulsion, design, desire, driving force, excuse, goal, grounds, guiding principle, hope, ideal, impetus, impulse, inspiration, intention, justification, kinetic, lodestar, mainspring, mobile, motivation, objective, pretext, purpose, rationale, reason, stimulation, vocation

motiveless accidental, adventitious, aimless, aleatory, arbitrary, casual, chance, coincidental, fortuitous, groundless, illogical, incidental, inexplicable, irrational, purposeless, random, serendipitous, stochastic, stray, unaccountable, unintended, unmotivated, unplanned

motorcycle autocycle, autorickshaw, bike, moped, motorbike, scooter, sidecar, superbike
See also list at **vehicle**.

motoring terms aquaplaning, autocade, automobilia, brake-fade, bump start, car alarm, carnet, carsickness, crash barrier, double declutch, double parking, driving licence, endorsement, garage, gas, grab, green card, gritter, handbrake turn, hard standing, hit-and-run accident, hitchhiker, hotting, hot-wiring, immobilizer, jack, joyride,

knock-for-knock, lighting-up time, lock, logbook, mileage, misfiring, MOT, motorcade, nearside, no-claims bonus, offside, oversteer, overtaking, parking meter, pile up, piston, pit, prang, registration number, roadholding, road test, shimmy, shunt, sideslip, skid, speed trap, stall, tailspin, tax disc, test drive, three-point turn, tow, traction, trade plate, traffic jam, turning circle, underseal, understeer, wheel wobble
See also lists at **registration**; **vehicle**.

mottled brindled, dappled, dotted, fly-spotted, freckled, grizzled, maculate, pepper-and-salt, peppered, roan, speckled, spotted, spotty, studded, tabby

mount ascend, back, bestride, board, climb on, embark, get on, go upstairs, hop in, horse, increase, jump in, mound, mountain, pile in, set up

mountain alp, barrow, ben, bluff, brae, butte, chain, cliff, climb, cordillera, crag, crest, downs, drumlin, dune, Everest, fell, foothill, heap, heights, highlands, hill, hillock, hilltop, hummock, hump, inselberg, knob, knoll, kop, kopje, massif, monticule, motte, mound, mount, Olympus, peak, pike, pile, pinnacle, precipice, range, ridge, roche moutonnée, saddle, scar, sierra, spur, summit, tor, tump, tumulus

mountainous alpine, altitudinous, Andean, cloud-capped, highland, hillocky, hilly, Himalayan, hummocky, monticulous, Olympian, orogenic, rolling, snow-capped, snow-clad, undulating, upland

mounted
may indicate a backword

mouthful bite, bolus, gobbet, helping, morsel, nibble, portion, seconds, serving, slice, sliver, titbit

move actuate, affect, convey, dispatch, disperse, displace, draw, drive, effort, gather, haul, hustle, impel, mobilize, motivate, nudge, propel, propose, pull, push, relocate, rush, scatter, send, shove, steps, throw, transfer, transport, transpose, tug, upset

movement activity, collectivism, communalism, communism, ecumenicalism, gesture, motion, socialism

moving active, agitated, ambulant, automotive, bustling, drifting, emotional, erratic, fleeting, flowing, flying, locomotive, mercurial, mobile, motile, motional, motivational, motive, motor, nomadic, peripatetic, relocating, restless, riding, running, rushing, scurrying, stirring, streaming, touching, transitional, travelling, wandering

mucilaginous gluey, glutinous, gory, mucous, snotty

mucus albumen, clot, glair, glue, gluten, gore, grume, mucilage, phlegm, pituita, pus, size

mud dirt, mire, muck, ooze, sediment, silt, slime, sludge, slush, swill

muddiness dirtiness, miriness, ooziness, slabbiness, sloppiness, slushiness, turbidity

muddled amiss, arsy-versy, askew, awry, chaotic, cockeyed, confused, haywire, higgledy-piggledy, jumbled, labyrinthine, scrambled, tangled, topsy-turvy, upside-down
may indicate an anagram

muddy dirty, marshy, miry, oozy, sedimentary, silty, slabby, sloppy, sludgy, slushy, squelchy, turbid, waterlogged

muffle baffle, deaden, drown, insulate, mute, silence, soundproof

muffled damped, deadened, dulled, flat, heavy, muted, nonresonant, silenced, smothered, soundproof, stifled

multiplication breeding, doubling, increase, proliferation, tripling

multiplicative increasing, manifold, multifold, multiple, multiplied, proliferative

multiplicity compositeness, count-lessness, diversity, infinity, many-sidedness, multifariousness, multifoldness, multiformity, multilateralism, multitudinousness, numerousness, pluralism, polyandry, polygamy, polygon, polygyny, polyhedron, polytheism, variety

multiply breed, burgeon, mushroom, proliferate, re-create

multitude billions, crowd, lots, many, millions, mob, myriads, plethora, scads, umpteen, wads

multitudinous legion, manifold, multifarious, multifold, multiple, numerous

mum ma, mother, quiet, sh, silent

mumble murmur, mutter, sigh, whisper

murder asphyxiate, assassination, bayonet, bomb, brain, burke, burn, bury alive, choke, do away with, drown, drowning, electrocute, eliminate, garrotte, gas, hanging, homicide, kill, knife, lance, manslaughter, pistol, poison, poleaxe, sabre, sandbag, shoot, smite, smother, spear, stab, stifle, strangle, strangulation, strike, suffocate, take out, wasting

murderous bloodthirsty, bloody, brutal, cannibalistic, cold-blooded, cruel, death-dealing, destructive, genocidal, gory, head-hunting, homicidal, internecine, man-eating, pathological, psychopathic, sanguinary, savage, slaughterous, trigger-happy

murk bleariness, blur, cataract, cloudiness, condensation, dinginess, drabness, dullness, filminess, fog, fret, fuzziness, greyness, haar, haze, indistinctness, miasma, mist, obscurity, opaqueness, peasouper, semitransparency, smog, smoke, steam, tarnish, vagueness, vapour

murky bleary, blurred, cloudy, distant, dusty, faint, filmy, foggy, frosted, fuzzy, hazy, ill-defined, indistinct, indistinguishable, low-definition, miasmal, milky, misty, muzzy, nebulous, obscured, opaque, remote, shadowy, smoggy, smoked, smoky, soft-focus, steamy, unclear, vague, veiled

murmur babble, blow, breathe, burble, buzz, chink, clink, clunk, crackle, croon, droning, fizz, flow, gurgle, hiss, hum, lap, moan, mumbling, mutter, patter, plash, plop, plunk, purl, purr, ripple, rustle, sigh, sizzle, sough, splash, splutter, sputter, squash, squish, susurration, swish, swoosh, tinkle, undertone, wheeze, whining, whirr, whisper
may indicate a homophone

muscularity brawn, endurance, hardiness, leanness, resilience, robustness, stalwartness, stamina, stringiness, tenacity, vigorousness, vitality, wiriness

muse conjecture, inspiration, meditate, ponder, query, question, speculate, suspect, think, wonder
See list of the nine muses.

music acid house, ambient, anthem, bhangra, calypso, cantata, gospel, harmony, heavy metal, hip-hop, house, hymn, hymnody, hymnology, kwela, macumba, marabenta, marabi, mass, mbaqanga, melodiousness, melody, merengue, musicality, musicalness, musicianship, oratorio, psalm, psalmody, punk, qawwali, ragga, rap, reggae, requiem, rock, rock and roll, salsa, ska, soca, son, soul, spiritual, techno, township jazz, trip-hop, tunefulness, zouk
See also list at **orchestra**.

musical harmonious, melodic, musicianly, musicophile, operetta, philharmonic, show, tuneful

musician artiste, balladeer, bandmaster, bard, bluesman, busker, cat, composer, conductor, funkster, instrumentalist, jazzman, kappelmeister, librettist, lyricist, maestro, minstrel, orchestrator, performer, player, popster, psalmist, repetiteur, soloist, swinger, syncopator, troubadour, virtuoso

---

THE NINE MUSES
CALLIOPE
CLIO
ERATO
EUTERPE
MELPOMENE
POLYHYMNIA
TERPSICHORE
THALIA
URANIA

---

mute dampen, deaden, dull, dumb, hush, lower, muffle, quieten, silence, soften, soft-pedal, soundproof, stifle, still, stop, subdue

muted distant, gentle, hushed, imperceptible, inaudible, indistinct, low, mumbled, murmured, muttered, pianissimo, piano, quiet, soft, subdued, unclear, weak, whispered

mutedness faintness, indistinctness, lowness, nonresonance, softness

mutilated
may indicate an anagram

mutilation amputation, castration, chopping, circumcision, curtailment, decapitation, docking, emasculation, excision, extirpation, fixing, lopping, severance

mutinous anarchist, counter-revolutionary, guerrilla, insubordinate, insurgent, insurrectionary, nihilist, rebellious, revolutionary, riotous, seditious, terrorist, treasonous

mutism deaf-mutism, dumbness, reticence, silence, speechlessness, taciturnity

mutter
may indicate a homophone

mutuality compensation, cooperation, dealing, give-and-take, interplay, reciprocity, repartee, retaliation, symbiosis, synergy, trade-off, transaction, two-way traffic

mysterious abstruse, allegorical, anagogical, anonymous, arcane, bewildering, cabbalistic, camouflaged, clandestine, complex, concealed, confusing, cryptic, difficult, disguised, enigmatic, esoteric, figurative, gnostic, hidden, incognito, indirect, inscrutable, insidious, intricate, knotty, labyrinthine, metaphorical, mystic, mystifying, oblique, occult, perplexing, problematic, puzzling, secret, secretive, symbolic, tropic, unintelligible, unknowable, unknown, unresolved

mysticism allegory, anagoge, cabbala, darkness, dimness, esoterica, esotericism, metaphor, mystery, occultism, oracle, secret, shadowiness, symbolism, unintelligibility

mystification abracadabra, complexity, confusion, difficulty, enigma, hocus-pocus, intricacy, mumbo jumbo, mystery, obfuscation, poser, problem, puzzle

mystify baffle, bamboozle, bewilder, confuse, deceive, perplex, puzzle, stump, stun

myth fable, fantasy, fictitious, folklore, legend
See also lists at **imaginary**; **legend**.

·N·

ABBREVIATIONS

N	en • name • née • nitrogen • north
NA	North Africa • not applicable • not available • sodium
NASA	National Aeronautics and Space Administration
NATO	North Atlantic Treaty Organization
NB	niobium • no ball • note well (Latin: *nota bene*)
NC	National Certificate • National Curriculum • no charge
NCO	noncommissioned officer
NCV	no commercial value
NE	neon • new edition • northeast
NI	National Insurance • nickel • Northern Ireland
NM	nanometre • nautical mile
NO	naval officer • nobelium • not out • number
NP	national park • neptunium • net proceeds • new paragraph
NS	nanosecond • near side
NSPCC	National Society for the Prevention of Cruelty to Children
NT	National Trust • New Testament • no trumps
NW	net worth • northwest
NY	New York
NZ	New Zealand

nadir base, baseline, bottom, crisis point, depression, depths, dregs, floor, lowest point, minimum, rock bottom, trough, zero hour

naive artless, callow, credulous, green, guileless, gullible, immature, inexperienced, ingenuous, innocent, trusting, unsophisticated, unworldly naïf, young

naivety artlessness, callowness, childhood, credulity, credulousness, golden age, greenness, guilelessness, gullibility, immaturity, inexperience, ingenuousness, innocence, naturalness, salad days, simple-mindedness, simplicity, unsophistication, unworldliness, youth

name agnomen, alias, allonym, appellation, call, celebrity, Christian name, cognomen, designate, diminutive, forename, hallmark, handle, maiden name, matronymic, moniker, nickname, nomen, nominate, noun, patronymic, pen name, praenomen, pseudonym, sobriquet, surname, trademark, tradename

nap catnap, forty winks, indentation, knub, nub, pile, pit, pock, protuberance, shag, snooze

narration account, allegory, anecdote, annals, ballad, cautionary tale, chronicle, conte, diary, docudrama, documentary, drama, epic, essay, fable, faction, fairy tale, fantasy, fiction, folk tale, history, journal, legend, metaphor, myth, parable, plot, record, reminiscence, reportage, saga, scenario, serial, simile, story, tale, travelogue, yarn

narrative autobiographical, biographical, complication, dénouement, development, documentary, epic, episode, factional, factual, fictional, heroic, imaginative, incident, kitchensink, leitmotiv, motif, mythological, picaresque, plot, romantic, scenario, storyline, structure, subject, subplot, theme, turning-point

narrow circumscribed, clinging, close(-fitting), compress, confine, constricted, contract, converge, cramped, figure-hugging, incommodious, limited, pent-up, pinch, restricted, slender, strait, straiten, taper, thin, tight, tighten

narrowing attenuation, bottleneck, contraction, convergence, funnel, shrinking, stenosis, stricture, taper, tapering

narrowly barely, closely, hardly, nearly, only just, tightly

narrow-minded blinkered, dogmatic, fanatical, fundamentalist, insular, intolerant, parochial, petty, small-minded

nasty
may indicate an anagram

nation country, kingdom, nationality, people, realm, state

national citizen, civic, colonial, communal, communist(ic), compatriot, cosmopolitan, democratic, federal, general, governmental, imperialistic, independent, international, interracial, nonaligned, republican, self-determining, self-governing, social, socialist, societal, state, subject, totalitarian, tribal

nationalism chauvinism, isolationism, jingoism, patriotism, protectionism, racism, xenophobia

native aboriginal, autochthonous, belonging, ethnic, genuine, inborn, indigenous, inhabitant, local, tribal

native land birthplace, cradle, fatherland, home, homeground, homeland, mother country, motherland, native soil

natural artless, biological, candid, direct, easy, expert, fool, frank, gifted, guileless, ingenuous, innate, instinctive, open, organic, simple-hearted, simpleton, talented, unaffected, unassuming, unfeigning, unforced, unpretentious, unsophisticated

naturalized accepted, acclimatized, assimilated, enfranchised, familiarized

naturalness artlessness, candidness, directness, easiness, frankness, honesty, openness, straightforwardness, unaffectedness, unpretentiousness

nature anatomy, appearance, aspect, attitude, attribute, biosphere, biota, body, breed, build, cast, character, complexion, composition, condition, constitution, demeanour, disposition, ecosphere, ecosystem, elements, environment, essence, expression, features, fettle, fitness, flora and fauna, health, hue, humour, innateness, look, makeup, materiality, mien, mood, mould, ontology, outdoors, pattern, personality, property, quality, quiddity, set, shape, soundness, stamp, strain, stripe, substantiality, suchness, temperament, thusness, trait, turn, type, wildlife

naughty
may indicate an anagram

nausea disgust, queasiness, repugnance, sickness, vomiting

nautical able-bodied, afloat, amphibian, amphibious, buoyant, marine, maritime, natatory, naval, sailorly, seaborne, seafaring, seaworthy, waterborne

navigate chart, circumnavigate, direct, plot, steer

navigation astronavigation, boating, compass reading, dead reckoning, helmsmanship, pilotage, plotting, sailing, seamanship, steering

near accessible, adjacent, adjoining, approaching, approximate, arm-in-arm, at hand, available, bordering on, bumper-to-bumper, cheek-by-jowl, close, close-run, contiguous, convenient, convergent, elbow-to-elbow, forthcoming, get-at-able, hand-in-hand, handy, home, hot, immediate, inseparable, intimate, local, neck-and-neck, neighbouring, next(-door), nigh, proximal, proximate, shoulder-to-shoulder, side-by-side, to hand, touching, vicinal, warm

nearness accessibility, adjacency, approach, approximation, appulse, availability, closeness, conjunction, convenience, convergence, handiness, immediacy, inseparability, intimacy, juncture, juxtaposition, propinquity, proximity, syzygy

necessary essential, fundamental, imperative, indispensable, needed, required, requisite, urgent, vital

necessitarianism determinism, fatalism, fatality, force majeure, predestination, predetermination

necessitate call for, cause, compel, demand, dictate, entail, involve, need, oblige, order, request, require, requisition, stipulate, want

necessitous bankrupt, brassick, broke, bust, craving, deprived, destitute, disadvantaged, hungry, lacking, longing for, needing, needy, penniless, pinched, poor, skint, starving, stony

necessity desideratum, essential, fundamental, imperative, must, necessary, need, precondition, prerequisite, requirement, requisite, urgency, want

neckwear ascot, band, bandanna, boa, bow tie, chemisette, choker, collar, comforter, cravat, dicky bow, Eton collar, fichu, fur, jabot, kerchief, muffler, neckband, neckcloth, neckerchief, necklace, neckpiece, scarf, shawl, stock, stole, tallith, tie, tippet, tucker, Windsor tie

need call, claim, craving, debt, demand, desire, destitution, gap, hardship, indigence, insufficiency, lack, lacuna, penury, poverty, privation, shortage, shortfall, slippage, want

needfulness breadline, crisis, desirability, duty, emergency, essentiality,

exigency, face-saving measures, indispensability, necessity, obligation, occasion, pinch, poverty, predicament, urgency, vitalness, want

needy destitute, hard up, indigent, necessitous, needful, poor, poverty-striken

negate abnegate, cancel, decline, deny, disallow, disavow, invalidate, prohibit, refuse, reject, say no, veto

negation abnegation, contradiction, counterargument, defeatism, denial, despondence, nay, naysaying, negative, negativism, no, noncorroboration, pessimism, rebuttal

negative abjuratory, abnegative, abrogative, contradictory, contrary, defeatist, defiant, despondent, nay, never, no, no-one, not, nowhere, obstructive, pessimistic, recusant, renunciative, renunciatory, repudiative, revocatory

negativeness defeatism, denial, fatalism, negation, negativity, nihilism, refusal

neglect disregard, forget, ignore, negligence, not heed, overlook

negligence carelessness, dereliction, disregard, forgetfulness, heedlessness, inattention, indiscretion, insouciance, neglectfulness, nonchalance, oblivion, remissness, thoughtlessness, unconcern, unmindfulness

negligent careless, disregardful, forgetful, heedless, inattentive, insouciant, neglectful, nonchalant, oblivious, remiss, thoughtless, uncaring, unconcerned, unmindful

negotiable concessionary, conciliatory, debatable, exchangeable, feasible, practicable, practical, pragmatic, provisional, provisory, workable

negotiate arbitrate, argy-bargy, bargain, barter, communicate, compromise, conciliate, confer, cooperate, deal, deliberate, discuss, do business, exchange views, haggle, hold talks, horse trade, jaw-jaw, make overtures, mediate, powwow, seek accord, seek agreement, settle, trade, use diplomacy, wrangle

negotiation arbitration, bargaining, bartering, communication, compromise, conciliation, dealing, diplomacy, discussions, exchange, haggling, horse trading, making terms, mediation, trade-off, treaty-making, wrangling *may indicate an anagram*

neighbour bystander, next-door neighbour, onlooker, touch

neighbourhood area, closeness, environs, ghetto, local, locality, manor, patch, precinct, surroundings, vicinity

nest bunch, den, eyrie, hideout, hotbed, lair, nestle, nidify, settle down, set up home, snuggery

neurosis anxiety, breakdown, phobia, psychosis

neurotic anxious, cycloid personality, cyclothyme, disturbed, dual personality, escapist, lunatic, multiple personality, neuropath, paranoid, psychoneurotic, psychopath, psychotic, schizoid, schizothyme, sociopath, split personality

neutrality balance, blandness, compromise, impartiality, independence, lukewarmness, moderation, mutuality, noninvolvement, reciprocity, symbiosis

new advanced, clean, contemporary, current, faddish, first, fresh, futuristic, in, innovative, inventive, latest, mint, modern, neological, neophytic, original, oven-fresh, postmodern, recent, replacement, revolutionary, state-of-the-art, topical, trendy, ultramodern, undeveloped, unexploited, ungathered, unopened, untapped, untouched, untrodden, up-to-date, virgin *may indicate an anagram*

newcomer amateur, baby, beginner, debutante, fledgling, fresher, freshman, greenhorn, immigrant, incomer, Johnny-come-lately, neophyte, new broom, new recruit, nouveau riche, novice, parvenu, rookie, tyro, upstart

newness blankness, cleanness, contemporaneity, currency, freshness, gimmickry, innovation, invention, mint condition, modernism, neology, neophilia, newfangledness, novelty, originality, purity, recentness, topicality, unfamiliarity, up-to-dateness, virginity

news breaking news, bulletin, column, current affairs, documentary, editorial, event, exclusive, exposé, eye-witness account, facts, feature, Fourth Estate, gossip, hard news, information, intelligence, item, journalism, leader, newscast, news conference, news flash, newsreel, press conference, press release, report, rumour, scoop, sportscast, story, straight news, update

newspaper broadsheet, daily, edition, extra, feuilleton, freesheet, giveaway, paper, rag, sheet, supplement, tabloid

newsworthy front-page, headline, important, newsy, significant

next following, later, latter, near, proximate, subsequent

night bedtime, blackness, dark, darkness, darktime, nightclub, nightlife, night school, night shift, night-time

nightwear bedgown, bed jacket, bedsocks, dressing gown, negligée, nightcap, nightclothes, nightdress, nightie, nightshirt, pyjamas, sleepwear

nil duck, love, nothing, nought, O, zero, zilch, zip

nimbleness alacrity, athleticism, briskness, flexibility, haste, nippiness, quickness, readiness, speed, suppleness, velocity

nine ennead, enneadic, enneagon, enneagonal, enneahedral, enneahedron, ninefold, niner, ninth, nonagenarian, nonagon, nonagonal, nonary, nonet, nonuple, nonuplet, novena, novenary

noble aristocrat, baron, baronet, blueblood, chivalrous, count, countess, decent, duchess, duke, earl, gent, gentleman, gentlewoman, grand duke, high-born, honourable, knight, lady, life peer, lord, magnanimous, marchioness, margrave, margravine, marquess, marquis, marquise, nob, optimate, patrician, peer, thane, titled, toff, upper class, virtuous, viscount, viscountess, well-bred

nobleness ancestory, breeding, distinction, dynasty, gentility, kingliness, line, lineage, nobility, pedigree, quality, virtue

nocturnal benighted, crepuscular, dark, dusky, nightly, night-time, twilight, vesperine

nomenclature addressing, appellation, baptism, calling, christening, classification, denomination, description, designation, identification, indication, naming, nicknaming, roll call, taxonomy, terminology

nonacceptance ban, bar, blackballing, blacklisting, boycott, circumscription, cold shoulder, ostracism, refusal, rejection, shunning, thumbsdown, veto

nonalcoholic alcohol-free, soft, unfermented

noncompliance defection, desertion, disloyalty, disobedience, disrespect, dissidence, insubordination, mutinousness, mutiny, nonconformity, treachery, treason

nonconforming bizarre, contrasting, different, distinct, eccentric, freakish, freaky, heretic, heterodox, idiosyncratic, incompatible, incongruous, inconsistent, individual, maverick, nutty, odd, outlandish, peculiar, rebellious, singular, unconformable, unconventional, unique, unorthodox, wacky, weird

nonconformism anarchism, Bohemianism, deviationism, eccentricity, heresy, heterodoxy, hippiedom, icono-

clasm, rebellion, revisionism, schism, unconventionality, unorthodoxy

nonconformist anarchic, atheistic, beatnik, Bohemian, breakaway, contrary, contumacious, defiant, deviationist, dissentient, dissenting, dissident, dropout, eccentric, free spirit, freethinker, Frondeur, heretical, heterodox, hippie, humanist, iconoclastic, independent, Jacobin, latitudinarian, malcontent, maverick, misfit, nonbelieving, nonconformer, nonconforming, opponent, outsider, protestant, radical, rationalist, rebel, rebellious, recalcitrant, recusant, renegade, revolutionary, schismatic(al), uncompliant, unconventional, unconventionalist, unorthodox

nonconformity contrast, difference, disaccord, disagreement, disparity, distinctness, diversity, eccentricity, freakishness, heresy, heterodoxy, idiosyncrasy, incompatibility, incongruity, inconsistency, individuality, peculiarity, singularity, unconformity, unconventionality, uniqueness, unorthodoxy

nonentity anonymity, figurehead, lightweight, mediocrity, nobody, nothing, pipsqueak, puppet, squirt, squit, stooge, subordinate, twerp, unknown, wimp

nonexistence emptiness, ethereality, immateriality, impalpability, incorporeality, intangibility, nonbeing, nonentity, nonhappening, nonoccurrence, nonsubsistence, nothing, nothingness, nullity, subjectivity, unbeing, unreality, unsubstantiality, vacuity, vacuum, void

nonexistent absent, blank, devoid, empty, imaginary, lacking, minus, missing, negative, null, unexisting, vacant, vacuous, void

nonfiction annals, autobiography, biography, commentary, confessions, critique, diary, discourse, dissertation, documentary, essay, factual, hagiography, history, journal, journalism, letter, memoirs, obituary, personal account, real, reference, report, résumé, review, study, thesis, travelogue, true

nonfulfilment deadlock, delay, desultoriness, failure, half measures, immaturity, imperfection, incompleteness, lack, loose ends, missing link, neglect, never-ending story, non sequitur, omission, oversight, perfunctoriness, procrastination, rough edges, scantiness, scrappiness, shortfall, sketchiness, skimpiness, sloppiness, stalemate, superficiality, underdevelopment

nonobservance avoidance, carelessness, casualness, disconformity, disregard, forgetfulness, gaucherie, inattention, indifference, neglect, negligence, nonadherence, noncompliance, nonconformity, noncooperation, obliviousness, oversight, rejection, remissness, slight, sloppiness, thoughtlessness

nonphysical immaterial, incorporeal, intangible, spiritual, transcendental

nonsense absurdity, amphigory, babble, Babel, balderdash, baloney, bilge, blah, bombast, bosh, bull, bunk(um), claptrap, crap, doggerel, double talk, drivel, empty talk, eyewash, gibberish, glossolalia, gobbledygook, Greek, hogwash, hooey, humbug, moonshine, piffle, poppycock, psychobabble, rigmarole, rot, rubbish, senselessness, tommyrot, tosh, trash, tripe, twaddle

nonsensical absurd, anserine, asinine, comic, crazy, droll, fanciful, farcical, fatuous, foolish, funny, humorous, idiotic, imaginative, jocular, laughable, ludicrous, mad, meaningless, merry, piffling, preposterous, ridiculous, senseless, silly, waggish

nonspecific blanket, broad, catch-all, dragnet, imprecise, inexact, loose, sweeping

nonuse abeyance, abstinence, avoidance, forbearance, neglect, redundancy, reserve, store, suspension, unemployment

noon 1200 hours, 12 o'clock, eight bells, meridian, midday, noontide

normal commonplace, conventional, customary, expected, habitual, natural, ordinary, orthodox, regular, routine, sane, sober, standard, traditional, typical, unexceptional, unsurprising, usual

notable A1, august, breathtaking, conspicuous, dignified, distinguished, earth-shaking, egregious, eminent, epoch-making, eventful, exalted, excellent, first-rate, formidable, front-page, gold-medal, impressive, influential, leading, memorable, monumental, newsworthy, noteworthy, outstanding, powerful, prestigious, prominent, remarkable, seismic, shattering, signal, sterling, stirring, superior, top-rank, unforgettable, world-shattering

notation bar, brace, characters, chart, interval, line, notes, paper, pause, score, script, sheet music, space, stave, symbols, time signature, tonic sol-fa

notch cleft, cog, crenation, crenel, crenellate, cut, dent, gash, gouge, groove, hack, incise, incision, incisure, indent, indentation, kerf, nick, nock, pink, score, serrate, serration, serrulation, slit, split, tooth

notched cogged, crenate, cut, dentate, incisural, indented, jagged, notchy, pinked, saw-toothed, scalloped, serrated, slit, split, toothed, uneven, zigzag

notch up accomplish, achieve, add to, gain, score, win

note A, accidental, annotate, B, breve, C, crotchet, D, demisemiquaver, do(h), dominant, E, F, fa(h), flat, G, harmonic, hemidemisemiquaver, jot, keynote, la(h), letter, me, mediant, memo(randum), mi, minim, natural, overtone, pitch, quaver, ray, re, record, remember, semibreve, semiquaver, semitone, sharp, so(h), sol, te, ti, tone, tonic, ut

notes adversaria, annotations, doodlings, dossier, jottings, marginalia, minutes, record, report, summary, writing

nothing aught, emptiness, naught, nihil, nix, nobody, none, O, vacancy, vacuum, void, zero, zilch, zip

nothingness blankness, emptiness, floccinaucinihilipilification, love, naught, nihility, nil, nonbeing, nonexistence, nothing, nothing whatever, nought, nowt, nullity, space, void, zero, zilch

notice ad(vertisement), bill, examine, mark, miss nothing, observe, poster, register, warning, watch

notional abstract, academic, conceptual, conjectural, esoteric, hypothetical, ideal, ideological, impractical, metaphysical, philosophical, speculative, theoretical, visionary

novel avant-garde, different, fresh, incomparable, inimitable, new, novella, off-beat, one-off, revolutionary, story, sui generis, transcendent, unheard-of, unique, unmatched, unparalleled, unprecedented
may indicate an anagram

nuclear power Chernobyl, core, fast-breeder reactor, fuel rod, gas-cooled reactor, magnox reactor, nuclear reactor, plutonium, Sellafield, thermal reactor, Three Mile Island, uranium, water-cooled reactor, Windscale

nucleus bull's-eye, core, focal point, focus, heart, heartland, hub, inner, inside, interior, kernel, keystone, lynchpin, marrow, midst, nub, nuclear, pivot, pivotal
may indicate the middle *letters of a word*

nude bare, ecdysiast, exhibitionist, in one's birthday suit, in the altogether, in the buff, in the raw, naked, naturist, plain, skinny-dipper, starkers, streaker, stripper, stripteaser, unclothed

nudity bareness, nakedness, undress

nuisance aggro, bother, bullying, harassment, hassle, trouble, victimization

null gone, lacking, missing, nonexistent, useless, worthless, vanished, void

number add, Arabic numeral, cardinal, character, cipher, constant, count, count heads, decimal, digit, enumerate, figure, finite number, gauge, group, infinite number, inventory, list, lots, many, measure, mob, multitude, no, notation, notch up, numeral, numerate, ordinal, plethora, poll, quantify, quantize, random number, reckon, Roman numeral, several, sign, spate, sum up, symbol, take stock, tally, tell, tot up, transfinite number, variable
See list of Roman numerals.

numberless boundless, countless, endless, immeasurable, incalculable, inexhaustible, infinite, innumerable, limitless, myriad, uncounted, untold

numbness anaesthesia, idleness, inactivity, insensibility, slowness, sluggishness, stagnation, stupor

numerable calculable, computable,

ROMAN NUMERALS						
I	1	XI	11		CI	101
II	2	XX	20		CD	400
III	3	XXX	30		P	400 (medieval)
IV	4	IL	49		ID	499
V	5	L	50		D	500
VI	6	LI	51		DI	501
VII	7	S	70 (medieval)		CM	900
VIII	8	R	80 (medieval)		M	1000
IX	9	IC	99		MD	1500
X	10	C	100			

countable, decidable, denumerable, enumerable, insoluble, measurable, mensurable, quantifiable, soluble, undecidable

numerical binary, decimal, denary, digital, even, figurate, fractional, integral, negative, numerary, numerate, numerative, numeric, odd, positive, ternary, whole

numismatics coin-collecting, numismatology

nurse attend, au pair, care for, Florence Nightingale, health visitor, look after, matron, midwife, ministering angel, nanny, nursemaid, sister, tend, tender, treat

nursery cloche, cold frame, conservatory, coolhouse, crêche, glasshouse, greenhouse, hothouse, infant school, jardinière, kindergarten, orangery, polytunnel, potting shed, propagator

nurture aliment, breast-feed, breed, cater, cultivate, farm, fatten up, feed, grow plants, incubate, look after, maintain, nourish, nurse, provision, purvey, raise, rearing, stock, suckle, sustain, tend, upbringing

nutcase basketcase, fruitcake, headcase, loony, nut

nutrition alimentation, diet, dietetics, food, sustenance

·O·

ABBREVIATIONS

O   blood group • duck • nil • ocean • octavo • October • office • old • order • ordinary • Orient • oxygen • ring • zero
OAP   old age pensioner
OBE   Officer of the Order of the British Empire • out-of-the-body experience
OCT   octave • octavo • October
OD   outside diameter • overdose • overdrawn • right eye (Latin: *oculus dexter*)
OHMS   On Her (His) Majesty's Service
OL   left eye (Latin: *oculus laevus*)
ONO   or near offer
OP   opposite prompt • opus • other people • outpatient • work
OS   osmium • outside • outsize • outstanding
OT   occupational therapy • Old Testament • overtime
OU   Open University • Oxford University
OXFAM   Oxford Committee for Famine Relief
OZ   ounce

obedience acquiescence, complaisance, compliance, conformity, deference, docility, dutifulness, goodness, malleability, meekness, nonresistance, obsequiousness, observance, passivity, pliance, readiness, servility, slavishness, submissiveness, subservience, tractability, willingness, yielding

obedient acquiescent, amenable, biddable, complaisant, compliant, conforming, deferential, disciplined, docile, dutiful, law-abiding, malleable, manageable, meek, obsequious, passive, pliant, resigned, servile, slavish, submissive, subservient, tame, tractable, trained, willing, yielding

obeisance bow, courtesy, curtsy, genuflection, grovelling, homage, humility, kneeling, kowtow, obsequy, prostration, respect, reverence, salaam, worship

obeisant courteous, humble, kneeling, respectful, reverential, worshipping

obey acquiesce, assent, comply, conform, consent, defer to, discharge, minister, serve, submit, yield

object aim, artefact, article, assail, challenge, combat, commodity, complain, contradict, contravene, controvert, counter, criticize, defend, defy, demur, deny, deprecate, disagree, dispute, dissent, expostulate, gadget, gainsay, gripe, grouse, impugn, item, kick, litigate, moan, negate, oppugn, protest, purpose, rebut, recipient, refute, remonstrate, retaliate, something, take exception, take issue, target, thing, thingumabob, thingumajig, thingummy, what's-its-name

objection argument, challenge, clamour, complaint, contradiction, contravention, controversion, controversy, defiance, demurral, denial, disagreement, disputation, dissent, dissidence, expostulation, fuss, impugnation, protest, rebuttal, refusal, refutation, rejection, remonstration

objectionability aggressiveness, argumentativeness, awkwardness, cantankerousness, contrariness, criticalness, defensiveness, defiance, discourtesy, fussiness, incivility, noncompliance, ungraciousness

objectionable aggressive, awkward, beastly, bellicose, bloody-minded, cantankerous, crabbed, quarrelsome, rude, uncivil, unpleasant, unwelcome

objective aim, bull's-eye, butt, crown, cup, destination, disinterested, end, finishing line, game, goal, laurels, mark, Mecca, neutral, prey, prize, quarry, quintain, scientific, target, trophy, winning post, wreath

obligatory binding, categorical, compulsory, imperative, incumbent on, inescapable, mandatory, peremptory, unavoidable, unconditional

oblige bind, call upon, command, commit, decree, engage, enjoin, expect, look to, obligate, order, pledge, require, saddle with, tie

obliged beholden, bound, committed, duty-bound, engaged, obligated, pledged, saddled, sworn, tied

oblique angle, bending, bevelled, biased, cater-cornered, convoluted, crooked, deflected, deviating, diagonal, digressive, distorted, divergent, dogleg, hairpin curve, hinted, implied, inclined, indirect, insinuated, kitty-cornered, leaning, listing, meandering, off-course, off-target, pitched, rhomboid, separatrix, sidelong, sideways, skew, skewed, skewwhiff, slanted, slash, slide, sloping, solidus, steep, stroke, tangent, tangential, thwart, tilting, transverse, turning, twisted, veiled, virgule, zigzag
See also list at **geometry**.

obliqueness bank, bias, camber, cant, convolution, crookedness, curvature, deflection, deviation, digression, divergence, inclination, indirection, list, meandering, pitch, skewness, slant, slide, slope, swerve, tangent, tilt, tip, transverseness, turn, twist, zigzag

obliquity bevel, bezel, bias, cant, declivity, edge, escarpment, hill, ramp, scarp, skewness, slant, slope, steepness, tangent, tilt, wedge

obliterate abrogate, annihilate, annul, black out, blot out, blue-pencil, bury, cancel, censor, conceal, cover up, cross out, deface, delete, demolish, destroy, efface, eliminate, eradicate, erase, expunge, exterminate, extirpate, liquidate, overprint, paint over, purge, raze, remove, rub out, rule out, score out, scratch out, scribble out, scrub, sponge off, strike out, submerge, vaporize, wash off, white out, wipe out

obliterated annihilated, buried, cancelled, deleted, demolished, destroyed, eliminated, eradicated, erased, expunged, exterminated, extirpated, forgotten, liquidated, unrecorded, vaporized

obliteration abrogation, annihilation, annulment, burial, cancellation, censorship, cessation, concealment, covering up, crossing out, defacement, dele, deletion, demolition, destruction, editing, effacement, elimination, eradication, erasure, expunction, extermination, extirpation, illegibility, interment, liquidation, oblivion, painting over, printing over, purge, removal, rubbing out, writing over

oblivion absorption, abstractedness, ataraxia, catatonia, coma, depersonalization, detachment, ecstasy, hypnosis, insensibility, introspection, narcosis, nonexistence, nothingness, rapture, senselessness, stupor, trance, unconsciousness, void, withdrawal

oblivious absorbed, abstracted, blind, catatonic, deaf, depersonalized, detached, distracted, ecstatic, hypnotic, insensible, introspective, preoccupied, rapturous, senseless, spaced-out, trance-like, unaware, unconscious, withdrawn

oblong rectangle
See also list at **geometry**.

obscene adult, atrocious, blue, dirty, filthy, indecent, lascivious, lewd, licentious, loathsome, pornographic, prurient, ribald, risque, rude, salacious, scabrous, scatological, smutty, vile

obscenity atrocity, dirty joke, indecency, lasciviousness, lewdness, licentiousness, outrage, porn, pornography, prurience, ribaldry, rudeness, salaciousness, scatology, smuttiness

obscure abstract, abstruse, allusive, ambiguous, arcane, baffle, bewilder, cabalistic, Cimmerian, cipher, cloudy, code, complex, complicate, confound, confuse, convoluted, cryptic, difficult, diffuse, disconcert, disregarded, disturb, elliptical, embarrass, enigmatic, equivocal, esoteric, faze, flummox, foggy, fuzzy, gnostic, humble, incomprehensible, indefinite, indirect, indistinct, involved, jibbering, Johnsonian, mix up, muddle, muddy, mumbo jumbo, murky, mysterious, mystify, neglected, non-plus, obfuscate, obfuscatory, obsidian, opaque, ornamental, overlooked, perplex, profound, purple, puzzle, recondite, stump, tortuous, unclear, unintelligible, unknown, unrecognized, weak, worry
may indicate an anagram

obscurity abstraction, abstruseness, allusion, ambiguity, anonymity, cloudiness, complexity, confusion, convolution, darkness, depth, difficulty, enigma, equivocalness, fogginess, gobbledegook, imprecision, inaccuracy, incomprehensibility, indefiniteness, indirectness, indistinctness, inexactness, inscrutability, jibberish, Johnsonese, muddle, mumbo jumbo, obfuscation, oblivion, obsidian, opacity, overcompression, paltriness, profundity, secrecy, tortuousness, unclearness, unintelligibility, vagueness, verbiage, weakness, wretchedness

observance accordance, accuracy, acknowledgment, attachment, attention, awareness, caring, ceremony, compliance, conformity, conscientiousness, custom, dependability, diligence, duty, faithfulness, fidelity, following, heeding, keeping, loyalty, obedience, recognition, regard, regularity, reliability, respect, ritual, vigilance, watchfulness

observant accurate, attentive, careful, compliant, conforming, conscientious, constant, dependable, devout, diligent, dutiful, exact, faithful, fastidious, heeding, literal, meticulous, obedient, pedantic, punctual, regarding, reliable, religious, responsible, scrupulous, watchful

observation comment, compliance, discovery, espionage, examination, inspection, look-see, note, once-over, opinion, peering, perusal, prying, recce, reconnaissance, remark, revelation, scan, scanning, scrutiny, study, supervision, surveillance, survey, voyeurism, watchfulness

observatory crow's nest, look out, planetarium, watchtower

observe abide by, acknowledge, adhere to, attend to, care, cling to, comply with, conform to, examine, follow, heed, keep, look at, notice, recognize, regard, see, show respect, stick to, watch

obsolete all over, annihilated, dead, defunct, destroyed, died out, ended, extinct, finished, kaput, obliterated, passed away, past, vanished, wiped out

obstacle accident, arrest, bar, barrier, block, blockade, botch, bottleneck, breakdown, bureaucracy, catch, Catch-22, check, cockup, contretemps, deadlock, delay, deterrent, difficulty, drag, drawback, embargo, filibuster, flaw, foul-up, glitch, hang-up, hazard, hiccup, hitch, hurdle, impasse, impediment, inconvenience, intervention, jam, lockout, malfunction, mix-up, problem, rub, sabbing, sabotage, snag, stay, stoppage, strike, teething troubles, tollgate, trouble, turnstile, vicious circle

obstetrician gynaecologist, midwife *See also list at* **occupation**.

obstinacy adamantine, bloody-mindedness, bull-headedness, callousness, contumacy, cussedness, disobedience, dourness, firmness, hardness, incorrigibility, indocility, inelasticity, inflexibility, intractability, mulishness, obduracy, pertinaciousness, perversity, pig-headedness, recalcitrance, refractoriness, resistance, rigidity, self-will, starchiness, stiff neck, stiffness, stubbornness, toughness, wrong-headedness

obstinate awkward, bloody-minded, callous, conservative, die-hard, dog-in-the-manger, firm, hard(line), headstrong, inflexible, intractable, mulish, obdurate, pertinacious, pig-headed, recalcitrant, refractory, rigid, self-willed, starchy, stiff, stubborn, tough, traditional, unbending, unmalleable, unyielding, wilful

obvious blatant, evident, glaring, lucid, manifest, patent, plain, unambiguous, undisguised

occasional casual, ceremonial, infrequent, interim, intermittent, part-time, passing, pro tem, provisional, sporadic, temporary

occult anagogic, arcane, astral plane, astrology, cabbalistic, charm, covert, cryptic, darken, dematerialize, eclipse, eeriness, encoded, enigmatic, esoteric, esoterica, etherealize, ghostliness, hermetic, hide, hypnotism, immaterialize, latent, magic, mesmerism, mysterious, mystify, numinousness, obscure, occlude, otherworldiness, paranormal, runic, secret, sorcery, spirituality, spiritualize, spirit world, supernatural, superphysical, supersensible, symbolic, voodoo, witchcraft

occultism alchemy, animism, anthroposophy, astral projection, astrology, cabbalism, esotericism, faith healing, fork bending, fortune telling, ghost dance, hermeticism, hypnotism, Kirlian photography, levitation, magic, mediumism, mesmerism, metapsychism, mind reading, mysticism, parapsychology, phrenology, poltergeistism, prophecy, psychography, psychokinesis, psychorrhagy, psychosophy, pyramidology, Rosicrucianism, scientology, shamanism, spiritism, spiritualism, spirit writing, supernaturalism, telaesthesia, telekinesis, telepathy, teleportation, telergy, theosophy, trance speaking, transcendentalism, ufology, voodooism, witchcraft

occultist adept, druid, ecstatic, esoteric, exorcist, faith healer, fakir, ghostbuster, mahatma, medium, mystic, psychic, psychometer, pyramidologist, spiritist, spiritualist, telekinetic, transcendentalist, ufologist, unspeller, yogi

occupation activity, annexation, bondage, business, career, conquest, craft, diversion, employment, field, job, line, livelihood, living, oppression, position, possession, post, profession, pursuit, residency, rule, seizure, situation, skill, subjection, task, tenancy, trade, vocation, work *See list of professions, trades, and occupations.*

occur act, come out, happen, perform, play, reappear, recur

occurrence case, episode, event, happening, incident, instance, juncture, milestone, moment, occasion, opportunity, point, stage

oceanic abyssal, billowing, breaking, briny, choppy, deep, estuarine, intertidal, littoral, marine, maritime, nautical, ocean-going, pelagic, rolling, seafaring, seaworthy, subaquatic, sublittoral, submarine, surging, swelling, terriginous, thalassic, tidal, turbulent

oceanography aquaculture, bathymetry, hydrography, marine biology, thalassography

odd asymmetric, bizarre, different, ir-

PROFESSIONS, TRADES, AND OCCUPATIONS

ABACIST
ABIGAIL
ABLE SEAMAN
ACCOMPANIST
ACCOMPTANT
ACCORDIONIST
ACCOUCHEUR
ACCOUCHEUSE
ACCOUNTANT
ACOLOTHIST
ACOLYTE
ACOLYTH
ACOUSTICIAN
ACROBAT
ACTOR
ACTOR
  MANAGER
ACTRESS
ACTUARY
ADJUDICATOR
AD-MAN
ADMINISTRATOR
ADMINISTRATRIX
ADSCRIPT
ADVERTISER
AEROLOGIST
AERONAUT
AGENT
AGRICULTURIST
AGROLOGIST
AGRONOMIST
AIR HOSTESS
AIRMAN
AIR STEWARD
ALCHEMIST
ALEWIFE
ALGEBRAIST
ALGERINE
ALLOPATHIST
ALLUMINOR
ALMONER
AMAH
AMANUENSIS
AMBULANCE
  MAN
ANAESTHETIST
ANALYSER
ANALYST
ANATOMIST
ANIMALCULIST
ANNOTATOR
ANNOUNCER
ANNUNCIATOR
ANTHROPOL-
  OGIST
ANTIQUARIAN
ANTIQUE
  DEALER
APHORIST
APIARIST

APOTHECARY
APPLE-GROWER
APPOSER
APPRENTICE
APRON-MAN
ARABIST
ARACHNOL-
  OGIST
ARBALISTER
ARBITER
ARBITRATOR
ARBITRATRIX
ARBORATOR
ARBORICULTUR-
  IST
ARBORIST
ARCH(A)EOL-
  OGIST
ARCHER(ESS)
ARCHITECT
ARCHIVIST
ARITHMETICIAN
ARMORIST
ARMOURER
ARMY OFFICER
ARQUEBUSIER
ARRESTOR
ART CRITIC
ART DEALER
ARTICLED CLERK
ARTIFICER
ARTILLERIST
ARTILLERYMAN
ARTISAN
ARTIST(E)
ASSAYER
ASSESSOR
ASSISTANT
  MASTER
ASSIZER
ASSURED
ASSURER
ASSYRIOLOGIST
ASTROLOGER
ASTRONAUT
ASTRONOMER
ATMOLOGIST
ATTENDANT
ATTORNEY
AUCTIONEER
AUDIO TYPIST
AUDIT CLERK
AUDITOR
AURIST
AUSCULTATOR
AUTHOR(ESS)
AUTOBIOGRA-
  PHER
AVIATOR
AWARDER

AYAH
BABU
BACTERIOL-
  OGIST
BAGMAKER
BAGMAN
BAGPIPER
BAILER
BAILIFF
BAILOR
BAKER
BALKER
BALLADIST
BALLERINA
BALLET DANCER
BALLET MASTER
BALLET
  MISTRESS
BALLOONIST
BALLPLAYER
BANDMASTER
BAND(S)MAN
BANK AGENT
BANK
  CASHIER
BANKER
BANK
  MANAGER
BANTAM-
  WEIGHT
BARBER
BARD
BARGEE
BARGEMAN
BARGEMASTER
BARKER
BARMAID
BARMAN
BARRISTER
BARROW BOY
BASEBALLER
BASKETMAKER
BASSOONIST
BATMAN
BATTI-WALLAH
BATTOLOGIST
BEACHCOMBER
BEADSWOMAN
BEARER
BEAUTICIAN
BEDESMAN
BEDMAKER
BEEFEATER
BEEKEEPER
BELLBOY
BELL-FOUNDER
BELL-HANGER
BELLHOP
BELLOWS-
  MAKER

BELL-RINGER
BEST BOY
BIBLIOGRAPHER
BIBLIOLOGIST
BIBLIOPEGIST
BIBLIOPOLIST
BILLIARD-MARKER
BILLIARD-PLAYER
BILL-STICKER
BINDER
BIOCHEMIST
BIOGRAPHER
BIOLOGIST
BIRD-CATCHER
BIRD-FANCIER
BIRDMAN
BIRD-WATCHER
BIT-MAKER
BLACKSMITH
BLADESMITH
BLASTER
BLEACHER
BLENDER
BLOCKMAKER
BLUEJACKET
BOATBUILDER
BOAT(S)MAN
BOATSWAIN
BODYGUARD
BODY SERVANT
BOFFIN
BOILERMAN
BOILERSMITH
BOMBARDIER
BONDMAID
BONDSERVANT
BONDSLAVE
BOND(S)MAN
BOND(S)-
  WOMAN
BONESETTER
BONZE
BOOKBINDER
BOOKHOLDER
BOOKIE
BOOKING
  CLERK
BOOKKEEPER
BOOKMAKER
BOOKMAN
BOOKSELLER
BOOTBLACK
BOOT-CATCHER
BOOTLEGGER
BOOTMAKER
BOOTS
BOSS
BOSUN
BOTANIST
BOTTLER

BOWMAKER
BOWMAN
BOW STREET
  RUNNER
BOXMAKER
BREWER
BREWSTER
BRICKLAYER
BRICKMAKER
BRIGAND
BROACHER
BROADCASTER
BROKER
BRUSHMAKER
BUCCANEER
BUGLER
BUILDER
BULLFIGHTER
BUREAUCRAT
BURGLAR
BURLER
BURNISHER
BURSAR
BUS
  CONDUCTOR
BUS DRIVER
BUSKER
BUTCHER
BUTLER
BUTTERWIFF
BUTTONS
CABBIE
CAB DRIVER
CABIN BOY
CABINET-MAKER
CABMAN
CADDY
CAFÉ OWNER
CALICO-PRINTER
CALKER
CALLBOY
CALLIGRAPHER
CAMBIST
CAMERAMAN
CAMPANOL-
  OGIST
CANDLEMAKER
CANNER
CAR DRIVER
CAREER GIRL
CARETAKER
CARICATURIST
CARPENTER
CARPET-FITTER
CARRIER
CAR SALESMAN
CARTER
CARTOGRAPHER
CARTOGRAPH-
  IST

CARTOONIST
CARTWRIGHT
CARVANEER
CARVER
CASEMAKER
CASEMAN
CASHIER
CASH-KEEPER
CASUAL
CATACLYSMIST
CAT BREEDER
CAT BURGLAR
CATECHIST
CATERER
CAT'S-MEAT-
 MAN
CAULKER
CELLARER
CELLARMAN
CELLIST
CENSOR
CERAM(IC)IST
CEROGRAPHIST
CHAIR-MAKER
CHAIR-MENDER
CHALK-CUTTER
CHAMBER-
 COUNSEL
CHAMBERMAID
CHANDLER
CHANTER
CHAPMAN
CHAR
CHARGEHAND
CHARIOTEER
CHARTOGRA-
 PHER
CHARWOMAN
CHAUFFEUR
CHEAPJACK
CHEESE-
 MONGER
CHEF
CHEMIST
CHICKEN-
 FARMER
CHIEF CASHIER
CHIFFONNIER
CHIMNEY-
 SWEEP(ER)
CHIROGRAPHIST
CHIROLOGIST
CHIROMANCER
CHIROPODIST
CHIROPRACTOR
CHIRURGEON
CHOIRBOY
CHOIRMASTER
CHORE(O)GRA-
 PHER

CHORIST(ER)
CHORUS GIRL
CHRONICLER
CHRONOGRA-
 PHER
CHRONOLO-
 GER
CHRONOLO-
 GIST
CHURCH-
 WARDEN
CIDERIST
CINDER-
 WENCH
CIRCUITEER
CIRCUIT RIDER
CITIZEN-SOLDIER
CIVIL ENGINEER
CIVIL SERVANT
CLAIM AGENT
CLAPPER BOY
CLAQUEUR
CLARIFIER
CLARINE(T)TIST
CLASSICS
 MASTER
CLEANER
CLEARSTARCHER
CLERGY(MAN)
CLERIC
CLERK
CLERK OF
 WORKS
CLICKER
CLINICIAN
CLIPPIE
CLOCKMAKER
CLOCK-SETTER
CLOG DANCER
CLOGMAKER
CLOTHIER
CLOTH MAKER
CLOTH-SHEARER
CLOTH-WORKER
CLOWN
COACH
COACH-BUILDER
COACHMAKER
COACHMAN
COAL-BACKER
COAL-FITTER
COALHEAVER
COALMAN
COAL-MASTER
COALMINER
COALOWNER
COAL-WHIPPER
CO-ASSESSOR
COASTGUARD
CO-AUTHOR

COBBLER
COCKLER
CODIFIER
CODIST
COFFEE-
 PLANTER
COFFIN-MAKER
COINER
COISTRIL
COLEOPTERIST
COLLAR-MAKER
COLLATOR
COLLECTOR
COLLIER
COLLOCUTOR
COLLOQUIST
COLOURIST
COLOUR
 SERGEANT
COLPORTEUR
COLUMNIST
COMBER
COMEDIAN
COMEDIENNE
COMETOGRA-
 PHER
COMIC
COMMIS-
 SIONAIRE
COMMIS-
 SIONER
COMPILER
COMPOSER
COMPOSITOR
COMPOUNDER
COMPRADOR
CONCHOLO-
 GIST
CONCIERGE
CONCORDIST
CONDER
CONDISCIPLE
CONDOTTIERE
CONDUCTOR
CONDUCTRESS
CONFEC-
 TIONER
CONFEDERATE
CONGRESS-
 MAN
CONJURER
CONSECRATOR
CONSERVATOR
CONSERVER
CONSTITUENT
CONTORTION-
 IST
CONTRABAND-
 IST
CONTRACTOR

CONTROLLER
CONVEYANCER
CONVEYOR
COOK
COOLIE
COOPER
CO-PILOT
COPPER
COPPERSMITH
COPYHOLDER
COPYIST
COPYWRITER
CORDWAINER
CORN
 CHANDLER
CORONER
CORSAIR
COSMOGON-
 IST
COSMOGRA-
 PHER
COSMOLOGIST
COSMONAUT
CO-STAR
COST CLERK
COSTER-
 (MONGER)
COSTUMIER
COTTON-
 SPINNER
COUNSEL(LOR)
COUNTER-
 CASTER
COUNTERFEITER
COURIER
COURTESAN
COURTIER
COUTURIER
COWBOY
COWFEEDER
COWHERD
COWKEEPER
COW-LEECH
COWMAN
COWPOKE
COXSWAIN
CRACKSMAN
CRAFTSMAN
CRAFTS-MASTER
CRANE DRIVER
CRANIOLOGIST
CRANIOSCO-
 PIST
CRAYONIST
CREW
CRIER
CRIMEWRITER
CRIMP
CRITIC
CROFTER

CROPPER
CROSSING-
 SWEEPER
CROUPIER
CRUSTACEOL-
 OGIST
CRYPTOGAMIST
CRYPTOGRA-
 PHER
CUB REPORTER
CULTIVATOR
CURATOR
CURER
CURRIER
CUSTODE
CUSTOMS
 MAN
CUTLER
CUTPURSE
CUTTER
CYMBALIST
CYPHER
CLERK
CYTOLOGIST
DAILY (HELP)
DAIRYMAID
DAIRYMAN
DANCE
 HOSTESS
DANCER
DANCING
 MASTER
DANCING
 MISTRESS
DANCING
 PARTNER
DANSEUR
DANSEUSE
DEALER
DECKHAND
DECORATOR
DECRETIST
DEEP-SEA
 DIVER
DEFENDER
DEIPNOSOPHIST
DELINEATOR
DELIVERY
 MAN
DEMOGRAPHER
DEMONOLO-
 GIST
DEMONSTRA-
 TOR
DENDROLOGIST
DENTIST
DERMATOLO-
 GIST
DESIGNER
DESK CLERK

DETECTIVE	DRAYMAN	EPIC POET	FELL-MONGER	FODDERER
DIAGNOSTI-	DREDGER	EPIGRAMMATIST	FELT-MAKER	FOLK-DANCER
CIAN	DRESS	EPITAPHIST	FENCE	FOLK-SINGER
DIALIST	DESIGNER	EPITOMIST	FENCING-	FOOTBOY
DIAMOND-	DRESSER	EPITOMIZER	MASTER	FOOTMAN
CUTTER	DRESSMAKER	ERRAND BOY	FERRYMAN	FOOTPAD
DIAMOND	DRILL SERGEANT	ESCAPOLOGIST	FICTOR	FOOTPLATEMAN
MERCHANT	DRIVER	ESSAYIST	FIDDLER	FORECASTER
DICE-MAKER	DROGMAN	ESSOINER	FIELD WORKER	FOREMAN
DIE-SINKER	DROVER	ESTATE AGENT	FIFER	FORESTER
DIET(ET)IST	DRUGGIST	ESTATE	FIGURANT	FORGEMAN
DIETITIAN	DRUM-MAKER	MANAGER	FIGURANTE	FORGER
DIGGER	DRUMMER(-BOY)	ESTIMATOR	FIGURE-MAKER	FORTUNE-
DIRECTOR	DRY CLEANER	ETHNOGRA-	FILE-CUTTER	TELLER
DIRECTRESS	DRYSALTER	PHER	FILER	FORWARDING
DIRECTRIX	DUSTMAN	ETHNOLOGIST	FILIBUSTER	AGENT
DISC JOCKEY	DUTY OFFICER	ETYMOLOGIST	FILING CLERK	FOUNDER
DISCOUNT-	DYER	EVANGELIST	FILM ACTOR	FOURBISSEUR
BROKER	ECCLESIASTIC	EXAMINANT	FILM DIRECTOR	FOWLER
DISCOUNTER	ECCLESIOLO-	EXAMINATOR	FILM EDITOR	FRAME-MAKER
DISCOVERER	GIST	EXCAVATOR	FILM EXTRA	FRAMER
DISHWASHER	ECOLOGIST	EXCERPTOR	FILM-MAKER	FREEBOOTER
DISPATCHER	EDITOR	EXCHANGE-	FILM PRODUCER	FREELANCE
DISPENSATOR	EDUCATIONAL-	BROKER	FILMSTAR	FREIGHTER
DISPENSER	IST	EXCHANGER	FINANCIER	FREIGHT-BROKER
DISSECTOR	EDUCATOR	EXCISEMAN	FINER	FRINGE-MAKER
DISTILLER	EGYPTOLOGIST	EXECUTIONER	FINESTILLER	FRIPPERER
DISTRAINER	ELECTRICIAN	EXECUTIVE	FINISHER	FRISEUR
DISTRAINOR	ELECTROPLATER	EXHIBITIONIST	FIRE BRIGADE	FROGMAN
DITCHER	ELECTROTYPIST	EXORCISER	FIRE EATER	FRUITERER
DIVA	ELECUTIONIST	EXORCIST	FIRE INSURER	FRUIT PICKER
DOC	EMBALMER	EXPERIMENTER	FIREMAN	FUELLER
DOCKER	EMBEZZLER	EXPLORATOR	FIREMASTER	FUGLEMAN
DOCKMASTER	EMBLAZONER	EXPLORER	FIRE-WORKER	FULLER
DOCTOR	EMBLEMATIST	EXPORTER	FIRST OFFICER	FUNAMBULIST
DOG BREEDER	EMBOWELLER	EXTORTIONER	FISH-CURER	FUND RAISER
DOG-FANCIER	EMBROIDERER	EXTRA	FISHER(MAN)	FURBISHER
DOG-LEECH	EMIGRATIONIST	EYE-SERVANT	FISHMONGER	FURNISHER
DOMESTIC	EMISSARY	FABLER	FISHWIFE	FURRIER
(SERVANT)	ENAMELLER	FABRICANT	FISH-WOMAN	GAFFER
DOMINIE	ENAMELLIST	FABULIST	FITTER	GALLEY-SLAVE
DON	ENCYCLO-	FACE-PAINTER	FLAG-MAKER	GALVANIST
DOORKEEPER	P(A)EDIST	FACTOR	FLATFOOT	GALVANOLO-
DOORMAN	ENGASTRIMUTH	FACTORY HAND	FLAUTIST	GIST
DOUGHBOY	ENGINE-DRIVER	FACTOTUM	FLAX-DRESSER	GAMEKEEPER
DOWSER	ENGINEER	FAITH HEALER	FLAX-WENCH	GAME
DRAFTSMAN	ENGINEMAN	FAKIR	FLAYER	WARDEN
DRAG(O)MAN	ENGRAVER	FALCONER	FLESHER	GANG
DRAMATIST	ENGROSSER	FAMILY	FLESH-MONGER	GANGER
DRAMATURGE	ENROLLER	DOCTOR	FLETCHER	GANGSTER
DRAMATURGIST	ENTERTAINER	FAMULIST	FLIER	GAOLER
DRAP(I)ER	ENTOMOLO-	FANCY-	FLIGHT CREW	GARDENER
DRAUGHTSMAN	GIST	MONGER	FLORIST	GASFITTER
DRAUGHTS-	ENTOMOTO-	FARMER	FLOWERGIRL	GASTRILOQUIST
WOMAN	MIST	FARMHAND	FLUNKEY	GATEMAN
DRAWBOY	ENTOZOOLO-	FARM LABOURER	FLUTIST	GAUCHO
DRAWER	GIST	FARRIER	FLUVIALIST	GAUGER
DRAWING-	ENTREPRENEUR	FASCIST	FLYFISHER	GAVELMAN
MASTER	ENVOY	FASHIONER	FLYING	GAZETTEER
DRAWLATCH	EPHEMERIST	FELLER	DOCTOR	GEAR-CUTTER

GEISHA GIRL
GEM-CUTTER
GENDARME
GENEALOGIST
GENETICIST
GENTLEMAN-
    FARMER
GEOGRAPHER
GEOLOGIST
GEOMETRICIAN
GERIATRICIAN
GHOSTWRITER
GIGOLO
GILDER
GILLIE
GIPSY
GIRDLER
GLADIATOR
GLASS-BENDER
GLASS-BLOWER
GLASS-CUTTER
GLASS-GRINDER
GLASSMAN
GLASS-WORKER
GLAZ(I)ER
GLEANER
GLEEMAN
GLEE-SINGER
GLOSSARIST
GLOSSER
GLOSSOGRA-
    PHER
GLOSSOLOGIST
GLOVER
GLUE-BOILER
GLUEMAKER
GLUER
GLYPHOGRA-
    PHER
GOATHERD
GODSMITH
GOLD-BEATER
GOLD-DIGGER
GOLDSMITH
GOLD-WASHER
GONDOLIER
GOSPELLER
GOSSIPER
GOVERNANTE
GOVERNESS
GOVERNOR
GP
GRAFFER
GRAFTER
GRAINER
GRAMMARIAN
GRAMMATI-
    CASTER
GRANGER
GRANTEE

GRANTOR
GRAVE-DIGGER
GRAVER
GRAZIER
GREASE-
    MONKEY
GREENGROCER
GRINDER
GRIP
GROCER
GROOM
GROUND-BAILIFF
GROUNDMAN
GUARD
GUARDIAN
GUARDSMAN
GUERRILLA
GUIDE(R)
GUIDON
GUILD
    (BROTHER)
GUITARIST
GUNMAN
GUNNER
GUN-RUNNER
GUNSLINGER
GUNSMITH
GYMNAST
GYMNOSO-
    PHIST
GYN(A)ECOL-
    OGIST
GYP
HABERDASHER
HACK
HACKLER
HACKNEY
    COACHMAN
HACKNEY-MAN
HAGIOGRAPHER
HAGIOLOGIST
HAIRDRESSER
HAIR STYLIST
HAKIM
HALIOGRAPHER
HALL PORTER
HAMMERER
HAND
HANDICRAFTS-
    MAN
HANDMAID(EN)
HANDYMAN
HARBOUR
    MASTER
HARDWARE-
    MAN
HARLEQUIN
HARMONIST
HARNESS-
    MAKER

HARPER
HARPIST
HARPOONER
HARPY
HARVESTER
HARVESTMAN
HATCHELLER
HATMAKER
HATTER
HAULIER
HAWKER
HAYMAKER
HEAD
HEAD COOK
HEAD
    GARDENER
HEAD PORTER
HEADSMAN
HEAD WAITER
HEALER
HEART
    SPECIALIST
HEAVER
HEDGE-PRIEST
HEDGE-WRITER
HELLENIST
HELMINTHOL-
    OGIST
HELMSMAN
HELOT
HENCHMAN
HERBALIST
HERBARIAN
HERBIST
HERBORIST
HERB-WOMAN
HERD
HERD(S)MAN
HERESIOGRA-
    PHER
HERITOR
HIEROGLYPHIST
HIEROGRAM-
    MATIST
HIEROLOGIST
HIEROPHANT
HIGGLER
HIGHWAYMAN
HIND
HIRED HAND
HIRED HELP
HIRELING
HIRER
HISTOLOGIST
HISTORIAN
HISTORIOGRA-
    PHER
HISTRION
HIVER
HODMAN

HOGHERD
HOG-RINGER
HOME HELP
HOMEOPATH
HOOPER
HOP-PICKER
HOPPO
HORNER
HORN PLAYER
HOROLOGIST
HORSE-BREAKER
HORSECOPER
HORSE-
    COURSER
HORSE
    DOCTOR
HORSE-
    KNACKER
HORSE-LEECH
HORSE-
    MILLINER
HORSE
    TRADER
HORTICULTURIST
HOSIER
HOSPITALLER
HOSPITAL
    NURSE
HOSTELLER
HOSTLER
HOTELIER
HOTEL-KEEPER
HOTEL
    MANAGER
HOUSE AGENT
HOUSEBOY
HOUSEBREAKER
HOUSE
    DECORATOR
HOUSE
    FURNISHER
HOUSEMAID
HOUSEMASTER
HOUSEMOTHER
HOUSEPAINTER
HOUSE
    STEWARD
HOUSE
    SURGEON
HOUSEWIFE
HUCKSTER
HUCKSTRESS
HUNTER
HUNTSMAN
HUSBANDMAN
HYDROGRA-
    PHER
HYDROPATHIST
HYGIENIST
HYMNOLOGIST

HYPNOTIST
HYPOTHECA-
    TOR
ICHTHYOLO-
    GIST
ILLUMINATOR
ILLUSIONIST
ILLUSTRATOR
IMMUNOLO-
    GIST
IMPORTER
IMPROPRIATOR
IMPROVER
INCUMBENT
INDEXER
INDUSTRIALIST
INFANTRYMAN
INGRAFTER
INKMAKER
INLAYER
INNHOLDER
INNKEEPER
INOCULATOR
INSCRIBER
INSPECTOR
INSTITUTIST
INSTITUTOR
INSTRUCTOR
INSTRUCTRESS
INSTRUMENT-
    ALIST
INSURANCE
    BROKER
INTELLIGENCER
INTENDANT
INTERAGENT
INTERN
INTERPRETER
INTERVIEWER
INVENTOR
INVOICE CLERK
IRON-FOUNDER
IRONIST
IRONMONGER
IRONSMITH
IRONWORKER
ISSUER
ITINERANT
IVORY-CARVER
IVORY-TURNER
IVORY-WORKER
JACK-SMITH
JAILER
JAILOR
JANITOR
JAPANNER
JERRY-BUILDER
JET PILOT
JEWELLER
JOBBER

JOB-MASTER
JOCKEY
JOINER
JOINT-
 EXECUTOR
JOINT-TRUSTEE
JONGLEUR
JOURNALIST
JOURNEYMAN
JOWTER
JUGGLER
JUNKMAN
JURISCONSULT
JURIST
JURYMAN
JUVENILE LEAD
KEELER
KEELMAN
KEEPER
KENNELMAID
KENNEL-MAN
KEYBOARDER
KILLER
KING'S
 COUNSEL
KIPPERER
KITCHENMAID
KNACKER
KNIFE-GRINDER
KNIFE-THROWER
KNITTER
LABOURER
LABOURING
 MAN
LACEMAKER
LACEMAN
LACKEY
LACQUERER
LADY'S MAID
LAMPLIGHTER
LAND AGENT
LANDER
LANDGIRL
LANDLADY
LANDLORD
LANDREEVE
LAND STEWARD
LAND
 SURVEYOR
LANGUAGE
 MASTER
LAPIDARY
LARCENER
LARCENIST
LARDERER
LASCAR
LATH-SPLITTER
LAUNDERER
LAUNDRESS
LAUNDRYMAID

LAUNDRYMAN
LAW OFFICER
LAWYER
LEADER-
 WRITER
LEADING LADY
LEADSMAN
LEATHER-
 DRESSER
LECTOR
LECTURER
LEDGER CLERK
LEECH
LEGIONARY
LEGISLATOR
LENDER
LETTER-CARRIER
LETTER-FOUNDER
LEXICOGRAPHER
LEXICOLOGIST
LIBRARIAN
LIBRETTIST
LIFEBOATMAN
LIGHTERMAN
LIGHTHOUSE-
 MAN
LIGHTKEEPER
LIME-BURNER
LINEN DRAPER
LINESMAN
LINKBOY
LINKMAN
LINOTYPER
LINOTYPIST
LIONTAMER
LIQUIDATOR
LITHOGRAPHER
LITHOLOGIST
LITHOTOMIST
LIVERYMAN
LOADER
LOAN AGENT
LOBSTERMAN
LOCK-KEEPER
LOCKMAKER
LOCKMAN
LOCKSMITH
LOGMAN
LOG-ROLLER
LOMBARD
LONGSHORE-
 MAN
LORRY DRIVER
LOSS ADJUSTER
LUMBER-DEALER
LUMBERER
LUMBERJACK
LUMBERMAN
LUMPER
LUTER

MACHINIST
MADRIGALIST
MAGI
MAGICIAN
MAGISTER
MAGISTRATE
MAGNETIST
MAID(-OF-ALL-
 WORK)
MAIDSERVANT
MAITRE D'HOTEL
MAJORDOMO
MAKE-UP ARTIST
MALACOLOGIST
MALE MODEL
MALE NURSE
MALTMAN
MALTSTER
MAMMALOGIST
MANAGER(ESS)
MAN-AT-ARMS
MANGLER
MANICURIST
MANNEQUIN
MANSERVANT
MANUAL
 LABOURER
MANUAL
 WORKER
MANUFAC-
 TURER
MARBLER
MARCHER
MARINER
MARKER
MARKET-
 GARDENER
MARSHAL
MASON
MASSEUSE
MASS
 PRODUCER
MASTER BAKER
MASTER-BUILDER
MASTER
 MARINER
MATADOR
MATCHMAKER
MATE
MATELOT
MATHEMA-
 TICIAN
MATRON
MD
MEALMAN
MEASURER
MEAT-HAWKER
MEATMAN
MEAT-
 SALESMAN

MECHANIC-
 (IAN)
MECHANIST
MEDAL(L)IST
MEDIC
MEDICAL MAN
MEDICAL
 OFFICER
MEDICINE MAN
MEDICO
MELODIST
MELODRAMA-
 TIST
MEMOIRIST
MEMORIALIST
MENDER
MENIAL
MENTOR
MERCATOR
MERCENARY
MERCER
MERCHANT-
 (MAN)
MERCHANT-
 TAILOR
MESMERIST
MESSENGER
METALLIST
METALLURGIST
METAL-MAN
METAL WORKER
METAPHYSI-
 CIAN
METEOROLO-
 GIST
METOPOSCO-
 PIST
METRICIAN
MEZZO
 SOPRANO
MICROSCOPIST
MIDWIFE
MILITIAMAN
MILKER
MILKMAID
MILKMAN
MILLER
MILLHAND
MILLINER
MILL-OWNER
MILLWRIGHT
MIME
MINER
MINERALIST
MINERALOGIST
MINIATURIST
MINISTER
MINISTRESS
MINSTREL
MINTER

MINTMASTER
MISCELLAN-
 ARIAN
MISCELLANIST
MISSIONARY
MO
MODELGIRL
MODELLER
MODISTE
MONEY-BROKER
MONEY-
 CHANGER
MONEYER
MONEY-LENDER
MONEY-
 SCRIVENER
MONGER
MONITOR
MONOGRA-
 PHER
MONOGRA-
 PHIST
MOONSHINER
MOOTMAN
MORISK
MORRIS-
 DANCER
MORTICIAN
MOSAIC-ARTIST
MOSAIC-
 WORKER
MOTHER-
 SUPERIOR
MOULDER
MUFFIN-MAN
MULE-SPINNER
MULETEER
MUMMER
MUMPER
MURALIST
MUSICAL
 DIRECTOR
MUSIC CRITIC
MUSICIAN
MUSIC MASTER
MUSIC
 MISTRESS
MUSIC
 PUBLISHER
MUSKETEER
MUSKETOON
MYOGRAPHIST
MYOLOGIST
MYSTERIARCH
MYSTIC
MYTHOGRA-
 PHER
MYTHOLOGIST
NAILER
NATURALIST

PROFESSIONS, TRADES, AND OCCUPATIONS continued

NAUTCH GIRL
NAVAL
  PENSIONER
NAVIGATOR
NAVVY
NECROLOGIST
NECRO-
  MANCER
NEEDLE-
  WOMAN
NEGOTIANT
NEGOTIATOR
NEOLOGIAN
NEOLOGIST
NEUROLOGIST
NEUROTOMIST
NEWSAGENT
NEWSBOY
NEWSCASTER
NEWS EDITOR
NEWSHAWK
NEWSPAPER-
  MAN
NEWSVENDOR
NEWSWRITER
NIGHT NURSE
NIGHT PORTER
NIGHT-
  WATCHMAN
NIGHTWORKER
NOMENCLA-
  TOR
NOSOLOGIST
NOTARY
NOVELIST
NUMISMATIST
NUMISMATOL-
  OGIST
NURSE
NURSEMAID
NURSER
NURSERYMAN
NUTRITIONIST
OBITUARIST
OBOIST
OBSTETRICIAN
OCULIST
ODD JOB MAN
OFFICE BOY
OFFICE JUNIOR
OFFICER
OFFICE STAFF
OILER
OILMAN
OIL PAINTER
ONEIROCRITIC
ONION-MAN
ONION-SELLER
OPERA SINGER
OPERATIVE

OPERATOR
OPHIOLOGIST
OPTHALMOL-
  OGIST
OPTICIAN
ORATOR
ORCHARDIST
ORCHESTRATOR
ORDAINER
ORDERER
ORDERLY
ORDINAND
ORDINATOR
ORGAN-BUILDER
ORGAN-
  GRINDER
ORGANIST
ORIENTALIST
ORNITHOL-
  OGIST
ORTHODONTIST
ORTHOGRA-
  PHER
ORTHOGRA-
  PHIST
ORTHOPEDIST
OSTEOLOGER
OSTEOLOGIST
OSTEOPATH
OSTLER
OTOLOGIST
OUTFITTER
OUTRIDER
OVARIOTOMIST
OVERLOOKER
OVERSEER
OWLER
PA
PACKER
PACKMAN
PAGE
PAGEBOY
PAINTER
PAINTER-
  STAINER
PALAEONTOL-
  OGIST
PALMIST
PAMPHLETEER
PANEGYRIST
PANEL-BEATER
PANTLER
PANTOMIMIST
PANTRYMAID
PAPERHANGER
PAPER-STAINER
PARGETER
PARK
  ATTENDANT
PARK-KEEPER

PARK-RANGER
PARLOURMAID
PARODIST
PARSON
PASQUILANT
PASQUILER
PASTOR
PASTRY-COOK
PATHFINDER
PATHOLOGIST
PATTERN-
  MAKER
PAVIER
PAVIOR
PAWNBROKER
PAYMASTER
PEARL-DIVER
PEARLFISHER
PEDAGOGUE
PEDANT
PEDDLER
PEDIATRICIAN
PEDIATRIST
PEDICURIST
PEDLAR
PELTMONGER
PENMAKER
PENMAN
PENOLOGIST
PEON
PERFORMER
PERFUMER
PERIODICALIST
PERRUQUIER
PETERMAN
PETROLOGIST
PETTIFOGGER
PEWTERER
PHARMA-
  CEUTIST
PHARMACIST
PHARMACOL-
  OGIST
PHILATELIST
PHILOLOGER
PHILOLOGIST
PHONOGRA-
  PHER
PHONOLOGIST
PHOTOGRA-
  PHER
PHRENOLOGIST
PHYSICIAN
PHYSICIST
PHYSIOGNO-
  MIST
PHYSIOGRA-
  PHER
PHYSIOLOGIST
PHYTOLOGIST

PIANIST
PIANO TUNER
PICADOR
PICAROON
PICKER
PICKPOCKET
PIEMAN
PILOT
PINKMAKER
PIPER
PIRATE
PITMAN
PITSAWYER
PLANISHER
PLANNER
PLANTER
PLANT
  MANAGER
PLASTERER
PLATELAYER
PLATER
PLATFORM-
  SPEAKER
PLAYER
PLAYWRIGHT
PLEADER
PLOUGHBOY
PLOUGHER
PLOUGHMAN
PLOUGH-
  WRIGHT
PLUMBER
PLUMBER'S
  MATE
PLURALIST
PLYER(FOR-HIRE)
PM
PNEUMATOL-
  OGIST
POACHER
POET(ASTER)
POINTSMAN
POLICEMAN
POLISHER
POLITICIAN
POLYPHONIST
POP ARTIST
PORK BUTCHER
PORTER
PORTIONIST
PORTRAITIST
PORTRAIT-
  PAINTER
PORTRAYER
PORTREEVE
PORTRESS
POSTBOY
POSTILER
POSTIL(L)ION
POSTMAN

POSTMASTER
POSTMISTRESS
POSTURF-
  MASTER
POSTWOMAN
POTBOY
POTMAKER
POTTER
POULTERER
POULTRY
  FARMER
PRACTISER
PRACTITIONER
PREACHER
PRECENTOR
PRECEPTOR
PRECEPTRESS
PREDICANT
PREFACER
PRELECTOR
PRELUDER
PRESCRIBER
PRESSER
PRESSMAN
PRESS OFFICER
PRESTIGIATOR
PRESTOR
PRIEST(ESS)
PRIMA
  DONNA
PRINTER
PRINT-SELLER
PRISON
  WARDER
PRIVATEER
PRIVATE EYE
PRIZE-FIGHTER
PRO
PROBATIONER
PROBATOR
PROCESS-
  SERVER
PROCURATOR
PROCURER
PROFESSIONAL
PROFESSIONAL
  (WO)MAN
PROFESSOR
PROFILIST
PROGRAMMER
PROGRAMME
  SELLER
PROMOTER
PROMPTER
PROMULGATOR
PRONOUNCER
PROOFREADER
PROPAGANDIST
PROPERTY
  MAN

PROPRIETOR	RAG	RINGMASTER	SCHOOL-	SHARE-BROKER
PROPRIETRESS	MERCHANT	RIVET(T)ER	MASTER	SHARECROPPER
PROPRIETRIX	RAILMAKER	ROADMAKER	SCHOOL-	SHARPER
PROSAIST	RAILWAY	ROADMAN	MISTRESS	SHARPSHOOTER
PROSPECTOR	ENGINEER	ROADMENDER	SCHOOL-	SHEARER
PROSTITUTE	RAILWAYMAN	ROADSWEEPER	TEACHER	SHEARMAN
PROTRACTOR	RANCHER	ROASTER	SCIENCE	SHEEPFARMER
PROVEDITOR	RANCHERO	ROBBER	MASTER	SHEPHERD(ESS)
PROVEDORE	RANGER	ROMANCER	SCIENTIST	SHIPBREAKER
PROVIDER	RAPPEREE	ROOFER	SCOURER	SHIP-BROKER
PROVISION	RAT-CATCHER	ROOTER	SCOUT	SHIPBUILDER
DEALER	RATER	ROPEDANCER	SCOUTMASTER	SHIP CHANDLER
PRUNER	RATTER	ROPEMAKER	SCRAPDEALER	SHIP-HOLDER
PSALMIST	READER	ROUGHRIDER	SCREENWRITER	SHIPMASTER
PSALMOGRA-	REALTOR	ROUNDSMAN	SCRIBE	SHIPMATE
PHER	REAPER	RUBBER-	SCRIP-HOLDER	SHIPOWNER
PSALMOGRA-	REAVER	GRADER	SCRIPTURE-	SHIPPER
PHIST	RECEIVER	RUBBER-	READER	SHIP'S BOY
PSYCHIATRIST	RECEPTION	PLANTER	SCRIPTWRITER	SHIP'S-
PSYCHO-	CLERK	RUGMAKER	SCRIVENER	CARPENTER
ANALYST	RECEPTIONIST	RUMOURER	SCRUTINEER	SHIP'S
PSYCHOLOGIST	RECITALIST	RUM RUNNER	SCULLERY-MAID	HUSBAND
PTERIDOLOGIST	RECRUITER	RUNER	SCULLION	SHIP'S MASTER
PUBLICAN	RECTOR	RUSTLER	SCULPTOR	SHIP'S MATE
PUBLICIST	REEVE	SACKER	SCULPTRESS	SHIPWRIGHT
PUBLICITY MAN	REFINER	SACRIST(AN)	SCYTHEMAN	SHOEBLACK
PUBLIC SPEAKER	REFORMIST	SADDLER	SEA-CAPTAIN	SHOEMAKER
PUBLISHER	REGENT	SAFEBLOWER	SEA-DOG	SHOER
PUDDLER	REGRATER	SAFEBREAKER	SEALER	SHOE-REPAIRER
PUGILIST	REHEARSER	SAFEMAKER	SEAMAN	SHOP
PULPITEER	RELESSEE	SAILING	SEAMSTER	ASSISTANT
PUNCTURIST	RELESSOR	MASTER	SEAMSTRESS	SHOPBOY
PUPIL	RELIEF	SAILMAKER	SEA-ROBBER	SHOPFITTER
PUPIL-TEACHER	RENTER	SAILOR	SEA-ROVER	SHOPGIRL
PUPPETEER	REP	SALES FORCE	SEASONER	SHOPKEEPER
PUPPET-PLAYER	REPAIRER	SALESMAN	SECOND MATE	SHOPSTEWARD
PURSER	REPORTER	SALES	SECRET AGENT	SHOPWALKER
PURVEYOR	REPRESENTATIVE	MANAGER	SECRETARY	SHOWGIRL
PYROLOGIST	REPRESENTER	SALESWOMAN	SEDITIONARY	SHOWMAN
PYTHONESS	REPUBLISHER	SALTER	SEED-	SHROFF
QUACK	RESEARCHER	SALVOR	MERCHANT	SHUNTER
QUALIFIER	RESETTER	SAMPLER	SEEDSMAN	SIDEROGRA-
QUARRIER	RESTAURATEUR	SAMURAI	SEER	PHIST
QUARRYMAN	RESTORER	SANDWICH	SEINER	SIDESMAN
QUARRY	RESURRECTION-	MAN	SEISMOLOGIST	SIGHTSMAN
MASTER	IST	SANSCRITIST	SEIZOR	SIGNALMAN
QUEEN'S	RETAILER	SAPPER	SELLER	SIGNWRITER
COUNSEL	RETAINER	SARTOR	SEMINARIST	SILENTIARY
QUERRY	REVIEWER	SATIRIST	SEMPSTER	SILKMAN
QUESTIONARY	REVOLUTION-	SAWBONES	SERF	SILK-MERCER
QUILL	ARY	SAWYER	SERVANT (GIRL)	SILK-
QUIZ-MASTER	REVOLUTIONIST	SAXOPHONIST	SERVER	THROW(ST)ER
RABBI(N)	REWRITER	SCARIFIER	SERVING-MAID	SILK-WEAVER
RACING DRIVER	RHETORICIAN	SCAVENGER	SERVING-MAN	SILVER-BEATER
RACING-TIPSTER	RIBBONMAN	SCENARIST	SERVITOR	SILVERSMITH
RACKETEER	RIDING-MASTER	SCENE-PAINTER	SETTER	SIMPLER
RADIOGRAPHER	RIGGER	SCENE-SHIFTER	SETTLER	SIMPLIST
RADIOLOGIST	RIGHT-HAND	SCHOLIAST	SEWER	SINGER
RAFTSMAN	MAN	SCHOOLMAN	SEXOLOGIST	SINGING-
RAGMAN	RINGER	SCHOOLMARM	SEXTON	MASTER

SINOLOGIST
SINOLOGUE
SIRCAR
SKETCHER
SKINNER
SKIPPER
SKIRMISHER
SKIVVY
SLATER
SLAUGHTERER
SLAUGHTER-
MAN
SLAVE
SLAVE-DRIVER
SLAVE-HOLDER
SLAVER
SLAVEY
SLEEPING
PARTNER
SLEUTH
SLIPPER
SLOP SELLER
SMALLHOLDER
SMELTER
SMITH
SMUGGLER
SNAKE-
CHARMER
SNARER
SNEAK THIEF
SNIPPER
SOAP-BOILER
SOAPMAKER
SOCAGER
SOCIAL
WORKER
SOCIOLOGIST
SOCMAN
SOIL
MECHANIC
SOLDIER
SOLICITOR
SOLOIST
SONNETEER
SORCERESS
SORTER
SOUTER
SOWER
SPACEMAN
SPEARMAN
SPECIAL AGENT
SPECIALIST
SPECTACLE-
MAKER
SPECTROSCO-
PIST
SPEECHWRITER
SPEEDCOP
SPENCER
SPICE-BLENDER

SPICER
SPINNER
SPORTSCASTER
SPORTSWRITER
SPOTTER
SPURRIER
SPY
SQUIRE
STABLEBOY
STABLEMAN
STAFF
STAFF NURSE
STAGE-DRIVER
STAGEHAND
STAGE
MANAGER
STAGER
STAINER
STAMPER
STAPLER
STARCHER
STATIONER
STATION-
MASTER
STATISTICIAN
STAY-MAKER
STEEPLEJACK
STEERER
STEERSMAN
STEERSMATE
STENOGRAPHER
STENOGRA-
PHIST
STEREOSCOPIST
STETHOSCOPIST
STEVEDORE
STEWARD(ESS)
STIPULATOR
STITCHER
STOCKBROKER
STOCKJOBBER
STOCKMAN
STOCKTAKER
STOKER
STONE-BORER
STONEBREAKER
STONECUTTER
STONEDRESSER
STONEMASON
STONESQUARER
STOREKEEPER
STOREMAN
STORER
STRATEGIST
STREET-SWEEPER
STREET-TRADER
STREET-WALKER
STREET-WARD
STRETCHER-
BEARER

STRIPPER
STRUMMER
STUNTMAN
SUB-
CONTRACTOR
SUBEDITOR
SUCCENTOR
SUGAR-REFINER
SUNDRIESMAN
SUPERCARGO
SUPERINTEN-
DENT
SUPERINTENDER
SUPERNUMER-
ARY
SUPERVISER
SUPPLIER
SURCHARGER
SURFACE-MAN
SURGEON
SUR-MASTER
SURVEYOR
SUTLER
SWABBER
SWAN-KEEPER
SWAN-UPPER
SWEEP(ER)
SWINDLER
SWINEHERD
SWITCHMAN
SWORDSMAN
SYCE
SYMPHONIST
SYNDICATE
SYNOPTIST
SYSTEM-
MAKER
SYSTEMS
ANALYST
TABLEMAID
TABLER
TABO(U)RER
TACTICIAN
TAILOR(ESS)
TALLIER
TALLOW
CHANDLER
TALLY CLERK
TALLYMAN
TAMER
TAMPER
TANNER
TAPSTER
TASKER
TASKMASTER
TASTER
TAVERNER
TAWER
TAX-COLLECTOR
TAXER

TAXIDERMIST
TAXI-DRIVER
TAXI-MAN
TEA-BLENDER
TEACHER
TEAMSTER
TEA PLANTER
TEATASTER
TECHNICIAN
TECHNOCRAT
TECHNOLOGIST
TELEGRAPH BOY
TELEGRAPHER
TELEGRAPHIST
TELEPHONIST
TELLER
TENTMAKER
TERMER
TEST ENGINEER
TESTER
TEST PILOT
THATCHER
THAUMATUR-
GIST
THEOGONIST
THEOLOGIAN
THEOLOGIST
THERAPEUTIST
THERAPIST
THESPIAN
THEURGIST
THIEF-CATCHER
THIMBLE-RIGGER
THRENODIST
THRESHER
THROWSTER
TICKET AGENT
TICKET
COLLECTOR
TICKET-PORTER
TIGHTROPE
WALKER
TILER
TILLER
TIMBERMAN
TIMBER TRADER
TIMEKEEPER
TINKER
TINMAN
TIN MINER
TINNER
TINSMITH
TIPSTER
TIRE-WOMAN
TOAST-
MASTER
TOBACCONIST
TOLL
COLLECTOR
TOLLER

TOLL-GATHERER
TOOLSMITH
TOOTH-DRAWER
TOPOGRAPHER
TORCH-BEARER
TORTURER
TOURIST AGENT
TOUT(ER)
TOWN CLERK
TOWNCRIER
TOWN
PLANNER
TOXICOLOGIST
TOXOPHILITE
TOYMAKER
TRACER
TRACKER
TRACTARIAN
TRADER
TRADESMAN
TRADESPEOPLE
TRADE
UNION(IST)
TRAFFIC COP
TRAFFICKER
TRAGEDIAN
TRAIN-BEARER
TRAINER
TRAMCAR-
DRIVER
TRAM
CONDUCTOR
TRAM-DRIVER
TRANSACTOR
TRANSCRIBER
TRANSLATOR
TRANSPLANTER
TRANSPORTER
TRAPPER
TRAVEL AGENT
TRAVELLER
TRAWLER(MAN)
TREASURER
TREASURESS
TREPANNER
TRIBUTARY
TRICHOLOGIST
TRIMMER
TRIPEMAN
TROUBADOUR
TRUCKER
TRUCKMAN
TRUMPETER
TRUSTEE
TUBMAN
TUMBLER
TUNER
TURNCOCK
TURNER
TURNKEY

PROFESSIONS, TRADES, AND OCCUPATIONS continued

TURNSPIT	VERSIFIER	WAREHOUSE-	WHETTER	WOOL-COMBER
TUTOR(ESS)	VET(ERINARIAN)	MAN	WHIP	WOOL-DRIVER
TYCOON	VETERINARY	WARPER	WHITENER	WOOL-DYER
TYLER	VETTURINO	WARRANTEE	WHITESMITH	WOOL-
TYMPANIST	VEXILLARY	WARRANTER	WHITESTER	GROWER
TYPE-FOUNDER	VICTUALLER	WARRENER	WHITEWASHER	WOOLLEN-
TYPESETTER	VIEWER	WARRIOR	WHITSTER	DRAPER
TYPIST	VINE-DRESSER	WASHER	WHOLESALER	WOOLMAN
TYPOGRAPHER	VINER	WASHER-	WIGMAKER	WOOL-SORTER
UNDERBEARER	VINTAGER	(WO)MAN	WINDOW-	WOOL-STAPLER
UNDERLETTER	VINTNER	WATCHKEEPER	CLEANER	WOOL-TRADER
UNDER-	VIOLINIST	WATCHMAKER	WINDOW-	WOOL-WINDER
MANAGER	VIOLIST	WATCHMAN	DRESSER	WORKER
UNDERSERVANT	VIOLONCELLIST	WATER-	WINEGROWER	WORKMAN
UNDERTAKER	VIRTUOSO	COLOURIST	WINEMAKER	WORKS
UNDERWRITER	VIVANDIÈRE	WATER DIVINER	WINE	MANAGER
UNIONIST	VOCABULIST	WATERGUARD	MERCHANT	WORKWOMAN
UPHOLSTERER	VOCALIST	WATERMAN	WINE-WAITER	WRAPPER
USHER(ETTE)	VOLCANIST	WAX-CHANDLER	WINNOWER	WRESTLER
USURER	VOLTIGEUR	WAXWORKER	WIREMAN	WRIGHT
VACHER	VOLUMIST	WEATHER	WIREWORKER	WRITER
VALET	WADSETTER	PROPHET	WITCH-	WRITING-
VALUATOR	WAGONER	WEAVER	DOCTOR	MASTER
VALUER	WAINWRIGHT	WEBSTER	WOODCARVER	XYLOPHONIST
VAMPER	WAITER	WEEDER	WOODCUTTER	YARDMASTER
VANMAN	WAITING-	WEIGHER	WOOD-	ZINCOGRAPHER
VARNISHER	WOMAN	WELDER	ENGRAVER	ZINC-WORKER
VASSAL	WAITRESS	WET NURSE	WOODMAN	ZOOGRAPHER
VENDER	WALKER-ON	WHALEMAN	WOOD-	ZOOGRAPHIST
VENDOR	WALLER	WHALER	MONGER	ZOOKEEPER
VENTRILOQUIST	WARD	WHARFINGER	WOOD-REEVE	ZOOLOGIST
VERGER	WARDEN	WHEEL-CUTTER	WOOD-	ZOOTOMIST
VERSEMONGER	WARDER	WHEELER	WORKER	ZYMOLOGIST
VERSER	WARDRESS	WHEELWRIGHT	WOOL-CARDER	

rational, irregular, lone, mismatched, single, strange, superfluous, unbalanced, uneven, unusual, weird *may indicate an anagram*

offal Bath chap, brains, brawn, calf's head, chitterlings, cowheel, cow's udder, elder, giblets, gore, guts, heart, innards, kidney, leftovers, liver, melts, neck sweatbread, ox cheek, oxtail, pig's feet, pig's fry, pig's head, pig's knuckles, rubbish, stomach sweatbread, sweatbread, thick seam, tongue, tripe, trotters, variety meat

offence affront, attack, crime, dudgeon, hostility, huff, hurt, indignity, insult, miff, transgression, umbrage, wrong

offend affront, aggravate, annoy, antagonize, arouse, bait, bother, break the

law, chafe, exasperate, fret, goad, grieve, harass, huff, incense, inflame, insult, irritate, miff, needle, nettle, outrage, pester, pinprick, pique, provoke, rankle, rile, ruffle, sin, sting, taunt, tease, torment, vex, work up, wound

offer advance, advertise, approach, auction, bait, bid, bribe, come-on, goad, hold out, induce, invitation, lure, persuade, proffer, proposal, proposition, spur, submit, suggest, volunteer

offering alms, appeasement, collection, conciliation, consecration, contribution, dedication, donation, expiation, gift, Maundy money, oblation, offertory, Peter's pence, present, propitiation, sacrifice, subscription, tithe, widow's mite

official alderman, ambassador, appa-

241

ratchik, authorized, bureaucrat, civil servant, clerk, commissioner, consul, councillor, counsellor, envoy, Eurocrat, formal, functionary, governmental, intendant, jobsworth, legal, magistrate, mandarin, marshal, mayor, minister, officer, peer, prefect, public, representative, secretary, senator, steward, tin god, vizier

officiate chair, control, direct, invigilate, minister, oversee, preside

officious busybodying, dictatorial, interfering, meddlesome, meddling, self-important, tampering

oil aviation fuel, crude oil, derv, diesel oil, ester, gas oil, grease, lather, lubricate, lubrify, methylated spirits, mineral oil, moisten, naphtha, oleaginize, oleum, paraffin, petrol, smooth, soap, wax

oil field offshore rig, oil platform, oil reserves, oil rig, oil well

oiliness adiposis, butteriness, creaminess, creepiness, fatness, fattiness, greasiness, lubricity, obsequiousness, pinguidity, richness, saponacity, sebaceousness, smarminess, soapiness, suaveness, unctuousness, waxiness

oily adipose, blubbery, buttery, butyraceous, butyric, cereous, creamy, creepy, fat, fatty, fleshy, greasy, lardy, milky, mucoid, obsequious, oleaginous, oleic, paraffinic, pinguid, rich, saponaceous, sebaceous, sleek, slick, slippery, slithery, smarmy, smooth, soapy, suety, tallowy, toadying, unctuous, unguinous, waxy

ointment abirritant, arquebusade, balm, balsam, brilliantine, chrism, collyrium, cream, demulcent, embrocation, emollient, eyewash, fomentation, inunction, lanolin, lenitive, liniment, lotion, macassar, nard, oil, paint, pomade, poultice, salve, spikenard, syrup, unction, unguent

old adamic, aged, age-old, ancestral, ancient, antediluvian, antiquarian, antiquated, antique, archaic, classic, crumbling, doddering, elderly, established, grey-haired, historical, immemorial, mature, mellow, Methuselah, moth-eaten, mouldering, musty, old-world, outdated, patriarchal, prewar, ripe, rooted, second-hand, senescent, senile, senior, stale, time-honoured, timeworn, traditional, used, venerable, veteran, vintage, worn

old age advanced years, anecdotage, decrepitude, dotage, elderliness, golden years, longevity, maturity, mellowness, pensionable age, retirement age, senescence, senility, seniority, third age, venerableness

old-fashioned antiquated, defunct, discarded, disused, old hat, outgrown, stale, unfashionable

old people ancestors, crumblies, elders, forebears, grandparents, Methuselah, pensioners, senior citizens, the elderly, wrinklies

omen augury, auspice, caution, forerunner, foretoken, harbinger, herald, indication, messenger, portent, precursor, prefigurement, presage, prognostication, sign, symptom, syndrome, type, warning

ominousness balefulness, fatefulness, foreboding, menace, portentousness

omission arrears, break, defalcation, default, deficiency, deficit, gap, insufficiency, interval, lack, lacuna, loss, need, oversight, shortfall, slippage, ullage, void, want

omnipresence appearance, attendance, diffusion, frequenting, permeation, pervasiveness, ubiquitousness

one ace, article, atom, atomic, entity, I, individual, integer, item, lone, module, monad, monadic, mono, person, persona, point, self, single, singleton, sole, solitary, solo, soul, unit, unity

oneness coherence, indissolubility, integrality, integrity, singleness, solidarity, undividedness, union, unity, wholeness

one-sided monochromatic, monolingual, one-piece, one-size, one-way, unicameral, unicellular, unidirectional, unilateral, uniplanar, unipolar, unisex

ongoing continuing, flowing on, inexorable, irreversible, moving, oncoming, onward, proceeding, profluent, unbroken

opaque black, blank, cloudy, coated, covered, dark, dense, foggy, impenetrable, impermeable, impervious, nontranslucent, nontransparent, solid, thick, windowless

opaqueness blackness, cloudiness, darkness, density, dimness, dirtiness, dullness, filminess, fogginess, fuzziness, haziness, impenetrability, impermeability, imperviousness, milkiness, mirroring, muddiness, murkiness, obfuscation, reflection, solidity, thickness, turbidity

open access, ajar, artless, barefaced, blunt, bold, brazen, breached, break, candid, clear, cleave, cleft, crack, crystal-clear, cut, daring, disclose, emphatic, erupt, explicit, explode, expose, extend, fissured, flaunting, forthright, fracture, frank, free, gaping, hack, hew, honest, ingenuous, leave ajar, naive, no-nonsense, open-faced, open-hearted, open-mouthed, outspoken, plain, plain-speaking, public, reveal, rupture, show, sincere, split, spread, straightforward, tear, torn, truthful, unbar, unblock, unbolt, unclosed, uncork, uncover, unfasten, unfold, unlatch, unlock, unreserved, unrestricted, unseal, unveil, unwrap, veracious, visible, wide-open

open-air alfresco, outdoor, out-of-door, outside

opened accessible, available, bare, clear, evident, extended, manifest, obvious, open-door, open-plan, patent, unbarred, unblocked, uncorked, uncovered, unenclosed, unfastened, un-

hindered, unimpeded, unlocked, unobstructed, unprotected, unrestricted, unsealed, vacant

opener bottle-opener, key, open sesame, passkey, password, tin-opener

opening aperture, bore, break, cavity, chasm, cleft, crack, crevice, cut, duct, fault, fissure, fracture, gap, gape, hole, hollow, interval, orifice, pass, passage, perforation, piercing, pricking, puncture, rupture, slot, space, split, tear

openness apparentness, artlessness, bluntness, candour, explicitness, forthrightness, frankness, glasnost, guilelessness, honesty, indiscretion, ingenuousness, lucidity, naivety, obviousness, open-heartedness, outspokenness, plainness, plain speaking, sincerity, straightforwardness, truth, unreservedness

operate
may indicate an anagram

operation action, agency, course, execution, exercise, force, implementation, measure, motion, movement, performance, play, power, procedure, process, strain, stress, surgery, swing, treatment, work

operational active, functional, going, running, usable, working

operative agent, armed, critical, crucial, effective, efficacious, efficient, established, important, influential, in force, in force, key, relevant, significant, switched on, valid, workable, worker, working

operator actor, controller, executive, manager, performer, programmer

opinionated closed, dogmatic, inflexible, intolerant, narrow-minded

opinionatedness bias, bigotry, blindness, closed mind, dogmatism, fanaticism, ignorance, illiberality, intolerance, narrow-mindedness, obscurantism, obsession, prejudice, rigorism, zealotry

opportunity certainty, chance, foothold, good odds, likelihood, luck, lucky break, occasion, odds on, open door, opening, possibility, probability, safe bet, scope, sure thing, toehold

oppose challenge, clash, collide, conflict, differ, dissent, face, fall out, feud, fight, object, protest, quarrel, rebut, resist, stand against, traverse

opposing antagonistic, antipathetic, challenging, competing, confrontational, contentious, defiant, different, disapproving, facing, fighting, hostile, inimical, objecting, opposite, resistant, rival

opposite antipodal, antithetic, confronting, contrapositive, contrariwise, contrary, contrasting, converse, diametric, eyeball-to-eyeball, face-to-face, facing, inverse, obverse, oncoming, other, polarized, reverse

oppositeness antithesis, confrontment, contradiction, contraposition, contrariety, contrariness, contrast, converse, inversion, obverse, opposure, polarity, reverse

opposition animosity, antagonism, antipathy, argument, aversion, balking, competitors, conflict, confrontation, contention, counteraction, defiance, disagreement, disapprobation, disapproval, dislike, enmity, filibuster, hate, hindrance, hostility, impugnation, inimicality, noncooperation, obstruction, opt-out, other side, other team, rebuff, recalcitrance, refusal, rejection, renitency, repugnance, resistance, rivalry, unfriendliness

oppositional adverse, alien, antagonistic, antipathetic, averse, contrary, counteractive, cross, disapproving, hostile, inimical, opposing, repugnant, rival, unfavourable, unfriendly, unpropitious

oppress browbeat, bully, crush, grind down, hector, hold down, hound, persecute, suppress, trample on, victimize

oppressive binding, bludgeoning, bulldozing, constraining, dictatorial, enforcing, forceful, hubristic, humid, muggy, overbearing, overweening, restraining, steamroller, strong-arm, violent

opulence abundance, bounty, comfort, cornucopia, ease, fleshpots, lavishness, luxury, plenty, plushness, profusion, sumptuousness, superfluity

opulent de luxe, diamond-studded, expensive, first-class, gilded, glittering, glitzy, lavish, luxurious, palatial, plush, ritzy, splendid, sumptuous

or alternatively, au, gold, yellow

oracle Cassandra, clairvoyant, Delphic oracle, doom merchant, medium, Nostradamus, occultist, prediction, prophet, Pythian oracle, pythoness, revelation, sage, seer, sibyl, soothsayer, sorcerer, telepathist, vaticinator, visionary, warlock, witch

oral
may indicate a homophone

orange amber, apricot, brassy, bronze, cadmium orange, carotene, carroty, clementine, coppery, flame-coloured, ginger, golden, goldfish, henna, mandarin, marigold, marmalade, nectarine, ochre, ochreous, old-gold, or, peach, pumpkin, raw sienna, reddish-yellow, saffron, sand, satsuma, sunflower, tan, tangerine, Titian

oratorical declamatory, demagogic(al), expressive, grandiloquent, rhetorical

oratory declamation, ranting, rhetoric, soap-box, speechifying, tubthumping

orbit ambit, beat, circle, circuit, circulate, cycle, eye socket, gyre, lap, loop, revolve, rotate, rounds, round trip, spin, spiral, tour, turn, walk, wheel

orbital ambagious, bypass, circuitous, circulatory, circumambient, circumlocutory, circumnavigable, deviating, indirect, meandering, oblique, revolutionary, ring road, rotatory, round-about, turning

orbiting circling, circularity, circulation, circumambulation, circumflexion, circummigration, circumnavigation, coil, ellipse, gyrating, gyre, helix, revolution, rotation, rounding, spinning, spiralling, turning, wheeling

orchestra band, chamber group, duo, ensemble, group, nonet, octet, quartet, quintet, septet, sextet, trio
See list of musical instruments.

orchestrate accompany, arrange, harmonize, melodize, organize, score, symphonize, syncopate

orchestration arrangement, chaconne, figure, instrumentation, musica ficta, passacaglia, passage, phrasing, sequence

ordain anoint, appoint, authorize, call, consecrate, frock, invest, read in, select, take vows

order align, alphabetize, arrangement, array, catalogue, classify, command, compose, degree, denomination, disposition, distribution, form, formalization, formation, grade, index, instruct, lawfulness, layout, line-up, list, manage, marshal, ordain, organization, pattern, prioritization, rank, request, schedule, scheme, setup, sort, structure, system, tidiness, uniformity

ordered accurate, alphabetized, arranged, arrayed, balanced, businesslike, classified, commanded, composed, disposed, formal(ized), hierarchical, indexed, methodical, meticulous, neat, organized, punctilious, ranked, regular, schematic, scientific, sorted, straight, structured, symmetrical, systematic, told, uniform, well-organized
may indicate an anagram

orderliness balance, cleanness, consistency, constance, continuity, correctness, custom, evenness, flatness, law, levelness, neatness, normality,

order, ordinariness, regularity, regulation, routine, rule, smoothness, steadiness, straightness, tidiness, tradition, uniformity

orderly attendant, balanced, cleaner, configurational, conformable, consistent, constant, continual, correct, creative, customary, dapper, dinky, even, everyday, flat, groomed, hospital porter, legal, level, methodical, metrical, neat, normal, ordinary, regular, routine, shipshape, sleek, slick, smart, smooth, spruce, steady, straight, systematic, tidy, traditional, trim, typical, uniform
may indicate an anagram

ordinariness averageness, mediocrity, normality, usualness

ordinary average, base, bearable, common(place), everyday, median, mediocre, middle-of-the-road, middling, moderate, passable, plebcian, so-so, tolerable, unheroic, vulgar, wet

organic biological, coherent, constitutional, fundamental, inherent, natural, organismal, organized, organological, systematic, vital

organism animal, animalcule, bacterium, body, creature, entity, germ, microbe, microorganism, plant, virus

organization arrangement, association, business, charting, company, corporation, group, management, method, planning, running, set up, structuring, system
may indicate an anagram

organizational formational, methodical, rational, schematic, systematic

organize arrange, control, coordinate, direct, manage, methodize, plan, put together, rationalize, schematize, standardize, systematize

organized methodized, planned, prearranged, rationalized, systematized
may indicate an anagram

orient accommodate, adapt, adjust,

MUSICAL INSTRUMENTS

ACCORDION
ADENKUM
(STAMPING TUBE)
AEOLIAN HARP
ALBOKA (HORNPIPE)
ALGHAITA (SHAWM)
ALPHORN (TRUMPET)
ALTOHORN
ANGEL CHIMES
ANGLE HARP
ANKLUNG (RATTLE)
ARGHUL (CLARINET)
ARPANETTA (ZITHER)
ATUMPAN
(KETTLEDRUM)
AULOI (SHAWM)
AUTOHARP
BAGANA (LYRE)
BAGPIPE
BALALAIKA (LUTE)
BANANA DRUM
BANDOURA (LUTE)
BANDURRIA (LUTE)
BANJO(LELE)
BARREL DRUM
BARREL ORGAN
BARYTON (VIOL)
BASSANELLO
(DOUBLE REED)
BASS DRUM
BASSET HORN
BASS HORN
BASSONORE
(BASSOON)
BASSOON
BATA (DRUM)
BELL CITTERN
BELLS
BHAYA
(KETTLEDRUM)
BIBLE REGAL
(ORGAN)
BICITRABIN (VINA)
BINIOU (BAGPIPE)
BIN (VINA)
BIRD SCARER
BIVALVE BELL
BIWA (LUTE)
BLADDER PIPE
BOARD ZITHER
BODHRAN (DRUM)
BOMBARDE
(SHAWM)
BOMBARDON
(TUBA)
BONGO DRUMS
BONNANG
(GONG)
BOUZOUKI (LUTE)
BOW HARP

BOWL LYRE
BOX LYRE
BUCCINA (TRUMPET)
BUGLE
BUISINE (TRUMPET)
BULL-ROARER
BUMBASS
BUMPA (CLARINET)
BUZZ DISK
CALLIOPE
(MECHANICAL
ORGAN)
CARILLON
CARNYX (TRUMPET)
CASTANETS
CELESTE
CELLO
CHAKAY (ZITHER)
CHALUMEAU
(CLARINET)
CHANG (DULCIMER)
CHANGKO (DRUM)
CHA PEI (LUTE)
CHENGCHENG
(CYMBALS)
CHIME (BAR)
CHINESE WOOD
BLOCK
CH'IN (ZITHER)
CHITARRA BATTENTE
(GUITAR)
CHITARRONE (LUTE)
CIMBALOM
(DULCIMER)
CIPACTLI (FLUTE)
CITTERN
CLAPPER BELL
CLAPPERS
CLARINET
(D'AMORE)
CLASSICAL GUITAR
CLAVE
CLAVICHORD
CLAVICOR (BRASS
FAMILY)
CLAVICYTHERIUM
(HARPSICHORD)
CLAVIORGAN
CLAW BELL
COBZA (LUTE)
COCKTAIL DRUMS
COG RATTLE
COLASCIONE (LUTE)
COMPONIUM
(MECHANICAL
ORGAN)
CONTRABASS
(DOUBLE BASS)
CONTRABASSOON
COR ANGLAIS

CORNEMUSE
(BAGPIPE)
CORNET(T)
CORNOPEAN
(BRASS FAMILY)
CORNU (TRUMPET)
COURTAUT (DOUBLE
REED)
COWBELL
CRECELLE (COG
RATTLE)
CROOK HORN
CROTALS
(PERCUSSION)
CRUMHORN
(DOUBLE REED)
CRWTH (LYRE)
CURTAL (DOUBLE
REED)
CYLINDRICAL
DRUMS
CYMBALS
CYTHARA ANGLICA
(HARP)
DA-DAIKO (DRUM)
DAIBYOSHI (DRUM)
DARABUKKE (DRUM)
DARBUK (DRUM)
DAULI (DRUM)
DEUTSCHE
SCHALMEI
(DOUBLE REED)
DHOLA (DRUM)
DIDGERIDOO
(TRUMPET)
DIPLICE (CLARINET)
DIPLO-KITHARA
(ZITHER)
DJUNADJAN (ZITHER)
DOBRO (GUITAR)
DOUBLE BASS
DOUBLE BASSOON
(CONTRA-
BASSOON)
DRUM
DUDELSACK
(BAGPIPES)
DUGDUGI (DRUM)
DULCIMER
DVOJACHKA (FLUTE)
DVOYNICE (FLUTE)
ENZENZE (ZITHER)
ERH-HU (FIDDLE)
EUPHONIUM (BRASS
FAMILY)
FANDUR (FIDDLE)
FIDDLE
FIDEL (FIDDLE)
FIDLA (ZITHER)
FIFE

FIPPLE FLUTE
FITHELE (FIDDLE)
FLAGEOLET (FLUTE)
FLEXATONE
(PERCUSSION)
FLUGELHORN
FLUTE
FRENCH HORN
FUJARA (FLUTE)
FUYE (FLUTE)
GADULKA (FIDDLE)
GAITA (BAGPIPE)
GAJDY (BAGPIPE)
GAMBANG KAYA
(XYLOPHONE)
GANSA GAMBANG
(METALLOPHONE)
GANSA JONGKOK
(METALLOPHONE)
GEIGENWERK
(MECHANICAL
HARPSICHORD)
GEKKIN (LUTE)
GENDER
(METALLOPHONE)
GITTERN
GLING-BU (FLUTE)
GLOCKENSPIEL
(METALLOPHONE)
GONG
GONG AGENG
GONG CHIMES
GONG DRUM
GONGUE
(PERCUSSION)
GRAND PIANO
GUITAR
GUITAR-BANJO
GUITAR-VIOLIN
GUSLE (FIDDLE)
HACKBRETT
(DULCIMER)
HANDBELL
HAND HORN
HANDLE DRUM
HAND TRUMPET
HARDANGERFELE
(FIDDLE)
HARMONICA
HARMONIUM
HARP
HARPSICHORD
HAWKBELL
HECKELCLARINA
(CLARINET)
HECKELPHONE
(OBOE)
HI-HAT CYMBALS
HORN
HU CH'IN (FIDDLE)

HULA IPU
(PERCUSSION)
HUMMEL (ZITHER)
HURDY GURDY
HURUK (DRUM)
HYDRAULIS
(ORGAN)
INGUNGU (DRUM)
ISIGUBU (DRUM)
JEW'S HARP
JINGLING JOHNNY
KACHAPI (ZITHER)
KAKKO (DRUM)
KALUNGU (TALKING
DRUM)
KAMANJE (FIDDLE)
KANTELEHARPE
(LYRE)
KANTELE (ZITHER)
KANUN (QANUN)
KAYAKEUM (ZITHER)
KAZOO (MIRLITON)
KELONTONG
(DRUM)
KEMANAK
(CLAPPERS)
KENA (QUENA)
KENONG (GONG)
KERAR (LYRE)
KETTLEDRUM
KHEN (MOUTH
ORGAN)
KHUMBGWE (FLUTE)
KISSAR (LYRE)
KIT (FIDDLE)
KITHARA (LYRE)
KOBORO (DRUM)
KO-KIU (FIDDLE)
KOMUNGO
(ZITHER)
KÖNIGHORN
(BRASS FAMILY)
KOTO (ZITHER)
LANGLEIK (ZITHER)
LANGSPIL (ZITHER)
LAP ORGAN
(MELODEON)
LAUNEDDAS
(CLARINET)
LIRA (FIDDLE)
LIRICA (FIDDLE)
LIRONE (FIDDLE)
LITHOPHONE
(PERCUSSION)
LITUUS (TRUMPET)
LONTAR (CLAPPERS)
LUR (HORN)
LUTE
LYRA (LYRE)
LYRE

MACHETE (LUTE)
MANDOBASS (LUTE)
MANDOCELLO
(LUTE)
MANDOLA (LUTE)
MANDOLINETTO
(UKULELE)
MANDOLIN (LUTE)
MANDOLONE (LUTE)
MARACAS
(PERCUSSION)
MASENQO (FIDDLE)
MAYURI (LUTE)
MBILA (XYLOPHONE)
MELLOPHONE
(HORN)
MELODEON
MELODICA
MIGYAUN (ZITHER)
MIRLITON (KAZOO)
MOKUGYO (DRUM)
MOOG
SYNTHESIZER
MORIN-CHUR
(FIDDLE)
MOROPI (DRUM)
MOSHUPIANE
(DRUM)
MOUTH ORGAN
MRIDANGA (DRUM)
MURUMBU (DRUM)
MUSETTE (BAGPIPE;
SHAWM)
MU YÜ (DRUM)
MVET (ZITHER)
NAKERS (DRUMS)
NAQARA (DRUMS)
NGOMA (DRUM)
NGURU (FLUTE)
NTENGA (DRUM)
NYCKELHARPA
OBOE
OBUKANO (LYRE)
OCARINA (FLUTE)
OCTAVIN (WIND)
O-DAIKO (DRUM)
OKEDO (DRUM)
OLIPHANT (HORN)
OMBGWE (FLUTE)
OPHICLEIDE (BRASS
FAMILY)
ORGAN
ORPHARION
(CITTERN)
ORPHICA (PIANO)
O-TSUZUMI (DRUM)
OTTAVINO
(VIRGINAL)
OUD (UD)
OUTI (LUTE)

P'AI HSIAO
(PANPIPE)
PAIMENSARVI
(HORN)
P'AI PAN (CLAPPERS)
PANDORA (CITTERN)
PANHUÉHUETL
(DRUM)
PANPIPE
PEACOCK SITAR
(LUTE)
PENORCON
(CITTERN)
PIAN(INO)
PIBCORN
(HORNPIPE)
PICCOLO
PICCO PIPE (FLUTE)
PIEN CH'ING
(LITHOPHONE)
PIFFARO (SHAWM)
PI NAI (SHAWM)
P'I P'A (LUTE)
PIPE
POCHETTE (KIT)
POMMER (SHAWM)
PSALTERY (ZITHER)
PU-ILU (CLAPPERS)
PUTORINO
(TRUMPET)
QANUN (ZITHER)
QUENA (FLUTE)
QUINTON (VIOL)
RACKET (DOUBLE
REED)
RAMKIE (LUTE)
RANASRINGA
(HORN)
RASPA (SCRAPER)
RATTLE
RAUSCHPFEIFE
(DOUBLE REED)
REBAB (FIDDLE)
REBEC (FIDDLE)
RECORDER
RESHOTO (DRUM)
RINCHIK (CYMBALS)
RKAN-DUNG
(TRUMPET)
RKAN-LING (HORN)
ROMMELPOT
(DRUM)
RONÉAT-EK
(XYLOPHONE)
ROTE (LYRE)
RUAN (LUTE)
SACKBUT
(TROMBONE)
SALPINX (TRUMPET)
SAMISEN (LUTE)

SAN HSIEN (LUTE)
SANTIR (DULCIMER)
SANTOOR
(DULCIMER)
SARANGI (FIDDLE)
SARINDA (FIDDLE)
SARON (DEMONG)
(METALLOPHONE)
SARRUSOPHONE
(BRASS)
SAVERNAKE HORN
SAW-THAI (FIDDLE)
SAXHORN
SAXOPHONE
SAXOTROMBA
SAXTUBA
SAZ (LUTE)
SCHRILLPFEIFE (FLUTE)
SERPENT
SHAING (HORN)
SI IAKLK
SHAKUHACHI
(FLUTE)
SHANAI (SHAWM)
SHAWM
SHENG (MOUTH
ORGAN)
SHIELD
(PERCUSSION)
SHIWAYA (FLUTE)
SHOFAR (HORN)
SHÔ (MOUTH
ORGAN)
SHOULDER HARP
SIDE DRUM
SISTRUM (RATTLE)
SITAR (LUTE)
SLEIGH BELLS
SLIDE TROMBONE
SLIT DRUM
SONAJERO (RATTLE)
SONA (SHAWM)
SOPILE (SHAWM)
SORDINE (KIT)
SORDONE (DOUBLE
REED)
SOUSAPHONE
SPAGANE
(CLAPPERS)
SPIKE FIDDLE
SPINET
SPITZHARFE (ZITHER)
SPOONS (CLAPPERS)
SRALAY (SHAWM)
SRINGARA (FIDDLE)
STOCK-AND-HORN
(HORNPIPE)
STRUMENTO DI
PORCO (ZITHER)
SURBAHAR (LUTE)

MUSICAL INSTRUMENTS continued

SURNAJ (SHAWM)
SWITCH
(PERCUSSION)
SYMPHONIUM
(MOUTH ORGAN)
SYRINX (PANPIPE)
TABLA (DRUM)
TABOR (DRUM)
TAIKO (DRUM)
TALAMBAS (DRUM)
TALLHARPA (LYRE)
TAM ÂM LA
(GONG)
TAMBOURINE
(DRUM)
TAMBURA (LUTE)
TAM-TAM (GONG)
TARABUKA (DRUM)
TAR (DRUM; LUTE)
TAROGATO
(CLARINET;
SHAWM)
TEPONAZTLI (DRUM)
TERBANG (DRUM)
THEORBO (LUTE)
THUMB PIANO
(JEW'S HARP)
TIBIA (SHAWM)

TIKTIRI (CLARINET)
TIMBALES (DRUM)
TIMPANI
TIN WHISTLE
TIPLE (SHAWM)
TIPPOO'S TIGER
(ORGAN)
TI-TZU (FLUTE)
TLAPANHUÉHUETL
(DRUM)
TLAPIZTALI (FLUTE)
TOM-TOM (DRUM)
TOTOMBITO
(ZITHER)
TRIANGLE
TRICCABALLACCA
(CLAPPERS)
TRO-KHMER (FIDDLE)
TROMBONE
TRO-U (FIDDLE)
TRUMPET
TSURI DAIKO (DRUM)
TSUZUMI (DRUM)
TUBA-DUPRÉ
TUBULAR BELLS
TUDUM (DRUM)
TUMYR (DRUM)
TUPAN (DRUM)

TURKISH CRESCENT
(JINGLING
JOHNNY)
TXISTU (FLUTE)
UCHIWA DAIKO
(DRUM)
UD (LUTE)
UJUSINI (FLUTE)
UKULELE
URUA (CLARINET)
UTI (LUTE)
VALIHA (ZITHER)
VIELLE (FIDDLE)
VIHUELA (GUITAR)
VINA (STRINGED
INSTRUMENT
RELATED TO SITAR)
VIOL
VIOLA (BASTARDA)
(VIOL)
VIOLA DA GAMBA
(VIOL)
VIOLA D'AMORE
(VIOL)
VIOLETTA (VIOL)
VIOLIN
VIOLONCELLO
VIOLONE (VIOL)

VIRGINAL
WHIP (PERCUSSION)
WHISTLE (FLUTE)
WOOD BLOCK
WURLITZER
XYLOPHONE
XYLORIMBA
(XYLOPHONE)
YANGCHIN
(DULCIMER)
YANGUM
(DULCIMER)
YUEH CH'IN (LUTE)
YUN LO (GONG)
YUN NGAO
(GONG)
YÜ (SCRAPER)
ZAMPOGNA
(BAGPIPE)
ZITHER
ZOBO (MIRLITON)
ZUMMARA
(CLARINET)
ZURLA (SHAWM)
ZURNA (SHAWM)

align, direct, E, east, point towards, steer

orientation adaptation, adjustment, alignment, bearings, collimation

original archetype, autograph, avant-garde, blueprint, chancy, creative, daring, enterprising, experimental, first, holograph, imaginative, innovative, invention, inventive, it, manuscript, model, modern, mould, new, novel, paradigm, pattern, pilot, pioneering, precedent, prototypal, reckless, risky, seminal, signature, source, strange, test case, unfamiliar, venturesome
may indicate an anagram

originality authenticity, avant-garde, beginning, creation, creativity, daring, dissimilarity, eccentricity, freshness, genuineness, idiosyncrasy, imagination, independence, individuality, initiation, innovation, inventiveness, modernism, newness, nonimitation, novelty, precedence, recklessness, risk, strangeness, unfamiliarity, uniqueness

originate auspicate, begin, conceive, create, design, devise, dream up, generate, imagine, initiate, innovate, invent, patent, pioneer, revolutionize, start

ornament adornment, alliteration, antithesis, arabesques, arrangement, assonance, beautify, boast, chef d'oeuvre, colour, cynosure, deck, decorate, elaborate, embellishment, embroidery, enhance, enrich, euphemize, euphuism, euphuize, festoon, figurativeness, floridness, flourish, floweriness, frills, garnish, gild, grace (note), hyperbaton, masterpiece, metaphor, overlay, overload, overstate, preciosity, purple passages, rant, rave, rhetoric, ring, simile, sing, trill, trimming, trope

ornate adorned, affected, beautified, bombastic, circumlocutory, coloured, convoluted, declamatory, decorated, diffuse, elaborate, eloquent, embellished, euphuistic, fancy, figurative, flamboyant, florid, flowery, frothy, fussy, fustian, garnished, gilded, grandiloquent, grandiose, highfalutin, high-flown, inflated, Johnsonian, Latinate, lofty, luxuriant, magniloquent, meretricious, metaphorical, oratorical, ostentatious, overloaded, pedantic, pompous, precious, pretentious, rhetorical, rich, sesquipedalian, showy, stately, stiff, stilted, tortuous, trimmed

ornithological avian, avicultural, bird-watching

orogenic mountain-building, orogenetic, orographic, orological, orometric

oscillate alternate, fluctuate, gyrate, nutate, pendulate, reciprocate, rotate, seesaw, shuttle, spin, sway, swing, teeter, vary, whirl, wibble-wobble, zigzag

oscillating alternating, back-and-forth, fluctuating, harmonic, libratory, nutational, periodic, reciprocal, seesaw, swinging, to-and-fro, up-and-down

oscillation agitation, alternation, Brownian movement, fluctuation, frequency, gyration, libration, nutation, pendulation, periodicity, reciprocation, shuttle, vibration

oscillator bob, cradle, metronome, pendulum, rocker, rocking chair, seesaw, shuttle, swing, teeterboard, vibrator

ostensible apparent, professed, superficial

ostentation display, flamboyance, show

ostentatious attention-seeking, flamboyant, flaunting, loud, showy

ostracism banishment, blackballing, deportation, exclusion, exile, expatriation, fugitation, outlawing, proscription, rustication, seclusion, the brushoff

ostracize ban, banish, blackball, brush off, cut, deport, exclude, exile, expatriate, extradite, fugitate, make unwelcome, outlaw, prohibit, proscribe, rusticate, seclude, snub, spurn, transport

otherwise
may indicate an anagram

otological audiological, aural, ENT, otalgic, otolaryngological, otorhinolaryngological, otoscopic

outcast abandoned, exile, expelled, flotsam, leper, pariah

outclassed beaten, bested, defeated, humbled, humiliated, outshone, ruined, trounced, worsted

outcry alarm, ballyhoo, banging, bawling, bedlam, chanting, clamour, clash, clatter, crash, din, hooting, howl, hubbub, hullabaloo, noisiness, objection, pandemonium, protest, racket, roar, row, rumpus, screaming, shemozzle, shouting, shriek, slamming, stamping, stramash, tumult, turmoil, ululation, uproar, vociferation, whoop, yelling

outdo beat, outbid, outdistance, outgo, outjump, outmanoeuvre, outmarch, outpace, outperform, outplay, outrace, outrank, outreach, outride, outrun, outshine, outstrip, outtrump, outvie, outwit, triumph over

outdoor alfresco, fresh-air, open-air, outside

outer exterior, external, outward, reflected, superficial, surface, visible, visual

outflow discharge, effluence, efflux, effusion, emanation, emission, evaporation, excretion, exhaust, exudation, flood, fountain, gush, gusher, inundation, jet, outfall, outflux, outpouring, perspiration, secretion, spill, spring, stream, sweating, transudation, voidance, waste, waterfall, well

outgoing chatty, emigratory, extrovert, gregarious, open, outward-bound, sociable, talkative

outlaw ban, banish, criminal, fugitive, vagabond

outlet anus, blowhole, chute, conduit, drain, drainpipe, exit, floodgate, flume, gargoyle, gutter, market, orifice, outfall, overflow, pore, release, sluice, spiracle, spout, tap, vent, weir

outline abbreviation, abridgement, abstract, blueprint, bones, brochure, chart, condensation, contour, contract, delineation, depiction, diagram, digest, draft, edge, emblem, engrave, epitomize, essentials, etch, frame, graph, illustrate, layout, limning, model, notes, pattern, picture, pilot scheme, plan, portrayal, précis, profile, project, proof, prospectus, prototype, reduction, representation, résumé, revision, rough out, sample, silhouette, skeleton, sketch, summarize, survey, syllabus, synopsis, trace, tracing

outlined abbreviated, abridged, brief, circumscriptive, delineative, depictive, descriptive, emblematic, impressionistic, marginal, peripheral, projectional, random, representative, sample, skeletal, summarized, thumbnail

out of
may indicate a hidden word

outside alfresco, beyond, external, extramural, hinterland, open-air, outback, outermost, outland, outlying, out-of-doors, outward
may indicate a split word

outsider alien, exile, foreigner, refugee, stranger

outsiders foreigners, non-members, others, strangers

outspoken abrupt, bluff, candid, curt, direct, frank, plain-spoken, straightforward

outspokenness abruptness, bluffness, candidness, curtness, directness, frankness, plain-spokenness, straightforwardness

out-talk bamboozle, filibuster, shout down, stonewall

outward displayed, external, facial, outer, projected, superficial, surface

over above, across, again, atop, bygone, completed, covering, done, ended, exhausted, extinct, extra, finished, gone, irrecoverable, maiden over, six balls, spent, superior, upside down

overact ad lib, barnstorm, ham, improvize, melodramatize, out-Herod Herod, overplay, send up, upstage

overacted affected, ballyhooed, bombastic, grandiloquent, histrionic, melodramatic, pretentious, teratologic

overacting ballyhoo, burlesque, caricature, hamming, histrionics, melodrama, puffery, travesty

overactivity excess, fidgetiness, hyperactivity, jumpiness, overambition, overexertion, overextension

overambitious arrogant, excessive, hubristic, overconfident, overenthusiastic, overextended, overloaded, overoptimistic, rash

overcast cloudy, dismal, glowering, louring

overcharge burn, clip, con, do, extort, fleece, inflate, mark up, overprice, oversell, profiteer, rack-rent, screw, sell dear, skin, sting, surcharge, swindle

overcharging exorbitance, extortionate price, overpricing, surcharge

overconfident arrogant, complacent, self-satisfied, smug, vain

overcrowd infest, outnumber, overman, overpopulate, overrun, overstaff, overwhelm, snow under, swamp

overdoing it effusiveness, overactivity, overdose, overestimation, overexpression, overextension, overindulgence, overload, overmeasure, overoptimism, overpayment, overpoliteness, overpraise, overstretching oneself, overweight

overdraft account score, bill, debt,

loan, mortgage, outstanding balance, red, tally, tick

overestimate exaggerate, hype, maximize, miscalculate, misjudge, overcharge, overpraise, overprice, overprize, overrate, overstate, overvalue, panegyrize

overestimated dear, exaggerated, expensive, misjudged, overpraised, overpriced, overrated, overvalued

overestimation arrogance, exaggeration, hubris, hype, hyperbole, idealism, megalomania, miscalculation, overoptimism, overrating, overstatement, overvaluation, rashness, vanity

overfed bloated, bursting, congested, crammed, gorged, overburdened, overstretched, replete, stuffed

overindulge binge, carouse, debauch, dissipate, gorge, overdo, squander, waste

overindulgence abandon, addiction, concupiscence, crapulence, drunkenness, excess, extravagance, gluttony, gourmandizing, greed, immoderation, incontinence, indiscipline, inordinateness, intemperance, overdoing, overeating, prodigality, uncontrol, unrestraint, wastefulness

overindulgent abandoned, addicted, concupiscent, crapulent, drunk, excessive, extravagant, gluttonous, gourmandizing, greedy, immoderate, incontinent, inordinate, intemperate, prodigal, uncontrolled, undisciplined, unrestrained, wasteful

overlie bridge, imbricate, jut, lap,

overarch, overhang, overlap, overshadow, shingle, span

overlooked blotted, disregarded, forgotten, ignored, neglected, omitted, swept clean, wiped away

overpower beat, bowl over, cripple, deaden, deflate, disarm, hamstring, knock out, KO, maim, muzzle, nobble, numb, overcome, overthrow, paralyse, prostrate, silence, smother, stifle, strangle, suffocate, switch off, wind

overrun beset, brimming, encroaching, flooding, infested, intrusive, inundated, invasive, overflowing, overgrown, overspread, plagued, swarming, teeming, trespassing

oversensitive highly strung, irascible, irritable, jumpy, nervy, temperamental, thin-skinned, touchy

overspend overdraw, overpay, pay through the nose

overstep brim over, exceed, flood, irrupt, leap-frog, overflow, overgo, overgrow, overpass, overreach, overrun, overspread, spill over

overthrown conquered, demolished, deposed, dethroned, oppressed, overset, overturned, revolutionary, subversive, subverted, suppressed, toppled, upset
may indicate an anagram

overturn
may indicate a backword

overview ball-park view, bird's-eye view, summary, survey

owed chargeable, coming to, in arrears, outstanding, payable, redeemable, unpaid, unsettled

·P·

P after (Latin: *post*) • four hundred (medieval Roman numeral) • page • pages • parking • pawn • pedal • penny • per • pint • soft (Italian: *piano*)

PA father • per annum • personal assistant • public address system

PACE Police and Criminal Evidence Act

PB lead

PC Parish Council • per cent • personal computer • petty cash • Police Constable • politically correct • postcard

PE physical education

PEI Prince Edward Island

PEP personal equity plan

PG page • parental guidance • paying guest

PH philosophy • public health

PHD Doctor of Philosophy

PI private investigator • professional indemnity

PIN personal identification number

PL place • Plimsoll line • Poet Laureate • programming language

PLC public limited company

PLO Palestine Liberation Organization

PM afternoon (Latin: *post meridiem*) • pipemma • postmortem • Prime Minister

PO petty officer • Post Office • postal order

POD payment on demand

POS point of sale

PP on behalf of (Latin: *per procurationem*) • pages • phosphorus • purl • very quietly (Italian: *pianissimo*)

PRO Public Record Office • public relations officer

PS postscript • private secretary

PT part • physical training • pint • platinum • port

PTO please turn over

PU plutonium

---

pacification accommodation, adjustment, agreement, ahimsa, appeasement, arbitration, armistice, cease-fire, cessation, compromise, conciliation, convention, détente, disarmament, entente, irenics, lull, mediation, moderation, mollification, moratorium, nonaggression pact, nonviolence, peacemaking, propitiation, rapprochement, reconciliation, satyagraha, test ban, treaty, truce, understanding

pacificatory appeasing, calming, conciliatory, content, disarming, dove-like, emollient, friendly, happy, irenic, lenitive, mediatory, negotiated, pacifiable, placatory, propitiatory, satisfying, soothing

pacifist civilian, conchie, conscientious objector, dove, mediator, neutral, noncombatant, peacekeeper, peacemaker

pacify accommodate, allay, alleviate, appease, assuage, calm, compose, conciliate, content, control, cool down, disarm, discipline, ease, harmonize, heal, mediate, mollify, placate, propitiate, quell, reconcile, restore, satisfy, smooth over, soothe, subdue, tranquillize

pack bag, bottle, box up, bundle, cage, can, cocoon, containerize, cover, crate up, enclose, entomb, envelope, flock, garage, herd, package, pot, pour in, reserve, rucksack, sheath, shelter, stable, store, surround, tin, wrap

packet boat, bundle, cover, document, envelope, file, folder, jacket, pack, packaging, parcel, sheath, wallet, wrapper

pageant exhibition, parade, performance, tableau

paid cleared, debt-free, discharged, liquidated, salaried, settled, waged

pain ache, affliction, agony, anguish, convulsion, cramp, discomfort, distress, dolour, flogging, hell, hurt, inflammation, irritation, lancination, malaise, martyrdom, misery, myalgia, neuralgia, nuisance, ordeal, pang, passion, pinprick, punishment, purgatory, smarting, soreness, sore spot, spasm, stab, stitch, suffering, tenderness, throbbing, throes, torment, torture, twinge

painful aching, acute, agonizing, biting, burning, chronic, cramping, distressing, excruciating, extreme, gnawing, grinding, gripping, harrowing, hurting, lancinating, pounding, purgatorial, racking, raw, scalding, searing, shooting, smarting, sore, splitting, stabbing, stinging, tender, throbbing, tingling, traumatic, unbearable

pain-relief anaesthetic, analgesia, numbing, sedative, soothing

paint brush, caricature, coat, colour, colourize, daub, describe, design, draw, dye, emulsion, form, gloss, gouache, illuminate, illustrate, ink in, outline, overpaint, picture, print, scumble, shade, shape, sketch, tint, tone, touch up, trace, underpaint, wash

pair bracket, couple, match, matchmake, mate, team, twin

palaeology archaeology, Assyriology, Egyptology, epigraphy, Sumerology

pale ashen, blanche, bleach, dim, enclosure, feeble, fence, ghastly, kingdom, limits, livid, pallid, post, sallow, stake, thin, waxen, weak, whiten

pander cater for, comply, matchmake, run after, serve, squire, stooge for

panorama conspectus, overview, survey, synopsis, world view

panting gasping, snorting, wheezing, winded

paper banknote, Bible paper, card, cardboard, cartridge paper, cellophane, certificate, computer paper, crepe paper, document, essay, foolscap, greaseproof paper, journal, newspaper, newsprint, notepaper, papier-mâché, pasteboard, pulp, quire, rag paper, ream, rice paper, sheet, stationery, thesis, tissue paper, toilet paper, tracing paper, typing paper, wallpaper, wrapping paper, writing paper

par average, dead-heat, deadlocked, drawn, equal, fifty-fifty, half-and-half, level-pegging, neck-and-neck, nip-and-tuck, quits, sameness, stalemated, standard, tied

parade esplanade, march, pageant, promenade, spectacle, strut

paragon ace, celebrity, champion, chart-topper, diva, expert, genius, highflier, laureate, mastermind, nonpareil, prima donna, prizewinner, prodigy, record-holder, specialist, superman, superstar, superwoman, victor, virtuoso, world-beater

parallel coextend, coextensive, collimate, concentric, equidistant, match, mirror, nonconvergent, nondivergent, run abreast

parallelism alignment, balance, co-extension, collimation, concentricity, correlation, correspondence, equality, equidistance, harmony, nonconvergence, nondivergence, uniformity

parallelogram parallelepiped, quadrilateral

paramedic ambulanceman, carer, chiropodist, dental hygienist, dental technician, dietician, dresser, hospital administrator, hygienist, medical auxiliary, midwife, nurse, nutritionist, occupational therapist, orderly, physiotherapist, radiographer, speech therapist, stretcher-bearer

parapsychological animist, astral, clairvoyant, extrasensory, occult, phantom, precognitive, psychic, psychokinetic, spiritual, supernatural, supersensible, telepathic

parapsychology clairvoyance, precognition, psychic phenomena, psychic research, psychokinesis, telepathy

parch dry up, mummify, preserve, shrivel, weazen, wilt, wither, wizen

pardon absolve, acquittal, be lenient, exculpation, forbear, forgive, give quarter, relax, relent, reprieve, sorry, spare, unbend

parenthood maternity, parentage, paternity

parity congruence, dead heat, deadlock, deuce, draw, equality, levelness, par, quits, stalemate, stasis, tie

parliamentary congressional, ecclesiastical, legislative, senatorial, synodal

parsimony cheeseparing, close-fistedness, minginess, miserliness, niggardliness, stinginess, tightfistedness, tightness, ungenerousness

part apportion, bisect, bit, break up, category, class, compartment, compartmentalize, cut up, depart, department, dismantle, dissect, divide, division, element, faction, fraction, fragment, half, instalment, limb, majority, minority, moiety, particle, partition, percentage, portion, proportion, role, say farewell, sectionalize, sector, segment, separate, sever, share, split, tithe, wave goodbye, whack

partial bitty, brashy, broken, crumbly, fragmented, headless, imperfect, inadequate, incomplete, in smithereens, insufficient, limbless, piecemeal, scrappy, unfinished

participate compete, enter, join in, play, take part

participation affiliation, association, character, collaboration, companionship, complicity, contribution, cooperation, co-sharing, duty, empathy, engagement, fellowship, function, inclusion, involvement, membership, mutualism, partaking, responsibility, role, sharing, sympathy

particle antielectron, antineutron, antiproton, antiquark, atom, baryon, bit, boson, cell, corpuscle, dot, electron, fermion, fragment, grain, granule, hadron, ion, kaon, K meson, lepton, meson, microdot, molecule, monad, muon, neutrino, neutron, nucleon, nucleus, parton, photon, pi meson, pinhead, pinpoint, pion, pixel, point, positron, proton, quantum, quark, seed, speck, tauon

particular article, chapter, definite, detail, determined, distinct, episode, fixed, fussy, indicated, individual, item, named, part, pinned down, single, singular, specific, stipulated

particularity amount, carefulness, definiteness, determination, distinctness, finickiness, fixing, indication, individuality, pinning down, quantity, singularity, specification, stipulation

parting adieu, centrifugence, decentralization, deployment, dismissal, division, fanning, farewell, golden handshake, goodbye, goodnight, leave-taking, sendoff, separation, splaying, spread, valediction
may indicate a split word

254

partisanship bias, clannishness, cliquishness, exclusiveness, factionalism, favouritism, one-sidedness, partiality, particularism, sectarianism, sectionalism, separatism

partner accompany, associate, boyfriend, cohabitant, cohabitee, colleague, common-law spouse, companion, consort, co-worker, date, escort, girlfriend, husband, live-in lover, lover, mate, other half, spouse, twin, wife, workmate

partnership alliance, association, coadministration, coagency, cochairmanship, collegialism, comanagement, common, confederation, co-ownership, copartnership, dividend, federalism, kitty, marriage, pool, profit-sharing, share, stock, store, tontine, union

part of
may indicate a hidden word

part of speech adjective, adverb, article, conjunction, copula, interjection, modifier, noun, participle, particle, preposition, pronoun, verb

party alliance, association, at-home, ball, band, banquet, barbecue, barnraising, beanfeast, beano, blowout, body, bop, bunch, cabal, camp, ceilidh, circle, clique, committee, company, crew, dance, denomination, dinner, disco, do, entertainment, event, faction, feast, federation, festivity, gala, gang, gathering, get-together, group, guild, hop, house-raising, house-warming, junta, knees-up, masquerade, mob, movement, orgy, partnership, rave, reception, sect, set, shindig, society, soirée, squad, team, troupe, wedding breakfast, wing

pass approve, become extinct, continue, die out, drag, elapse, end, expire, finish, flash by, flow, fly, graduate, hand on, intervene, make the grade, move through, omit, overtake, passport, pathway, permit, predicament, proposition, qualify, roll on, skirt, sleight of hand, succeed, throw

passage alley, beat, crossing, journey, lane, movement, passing, path, patrol, perambulation, round, section, transcursion, transduction, transference, transfusion, transit, transmission, traversing, trip, voyage

passageway aisle, artery, conduit, corridor, doorway, entrance, exit, gangway, gorge, hallway, mousehole, pass, pipe, pipeline, postern, rabbithole, sewer, tunnel, vein, windpipe

passing acceptable, crossing, dying, elapsing, hasty, moving, overtaking, proceeding, ratification, transducing, transferring, transitional, traversing, vanishing

passionate ardent, committed, devoted, ecstatic, effusive, emotional, enthusiastic, envious, excitable, fanatical, fervent, fiery, heated, hot-headed, hysterical, impassioned, impetuous, inflamed, inspired, intense, jealous, loving, manic, melodramatic, mercurial, obsessed, OTT, raging, rapturous, raving, seething, spirited, temperamental, torrid, touchy, unstable, vehement, vigorous, volatile, zealous, zestful

passport clearance, documentation, papers, pass, permit, safe conduct, visa

past ancient (history), ancient times, antiquity, bygones, early, eld, elder, ex, finished, former times, golden age, gone, historical, history, long ago, old, olden days, over, prehistoric, prehistory, primal, primeval, primitive, protohistoric, protohistory, time immemorial, yesterday, yesteryear

paste adhesive, batter, emulsion, glair, glaze, glue, pâté, pulp, punch, simulation, size, spread, stick

pastime activity, amusement, entertainment, hobby, recreation

pastry cake, cheese, choux, Danish, filo, flaky, fleur, Genoese, puff, shortcrust

path berm, by-path, calling, direction,

footpath, lane, passage, pavement, road, rut, towpath, track, trail, way

pathology bacteriology, epidemiology, etiology, nosology, parasitology

patience composure, disregard, forbearance, indulgence, overlooking, solitaire, stoicism, tolerance

patient case, in-patient, invalid, long-suffering, out-patient, persistent, stoic, tolerant, unhurried

patronage abetment, advocacy, aegis, auspices, backing, championship, countenance, encouragement, fosterage, seconding, sponsorship, subsidization, support, tutelage

pattern array, conformity, correlation, correspondence, crewel work, crochet, design, detail, embroidery, fancywork, filigree, flourish, fluting, gilding, gold leaf, illumination, illustration, lacework, lettering, match, model, mosaic, mould, needlework, ormolu, patchwork, pokerwork, pyrography, scrollwork, smocking, structure, system, tapestry, tattooing

pauper bag lady, bankrupt, beggar, bum, church mouse, down-and-out, homeless person, indigent, insolvent, lazar, mendicant, poor relation, slum-dweller, squatter, tramp, vagrant

pause adjourn, armistice, break, breather, breathing space, caesura, ceasefire, cooling-off period, day off, delay, fall asleep, fermata, gap, hang fire, hold back, holiday, interim, interlude, interruption, interval, lacuna, leisure, letup, lull, moratorium, nap, recess, respite, rest, sleep, stay, stop, suspend, suspension, time off, time-out, truce, vacation

pay advance, alimony, allowance, annuity, barter, bonus, bursary, commission, compensate, credits, disburse, discharge, dividend, earnings, emolument, expend, fee, fellowship, fringe benefit, gate money, give, gratuity, honorarium, honour, ill-gotten gains, income, indemnify, maintenance, make amends, make reparation, payoff, payout, pay packet, pension, perk, perquisite, pin money, pocket money, proceeds, profits, receipts, redeem, remit, remuneration, repay, requite, restitute, retaliate, returns, revenue, reward, royalty, salary, scholarship, settle up, spend, stipend, subscribe, takings, tip, tontine, trade, wage, winnings

payable due, owed, redeemable, refundable, remittable

pay back compensate, get even, indemnify, recompense, refund, reimburse, repay, restitute, retaliate

paying atoning, compensatory, disbursing, expending, redemptive, retributive, spending, suffering

payment clearance, contribution, defrayment, deposit, disbursement, discharge, donation, earnest, expenditure, handsel, instalment, liquidation, offering, outlay, payoff, premium, quittance, receipt, receivables, release, remittance, satisfaction, settlement, subscription, tribute

peace ahimsa, amity, amnesty, angel, armistice, avoidance, broken arrow, cease-fire, cessation, Christ, coexistence, concord, demob, demobilization, disarmament, dove, Eirene, friendship, golden times, harmony, indifference, Irene, irenics, lamb, neutrality, nonaggression, nonalignment, nonintervention, noninvolvment, nonviolence, olive branch, pacifism, palmy days, Pax (Romana), Peace Corps, peace pipe, peace sign, peacetime, quiescence, quiet, repose conciliation, rest, restfulness, serenity, silence, stillness, surrender, tranquillity, truce, white flag

peaceful agreeable, calm, civilian, conciliatory, dovelike, easy-going, golden, good-natured, halcyon, harmonious, innocent, irenic, law-abiding, mild, neutral, nonaggressive, nonaligned, nonviolent, pacifist, palmy, passive, peaceable, peacelike, piping, placatory, quiet, serene, still, tolerant, tranquil

peace offering amnesty, atonement, blood money, calumet, compensation, irenicon, mercy, olive branch, pardon, peace pipe, reparation, restitution, wergild, white flag

peak acme, apex, culminate, droop, knap, languish, pinnacle, protrude, summit, top, zenith

peal carillon, clang, handbell, ring

pealing chiming, repeating, resounding, ringing

peculiar
may indicate an anagram

pedantic authoritative, close, cogent, exacting, forceful, fussy, hair-splitting, lawful, legal, legitimate, literal-minded, meticulous, nit-picking, quibbling, rigid, rigorous, severe, strict, weighty

pedantry authority, fussiness, lawfulness, literal-mindedness, precision, rigidity, rigour, severity, strictness, subtlety, weight

pedestrian crossing Belisha beacon, panda crossing, pelican crossing, zebra crossing

pedlar bagman, barrow boy, chapman, cheap-jack, colporteur, costermonger, Gypsy, hawker, huckster, market trader, peddler, rag-and-bone man, stall-keeper, sutler, tinker, traveller
See also list at **occupation**.

peel bark, decorticate, desquamate, excoriate, exfoliate, exuviate, flake, moult, pick off, rind, scale, scalp, scrape, shed, shell, skin, slough, strip, undress

peeling abscission, decortication, desquamation, ecdysis, excoriation, exfoliation, exfoliatory, exuvial, exuviation, moulting, shedding, sloughy, undressing

pen author, ballpoint, biro, cage, compose, confine, coop, corral, enclosure, fold, hutch, kennel, nib, paddock, pigsty, plume, poet, prison, quill, scribble, scribe, write, writer

penalize avenge, condemn, exact retribution, fix, pay back, punish, retaliate, sentence, settle

penalty compensation, condemnation, costs, damages, fine, liability, obligation, payment, penance, price, punishment, ransom, restitution, restoration, sentence

penance asceticism, atonement, breast-beating, flagellation, mortification, prostration, punishment, purgation, purification, reparation, self-mortification, sentence

pendulum bob, metronome, oscillator, pendant

penetrating acute, infiltrating, intervening, osmotic, percolating, permeating, piercing, transudating

peninsula bill, cape, foreland, head, headland, hook, mull, neck, point, projection, promontory, sandspit, spit, spur, tongue

penitence apology, compunction, confession, contrition, conversion, guilt, pangs, qualms, recantation, reformation, regretfulness, remorsefulness, repentance, scruples, self-reproach, shamefulness, sorriness, soul-searching

penitent apologetic, ashamed, compunctious, conscience-stricken, contrite, guilty, lamenting, regretful, remorseful, repentant, rueful, self-condemning, sorrowful, sorry

penology criminology, penal code

pensioner crumbly, dodderer, dotard, geriatric, greybeard, Methuselah, old fogy, oldie, old person, oldster, senior citizen, veteran, wrinkly

people bourgeoisie, commonalty, family, folk, grass-roots, great unwashed, have nots, hoi-polloi, humanity, humankind, kin, lower orders, plebeians, plebs, populace, populate, population, proletariat, settle, the common people, the commons, the masses, vulgar herd, working-classes

perceptive aware, delicate, fastidious, insightful, meticulous, refined

perfect A1, absolute, accomplish, accurate, achieve, ameliorate, A-OK, archetypal, best, blameless, blemish-free, brilliant, classic, complete, consummate, correct, crown, dazzling, define, detail, elaborate, entire, exact, excellent, execute, exemplary, expert, faultless, finished, flawless, fulfilled, ideal, immaculate, impeccable, impeccant, improve, indefectible, infallible, innocent, intact, irreproachable, masterly, matured, number-one, particularize, peerless, pinpoint, polish, precise, proficient, pure, ready, realize, rectify, refine, ripen, saintly, set, skilled, sound, spotless, spot on, square, sublime, superb, supreme, top, total, transcendent, trim, true, unbroken, uncontaminated, undamaged, unequalled, unmarred, unmatched, unrivalled, unscarred, unscathed, unspoiled, unstained, unsurpassable, utter, whole

perfection accuracy, acme, archetype, brilliance, capstone, completeness, completion, consummation, correctness, excellence, faultlessness, flawlessness, idealness, immaculacy, impeccability, impeccancy, indefectability, infallibility, innocence, irreproachability, masterpiece, paragon, pattern, peak, pinnacle, preciseness, purity, quintessence, sainthood, sinlessness, soundness, spotlessness, standard, summit, transcendence, ultimate, wholeness, zenith

perfectionist choosy, demanding, exacting, expert, fastidious, fussy, hairsplitting, maestro, master, meticulous, particular, pedant(ic), picky, precise, punctilious, purist, quibbling, scrupulous, stickler

perform acquit, act, carry out, execute, fulfil, meet, play, practise, pretend, satisfy, suffice

performance acquittal, benefit, bill, command performance, composition, concert, convention, custom, debut, discharge, execution, exhibition, fulfilment, gig, improvisation, instrumentation, jamming, matinée, orchestration, play, practice, premiere, presentation, preview, procedure, production, prom, recital, routine, satisfaction, show, sufficiency, usage

perfume aftershave, aromatize, burn incense, cense, cologne, deodorant, embalm, fragrance, odour, scent, smell, spray, thurify

perfunctory casual, desultory, indifferent, lackadaisical, offhand, superficial

period ancien régime, break, breather, Classical Age, Dark Ages, eon, epoch, era, fit, full stop, heroic age, Industrial Revolution, interval, menstruation, Middle Ages, olam, pause, Renaissance, space, span, spell, stretch, term, time, timespan

periodic annual, biannual, biennial, bulletin, cyclic, daily, discontinuous, fitful, hourly, intermittent, irregular, iterative, journal, magazine, millennial, monthly, newsletter, quinquennial, recurrent, regular, repetitive, returning, seasonal, sporadic, weekly, yearly

periodicity recurrence, regularity, repetition, return

periphery border, circumference, fringe, outline, surroundings

perjurious cooked-up, defamatory, framed, libellous, misrepresented, perjured, planted, put-up, slanderous, trumped-up

permanence abidance, changelessness, conservation, constancy, continuance, continuity, dependability, durability, endurance, entrenchment, environmentalism, establishment, eternity, everlastingness, finality, firmness, fixedness, immobility, immortality, immutability, imperishability, indestructibility, perpetuity, perseverance, persistence, preservation, reliability, rigidity, solidity, stability, steadfastness, steadiness, subsistence, survival

permanent abiding, ceaseless, changeless, conserved, constant, continual, continuous, deathless, dependable, durable, enduring, entrenched, established, eternal, evergreen, everlasting, fixed, immortal, immovable, immutable, imperishable, incessant, incorruptible, indestructible, invariable, inviolable, lasting, perennial, perpetual, persevering, persistent, preserved, reliable, stable, steadfast, surviving, sustained, unalterable, unbreakable, unceasing, unchanging, undying, unfailing, unremitting

permission approbation, approval, authority, authorization, avowal, blank cheque, blessing, carte blanche, clearance, concession, connivance, consent, credential, declaration, dispensation, empowerment, enablement, endorsement, endowment, equipment, evidence, free hand, go ahead, green light, indulgence, investment, justification, leave, leniency, licence, mandate, nonliability, permit, reference, rights, sanction, say-so, testimonial, the thumbs-up, visa, warrant

permissive allowing, indulgent, lax, lenient, liberal, loose, tolerant

permit allow, approve, authorize, bless, certificate, charter, chit, clear, consent, countenance, credentials, diploma, docket, empower, enable, endorsement, facilitate, grant, green card, imprimatur, legalize, legitimize, let, licence, license, pass, passport, patent, recommendation, reference, release, sanction, seal, signature, testimonial, ticket, tolerate, visa, voucher, waiver, warrant

permitted above board, acceptable,

allowed, approved, authorized, lawful, legal, legitimate, licit, patent

perpendicular normal, orthogonal, rectangular, right-angled, square, upright, vertical

perpetuate eternalize, immortalize, maintain, memorialize, preserve

perplexed
may indicate an anagram

persecute bully, harass, oppress, plague, torture

perseverance determination, doggedness, insistence, obstinacy, patience, persistence, pertinacity, plodding, resolution, stubbornness, tenacity

persevere iterate, peg away, persist, plod, repeat, slog away

persevering assiduous, determined, diligent, dogged, enduring, faithful, industrious, obstinate, patient, persistent, plodding, resolute, sedulous, slogging away, staunch, strenuous, stubborn, surviving, tenacious

persist endure, hold out, persevere, soldier on, stand firm, stiffen

person Adamite, body, creature, customer, earthling, everyman, human, I, individual, John Doe, mortal, one, party, somebody, soul, tellurian

personable agreeable, appealing, attractive, blooming, charming, elegant, enchanting, peachy, rosy, tasteful, tidy, trim

personality celebrity, character, charisma, identity, nature, star, VIP

personnel band, cadre, cast, company, complement, crew, employees, gang, hands, labour, manpower, organization, payroll, squad, staff, team, workers, workforce

persuadability credulity, docility, impressibility, pliability, pliancy, softness, suggestibility, susceptibility, tractability, willingness

persuadable credulous, docile, egged

on, encouraged, incited, induced, inspired, motivated, pressured, receptive, spurred on, tractable

persuade advise, brainwash, cajole, cause, coax, convert, convince, counsel, dispose, engage, enlist, evangelize, impel, incline, indoctrinate, induce, influence, insist, instigate, lobby, motivate, move, preach, pressure, prevail upon, procure, prompt, proselytize, push into, revive, save, sweet-talk, urge, wheedle, win over

persuasion brainwashing, clout, evangelism, inclination, indoctrination, inducement, influence, insistence, lobbying, patter, preference, pressure, prompting, proselytizing, revivalism, sales pitch, spiritual rebirth

persuasive addictive, alluring, attractive, bewitching, charismatic, cogent, compelling, convincing, effective, encouraging, fascinating, hortatory, hypnotic, impressive, inducing, influential, inviting, irresistible, magnetic, mesmeric, motivating, stimulating, tantalizing, tempting, winning

perversion abasement, abuse, barbarism, brutalization, coarsening, corruption, debasement, deformation, degradation, dehumanization, depravation, devaluation, distortion, misuse, subversion, vitiation, vulgarization

pervert abase, abuse, barbarize, brutalize, corrupt, debase, debauch, deform, degrade, dehumanize, denature, deprave, deviant, distort, lower, misuse, ruin, sex criminal, subvert, twist, vitiate, vulgarize, warp
may indicate an anagram

pessimist fatalist, grouch, grouser, killjoy, misery, moaner, sourpuss, spoilsport

pessimistic anxious, defeatist, dreading, gloomy, hopeless

pest beast, boor, bug, hooligan, lout, nuisance, oaf, parasite, troublemaker, vermin

pet hate abomination, anathema, bête noire, bugbear, phobia

petroleum crude, diesel oil, fossil oil, four-star, fuel oil, kerosene, motor oil, paraffin, petrol, two-star, unleaded, white gas

petting bundling, caress, cuddle, embrace, fondling, hug, kissing, lovebite, necking, nibble, osculation, peck, smacker, smooching, squeeze

pharmacological chemical, pharmaceutic, therapeutic

pharmacologist chemist, dispenser, pharmaceutist, pharmacist

pharmacology chemotherapy, dosology, pharmaceutics, pharmacy, posology

philanthropic aid-giving, alms-giving, altruistic, beneficent, benevolent, big-hearted, charitable, communistic, compassionate, enlightened, generous, gracious, humane, humanitarian, idealistic, kind, liberal, munificent, public spirited, reforming, socialistic, utilitarian, visionary

philanthropist aid worker, almoner, altruist, benefactor, Benthamite, do-gooder, good neighbour, Good Samaritan, helping hand, humanitarian, idealist, internationalist, missionary, social worker, utilitarian, utopian, visionary, volunteer, welfare worker

philanthropy altruism, beneficence, benevolence, brotherly love, charity, compassion, dedication, do-gooding, generosity, goodwill, grace, helpfulness, humaneness, humanitarianism, kindness, liberality, munificence, open-handedness, unselfishness, welfarism

philosopher academic, analyst, armchair critic, cosmologist, dialectician, doctrinarian, dreamer, hypothecator, hypothesizer, idealist, ideologue, inquirer, investigator, logician, metaphysician, moralist, researcher, searcher, sophist, speculator, surmiser, syllogist, theorist, thinker, visionary

philosophical analytical, cool, detached, logical, objective, resigned, stoical, thoughtful, tolerant

philosophize analyse, brood, challenge, cogitate, conceptualize, consider, contemplate, deliberate, dream, examine, excogitate, hypothesize, idealize, inquire, introspect, investigate, look into, muse, ponder, query, question, ratiocinate, reflect, ruminate, scrutinize, search, soul-search, speculate, suppose, surmise, think about, wonder

philosophy attitude, doctrine, judgment, opinion, outlook, principle, reasoning, thesis, thought, viewpoint

phonetic aspirate, guttural, nasal, phonic, throaty, tonal, tonic, twangy *may indicate a homophone*

photocopy duplicate, facsimile, photogravure, Photostat, replica, Xerography, Xerox

photograph action sequence, close up, daguerreotype, film, focus, hologram, long shot, pan, photo, Photofit, photomontage, photomural, pin-up, portrait, radiograph, shadowgraph, shoot, slide, snap, snapshot, take, transparency, video, X-ray, zoom in

photographic camera-shy, photogenic, photosensitive, pictorial, realistic

photography aerial photography, astrophotography, black-and-white photography, cinematography, colour photography, fashion photography, flash photography, holography, infrared photography, macrophotography, microphotography, photojournalism, phototopography, portraiture, radiography, stereophotography, telephotography, time-lapse photography, underwater photography, wildlife photography

phrasing circumlocution, locution, metaphor, paraphrase, periphrasis, phraseology, trope, wording

physically dynamically, materially, mechanically, really, solidly

physics acoustics, aerodynamics, dynamics, electroacoustics, electrodynamics, hydrodynamics, kinematics, mechanics, optics, statics, thermodynamics, ultrasonics

physiology anatomy, biology, build, structure

pick abstract, anthologize, appoint, approve, axe, chip, cream, cull, delegate, designate, detail, discriminate, distinguish, earmark, excerpt, gather, glean, highlight, identify, isolate, pass, plectrum, pluck, preselect, recommend, reserve, scrape, separate, sift, single out, skim, winnow

pictorial calligraphic, diagrammatic, graphic, iconic, illusionist, linear, mosaic, optical, photographic, tabular

picture altarpiece, animation, aquarelle, aquatint, brass rubbing, canvas, caricature, cartoon, collage, comic, daub, delineation, diagram, doodle, draft, drawing, encaustic, fresco, frottage, graffito, grisaille, icon, illumination, illustration, image, impasto, likeness, masterpiece, miniature, montage, mural, old master, outline, painting, photogravure, plate, postcard, poster, print, reproduction, scribble, silhouette, silverpoint drawing, sketch, study, tableau, tracing, vignette, visualize, wash, woodcut, work of art

piece addition, band, bar, bit, bite, bolt, branch, category, chip, chunk, class, clod, coil, crumb, cutlet, department, division, dollop, drop, faction, finger, flake, fraction, fragment, gun, helping, hunk, insertion, line, lump, measure, morsel, off-cut, parcel, part, patch, portion, rag, rasher, roll, run, scale, scrap, section, sector, segment, shard, shred, slab, slice, sliver, smidgin, snippet, sod, speck, splinter, streak, string, strip, stripe, swatch, tranche, unit, wedge, wisp, wodge

pill cachet, capsule, dragee, gel, lozenge, pastille, powder, tablet, troche

pillar column, pier, pilaster, shaft

pimple acne, blackhead, boil, bubo, carbuncle, pustule, spot, swelling, whitehead, zit

pioneer discover, explore, found, frontiersman, guide, inaugurate, influence, initiate, innovate, invent, map out, open up, pilot, popularize, reconnoitre, spearhead, trailblazer, trendsetter

piquancy acuity, aroma, asperity, bite, bitterness, flavour, gaminess, kick, penetration, poignancy, pungency, raciness, smokiness, sourness, spiciness, sting, tanginess, tartness, zest

piquant appetizing, aromatic, biting, bitter, cured, flavourful, gamy, herby, hot, kippered, minty, peppery, pickled, pungent, racy, salty, savoury, seasoned, sharp, smoky, sour, soused, spiced, spicy, stinging, strong, tangy, tart

piracy bootlegging, copying, counterfeiting, faking, plundering, stealing

pitch angle, apex, bitumen, encamp, field, inflection, intonation, key, plunge, pronunciation, sales-talk, spiel, stress, tar, throw, tilt, timbre

pitiful affecting, distressing, grievous, heart-breaking, heart-rending, moving, pathetic, ruthful, sad, tear-jerking, touching

pitiless barbarous, brutal, callous, cold (blooded), coldhearted, cruel, flinty, hard(hearted), harsh, heartless, impassive, obdurate, remorseless, ruthless, sadistic, severe, soulless, stonyhearted, tough, uncaring, unfeeling, unforgiving, unpitying, unresponsive, unsympathetic, vengeful, vindictive

pitilessness callousness, cruelty, flintiness, hardheartedness, hardness, heartlessness, inclemency, inhumanity, intolerance, mercilessness, remorselessness, ruthlessness, severity

pity benevolence, caring, charity, commiserate, compassion, condolence, empathize, feel for, gentleness, humanity, kindness, mercifulness, softheartedness, support, sympathy, tenderheartedness, tenderness, understanding, warmheartedness

pitying caring, charitable, clement, comforting, commiserative, compassionate, condolent, consoling, forbearant, forgiving, gentle, humane, kind, kindhearted, lenient, merciful, sympathetic, tenderhearted, understanding, yielding

pivot fulcrum, gudgeon, hinge, hingle, pin, pintle, pole, radiant, rotate, rowlock, swivel, trunnion

placing establishment, fixation, installation, locating, placement, posting, settling, siting, situating, stationing

plagiarism cheating, copying, cribbing, fake, imitating, lifting, misappropriation, pastiche

plagiarize bootleg, cheat, copy, crib, imitate, lift, pirate

plain austere, clear-cut, definite, dignified, direct, distinguished, explicit, perspicacious, restrained, simple, stark, straightforward, unadorned, unambiguous

plainness asceticism, asceticism, austerity, prudery, puritanism, restraint, self-denial, simplicity, Spartanism

plan agenda, aim, almanac, amendment, announcement, approach, arrange, brainchild, brainstorm, brainwave, budget, calculate, centralize, contrive, design, envisage, expect, forecast, foresee, idea, intend, intention, invention, itinerary, map, methodize, motion, notice, order, organize, prearrange, predetermine, predict, prepare, preview, programme, project, proposal, proposition, prospectus, publication, rationalize, resolution, resolve, schedule, scheme, suggestion, systematize, timetable

plane aero, aircraft, bore, chisel, glide, level, router, sand, shape, smooth
See also list at **aviator**.

planet asteroid, earthgrazer, planetoid, wandering star
See list of planets and their satellites.

planned contrived, designed, intended, intentional, meant, methodical, orderly, organized, premeditated, prepared, rational, schematic, systematic, worked out

planning centralization, conspiratorial, contrivance, contriving, cunning, ingenious, intriguing, involved, Machiavellian, order, organization, plotting, purposeful, rationalization, resourceful, scheming, systematization, wheeler-dealing

planometer planimeter, ruler, spirit level

plant air plant, annual, bed out, biennial, bud, bush, cactus, cereal, climber, engraft, ephemeral, epiphyte, establish, evergreen, factory, flower, frame-up, garden plant, graft, herb, house plant, hydrophyte, implant, insert, liana, machinery, parasite, perennial, pot plant, sapling, seedling, shrub, spy, succulent, transplant, tree, twiner, vegetable, vine, weed, wort, xerophyte

plantlike grassy, herbaceous, herbal, leafy, overgrown, vegetable, vegetal, vegetative, verdant, weedy

plants flora, greenery, growth, herbage, vegetation, verdure

plastic surgery cosmetic surgery, facelift, liposuction

plate charger, coat, dish, gild, illustration, panel, platter, salver, saucer, tray

plausibility credibility, likelihood, possibility, probability, reasonability, verisimilitude

plausible believable, credible, likely, persuasive, possible, probable, reasonable

play act, compete, depict, dialogue, docudrama, dumbshow, duodrama, farce, fiddle with, fool about, fun, happening, improvisation, improvise, jam, join in, kitchen-sink drama, leisure, libretto, lines, masque, melodrama, mime, monodrama, move, pantomime, perform, piece, playlet, pretend, psychodrama, radio play, recreation, render, riff, rock, room, screenplay, script, show, sketch, swing, teleplay, text, vehicle, work
See also list at **theatre**.

play down constrain, curtail, de-

PLANETS AND THEIR SATELLITES	
MERCURY	
VENUS	
EARTH	MOON
MARS	PHOBOS, DEIMOS
JUPITER	METIS, ADRASTEA, AMALTHEA, THEBE, IO, EUROPA, GANYMEDE, CALLISTO, LEDA, HIMALIA, LYSITHEA, ELARA, ANANKE, CARME, PASIPHAË, SINOPE
SATURN	MIMAS, ENCELADUS, TETHYS, TELESTO, CALYPSO, DIONE, RHEA, HELENE, TITAN, HYPERION, IAPETUS, PHOEBE, JANUS, PAN, ATLAS, PROMETHEUS, PANDORA, EPIMETHEUS
URANUS	MIRANDA, ARIEL, UMBRIEL, TITANIA, OBERON, CORDELIA, OPHELIA, BIANCA, CRESSIDA, DESDEMONA, JULIET, PORTIA, ROSALIND, BELINDA, PUCK
NEPTUNE	TRITON, NEREID, NAIAD, THALASSA, DESPINA, GALATEA, PROTEUS
PLUTO	ACHILLES, ADONIS, AMOR, APOLLO, ASTRAEA, ATEN, CERES, CHARON, CHIRON, EROS, EUNOMIA, EUPHROSYNE, HEBE, HERMES, HIDALGO, HYGIEA, ICARUS, IRIS, JUNO, PALLAS, VESTA

emphasize, deprecate, dilute, diminish, disregard, moderate, reduce, restrain, underplay

playing card ace, club, court card, deuce, diamond, face card, heart, jack, joker, king, knave, picture card, queen, spade, wildcard, X
See also list at **game**.

plea apology, argument, claim, cry, defence, entreaty, excuse, pleading, request

plead apologize, argue, beg, canvass, entreat, explain, implore, justify, persuade, prevail upon, rationalize, request, vindicate

pleasant acceptable, agreeable, appealing, blissful, charming, comfortable, comforting, congenial, convivial, cosy, cuddly, cushy, delectable, delicious, delightful, divine, dulcet, easeful, Elysian, enjoyable, euphonious, fragrant, fresh, gratifying, heart-warming, heavenly, idyllic, inviting, likable, lovable, lovely, melodious, mouth-watering, nice, palatable, paradisiacal, perfumed, pleasing, pleasurable, refreshing, relaxing, restful, satisfying, scrumptious, smooth, snug, soft, soothing, sublime, sumptuous, sweet, tasteful, voluptuous, warm, welcome

pleasantness agreeableness, appeal, bliss, charm, delightfulness, heaven, loveliness, niceness, pleasurableness

pleased chuffed, comfortable, content, cosy, delighted, euphoric, gratified, gruntled, happy, high, relaxed, satisfied, warm

pleasure amusement, bliss, carnality, comfort, contentment, conviviality, creature comforts, delight, dissipation, diversion, ease, enjoyment, entertainment, epicureanism, eroticism, euphoria, felicity, fragrance, fun, gourmandising, gratification, happiness, hedonism, indulgence, loveliness, luxury, orgasm, profligacy, satisfaction, self-indulgence, sensualism, sensuousness, sweetness, tastiness, titillation, voluptuousness, well-being, zest

pleasure-loving epicurean, fun-loving, gourmand, gourmet, hedonistic, self-indulgent, sensual, voluptuous

pleat corrugation, crease, crimp, crinkle, crumple, flounce, furrow, gather, plait, pucker, ripple, ruche, ruck, ruffle, rumple, shirr, tuck, wrinkle

plebeian bourgeois, cheap, churl, common, country bumpkin, country cousin, everyman, hick, hillbilly, husband man, little man, low, man-in-the-street, Mr Nobody, ordinary, peasant, pleb, plebby, prole, proletarian, provincial, regular guy, rustic, serf, tacky, titleless, underling, villein, vulgar, yokel

plentiful abundant, affluent, ample, bottomless, bountiful, copious, endless, fat, fertile, great, inexhaustible, lavish, liberal, lush, luxuriant, opulent, profuse, prolific, rank, rich, riotous, unmeasured

plenty abundance, affluence, amplitude, banquet, copiousness, cornucopia, extravagance, feast, fecundity, fertility, flood, fullness, galore, lashings, lots, lushness, luxuriance, luxury, oodles, orgy, outpouring, plenitude, prodigality, productivity, profusion, proliferation, prolificacy, riches, riot, shower, spate, stream, wealth

pliancy acclimatization, accommodation, adaptability, adjustment, assimilation, flexibility, malleability, naturalization, plasticity, rehabilitation, softness

pliant acrobatic, adaptable, athletic, bendable, doughy, ductile, elastic, extensile, flexible, giving, impressible, lissom, lithe, loose-limbed, malleable, melting, mouldable, pasty, plastic, putty-like, shapable, springy, stretchable, supple, tractile, waxy, willowy, yielding

plight betroth, catch-22, corner, crisis,

dilemma, emergency, exigency, fix, hole, jam, pickle, pinch, pledge, predicament, pretty pass, quandary, trouble

plot allotment, brew, cabal, concoct, conspiracy, countermine, ensnare, fit-up, frame(-up), game, hatch, intrigue, land, machination, manipulation, manoeuvre, map (out), plan, ploy, racket, scheme, story(line), trap, undermine, web

plug block, dam, power point, publicity, socket, stop up

plunder booty, depredate, despoil, forage, freeboot, loot, pillage, raid, ransack, sack, spoliate

plundering banditry, brigandism, bucaneering, depredation, despoliation, foraging, foray, freebooting, grave-robbing, looting, outlawry, pillaging, privateering, raiding, ransacking, sacking, spoliation

plural majority, many, more, most, multiple, multitudinous, numerous, several, some, upwards of

plurality a handful, a number, many, more, several, some

pluralize clone, increase, multiply, proliferate, propagate, replicate

plutocrat capitalist, fat cat, merchant, millionaire

poem alba, aubade, ballad(e), bucolic, cento, chanson, clerihew, complaint, dirge, dithyramb, eclogue, elegiac poem, elegy, encomium, epic, epigram, epithalamium, epode, georgic, haiku, hymn, idyll, lay, limerick, lyric, madrigal, monody, nursery rhyme, ode, palinode, pastoral, prothalamion, psalm, rhyme, rondeau, ro(u)ndel, roundelay, saga, satire, sestina, song, sonnet, tanka, tenzone, threnody, triolet, verse (epistle), vilanelle, virelay

poeticism alliteration, anaphora, antonomasia, apostrophe, archaicism, assonance, chiasmus, conceit, consonance, elision, epistrophe, epithet, eu-

phony, imagery, inversion, irony, kenning, metaphor, metonymy, onomatopoeia, parallelism, paronomasia, pathetic fallacy, peraphrasis, personification, poetic licence, prosopopoeia, pseudostatement, pun, repetition, simile, synaesthesia, synecdoche, trope

poetry balladry, ditties, doggerel, folk poetry, jingles, light verse, macaronics, numbers, poesy, poetics, rhyme, song, verse, versification

point aim, compass point (N,S,E,W), cusp, design, dot, end, full stop, idea, indicate, instant, intent, intention, issue, juncture, location, meaning, moment, object, occasion, plan, prong, purpose, spike, spot, sting, tine, tip, use, value, vertex, worth

poise balance, calmness, confidence, insouciance, nonchalance, polish, sangfroid

poison adulterate, arsenic, besmirch, bespoil, carbon monoxide, carcinogen, contaminate, cyanide, drug, exhaust fumes, hemlock, infect, insecticide, intoxicate, Paraquat, pollute, prussic acid, rat poison, ratsbane, rotenone, spoil, strychnine, taint, toxin, venom, warfarin, weedkiller

poisoning contagion, infection, poisonousness, pollution, toxicity, venomousness

pole Antarctic, Arctic, caber, N, north, S, shaft, south, staff, totem

police airport police, boys in blue, CIA, CID, control, constabulary, FBI, filth, fuzz, gendarmerie, international police, Interpol, mounted police, Mounties, regulate, Scotland Yard, the law, the thin blue line

police car Black Maria, panda, patrol, police van, squad

police officer bizzy, bobby, busy, chief constable, commissioner, constable, cop(per), detective, dick, flatfoot, inspector, law-enforcer, lieutenant, Mountie, patrolman, peeler, pig, plainclothes, plod, policeman, private detective, private police, provost marshal, rozzer, security officer, sergeant, superintendent

policy actions, address, approach, attack, counteractions, countermeasures, diplomacy, foresight, forethought, formula, mandate, manifesto, measures, platform, procedure, prospectus, reactions, rule, statesmanship, steps, strategy, system, tactics, ticket, way

polished burnished, enamelled, glacé, glassy, glazed, gleaming, glossy, lacquered, mirror-like, perfected, refined, shiny, varnished, waxed

polishing buffing, burnishing, dressing, refining, rubbing, sanding, shining, smoothing

political affiliated, associated, bipartisan, communistic, factional, green, independent, leftist, left-wing, liberal, middle-of-the-road, nationalistic, nonpartisan, particular, partisan, party-minded, politicized, popular, radical, red, right-wing, sectarian, sectional, separatist, socialistic, true-blue

political party centre, Conservative, Green, Labour, left, Liberal Democrats, Plaid Cymru, right, Scottish National, Sinn Féin, Tory, Ulster Unionist, Whig

politician activist, anarchist, anarcho-syndicalist, backbencher, cabinet minister, canvasser, centrist, commie, communist, comrade, democrat, diplomat, dry, ecologist, fascist, hard-liner, independent, junior minister, leftie, leftist, left-winger, lefty, liberal, life peer, loyalist, Marxist, minister, moderate, nationalist, Nazi, neo-Nazi, Parliamentarian, party chairman, party manager, party member, party whip, party worker, peer, populist, radical, reactionary, Red, revolter, rightist, right-winger, secretary, sectarian, softsoaper, smooth-talker, socialist, stalwart, syndicalist, Trot(skyist), undersecretary, wet, whip

politics diplomacy, public affairs, statecraft, statesmanship

pollution adulteration, contamination, dirtying, effluvium, mephitis, pollutant, spoiling

polymer nylon, plastic, polyester, polypropylene, polystyrene, polythene, polyurethane

pomade brilliantine, hair conditioner, pomatum, setting lotion

pomp circumstance, formality, majesty, pageantry, parade, pride, solemnity, starchiness, state, stiffness

pomposity bombast, grandiloquence, pontification, self-importance, stuffiness, turgidity

pompous bombastic, grandiloquent, long-drawn-out, pontificating, self-important, stuffy, turgid, windy

ponderous burdensome, cumbersome, onerous, oppressive, taxing, unwieldy

poor bad, cheap, coarse, contemptible, corrupt, crappy, crummy, decaying, deplorable, deprived, despicable, destitute, diseased, disgraceful, disgusting, duff, foul, grievous, grotty, grubby, gungy, hand-to-mouth, hard up, hateful, impecunious, indigent, jerry-built, lamentable, lousy, lowpaid, makeshift, mean, measly, miserable, moneyless, mouldy, nauseating, necessitous, needy, patchy, penniless, penurious, pitiful, poisoned, poverty-stricken, putrid, reprehensible, revolting, rotten, sad, scratch, scruffy, shabby, shameful, shoddy, stale, stinking, straitened, subnormal, substandard, tatty, undercapitalized, underfinanced, underfunded, underpaid, underprivileged, vulgar, wanting, woeful, worthless, wretched, yucky

popular beloved, best-selling, chart-topping, entertained, feted, liked, welcome

popularize commercialize, mass-produce, publicize, vulgarize

popular music charts, easy listening, hit, pop, rock (and roll)

portion allocation, allotment, allowance, batch, bunch, chunk, dividend, dole, dollop, dosage, dose, fraction, gob, helping, hunk, load, lot, majority, mass, measure, minority, pack, packet, parcel, part, piece, pittance, plot, proportion, quantum, quorum, quota, ratio, ration, share, slice, stint, whack

pose assume, baffle, bluff, model, place, play act, posture, pretend, show off, stance, swank

position arrange, category, class, classification, degree, echelon, grade, job, level, location, office, order, place, pose, post, rank, rating, set up, status, subordination

possess buy, command, enjoy, have, hold, keep, occupy, own

possessed bedevilled, belonging to, bewitched, hag-ridden, held, owned

possessing enjoying, having, holding, landowning, occupying, owning, possessory, proprietorial

possession accoutrements, appropriation, appurtenances, belongings, claiming, colony, control, custody, dependency, dominion, effects, enjoyment, estate, freehold, gear, goods, grasp, grip, heritage, holding, impedimenta, landowning, lordship, luggage, occupation, ownership, paraphernalia, patrimony, plantation, property, proprietorship, protectorate, retention, sovereignty, stuff, taking, temporalities, tenancy, tenure, things, trappings

possibility ability, availability, capacity, chance, contingency, eventuality, feasibility, likelihood, odds, opportunity, plausibility, potential, promise, prospect, viability, virtuality

possible able, accessible, achievable, admissible, approachable, attainable, available, believable, capable, conceivable, credible, doable, feasible, flexible, imaginable, likely, operable, performable, potential, practical, reachable, realizable, reasonable, tenable, thinkable, viable, workable
may indicate an anagram

post after, airmail, dead-letter office, express delivery, fax, forward, forwarded mail, inland post, international mail, job, letter post, metered mail, overseas mail, parcel post, pole, position, postal service, poste restante, post office, recorded delivery, registered mail, returned-letter office, sea mail, sorting office, special delivery, surface mail, telex

post-mortem autopsy, embalmed, fossilized, funereal, mummified, posthumous, post-obit

postpone balk, delay, demur, hesitate, procrastinate, shelve

postponed adjourned, blocked, deferred, detained, extended, halted, held-up, hindered, (log-)jammed, mothballed, obstructed, prolonged, prorogued, protracted, remanded, restrained, stalled, stonewalled, suspended, tabled

postponement adjournment, deferment, delay, extension, filibuster, procrastination, prolongation, prorogation, protraction, shelving, stonewalling

pot amphora, ampulla, bain-marie, boiler, bowl, brazier, cafetière, cake tin, casserole, cauldron, chamber pot, coffeepot, coffee urn, crock, cruse, cup, double boiler, ewer, fish kettle, frying pan, honeypot, jamjar, jar, jug, kettle, kitty, marijuana, mug, pan, percolator, pipkin, pitcher, roaster, roasting tin, ruin, saucepan, skillet, steamer, teapot, urn, vase, vessel, warming pan, wok

potent compelling, convincing, effective, extreme, fervent, fierce, forceful, formidable, high-powered, intense, mighty, persuasive, powerful, puissant, redoubtable, vehement, weighty

potential ability, auspices, capability,

capacity, dormant, eventual, future, hope, omen, possibilities, possible, promising, prospective, undeveloped, virtual
may indicate an anagram

poultry fowl, game, grouse, partridge, pheasant

poverty abjectness, bankruptcy, breadline, coarseness, contamination, contemptibleness, corruption, depression, deprivation, destitution, difficulties, dire straits, dirtiness, disgrace, disorder, disreputability, distress, grottiness, grubbiness, hand-to-mouth existence, hardship, impecuniousness, impoverishment, indecency, indigence, lack, lousiness, lowness, low pay, meanness, melancholy, misery, necessitousness, need, negative equity, obscenity, pauperism, pennilessness, penury, pestilence, pitifulness, poison, poverty trap, privation, recession, reduced circumstances, rottenness, sadness, sickness, sleaze, sleaziness, slender means, slump, sordidness, squalor, stink, subsistence level, taint, want, woe, wretchedness

powder ash, attritus, chalk, coaldust, crumble, dirt, dredge, dust, dustball, efflorescence, flour, fluff, grind, gunpowder, kittens, lint, pounce, pulverize, pussies, rouge, sand, sawdust, scatter, slut's wool, smut, soot, sprinkle

powderiness bloom, chalkiness, dustiness, efflorescence, flouriness, pulverulence

powdery calcareous, chalky, dirty, dusty, flocculent, pulverulent, scobiform, sooty

power ability, ascendancy, authority, charisma, control, cube, drive, effort, electrify, endeavour, endurance, energize, energy, exertion, exponent, force, forcefulness, government, greatness, hegemony, index, influence, magic, mana, might, muscle, omnipotence, oomph, persuasion, potency, predominance, prevalence, puissance, punch, sovereignty, square, stamina, strength, superiority, sway, virility

powerful almighty, athletic, authoritative, brawny, brutal, bullying, burly, charismatic, cogent, compelling, compulsive, effectual, efficient, empowered, endowed, enduring, forceful, great, hardy, hegemonic, indefatigable, influential, lean, mighty, muscular, omnipotent, plenipotentiary, potent, predominant, prevailing, prevalent, proficient, puissant, resilient, robust, rough, sinewy, sovereign, stalwart, strapping, stringy, strong, superior, tenacious, unflagging, untiring, vicious, virile, weather-beaten, wiry

powerless broken down, deactivated, deposed, disfranchised, disqualified, dud, duff, good-for-nothing, impotent, in abeyance, incapable, incompetent, ineffective, inefficient, inept, inoperative, invalid, kaput, mothballed, suspended, switched off, unable, unauthorized, unemployed, unfit, unworkable, useless, weak, worthless

powerlessness decrepitude, disqualification, fragility, frailty, impotence, inability, incapability, incapacity, incompetence, ineffectiveness, inefficiency, ineptitude, inutility, invalidation, unfitness, uselessness

practical businesslike, down-to-earth, expedient, functional, hard-headed, level-headed, manual, matter-of-fact, mechanical, no-frills, no-nonsense, operational, operative, pragmatic, realistic, sensible, serviceable, sound, useable, utilitarian, workable

praise acclaim, adulation, apotheosis, boost, commend, compliment, congratulate, deify, eulogize, exalt, extol, flattery, glorify, glory, hero-worship, honour, hype, idolatry, idolize, laud, lionization, magnify, panegyrize, puff up, trumpet, wax lyrical

praiseworthy admirable, commendable, creditable, deserving, estimable, laudable, meritorious, unimpeachable, worthy

pray beseech, chant, give thanks, impetrate, implore, incant, invoke, petition, request, rogate, supplicate

prayer alenu, allocution, anamnesis, Ave Maria, benediction, berakah, blessing, comprecation, devotion, dharani, epidesis, eulogia, gayatri, geullah, grace, Hail Mary, impetration, intention, intercession, invocation, kol nidre, Kyrie Eleison, mantra, motzi, nembutsu, nishmat, om, orison, petition, request, rogation, rosary, supplication, vigils

prayer book breviary, canon, farse, lectionary, machzor, menaion, missal, ordinal, pontifical, rubric, siddur

preach baptize, convert, convince, crusade, evangelize, heresy-hunt, persecute, preachify, proselytize, sermonize, witch-hunt

precede antecede, antedate, anticipate, forerun, foreshadow, front, go before, guide, head, indicate, lead, pilot, predate, pre-empt, spearhead

precedence antecedence, anteposition, anteriority, pre-emption, priority

precedent antecedent, criterion, example, forerunner, formula, lead, model, paradigm, pattern, prototype, standard, yardstick

preceding antecedent, anterior, earliest, first, leading, precessional, pre-emptive

precept act, admonition, advice, article, charge, code, command, constitution, convention, custom, direction, example, form, formula, guideline, injunction, instruction, judgment, law, legislation, mandate, maxim, moral, norm, order, practice, prescription, principle, regulation, remedy, rule, statute, tenet, text, warning, warrant, writ

precipitation cloudburst, deluge, dew, downpour, drizzle, flood, flurry,

hastening, hurrying, pluviosity, rain, raindrop, rainfall, raininess, rainstorm, rainwater, rushing, shower, snowfall, spate, wetness

preclude exclude, forestall, pre-empt, prevent

precognition clairvoyance, divination, premonition, presentiment, second sight, sixth sense, telepathy

precursor ancestor, announcer, avant-garde, discoverer, explorer, forebear, forerunner, founding father, frontiersman, harbinger, herald, innovator, inventor, leader, messenger, pathfinder, pilot, pioneer, scout, trailblazer, trendsetter, vanguard

precursory ancestral, baptismal, basic, elementary, inaugural, initial, introductory, preceding, precursive, prefatory, preliminary, proemial

predecessor ancestor, eldest, firstborn, forebear, forefather, senior

predetermination decree, destiny, doom, fate, foreordination, karma, kismet, lot, predestination, preordination, will

predetermine appoint, decree, destine, doom, foreordain, intend, predestine, preordain

predicament bind, catch-22, cleft stick, difficulties, dilemma, fine mess, fix, hole, hot water, how-do-you-do, jam, mess, muddle, no-win situation, pickle, pinch, plight, pretty pass, problem, scrape, situation, snafu, snarl-up, sorry plight, spot, squeeze, tangle, tricky spot, trouble

predict announce, augur, believe, betoken, estimate, forebode, forecast, foresee, foreshow, foretell, guess, harbinger, herald, hint, indicate, lower, menace, notify, portend, presage, presume, prognosticate, promise, prophesy, raise expectations, reckon, represent, reveal, signify, speculate, suggest, think, threaten, typify, warn

predictable certain, common, customary, expected, foreseeable, likely, ordinary, plain, possible, potential, probable, run-of-the-mill, straightforward, sure, unsurprising, usual

predicted forecast, foreseen, foretold, prophesied

predicting apocalyptic, cautionary, clairvoyant, fatidic, foreboding, foreseeing, heralding, mantic, oracular, precursory, prefiguring, premonitory, prescient, presentient, prophetic, sibylline, signifying, vatic, weather-wise

prediction apocalypse, expectation, feeling, foreboding, forecast, foresight, foretelling, forewarning, fortune, horoscope, hunch, prefiguration, premonition, presage, presentiment, prognosis, prophecy, prospect, revelation

predictive anticipant, anticipatory, clairvoyant, expectant, farsighted, intuitive, longsighted, precognitive, prescient, prognostic, prophetic, prospective, statistical, telepathic

preface foreword, frontispiece, introduce, introduction, opening, overture, preliminaries, prelude, proem, prologue

prefer approve, choose, fancy, favour, incline, intend, lean (towards), like best, predispose oneself, select, tend, want

preference bias, choice, desirability, fancy, favour, favouritism, inclination, leaning, liking, partiality, predilection, preferability, prejudice, taste, tendency

prefix affix, preface, prefixion, prothesis

pregnant antenatal, breeding, broody, enceinte, expecting, fecundated, fertilized, gravid, impregnated, in the club, meaningful, perinatal, pivotal, preggers, up the spout

prehistoric age Bronze Age, Chalcolithic period, Iron Age, Mesolithic period, Neolithic period, Palaeolithic period, Stone Age
See also list at **geological**.

prejudge bias, forejudge, precondemn, prejudice

prejudgment fixation, foregone conclusion, obsession, preconception, predetermination, presupposition

prejudice bias, bigotry, discrimination, inequity, insularism, intolerance, jaundice, narrow-mindedness, one-sidedness, parochialism, partisanship, pettiness, prejudgment, unfairness

prejudiced ageist, anti-semitic, biased, bigoted, class conscious, contemptuous, despising, dogmatic, fundamentalist, narrow-minded, racially prejudiced, sexist, snobbish, undemocratic, xenophobic

premature anticipatory, beforehand, early, expectative, foresighted, forward, half-baked, half-cocked, hasty, impetuous, overhasty, precipitate, precocious, pre-emptive, preparatory, prevenient, prophetic

prematurity anticipation, expectation, foresight, haste, impetuosity, precipitance, precociousness, pre-emption, preparation, prevenience

premeditate contrive, fix, frame, plan, prearrange, preconceive, preconcert, preset

premeditation agenda, forethought, intention, plan, plot, prearrangement, preparation, project, resolve

premiere debut, first night, flotation, inaugural address, launch, maiden speech, maiden voyage, main, principal, opening ceremony, unveiling

premise assume, axiom, defend, excuse, explain, justify, philosophize, postulate, theorize

premonition augury, divination, foreboding, forewarning, omen, presentiment

preordain destine, doom, fate, ordain, predestine, predetermine

preparation anticipation, avantgardism, breakthrough, cocking, con-

sultation, development, discovery, exploration, flotation, foresight, forethought, foundation, groundwork, inauguration, innovation, launching, leap, loading, organization, pioneering, planning, prearrangement, priming, promotion
may indicate an anagram

preparations arrangement, basis, blueprint, foundation, framework, groundwork, measures, outline, pilot, plan, preliminaries, prototype, spadework, steps

preparatory basic, developmental, elementary, exploratory, foundational, introductory, precautionary, preliminary, provisional, stopgap

prepare adjust, anticipate, arrange, array, assemble, cock, commission, exercise, expect, fix, focus, foresee, gear up, get ready, introduce, limber up, make operational, make ready, mobilize, order, practise, precipitate, prime, rehearse, reserve, rev up, stand by, stoke up, stow, take steps, tee up, train, tune, warm up, wind

prepared accoutred, alert, all set, armed, briefed, dressed, equipped, experienced, forearmed, forewarned, furnished, groomed, instructed, keyed up, mobilized, on stand-by, organized, practised, primed, qualified, ready, spoiling for, standing by, teed up, trained, tuned, tutored, unsurprised, vigilant, waiting, well-appointed, well-rehearsed
may indicate an anagram

preparedness fitness, maturity, mellowness, peak, readiness, ripeness, shipshape condition

prerogative authority, birthright, claim, demand, primogeniture, privilege, right, title

presageful augural, auspicial, fateful, favourable, fortunate, haruspical, inauspicious, ominous, portentous, promising, propitious, significant, unfavourable

prescription confection, course, decree, dose, essence, excipient, formula, galenical, prerogative, ruling, vehicle

presence actuality, attendance, being, closeness, existence, manifestation, materialness, ontology, poise, reality, self-confidence, solidity, spectre, thusness

present actual, attending, contemporary, current, disclose, display, exhibit, existent, expose (oneself), extant, fashionable, gift, instant, issue, launch, make apparent, manifest, material, modern, now, publish, put forward, real, realize, release, reveal, screen, show, solid, today, topical, treat, up-to-date

preservation boiling, canning, conservation, continuation, curing, dehydration, deliverance, desiccation, ecology, economy, frugality, hygiene, insulation, irradiation, maintenance, marination, mummification, packaging, permanence, perpetuation, pickling, processing, prolongation, protection, provision, redemption, refrigeration, reservation, retention, safekeeping, salvation, saving, service, smoking, sterilization, storage, support, taxidermy, tinning

preservative alcohol, amber, aspic, bottle, brine, camphor, can, creosote, formaldehyde, ice, jar, marinade, mothball, pickle, plastic, refrigerator, salt, spice, tin, vacuum flask, varnish

preserve bolster, bottle, bottled fruit, can, chutney, conserve, continue, creosote, cure, defend, dehydrate, dry, embalm, finalize, fix, freeze, guard, immortalize, irradiate, jam, jelly, keep, kipper, maintain, marinate, marmalade, mummify, paint, perpetuate, pickle, process, prolong, protect, refrigerate, rescue, safeguard, salt, save, season, service, smoke, souse, spare, stabilize, store, stuff, supply, support, sustain, tin, uphold, varnish, waterproof, whitewash

preserved alive, bottled, canned,

cherished, conserved, corned, cured, dehydrated, desiccated, dried, embalmed, fresh, frozen, intact, kept, marinated, mothballed, mummified, perfect, pickled, potted, protected, salted, saved, smoked, soused, stored, stuffed, tinned, treasured, undecayed, whole

preserving conservational, conserving, ecological, energy-saving, environment-friendly, green, hygienic, preventive, prophylactic, protecting, redemptive, salubrious

press broadsheet, crush, flatten, Fleet Street, goad, iron, newspapers, push, rags, tabloids, urge

press on climb, drive on, forge ahead, gain ground, gain height, gather way, keep on, make leeway, push on, rise

prestige augustness, dignity, kudos, reputation, style

prestigious august, commanding, dignified, high-falutin, high-flying, impressive, mighty, stylish

presume assume, be impertinent, suppose, take liberties

presumptuousness familiarity, impertinence, licentiousness

pretence affectation, ambiguity, ambivalence, apparentness, artificiality, attitudinizing, bluff, cheating, concealment, deception, dissimulation, evasion, excuse, feigning, flimflam, flummery, gammon, hollowness, humbuggery, imitation, impersonation, imposture, insincerity, jiggery-pokery, make-believe, meretriciousness, ostensibility, play-acting, pose, posture, pretext, representation, sham, shift, show, speciousness, subterfuge, tokenism, uncandidness, unfrankness

pretend affect, attitudinize, bluff, conceal, cry, deceive, delude, dissemble, dissimulate, evade, feign, feint, gammon, humbug, imitate, impersonate, play-act, play possum, pose, posture,

put on, represent, shift, show, shuffle, soft-soap, sweet-talk, whitewash

pretender actor, attitudinizer, bluffer, charlatan, claimant, deceiver, exhibitionist, humbug, hypocrite, poser, poseur, swank

pretending affecting, apparent, attitudinizing, bluffing, dissembling, dissimulating, feigning, masquerading, ostensible, play-acting, posing, posturing, seeming, so-called

pretentious affected, artificial, bluffing, deceptive, false(-faced), hollow, hypocritical, insincere, mealy-mouthed, meretricious, phoney, play-acting, posing, posturing, pretending, sanctimonious, showy, tokenistic, unctuous, unnatural

pretentiousness artifice, euphemism, falsity, pose, posture, sanctimoniousness

prevail compel, control, dominate, fascinate, force, have sway, hypnotize, master, mesmerize, obtain, outweigh, overbear, overcome, override, predominate, reign, rule, run, subdue, subjugate, tyrannize

prevailing accepted, common, communal, dominant, popular, predominant, prevalent, public, unrestricted, widespread

preview omen, premonition, taster, trailer, warning

prey criminal, deserter, escapee, feed on, fugitive, game, grab, lost child, missing person, oppress, quarry, victim

price amount, appraise, assess, bounty, charge, cheapness, consequence, cost, dearness, estimate, evaluate, figure, quotation, rate, tariff, value

priced assessed, rated, valued, worth

pride arrogance, courage, honour, hubris, lions, proudness, self-confidence, self-esteem, self-importance, self-regard, self-respect, spirit

priest almoner, archbishop, Arch Druid(ess), ayatollah, beadle, bishop, Brahman, canon, cardinal, chaplain, chief rabbi, churchwarden, clergy-(wo)man, cleric, curate, deacon(ess), dean, dhammaduta, divine, ecclesiastic, Grand Lama, guru, hakam, hazzan, hierophant, imam, Kalif, kohen, lama, maftir, minister, ministress, monsignor, muezzin, mukdam, mullah, ordinand, parson, pastor(ess), patriarch, pontif, poonghie, pope, priestess, pundit, qadi, rabbi, rector, Rev, Reverend, scribe, sexton, verger, vicar, witch-doctor, zen-ji

priesthood abbacy, archdiocese, bishopric, Brahminism, cardinalship, chaplaincy, clericalism, curacy, deaconship, deanship, diocese, ecclesiasticism, episcopate, hierocracy, holy orders, investiture, ordination, papacy, parish, pastorate, pastorship, pontificate, popedom, prelature, primacy, province, rabbinate, rectorship, sacerdotalism, see, the Church, the clergy, the cloth, the ministry, vicarship

priestly canonical, churchly, clerical, diocesan, druidic, ecclesiastic, episcopal, hieratic, hierocratic, hierophantic, ministerial, papal, parochial, pastoral, pontifical, prelatic, presbyteral, rabbinic, sacerdotal

primal antediluvian, central, early, fundamental, prehistoric, prelapsarian, primeval, primitive, primordial

primary chief, elder, first, foremost, headmost, leading, original, pre-eminent, senior, superior, supreme

primate anthropoid, bishop, hominid, official, pongid, prosimian, simian

prime aboriginal, earliest, educate, eminent, first, heyday, main, number, original, pinnacle, prepare, primal, primeval, primitive, primordial, pristine, valuable

primeval ancient, antique, archaic, fossil, original, prehistoric, primitive

print clone, copy, duplicate, edition, facsimile, fingerprint, footprint, impress, imprint, mark, offprint, photocopy, publication, replica, reprint, screen-print, stamp, trace, type(face)

prior abbot, above-mentioned, advanced, aforementioned, aforenamed, aforesaid, before, earlier, elder, eldest, erstwhile, ex, first, foregoing, foremost, former, forward, last, late, leading, onetime, previous, primal, senior

priority antecedence, anteriority, dominion, forefront, importance, pole position, precedence, pre-eminence, pre-existence, preference, prerogative, previousness, primacy, privilege, seniority, superiority, supremacy, the lead, urgency, vanguard

prison borstal, bucket, can, cell, chokey, clink, compound, concentration camp, cooler, detention centre, dungeon, glasshouse, Gulag, jail, jug, labourcamp, lockup, nick, oubliette, pound, prison camp, quod, reformatory, slammer, stir

prisoner captive, con, convict, detainee, hostage, inmate, jailbird, lifer

privacy retreat, sanctum, seclusion, secrecy

private clandestine, concealed, covert, GI, hidden, internal, intimate, inward, personal, secret, soldier

prize award, blue ribbon, Booker Prize, certificate, crown, cup, esteem, force open, jackpot, kitty, lever, medal, Nobel Prize, pot, prize money, regard, shield, trophy, value, wooden spoon

probability anticipation, chance, expectation, forecast, liability, likelihood, odds, outlook, predictability, prediction, presumption, prognosis, proneness, prospect

probable anticipated, apparent, apt, evident, expected, indubitable, liable, likely, ostensible, predictive, presumable, prone, prospective, tending, undoubted, unquestionable

probity carefulness, decency, dependability, ethics, fairness, fastidiousness, good character, goodness, high ideals, high-mindedness, honourableness, impartiality, incorruptibility, integrity, meticulousness, morality, nobleness, principles, reliability, repute, respectability, scrupulousness, sincerity, soundness, trustworthiness, uprightness, veracity

problem anxiety, brainteaser, braintwister, conundrum, crux, dilemma, enigma, Gordian knot, headache, imbroglio, maze, nodus, nonplus, perplexity, poser, puzzle, quandary, vexed question, worry

problematic baffling, challenging, complex, complicated, confusing, convoluted, debatable, delicate, demanding, difficult, enigmatic, esoteric, exacting, hairy, illegible, impenetrable, indecipherable, intricate, involved, knotty, labyrinthine, moot, mysterious, obfuscating, obscure, pernickety, perplexing, puzzling, quizzical, recondite, riddling, sticky, thorny, ticklish, tough, tricky, troubling, unclear, undecided, unintelligible

procedure beadledom, bureaucracy, drill, method, MO, modus operandi, operation, petty officialdom, policy, practice, red tape, routine, system

proceed advance, circulate, go (forward), journey, move (along), pass on, patrol, progress, roll, travel, voyage, weave

process convert, follow, march, method, operation, procedure, sort, succession, system, transform, treat *may indicate an anagram*

procession caravan, cavalcade, column, cortège, crocodile, file, gridlock, line, march past, motorcade, pageant, parade, promenade, queue, series, sequence, stream, tailback, train

proclaim announce, blast, blazon, cry, declaim, declare, herald, notify, pronounce, publish, trumpet

procrastinating delaying, lazy, neglectful, negligent, postponing, remiss, sluggish

produce accomplish, arrange, bear, beget, breed, bud, build, cause, commodity, compose, construct, create, crop, cultivate, design, develop, direct, educate, effect, egg, engender, engineer, execute, fabricate, farm, fashion, father, find, forge, generate, germinate, give birth, goods, grow, harvest, hatch, income, innovate, invent, machine, make, manufacture, mass-produce, merchandise, mill, mother, mould, multiply, offspring, originate, output, prefabricate, present, process, pullulate, raise, rear, reproduce, reveal, revenue, seed, shape, show, sire, sow, spawn, stage, structure, supply, synthesize, teem, train, uncover, unfold, wares, yield

producer angel, auteur, backer, director, exhibitor, impresario, patron, playbroker, promoter, ringmaster, showman, stage manager, theatrical agent

product artefact, article, by-product, compound, concoction, confection, consequence, creation, creature, decoction, effect, end-product, essence, extract, issue, item, manufacture, object, offshoot, outcome, output, result, spin-off, thing, turnout, waste

production accomplishment, achievement, composition, conception, concert, concoction, craftsmanship, creation, design, enactment, enterprise, execution, formulation, handiwork, invention, making, organization, performance, planning, preparation, presentation, project, show, skill, spectacle, structure

productive creative, fecund, fertile, formative, fruitful, high-yielding, innovative, interest-bearing, inventive, lucrative, original, paying, profitable, prolific, remunerative, rich, worthwhile

productiveness fecundation, fertilization, fructification, imaginativeness, inventiveness, pollination, procreation, propagation, reproduction, resourcefulness

productivity effort, endeavour, output, throughput, turnout

professional authority, doyen, efficient, expert, guru, industrial, occupational, pundit, savant, specialist, vocational, white collar *See also list at* **occupation**.

proficiency ability, accomplishment, adroitness, competence, deftness, dexterousness, efficiency, expertise, gift, handiness, masterfulness, skilfulness, talent, versatility

proficient accomplished, adroit, competent, deft, dexterous, efficient, expert, gifted, handy, masterful, skilled, talented, versatile, wicked

profile alto-relievo, bas-relief, contour, delineation, description, elevation, embossment, form, outline, projection, relievo, silhouette, summary

profit advantage, capitalize on, clear, dividends, emolument, gains, gross, interest, net, percentage, prosper

profitable advantageous, beneficial, edifying, fruitful, gainful, lucrative, money-making, paying, productive, profit-making, remunerative, rewarding, salutary, valuable, worthwhile

profundity acuity, astuteness, depth, discernment, insight, penetration, perspicacity, sagacity, understanding, wisdom

profuse abundant, bounteous, copious, prolific, rich, wasteful

profuseness abundance, bags, barrels, heaps, loads, oodles, plenty, rifeness, tons

progeny baby, brood, child, issue, kid, litter, nipper, offspring, spawn, sprog, young

progress advance, develop, evolve,

headway, preferment, proceed, recover, recuperate, rolling on, travel, wade through

prohibition ban, bar, embargo, forbiddance, interdiction, proscription, taboo, veto

project beetle, hover, jut, overhang, overlie, plan, throw, undertaking

projectile ballistic, ejective, explosive, expulsive, jaculatory, missile, trajectile

projecting beetle-browed, forecasting, jutting, overhanging, sticking out

projection balcony, cape, forecast, fortification, headland, jetty, ledge, mountain, ness, outcrop, overhang, overlie, peak, peninsula, pier, point, prediction, promontory, protruberance, shelf, spit

proliferate boom, brim, bristle with, crawl with, exuberate, flow, luxuriate, multiply, mushroom, overflow, populate, prosper, riot, shower, stream, superabound, swarm, teem

prominence cachet, clout, distinction, eminence, esteem, exaltedness, glory, importance, impressiveness, knob, kudos, mark, outgrowth, position, prestige, primacy, protruberance, repute, salience

prominent eminent, important, jutting out, noted, noticeable, outstanding, protuberant

promiscuity debauchery, decadence, defloration, depravity, easy virtue, fornication, free love, harlotry, incontinence, lasciviousness, libertinism, licentiousness, lubricity, mixing, muddle, nymphomania, permissiveness, priapism, salaciousness, satyriasis, seduction, unchastity, venery, wantonness, wenching, whoring, whorishness, wife swapping, womanizing

promise adjuration, affidavit, affirm, assurance, authorization, betrothal, bond, certificate, commitment, compact, confirm, contract, covenant, deposition, engagement, gentleman's agreement, guarantee, handshake, insurance, intention, oath, obligation, permit, pledge, profession, proffer, swear, testify, testimony, tie, understanding, undertake to, vow, warrant, word

promised assured, betrothed, bound, committed, engaged, on oath, pledged, professed, spoken for, sworn

promised land Canaan, El Dorado, Elysian Fields, Erewhon, eternal life, Heaven, Israel, Shangri-la, the millennium, Utopia, Valhalla
See also list at **imaginary**

promote advance, aid, elevate, enhance, enshrine, exalt, heighten, perk up, publicise, sublimate

promoted advanced, advertised, apotheosized, beatified, canonized, deified, elevated, enshrined, exalted, lionized

pronounced
may indicate a homophone

proof affirmation, ascertainment, attestation, bombproof, bulletproof, certainty, childproof, circumstantiation, clarification, confirmation, corroboration, demonstration, determination, establishment, evidence, failsafe, fireproof, foolproof, illustration, invulnerable, justification, leakproof, mothproof, QED, ratification, rustproof, settlement, shatterproof, showerproof, steadfast, substantiation, support, testimonial, trial, verification, waterproof, weatherproof

propaganda advertising, agitprop, brainwashing, consciousness-raising, hard selling, indoctrination, pamphleteering, PR, promotion, publicity

propagate bed out, beget, breed, bud, compost, crop, cultivate, deadhead, deblossom, debud, delve, dib, dibble, dig, dust, engender, fertilize, fork, generate, graft, hatch, hoe, incubate, layer, lop, mow, mulch, plant, pollinate, pot, procreate, produce, prune, puddle in,

raise, rake, rear, rotavate, seed, sow, spade, spawn, stake, thin, tie in, topdress, train, transplant, trench, water, weed

propagation birth, breeding, coition, conception, copulation, fecundation, fertilization, florescence, flowering, fructification, fruition, generation, genesis, germination, gestation, hatching, impregnation, incubation, natality, nativity, parturition, pollination, pregnancy, procreation, sex, sexual intercourse, spawning

propagator begetter, cultivator, dam, fertilizer, parent, pollinator, procreator, sire

propel drive, impel, jaculate, kick, launch, move, pedal, pole, project, push, row, shove, thrust, traject, treadle, wheel

propellant ejector, emitter, explosive, radiator

properness correctness, decency, etiquette, honesty, honour, integrity, probity, propriety, seemliness

property acreage, allotment, apartment, belongings, building, bungalow, castle, chalet, characteristic, chattels, claim, common, copyright, cottage, dependency, domain, dominion, estate, farm, flat, goods, grounds, hacienda, homestead, house, land, living, lot, manor, mansion, parcel, patent, penthouse, plantation, plot, possession, quality, ranch, receipt, right, small holding, tenement, territory, tract, villa

prophesy divine, dowse, forecast, foresee, foretell, gamble, intuit, predict, soothsay, tell fortunes, vaticinate

prophylaxis antisepsis, bactericide, contraception, disinfectant, disinfection, fumigant, germicide, hygiene, immunization, inoculation, insecticide, isolation, preventive, quarantine, sanitation, sterilization, vaccination

proportion percentage, balance,

equalize, modify, ratio, relationship, rhythm, symmetry

propulsion bunt, butt, drive, impetus, impulsion, jaculation, kick, momentum, propelling, pulsion, push, shove, shunt, thrust

propulsive driving, motive, propellant, pulsive, pushing, shoving

prospect ambition, aspiration, design, desire, enterprise, explore, hope, plan, project, proposal, pursuit, purview, search for, study, undertaking, view

prosper accomplish, achieve, blossom, compass, effect, flourish, flower, thrive

prosperity affluence, blessings, boom, comfort, ease, fame, fortune, glory, golden age, good times, halcyon days, heyday, honeymoon period, luxury, palmy days, plenty, prestige, salad days, security, success, thriving, wealth, welfare, well-being

prosperous affluent, at ease, auspicious, blessed, blissful, booming, comfortable, cosy, famous, fat, favourable, flourishing, fortunate, golden, halcyon, lucky, luxurious, opulent, palmy, profiteering, promising, propitious, rich, rising, rosy, successful, thriving, upwardly mobile, wealthy, well-heeled, well-off, well-to-do

prostitute call-girl, courtesan, devalue, fille de joie, gigolo, importune, mercenary, pander, pimp, procure, rent boy, sex worker, solicit, streetwalk, tart, tom, whore

prostitution brothel-keeping, degradation, harlotry, importuning, oldest profession, pandering, pimping, procuring, selling out, soliciting, streetwalking, vice, whoredom

prostration grovelling, proneness, reclining, recumbency, supineness

protect armour, buffer, care for, champion, chaperon, cherish, conceal, conserve, cover, cushion, defend, deliver, enclose, entrench, envelop, escort, flank, fortify, foster, guard, harbour, hide, house, insulate, keep, lag, mind, monitor, mother, nurse, patrol, patronize, police, preserve, rescue, retreat, safeguard, screen, secure, shade, shelter, shepherd, shield, spare, store, strengthen, support, tend, vouch for, ward, watch over

protected bandaged, concealed, enclosed, exempt, hidden, immune, screened, sheathed, shielded, swathed

protection aegis, aid, armour, asylum, bastion, buffer, bulwark, charge, contraception, convoy, cover, cushion, custodianship, custody, defence, ditch, escort, guard, guardianship, haven, hope, immunity, impregnability, insurance, invulnerability, mainstay, moat, palisade, patronage, precaution, prophylaxis, protectorate, provision, refuge, safeguard, safekeeping, sanctuary, screen, shelter, shield, stockade, support, surety, surrogacy, surveillance, tutelage, umbrella, vetting, ward, wardship

protest agitate, boycott, challenge, clamour, complain, contradiction, counteraction, defiance, defy, demo, demonstrate, denial, deprecate, detract, disagree, disapprobation, disapproval, disavowal, disclaimer, dissatisfaction, dissent, gainsay, march, mutiny, negation, negativity, objection, occupy, oppose, opposition, outcry, picket, rally, recalcitrance, recusance, refutation, renunciation, repudiate, resist, say no, strike, warn

protester demonstrator, dissident, marcher, recalcitrant, recusant, reformer, striker, suffragette, suffragist

protesting challenging, contradictive, counteractive, critical, defiant, denying, deprecatory, disapproving, disobedient, dissatisfied, dissenting, negating, noncompliant, nonconformist, objecting, opposing, recalcitrant, recusant, refractory, unconsenting

prototype blank, blueprint, cast, die,

dummy, example, format, formula, frame, jig, matrix, model, mould, paradigm, pattern, punch, stamp, stencil, template

prototypical custom-built, designer, dummy, exemplary, generic, model, original, paradigmatic, ready-made, tailor-made

protract carry on, endure, extend, follow up, further, hang on, maintain, perpetuate, persevere, persist, prolong, pursue, resume

protracted drawn-out, enduring, extended, interminable, lasting, lengthened, persistent, prolonged, unceasing, unrelenting, unremitting

protraction addition, endurance, extension, furtherance, long duration, perpetuation, perseverance, persistence, prolongation, pursuit, survival

protrude be conspicuous, jut out, overhang, poke out, project, stand out, stick out, swell

protuberance antenna, beak, brow, bugle, bump, conk, face, forehead, hooter, nose, proboscis, protrusion, snoot, snout, swelling, trunk

protuberant beaked, bumpy, jutting out, protrudent, proud, sticking out, swelling

proud arrogant, courageous, highhatted, hoity-toity, honourable, hubristic, noble, self-confident, self-esteeming, self-important, self-regarding, spirited, supercilious

prove affirm, ascertain, attest, authenticate, back up, certify, circumstantiate, clarify, clinch, confirm, corroborate, countersign, demonstrate, determine, endorse, establish, evidence, evince, fix, illustrate, justify, ratify, rise, settle, show, substantiate, support, sustain, test, try, validate, verify

proved ascertained, attested, authenticated, certified, confirmed, corroborated, demonstrated, determined, established, shown, substantiated, validated, verified

proven affirmed, borne out, corroborative, evidential, justified, probative, probatory, ratified, relevant, settled, shown, tried (and tested)

proverbial aphoristic, axiomatic, banal, clichéd, commonplace, enigmatic, epigrammatic, gnomic, hackneyed, moralistic, oracular, perceptive, pithy, platitudinous, sententious, stereotyped, stock, trite, witty

provider baker, bursar, butcher, butler, creditor, donor, drysalter, feeder, fishmonger, giver, greengrocer, grocer, lender, middleman, milkman, panderer, poulterer, procurer, purser, quartermaster, retailer, shopkeeper, steward, storekeeper, supplier, treasurer, victualler, vintner, waiter, waitress, wholesaler

provision accommodate, afford, arm, assistance, board, budget, bunker, cater, clothing, delivery, distribution, entertainment, equip, feed, find, fit out, fix up, forage, furnish, hoard, keep, kit out, lend, logistics, maintenance, make ready, man, measure, offer, pandering, precaution, preparation, present, procuring, provide, purvey, rations, refill, reserves, self-service, serve, service, staff, step, stock, stockpile, stores, supplies, support, takeaway, topping-up, victualling

provisional all-in, catered, conditional, equipped, furnished, given, interim, limited, offered, prepared, provided, qualified, ready, staffed, stocked, supplied, temporary, victualled, well-appointed

provisioning appointment, armament, array, catering, commission, equipping, fitting out, furnishing, gear, kit, logistics, marshalling, outfit, providing, supply

provisions comestibles, food, groceries, grub, nosh, provender, sustenance, victuals

prude censor, moral guardian, prig, Victorian

prudence anticipation, care, caution, circumspection, farsightedness, forethought, insight, longsightedness, perspicacity, plan, precaution, premeditation, preparation, providence, readiness, sagacity, wisdom

prudent careful, cautious, circumspect, provident, sagacious, wise

prying curiosity, gossipy, meddlesome, meddling, nosy, officious, prurient, rubbernecking, snooping, tittletattle, voyeurism

psychiatrist alienist, headshrinker, neuropsychiatrist, psychoanalyst, psychotherapist, shrink, trick-cyclist

psychic astrologer, augur, auspex, clairaudient, clairsentient, clairvoyant, cosmic, crystal gazer, diviner, extrasensory, fortune teller, haruspex, magical, medium, mental, occult, oracle, palmreader, parapsychological, prophet, psychokinetic, psychological, psychosensory, pythoness, radiaesthetic, seer, sibyl, soothsayer, spiritualis(tic), subconscious, telaesthetic, telekinetic, telepathic, telergic, transcendental, vates, wise woman

psychological emotional, in the mind, instinctive, mental, personal, psychiatric, spiritual

psychologist analyst, behaviour therapist, counsellor, dramatherapist, hypnotherapist, narcotherapist, psychoanalyst, psychotherapist

psychology behaviourism, character, ethology, mentality, nature, personality, psychoanalysis, psychodynamics

psychosis breakdown, neurosis, psychopathy

public common people, communal, customers, general, governmental, grass roots, hoi polloi, masses, mob, multitude, municipal, open, populace, prominent, published, rabble, state-owned, unrestricted, vox populi

publication announcement, ban, book, broadcasting, bulletin, circulation, communiqué, declaration, decree, disclosure, dissemination, divulgence, edict, encyclical, journal, magazine, manifesto, newsletter, notification, organ, periodical, proclamation, promulgation, pronouncement, pronunciamento, publishing, report, sermon, speech, statement, ukase, ventilation

publicity advertising, blurb, circulation, coverage, currency, fame, infamy, limelight, manifestation, notoriety, openness, PR, public eye, publicness, puff, spotlight

publicize advertise, announce, ballyhoo, bill, boost, celebrate, emphasize, feature, headline, highlight, pamphleteer, pinpoint, placard, plug, proclaim, promote, propagandize, puff, push, request, sell, splash, spotlight, tout

publicizer advertiser, announcer, barker, copywriter, crier, herald, hidden persuader, image-maker, messenger, pamphleteer, press agent, proclaimer, promoter, propagandist, PR person, publicist, publicity agent, sandwichman, spieler, tout

public spirit Benthamism, citizenship, civism, communism, humanitarianism, reformism, social conscience, socialism, utilitarianism

publish circulate, cover, distribute, issue, print, put out, report, serialize, syndicate, write up

published aired, announced, broadcast, circularized, circulating, communicated, current, declared, disclosed, disseminated, distributed, exposed, open, printed, proclaimed, public, revealed, televised, ventilated

pull attraction, drag, draught, draw, flick, flip, hale, handle, haul, heave, hitch, jerk, jig, joggle, jolt, kedge, knob, lug, magnetism, pluck, rowing, snatch, strain, tow, trail, train, trawl, trice, tug, tweak, twitch, warp, wrench, yank, yerk

pulp agar, aspic, bonnyclabber, crush, curd, dough, fiction, fool, gel, gelatin, jam, jelly, junket, liquidize, lurid, mousse, mush, pap, paste, pith, pudding, purée, sensational, squash, stodge, syrup, treacle

pulper blender, curdler, emulsifier, food processor, macerator, masher, pulp engine, thickener

pulpiness creaminess, doughiness, flabbiness, fleshiness, juiciness, mushiness, overripeness, pastiness, pithiness, sappiness, sogginess, sponginess, squashiness, stodginess, succulence

pulpy amylaceous, creamy, doughy, flabby, mushy, soggy, soupy, spongy, squashy, starchy, stodgy

pulverization atomization, attrition, beating, brecciation, comminution, contusion, crumbling, crushing, decomposition, disintegration, flaking, fragmentation, frosting, granulation, grating, grinding, levigation, limation, mashing, micronization, milling, multure, pounding, powdering, sharding, shredding, smashing, trituration

pulverize atomize, bray, brecciate, comminute, disintegrate, fragment, levigate, micronize, pestle, powder, shard, triturate

pulverized comminuted, crushed, disintegrated, granulated, grated, ground, levigated, pestled, powdered, sharded, shredded, sifted, triturated *may indicate an anagram*

punctuate break, dash, dot, hyphenate, interrupt, stress, underline

punctuation accent, apostrophe, asterisk, blank, braces, brackets, break, breve, caret, cedilla, circumflex, colon, comma, dagger, dash, diacritic, dieresis, ellipsis, em rule, en rule, exclamation mark, full stop, hacek, hamse, hyphen, indention, index, interrobang, inverted comma, macron, obelus, para-graph, parentheses, pause, period, point, query, question mark, quotation mark, quotes, semicolon, solidus, stroke, swung dash, tilde, umlaut, underlining, virgule

pungent mordant, piquant, sharp

punish admonish, afflict, amerce, ban, banish, bind over, blackball, cashier, castigate, chasten, chastise, chide, correct, degrade, demote, deport, discipline, drum out, exile, expel, fine, gate, hurt, impose, imprison, inflict, keelhaul, lock up, mulct, ostracize, outlaw, persecute, picket, pillory, proscribe, rebuke, reprimand, reprove, scold, send down, shame, spread-eagle, strafe, suspend, tell off, unfrock, victimize, visit

punishable amerceable, condemned, liable, mulctable

punished beaten, castigated, disciplined, executed, fined, gated, imprisoned, tortured

punishing arduous, back-breaking, demanding, exhausting, gruelling, hard, laborious, painful, strenuous, taxing, torturous

punishment admonition, amercement, banishment, belt, bilboes, binding over, birch, blackballing, cane, castigation, cat-o'-nine-tails, chain, chastening, chastisement, chiding, club, confinement, correction, cosh, cowhide, cudgel, demotion, deodand, deportation, detention, discipline, downgrading, dressing-down, drubbing, ducking stool, dunce's cap, dusting down, example, expulsion, ferule, fetters, fining, gating, horsewhip, house arrest, imprisonment, incarceration, internment, irons, keelhauling, knout, lash, lesson, mulct, ostracism, outlawing, penalization, persecution, pillory, proscription, quirt, rebuke, reprimand, reproof, rod, ruler, sandbag, scolding, scourge, sentence, shame, stick, stocks, strap, suspension, switch, tawse, telling off, thong, ticking off, unfrocking, victimization, whip

punitive admonitory, castigatory, corrective, disciplinary, instructive, penalizing, punishing, retaliatory, retributive, revengeful, vindictive

purchase acquire, acquisition, afford, bargain, bribe, buy, find, foothold, get, invest in, leverage, obtain, order, procure, rip-off, shopping, snap up, speculate, teleshop

purchaser bargain-hunter, bidder, buyer, client, clientele, consignee, consumer, customer, emptor, haggler, investor, offerer, patron, shopper, speculator, spender, taker, teleshopper, transferee, vendee

pure blank, celibate, chaste, cleansed, clear, continent, faultless, godly, immaculate, innocent, maidenly, neat, pedigreed, perfect, pious, Platonic, purebred, purified, refined, religious, righteous, saintly, sanctified, sinless, snowy, spotless, stainless, sublimated, temperate, thoroughbred, unadulterated, unblemished, uncoloured, uncontaminated, undefiled, undiluted, unfallen, unflavoured, unfragranced, unpolluted, unseasoned, unspiced, unspoilt, unsullied, untarnished, untinged, untouched, unwedded, vestal, virgin, virginal, virtuous, white

purebred pedigree, thoroughbred

purgative aperient, cathartic, diuretic, emetic, enema, evacuant, expectorant, laxative, nauseant

purification Asperges, cleansing, clearance, decontamination, dialysis, disinfection, disinfestation, elimination, expulsion, flushing, lustration, purgation, purging, riddance, sterilization, washing

purified antiseptic, aseptic, cleansed, dainty, deodorized, disinfected, nice, polished, scrubbed, shining, snow-white, spick-and-span, sterile, sterilized

purify antisepticize, catheterize, censor, clarify, cleanse, decontaminate, dialyse, disinfect, distil, elevate, elutriate, expurgate, filter, flush out, freshen, fumigate, lave, leach, lixivate, lustrate, percolate, purge, refine, sanitize, sieve, sift, sterilize, strain, sublimate, wash, weed out

purifying ablutionary, cleansing, detergent, disinfectant, germicidal, hygienic, lustral, purging, purificatory, sanitary, sterilizing

purity chastity, clarity, cleanness, clearness, faith, faultlessness, flawlessness, freshness, godliness, high-mindedness, holiness, honour, immaculacy, innocence, integrity, modesty, morality, moral rectitude, perfection, piety, primness, pudency, rectitude, righteousness, sanctity, simplicity, sinlessness, spotlessness, stainlessness, virginity, virginity, virtue, virtue

purple amaranth(ine), amethyst(ine), aubergine, beetroot, bishop's purple, cobalt violet, damson-coloured, foxglove, fuchsia, funeral colour, gentian violet, heather, heliotrope, hyacinthine, imperial purple, indigo, lavender, lilac, magenta, maroon, mauve(ine), methyl violet, mourning colour, mulberry, murrey, nobility, ornate, Parma violet, permanent magenta, plum-coloured, puce, purple-blue, purple-red, purplish, purply, purpure, regal, royal, Thalo purple, Thio violet, Tyrian purple, violaceous, violet, Windsor violet *See also list at* **colour**.

purpose aim, design, end, function, goal, meaning, object, point, reason, significance, target

purposive aimed, designed, functional, intentional, meaningful, planned, proposed, reasoned, schematic, significant, targeting, teleological

pursue chase, chevy, chivy, dig for, fish for, follow, harass, harry, hunt for, oppress, persecute, quest after, search for, seek, shadow, tail

pursued chased, followed, hounded, hunted, sought

pursuer chaser, dogger, follower, quester, researcher, searcher, seeker, shadow, sleuth, tail

pursuit battue, beat, casting, chase, dragnet, drive, gunning, hounding, hunt, manhunt, paper chase, persecution, perseverance, persistence, quest, race, search, shooting, steeplechase, tally-ho, witch-hunt

purulent festering, mattering, pussy, running, suppurative

pus discharge, festering, ichor, matter, mucopus, purulence, pussiness, pustule, sanies, seropus, suppuration

push ambition, assert oneself, attack, defy, demonstrate, drive, ease along, effort, impel, pitchfork, pitch forward, profit by, propaganda, propulsion, protest, react, send flying, shoulder, shove, show willingness, thrust

pusher connection, drug dealer, drug peddler, go-getter, hustler, propellant

put off delay, disaffect, disgust, disincline, indispose, postpone, render averse, repel, set against, turn against

putrefaction decay, mortification, necrosis, rottenness

putrid decaying, decomposed, gamy, high, off, putrescent, rancid, rotten, rotting, sour, tainted

puzzle baffle, bewilder, cipher, code, conundrum, enigma, mystery, paradox, ponder, problem, riddle, secret, think *may indicate an anagram*

·Q·

ABBREVIATIONS

Q   quart • queen • question
QC   lawyer • quality control • Queen's Counsel
QED   which was to be proved (Latin: *quod erat demonstrandum*)
QT   quart • quiet
QV   cross reference (Latin: *quod vide*)
QY   query

quadrilateral four-sided, foursquare, oblong, parallelogram, quadrangle, quadrate, rectangle, rectangular, rhombus, square, tetragon, tetrahedral, tetrahedron, trapezium, trapezoid

quadrisection quadripartition, quartering

quadruplication fourfoldness, quadruplicature, quadrupling

qualification ability, acceptability, adequacy, applicability, appositeness, appropriateness, aptness, capability, condition, degree, deservedness, diploma, dueness, efficacy, eligibility, entitlement, fitness, meritedness, proficiency, propriety, relevance, restriction, sufficiency, suitability, worthiness

qualifications authorization, baccalaureate, background, certification, credentials, degree, diploma, documentation, examinations, experience, expertise, history, licence, licentiate, permit, record, references, skills, testimonial

qualified able, acceptable, appropriate, apt, capable, competent, deserved, eligible, equipped, experienced, fit, merited, practised, prepared, proficient, skilled, suitable, suited, tempered, versed, well-adapted, worthy

quantitative counted, measured, numbered, sized, weighed

quantity altitude, amount, amplitude, breadth, bulk, capacity, depth, dimension, extent, heaviness, height, length, lightness, magnitude, mass, measurement, multitude, proportions, thickness, thinness, volume, weight, width *See also list at* **measure**.

quarrel affray, aggro, altercation, argue, argument, bicker, bother, brawl, chastisement, clash, conflict, disagree, dissent, feud, fight, fisticuffs, insult, nag, offend, row, scrap, scuffle, set-to, spat, squabble, strife, tiff, vendetta, wrangle

quarter area, district, fourth, mercy, note, pity, quadrant, region, twenty-five percent

quartered four-handed, four-part, four-stroke, quadrifid, quadripartite, quadrisected, quarterly

queer
may indicate an anagram

question analyse, appeal, ask, canvass, challenge, check, confusion, difficulty, doubt, entreaty, examine, hunt, inquire, inspect, interpellate, interview, investigate, plea, plead, poll, probe, problem, pry, puzzle, query, quest, quiz, request, research, seek, sound out, test, try, uncertainty

questionable ambiguous, arguable, at issue, beyond belief, borderline, chancy, controversial, debatable, deceptive, disputable, dodgy, doubtful, dubious, equivocal, exceptional, extraordinary, fanciful, implausible, improbable, incredible, moot, risky, shady, spurious, suspicious, unbelievable, uncertain, unlikely, unreliable, untrustworthy, unverifiable, wild *may indicate an anagram*

questioned analysed, asked, canvassed, challenged, (cross-)examined, grilled, inspected, interrogated, investigated, polled, probed, pumped, quizzed

questioning analysis, argument, challenge, cross-examination, curious, doubting, elenctic, exploratory, fact-finding, grilling, inquest, inquiry, inquisition, inquisitive, inspection, interpellant, interpellation, interrogation, introspective, investigative, knowledge-seeking, pleading, poll, probe, prying, pumping, querying, quest, requesting, research, review, scrutiny, search, study, survey, wondering

question mark interrogation mark, interrogation point, query

questionnaire audition, catechism, census, checklist, examination, hearing, interview, poll, question paper, quiz, test, trial, viva

queue fall in, file, line, march past, parade, promenade

quibble cavil, equivocate, filibuster, hedge, nit-pick, palter, pettifog, prevaricate, pussyfoot, shuffle, split hairs

quibbling captiousness, cavilling, equivocal, hair-splitting, hedging, jiggery-pokery, nit-picking, paltering, pettifoggery, prevarication, pussyfooting, shuffling, subtlety

quick-wittedness acuity, acumen, alacrity, brightness, flair, liveliness, mental agility, sharpness

quiescent calm, composed, dormant, hushed, impassive, inactive, leisured, pacific, peaceful, reposing, restful, serene, silent, smooth, soundless, still, tranquil, unagitated, unmoving, unstirring

quietness aside, faintness, muteness, mutter, noiselessness, nuance, peace, silence, taciturnity, undertone, whisper

quintessence archetype, concentrate, distillate, elixir, embodiment, epitome, extract, flower, heart, incarnation, personification, soul, spirit

quintessential archetypical, consummate, peerless, singular, unique

quit abscond, absent oneself, cease, debouch, decamp, disappear, elope, emigrate, escape, expatriate, flit, give up, leave, march out, relocate, resign, slip away, stop, take wing, up sticks, vanish

quitter defeatist, dropout, failure, fly-by-night

·R·

ABBREVIATIONS

R	eighty (Medieval Roman numeral) • King (Latin: *Rex*) • King and Emperor (Latin: *Rex et Imperator*) • queen (Latin: *Regina*) • radius • railway • ray • reverse • right • river • rook • Royal • run • street (French: *rue*)
RA	artist • radium • Royal Academy
RAC	Royal Armoured Corps • Royal Automobile Club
RAD	radiator • radical
RADA	Royal Academy of Dramatic Art
RADAR	radio detection and ranging
RAF	Royal Air Force
RALL	becoming slow (Italian: *rallentando*)
RAM	random-access memory
RB	rubidium
RC	Red Cross • Reserve Corps • Roman Catholic
RCA	Radio Corporation of America
RCP	Royal College of Physicians
RD	road • Royal Dragoons
RE	about • again • concerning • religious education • Royal Engineers
RECT	receipt • rectangle • Rector
REF	referee • reference
REG	regiment • register • registrar • regular
REL	relative • religion
REME	Royal Electrical and Mechanical Engineer
REP	repeat • repertory company • reporter • representative
RES	residence • resolution
REV	revenue • Reverend • revolution
RF	radio frequency • rutherfordium
RH	rhesus • rhodium • right hand • Royal Highness
RI	Queen and Empress (Latin: *Regina et Imperatrix*) • religious instruction • Royal Institution
RIBA	Member of the Royal Institute
RIP	rest in peace (Latin: *requiescat in pace*)
RIT	holding back (Italian: *ritardando*)
RK	religious knowledge
RM	Royal Mail • Royal Marines
RN	radon • Royal Navy
RO	record office • run out
ROM	read-only memory • Roman
RP	Received Pronunciation • Regius Professor • reply paid
RR	Right Reverend • Rolls-Royce
RSVP	please reply (French: *répondez s'il vous plaît*)
RV	rateable value • Revised Version

race autocross, colour, compete, contest, ethnic, marathon, motocross, orienteering, origin, rally, rallycross, run, speedway, steeplechase, the dogs, the turf

racial ethnic, ethnological

racism anti-Semitism, apartheid, bigotry, colour prejudice, racialism, segregation, xenophobia

rack deck, floor, frame, layer, level, pain, scaffolding, shelf, shelving, storey, strain, torture, wring, wrest

radiate diffuse, disperse, emanate, irradiate, ray, scatter

radiating gleaming, radial, rayed, spoked

radiation diffusion, dispersion, emanation, fallout, glow, radiance, radius, ray, scattering, spoke

radio AM, bleep, broadcast, cat's whisker, crystal set, FM, LW, MW, pager, personal stereo, radiopager, receiver, signal, stereo, transistor radio, UHF, VHF, walkie-talkie, Walkman, wireless

radioactivity activity, decay, emission, half-life, mean life

rage anger, bluster, boil, breathe fire, burn, chafe, fad, fight, fret, frown, fulminate, fume, fury, glare, glower, go berserk, growl, look daggers, lour, quarrel, raise Cain, raise hell, rampage, rant, rave, scowl, seethe, simmer, sizzle, smoke, smoulder, snap, snarl, stew, storm, trend
may indicate an anagram

rail bar, berate, broad gauge, complain, handrail, harangue, metals, narrowgauge, object, protest, railing, roadbed, sleeper, standard gauge

railway BR, cablecar, cog railway, el, elevated railway, funicular, light railway, line, main-line, metritis, metro, monorail, rack railway, railroad, RY, subway, telpher, track, tramline, tramway, tube, underground

railway station depot, halt, platform, railhead, terminus, whistle stop

railway worker engine driver, fireman, guard, inspector, lengthman, motorman, platelayer, pointsman, porter, railwayman, signalman, station manager

rain drizzle, mizzle, pelt, pour, precipitate, shower, spit, stream, teem

rainbow double rainbow, fogbow, spectrum

rainy drizzly, pluvial, showery, torrential, wet

raise boost, build, buoy up, elevate, erect, exalt, heft, heighten, heist, help up, hike, hoick, hoist, hold up, jack up, lever, levitate, lift, mount, nurture, payrise, prop up, rouse, shoulder, support, uphold, uplift, waken

raised elevated, hoisted, levitated, lifted, upcast, upraised, upreared, upstanding, vertical
may indicate a backword

raising antigravity, ascent, attollent, elevation, erection, escalation, heave, hoist, levitation, lifting, rearing, sublevation, upcast, upheaval, uplift, upthrow, upthrust

rally banter, collect, demo, demonstration, encourage, gathering, mass meeting, motocross, motor race, protest, recover, regroup, run, sit-in, tease

ramble
may indicate an anagram

random accidental, adventitious, aleatoric, casual, catch-as-catch-can, chancy, coincidental, contingent, dicey, epiphenomenal, fluky, fortuitous, haphazard, hit-or-miss, iffy, incalculable, incidental, indeterminable, noncausal, risky, serendipitous, sink-or-swim, stochastic, uncertain, unexpected, unforeseeable, unforeseen, unpredictable

range Aga, area, array, chain, compass, cordillera, coverage, field, gamut, grasp, radius, reach, ridge, scope, spectrum, sphere, stove, stretch, sweep

ranging free-range, travelling, unconfined, unfettered, untethered

rank authority, caste, circumstance, class, coarse, echelon, estate, footing, foul, grading, hierarchy, level, order, place, position, precedence, putrid, smelly, sphere, standing, station, status, stinking, value

ranked authoritative, classed, classified, ecclesiastical, hierarchic, leading, ordered, preceding, rated

rant babble, blah, blarney, blather, crack jokes, drivel, drool, flatter, gabble, gag, garble, gibber, gush, jabber, jaw, joke, prate, prattle, pun, quip, rave, rhapsodize, romance, spiel, twaddle, vapour, waffle, yackety-yak, yammer

rape abuse, force, indecently assault, interfere with, ravish, violate

rarefaction adulteration, attenuation, dilation, dilution, etherealization, expansion, extension, thinning, weakness

rarefied adulterated, attenuated, dilative, diluted, etherealized, expansive, extending, extensive, thinning, watered-down, weak

rarity infrequency, intermittence, scarcity, sporadicalness, thinness, unusualness

rash allergic reaction, audacious, bold, breakneck, capricious, careless, couldn't-care-less, danger-loving, daredevil, death-defying, desperate, devil-may-care, do-or-die, flippant, foolhardy, foolish, frivolous, gung ho, harebrained, hasty, headlong, heedless, hotheaded, ill-considered, impatient, impetuous, improvident, imprudent, impulsive, incautious, inconsiderate, indiscreet, injudicious, irresponsible, madcap, outbreak, overconfident, precipitate, reckless, regardless, series,

slapdash, spate, thoughtless, trigger-happy, uncircumspect, unwary, wild *may indicate an anagram*

rashness adventurousness, audacity, brinkmanship, capriciousness, carelessness, daredevilry, daring, desperation, excitability, flippancy, folly, foolhardiness, frivolity, heedlessness, impatience, impetuousness, imprudence, impulsiveness, indiscretion, levity, overconfidence, presumption, recklessness, temerity

ratify autograph, countersign, endorse, initial, inscribe, sign, undersign

ratio fraction, percentage, proportion, relationship

rational analytical, balanced, clear-headed, coherent, impartial, intelligent, intelligible, judicious, level-headed, logical, lucid, objective, plausible, pragmatic, ratiocinative, realistic, reasonable, sane, sound, well-reasoned

rationality coherence, common sense, intelligence, intelligibility, lucidity, reasonableness, wits

rationalize clarify, construe, deduce, define, demonstrate, downsize, economize, elucidate, evaluate, exemplify, explain, expound, illuminate, illustrate, infer, interpret, justify, make excuses, organize, reason, reform, restructure, show, streamline, syllogize, systematize, think through, vindicate

rattle babble, castanets, chatter, chug, clack, clatter, clicking, disturb, knocking, maracas, racket, sputter, ticking

raw artless, awkward, callow, coarse, credulous, crude, fresh, gauche, grazed, green, gullible, immature, inexperienced, ingenuous, innocent, naive, sore, uncooked, unrefined, unripe, unseasoned, unskilled, unsophisticated, untested, untrained

reach arrive, attain, carry, come to, extend, get there, go, grasp, make it, outreach, outstretch, span, stretch

react activate, answer, bounce back,

echo, exchange, grimace, interact, invert, kick back, neutralize, rebuff, recalcitrate, recoil, respond, retroact, return, reverberate, shrink, shudder

reaction answer, echo, rebuff, recoil, reflex, reflux, repercussion, response, retroaction, return, reverberation

reactionary conservative, counter-revolutionary, old-fashioned, traditionalist
may indicate a backword

reactive antiphonal, echoing, interactive, interlocutory, knee-jerk, reactionary, rebuffed, recalcitrant, recoiling, reflexive, refluent, repercussive, responsive, retortive, retroactive, returning, reverberatory, revulsive

ready-made convenience, instant, prefabricated, processed

real actual, authentic, corporeal, de facto, empirical, entelechial, existing, factual, genuine, historical, honest-to-God, indisputable, known, material, occurring, phenomenal, physical, positive, provable, solid, substantial, tangible, true, undeniable, valid, veritable

realism authenticity, naturalism, pragmatism, verisimilitude

realist naturalist, photorealist, pragmatist, verist

realistic authentic, convincing, eidetic, expressive, faithful, genuine, graphic, impressionistic, lifelike, natural, naturalistic, photographic, picturesque, truthful

reality actuality, authenticity, basics, corporeality, crunch, entelechy, existence, fact, facticity, factuality, fundamentals, historicity, home truths, materiality, matter, necessity, occurrence, practicality, presence, solidity, substance, substantiality, substantivity, tangibility, truth, validity

realizable achievable, attainable, feasible, likely, plausible, possible, practicable, probable

realize apprehend, conclude, conjecture, deduce, get, grasp, hit one, hypothesize, infer, intuit, invent, originate, perceive, premise, remember, see, speculate, strike one, suppose, surmise, theorize, understand

reappearance recurrence, reincarnation, reissue, repeat, republication, resurrection, return, second coming

rear afterpart, afterthought, back, background, backside, backstage, behind, bottom, bring up, bum, buttocks, caudal, coda, derriere, dorsal, end, endpiece, epilogue, fundament, haunches, heel, hind, hindmost, hindquarters, hinterland, last, lumbar, mizzen, posterior, postern, postscript, raise, rump, sitter, sit-upon, stern, tail, trail, train, upend, uprise, wake
may indicate the last letter(s) of a word

rearrange adjust, realign, regroup, reorder, reorganize, restructure, shake up

reason aim, analyse, answer, basis, deduce, excuse, explanation, generalize, grounds, idea, induce, infer, intellect, intelligence, judge, judgment, key, logicalize, mind, motive, object, occasion, opportunity, perceive, perception, pretext, purpose, ratiocinate, rationale, rationality, rationalize, sanity, sense, synthesize, think, understanding, wisdom

reasoning analysis, deduction, generalization, ideological, induction, inference, intellectual, intelligent, judgmental, knowledgeable, logic(al), perceptive, philosophical, ratiocination, rational, rationality, sane, sensible, syllogism, wise

rebel commie, dissident, freedom fighter, heretic, leftie, mutineer, oppose, pinko, resist, revolt, revolutionary, secessionist
may indicate an anagram

rebellion civil disobedience, guerrilla warfare, insurgence, insurrection, mutiny, nonconformity, passive resistance, revolt, revolution, terrorism, uprising

rebirth re-education, reformation, regeneration, renaissance, revolution

rebuke criticism, crushing reply, rebuff, reprimand, retort

rebut challenge, contest, contradict, contravene, controvert, counter, defy, demur, deny, deprecate, disagree, disprove, dissent, gainsay, impugn, object, obstruct, protest, question, refute, rejoin, retort

rebuttal antithesis, challenge, contradiction, contrary, contravention, defiance, demur, demurral, denial, disagreement, dissent, objection, opposite, protest, refutation, rejoinder, retort, reverse

recant abjure, abrogate, apologize, apostatize, back down, backpedal, convert, crawl, cringe, deny, disavow, disclaim, forswear, negate, recall, refute, renege, renounce, repent, repudiate, rescind, retract, revoke, turn, unsay, withdraw

recantation abjuration, abrogation, apology, apostasy, denial, disavowal, disclaimer, forswearing, negation, recall, renunciation, repudiation, retraction, revocation, withdrawal

receding backsliding, declining, ebbing, lapsing, recessive, refluent, regressive, relapsing, retractile, retreating

receipt acceptance, counterfoil, stub, voucher

receivable collectable, compensatory, gettable, hereditary, pensionary, primogenitary, takable

receive accept, accrue, acknowledge, acquire, admit, bring in, clear, collect, come into, earn, entertain, fence, gain, get, greet, gross, host, inherit, net, obtain, pocket, receipt, secure, succeed to, take home, usher in, welcome

received accepted, acknowledged, acquired, collected, entertained, gained, gotten, inherited, receipted, secured, taken, welcomed

receiving acceptance, acquisition, bequest, birthright, getting, given, heirloom, heirship, hereditament, heritage, inheritance, legacy, paid, patrimony, pensioned, primogeniture, receivership, recipience, succession, taking, wage-earning
may indicate a split word

reception admission, aloha, drawing room, entertaining, greeting, handshake, hello, hospitality, living room, lobby, party, red-carpet, sitting room, welcoming

receptive accessible, bright, clever, hospitable, inviting, open(-minded), perceptive, quick, recipient, welcoming

recession boom/bust cycle, deflation, depression, disinflation, hollow, inflation, retreat, slump, stagflation, stagnation, withdrawal

recipient acceptor, acquirer, annuitant, beneficiary, consignee, earner, pensioner, lessee, licensee, payee, receiver

reciprocal alternative, balancing, bartered, changed, compensatory, compromising, counteracting, exchanged, give-and-take, interacting, interchangeable, interplaying, reacting, recoiling, requited, retaliatory, seesaw, swapped, trade-off

reciprocate alternate, balance, barter, change, compensate, compromise, counteract, counterchange, counterstrike, exchange, interact, interchange, interplay, interrelate, react, recoil, repay, requite, respond, retaliate, retort, return, seesaw, swap, take turns, trade off

reciprocity backscratching, coadjuvancy, compromise, concession, correlation, exchanging favours, interaction, interplay, mutualism, networking, participation, sharing, symbiosis

recognition acknowledgment, applause, awareness, credit, identification, perception, praise, reward, testimonial, tribute, understanding

recognizability cognizability, definiteness, distinctiveness, distinguishability

recognizable defined, distinct, distinguishable, identifiable, knowable, unmistakable

recognize ascribe, attribute, conceive, detect, discern, distinguish, identify, ken, perceive, spot

recoil backfire, backlash, boomerang, bounce back, bound back, cannon, echo, elasticity, flinch, kick back, mirror, oscillate, rebound, reflect, reflection, reflex, refluence, reflux, repercussion, resilience, resonance, resound, return, reverberation, reversion, revert, ricochet, shrink, spring back, swing back, uncoil

recoiling backfiring, bouncing, elastic, jumping, rebounding, reflective, repercussive, resilient, resonant, reverberative, springy, shrinking, vibrating

recommendation advice, approval, command, credential, encouragement, reference, suggestion, testimonial

recompense apologize, appease, atone, compensate, expiate, indemnify, make amends, propitiate, reconcile

reconsider redo, re-examine, reflect, rethink, review

record account, album, annals, archives, bill, calendar, card, cartulary, cashbook, cassette, catalogue, CD, chequebook, chronicle, copy, counterfoil, cutting, database, diary, directory, disk, docket, documentation, dossier, empanel, enrol, entry, EP, file, film, form, Hansard, history, index, input, inscribe, inventory, invoice, item, jotter, journal, ledger, list, log, logbook, LP, memo, memoir, microcard, microfiche, microfilm, minidisk, minutes, narrate, narrative, note, notebook, notepad, papers, photocopy, photograph, picture, portfolio, portrait, print, receipt, recite, recount, register, relate, reminder, report, represent, representation, return, rollbook, scrapbook, single, sketch, snapshot, statement, stub, table, tablet, tabulate, tally, tape, videodisc, videotape, vinyl, voucher

recount chronicle, cover, detail, dramatize, narrate, recapitulate, recite, record, relate, reminisce, repeat, report, review, tell, testify

recover bounce back, convalesce, cool off, get well, mend, rally, reawaken, recuperate, repose, rest, revive, salvage, survive

recovery comeback, recapturing, reclaiming, recoupment, regaining, retrieval, salvation

recreational amusing, enjoyable, entertaining, leisurely, relaxing

recruit cadet, conscript, draft, helper, mobilize, rookie, round up

rectification adjustment, amendment, correction, editing, mending, recension, redaction, repair, revision

rectify adjust, amend, compensate for, correct, edit, fine-tune, fix, mend, patch, put right, rationalize, redact, redress, reform, regularize, remedy, repair, revise, sort out, straighten, streamline

recuperation abreaction, catharsis, convalescence, cure, easing, healing, mending, rallying, recovery, relief, upturn

recurrent ceaseless, cyclical, haunting, incessant, periodic, reappearing, regular, returning, unremitting

red alizarin, blood-red, cadmium red, cadmium scarlet, carmine, carnation, cerise, cherry, cinnabar, cochineal, Communist, coral, cramoisy, crimson (lake), cyclamen, damask, dragon's blood, flame-red, fuchsia, Grumbacher

red, gules, henna, Indian red, kermes, magenta, maroon, murex, murrey, oxblood, peach-coloured, pink, red lead, red ochre, revolutionary, rosaniline, roseate, rose madder, rosy, rouge, ruby, ruddle, russet, rust, salmon, scarlet, shocking pink, Socialist, solferino, sore, Thalo red, Venetian red, vermeil, vermilion, Windsor red
See also list at **colours**.

redden blush, colour, crimson, flush, glow, incarnadine, mantle, raddle, rouge, rubefy, rubricate, ruddle

red-faced blooming, blowzy, blushing, feverish, fiery, florid, flushed, flushing, glowing, red-cheeked, reddened, rosy-cheeked, rouged, rubescent, rubicund, ruddy, sanguine, sunburnt

red-haired auburn, carroty, chestnut, ginger-haired, sandy, Titian

redness blush, floridness, flush, glow, rosiness, rubefaction, rubescence, rubicundity, ruddiness, rufescence

reduce cut back, decimate, diminish, eliminate, pare, prune, rarefy, rationalize, scale down, thin, trim, weed

reduced abbreviated, abridged, chopped, condensed, corroded, curtailed, cut-price, cut-rate, decapitated, decimated, decreased, devalued, diminished, discounted, docked, eroded, headless, lessened, lopped, minus, mutilated, severed, shortened

reel dance, pirouette, roll, round, spin, swirl, turn, twirl, wheel, whirl, whirlabout

reeling
may indicate an anagram

reference book ABC, almanac, atlas, A–Z, Baedeker, Bradshaw, catalogue, chart, dictionary, directory, encyclop(a)edia, ephemeris, Fodor, gazetteer, guidebook, handbook, index, itinerary, manual, map, Michelin, plan, road map, telephone directory, the-saurus, timetable, travelogue, vade mecum, yearbook, Yellow Pages

refine cultivate, distil, perfect, polish, purify

refined aesthetic, appreciative, civilized, cleansed, courteous, critical, delicate, dignified, discriminating, distingué, elegant, genteel, gentlemanly, graceful, ladylike, polished, purified, sophisticated, subtle, tasteful, U, urbane, well-bred, well-finished, well-mannered, well-spoken

refinement condensation, cultivation, detail, discrimination, distillation, elegance, extraction, purification, separation, sublimation, subtlety, vaporization

reflection cat's eye, contemplation, image, indication, likeness, looking glass, mirror, notion, reflector, representation, speculum

reformism antifascism, antiracism, Black Power, chiliasm, communism, ecology, extremism, Fabianism, feminism, gradualism, Greenpeace, humanism, idealism, liberalism, Marxism, meliorism, millenarianism, peace movement, perfectionism, progressivism, prohibitionism, radicalism, revolution, socialism, suffragism, Utopianism

refractory arbitrary, contrary, contumacious, crotchety, disobedient, incorrigible, intractable, irascible, irrepressible, perverse, recalcitrant, restive, uncontrollable, ungovernable, unmanageable, unpersuadable, unruly, wayward

refrain abstain, avoid, chorus, defer, delay, eschew, forbear, idle, pass up, procrastinate, repress, retard, sit back, tune

refresh aerate, air, animate, brace, cheer, clean, cool, ease, enliven, exhilarate, feed, fortify, freshen, invigorate, reanimate, recreate, recruit, reinvigorate, rejuvenate, relieve, renew, renovate, repair, restore, resuscitate, revitalize, revive, spruce up, stimulate, strengthen, tidy, ventilate, vitalize

refreshed braced, enlivened, exhilarated, fortified, invigorated, perked up, recovered, rested, restored, revitalized, revived, stimulated

refresher break, holiday, repose, rest, restorative, reviver, stimulant, tonic, vacation

refreshment aeration, animation, ease, exhilaration, invigoration, reanimation, recovery, recreation, recruitment, recuperation, reinvigoration, rejuvenation, relief, renewal, renovation, repair, repose, rest, restoration, resuscitation, revitalization, revival, stimulation, ventilation, vitalization

refreshments drink, food, pick-me-up, refection, snack, sustenance

refrigerant coolant, liquid oxygen, lox

refrigerator chill cupboard, chilled counter, cool box, deep-freeze, Esky, freezer, fridge, fridge-freezer, ice bucket, ice pack

refuge acropolis, ark, asylum, bastion, blockhouse, bolt hole, cache, chamber, citadel, cubbyhole, fortress, foxhole, haven, hermitage, hide-out, hid(e)yhole, home, ivory tower, keep, priest hole, recourse, resort, retreat, rock, safe harbour, safe house, sanctuary, sanctum (sanctorum), shelter, stronghold, temple, ward

refurbish gentrify, modernize, recondition, redecorate, refashion, refit, remodel, renew, renovate, restore, revamp, upgrade

refusal denial, denigration, negation, nonacceptance, noncompliance, noncooperation, recalcitrance, red light, rejection, repulsion, resistance, thumbs down, unwillingness

refuse avoid, bilge, bits, blench, castoff, complain, compost, contradict, crumbs, debris, decline, demur, deny, dirt, disapprove, disposable, dross, duck, elude, fight, flinch, jib, junk, leftovers, litter, lumber, muck, negate, neglect, object, oppose, protest, recoil, reject, repel, repulse, resist, rubbish, say no, scrap, shavings, shirk, shrink from, spoilage, stuff, sweepings, throwaway, turn down, wastage

refused denied, ejected, excluded, rejected, withheld

refusing adverse, disagreeing, dissenting, negative, nonaccepting, opposed, opting out, recalcitrant, resistant, uncompliant, unconsenting, unconvinced, uncooperative, unreconciled, unwilling

refutability confutability, defeasibility, disprovability, groundlessness, unsoundness, weakness

refutable confutable, defeasible, disprovable, faulty, flawed, groundless, inconclusive, objectionable, unfounded, unsound, weak

refutation abrogation, annulment, confounding, disaffirmation, disallowal, disconfirmation, discrediting, dismissal, disproof, disproval, invalidation, naysaying, negation, nullification, subversion, undermining

refute abrogate, annul, belie, confound, confute, crush, defeat, deflate, demolish, destroy, disallow, disconfirm, discredit, dismiss, dispose of, disprove, explode, expose, floor, forbid, invalidate, negate, nullify, outsmart, outwit, overthrow, overturn, quash, shout down, show up, silence, squash, undermine

refuting answering, contradictory, contravening, counteractive, disclaiming, disowning, rebutting, repudiating, responding, retaliatory

regards compliments, devoirs, good wishes, greetings, respects, salutations

region area, belt, continent, ground, island, islet, landmass, peninsula, place, section, sector, space, terrain, territory, zone

regional antipodean, areal, continental, eastern, geographical, highland, insular, latitudinal, local, longitudinal, lowland, northern, Occidental, Oriental, peninsular, provincial, southern, spatial, subtropical, territorial, topographic, tropical, western, zonal

regionalism nationalism, parochialism, patriotism, provincialism

regions back-country, backwater, backwoods, borders, brush, bush, corridor, countryside, green belt, heartland, hickdom, highlands, hinterland, lowlands, march, outback, outpost, provinces, virgin territory, wasteland, wilderness, yokeldom

regions of the world Antipodes, developed world, Far East, Middle East, New World, Occident, Old World, Orient, Third World

register book, cadaster, catalogue, census, docket, empanel, enlist, enrol, enter, itemize, list, panel, payroll, poll, range, realize, record, reserve, roll, roster, rota, score, scroll, tabulate, tally, till, understand

registration accounts, booking, bookkeeping, cataloguing, empanelment, enlistment, enrolment, entry, filing, indexing, listing, recording, record-keeping, registry, reservation *See list of international car registrations.*

regress backslide, decline, fall off, lapse, lose ground, recidivate, relapse, retrocede, retroflex, retrograde, retrogress, return, revert, slip back

regressive atavistic, compensatory, reactive, recessive, recidivist, reflexive, restitutive, retroactive, retrograde, retrospective, retroverse, reversionary

regular annual, automative, changeless, clockwork, commensurate, conforming, consistent, constant, correspondent, customary, daily, equipol-

lent, even, even-sided, featureless, flat, frequent, habitual, homeostatic, homogeneous, hourly, invariable, invariant, isochronal, level, measured, metronomic, monotonous, monthly, mundane, oscillatory, periodic, phasic, predictable, proportionate, recurrent, regimented, reliable, repeating, repetitive, returning, revolving, rhythmic, routine, serial, smooth, stable, standardized, steady, symmetrical, tantamount, tidal, timed, unchanging, undeviating, uniform, unvaried, usual, weekly, well-ordered, yearly

regularity alternation, automation, beat, changelessness, conformity, consistency, constancy, equilibrium, evenness, flatness, frequency, homeostasis, homogeneity, invariability, levelness, measure, monotonousness, oscillation, pattern, periodicity, phasing, precession, pulsation, reciprocity, recurrence, regimentation, repetition, return, rhythm, routine, serialization, smoothness, standardization, swing, symmetry, tempo, throb, tick, timing, treadmill, undulation, uniformity

regulate adjust, balance, control, dictate, flatten, govern, normalize, order, organize, rationalize, rule, serialize, standardize, steady, systematize, time

rehearsal draft, dry run, dummy run, hearing, mock-up, model, practice, road test, sketch, test flight, trial, tryout

rehearse mock up, model, practise, run through, simulate, sketch, try out

reject ban, bar, blackball, blacklist, boycott, cold shoulder, decline, deselect, disallow, discard, disregard, exclude, failure, faulty goods, ignore, ostracize, prohibit, rebuff, refuse, repel, repulse, return, spurn, veto, vote against

rejected annulled, cancelled, cast out, challenged, contested, contravened, countermanded, declined, denied, deprecated, disallowed, disavowed, dis-

rejected

INTERNATIONAL CAR REGISTRATIONS

REGISTRATION	COUNTRY	REGISTRATION	COUNTRY
A	Austria	MW	Malawi
AL	Albania	N	Norway
AUS	Australia	NIG	Niger
B	Belgium	NL	Netherlands
BDS	Barbados	NZ	New Zealand
BG	Bulgaria	P	Portugal
BR	Brazil	PA	Panama
BRG	Guyana	PAK	Pakistan
BRN	Bahrain	PE	Peru
BS	Bahamas	PI	Philippines
C	Cuba	PL	Poland
CDN	Canada	PY	Paraguay
CH	Switzerland	R	Romania
CI	Côte d'Ivoire	RA	Argentina
CO	Colombia	RB	Botswana
CR	Costa Rica	RC	China
CY	Cyprus	RCA	Central African Republic
D	Germany	RCB	Congo
DK	Denmark	RCH	Chile
DZ	Algeria	RH	Haiti
E	Spain	RI	Indonesia
EC	Ecuador	RIM	Mauritania
F	France	RL	Lebanon
FL	Liechtenstein	RM	Malagasy Republic
GB	Great Britain	RMM	Mali
GCA	Guatemala	ROK	South Korea
GH	Ghana	RU	Burundi
GR	Greece	RWA	Rwanda
H	Hungary	S	Sweden
HK	Hong Kong	SD	Swaziland
HKJ	Jordan	SF	Finland
I	Italy	SGP	Singapore
IL	Israel	SME	Surinam
IND	India	SN	Senegal
IR	Iran	SYR	Syria
IRL	Ireland	T	Thailand
IRQ	Iraq	TG	Togo
IS	Iceland	TN	Tunisia
J	Japan	TR	Turkey
JA	Jamaica	TT	Trinidad and Tobago
KWT	Kuwait	U	Uruguay
L	Luxembourg	USA	United States of America
LAO	Laos	VN	Vietnam
LB	Liberia	WAL	Sierra Leone
LS	Lesotho	WAN	Nigeria
M	Malta	WS	Western Samoa
MA	Morocco	YV	Venezuela
MAL	Malaysia	Z	Zambia
MEX	Mexico	ZA	South Africa
MS	Mauritius		

believed, discarded, disclaimed, dismissed, disobeyed, disowned, disproved, disused, excluded, ineligible, invalidated, negated, nullified, obstructed, prohibited, questioned, rebutted, recanted, redundant, refused, refuted, renounced, repealed, repudiated, rescinded, retracted, returned, reversed, snubbed, thrown away, turned down, unacceptable, unqualified, unrequited, unselected, unsuitable, unusable, unwanted, vetoed

rejection apostasy, avoidance, black-balling, boycott, brush-off, cold shoulder, declining, denial, disallowance, disapproval, disassociation, disavowal, disbelief, disclaimer, disclamation, disobedience, disownment, dissociation, ejection, exception, exclusion, exemption, expulsion, invalidation, nonacceptance, nonbelief, nonobservance, prohibition, rebuff, recusance, recusancy, refusal, renunciation, repudiation, repulse, slight, snub, spurn, unbelief, veto

rejoice banquet, carouse, celebrate, exult, feast, glory, jubilate, make merry, rave, revel, roister, triumph

rejoicing anniversary, applause, banquet, beano, celebration, celebratory, cheering, cheery, delight, ecstatic, euphoric, exultant, exultation, feast, festival, festivities, field day, flag-waving, gaudy, glorious, happiness, happy, high, holiday, jolliness, jollity, jolly, joyful, jubilant, jubilation, jubilee, mafficking, merriment, ovation, party, rave, revel, roistering, street party, triumphant

related accompanied, added, affiliated, agnate, akin to, allied, apposite, associated, attached, bonded, bound, cognate, combined, connected, consanguineous, germane, implicated, involved, joined, kindred, linked, merged, paired, pertinent, relevant, spliced, tied, twinned, wedded

relatedness addition, adjunct, affiliation, affinity, agreement, alliance, appositeness, association, attachment, bearing, bond, combination, connectedness, consanguinity, correlation, correspondence, friendship, germaneness, homology, implication, interconnection, involvement, kinship, liaison, link, linkage, merger, mutuality, parallel, partnership, pertinence, propinquity, rapport, relationship, relevance, similarity, tie-up

relate to affect, answer to, appertain, apply to, associate, bear upon, bracket, connect, contrast, correspond, couple, cross-refer, deal with, empathize, fit, interest, juxtapose, liaise, link, match, pertain, reconcile, refer to, tie up, touch upon, understand

relax calm, deregulate, doze, drowse, kill time, laze, let up, lie idle, loll, loosen, lounge, mitigate, nap, recline, repose, rest, sit back, slacken, sleep, snooze, unwind

relaxed at ease, carefree, casual, comfortable, content, cool, derestricted, easeful, easygoing, eudemonic, floppy, gentle, idle, laid-back, lazy, leisurely, nonchalant, painfree, peaceful, quiet, resting, slack, tranquil, troublefree, unhurried

relegate ascribe, banish, demote, discharge, dismiss, downgrade

relegation banishment, demotion, discharge, dismissal, downgrading, layoff, redundancy

relief aid, alms, assistant, auxiliary, cameo, carving, charity, comfort, embossment, help, intaglio, lull, outline, painkiller, profile, reassurance, reinforcements, relaxation, release, repose, rest, support

relieve abate, allay, alleviate, anaesthetize, appease, assuage, calm, comfort, console, cover for, diminish, ease, lessen, let go, liberate, lighten, mitigate, moderate, mollify, pacify, palliate, quiet, reassure, refresh, reinforce, relax, replace, restore, sedate, soften, solace, soothe, stand in for, take over from, temper, tranquillize

relieving assuaging, balsamic, calming, comforting, consoling, curative, easing, helping, hypnotic, palliative, reassuring, refreshing, relaxing, remedial, restorative, sedative, soothing

religion belief-system, canon, chapter, church, credo, creed, cult, denomination, doctrine, dogma, faction, faith,

religionist

RELIGIOUS MOVEMENTS			
ABECEDARIANS	BAHAISM	HUGUENOTS	PLYMOUTH
ABELIANS	BAPTISTS	HUMANISM	BRETHREN
ABELITES	BASILIDEANS	I AM	PRESBYTERIANISM
ABODE OF LOVE	BENEDICTINES	ISLAM	PROTESTANTISM
ABRAHAMITES	BERNARDINES	JAINISM	PURITANS
ABSTINENTS	BON	JANSENISM	QUAKERS
ABYSSINIAN	BOSCI	JEHOVAH'S	REDEMPTORISTS
CHURCH	BUCI IANITES	WITNESSES	ROMAN
ACOEMETI	BUDDHISM	JUDAISM	CATHOLICISM
ADAMITES	CALIXTINES	JUMPERS	SALVATION ARMY
ADMADIYA	CALVINISM	KEGON	SHAKERS
ADVENTISTS	CATHOLICISM	LAMAISM	SHINTO
AGONIZANTS	CHRISTIANITY	MAR THOMA	SIKHISM
AHMADIYA	CHRISTIAN SCIENCE	METHODISM	SPIRITUALISM
AINU	CHUNTOKYO	MOHAMMEDANISM	STUDITES
AJIVIKA	CONGREGATION-	MORAVIAN	TAOISM
AMARITES	ALISM	BRETHREN	THAGS
AMBROSIANS	COVENANTERS	MORMONS	THUGS
ANABAPTISTS	FRANKISTS	NICHIREN	UNITARIANISM
ANGLICANISM	FUNDAMENTALISM	NOSAIRIS	VOODOO
ANTIPAEDOBAPTISTS	GIDEONS	PANTHEISM	WAHABIS
ARMINIANISM	HICKSITES	PARSEES	ZEN
BABISM	HINDUISM	PARSIS	ZIONISM

manifesto, movement, order, persuasion, sect, superstition
See list of religious movements.

religionist Bible-basher, crusader, evangelist, fanatic, formalist, fundamentalist, ghazi, god squad, iconoclast, preacher, precisian, pulpiteer, salvationist, sermonizer, televangelist, TV evangelist, witch-hunter, zealot

religiosity Bible-bashing, bibliolatry, churchiness, crusading, fanaticism, fundamentalism, heresy-hunting, overpiety, preachiness, salvationism, unctuousness, witch-hunting

religious anchoretic, ardent, ascetic, Bible-worshipping, canting, cherubic, churchgoing, churchy, crusading, devout, evangelical, faithful, fanatical, fervent, formalistic, fundamentalist, God-fearing, godly, holier-than-thou, holy, humble, militant, missionary, monastic, mystic, orthodox, otherworldly, overreligious, Pharisaic, pious, practising, prayerful, preachy, priest-ridden, reverent(ial), ritualistic, saintly, sanctimonious, self-righteous, self-sacrificing, seraphic, spiritual, strict, theopathic, transcendent, unctuous, witch-hunting, worshipful, zealous

religiousness deism, devotion, faithfulness, fervour, humility, mysticism, observance, piety, puja, reverence, ritualism, sanctimony, self-sacrifice, spirituality, strictness, theism, zeal

relinquish abdicate, abnegate, abstain, assign, avoid, cast off, cede, discard, divest, doff, drop, forfeit, forgo, forswear, hand over, jettison, junk, loose, lose, recant, release, renounce, repudiate, resign, scrap, shed, shred, slough, surrender, tear up, tergiversate, transfer, unclench, waive, yield

relinquished abandoned, apostatical, cancelled, castaway, derelict, deserted, dropped, forgone, forsaken, invalid, jilted, scrapped, stranded, surrendered, void, waived

relinquishment abandonment, abdication, abnegation, abolition, abrogation, absence, abstinence, annulment, avoidance, cancellation, cession, defection, departure, dereliction, desertion, desuetude, discontinuance, disuse, evacuation, forfeit, recantation, renunciation, resignation, retirement, schism, secession, strike, surrender, transfer, truancy, withdrawal, yielding

reluctant averse, cautious, dissenting, opposed, protesting, resistant, sceptical, sulky, unenthusiastic, unwilling, wary

remain abide, mark time, stay, tread water, wait

remainder aftereffect, afterglow, bits, butt, debris, fag end, footprint, fossil, fragments, frustum, husk, memorabilia, record, relic, reminder, remnant, rest, result, ruins, scrag end, shell, souvenir, stub, stump, survival, trace, track, trail, vestige, wreckage

remaining deposited, extant, left, precipitated, residual, resultant, sedimentary, spare, superfluous, surviving, vestigial

remains corpse, crumbs, leavings, left-overs, rejects, seconds, sweepings

remedial analeptic, analgesic, antidotal, antiseptic, balsamic, beneficial, cathartic, cleansing, corrective, counteracting, curative, febrifugal, healing, helpful, medicinal, palliative, panacean, restorative, soothing, stimulative, therapeutic, tonic

remedy aid, alleviate, amendment, amends, answer, antidote, atonement, correct, corrective, cure, demulce, ease, elixir, expiation, fix, heal, help, mend, moderator, neutralize, palliate, panacea, prescription, recovery, recuperation, redress, relief, relieve, restitution, restore, solution, soothe, specific, succour, treat
may indicate an anagram

remember antiquarianize, archaize, conjure up, hark back, identify, memorize, recall, recapture, recognize, recollect, reflect, regress, relive, reminisce, reprise, retrace, review

remembrance déjà vu, flashback, harking back, memorial, nostalgia, recalling, reminiscence, reviewing, rosemary

remind haunt, jog someone's memory, nag, prompt, recapitulate, review

reminder album, cue, diary, memo, memorandum, mnemonic, note, prompt, record, scrapbook

remorse contrition, embarrassment, guilty conscience, penitence, qualms, regret, self-reproach, shame

removal asset-stripping, cancelling, catharsis, cleaning out, clearance, cut, deduction, deletion, depletion, displacement, draining, egress, elimination, emptying, eradication, erasure, evacuation, exhaustion, extraction, extrication, moving, plucking out, pulling up, purging, ripping out, scouring out, subtraction, unfouling, uprooting, voidance

remove amputate, clip, curtail, decapitate, deduct, denude, detract, displace, distance, dock, draw out, eliminate, extract, extricate, flake, flay, lop, move, pare, peel, pluck, prune, pull out, retreat, rip out, root out, rule out, shear, shift, skin, strip, subtract, tear out

remunerate bribe, compensate, distribute, pay, reward, tip

remuneration bonus, commission, earnings, emolument, enticement, expenses, fee, golden handshake, honorarium, incentive, income, inducement, pay, payment, payoff, pension, perk, perquisite, redundancy pay, retainer, salary, wages

renaissance reanimation, rebirth, reincarnation, resurrection, revival, revivification

renew change, freshen, modernize, rebuild, reconstruct, recycle, redesign, refresh, refurbish, regenerate, rehash, reheat, reissue, rejuvenate, remake, renovate, repaint, replay, replenish, reprint, reprocess, rerun, restart, restore, resume, resurrect, revise, revive, update, upgrade

renewable energy biodiesel, biofuels, biomass, geothermal energy, hydroelectricity, photovoltaic cell, solar energy, tidal energy, tidal power, water mill, water turbine, wave power, wind generator, windmill, wind power, wind pump, wind turbine

renewal addition, change, new leaf, new look, reconstruction, refurbishment, regeneration, rejuvenation, remake, renovation, reorganization, repainting, restoration, resurrection, revival, revivification, updating

renewed changed, freshened, modernized, reconstructed, redesigned, refilled, refreshed, refurbished, regenerated, rejuvenated, remade, renovated, repainted, replenished, restored, resurrected, revived, revivified, touched up

renounce abjure, abrogate, abstain, annul, apostasize, cancel, countermand, demur, deny, forebear, forgo, forswear, go without, invalidate, nullify, recant, relinquish, repeal, repudiate, rescind, retract, revoke, swear off, take back, tergiversate

renowned celebrated, fabled, famous, illustrious, sung

renunciation abjuration, abrogation, annulment, cancellation, countermand, denial, forswearing, invalidation, nullification, recantation, refusal, rejection, relinquishment, repeal, repudiation, rescindment, retraction, revocation, swearing-off

repair adjust, amend, correct, darn, emendation, fix, go, leave, maintain, mend, patch, put right, reactivate, reassemble, reconditioning, rectify, redintegration, refit, reintegration, remedy, renewal, renovation, reparation, restoration, service, visit
may indicate an anagram

repairable curable, medicable, mendable, operable, recoverable, rectifiable, redeemable, restorable, retrievable, treatable

repaired correct, fixed, hurried off, mended, patched, rebuilt, reclaimed, reconditioned, reconstituted, reconstructed, recovered, rectified, remade, renewed, renovated, restored, right, salvaged

reparation amends, apology, appeasement, atonement, compensation, expiation, indemnity, propitiation, recompense, reconciliation

repayment atonement, compensation, indemnity, payback, recompense, refund, reimbursement, restitution, settlement, vengeance

repeat bis, copy, curtain call, ditto, double, duplicate, echo, encore, imitate, mimic, mirror, parrot, plagiarize, practise, redo, rehash, rehearse, reissue, reiterate, remake, repetition, replay, replicate, reprint, reproduce, rerun, reshowing, restate

repeated doubled, duplicated, echoed, frequent, imitative, mirrored, parrotlike, plagiarized, recurrent, redone, remade, replicated, reproduced

repel annoy, antagonize, coldshoulder, cut, deter, disgust, disincline, displease, drive away, enrage, grate, head off, jar, nauseate, offend, rebuff, refuse, reject, repulse, revolt, scandalize, shock, sicken, slight, snub, spurn, torment, turn back, upset

repent apologize, recant, reform, regret

repercussion aftermath, backlash, causality, chain reaction, consequence, domino theory, effect, knock-on effect, result, reverberation, snowball effect

repetition anaphora, copying, ditto, duplication, echo, echolalia, epistrophe, imitation, plagiarism, practising, recital, recurrence, reecho, rehearsal, repeating, replication, reproduction

repetitious doubling, duplicative,

echoing, harping, iterative, otiose, pleonastic, prolix, recapitulative, redundant, reiterant, reproductive, stuck-in-a-groove, tautological, wordy

repetitiveness daily grind, familiarity, habit, humdrum, invariability, monotony, regularity, repetition, routine, rut, tedium, uniformity

replace banish, cast out, deport, depose, dethrone, eject, evict, exchange, exile, expel, ostracize, oust, overthrow, restore, substitute, supplant, turn out, unseat, usurp

replaced deposed, exchanged, overthrown, put back, removed, supplanted, transferred

replacement coup, deposition, overthrow, restoration, substitution, supplantation, takeover, unseating

replenish fill (up), refill, refresh, refuel, reinforce, reload, restock, resupply, revictual, revitalize, top up

replica clone, copy, double, duplicate, photocopy, print

reply answer, confutation, feedback, refutation, respond, response, retort

report appraisal, bang, bell, broadcast, circulate, cover, crack, crash, disclose, document, inform, narrate, publicize, publish, recount, statement, transmit, write

reported *may indicate a homophone*

reporting coverage, doorstepping, giving an account, informing, journalism, newscasting, newspapering, reportage, sportscasting

repose ataraxia, composure, contemplation, death, nirvana, peace, placidity, quiescence, quietness, rest, satori, serenity, silence, sleep, slumber, tranquillity

represent act for, aid, arbitrate, assist, copy, delineate, depict, duplicate, embody, epitomize, evoke, help, imitate, impersonate, incarnate, manifest, mediate, mirror, negotiate, personify, portray, present, realize, reflect, render, reproduce, resemble, speak for, stand for, substitute for, symbolize, typify

representation advocacy, copy, delegation, delineation, depiction, description, doppelgänger, double, drawing, duplicate, embodiment, epitome, evocation, exemplar, facsimile, figuration, hieroglyphics, imitation, impersonation, impression, incarnation, indication, likeness, lithograph, lookalike, manifestation, notation, outline, personification, photocopy, pictogram, picture, portrait, portrayal, presentation, quintessence, realism, realization, reflection, rendering, replica, runes, semblance, similarity, sketch, spitting image, symbolization, tracing, type, typification, writing

representational abstract, archetypal, artistic, characteristic, delineatory, depictive, descriptive, diagrammatic, emblematic, evocative, exemplary, figurative, graphic, hieroglyphic, iconic, illustrative, imitative, impressionistic, like, naturalistic, non-representational, photogenic, photographic, pictorial, portraying, quintessential, realistic, reflecting, similar, surrealistic, symbolic, true-to-life, typical, vivid

representative accountant, adviser, agency, agent, ambassador, attorney, consultant, counsellor, cross-section, delegate, deputy, envoy, example, mouthpiece, ombudsman, peacemaker, pleader, propitiator, proxy, publicist, rep, replacement, sample, specimen, spokesperson, stand-in, substitute

reprinted rehashed, reissued, remade, reprocessed

reproduce breed, clone, copy, counterfeit, duplicate, echo, photocopy, repeat, replicate, reprint

reproduced copied, duplicated, printed, reappearing, reborn, recreated, renascent, renewed, repeated, resurgent, resurrectional

reproduction blueprint, breeding, carbon copy, caricature, cartoon, draft, duplication, multiplication, photocopy, photograph, print, proliferation, publishing, reconstruction, regeneration, repetition, replication, sketch, spawning

reproductive generative, genetic, genital, germinal, in season, on heat, originative, procreative, seminal, sexual, spermatic

reptilian chelonian, cold-blooded, crocodilian, lacertilian, lizardlike, reptiliform, saurian, scaly, serpentine, squamous, turtlelike
See list of reptiles.

repulse brush-off, cold shoulder, dismissal, ejection, expulsion, push away, rebuff, refusal, rejection, snub, spurning

repulsion disgust, driving away, recoil, repellence, repulsiveness

repulsive abhorrent, antipathetic, appalling, disgusting, foul, hideous, horrible, loathsome, nauseating, noisome, obnoxious, obscene, offensive, off-putting, repellent, repugnant, sickening, ugly

reputable above board, approved, creditworthy, distinguished, eminent, famous, honourable, honoured, renowned, respected, trustworthy

repute confidence, prestige, probity, reliability, standing, trust

reputed alleged, supposed

request accost, adjuration, adjure, appeal, application, apply, approach, ask-

---

REPTILES

ADDER	GABOON VIPER	PIT VIPER
AGAMA	GALÁPAGOS GIANT	POND TURTLE
ALLIGATOR	TORTOISE	PUFF ADDER
AMPHISBAENA	GARTER SNAKE	PYTHON
ANACONDA	GAVIAL	RACER
ANOLE	GECKO	RAT SNAKE
ASP	GILA MONSTER	RATTLESNAKE
BASILISK	GLASS SNAKE	RINGHALS
BEARDED LIZARD	GRASS SNAKE	RUSSELL'S VIPER
BLACK SNAKE	GREEN TURTLE	SAND LIZARD
BLIND SNAKE	HARLEQUIN SNAKE	SEA SNAKE
BLINDWORM	HAWKSBILL TURTLE	SIDEWINDER
BOA CONSTRICTOR	HOGNOSE SNAKE	SKINK
BOOMSLANG	HORNED TOAD	SLOW-WORM
BOX TURTLE	HORNED VIPER	SMOOTH SNAKE
BULL SNAKE	IGUANA	SNAKE
BUSHMASTER	JACARÉ	SNAPPING TURTLE
CAYMAN	KING COBRA	SOFT-SHELLED TURTLE
CHAMELEON	KING SNAKE	SPHENODON
CHUCKWALLA	KOMODO DRAGON	TAIPAN
COBRA	KRAIT	TERRAPIN
COPPERHEAD	LEATHERBACK	TOKAY
CORAL SNAKE	LIZARD	TORTOISE
COTTONMOUTH	LOGGERHEAD TURTLE	TREE SNAKE
CROCODILE	MAMBA	TURTLE
DIAMONDBACK	MANGROVE SNAKE	VINE SNAKE
RATTLESNAKE	MATAMATA	VIPER
DIAMONDBACK TERRAPIN	MILK SNAKE	WART SNAKE
FER-DE-LANCE	MOCCASIN	WATER MOCCASIN
FLYING LIZARD	MOLOCH	WATER SNAKE
FLYING SNAKE	MONITOR LIZARD	WHIP SNAKE
FRILLED LIZARD	MUGGER	WORM LIZARD

ing, begging, beseech, bid, bug, cajole, claim, coax, court, cry, desire, entreaty, favour, hawk, hustle, implore, importunity, insist, invite, invocation, invoke, move, offer, persuade, pester, petition, prayer, proposition, requirement, solicit, suggestion, suit, supplication, tout, urge, want, wish, woo

requesting adjuratory, asking, incantational, insistent, invocational, propositional, urgent

require be without, demand, lack, need, want

required absent, booked, compulsory, demanded, desired, earmarked, essential, indispensable, lacking, missing, necessary, needed, obligatory, ordered, prerequisite, requested, requisite, reserved, vital, wanted

requirement a must, command, condition, desideratum, essential, indent, injunction, necessaries, necessity, needs, order, proviso, request, requisite, requisition, specification, standards, stipulation, ultimatum

research analysis, blueprint, concert, contrive, document, draft, improvise, investigation, organize, outline, plan, plot, prearrange, predetermine, sketch, study

resemble accord, agree, coincide, compare, correspond, evoke, favour, look like, match, parallel, suggest, tally

resent bear malice, begrudge, object to, suffer, take offence

resentful acerbic, acrimonious, affronted, aggravated, annoyed, bileful, bitter, caustic, disapproving, discontented, displeased, envious, exasperated, grudging, hurt, ill-humoured, impatient, indignant, insulted, irritated, jealous, malicious, nettled, offended, pained, peeved, piqued, provoked, putout, reproachful, riled, shirty, sore, spiteful, splenetic, stung, vexed, virulent, worked-up, wrought-up

resentment acidity, acrimony, aggravation, animosity, annoyance, asperity, bitterness, disapprobation, disapproval, discontent, displeasure, dissatisfaction, envy, exasperation, gall, grudge, heartburning, ill humour, irritation, jealousy, malice, peevishness, pique, rancour, soreness, spleen, vexation

reserve aloofness, backwardness, book, coldness, constraint, coolness, diffidence, keep, modesty, nature reserve, order, quietness, reluctance, reservation, restraint, reticence, sanctuary, shyness, standoffishness, withhold

reserved aloof, backward, booked, cold, constrained, cool, diffident, low-profile, modest, ordered, quiet, reluctant, restrained, reticent, retiring, shy, standoffish, subdued, unapproachable, unassuming, unheard, unseen, untouchable

reserves backup, emergency funds, nest egg, reinforcements, safeguard, stand-by, store

reside dwell, exist in, inhabit, lie within, live in, occupy

residence abode, domicile, habitat, habitation, home, house, inhabitance, occupancy

resident at home, citizen, colonial, colonized, domiciled, dwelling, householder, in, inhabitant, in-house, in occupation, live-in, naturalized, occupier, settled, tenant

residue alluvium, ashes, bilge, castoffs, chaff, clippings, crumbs, deposit, detritus, dirt, dregs, dross, filings, grounds, husks, jumble, junk, lees, leftovers, litter, loess, lumber, moraine, offcuts, peelings, powder, precipitate, refuse, remnants, residual, rubbish, sawdust, scoria, scraps, scum, scurf, sediment, sewage, shavings, silt, slag, slough, sludge, stubble, sweepings, trimmings, waste

resign abandon, abdicate, depart, desert, drop, forgo, give up, leave, quit, relinquish, renunciate, retire, stand down, surrender, vacate, withdraw

resignation abandonment, abdication, acceptance, acquiescence, departure, quitting, relinquishment, renouncement, renunciation, retirement, surrender, withdrawal

resigned accepting, acquiescent, indifferent, passive, phlegmatic, sanguine, stoical, submissive

resilience adaptability, bounce, cheerfulness, elasticity, endurance, recoil, reflex, strength, toughness

resin amber, asphalt, bitumen, gum, japan, resina, resinoid, rosin, tar, varnish

resinous asphaltic, bituminous, gummy, japanned, pitchy, rosiny, tarry, varnished

resist challenge, confront, contend with, defy, deprecate, dissent, endure, harden, hinder, last, object to, obstruct, oppose, protest, rebuff, refuse, repel, repulse, stand against, stiffen, strike, survive, toughen, walk out, withstand

resistance challenge, defiance, deprecation, dissent, immunity, negativeness, noncooperation, objection, opposition, protest, rebuff, refusal, reluctance, renitency, repellence, repulse, stand, unwillingness

resistant bulletproof, challenging, defiant, deprecative, dissenting, hardcore, hard-headed, hard-nosed, hard-shell, invincible, noncooperative, obstructive, proof, protesting, reactionary, reluctant, renitent, repellent, unbeatable, unbowed, undefeated, unquelled, unsubdued, unsubmissive, unwilling, withstanding

resolute concentrated, courageous, decided, decisive, deliberate, determined, firm, hell-bent, intent, obsessed, plucky, purposeful, resilient, resolved, set, single-minded, steadfast, stouthearted

resolution conciliation, conclusion, decidedness, decisiveness, declaration, determination, doggedness, ending, intention, outcome, purposefulness, resolve, settlement, solution

resolve callousness, conclude, cynicalness, decide, design, determine, engage, fix, hardheartedness, inflexibility, intend, mean to, obdurateness, obstinacy, project, promise, purpose, seal, settle, shoulder, single-mindedness, solve, sort out, sternness, stubbornness, terminate, threaten, undertake, unfeelingness, unyieldingness, will

resonance buzzing, echo, hollowness, humming, oscillation, rebounding, recurrence, reflection, resounding, reverberation, vibration, whirring

resonant buzzing, carrying, echoing, hollow, humming, lingering, persisting, pulsating, reboant, rebounding, resounding, reverberating, stentorian, vibrating, whirring

resonate boom, buzz, echo, hum, oscillate, rebound, recur, resound, reverberate, vibrate, whir

resort betake oneself, go, haunt, have recourse, head for, help, leave for, seaside, spa, tourist town

resound alliterate, beat, drum, echo, hammer, oscillate, pound, pulse, reverberate, rhyme, throb, thrum, vibrate

resource deposits, fountain, gasfield, mine, oilfield, quarry, reserve, seam, source, supply, vein

respect admire, appreciate, appreciation, approbation, approval, attention, authority, consideration, esteem, favour, honour, prestige, prize, recognition, regard, relation, repute, treasure, value

respectable estimable, laudable, praiseworthy, reputable, upright, venerable, worthy

respected admired, appreciated, esteemed, honoured, prestigious, prized, revered, reverenced, time-honoured, valued

respectful appreciative, attentive, bootlicking, ceremonious, compliant, considerate, courteous, deferential, dutiful, fawning, gracious, honorific, humble, ingratiating, kowtowing, obeisant, obsequious, polite, regardful, servile, submitting

respectfulness attentions, comity, courtesy, deference, devotion, humbleness, humility, loyalty

respond answer, counteract, react, rebuff, recoil, reply, retaliate, retort, riposte, understand

response effect, fall-back, reaction, rebuff, recoil, reflex, repercussion, reply, retort, retreat, retroaction, riposte

restless excited, fevered, feverish, fidgety, flustered, fluttering, fluttery, fussing, itchy, twitchy

restlessness agitation, aimlessness, desultoriness, excitability, fever, feverishness, fiddling, fidgetiness, fret, inattention, insomnia, itchiness, jumpiness, nervousness, pottering, sleeplessness, the fidgets, twitchiness, unease, unrest, wakefulness

restoration amends, atonement, compensation, deliverance, derestriction, provision, rebuilding, recall, reclamation, reconstitution, reconstruction, reconversion, recovery, redemption, redress, re-establishment, rehabilitation, reinstallation, reinstatement, reinstitution, reinvestment, remodelling, reparation, replacement, replenishment, rescue, restitution, resumption, retrieval, returning, revival, salvation, strengthening, transfer

restorative analeptic, curative, healing, medicated, recuperative, redemptive, remedial, reparative, reviving, sanative

restore atone, compensate, overhaul, rally, reappoint, reassemble, rebuild, recall, recommence, reconstitute, reconstruct, recover, redeem, redo,

re-establish, reform, reformulate, rehabilitate, reinforce, reinstall, reinstate, reinstitute, reintroduce, relaunch, remake, reorganize, reorient, replace, replenish, reprogramme, rescue, restart, restock, resume, retrieve, return, revalidate, revive, salvage, save, service, start afresh, strengthen, undo, unmake

restrain anchor, ban, bar, bind, box in, brake, censor, chain, check, circumsribe, coerce, constrain, constrict, control, curb, curtail, cut, demarcate, discipline, drag, exclude, fetter, handcuff, hem in, hinder, impede, interdict, keep out, leash, limit, muzzle, oppress, patrol, police, pressure, prevent, prohibit, punish, quash, quell, regulate, rein, repress, restrict, retard, retrench, rope, shackle, slow, squeeze, stifle, stipulate, stop, straitjacket, suppress, tether, tie, veto

restraining authoritative, circumscriptive, coercive, conditional, constrictive, disciplined, exclusive, frozen, injunctive, interdictive, interventional, limiting, monopolistic, narrow, oppressive, preventive, prohibitive, restrictive, severe, slow, stifling, strict, suppressive

restraint anchor, apron strings, authority, bar, bolt, bond, brake, catch, censorship, chain, check, circumscription, clamp, clasp, composure, constraint, constriction, control, coolness, crackdown, crushing, curb, curtailment, discipline, D-notice, doorstop, exclusivity, fetter, handcuffs, hasp, hindrance, impediment, injunction, interdict, knot, latch, lead, leash, limitations, lock, muzzle, obstacle, padlock, prevention, prohibition, quashing, quelling, rein, requirement, retardation, retrenchment, rope, self-control, shackles, smashing, smothering, squeeze, stifling, stipulation, straitjacket, tether, throttling, tie, veto

restricted choice, elite, limited, private, secret, select

result answer, arise, difference, emanate, ensue, equation, flow, issue, product, remainder, score, solution, spring, sum, tally, total, turn out
may indicate an anagram

retailer baker, butcher, dealer, distributor, florist, (green)grocer, haberdasher, mercer, merchant, middleman, milliner, monger, newsagent, provisioner, regrater, shopkeeper, storekeeper, tailor, tobacconist, tradesman, wholesaler
See also list at **occupation**.

retain buttonhole, employ, grab, keep, remember

retained bound, circumscribed, clasped, clutched, contained, detained, employed, fast, fenced in, glued, grasped, gripped, gummed, held, imprisoned, kept, penned, pinioned, pinned, preserved, refused, remembered, saved, stapled, strangled, stuck, walled in, withheld
may indicate a split word

retaliate answer, avenge, boomerang, counter, hit back, parry, punish, react, reciprocate, recoil, recoup, repay, requite, resist, retort, riposte, round on

retaliation an eye for an eye and a tooth for a tooth, backlash, boomerang, comeback, comeuppance, counteraction, counterblast, counterplot, counterstroke, counter suit, dueness, just deserts, justice, Nemesis, punishment, reciprocation, redress, rejoinder, reparation, repayment, reprisal, retort, retribution, revenge, riposte, talion, vengeance

retaliatory argumentative, commutative, compensatory, convertible, counterblasted, countercharged, counterstated, exchangeable, interchangeable, interjecting, punitive, rebutted, reciprocal, recriminatory, refutative, refutatory, retaliative, retributive, revengeful, substitutive, vengeful, vindictive

retention adhesion, clasp, clinging

on, grabbing, grip, hanging on, holding, persistence, prehension, retainment, seizure, stickiness, stranglehold, tenaciousness, viscidity

retentive adhesive, clasping, clinging, clogged, cohesive, constipated, costive, firm, grasping, gripping, indissoluble, parsimonious, retaining, tenacious, tight-fisted, vicelike

rethink have second thoughts, reconsider, revise

retract backtrack, recant, sheathe, withdraw

retreat back out, disengagement, fall back, give ground, haven, hideaway, pull back, recess, refuge, resign, retire, run away, sanctuary, withdraw, withdrawal

retribution comeuppance, doomsday, judgment, just deserts, justice, Nemesis, reckoning, repayment, reprisal, requital, retaliation, vengeance

retroactive backward-looking, nostalgic, reactionary, retrospective

retrospect anecdote, autobiography, flashback, hindsight, history, looking back, memoirs, remembrance, reminiscence, reprise, review

retrospective backward-looking, diachronic, remembering, reminiscing, retroactive

return atone, comeback, commute, deliver, extradite, go back, homecoming, kick back, make restitution, ransom, reappearance, reappoint, rebirth, rebound, recall, recoil, recurrence, recursion, recycle, redeem, reenthrone, re-entry, reestablish, regress, rehabilitate, reincarnation, reinstate, reinvest, relapse, remember, remuneration, renaissance, renewal, repatriate, replace, reprise, requite, rescue, restoration, restore, retrocede, revert, revival, round (trip), shuttle, swing, yield
may indicate a backward

returning atonement, deliverance, extradition, ransom, reappointment, recycling, redemption, reenthronement, reestablishment, rehabilitation, reinstatement, reinvestment, repatriation, replacement, requital, rescue, restitution, restoration, retrocesson, reversion

reuse reclaim, recycle, reprocess, salvage

reveal accentuate, advertise, betray, bring forth, communicate, disclose, divulge, emphasize, enhance, evidence, evince, explain, expose, express, highlight, illuminate, indicate, inform, lay bare, manifest, open up, point up, proclaim, promote, publicize, publish, show, solve, spotlight, spread out, uncover, unearth, unfold, unfurl, unmask, unveil

revelatory apocalyptic, epiphanic, explanatory, explicatory, expository, interpretive, manifesting

revenge poetic justice, punishment, reprisal, requital, retaliation, retribution, vengeance

revenue bonus, credits, earnings, gain, incomings, interest, premium, proceeds, profits, receipts, return, royalties, takings, turnover

reverberation alliteration, assonance, beat, drumming, echo, hammering, oscillation, pulse, resonance, rhyme, rhythm, throb, vibration

reverberatory alliterative, assonant, beating, chanting, chiming, drumming, hammering, oscillatory, pulsating, resonant, rhyming, rhythmical, throbbing, vibrational

revere admire, adore, apotheosize, cherish, deify, hero-worship, honour, idolize, lionize, venerate, worship

reverent admiring, adoring, adulatory, awestruck, deifying, devout, idolizing, venerative, worshipping

reversal abjuration, abnegation, about-face, abrogation, apostasy, back-pedalling, backtracking, backup, cassation, denial, disavowal, disclamation, disownment, ebb, forswearing, inver-

sion, palinody, recantation, refluence, reflux, regurgitation, reneging, renunciation, repentance, repudiation, retraction, reversing, revocation, second thoughts, self- contradiction, tergiversation, treason, turnaround, U-turn, voidance

reverse abjure, abnegate, abrogate, apostasize, archaize, back, backfire, backslide, backtrack, betray, boomerang, B side, contradict oneself, converse, counteract, countermarch, desert, disavow, disclaim, disown, double back, ebb, equivocate, flip side, forswear, invert, opposite, react, rear, recant, recede, recidivate, recoil, regress, regurgitate, relapse, renege, renounce, repent, repudiate, retire, retract, retreat, retrogress, revert, revoke, revolt, ricochet, tergiversate, think again, turn, unsay, vacillate, waver, withdraw

reversed backfired, back-to-front, counter, inside-out, reacted, recanted, regressed, retired, retracted, retreated, returned, reverted, upside-down *may indicate a backword*

reversible recoverable, restorable, retrievable, returnable

reversion about-turn, apostasy, atavism, backfire, backlash, backsliding, counteraction, counter-reformation, counter-revolution, reaction, recantation, recession, recidivism, recoil, regression, relapse, repentance, retirement, retraction, retreat, retroaction, retroflexion, retrogression, retrospection, retroversion, return, ricochet, U-turn, volte-face, withdrawal

revival boom, comeback, palingenesis, prosperity, rally, reactivation, reanimation, reappearance, reawakening, rebirth, recovery, recruitment, recurrence, refreshment, regeneration, rejuvenation, renaissance, renewal, respiration, resurgence, resurrection, resuscitation, revitalization, revivification

revive reanimate, reawaken, refresh, regenerate, reinvigorate, rejuvenate, rekindle, renew, resurrect, resuscitate, revitalize

revoke abrogate, apostatize, cancel, deny, disavow, disclaim, negate, recant, repudiate

revolt defend oneself, disgust, fight off, horrify, mutiny, rebel, rise up

revolution breakaway, circle, coup (d'état), guerrilla warfare, insurgence, insurrection, mutiny, orbit, putsch, rebellion, resistance, revolt, rotation, sans-culottism, schism, secession, sedition, terrorism, transformation, turn, uprising
may indicate an anagram or *a backword*

reward acclaim, acclamation, acknowledgment, award, bounty, bouquet, credit, decorate, favour, gratitude, honours, praise, present, prize, recognize, recompense, remunerate, satisfy, thanks, tribute

rewarded acclaimed, acknowledged, credited, paid, praised, recognized

rewarding advantageous, gainful, lucrative, money-making, paying, profitable, remunerative, satisfying, worthwhile

rhetorician classicist, demagogue, euphuist, orator, phrasemonger, purist, speaker, stylist, wordsmith, wordspinner

rheumy chylific, humoral, ichorous, lachrymal, phlegmy, purulent, pussy, sanious, serous, suppurating, tearlike, weeping

rhythm beat, drumbeat, heartbeat, metre, pulse, syncopation, tempo, timing

ribald barbarius, bawdy, blue, coarse, crude, filthy, immoral, indecent, lewd, obscene, provocative, rabelaisian, rude, scatalogical, smutty, unmentionable, unprintable, unquotable

riddle enigma, mystery, pelt, pepper, puzzle, sieve, strafe

ridicule burlesque, caricature, deride, despise, guy, humiliate, imitation, impersonation, irony, jeer, lampoon, mockery, pan, parody, pasquinade, rag, roast, sarcasm, satirize, scoff, scorn, send-up, skit, sneer, snort, squib, take-off, taunt, tease

ridiculing derisive, ironic, mocking, sarcastic, satirical

ridiculous absurd, asinine, bizarre, burlesque, clownish, comic, comical, daft, derisory, droll, eccentric, farcical, far-fetched, fatuous, foolish, funny, hilarious, humourous, knock-about, laughable, nutty, preposterous, priceless, rib-tickling, risible, rum, side-splitting, slapstick, witty, zany
may indicate an anagram

right accurate, authority, birthright, claim, correct, decent, desert, direct, due, entitlement, equitable, fair, fix, just, justified, mend, prerogative, proper, R, rectitude, repair, straight, true

righteousness godliness, integrity, probity, rectitude, uprightness, virtue

right-handed dextral, dextrorotary

right-minded decent, law-abiding, sane, sober, sporting

ring band, bend, blare, carillon, chime, chink, circle, circumambulate, circummigrate, circumnavigate, circumvent, clang, clink, compass, curve, ear-ring, flank, gird, girdle, jangle, jingle, knell, lap, loop, O, peal, ping, skirt, sound, surround, tinkle, tintinnabulate, toll, twang, wedding ring
See also list at **jewellery**.

ringing blare, campanology, carillon, chime, chink, clang, clink, ding-dong, fanfare, flourish, jingle, knell, loud, pealing, pinging, pip, resounding, sounding, ting-a-ling, tinkle, tintinnabular, tintinnabulation, toll, tucket
may indicate a split word

ringroad bypass, detour, orbital, scenic route

rise ascend, climb, culminate, get up, grow, incline, increase, mount, peak, originate, progress, rear up, shoot up, uprise

rising airborne, anabatic, ascendant, ascensional, bullish, buoyant, escalating, floating, lifting, mounting, rampant, rearing, rocketing, soaring, upcoming, upgoing, uprising, zooming *may indicate a backword*

risk chance, danger, dare, defy, gamble, hazard, speculate, venture

rite almsgiving, blessing, ceremony, chalukah, confession, hymn-singing, penitence, potlatch, praise, prayer, psalm-singing, puja, ritual, sacrifice, supplication, thanksgiving

ritual ceremony, convention, correctness, custom, drill, form, formality, formula, habit, liturgy, mass, observance, procedure, protocol, rite, routine, sacrament, service, smartness, traditional

ritualistic ceremonial, chrismal, festive, fetishistic, libational, liturgical, oblational, sacral, sacramental, sacrificial, symbolic, totemistic

river affluent, beck, bourn, branch, brook, brooklet, burn, canal, confluence, creek, cut, Dee, distributary, Exe, feeder, flower, freshet, gill, millstream, rill, rillet, rivulet, runnel, sike, stream, streamlet, tributary, wadi, watercourse, waterway

road A, AI, alley, artery, Autobahn, autoroute, autostrada, avenue, B, boulevard, box junction, bridge, bypass, byway, camber, carriageway, causeway, chicane, circus, clearway, close, court, crescent, crossroads, cul-de-sac, dead end, dirt, drive, farm track, feeder, filter, flyover, hairpin bend, hard shoulder, highway, interchange, intersection, junction, lane, M, main, mews, M1, motorway, overpass, path, place, ring, roundabout, route, row, side, single track, slip, street, terrace, thoroughfare, T-junction, toll, track, trunk, underpass, wynd

robe bathrobe, caftan, cassock, chiton, clothe, drape, dress, gown, himation, housecoat, jacket, kimono, negligée, pallium, peignoir, sari, toga, tunic, wrapper

rock bob, boulder, bounce, careen, dance, flutter, lump, lurch, mineral, monolith, nod, pebble, pitch, reel, rock' n' roll, roll, shake, stagger, stone, swag, sway, swing, totter, tumble, undulation, waddle, waggle, wave, waver

rocky flinty, granite, gravelly, gritty, lapideous, lithic, lithoid, lumpy, marble, pebbly, rock-hard, stone

rogue bad egg, bad influence, bad lot, blackguard, black sheep, bounder, cad, ne'er-do-well, scoundrel, shit, ugly customer, undesirable

role antagonist, bit part, cameo, character, function, part, position, protagonist, support, vignette, walk-on

roll bap, bowl, crank, furl, reel, revolve, rotate, rumble, screw, scroll, spin, trill, troll, trundle, twist, wamble, wind, yarn

romance affair, amour, amourette, daydream, entanglement, fairy tale, fantasy, flirtation, intrigue, liaison, love affair, novel, relationship, seduction

roof canopy, ceiling, dome, eaves, flat roof, gable, gambrel roof, hipped roof, imbricated roof, lid, mansard roof, pitched roof, plaster, thatch, tile, top

room accommodation, airspace, amplitude, bathroom, bedroom, berth, berthage, capacity, clearance, compartment, headroom, kitchen, latitude, leeway, lounge, margin, play, scope, seating, seaway, storage, stowage, swing, windage

rot contaminate, decay, infect, mildew, mould, nonsense, pollute, putrefaction

rotary centrifugal, centripetal, circling, circulatory, circumgyratory, circumrotatory, cyclic, cyclonic, dizzy, giddy, gyratory, orbital, pivotal, torsional, trochilic, turbinated, vertiginous, vortical
may indicate a palindrome

rotate circle, circuit, circulate, circumnutate, circumvolve, gyrate, gyre, hinge, orbit, pirouette, pivot, revolve, spin (round), swing (round), swivel, turn, twirl, waltz, wheel, whirl

rotation circuition, circulation, circumference, circumnavigation, circumnutation, circumrotation, circumvolution, cycle, full circle, gyration, orbit, revolution, revs, spin, turbination, volution

rotator airscrew, autogyro, bobbin, capstan, centrifuge, circular saw, drill, fan, gyro(scope), impeller, prop, propeller, rotor, screw, spindle, spin-dryer, spinning top, spit, spool, treadmill, turbine, turnspit, turntable, ultracentrifuge, wheel, whisk, winder, windmill

rough aggressive, chafing, coarse, corrugated, craggy, crinkly, crude, crumpled, fibrous, fretting, galling, grained, granular, grating, grinding, gritty, hairy, heavy-going, heavy-handed, homespun, impassable, impenetrable, inequal, irregular, linsey-woolsey, muricate, nonuniform, ragged, rasping, ribbed, rippled, roughcast, roughhewn, rude, ruffled, rugged, rugose, textured, tough, tweedy, twilled, undulatory, uneven, unnavigable, unpolished, unrefined, unsifted, unsmooth, vague, violent, woolly, wrinkled

roughen break, coarsen, corrugate, crack, crease, crenate, crinkle, crumple, emboss, engrail, fold, furrow, gnarl, granulate, grate, hack, indent, kink, knot, mill, notch, pothole, roughcast, rough-hew, ruffle, rumple, sandpaper, serrate, stud, tangle, tousle, wrinkle
may indicate an anagram

roughness aggression, bristliness, brokenness, bumpiness, choppiness, clumsiness, coarseness, corrugation, cragginess, crudeness, deckle edge, granulation, hairiness, hispidity, horripilation, inequality, irregularity, jaggedness, joltiness, knobbliness, lumpiness, nodosity, nonuniformity, nubbiness, raggedness, rudeness, ruggedness, rugosity, saw edge, scabrousness, scaliness, scraggliness, scratchiness, serration, shagginess, sketchiness, spininess, toughness, turbulence, unevenness, vagueness, villosity, violence, wrinkliness

round ambit, ammunition, approximate, bell-shaped, bowl, bulbous, circle, circuit, circumambulation, circumnavigation, conical, convex, cylindrical, egg-shaped, gibbous, globose, groove, hemispherical, lap, madrigal, orbicular, orbit, ovoid, part-song, perfected, revolution, rotund, rut, spherelike, spherical, tubular, turn
may indicate a backword

rounded chubby, complete, corpulent, curvaceous, curvy, fat, fleshy, mature, obese, overweight, paunchy, pear-shaped, plump, podgy, portly, pot-bellied, shapely, sinuous, stout, tubby, undulatory, wavy

roundness circularity, convexity, curvaceous, cylindricality, gibbousness, globosity, orbicularity, plumpness, rotundity, sphericity

rout break, crush, destroy, drub, flatten, KO, lick, overwhelm, send packing, thrash, trample underfoot, trounce, whip, whitewash, wipe out

route access, approach, beat, bypass, circuit, circumference, circumlocution, course, dadit, detour, direction, drive, itinerary, lane, line, march, orbit, passage, path, road, run, track, trail, trajectory, way

rove divagate, excurse, pererrate, straggle, wander

rub abrasion, brush, buff, burnish,

chafe, curry, dress, furbish, irritation, levigate, massage, obstacle, polish, predicament, sand, sandblast, sandpaper, scour, scrub, smooth, wax

rubber caoutchouc, ebonite, elastomer, eraser, gutta-percha, latex, neoprene, vulcanite

rubbish baloney, bosh, bunkum, criticize, debris, garbage, hogwash, hokum, hooey, junk, refuse, scraps, trash
may indicate an anagram

rude barefaced, bawdy, bluff, brash, cheeky, coarse, contemptuous, crude, derisive, disrespectful, inhospitable, obscene, offensive, primitive, raw, rough, sassy, simple

rudeness contempt, derision, disrespectfulness, harshness, obscenity, offence, plainness, ridicule, roughness, simplicity, vulgarity

rudiment base, basics, bedrock, beginnings, building blocks, egg, element, first step, foundation, fundamentals, germ, groundwork, hypothesis, preparation, principle, raw material, root, seed, spadework, spore

rudimentary basic, elementary, fundamental, immature, rudimental, undeveloped

ruin apocalypse, bankruptcy, bedevil, blow, breakdown, break-up, calamity, cataclysm, catastrophe, clobber, collapse, crack-up, crash, death knell, débâcle, deface, dilapidation, disaster, dish, doom, downfall, failure, flatten, floor, hamstring, hobble, insolvency, knock flat, KO, loss, mar, meltdown, mutilate, perdition, ruination, scupper, sink, smash, spifflicate, spoil, trash, trounce, upheaval, waste, Waterloo, wreck, write-off
may indicate an anagram

rule act, adjudicate, bylaw, colonize, commandment, control, covenant, decide, declare, decree, deem, determine, directive, edict, enactment, establish, fiat, find, govern, injunction, judge, law, lay down, mandate, occupy, ordain, order, ordinance, prescribe, prescription, principle, pronounce, regulate, regulation, reign, resolve, ruler, settle, statute, ukase

ruler autocrat, Big Brother, captor, despot, dictator, duce, jack-in-office, martinet, monarch, oppressor, petty tyrant, satrap, shogun, slide rule, tin god, tyrant, warlord

ruling authoritative, commanding, controlling, dominant, influential, masterful, powerful, reigning, sovereign, supreme

rum
may indicate an anagram

run abscond, be off, blur, bolt, charge, coop, course, dash, decamp, depart, desert, disembogue, drain, drip, duration, elope, escape, flee, flood, flow, fly, go, hurry, inundate, jog, leave, make off, mingle, overflow, part company, pour, quit, race, retire, retreat, rush, scamper, scoot, score, scurry, slop, snag, spill, sprint, withdraw

rung level, notch, peg, stage, step

·S·

ABBREVIATIONS

S	Mr (Italian: *signor*) • on (French: *sur*) • school • second • seven (medieval Roman numeral) • shilling • soh • spades • sulphur
SA	Salvation Army • sex appeal • south • South Africa • South America • undated (Latin: *sine anno*)
SAD	seasonal affective disorder
SAE	stamped addressed envelope
SAM	Samaritan • Samuel
SAT	Saturday • standard assessment task
SB	Sam Browne (military belt) • Special Branch
SC	self-contained • small capitals • social club • Special Constable
SD	semi-detached • special delivery
SDI	Strategic Defense Initiative
SDP	Social Democratic Party
SE	London district • selenium • southeast • stock exchange
SEC	second • secondary • secretary • section
SERPS	State Earnings-Related Pension Scheme
SF	science fiction • strongly accented (Italian: *sforzando*)
SG	Secretary General • specific gravity
SI	silicon • Star of India
SIT	sitting room • situation
SM	sadomasochism • sales manager • Sergeant Major
SN	tin
SO	standing order • Symphony Orchestra
SOC	socialist • society
SOCO	scene-of-crime officer
SOE	Special Operations Executive (WW2)
SOL	solicitor • solution
SOS	save our souls • Secretary of State
SP	special • without issue (Latin: *sine prole*)
SQ	sequence • Squadron • Square
SRN	State Registered Nurse (now RGN)
SS	secret service • sections • ship • Nazi paramilitary organization (German: *Schutzstaffel*)
ST	Saint • stanza • statute • Summer Time
STE	French Saint
SUB	subeditor • subscription • submarine

---

sacred consecrated, holy

sacred object ark, aronha-kodesh, asperger, asterisk, beadroll, black stone, Bo tree, bugia, candle, chalice, crucifix, Holy Grail, holy water, icon, incense, menorah, phylactery, prayermat, prayer shawl, prayerwheel, relic, rosary beads, tallith, Torah scrolls

sacrifice abandon, abandonment, burn, crucifixion, crucify, immolate, immolation, martyr, martyrdom, oblation, offering, relinquishment, renunciation

sacrificial conciliatory, consecrated, contributory, donated, expiatory, martyred, oblatory, propitiatory

sad crestfallen, desolate, disconsolate, distressed, doleful, dolorous, downhearted, forlorn, grief-stricken, heartbroken, heavyhearted, inconsolable, languishing, miserable, mournful, pining, sorrowful, tearful, tormented, ululant, unhappy, woebegone, wretched

safe assured, bank vault, benign, certain, clear, defended, dependable, drinkable, edible, garrisoned, guaranteed, guarded, harmless, immunized, imprisoned, innocent, innocuous, intact, lockbox, nonflammable, nontoxic, patronized, potable, preserved, protected, reliable, risk-free, salubrious, screened, secure, sheltered, shielded, snug, sound, spared, strongbox, sure, tame, trustworthy, undamaged, unexposed, unharmed, unhazardous, unhurt, uninjured, unmolested, unpolluted, unscathed, unthreatened, unthreatening, warranted

safeguard attend to, baby-sit, care for, chaperone, check, inspect, invigilate, nurse, survey, watch over

safety assurance, avoidance, certainty, confidence, deliverance, faith, guarantee, harmlessness, immunity, impregnability, invulnerability, protection, rescue, security, warranty, welfare

sage academic, counsellor, guru, herb, highbrow, intellectual, know-all, mage, mentor, pundit, savant, Socrates, wise man

said
may indicate a homophone

sail back, cast off, crab, cruise, embark, gybe, launch, luff, pay off, race, scud, spread canvas, tack, veer, weigh anchor, yaw

sailor AB, admiral, argonaut, boatswain, bosun's mate, buccaneer, cabin boy, captain, circumnavigator, coastguardsman, coxswain, deckhand, fisherman, foretopman, hearty, helmsman, Jack, leadsman, marine, mariner, matelot, naval officer, navigator, old salt, pilot, pirate, privateer, quartermaster, reefer, RN, sea dog, seafarer, seaman, shipmate, ship's master, ship's steward, skipper, steersman, tar, whaler, wheelman

saint acolyte, altruist, believer, bodhissatva, catechumen, charismatic, convert, devotee, disciple, fakir, friend, good neighbour, Good Samaritan, helper, holyman, Holy Mary, Madonna, marabout, martyr, monk, mystic, neophyte, nun, Our Lady, patron saint, philanthropist, pilgrim, priest, redeemed soul, rescuer, sadhu, the Virgin, well-wisher, white knight, worshipper

salad coleslaw, macedoine
may indicate an anagram

sale auction, bazaar, car-boot, clearance, closing-down, Dutch auction, fair, jumble, roup, selling off, sell-out, transaction

saleable available, marketable, merchantable, vendible

salesman agent, rep, representative, shop assistant, shopwalker, traveller

salesmanship hard sell, patter, pitch, service, spiel

saliva dribble, drivel, foam, froth, salivation, slabber, slaver, slobber, spit, spittle

salivate dribble, drivel, drool, slabber, slaver, slobber, spit, splutter

sallow bilious, jaundiced, pale, sickly, wan, yellowish

sally break-out, breakthrough, offensive, sortie, thrust

salubrity fitness, health, healthiness, nutritiousness, well-being, wholesomeness

salutation advances, appeal, court, exhortation, greeting, hail, invocation, peroration, praise, salaam, suit, valediction, welcome

salute address, applaud, banners, chair, cheer, drum roll, fanfare, fête, flags, fly-past, garland, greet, lionize, march-past, mob, present arms, salvo, tattoo, tickertape, tribute, triumph, welcome

same absorbed, agreed, assimilated, coalescent, consubstantial, homogeneous, homoousian, idem, identical, indistinguishable, isotrophic, matching, merging, one, redundant, repeated, repetitious, selfsame, solid, tautologic, undifferentiated, united, unvarying, verbatim

sameness agreement, assimilation, coalescence, identicalness, indistinguishability, isotrophy, mergence, oneness, repetition, selfsameness, solidarity, tautology, uniformity, unity

sanatorium health farm, hot springs, spa, thermae

sandpaper emery paper, file, glasspaper

sandwich burger, butty, club sandwich, hot dog, poor-boy, sarnie, toasted sandwich

sane compos mentis, normal, reasonable, sober, sound, together

sanity normality, sobriety, stability

satellite asteroid, dependant, entourage, groupie, hanger-on, moon, planet, spaceship, Sputnik, star, sun

satirize caricature, lampoon, parody, send up, take off

satisfaction comfort, complacency, contentedness, ease, enjoyment, equanimity, fulfilment, gratification, happiness, pleasure, satiation, serenity, smugness, thankfulness

satisfactory acceptable, adequate, enough, fair, OK, passable, permissible, so-so, sufficient, tolerable, worthwhile

satisfied comfortable, complacent, content, fulfilled, full, gratified, happy, pleased, satiated, serene, smug, thankful, uncomplaining

satisfy content, fill, fulfil, gratify, indulge, please, quench, sate, satiate, slake

sauce aïoli, apple sauce, barbecue sauce, béarnaise sauce, béchamel sauce, bolognese sauce, bordelaise sauce, bourguignonne, bread sauce, brown sauce, catsup, chaudfroid, cheek, cheese sauce, cranberry sauce, demiglace, dip, fondue, French dressing, gravy, hollandaise sauce, horseradish sauce, impertinence, ketchup, mayonnaise, milanese sauce, mint sauce, onion sauce, roux, salad cream, salad dressing, sauce espagnole, sauce suprême, soy sauce, Tabasco sauce, tartare sauce, velouté, vinaigrette, white sauce, Worcester sauce

sauciness brass, cheek, disrespect, freshness, impertinence, impudence, pertness, sassiness

saunter amble, crawl, creep, drip, hirple, hobble, idle, inch along, laze, limp, mince, ooze, plod along, scuff, shamble, shuffle along, stroll, toddle along, traipse, trickle, trudge

sausage banger, bologna sausage, boloney, bratwurst, chipolata, Cumberland sausage, frankfurter, garlic sausage, herb sausage, liver sausage, polony, salami, sausagemeat, saveloy, Vienna sausage, wienerwurst

save cut costs, deliver, economize, emancipate, keep, liberate, release, reprieve, rescue, reserve, retrench, scrape, scrimp

say
may indicate a homophone

scale delaminate, desquamate, exfoliate, extent, flake, peel, ranking, scope, sequence, shave, strip

scales balance, calibrator, scale, steelyard, weighbridge, weighing machine

scant few, meagre, sparse

scar blemish, cicatrix, mark, pimple, pockmark, spot, stain, weal, welt, zit

scarce few, infrequent, nonexistent, rare, short, sparse, unavailable, unobtainable, unprocurable

scarcity dearth, deprivation, diminution, drought, famine, leanness, need, paucity, poverty, shortage

scatter broadcast, disperse, disseminate, dot about, sow, space out, spread, sprinkle, string out
may indicate an anagram

scenery backcloth, backdrop, cyclorama, decor, flat, landscape, surroundings

sceptical agnostic, cynical, distrustful, doubting, journalistic, philosophical, Pyrrhonist, scientific

scheme conspire, contrive, devise, intrigue, plan, plot, wangle
may indicate an anagram

schoolroom campus, classroom, common room, dormitory, formroom, gymnasium, hall, laboratory, language laboratory, library, sanatorium, schoolhouse, staffroom, workshop

science biochemistry, biology, chemistry, electromagnetism, geophysics, mechanics, nucleonics, physics, technology, thermodynamics

scope berth, clearance, elbowroom, latitude, leeway, leverage, manoeuvrability, microscope, opportunity, oscilloscope, play, range, room, telescope

score count, mark, scratch, tally

scorn abuse, answer back, asperse, belittle, blackening, challenge, confront, contempt, dare, debasement, defame, defilement, degradation, denigrate, depreciate, derision, despise, disagree, disdain, disobey, disparage, disregard, dissent, ignore, insult, oppose, rebel, refuse, resist, revilement, run down,

scurrility, slight, spurn, tarnishing, taunt, threaten, trivialize, usurp, vilification

scornful contemptuous, contumelious, derisive, mocking, ridiculing, sarcastic, scoffing, sneering

scrambled
may indicate an anagram

scraping grazing, scouring, scratch, scratching, scrubbing, scuff, scuffing

scream gasp, groan, ouch, ow, shriek, squeal, whimper, whine

screen blind, buffer, camouflage, cloak, cover, curtain, guard, mask, shutter, veil

scrutinize fix upon, heed, nit-pick, study, survey

sculpt carve, cast, chip, chisel, cut, form, model, mould, shape, whittle

sculpted
may indicate an anagram

sculptor carver, caster, chaser, engraver, etcher, figurist, lapidary, modeller, monumental mason, moulder, statuary

sculptural anaglyptic, ceroplastic, glyptic, graven, marmoreal, monumental, moulded, plastic, toreutic

sculpture anaglyptics, aquatint, bust, cameo, carving, caryatid, casting, chasing, cire-perdue, embossing, engraving, etching, figure, figurine, group, head, intaglio, medal, medallion, modelling, moulding, plastic art, relief, statuary, statue, statuette, stonecutting, torso, waxwork

sea brine, high seas, main, ocean, ocean blue, seven seas, the billow, the deep

seafront esplanade, marina, prom, promenade, shore, strand

seaside beach, coastal, littoral, shoreline, tideline, waterfront, waterside

season acclimatize, accustom, anneal, autumn, cure, curry, discipline, dry, fall, flavour, harden, interval, inure, kipper, marinate, mature, pepper, period, pickle, salt, smoke, souse, spell, spice, spring, summer, term, toughen, winter

seasonable appropriate, convenient, opportune, providential, seemly, suitable, timely, welcome, well-timed

seasoned accustomed, curried, flavoured, hardened, inured, matured, salted, spiced, toughened

seasoning additive, chutney, condiment, curry, dressing, flavouring, garlic, garnish, gherkin, ketchup, marinade, mayonnaise, onion, pepper, pickle, relish, salt, sauce, vinaigrette

secluded cloistered, deserted, desolate, hidden, isolated, private, quiet, remote, sequestered, uninhabited

secondary by-side, incidental, low-level, minor, peripheral, subsidiary

secrecy blackout, censorship, concealment, confidentiality, cover-up, misinformation, privacy, silence, suppression

secret censored, classified, closed, confidential, hush-hush, intimate, isolated, off-the-record, private, privy, restricted, sealed, secluded, suppressed, top-secret, undisclosed, undivulged, unrevealed, unspoken, untold

secrete cry, discharge, eject, emanate, emit, excrete, exude, lacrimate, lactate, liberate, perspire, produce, release, salivate, sweat, transude, void, weep

secretion crying, discharge, ejection, emanation, emission, excretion, exudation, lacrimation, lactation, perspiration, release, salivation, sweating, transudation, voidance, weeping

secretive cabalistic, clandestine, cloak-and-dagger, close, conspirational, covert, furtive, reticent, silent, sly, stealthy, surreptitious, undercover, underhand

secretiveness cabal, clandestineness,

conspiracy, counterintelligence, covertness, espionage, furtiveness, intrigue, mole, omertà, plot, shiftiness, spy, stealth

secretory salivary, sudatory, sweaty

sections catalogue, chapters, chart, checklist, code, divisions, glossary, index, inventory, items, list, register, schedule, table, tally, themes, topics

secure anchor, defend, deterrent, guard, immune, impregnable, invulnerable, lock away, patrol, police, protect, protective, safe, safeguard, safekeep, shelter, shield, support, sure

security accept responsibility, answer for, assure, attest to, certify, chit, commit oneself, contract, insure, IOU, pawn ticket, premium, promissory note, secure, take on, underwrite, voucher, vouch for

sedentary bedridden, bent, crouching, dormant, housebound, hunched, passive, prostrate, shut-in, sitting, squatting, stay-at-home, stooping, supine

sediment bedrock, boulder, chesil, clay, delta, deposit, granules, gravel, loess, mud, ooze, pebbles, rock, sand, shingle, silt, stone

seditionist anarchist, collaborator, conspirator, extremist, fifth columnist, freedom fighter, guerrilla, Guy Fawkes, infiltrator, insurgent, insurrectionist, Luddite, nihilist, partisan, quisling, revolutionary, rioter, saboteur, spy, subversive, tergiversator, terrorist, traitor, urban guerrilla

see behold, catch on, descry, discern, discover, distinguish, espy, glimpse, look at, meet, notice, perceive, recognize, sight, sightsee, spectate, spot, twig, understand, watch, witness

seedy dog-eared, down-at-heel, moth-eaten, shabby, tacky, tatty

seeing aware, clear-sighted, discerning, eagle-eyed, far-sighted, glaring, goggle-eyed, hawk-eyed, imaginative, looking, noticing, observant, perceptive, perspicacious, pop-eyed, sharp-eyed, sighted, staring, vigilant, visionary, watchful, watching

seep dribble, drip, exude, leak, ooze, percolate, perspire, sweat, trickle, weep

seepage draining, percolation, permeation

segregate boycott, cold-shoulder, detach, discriminate against, divide, ghettoize, isolate, ostracize, quarantine, remove, seclude, sequester, shun, slight, snub

segregation boycott, discrimination, ghettoization, ostracism, preclusion, seclusion, sequestration

select accept, adopt, choose, coopt, decide, determine, differentiate, discern, discriminate, distinguish, elect, judge, opt, plump for, prefer, sort

selecting choosing, choosy, deciding, decisive, discerning, discretional, discriminating, eclectic, exercising choice, favouring, optional, particular, picky, preferential, selective, showing preference, volitional

selection adoption, anthology, appointment, assortment, choice, commission, decision, designation, determination, discretion, discrimination, eclecticism, elite, excerpts, gleanings, judgment, nomination, pick, range, shortlist, variety

self-abasing deferent, diminishing, dispirited, self-abnegating, self-deprecating, self-doubting, self-effacing, self-submitting, submitting

self-absorbed egotistic, narcissistic, self-centred, self-devoted, selfish, self-loving, self-obsessed, self-worshipping, vain

self-admiration narcissism, self-endearment, self-esteem, self-worship, smugness, superciliousness, vaingloriousness

self-assured appointed, authorized, autocratic, bossy, commissioned, controlling, domineering, high-handed, imperious, lordly, mandated, powerful, self-confident, superior

self-deception delusion, make-believe, wishful thinking

self-indulgence carnality, epicureanism, hedonism, luxury, pleasure-seeking, self-gratification, sensuality, sybaritism, voluptuousness

self-interest egocentricsm, egotism, me-ism, self-centred, self-centredness, selfishness, solipsism

selfish acquisitive, ambitious, avaricious, cold-hearted, covetous, envious, greedy, individualistic, jealous, materialistic, mean, mean-spirited, miserly, money-grubbing, monopolistic, niggardly, opportunistic, parsimonious, possessive, self-centred, self-indulgent, self-interested, self-pitying, self-seeking, self-serving, stingy, uncharitable, ungenerous

self-reliant confident, determined, dogged, intrepid, persevering, resolute, self-assured, steadfast, tenacious, unafraid, unfearing

self-restrained abstemious, abstinent, ascetic, celibate, chaste, continent, cool, costive, dieting, economical, fasting, forbearing, formal, frugal, inhibiting, introversive, Lenten, moderate, modest, parsimonious, pent up, plain, prohibited, pure, puritanic, quiet, refraining, renunciative, repressive, reserved, restrictive, self-controlled, self-denying, self-disciplined, self-sufficient, shy, sober, sparing, spartan, stiff, stinting, strait-laced, strict, teetotal, temperate, uptight

self-restraint abstinence, asceticism, avoidance, celibacy, chastity, constraint, continence, dieting, embarrassment, eschewal, fasting, forbearance, formality, inhibition, introversion, moderation, modesty, prohibition, purity, quietness, renunciation, repression, reserve, restriction, self-abnegation, self-control, self-denial, self-discipline, self-sufficiency, shyness, soberness, spartanism, stiffness, teetotalism, temperance, veganism, vegetarianism

self-righteousness affectation, genteelism, gravity, Grundyism, mealy-mouthedness, narrow-mindedness, overmodesty, pietism, priggishness, primness, prudery, puritanism, sanctimony, seriousness, shockability, smugness

self-satisfaction complacency, self-congratulation, smugness, solipsism

sell auction, barter, canvass, carry, convey, deal, dump, encash, exchange, flog, gain, handle, hawk, lose, market, merchandise, peddle, promote, push, realize, reduce, remainder, retail, solicit, stock, tout, trade, transfer, undercut, unload, vend, wholesale

seller auctioneer, bear, consignor, transferor, vendor

selling advertisement, auction, barter, conveyance, deal, dealing, disposal, distribution, exchange, marketing, merchandising, peddling, promotion, retail, trade, traffic, transaction, transfer, vending, wholesale

semantic lexical, linguistic, philological, semiotic, verbal

semiliquid colloid, emulsion, emulsoid, glop, goo, guck, gunge, gunk, incrassate, inspissate, paste, semifluid, slime, sticky, viscid, viscous

semiliquidity erassitude, gaum, semifluidity, spissitude, stickiness, viscidity, viscosity

send address, consign, direct, dispatch, forward, mail, pack off, post, redirect, shake off, shoo off, transmit

seniority lead, pre-eminence, superiority, supremacy

sensate audible, noticeable, palpable, perceptible, tactile, tangible, visible

sensation agitation, awareness, consciousness, emotion, excitement, experience, feeling, hearing, impression, perception, reaction, receptivity, response, sensum, sentience, sentiment, sight, smell, taste, thrill, touch

sense detect, experience, feel, hear, horripilate, itch, notice, perceive, prickle, react, realize, respond, see, smell, taste, tickle, tingle, touch

sensible aware, feeling, percipient, practical, rational, reasonable, sane, sensitive, sentient

sensitive affectible, amicable, aware, bathetic, caring, compassionate, cordial, delicate, emotional, empathetic, feeling, fond, friendly, highly strung, impressible, impressionable, maudlin, mawkish, nostalgic, overcome, overwhelmed, overwrought, perceptive, receptive, responsive, romantic, sentient, sentimental, sloppy, soft-hearted, suggestible, susceptible, sympathetic, tearful, tender, warm

sensitiveness affectibility, awareness, commiseration, compassion, delicacy, empathy, impressibility, impressionability, pity, receptivity, responsiveness, sensibility, sentimentality, suggestibility, susceptibility, sympathy, tenderness

sensitivity delicacy, feelings, hyperaesthesia, prickliness, susceptibility, tenderness, thin skin, ticklishness, touchiness, vulnerability

sentence bird, fistful, handful, lag, life, porridge, stretch, time

separable breakable, discernible, dissolvable, distinguishable, divisible, fissionable, partiable, resolvable, scissile, severable, tearable

separate anarchic, apart, discrete, dissociated, divide, independent, isolated, nonassimilated, nonconforming, part, rebellious, removed, splay, split, unaffiliated

separateness apartheid, detachment, dichotomy, difference, disaffiliation, discreteness, dissociation, division, immiscibility, independence, insularity, isolation, isolationism, nationalism, nonassimilation, nonconformity, noninvolvement, partition, segmentation, segregation, separatism, severalty

separates accessories, add-ons, coordinates, peripherals

separation apartheid, Balkanization, banishment, blackball, blacklist, boycott, breakage, concealment, decomposition, deportation, detachment, deviation, disconnection, discontinuity, disintegration, disjunction, dislocation, dispersion, disruption, dissection, dissolution, disunion, divergence, divorce, estrangement, exclusion, exile, expulsion, fission, fragmentation, isolation, liberating, loneliness, loosening, ostracism, parting, purdah, quarantine, rejection, resolution, retreat, scattering, schism, seclusion, segregation, separability, separating, severance, shattering, solitariness, split, splitting, spreading, uncoupling, unfastening

separator border, caesura, comma, dash, diaeresis, dividing line, full stop, hyphen, interface, partition, slash, solidus, umlaut

sequel aftermath, coda, consequence, continuation, development, epilogue, follow-up, postlude, postscript, series, upshot

sequence consecutiveness, following, procession, progression, serialization, succession

sequential consecutive, continuous, following, progressive, sequacious, serial, succeeding, successional

serenity calmness, collectedness, composure, coolness, disinterest, imperturbability, inexcitability, insouciance, tranquillity

series alternation, chain, course, cycle, line, rotation, run, string, train

serious elevated, grand, grave, heavy, important, impressive, intense, lofty, majestic, significant, solemn, solid, sublime, weighty

seriousness attention, elevation, eloquence, grandeur, gravity, importance, impressiveness, loftiness, prominence, significance, solemnity, sublimity, weight

servant amah, assistant, attendant, au pair, ayah, bailiff, butler, chamberlain, chambermaid, char, charwoman, chauffeur, cook, daily help, dishwasher, domestic, driver, drudge, employee, factotum, farmhand, flunky, follower, footman, gardener, gentleman's gentleman, groom, handmaiden, handyman, help, henchman, hireling, house boy, housekeeper, housemaid, inferior, labourer, lackey, lady-in-waiting, liegeman, maid, maidservant, major-domo, manservant, menial, minion, nannie, nursemaid, orderly, parlourmaid, retainer, servitor, skivvy, stableboy, steward, subaltern, subordinate, underling, wench, worker

serve accompany, assist, attend, cater for, char, clean for, follow, help, look after, minister to, obey, oblige, pander to, tend, wait on, work for

servile abject, compliant, deferential, dependent, menial, slavish, submissive, subservient

servility abjectness, compliance, deference, helotism, menialness, peonage, pliancy, serfdom, slavery, slavishness, submission, subservience

session bout, go, innings, phase, shift, spell, stint, tenure, term, turn, watch, whack

setback blow, hindrance, hitch, obstacle, reversal, snag, stumbling block, upset
may indicate a backward

set in
may indicate a split word

set out be off, board, cast off, embark, emerge, get off, hop on, issue forth, jump on, march off, mount, move off, sally forth, set forth, set sail, start out, strike out, take off, weigh anchor

settle bill, board, burrow, charge, colonize, crash, domicile, dwell, encamp, ensconce oneself, gatecrash, immigrate, inhabit, invoice, locate, lodge, move in, nest, nestle, pay up, people, perch, pioneer, populate, quarter, reside in, roost, square up, squat, stable, trespass

settlement hamlet, municipality, suburbs, town, village

settler colonizer, immigrant, incomer, pioneer, precursor

seven diminished seventh, heptad, heptadic, heptagon, heptagonal, heptahedral, heptahedron, heptameter, heptangular, Heptateuch, heptatonic, septenary, septennial, septet, septuagenarian, septuple, septuplet, septuplicate, seven days, sevener, sevenfold, seventh, week

sever bite, blow up, break, break up, cannibalize, carve up, chip, chop, cleave, crack, crumble, crunch, cut, decay, decompose, degrade, demobilize, destroy, detach, disassemble, disband, disconnect, disengage, disentangle, disintegrate, dislocate, dismantle, dispel, disperse, displace, dissolve, disunite, divorce, eject, expel, fracture, gash, grind, hack, hew, lacerate, ladder, liberate, loosen, mash, mince, pulverize, relax, release, rend, rip, rive, rupture, saw, scatter, shatter, shiver, shred, slacken, slash, slice, slit, smash, snap, splinter, stab, sunder, tear, throw, unbind, unbutton, unclasp, uncouple, undo, unfasten, unfetter, unhitch, unlock, unpick, unplug, unravel, unseat, untie, unzip, wrench

severe authoritarian, autocratic, bossy, brutal, callous, censorious, coercive, cruel, despotic, dictatorial, dominating, domineering, Draconian, exacting, exploitative, Fascist, fastidious, firm, formal, fundamentalist, hard, hard-headed, hardhearted, harsh, heavy-handed, inflexible, inhumane, inquisitorial, intolerant, merciless, militaristic, obstinate, oppressive, orthodox, pedantic, pitiless, repressive, rigid, rigorous, stern, strict, stringent, stubborn, totalitarian, tough, tyrannical, unbending, uncharitable, uncompromising, undemocratic, unforgiving, unsparing

severity asperity, authority, bigotry, bullying, callousness, clampdown, cruelty, discipline, fastidiousness, firmness, formality, fundamentalism, hardness, harshness, inclemency, inflexibility, inhumanity, intolerance, meticulousness, obstinacy, orthodoxy, pedantry, pitilessness, power, regimentation, restraint, rigidity, rigorousness, ruggedness, sternness, strictness, stringency, stubbornness, toughness, uncharitableness

sewer cesspool, drain, needle, tailor

sex bonking, coition, consummation, copulation, coupling, fornication, intercourse, intimacy, mating, pairing, procreation, propagation, reproduction, rumpy-pumpy, screwing, wedlock

sexual assault child abuse, date rape, flashing, gang rape, gross indecency, pederasty, rape, ravishment, sadism, violation

sexuality bisexuality, desire, heterosexuality, homosexuality, lesbianism, libido, orientation, preference, sexiness

shadow contour, figure, follow, form, framework, profile, relief, shape, silhouette, trace, track

shady clouded, cloudy, dark, dim, dirty, grimy, murky, obfuscated, obscure, shadowy, suspicious

shake beat, didder, drum, falter, fidget, go pitapat, jerk, jigger, jigget, jiggle, judder, palpitate, pulsate, pulse, quake, quaver, quiver, shiver, shudder, squirm, thrill, throb, tremble, tremor, twitch, twitter, vibrate, wag, waggle, wiggle, wriggle
may indicate an anagram

shaking quavering, quivering, succussion, tremulousness, vibration

shaky aguey, doddering, juddering, quaky, quavery, quivery, shaking, shivery, shuddering, succussatory, succussive, unsteady, vibratory, wobbly

shallow shoal, superficial, trivial

shallowness cursoriness, dusting, lightness, shoaliness, slightness, sprinkling, superficiality, superficies, surface, triviality

shame contrition, defile, degrade, demean, desecrate, disappointment, discredit, disgrace, dishonour, embarrass, humiliation, lower oneself, mortify, qualms, regret, remorse

shape build, carve, cast, chisel, compose, construct, create, cut, elaborate, evolve, fabricate, fashion, figure, forge, form, formulate, frame, hammer out, hew, make, manufacture, model, mould, produce, raise, round, sculpt, shape, style, tailor, turn, unify

shaped concrete, fictile, isomorphic, morphogenic, morphologic, plastic, Platonic, solid

shapeless amoebic, amorphous, blobby, blurred, featureless, formless, fuzzy, hazy, ill-defined, incomplete, indefinite, misty, obscure, raw, shadowed, unclear, uncut, undefined, undeveloped, unfinished, vague

shapelessness amorphousness, blurriness, chaos, featurelessness, fogginess, formlessness, fuzziness, haziness, incompleteness, mistiness, obscureness, obscurity, rawness, unclearness, undevelopment, vagueness

share communalize, communize, contribute, cooperate, go Dutch, internationalize, involve oneself, join, join in, nationalize, part, partake of, participate, portion, socialize

shared blended, common, compatible, cooperative, dovetailed, intermediary, interpenetrative, permeated, same

sharp acicular, acid, acuminate, acerbic, clever, conic, cultrate, cutting, ensiform, hastate, honed, intelligent, keen-edged, knife-edged, lanceolate, mucronate, pointed, pyramidal, razor-edged, sagittal, saw-edged, smart, sour, swordlike, tapered, tapering, unblunted

sharpen barb, edge, file, grind, hone, notch, oilstone, point, sandpaper, serrate, spur, strap, strop, taper, whet

sharpness acumination, bristliness, denticulation, dentition, mucronation, pointedness, prickliness, serration, spininess, thorniness

shave depilate, deplume, desquamate, excoriate, exfoliate, exuviate, flay, fleece, pare, peel, pluck, scalp, shear, skin, tonsure

shed flayed, go bald, moulted, recede, scalped, shaven, skinned, slough off

shedding depilation, desquamation, excoriation, exfoliation, exuviation, skinning

shelter asylum, awning, booth, bothy, camp, cover, deri, dive, dock, eyeshade, ghat, harbour, haven, hedge, hole, hovel, huddle, hut, hutch, joint, kiphouse, lean-to, lee, marina, outhouse, pigsty, port, quay, retreat, roof, safe house, screen, shack, shade, shanty, shed, shield, slum, squat, stockade, sunshade, windbreak

shine dazzle, gleam, glitter, gloss, glow, sheen, sparkle, twinkle

shirk make excuses, malinger, scrimshank, skive

shirking apathy, cop-out, inaction, inactivity, passivity, skiving

shirt blouse, bustier, dress shirt, evening shirt, halter, middy blouse, overblouse, polo shirt, smock, sweat shirt, tank top, top, T-shirt

shock blow, bombshell, eye-opener, facer, fright, horror, jolt, jump, mass, mop, mane, start, surprise, thatch, thunderbolt, turn

shoddiness badness, bad taste, baseness, cheapness, commonness, crumminess, gaudiness, inferiority, kitsch, lowness, meanness, paltriness, pettiness, pokiness, poorness, scruffiness, second-ratedness, shabbiness, vulgarity, worthlessness

shoddy base, crummy, gaudy, inferior, jerry-built, lousy, low, low quality, mangy, mean, paltry, poky, poor, scruffy, scummy, second-rate, shabby, shopsoiled, tacky, tatty, tawdry, tinpot, trashy, twopenny, unmarketable, unsaleable, useless, valueless, worthless

shoot blast, blow away, bombard, cannonade, detonate, discharge, explode, fell, fire, gun, hit, let fly, loose off, pistol, plug, strike, volley

shop browse, buy, expend, market, order, purchase, require, spend, spree, teleshop

short amiss, brief, compendious, concise, curt, deficient, diminutive, dumpy, half-done, inadequate, incomplete, insufficient, lacking, little, low, minus, missing, needy, pug-nosed, retroussé, scanty, scarce, skimpy, snub, squat, stocky, stubby, stumpy, stunted, succinct, summary, synoptic, terse, thickset, transient, unfinished, unfulfilled, unreached, vain, wanting

shortcoming blemish, defalcation, default, defect, deficiency, failure, fault, imperfection, inadequacy, inferiority

shorten abbreviate, abridge, abstract, axe, bob, capsulize, clip, compress, condense, crop, curtail, cut short, decapitate, digest, dock, elide, encapsulate, epitomize, foreshorten, lop, mow, poll, prune, reap, reduce, retrench, shave, shear, skimp, slash, stunt, summarize, telescope, trim, truncate

shortened clipped, compacted, contracted, curtailed, mown, reduced, sawn-off, shorn, summarized, synopsized, truncated

shortening abbreviation, abridgement, capsulization, compression, curtailment, decapitation, elision, encapsulation, epitomization, reduction, retrenchment

shortfall cursoriness, dearth, deficit, famine, incompleteness, insufficiency, lack, loss, need, noncompletion, perfunctoriness, requirement, scarcity, shortage, want

shortness brevity, briefness, compendiousness, conciseness, curtness, diminutiveness, dumpiness, littleness, lowness, scantiness, skimpiness, snubness, squatness, stockiness, stubbiness, stumpiness, stuntedness, succinctness, terseness, transience

short-sighted myopic, near-sighted

shot bombardment, bowshot, cannonade, detonation, discharge, ejection, fusillade, gunshot, salvo, spray, stoneshot, tattoo, volley

shout bawl, bellow, blare, boom, bray, cachinnate, catcall, caterwaul, cry, exclaim, howl, roar, scream, screech, shriek, shrill, squawk, thunder, trumpet, ululate, whistle, yell, yowl

shovel dredge, dredger, Persian wheel, pickaxe, rake, scoop, shadoof, spoon, toothpick

show act, advertise, appearance, ballet, carnival, circus, concert, demonstrate, demonstration, disclose, display, exhibit, exhibition, expose, façade, fête, fireworks, gala, highlight, illuminate, illustrate, image, indicate, manifest, manifestation, march, mask, mime, mirror, open, opera, pageant, parade, perform, persona, play, present, promenade, reflect, reveal, scene, spectacle, sport, spotlight, stage-manage, stunt, tableau, tattoo, tournament, uncover, unmask, window-dress

showbusiness burlesque, entertainment industry, Hollywood, music hall, showbiz, variety, vaudeville, West End

showiness demonstrativeness, ostentation, pretension, showmanship

side

show off boast, flaunt oneself, peacock, prance, preen oneself, promenade, strut, swagger, swank, upstage *may indicate an anagram*

showpiece antique, collectable, curio, example, exhibit, mock-up, museum piece, pride, specimen

showy brilliant, demonstrative, eye-catching, highlighted, high-profile, illuminated, lucid, ostentatious, outstanding, pretentious, prominent, remarkable, shameless, spectacular, spotlighted, stark, striking, visual, vivid

shriek catcall, creak, pipe, scream, screech, squeak, squeal, whistle, wolf-whistle

shrill acute, bleeping, creaky, ear-piercing, high-pitched, piping, reedy, sharp, squeaky, tinny, whistling

shrillness bleep, catcall, creak, falsetto, high note, high pitch, piping, scream, screech, shriek, squeak, squeal, whistle, whistling, wolf whistle

shrine cella, cromlech, dagoba, marae, naos, reliquary, sanctuary, stupa, tabernacle, tope

shrink abbreviate, abridge, avoid, belittle, circumscribe, clip, compact, compress, concentrate, condense, constrict, contract, cramp, crush, curtail, cut, decrease, deflate, diminish, dock, economize, emaciate, file, flatten, flinch, grind, jib, lessen, limit, miniaturize, minimize, narrow, pare, pinch, press, prune, psychiatrist, reduce, restrict, retrench, sear, shave, shear, shorten, shrivel, shy away, slash, slim, squeeze, strangle, stunt, telescope, thin, tighten, trim, waste, whittle away, wither

shrinking astringent, circumscriptive, collapsing, compressive, constricting, constringent, contracting, cramping, crushing, decreasing, deflationary, emaciating, gathering, lessening, limiting, narrowing, pinching, puckering, pursing, reducing, restricting, searing,

shortening, shrivelling, slimming, strangling, stunting, styptic, tabescent, thinning, tightening, waning, wasting

shunned blackballed, blacklisted, cold-shouldered, disbarred, exiled, outcast, struck off

shy back off, balk at, bashful, blench, blink, chuck, demur, diffident, draw back, embarrassed, flinch, frightened, funk, hang back, hurl, introverted, jib, lob, mouselike, refuse, retiring, retreat, self-conscious, shrink, shrinking, silent, start, taciturn, throw, timid, timorous

shyness agoraphobia, anthropophobia, bashfulness, blenching, blinking, diffidence, disposition, embarrassment, escapism, flinching, introversion, isolationism, jibbing, modesty, neutrality, nonintervention, noninvolvement, recoil, refusal, reluctance, retirement, retiring, retreat, revulsion, self-consciousness, shrinking, timidity, timorousness, unwillingness, withdrawal

sick bedridden, chronic, comatose, confined, critical, feverish, groggy, headachy, hospitalized, ill, incurable, indisposed, inoperable, moribund, off-colour, poorly, prostrate, quarantined, queasy, serious, taken ill, terminal, unwell, vomit, wasting away *may indicate an anagram*

sicken ail, collapse, deteriorate, droop, drop, fail, faint, feel ill, flag, languish, peak, pine, sink, suffer, vomit, weaken

sickening emetic, purgative

sickness anaemia, anorexia, asthenia, burnout, caducity, debility, decrepitude, deflation, depletion, disease, dissipation, dizziness, enervation, exhaustion, faintness, fatigue, flagging, frailty, giddiness, illness, infirmity, lameness, paleness, senility, shakiness, sickliness, thinness, tiredness, vertigo, waning, weakliness, weariness

side bilateral, cheek, collateral, edge, facing, far side, flank, flanking, hillside,

321

hip, jaw, jowl, lateral, laterality, lee, left, near side, oblique, offside, port, profile, quadrilateral, ribs, right, sideboards, sidelong, skirting, snobbery, spin, starboard, temple, windward

sidestep avert, avoid, deviate, gee, haw, jib, passage, shy, sidle, turn away

siege blockade, encirclement, encroachment, infringement, inroad, investment

sign autograph, banner, brand, cipher, clue, code, connotation, cue, emblem, equal sign, evidence, fingerprint, hieroglyphics, image, indicator, key, lead, marker, meaning, omen, password, placard, poster, representation, rune, scent, shibboleth, sigla, signal, signature, signpost, symbol, symptom, syndrome, token, traces, track, trail

signal alarm, alarum, alert, announce, beacon, bell, bleep, call, command, communicate, cry, declare, flare, foghorn, gong, hail, heliograph, herald, honk, hooter, horn, indication, inform, knell, light, manifestation, message, pips, pointer, proclaim, publish, rocket, semaphore, shout, siren, summon, warn, warning, whistle, wigwag

signalling announcing, calling, commanding, hailing, inviting, proclaiming, publishing, shouting, summoning, warning

significance drift, import, importance, meaning, pith, purport, sense, seriousness, substance, tendency, trend

significant consequential, important, meaty, of moment, pithy, serious, substantial, weighty

signify betoken, blazon, characterize, connote, denote, disclose, emphasize, highlight, imply, indicate, intimate, mean, represent, reveal, signalize, suggest, symbolize, symptomize, typify

signifying connotative, demonstrative, denotative, directional, disclosing, evidential, explanatory, expressive, identifying, indicative, interpretive, meaningful, ominous, pointing, presageful, prophetic, representative, revealing, signalizing, signalling, significative, suggestive, symbolic

signs autograph, blaze, countersign, demarcate, direct, gesture, guide, indicate, initial, mark, point to, signal, signpost

silence calm, closeness, confidentiality, discretion, drown, dumbness, faintness, gag, hush, inaudibility, lull, muffle, mute, mutedness, muteness, muzzle, noiselessness, peace, quell, quieten, quietude, reserve, rest, reticence, sh, shush, smother, softness, soundlessness, speechlessness, stifle, still, stillness, stop, subdue, taciturnity, voicelessness, wordlessness

silencer cork, damper, double-glazing, earplugs, filter, mute, soft pedal, soundproofing

silent aphasic, aphonic, calm, dumb, dumbfounded, faint, hushed, inaudible, mum, mute, muted, noiseless, peaceful, quiescent, quiet, reserved, reticent, soft, soundless, soundproof, speechless, still, stilly, tacit, taciturn, tight-lipped, unspoken, voiceless, withdrawn, wordless

similar akin, alike, allied, analogous, approximate, close, coincidental, commensurable, comparable, connected, corresponding, equivalent, homogeneous, homographic, homoiousian, homonymic, homophonic, identical, like, matching, near, parallel, related, resembling, same, symmetrical, synchronous, synonymous

similarity accordance, affinity, agreement, aping, approximation, assimilation, closeness, coincidence, comparability, conformity, copying, correspondence, equality, equivalence, homogeneity, homograph, homoiousia, homonym, homonymy, homophone, imitation, kinship, likeness, mimicking, nearness, parallel, parallelism, parity, portrayal, proportionality, resemblance, sameness, semblance, similitude, synchronicity, synonymousness, synonymy, uniformity

simple apodeictic, apodictic, articulate, ascetic, austere, backward, bald, bare, basic, clean, clear, clinical, common, common-or-garden, comprehensible, direct, distinct, downright, easy, elemental, elementary, everyday, exoteric, explained, explicit, forthright, fundamental, homespun, homy, humble, intelligible, interpreted, intrinsic, irreducible, legible, limpid, lowly, lucid, matter-of-fact, mere, minimal, modest, monolithic, mundane, no frills, obvious, one, ordinary, perspicuous, plain, popularized, prosaic, pure, quotidian, readable, self-evident, self-explanatory, severe, sheer, single, spare, Spartan, stark, straightforward, stupid, transparent, unadorned, unadulterated, unaffected, unassuming, unblended, uncomplicated, unelaborate, unified, uniform, unintelligent, unmingled, unmixed, unostentatious, unpretentious, utter, workaday

simplicity absoluteness, articulateness, asceticism, austerity, baldness, bareness, clarity, cleanness, clearness, clinicalness, commonness, decipherability, directness, distinctness, easiness, explicitness, facility, homeyness, homogeneity, humbleness, intelligibility, legibility, limpidity, lowliness, lucidity, minimalism, mundaneness, nakedness, neatness, obviousness, oneness, ordinariness, perspicuity, plainness, purity, self-evidence, severity, spareness, starkness, straightforwardness, transparency, unaffectedness, unambiguousness, uniformity, unostentatiousness, unpretentiousness

simplify articulate, clarify, elucidate, explain, explicate, facilitate, interpret, popularize, sort out, spell out, unify, unravel, unscramble

simulated aped, artificial, copied, counterfeit, cultured, duplicated, ersatz, false, imitated, imitation, mimicked, mocked, phoney, pseudo, replicated, spurious, synthetic

simultaneity accompaniment, coevality, coexistence, coincidence, concomitance, concurrence, contemporaneousness, synchronicity

simultaneous coeternal, coeval, coexistent, coincident, concomitant, concurrent, contemporary

sin assassinate, atrocity, blasphemy, crime, desecration, enormity, err, felony, go astray, illegality, impiety, impropriety, indiscretion, iniquity, injustice, kidnap, malpractice, misconduct, misdemeanour, murder, negligence, outrage, peccadillo, profaneness, rob, sacrilege, slip, steal, transgress, transgression, trespass, ungodliness, vice, wickedness, wrong, wrongdoing

sinful bad, criminal, deadly, devilish, evil, heinous, illegal, mortal, murderous, naughty, wicked

sing carol, chant, cheep, chirp, chirrup, chorus, croon, hoot, incant, lilt, peep, quaver, trill, tweet, twitter, vocalize, warble, yodel

singer belter, canary, crooner, songster, vocalist

single alone, bachelor, celibate, chaste, divorced, divorcee, loner, maiden aunt, separated, singleton, spinster, unmarried, widow, widowed, widower

singleness individuality, oneness, uniqueness

single out detach, isolate, pick out, separate

singular distinct, individual, once-in-a-lifetime, one-off, only-begotten, particular, special, unique

singularity distinctiveness, identity, individuality, particularity, specialness, uniqueness

sink descend, drain, gravitate, settle, washbasin

sinkage cadence, catenary, decline,

decrease, decurrence, depression, downgrade, droop, drowning, gravitation, immersion, lapse, lowering, sag, slump, submergence, subsidence

sit alight, bend, crouch, drape oneself, duck, hunch, land, lie down, park oneself, perch, prostrate, recline, scrooch down, seat oneself, spreadeagle, squat, stoop, supinate

situate deploy, direct, fix, install, locate, orientate, place, position, post, put, set, site, stand, station

situated appointed, employed, located, orientated, placed, pointed, positioned, seated, set, sited, stationed

situation altitude, aspect, bearings, circumstances, condition, direction, frontage, geography, job, latitude, locale, location, longitude, office, orientation, place, point, position, post, scene, seat, setting, side, site, spot, state, topography, venue

six half-a-dozen, hexachord, hexad, hexadecimal, hexadic, hexagon, hexagonal, hexagram, hexahedral, hexahedron, hexameter, hexangular, hexapod, Hexateuch, hexatonic, sexagenarian, sexagenary, sexennial, sexpartite, sextet, sextile, sextuple, sextuplet, sextuplicate, sixain, sixer, sixfold, six-footer, six-shooter, sixth, sixth form, sixth sense, threescore

sixth sense clairaudience, clairsentience, clairvoyance, cosmic consciousness, crystal vision, ESP, feyness, foresight, insight, intuition, metapsychosis, precognition, premonition, psi faculty, psychometry, second sight, telekinesis, telepathy, third eye

size accommodation, altitude, amount, amplitude, area, azimuth, breadth, bulk, burden, calibre, capacity, circumference, content, coordinates, coverage, cubature, declination, degree, depth, diameter, dimension, displacement, distance, dosage, expanse, extent, gauge, girth, glue, height, latitude, length, limit, longitude, magnitude,

mass, measurement, proportion, quantity, radius, range, reach, room, scale, scantling, scope, space, spread, stowage, tankage, tonnage, value, volume, weight, width

skeletal bony, osseous, ossicular, ossiferous, ossified, osteal

skeleton bone, bones, carapace, cartilage, chrondroblast, endoskeleton, exoskeleton, framework, horn, keratin, ligament, ossicle, ossification, osteoblast, outline, preliminary, sketch, tendon

sketch act, draft, draw, mock-up, rough, scene, skit

skilful A1, able, accomplished, ace, adaptable, adept, adroit, agile, apt, clever, competent, crack, cunning, deft, dexterous, diplomatic, efficient, excellent, first-rate, gifted, green-fingered, ingenious, intelligent, magisterial, masterful, nimble, panurgic, proficient, quick-witted, resourceful, shrewd, slick, smart, sound, superb, sure-footed, talented, topflight, topnotch, versatile, wise, wizard

skill ability, accomplishment, acquirement, adaptability, address, adeptness, adroitness, aptitude, art, attainment, capability, capacity, cleverness, competence, control, craft, craftsmanship, deftness, delicacy, dexterity, discretion, discrimination, ease, efficiency, excellence, execution, experience, expertise, exploitation, facility, faculty, finesse, flexibility, fluency, forte, grace, handiness, ingenuity, knowledge, mastery, métier, nous, professionalism, proficiency, prowess, resourcefulness, sagacity, sharpness, sophistication, speciality, stratagem, strength, style, tact, tactics, talent, technique, touch, trick, versatility, virtuosity

skin coating, cortex, cuticle, epidermis, exoskeleton, film, flay, hull, husk, veneer

skirted edged, fringed, valanced

sky clouds, firmament, heavens, space, welkin

sky-diver aeronaut, faller, free-faller, hang-glider, parachutist

skyscraper high-rise flats, tower block

slang argot, back slang, cant, colloquialism, dog Latin, pig Latin, rhyming slang

slant bank, cant, lean, list, pitch, tilt, tip

slapstick burlesque, farce, knockabout

slaughter annihilation, battle, battue, bloodbath, burn, butcher, butchery, carnage, decimation, demolish, destroy, destruction, ethnic cleansing, extermination, Final Solution, genocide, gun down, holocaust, kill, killing, liquidation, massacre, mass destruction, mass murder, mow down, noyade, nuke, pogrom, poleaxe, purge, ravage, scorch, shoot down, slay, the Holocaust, war, wipe out

slaughterhouse abattoir, arena, battleground, bullring, knacker's yard, shambles

slave bondservant, captive, serf, slavegirl, thrall, vassal

sled bobsled, bombardier, dogsled, drag, dray, jumper, luge, sledge, sleigh, snowboard, snowmobile, toboggan, troika

sleep aestivation, bye-byes, catalepsy, catnap, coma, dormancy, doze, doziness, dreamland, drowsiness, heaviness, hibernation, hypnosis, insensibility, kip, Morpheus, nap, nod off, oblivion, oscitancy, repose, rest, sandman, shut-eye, siesta, slumber, snooze, somnolence, stupor, trance, unconsciousness, yawn

sleepy aestivating, anaesthetized, comatose, doped, dopy, dormant, dozing, dozy, dreaming, drowsy, drugged, fuzzy, heavy-eyed, hibernating, hypnotized, insensible, narcotized, out cold, resting, sedated, slumberous, somnolent, soporific, torpid, unconscious, woozy, yawning

slice chip, collop, cut, disc, flake, lath, pane, panel, paring, plank, plaque, rasher, scale, shaving, slab, slat, slate, sliver, squama, tablet, tile, wafer

slide acclivity, coast, declivity, dip, glide, glissade, inclination, incline, list, oscillate, precipice, sideslip, skid, skim, slidder, slip, slither, slope, swing, tilt, toboggan, wobble

slim diet, lose weight, reduce, slenderize

slime glop, goo, gook, guck, gunge, gunk

slimming calorie-counting, dieting, reducing, slenderizing, weight-watching

slope pitch, sheer, slant, sweep, tack

slough cast, desquamate, ecdyse, exuviate, moult, shed

slow ambling, clumsy, crawling, creeping, dragging, dull, faltering, flagging, halting, hobbling, limping, lumbering, plodding, sauntering, shambling, shuffling, slouching, snail-paced, staggering, strolling, stupid, tottering, waddling

slow down arrest, back-pedal, brake, check, curb, decelerate, delay, detain, ease off, hinder, impede, moderate, obstruct, reef, rein in, relax, retard, slacken off, stay

slowness amble, circumspection, crawl, creeping, dawdle, deliberation, dilatoriness, dragging, Fabianism, gradualism, hobble, indolence, inertia, inertness, jog, languor, laziness, leisureliness, lentitude, lethargy, limp, lumbering, methodicalness, meticulousness, patience, piaffer, plod, pottering, restraint, saunter, shamble, shuffle, slackness, sloth, slouch, sluggishness, stroll, trot, trudge, unhurriedness, waddle, walk

sly acute, arch, artful, astute, beguiling, cagey, calculating, canny, cautious, clandestine, clever, conspiring, contriving, covert, crafty, crooked, cunning, deceitful, devious, dishonest, disingenuous, equivocal, experienced, feline, flattering, fly, foxy, guileful, hypocritical, imaginative, ingenious, insidious, insincere, intelligent, intriguing, inventive, knavish, knowing, knowledgeable, Machiavellian, pawky, perfidious, planning, plotting, practising, rascally, reserved, resourceful, reticent, scheming, secret, serpentine, sharp, shifty, shrewd, skilful, slick, slippery, smart, sophistic, sophistical, sophisticated, stealthy, strategical, subtle, tactical, temporizing, timeserving, tricksy, tricky, underhand, urbane, vulpine, wary, well-laid, wily, wise

small infinitesimal, insignificant, minute, petty, tiny

smaller abbreviated, abridged, boiled-down, circumscribed, clipped, closed-up, collapsed, compact, compressed, concentrated, condensed, constricted, contracted, crushed, curled-up, curtailed, decreased, drawn-in, emaciated, flat, gathered, huddled, miniaturized, narrowed, pinched, pruned, puckered, pursed, reduced, rolled-up, scaled-down, seared, shorn, shortened, shrivelled, shrunk, smocked, squeezed, stunted, telescoped, trimmed, tucked, wasted, withered, wizened

smile beam, chortle, chuckle, crow, giggle, grin, guffaw, laugh, purr, rejoice, sing

smoky cloudy, foggy, misty, smoggy, steamy, vaporing

smooth allay, alleviate, ameliorate, appease, assuage, bald, buff, butter, calm, charm, clean-shaven, close-woven, coat, comb, cottony, creepy, downy, even, fine, fine-grained, fine-woven, flatten, fleecy, flush, frictionless, glabrous, glacé, glaze, glib, grease, hairless, harrow, ingratiating, iron, level, levigate, lubricate, mangle, mitigate, mow, oil, pacify, paint, pave, peachlike, plane, plush, polish, press, rake, refined, roll, rub, sand, satiny, shave, silken, silky, sleek, slick, slimy, slippery, slithery, smarmy, soft, soothe, sophisticated, starch, streamlined, suave, sycophantic, toady, unctuous, urbane, varnish, velvety, wax, waxy, woolly

smoothness calm, calmness, downiness, evenness, finish, flatness, fleeciness, flushness, glassiness, glossiness, greasiness, horizontality, levelness, levigation, lubrication, lustre, oiliness, peacefulness, plushiness, quiescence, regularity, serenity, shininess, silkiness, sleekness, slickness, slipperiness, slitheriness, softness, stillness, unctuousness, uniformity

snag aggravation, annoyance, catch, complication, dead end, deadlock, drawback, halt, hindrance, hitch, hurdle, impasse, inconvenience, obstacle, obstruction, pitfall, stalemate, stop, teething troubles

snake adder, asp, betrayer, double-crosser, Judas, python, serpent, turncoat, twister, viper, traitor

snaky anguine, colubriform, colubrine, serpentiform, serpentine, sinuous, twisting, viperish, winding

snare ambush, catch, decoy, divert, entangle, gin, hijack, kidnap, lure, net, trap, waylay

snipe game bird, pick off, pot, potshot, torpedo

snow avalanche, blizzard, cocaine, freeze, hail, hailstone, ice over, slush, snowball, snowdrift, snowflake, snowman, Snow Queen, spindrift, whiteout

soar ascend, climb, mount, rise

sob bawl, blub, blubber, cry, fret, gasp, groan, howl, keen, lament, mewl, moan, pule, sigh, ululate, wail, weep, whimper, whine, yammer

sober abstemious, abstinent, calm,

clear-headed, composed, dignified, dry, grave, prohibitionist, restrained, serious, steady, strict, teetotal, temperate, unfuddled

sobriety abstemiousness, abstinence, teetotalism, temperance

sociability affability, amiability, amicability, Bohemianism, clubbishness, communicativeness, companionability, conviviality, cordiality, friendliness, geniality, graciousness, gregariousness, hospitality, joviality, kindness, neighbourliness, relaxedness, socialness, warmth

sociable affable, affectionate, amiable, amicable, Bohemian, cheerful, civil, clubbish, communicative, companionable, convivial, cordial, courteous, easy-going, extrovert, free-and-easy, friendly, genial, gracious, gregarious, hail-fellow-well-met, hearty, hospitable, inviting, jolly, jovial, lively, matey, merry, neighbourly, outgoing, pally, party-minded, relaxed, smiling, social-minded, urbane, warm, welcoming

socialize civilize, gather, industrialize, interact, make merry, organize, party, rage, rave, reform, urbanize

social services community service, DSS, social security, social work, welfare state

societal clannish, communal, cultural, customary, ethnic, familial, federal, folk, national, racial, received, traditional, tribal

society association, clan, class, club, collectivity, community, elite, family, group, high society, nation, people, race, the public, tribe

sociological behavioural, communal, educational, environmental, social, societal, sociobiological, socioeconomic

sociologist demographer, social psychologist, social scientist, social worker, sociobiologist

soft easygoing, feeble, flabby, flaccid, flimsy, floppy, fluffy, fluid, gentle, lax, lenient, limp, loose, muted, nonrigid, p, pp, quiet, relaxed, rubbery, slack, soppy, sprung, tender, unstrung

soften bend, chew, cushion, drench, featherbed, flop, fluff, grease, impress, knead, liquefy, loosen, lubricate, macerate, mash, massage, mature, mellow, melt, mould, oil, pad, plump, pulp, pulverize, relax, ripen, sag, shape, slacken, spring, squash, steep, tenderize, unbend, unstiffen, wax, whip

softhearted compassionate, complaisant, delicate, easygoing, gentle, kind, lax, lenient, mellow, mild, relaxed, sympathetic, tender, warmhearted

softness bendability, extendibility, extensibility, flabbiness, flaccidity, flexibility, floppiness, fluffiness, gentleness, give, impressibility, laxness, lenience, limberness, limpness, litheness, looseness, malleability, nonrigidity, pliability, rubberiness, slackness, suppleness, tractability, weakness

soft option breeze, cinch, doddle, picnic, plain sailing, pushover, sinecure, sitting duck, snap, walkover

soil alluvium, clay, dirty, earth, gravel, loam, mar, mud, regolith, sand, silt, spoil, stain, subsoil, topsoil

solecism clumsiness, crack, dysphemism, epigram, gag, howler, joke, laugh, malapropism, pun, quip, riddle, scream, spoonerism, vulgarism, wellerism, wisecrack, witticism

solemn deadpan, dour, frowning, glum, grave, grim, humourless, long-faced, pensive, poker-faced, sedate, serious, severe, sober, sombre, staid, stern, stony-faced, straight-faced, sullen, thoughtful, unsmiling

solemnity dourness, gloom, gravitas, gravity, grimness, humourlessness, severity, staidness, sternness, sullenness, thoughtfulness

solicit accost, appeal, beg, bother,

busk, cadge, canvass, freeload, hustle, mooch, pester, scrounge, sponge, tap

solicitation appealing, begging, bothering, busking, cadging, canvassing, freeloading, fund-raising, mendicancy, mooching, pestering, scrounging, sponging

solicitous anxious, attentive, caring, concerned, considerate, courteous, gallant, indulgent, mindful, protective, worried

solicitude anxiety, attendance, care, consideration, courtesy, gallantry, indulgence, protection, spoiling

solidification arteriosclerosis, calcification, crystallization, fossilization, glaciation, granulation, hardening, lapidification, ossification, petrifaction, sclerosis, setting, steeling, tempering, vitrification, vulcanization

solidify calcify, candy, concentrate, condense, crystallize, emulsify, firm, fossilize, freeze, gel, glaciate, granulate, jell, ossify, petrify, set, stabilize, stiffen, thicken, vitrify

soliloquize apostrophize, monologize, talk to oneself, think aloud

soliloquy apostrophe, aside, monodrama, monody, monologue, ravings

solitary alone, aloof, antisocial, isolated, lone, reclusive, sole, standoffish, unsociable

solo alone, independent, one-man, one-woman, single-handed, unaccompanied, unaided, unassisted, unchaperoned

solution answer, antidote, clearing up, conclusion, contrivance, decoction, decoding, denouement, discovery, emulsion, explanation, infusion, interpretation, issue, measure, outcome, plan, reason, remedy, resolution, resolving, resource, result, sorting out, suspension, unscrambling, upshot, working out

solve clear up, conclude, contrive, decode, discover, equate, explain, interpret, measure, plan, reason, remedy, resolve, score, sort out, sum, total, unscramble, work out

solved concluded, decoded, sorted out, unscrambled, worked out

solvency credit-worthiness, independence, self-sufficiency, solidity, soundness, substance

solvent anticoagulent, credit-worthy, dissolvent, liquifier, resolvent, solid, sound, thinner

song air, anthem, aubade, barcarolle, berceuse, calypso, cantide, carol, cavatina, chanson, chant, chorale, chorus, glee, hymn, lay, lilt, lullaby, lyric, madrigal, plainchant, psalm, round, roundelay, serenade, shanty, solo, spiritual, strain, tune, yodel

songbird bunting, crow, finch, flycatcher, jackdaw, lark, magpie, nightingale, oriole, passerine, pipit, raven, rook, shrike, sparrow, starling, thrush, tit, wagtail, warbler, weaverbird, wren *See also list at* **birds**.

soothe assuage, calm, lull, pacify, tranquillize

soothing alleviative, analgesic, anodyne, assuaging, bland, calming, comforting, demulcent, disarming, easing, emollient, hypnotic, lenitive, lubricating, mesmeric, narcotic, nonirritant, pacificatory, pain-killing, peaceful, quiescent, quiet, sedative, smooth, soft, soporific, still, tranquillizing

sophism antilogy, fallacy, paradox, solecism

sophistic baseless, casuistic, circular, contradictory, contrived, distorted, dubious, empty, equivocal, erroneous, fallacious, faulty, fictitious, flawed, groundless, illogical, illusory, inconsequential, inconsistent, invalid, irrational, jesuitic, logic-chopping, misapplied, misinformed, misleading, paradoxical, paralogistic, pseudosyllogistic, rhetorical, solecistic, specious, spurious, superficial, tortuous, unfounded, unreasonable, unsound, untenable

sophistry casuistry, circularity, distortion, equivocation, fallaciousness, illogicality, inconsistency, jesuitry, logic-chopping, misapplication, moonshine, philosophism, sleight, solecism, speciousness, subterfuge

soporific anaesthetic, barbiturate, morphine, narcotic, nepenthe, nightcap, opiate, sedative, sleeping pill, somnifacient

sore aggrieved, allergic, angry, blister, inflamed, itchy, nettled, offended, painful, peeved, raw, resentful, sensitized, tender, ticklish, tingling

soreness allergy, itchiness, rawness, tenderness, ticklishness, tingling

sorrow agony, anguish, bleed for, desolation, distress, dolour, downheartedness, grief, grieve, heartache, heartbreak, heavyheartedness, lament, languishment, misery, mourning, pain, regret, sadness, suffering, torment, unhappiness, weep for, woe, wretchedness

sort analyse, arrange, assort, breed, codify, divide, genre, grade, ilk, index, kidney, kind, order, organize, rank, rate, species, subdivide, tabulate, type, variety
may indicate an anagram

sound able-bodied, beat, blow, bow, din, fiddle, fit, healthy, lip, noise, pick, pluck, recovered, strong, strum, tongue, toot, trumpet, twang, well, whistle
may indicate a homophone

soup bisque, borscht, bouillabaisse, bouillon, broth, clear soup, cock-a-leekie, consommé, cream soup, gazpacho, gravy, gruel, gumbo, julienne, minestrone, mulligatawny, porridge, potage, purée, Scotch broth, slops, stew, stock, vichysoisse
may indicate an anagram

sour acidic, acidify, acrid, bitter, crabbed, crotchety, curdle, ferment, go bad, irritable, moulder, off, sharpen, spoil, turn

source authority, birthplace, breeding ground, bud, channel, cradle, egg, embryo, fertile soil, fount, fountain, fountainhead, germ, grapevine, hatchery, home, hotbed, incubator, mainspring, mine, nest, nucleus, nursery, origin, primordial soup, protoplasm, provenance, quarry, root, seed, wellhead, wellspring, womb

sourness acerbity, acidity, acidulousness, astringency, bitterness, dryness, greenness, sharpness, tartness, unripeness, vinegariness

sovereign Caesar, caliph, crown prince, crown princess, emperor, empress, Kaiser, Kaiserin, khan, king, maharajah, mikado, Mogul, monarch, nabob, Pharaoh, pound, prince, prince regent, princess, queen, queen mother, queen regent, rajah, rani, Regina, Rex, shah, sultan, tsar, tsarina

sow cast, disperse, disseminate, distribute, fling, foster, initiate, litter, scatter, seed, strew

space area, blank, breadth, break, capacity, circumference, clear, cosmos, depth, diameter, dimension, expanse, extent, gap, heavens, height, hole, interspace, interval, lacuna, length, make room, measure, pause, proportion, separate, size, surface, tract, universe, void, volume, width
See also list at **astronomer**.

spacecraft Apollo, Atlantis, Challenger, Columbia, Discovery, lunar module, Mir, module, Salyut, Skylab, space capsule, spacelab, space laboratory, space platform, space probe, spaceship, space shuttle, space station

spaced discontinuous, interspaced, interstitial, intervallic, parted, removed, separate

spacious airy, ample, amplitudinous,

broad, capacious, cavernous, commodious, deep, enormous, expansive, extended, great, high, immense, lofty, long, outsized, roomy, sizeable, vast, voluminous, wide

spaciousness capaciousness, expansiveness, extensiveness, immensity, roominess, vastness, voluminousness

sparse dispersed, dotted about, empty, exiguous, infrequent, intermittent, light, little, low-density, meagre, measly, minimal, niggardly, occasional, rare, scant, scarce, scattered, sporadic, sprinkled, strung out, tenuous, thin, uncommon, underpopulated, understaffed, vacuous, void

sparseness airiness, buoyancy, delicacy, emptiness, ethereality, fineness, flimsiness, gaseousness, immateriality, insubstantiality, lightness, rarity, scarcity, slightness, tenuity, thinness, vacuity, voidness, volatility, windiness, wispiness

spasm convulsion, fit, jerk, jump, paroxysm, rictus, seizure, throes, tic, twitch, vellication

spatial cosmic, cubic, dimensional, flat, proportional, radial, space-time, spatiotemporal, stereoscopic, superficial, surface, two-dimensional, volumetric

speak articulate, blurt out, cite, declare, ejaculate, enunciate, exclaim, express, interject, interrupt, mention, phrase, proclaim, pronounce, quote, recite, relate, respond, rhyme, say, state, talk, tell, utter, verbalize, vocalize, vociferate, voice

speaking articulate, fluent, loquacious, outspoken, talkative, voluble, well-spoken

specification bounding, bounds, check, circumscription, conditions, confinement, control, definition, delimitation, demarcation, determination, limitation, mandate, prescription, proscription, qualification, restriction

specify bind, check, circumscribe, confine, control, define, delimit, demarcate, determine, frame, indicate, limit, measure, oblige, particularize, prescribe, proscribe, qualify, quantify, require, reserve, restrain, restrict, stipulate

spectacle apparition, emanation, ghost, hallucination, hologram, marvel, miracle, mirage, pretence, prodigy, revelation, seeming, sight, vision

speculate conjecture, estimate, gamble, guess, hypothesize, invest, prospect, risk, venture

speculation conjecture, estimation, guesswork

speculative chancy, conceptual, conjectural, deliberative, dreamy, fanciful, introspective, inventive, meditative, musing, notional, pondered, profound, risky, suppositional, theoretical

speech accent, address, broadcast, cant, chat, chinwag, colloquy, conversation, dialect, dialogue, diatribe, discourse, dissertation, earful, encomium, eulogy, exhortation, harangue, homily, idiom, invective, jargon, language, langue, lecture, monologue, mouthful, natter, obloquy, obsequies, oration, panegyric, parlance, parole, patois, patter, peroration, rabbit, rap, reading, recital, sermon, slang, speaking, spiel, talk, talking, tirade, tongue, valedictory , vernacular, vocabulary, yakkety-yak
may indicate a homophone

speech defect aphasia, babbling, dysphasia, dysphemia, lallation, lisping, paraphasia, sibilation, stammer, stutter

speechless agog, choked, dumb, dumbfounded, gagged, gobsmacked, inarticulate, mum, mute, reticent, silenced, silent, taciturn, tongue-tied

speechmaker declaimer, demagogue, expositor, lecturer, orator, pontificator, preacher, pulpiteer, rabble-rouser, ranter, reader, rhetorician, sermonizer, spokesperson, tub-thumper

speed accelerate, bolt, bowl along, bustle, careen, career, chase, dash, expedite, fidget, flit, fly, fret, fume, hasten, hurry, hurtle, hustle, lope, precipitate, race, rattle along, run, rush, scamper, scoot, scour, scurry, scuttle, skirr, sprint, spurt, streak, sweep along, tear off, thunder along, whirl, whisk, whizz, wing, zip, zoom

speed agility, breakneck speed, briskness, career, celerity, fastness, fleetness, flurry, hastiness, hurry, instantaneity, knot, Mach number, nimbleness, promptness, quickness, racing, rapidity, rashness, speediness, swiftness, velocity

spell abracadabra, abraxas, allure, attraction, charm, conjuration, curse, evil eye, glamour, glossolalia, hex, hocus pocus, incantation, jinx, mumbo jumbo, open sesame, paternoster, pentagram, period, philtre, rune, stretch, wanga, weird, whammy, write out

spelling orthography, phonetic spelling

spend fritter, idle, kill, squander, waste, while away

spendthrift extravagant, prodigal, profligate, squanderer, waster, wastrel

sphere ambit, area, arena, bailiwick, ball, balloon, bead, branch, bubble, bulb, business, concern, course, discipline, domain, drop, egg, field, forte, globe, globule, interest, jurisdiction, line, marble, métier, orb, orbit, pale, pea, pellet, pigeon, pill, province, realm, scope, spheroid, territory, theatre

spiky acanthoid, awned, barbed, brambly, briery, bristly, hispid, prickly, pricky, spiked, spiny, star-shaped, stellate, stinging, thistly, thorny

spin attitude, bias, braid, extrude, plait, slant, turn, twiddle, twist

spinning braiding, circling, interbraiding, intertwining, orbiting, plaiting, rotating, spiralling, twining, twirling, twisting, whirling

spirit astral body, atman, ego, geist, ghast, ghost, ghoul, gin, hooch, id, kamarupa, linga sharira, liquor, phantom, psyche, soul, spectre, superego, the subconscious, the unconscious, third eye, vodka, whisky

spiritual airy, alien, astral, creepy, disembodied, eerie, eldritch, elemental, ethereal, extramundane, extraterrestrial, ghostly, holy, immaterial, incorporeal, intangible, otherworldly, phantasmal, religious, shadowy, spectral, spooky, strange, supramundane, transmundane, uncanny, unearthly, unworldly, weird

spleen bile, bitterness, crabbedness, moroseness, rancour, sour grapes, sullenness

splenetic bilious, bitter, crabbed, grumpy, harsh, morose, rancorous, sarcastic, sullen

split abscission, amputation, breach, break, castration, chasm, cleavage, cleft, crack, curtailment, cutting, decapitation, figgure, gap, gash, hole, incision, laceration, ladder, offcut, opening, rent, resection, retrenchment, rift, rip, rupture, scission, section, slit, slot, tear

spoils booty, loot, pillage, plunder, scalp, swag, winnings

sponge absorbent, adsorbent, blotter, blotting paper, parasitize, use

spongelike calcareous, fibrous, poriferan, poriferous, spongy

spontaneity extemporization, flash, hunch, idea, impromptu, improvisation, impulsiveness, inspiration, instinct, intuition, involuntariness, knee-jerk reaction, reflex, snap decision, surprise, winging it

spontaneous ad hoc, ad lib, automatic, emotional, extemporized, impetuous, impromptu, improvised, impulsive, incautious, instinctive, intuitive, involuntary, kneejerk, natural, off-the-cuff, on the spot, rash, snap, spur-of-the-moment, sudden, uncontrived, unforced, unguarded, unmotivated, unprompted, unprovoked, unrehearsed, unstudied, untaught, voluntary, willing, winging it

sport bout, contest, division, event, game, knockout, league, match, meeting, round, set, tournament
See list of sports.

sporting acrobatic, agonistic, athletic, competitive, gymnastic, sportive, sporty

sportsground alley, arena, course, court, field, green, ground, links, pitch, ring, stadium, track, venue

sportsman athlete, challenger, contender, defender, opponent, player

spot blot, blotch, crud, defect, detect, disfigurement, distortion, flaw, imperfection, mark, notice, pick out, pockmark, scar, see, smear, smudge, spatter, speck, stain, stigma, tarnish, weal, welt

spotless blank, clean, immaculate, perfect, pure, stainless, unadulterated, uncontaminated, undefiled, unmixed, unmuddied, unpolluted, unsoiled, unstained, unsullied, untainted, untarnished, untouched, virginal

SPORTS

AIKIDO	FOXHUNTING	PENTATHLON
AMERICAN FOOTBALL	FREESTYLE WRESTLING	PETANQUE
ANGLING	GOLF	PIGEON RACING
ARCHERY	GREYHOUND RACING	PING-PONG
ASSOCIATION FOOTBALL	GYMKHANA	POINT-TO-POINT
ATHLETICS	GYMNASTICS	POLE VAULT
BADMINTON	HAMMER THROW	POLO
BASEBALL	HANDBALL	RACKETS
BASKETBALL	HANG-GLIDING	RALLY
BEARBAITING	HARNESS RACING	REAL TENNIS
BIATHLON	HOCKEY	RODEO
BLOOD SPORTS	HORSE RACING	ROUNDERS
BOBSLEDDING	HORSE TRIALS	ROWING
BOULES	HURDLING	RUGBY LEAGUE
BOWLING	HURLING	RUGBY UNION
BOWLS	ICE HOCKEY	SEPAK TAKRAW
BOXING	ICE SKATING	SHINTY
BULLBAITING	JAVELIN THROW	SHOOTING
BULLFIGHTING	JUDO	SHOT PUT
CABER TOSSING	JUJITSU	SKATEBOARDING
CANOEING	KABADDI	SKIING
CLAY-PIGEON SHOOTING	KARATE	SKYDIVING
COCKFIGHTING	KARTING	SPEEDWAY
COURSING	KENDO	SQUASH RACKETS
CRICKET	KUNG FU	STEEPLECHASE
CROQUET	LACROSSE	STOCK-CAR RACING
CURLING	LONG JUMP	SWIMMING
DECATHLON	MARATHON	TABLE TENNIS
DISCUS THROW	MARTIAL ARTS	TAE KWON-DO
DRAG RACING	MOTO-CROSS	TENNIS
DRESSAGE	MOTORCYCLE RACING	TOBOGGANING
EQUESTRIANISM	MOTOR RACING	TRIPLE JUMP
ETON WALL GAME	MOUNTAINEERING	TUG OF WAR
FALCONRY	NETBALL	VOLLEYBALL
FENCING	ORIENTEERING	WATER POLO
FIVES	PARACHUTING	WATER SKIING
FLAT RACING	PATO	WEIGHT LIFTING
FOOTBALL LEAGUE	PELOTA	WRESTLING

spouse blushing bride, bride, bridegroom, groom, helpmate, helpmeet, husband, other half, partner, soul mate, wife

sprawled astray, drifting, loose, lounging, spread-eagled, straggling, wandering

spread diffuse, disperse, diverge, gush, intumescence, radiate, scatter, spiral, sprawl, surge, swell, upsurge

spring bob, bound, brook, budtime, coil, Easter, flowery, fountain, gush, hairspring, jet, juicy, jump, leap, mainspring, Maytime, pop up, sappy, seedtime, spout, springtime, start up, stream, upshoot, vernal, vernal season, well, young

sprinkle affusion, asperge, atomize, bespatter, clash, dabble, dot, dredge, dust, flour, freckle, mist, paddle, pepper, powder, scatter, shower, slobber, slop, slosh, smatter, sparge, spatter, speck, speckle, splash, splatter, spot, spray, stud

sprinkler aerosol, aspergillum, atomizer, sparger, sprayer, sprinkler, vaporizer, watering can, water pistol

spruce conifer, dapper, natty, neat, orderly, spick-and-span, tidy, well-groomed

spun braided, extruded, plaited, twined, twirled, twisted, whirled

spurious apocryphal, artificial, bogus, casuistic, charlatan, factitious, forged, hollow, humbug, illegitimate, imposturous, phoney, quackish, sophistic, specious, unauthentic, ungenuine, unreal

spuriousness artificiality, bogusness, casuistry, charlatanism, counterfeiting, factitiousness, falseness, forgery, hollowness, humbug, illegitimacy, imposture, Jesuitism, mountebankery, phoniness, quackery, sophistry, speciousness, unauthenticity, ungenuineness, unrealness

squalor dirt, dirtiness, filth, foulness, grime, gunge, mephitis, miasma, pollution, seediness, smog, smoke, sordidness

squatness chunkiness, dumpiness, lumpishness, squareness, stockiness

squinting boss-eyed, cockeyed, crosseyed, nystigmatic, strabismic, walleyed

stab attempt, bayonet, cut, effort, impale, knife, lance, lunge, pierce, run through, slash, spear, thrust, try

stability balance, calm, changelessness, consistency, constancy, deathlessness, durability, equilibrium, firmness, fixedness, flow, immobilization, immutability, indestructibility, inflexibility, invariability, irreversibility, permanence, reliability, rootedness, routine, rut, secureness, solidity, soundness, stasis, steadfastness, steadiness, strength, trend, unchangeableness

stabilized anchored, balanced, chained, established, fixed, grounded, moored, rooted, settled, tethered, tied

stabilizer aerofoil, aileron, ballast, beam, buttress, centreboard, counterbalance, counterweight, crossbeam, fin, joist, keel, prop, spoiler, support

stable aground, balanced, barn, calm, consistent, constant, continuing, dependable, durable, enduring, equable, equiponderant, evergreen, firm, homeostatic, immobile, immutable, imperishable, incommutable, incontrovertible, indefeasible, indelible, indestructible, indisputable, indissoluble, inextinguishable, inflexible, intransmutable, invariable, irreversible, irrevocable, pen, perpetual, pound, predictable, reliable, rocklike, secure, self-regulating, solid, sound, stall, static, steadfast, steady, stiff, strong, sty, symmetrical, unchangeable, unshakable, unvarying, well-founded

stage heat, lap, leg, phase, podium, rostrum, round, the boards, wings
See also list at **theatre.**

stagnate idle, vegetate

stairs companion way, escalator, fire escape, landing stage, perron, stepladder, steps

staleness overripeness, rankness, rottenness, sourness, spoilage

stall aquarium, aviary, barn, barrow, battery, bird cage, booth, byre, cage, cattery, coop, counter, cowshed, dovecote, fold, halt, henhouse, kennel, kiosk, menagerie, newsstand, pigeon loft, pound, run, stable, stand, stop, sty, zoo

stamina backbone, bottle, courage, endurance, fortitude, gameness, grit, guts, pluck, staying power, strength

standardize align, allocate, assimilate, average out, balance, clone, coalesce, consubstantiate, conventionalize, distribute, divide, equalize, equate, flatten, generalize, homogenize, join, level, liken, merge, normalize, order, pair, parallel, proportion, regularize, regulate, share out, smooth, smooth out, stereotype, symmetrize, synchronize, synthesize, twin, unify, unite

star black hole, celebrity, celestial body, heavenly body, luminary, neutron star, nova, orb, pulsar, quasar, red giant, sphere, supernova, white dwarf, white hole
See also list at **astronomer**.

starry starbright, star-spangled, star-studded

start ascent, begin, blastoff, boarding, bully off, bundle, commence, embarkation, emplanement, enplanement, entrainment, get moving, get underway, initiative, jerk, jump, kick off, launch, liftoff, opening, outset, sally forth, set afloat, set going, set sail, shock, startle, takeoff

state affirm, archduchy, argue, aspect, attest, bailiwick, bishopric, borough, canton, category, circumstances, city-state, claim, class, colony, commonwealth, condition, confederation, constituency, country, county, denote, dependency, diocese, district, division, dominion, duchy, dukedom, echelon, electorate, empire, establish, estate, evince, federation, fettle, footing, form, hold, hundred, hypothesize, imply, kingdom, lot, maintain, mandate, order, palatinate, parish, place, position, postulate, posture, precinct, principality, propose, protectorate, prove, province, rank, realm, region, repair, republic, riding, role, say, shire, show, situation, soke, standing, status, structure, suggest, superpower, territory, wapentake, ward

stated admitted, affirmed, alleged, announced, asserted, attested, avowed, confessed, declared, disclosed, proclaimed, professed, pronounced, read, released, submitted, uttered
may indicate a homophone

stateliness condescension, hauteur, loftiness, nobility

stately aristocratic, august, authoritative, condescending, elevated, grand, grave, high-and-mighty, high-handed, high-nosed, imperious, imposing, kingly, lofty, lordly, majestic, noble, pompous, princely, queenly, regal, royal, sedate, solemn, sombre, statuesque, venerable, worthy

statement announcement, bill, creed, declaration, dictum, enunciation, invoice, manifesto, maxim, predication, prepared text, proclamation, profession, pronouncement, proposition, say, say-so, stance, stand, submission, supposition, thesis, utterance, word

statistical actuarial, psephological

statistics averages, figures, indexes, psephology, tables

steadfastness confidence, determination, endurance, fortitude, intrepidity, perseverance, resoluteness, self-reliance, tenacity

steady constant, continual, dependable, firm, immovable, indefatigable, iterated, regular, reiterated, reliable, renewed, repeated, self-controlled, self-possessed, solid, staunch, unceasing, unchangeable, undrooping, unfailing, unfaltering, unflagging, unremitting, untiring, unwavering, unwearied, vigilant

steal appropriate, boost, borrow, burglarize, fiddle, filch, hijack, housebreak, hustle, lift, mug, nick, nobble, pickpocket, pilfer, pinch, poach, purloin, ram-raid, rob, scrounge, shoplift, skyjack, snaffle, snatch, snitch, swipe, thieve

stealing boosting, borrowing, burglary, cattle raiding, fiddling, filching, hijacking, housebreaking, hustling, kleptomania, larceny, lifting, light-fingeredness, mugging, nicking, pickpocketing, pilfering, pinching, piracy, poaching, purloining, purse-snatching, ram-raiding, robbing, rustling, safecracking, scrounging, scrumping, shoplifting, skyjacking, snatching, snitching, swiping, taking, theft, thieving

steam cloud, condensation, fog, haze, mist

steeple barbican, belfry, campanile, flèche, lighthouse, minaret, pagoda, pile, spire, tower, turret, watchtower, windmill, ziggurat

stench effluvium, exhalation, fetidness, frowstiness, frowziness, fug, fustiness, gas, hum, malodour, mephitis, miasma, mustiness, niff, osmidrosis, pong, reek, smelliness, staleness, stink, sweatiness, whiff

step bridgeboard, doorstep, footrest, jump, kickstool, leap, level, rest, riser, round, rundle, rung, scale, spoke, spurt, stage, stair, stave, stepping-stone, stepstool, stride, string, tread

sterilize aerate, antisepticize, boil, chlorinate, cleanse, conserve, decontaminate, disinfect, drain, dry, freshen, fumigate, immunize, inoculate, isolate, pasteurize, preserve, purify, quarantine, sanitize, vaccinate, ventilate

sterilized castrated, gelded, infertile, neutered, spayed, vasectomized

stew
may indicate an anagram

stick adhere, affix, agglutinate, branch, cement, clamp, clasp, clench, clinch, cling on, clutch, embrace, glue, grapple, grasp, grip, gum, hug, join, paste, show tenaciousness, solder, staple, twig, unite, weld

stillness doldrums, horse latitudes, hush, lull, windlessness

stimulate awaken, bring out, contrive, draw out, elicit, encourage, engineer, evoke, excite, foment, hasten, incite, induce, influence, inspire, kindle, manage, motivate, plan, precipitate, procure, provoke, set off, spark off, tempt, trigger off

stimulating arch, exciting, interesting, intriguing, lively, medicinal, poignant, provocative, restorative, spirited, thought-provoking, titillating

stimulation archness, harshness, liveliness, poignancy, roughness, spirit, titillation, zest

stimulus buzz, fillip, fluttering, formication, frisson, goad, gooseflesh, heebie-jeebies, heightener, horripilation, itch, kick, prickle, prod, sop, spur, stimulant, stimulation, thrill, throb, tickle, tingle, titillation, tonic

stink BO, hum, niff, pong, reek, smell, whiff

stinking ammoniacal, asphyxiating, fetid, foul-smelling, frowsty, frowzy, fuggy, fusty, malodorous, mephitic, miasmic, musty, niffy, noisome, offensive, overpowering, pongy, rank, reeking, smelly, stale, sulphurous, sweaty, unventilated, unwashed, unwholesome, whiffy

stir
may indicate an anagram

stock market bourse, change, commodity exchange, securities market, share shop, Stock Exchange, The City *See also list at* **economic**.

stocky beefy, brawny, burly, chunky, elephantine, heavy, heavyset, hefty, hulking, lumbering, lumpish, lusty, meaty, square, squat, stout, strapping, thickset, well-built

stoicism coldness, indifference, philosophicalness, phlegm, sanguinity

stolen hot, ill-gotten, knock-off, nicked, off the back of a lorry, pilfered, purloined, rip-off

stomach ache bellyache, colic, dyspepsia, grips, gut-ache, heartburn, hunger pains, indigestion, pyrosis, tummy ache, ulcer

stone boulder, chuck, gem, gravel, hurl at, jewel, kernel, lapidate, pebble, pelt, pip, rock, shingle, shy, sling, throw at, tombstone

stop airport, bandage, bar, blockade, blockage, block up, breakdown, breaking off, bung, bus stop, cap, cease trading, check, checkmate, choke, clog, closedown, close down, closure, conclusion, congest, constipate, constrict, contract, cork, dam, deadlock, defeat, dismissal, draw, end, erase, failure, finish, give up, glitch, go bankrupt, guillotine, halt, hanging up, harbour, hinder, hindrance, hitch, holdup, interruption, lay-by, obstruct, occlude, petrol station, plug, quit, railway station, resign, retire, retirement, ringing off, shut down, stalemate, stand down, standstill, staunch, stay, stoppage, strangle, strike, taxi rank, terminal, terminus, throttle, top, waiting room, walk out, wind up

stopped bandaged, blocked, bunged up, capped, choked up, clogged, congested, constipated, constricted, corked, costive, dammed, full, halted, impassable, impenetrable, jammed, obstructed, occluded, packed, plugged, staunched, stuffed, stuffed up

stopper bandage, bung, cap, choke, clot, cork, covering, damper, faucet, lid, peg, pin, piston, plug, seal, spigot, stop, stuffing, tampion, tampon, tap, top, tourniquet, trip switch, valve, wadding, wedge

storage accommodation, accumulation, armoury, arsenal, bank, barn, bottling, box, boxroom, bunker, buttery, cabinet, cellar, chamber, chest, coffer, conservation, container, cupboard, depository, depot, dock, drawer, entrepot, exchequer, freezer, garage, garnering, gathering, gunroom, hold, holdall, larder, magazine, memory, moneybox, pantry, portmanteau, preservation, protection, refrigerator, reservoir, room, safe, shed, shelf, silage, silo, space, stable, stabling, stillroom, stockroom, storehouse, storeship, stowage, strongbox, strongroom, suitcase, till, treasury, trunk, vault, warehousing, wharf

store accumulation, amass, amount, assets, augment, backlog, bagful, board, bottle, boutique, bucketful, buildup, bulk-buy, bundle, bury, cache, capital, charity, conceal, conserve, corner shop, crop, deposit, file, fill, fuel, fund, garner, gather, glean, harvest, haystack, heap, hide, hiding-place, hive, hoard, holding, hypermarket, increase, invest, investment, keep, kitty, leave, load, mass, merchanidse, mow, pack, packet, pick, pickle, pool, preserve, property, provision, quantity, reap, refill, refuel, replenish, reserve, reserves, reservoir, retail outlet, retain, save, savings, secrete, shop, stack, stock, stock-in-trade, stockpile, stow, supermarket, superstore, supply, treasure, trousseau, vintage

stormy inclement, tempestuous, thundery
may indicate an anagram

straight candid, direct, heterosexual, honest, horizontal, linear, perpendicular, plumb, rectilinear, right, rigid, sober, true, unbent, uncurled, vertical

straighten disentangle, flatten out, iron out, neaten, unbend, uncoil, uncurl, unfold, unfurl, unravel, unroll, unscramble, untangle, untwist
may indicate an anagram

straightforward candid, clear, direct, forthright, frank, guileless, ingenuous, open, open-hearted, plain, simple, uncomplicated

straightness directness, linearity, perpendicularity, rectilinearity

strain acid, angst, anxiety, bitterness, fear, gall, pressure, sourness, sprain, stress, torment, worry

strait bottleneck, channel, chink, corridor, crack, ditch, gully, isthmus, narrows, passage, peninsula, ravine, spit, straits, tunnel

strange abnormal, bizarre, eccentric, odd, oddball, quaint, unexpected, weird
may indicate an anagram

stratagem ambush, art, artifice, blind, catch, cheat, con, confidence trick, contrivance, deception, device, ditch, dodge, evasion, excuse, expedient, feint, flimflam, fraud, game, lie, machination, manoeuvre, move, net, Parthian shot, pitfall, plan, plot, ploy, pretext, red herring, resort, resource, ruse, scam, sham, shift, smoke screen, stalking-horse, strategy, subterfuge, swindle, tactics, trap, Trojan horse, web, wile, wrinkle

strength assertiveness, athleticism, backbone, beefiness, brawn, burliness, determination, durability, force, fortification, guts, impenetrability, impregnability, invincibility, inviolability, manliness, might, musculature, potency, power, protection, resilience, resistance, resolution, resourcefulness, sinews, spunk, stability, stamina, steadfastness, stoutheartedness, survivability, tenacity, toughness, virility

strengthen anneal, boost, brace, build up, buttress, confirm, emphasize, entrench, fortify, harden, invigorate, mercerize, protect, refresh, reinforce, reinvigorate, revive, stress, support, sustain, tan, temper, toughen, underline, underscore, vulcanize

strengthened braced, buttressed, durable, fortified, hard-wearing, heavy-duty, protective, reinforced, resistant, restored, revived, stout, substantial, tough, toughened, well-armed, well-built, well-protected

stridency blare, blast, brassiness, bray, cacophony, clamour, discordance, dissonance, harshness, howl, raucousness, skirl, squawk, stridor, tantara, ululation, wail, yawp, yell, yelp

strident blare, blaring, blast, brassy, bray, braying, cacophonous, clamorous, clash, discord, discordant, dissonant, ear-splitting, flat, grating, grind, harsh, howl, howling, inharmonious, jangle, jar, jarring, loud, metallic, penetrating, rasp, raucous, skirl, squawk, ululant, ululate, unmelodious, unmusical, wail, yawl, yawp, yell, yelp

strike beat up, boycott, bring down, butt, close with, demonstration, fall upon, flail, go berserk, go for, go-slow, grapple with, hammer, hit, industrial action, jump, kick, knock down, lace into, lay into, lay low, lockout, maul, mug, picket, pitch into, poke, pounce upon, punch, push, round on, run amok, sail into, savage, set on, sit-in, swipe, tear into, walkout, work-in

striking biting, bold, bright, brilliant, concentrated, daring, dazzling, glaring, heady, hot, intoxicating, loud, mordant, neat, piquant, pungent, pure, sharp, spicy, stark, strong-smelling, strong-tasting, undiluted

strip band, belt, denude, disrobe, peel, ribbon, skin, undress, unwrap

striped banded, barred, jaspé, lined,

marbled, paned, panelled, reticulate, streaked, striate, veined

strong amazonian, athletic, beefy, brawny, burly, feisty, fit, hardy, healthy, Herculean, lusty, manly, muscular, powerful, red-blooded, robust, sinewy, sound, stalwart, stout, strapping, sturdy, tough, vigorous, virile

strong-willed adamant, cast-iron, grim, hard, implacable, inexorable, inflexible, intransigent, merciless, obstinate, relentless, ruthless, steely, stern, stubborn, unbending, uncompromising, unyielding

structural architectonic, architectural, constructional, edificial, erected, fabricated, foundational, infrastructural, mechanical, organizational, precast, prestressed, substructural, superstructural, tectonic, textural

structure architectonics, architecture, arrange, arrangement, bridge, building, bulkhead, construction, dam, design, draw up, embankment, formula, invent, organization, organize, pattern, plan, prepare, pylon, railway, road, runway, tectonics, tunnel

structuring building, creation, forging, formation, making, moulding, patterning, production, shaping

stubborn callous, case-hardened, determined, difficult, hard-boiled, hardhearted, immutable, inflexible, intractable, intransigent, obdurate, obstinate, single-minded, stony-hearted, thick-skinned, unalterable, unbending, ungiving, unyielding

study con, discover, find out, grasp, learn, take in

stuff cram, fill, fill up, gear, insert, jam, junk, make full, materials, matter, pack, pack in, pad, pour in, squeeze in, things, top up

stuffing filling, lining, packing, padding, wadding
may indicate a hidden word

stupid backward, brainless, cretinous, dense, dim, dim-witted, doltish, dull, feeble-minded, idiotic, imbecilic, mindless, moronic, obtuse, senseless, simple, slow, thick, unintelligent, vacant, vacuous
may indicate an anagram

stupidity backwardness, blockheadedness, brainlessness, denseness, dimness, dim-wittedness, dull-wittedness, feeble-mindedness, hebetude, idiocy, imbecility, mindlessness, obtuseness, senselessness, simple-mindedness, slowness, stolidity, thick-headedness, thickness, unreason, vacancy, vacuity

style affectation, approach, character, couch, express, fashion, formulate, frame, idiom, idiosyncrasy, manner, mannerism, mode, overwrite, peculiarity, phrase, present, put, quality, speciality, state, strain, technique, tenor, tone, vein, way, word

styled arranged, bespoke, curled, designed, designer, made-to-measure, permed, planned, ready-made, ready-to-wear, sartorial, snazzy, tailored, tailor-made, trimmed

stylish chic, elegant, fashionable, graceful, sophisticated

stylishness charm, chic, élan, elegance, flair, grace, panache

subconscious repressed, subliminal, suppressed, unconscious

subject apprentice, apprenticed, browbeat, business, captive, citizen, colonize, compulsory, dependent, disenfranchise, employ, employable, employed, exploit, gist, henpeck, humble, humiliate, indenture, indentured, in harness, involuntary, issue, junior, kick around, lower, meaning, obedient, point, railroad, regiment, servile, subdue, subjugate, subordinate, subservient, substitute, symbiotic, tame, thesis, topic, trample on, tutor, unfree

subjection allegiance, apprenticeship, bondage, captivity, constraint, defeat, dependence, disenfranchisement, employment, enslavement, feudalism, indentureship, inferiority, juniority, obedience, peonage, serfdom, service, servility, servitude, slavery, subjugation, subordination, subservience, symbiosis, thraldom, tutelage, vassalage, villeinage, wardship

subjective biased, personal

subjectivity bias, prejudice

subletly delicacy, distinction

submergence detrusion, ducking, oppression, plunging, pushing under, sinking, sousing, suppression

submission abandonment, abdication, acquiescence, agreeing, apathy, appeasement, assent, bow, capitulation, cession, collaboration, compliance, concession, consent, cop-out, curtsy, deference, fatalism, genuflection, grovelling, homage, humility, inactivity, kneeling, kowtow, lethargy, masochism, nonresistance, obedience, obeisance, passivity, prostration, resignation, resigned, sell-out, servitude, slavishness, subservience, succumbing, supineness, surrender, tameness, yielding

submissive disinterested, intimidated, obedient, passive, resigned, subservient, timid, uncomplaining

submit abdicate, abide, accept, acquiesce, allow, appease, assent, bow to, capitulate, comply, concede, consent, crawl, defer to, disregard, eat dirt, give in, give way, grant, grovel, ignore, knuckle under, obey, overlook, pass up, relent, relinquish, resign, resign oneself, retire, retreat, stand down, step aside, surrender, withdraw, yield

submitting accommodating, acquiescent, agreeable, amenable, assenting, bending, biddable, boot-licking, concessionary, crawling, cringing, crouching, docile, fatalistic, humble, malleable, masochistic, meek, obedient, pliant, prostrate, resigned, servile, slavish, soft, subdued, subservient, surren-

dering, sycophantic, toadying, tractable, unresisting, weak-kneed

subnormality backwardness, cretinism, feeblemindedness, idiocy, imbecility, mental handicap, retardation

subordinate ancillary, apprentice, assistant, auxiliary, conscript, criminal, dependent, employee, fag, flunkey, helper, humble, inferior, junior, lackey, learner, minion, minor, right-hand man, second-class, second-division, second fiddle, secretary, servant, sidekick, stooge, student, subaltern, subject, subservient, subsidiary, substitute, sycophant, tool, tributary, underling, untouchable

subsidy advance, aid, allowance, bestowal, bursary, contribution, credit, donation, dowry, endowment, fellowship, funding, grant, loan, scholarship, settlement, sponsorship, stipend, subvention

substitute act for, acting, additional, alternate, analogy, appear for, back up, bandage, cover for, deputy, double for, doublet, equivalent, fill in, foster, ghostwrite, guilt-offering, lookalike, makeshift, metaphor, negotiate for, pacemaker, prosthesis, provisional, proxy, relieve, remount, replace, replacement, representation, reserve, sacrifice, second, soundalike, stand in, stopgap, succedaneum, surrogate, symbol, synonym, temporary, transplant, understudy

substitution alternation, alternative, change, commutation, compensation, compromise, deputing, equivalence, exchange, expedient, expiation, replacement, representation, shuffle, stopgap, supersession, supplanting, surrogation, swap, switch, vicariousness

substitutive alternative, back-up, foster, locum, relief, reserve, stand-in, substitutable, surrogate

subsume add to, categorize as, class with, count with, enter, enumerate with, list, number with, place under, put in, reckon among

subterfuge blag, cavil, contrivance, dodge, misinformation, propaganda, quibble, quip, quirk, ruse, scam, scheme, shuffle, stratagem, trick

subtle delicate, discriminating, elegant, fastidious, pastel, refined, restrained, tasteful

subtlety delicacy, discrimination, elegance, fastidiousness, finesse, refinement, restraint

subtract abbreviate, abridge, abstract, allow, cancel, condense, cull, cut, decimate, decrease, deduct, delete, detract from, devalue, diminish, discount, eliminate, eradicate, erase, except, exclude, extirpate, extract, leave out, obliterate, offset, omit, remove, rip out, take out, thin out, uproot, weed, withdraw

subtracted abstracted, deducted, deleted, ejected, eliminated, eradicated, erased, excepted, excluded, expelled, extracted, obliterated, removed, withdrawn

subtraction abstraction, bowdlerization, cut, decimation, decrease, deduction, deletion, detraction, devaluation, diminution, discount, discounting, editing, ejection, elimination, eradication, erasure, exception, exclusion, expulsion, expurgation, extraction, minus, obliteration, offset, removal, retrenchment, shrinkage, withdrawal

subtractive abstract, deductive, eradicable, extirpative, reductive, removable

suburb built-up area, dormitory suburb, garden suburb, green belt, outskirts, subtopia, suburbia

subversion agitation, agitprop, anarchy, cabal, conspiracy, espionage, faction, fifth columnism, infiltration, intrigue, lese-majesty, plot, sabotage, sedition, spying, terrorism, treason

subversive anarchic, breakaway, conspiratorial, factional, insurgent, insurrectional, mutinous, rebellious, revolutionary, schismatic, seditious, treasonable

succeed accomplish, come after, consecutive, ensue, follow, inherit, make good, relieve, replace, result from, run on, substitute, supersede, supervene, supplant, usurp, win, work out

succeeding another, arranged, close, consecutive, consequent, ensuing, following, last, late, latter, near, next, ordered, proximate, pursuant, second, sequential, subsequent, successional

success accomplishment, achievement, affluence, ascendancy, attainment, breakthrough, celebration, celebrity, fame, feat, fortune, happiness, killing, luck, luxury, mastery, name, plenty, prosperity, riches, sensation, smash, stardom, thriving, wealth

successful best-ever, best-selling, certain, chart-topping, crowning, effective, efficacious, famous, favourable, flourishing, fortunate, fruitful, lucky, masterly, never-failing, prosperous, rising, surefire, surefooted, thriving, wealthy, winning

succession arrangement, chain, continuation, course, cycle, entourage, flow, flux, following, hierarchy, list, order, pecking order, procession, progress, progression, queue, retinue, rota, run, sequence, series, subsequence, suite, tailback, train, turn, wake

successor beneficiary, descendant, heir, heiress, inheritor, replacement, substitute

succumb apologize, bend, bow, brown-nose, collapse, crawl, cringe, crouch, curtsy, do homage, drop, eat dirt, endure, faint, grovel, kneel, knuckle under, kowtow, sag, stomach, stoop, submit, suffer, tire, toady, wilt

suck aspirate, detect, drain, draw off,

inhale, inspire, siphon off, smell, suckle, vacuum

sucking aspiration, draining, draught, drawing, inhalation, milking, siphoning, suction, tapping, vacuuming

suffering aching, afflicted, black-and-blue, bleeding, blistered, distressed, hurting, in agony, martyred, raw, sore, tormented, tortured, traumatized, wincing, writhing

suffice answer, content, do, fill, fulfil, meet requirements, pass muster, qualify, quench, reach, refill, replenish, sate, satisfy, serve, settle, stand, support, work

sufficiency acceptability, adequacy, assets, autarky, competence, completion, contentment, enough, fulfilment, minimum, pass, qualification, quorum, repletion, requirement, satiety, satisfaction, self-sufficiency

sufficient acceptable, adequate, commensurate, competent, complete, contenting, enough, equal to, fitting, hand-to-mouth, makeshift, measured, provisional, satisfactory, satisfying, self-sufficient, sufficing, suitable

suggestibility adaptability, compliance, docility, gullibility, impressibility, malleability, receptivity, susceptibility, tractability, willingness

suggestible adaptable, compliant, docile, easily led, gullible, impressible, malleable, receptive, soft, susceptible, tractable, willing

suggestion dash, hint, idea, inkling, intimation, iota, jot, proposal, smattering, soupçon, sprinkling, suspicion, taste, thought, tinge, tip, touch, trace, warning

suicide felo-de-se, hara-kiri, kamikaze, parasuicide, self-destruction, self-immolation, self-slaughter, seppuku, suttee, topping oneself

suit boiler suit, catsuit, club, coordinates, costume, courtship, coveralls, diamond, dress suit, ensemble, fit, heart, jump suit, leotard, lounge suit, outfit, pinstripe suit, separates, shell suit, spade, tracksuit, trouser suit, tweeds, tweed suit, wooing

suitability aptness, fitness, pertinence, relevance, relevancy

suitable appropriate, apt, fit, fitting, pertinent, relevant

sulk brood, fret, moan, mope, pout, whine, whinge

sullen atrabilious, black, blue, cheerless, dark, dejected, depressed, dismal, dour, gloomy, glum, grim, ill-humoured, ill-natured, melancholy, moody, morose, pouting, saturnine, serious, sombre, sour, stern, sulky, surly

sullenness atrabiliousness, dejection, down in the dumps, glumness, grimness, grumpishness, huff, melancholy, moaning, moodiness, mopiness, moroseness, mumpishness, pouting, sighing, sourness, sternness, sulkiness, surliness, the blues, the hump, the sulks, unsociability, whininess

sum aggregate, calculation, complex, corpus, ensemble, summation, system, total

summariness brevity, briefness, brusqueness, compactness, compendiousness, conciseness, laconism, pithiness, pointedness, shortness, succinctness, terseness

summarize abbreviate, abridge, abstract, condense, contract, digest, encapsulate, epigrammatize, epitomize, outline, pot, précis, recap, recapitulate, reduce, resume, shorten, sketch, sum up, synopsize, truncate

summary abbreviation, abridgement, abstract, bird's-eye view, brief, brusque, capsule, compact, compendious, compendium, concise, conspectus, curt, digest, drift, ellipsis, epigrammatic, epitome, gist, irreducible, laconic, outline, overview, pithy, pointed, précis, recap, recapitulation, résumé, review, rundown, short, sketch, succinct, survey, synopsis, terse, thumbnail sketch

summer aestivation, dog days, flaming June, haymaking, heat-haze, heat wave, hot spell, Indian summer, midsummer, summertide, summertime

summit acme, apex, apogee, brow, climax, crest, culmination, cusp, exosphere, extremity, heaven, height, high ground, limit, maximum, meridian, peak, pinnacle, pitch, point, pole, ridge, seventh heaven, sky, tip, top, vertex, zenith

summons call, citation, order, subpoena, warrant, writ

sun daystar, drought, dry spell, heat, heatwave, Helios, Hyperion, Indian summer, midnight sun, scorcher, sizzler, Sol, solar flare, sunlight, sunshine, sunspot

sunny bright, clear, cloudless, daylight, fine, good-natured, hot, pleasant

superficial cursory, empty, flat, flimsy, foolish, frivolous, hasty, idle, light, lightweight, meaningless, one-dimensional, petty, silly, skin-deep, slight, surface, thin, trifling, trivial, unimportant

superfluity accessory, bonus, diffuseness, duplication, excrescence, extra, frill, glut, leftovers, luxury, nonessential, overemployment, overfulfilment, overkill, oversupply, perk, perquisite, pleonasm, redundancy, remainder, spare, supererogation, surfeit, surplus, tautology

superfluous circuitous, excess, extra, leftover, luxury, needless, nonessential, otiose, pleonastic, rambling, redundant, remaining, residual, spare, supererogatory, surplus, tautologous, unnecessary

superior above, ahead, arch, better, bigwig, boss, captain, chief, commander, eclipsing, elder, exceeding, executive, finer, foreman, gaffer, general, governor, greater, head, headmaster, headmistress, higher, higher-up, leader, leading, manager, master, outclassing, over, overtopping, principal, ruler, senior, super, superintendent, surpassing

superiority altitude, ascendency, domination, eminence, excellence, greatness, incomparability, influence, inimitability, leverage, loftiness, majority, paramountcy, perfection, precedence, predominance, preeminence, preponderance, prepotence, prestige, primacy, priority, prominence, quality, seniority, sublimity, success, supremacy, transcendence, virtuosity

supernatural ghostly, other-worldly, paranormal, preternatural, spooky

supplementary accessory, additional, ancillary, auxiliary, extra, subsidiary

supplement augment, follow-up, postscript, sequel

supplies ammunition, equipment, machinery, material, munitions, provisions, resources, stock

support abut, abutment, advice, advocate, alleviate, back, back up, bear, benediction, benefit, bolster, boost, brace, bracket, bulwark, buttress, care for, carry, champion, comfort, commend, counsel, deliverance, doctor, ease, embank, favour, frame, guidance, hearten, hold up, intercession, join, kindness, lift, look after, ministration, nurse, offices, post, prayer, prop, rampart, recommend, reinforce, relief, relieve, remedy, rescue, restore, revive, scaffold, second, service, shore up, strengthen, strengthening, succour, tend, treat, truss, underpin, underpinning, uphold, wall

supportable acceptable, average, bearable, endurable, manageable, passable, so-so, sufferable, tolerable

supported assured, attested, authenticated, backed, certified, confirmed, corroborated, endorsed, established, ratified, reinforced, seconded, substantiated, supported, validated, verified

supporter abutment, angel, backbone, balustrade, base, basement, beam, bedrock, brace, bracket, bulwark, buttress, carer, caryatid, chassis, column, comfort, cornerstone, crossbar, embankment, fan, foundation, framework, friend, fulcrum, girder, good Samaritan, groundwork, helpmate, keystone, lintel, mainstay, mantelpiece, mounting, neighbour, pedestal, pier, pilaster, pile, pillar, post, prop, rafter, rampart, scaffolding, shaft, shelf, skeleton, stand, stem, struct, substructure, succourer, table, transom, tripod, undercarriage, underframe, underlay, underpinning, wall

supporting advocating, backing, championing, for, in favour, pro, recommending, supportive

supportive advocatory, ancillary, attending, auxiliary, basal, benevolent, caring, collaborative, comforting, contributory, cooperative, corroborative, discipular, empathetic, encouraging, favourable, fostering, foundational, ground, guardian, heartening, helpful, intercessional, kindly, maintaining, ministering, morale-boosting, nurturing, patronal, preferential, reassuring, retaining, stipendiary, subsidiary, substitute, succouring, sustaining, sympathetic, tending, understanding, upholding, well-disposed

suppose affirm, assert, assume, believe, conceive, conclude, conjecture, deduce, divine, draft, dream, fancy, gather, guess, guesstimate, hypothesize, imagine, infer, intuit, let, opine, outline, plan, posit, postulate, predicate, premise, presume, presuppose, presurmise, pretend, reason, sketch, speculate, surmise, suspect, take it, theorize, think, understand

supposed abstract, alleged, assented, assumed, fabled, fanciful, given, granted, imagined, inferred, mooted, presumed, putative, quasi, reputed, so-called, suppositive, taken, titular, topical, understood, unreal

supposition affectation, argument, assumption, attitude, conceit, condition, conditions, explanation, fancy, hypothesis, idea, ideality, model, notion, opinion, orientation, position, postulation, premise, presumption, presupposition, pretence, proposal, stand, standpoint, stipulation, submission, suggestion, theorem, theory, thesis, topic

suppositional academic, allusive, armchair, assumptive, blue-sky, conjectural, gratuitous, guessing, guesstimating, hinting, hypothetical, intuitive, moot, notional, postulatory, presumptive, propositional, putative, speculative, stimulating, suggestive, surmised, theoretical, thought-provoking, unverified

suppress abuse, censor, coerce, conceal, cover up, enslave, exploit, expurgate, extort, harass, hide, hush up, misgovern, mishandle, misrule, oppress, persecute, repress, restrain, restrict, subject, subjugate, terrorize, torment, torture, tyrannize, victimize

suppression censorship, coercion, concealment, exploitation, expurgation, extortion, harassment, hiding, inquisition, oppression, persecution, repression, restriction, silencing, subjection, subjugation, victimization

surface cement, coating, cobble, concrete, external, façade, facing, gravel, macadamize, pave, skin, tar, tarmac, top layer

surgery amputation, brain surgery, dental surgery, division, excision, grafting, keyhole surgery, neurosurgery, op, open-heart surgery, operation, perfusion, plastic surgery, psychosurgery, suture, transfusion, transplantation

surpassing better, greater, higher, over-extended, overlong

surplus abundance, bonus, carried over, dividend, excess, extra, extras, glut, leftovers, otiose, outstanding, overabundant, overgrowth, overload, overloaded, owed, pleonasm, pleonastic, redundancy, spare, spares, superfluity, surfeit, unused, unwanted

surprise alarm, amaze, astonish, astound, baffle, catch off guard, discover, frighten, improbability, jolt, miscalculation, misjudgment, spring on, startle, take aback, take unawares, unexpectedness, unpredictability, unpreparedness, unreadiness

surprised ambushed, startled, trapped, unaware, unprepared, unsuspecting

surprising abnormal, amazing, astonishing, astounding, freakish, freaky, odd, peculiar, serendipitous, shocking, staggering, sudden, unannounced, unanticipated, unbelievable, unexpected, unforeseen, unprecedented, unpredictable, unusual

surround border, circle, contain, edge, encircle, enclose, encompass, enfold, envelop, environ, frame, outlie, outline

surrounded circumambient, circumscribed, encircled, enclosed, encompassed, enfolded, enveloped, girded, hemmed-in, roundabout, wrapped
may indicate a split word

surrounding around, background, environmental, neighbourhood, outlying, perimetric, peripheral

surroundings area, arena, backdrop, background, circumstances, confines, environment, environs, green belt, locale, location, neighbourhood, outposts, outskirts, perimeter, periphery, precincts, scene, scenery, setting, situation, stage, suburb, vicinity

susceptible agitated, allergic, delicate, docile, excitable, gullible, hot-blooded, hyperactive, impressionable, irritable, irritated, jumpy, over-

sensitive, perceptive, responsive, stirred, temperamental, tender, tetchy, thin-skinned, thrilled, touchy

suspend dangle, drape, droop, fasten, hang, hang down, hook up, postpone, put on hold, put up, stop, swing, trail

suspended abrogated, dangling, deactivated, hanging, in abeyance, in reserve, on hold, on ice, pendent, pending, pendulous, pensile, powerless, sagging, swinging, switched off

suspension dangle, dangling, drape, droop, hang, hanging, pendency, pendulousness, pensileness, sag, swing

suspicion agnosticism, atheism, caution, conjecture, denial, disbelief, distrust, doubt, incredulity, rejection, scepticism

sustain coddle, cosset, keep, maintain, mother, nourish, nurture, pamper, protect, provide for, support, sympathize

sustenance care, daily bread, keep, livelihood, living, maintenance, manna, mothering, nourishment, nurture, provision, subsistence, support, sustainment, sympathy, upkeep

swank show off, strut, swagger

swearing Anglo-Saxon, billingsgate, coprolalia, cursing, effing and blinding, expletive, foul mouth, four-letter word, profanity, scatology, shouting, the f-word, vulgarism

sweat exudation, glow, perspiration, steam, sudation, sudor, swelter, wilt

sweater Aran sweater, cardie, cardigan, cashmere sweater, crew-neck, Fair Isle, fisherman's jersey, Guernsey, jersey, jumper, knit, polo-neck, pullover, ski sweater, slipover, turtleneck, twinset, V-neck, woolly

sweaty clammy, diaphoretic, glowing, perspiring, sticky, sudatory, sudoric, sweating, wilting

sweet ambrosial, barley sugar, bittersweet, boiled sweet, bonbon, butterscotch, candied, caramel, cloying, comfit, confectionary, crystallized, crystallized fruit, fondant, fudge, gentle, glazed, gobstopper, gum, gumdrop, honeyed, iced, jelly bean, jujube, kindly, liquorice, liquorice allsort, lollipop, marshmallow, marzipan, nectared, peppermint, praline, saccharine, sentimental, sickly, sugared, sweet-and-sour, sweetie, sweetmeat, syrupy, taffy, toffee, toffee apple, treacly

sweeten candy, glaze, honey, ice, mull, sugar, sugar-coat

sweetener ambrosia, aspartame, bribe, conserve, cyclamate, delicacies, glacé fruit, honey, honeydew, jam, jelly, marmalade, molasses, nectar, preserve, saccharine, sucrose, sugar, sweetmeats, syrup, treacle

sweetness benevolence, cloying, fragrance, freshness, gentleness, kindness, melodiousness, pleasantness, saccharinity, sickliness, smoothness, sugariness, syrupiness, tenderness, thoughtfulness

swelling bulge, enlargement, extension, tumour

swerve break, crabwalk, drift, leeway, leg break, pitch, roll, shift, sideslip, sidestep, skid, swing, veer, yaw

swift agile, alacritous, all-out, breakneck, cantering, charging, darting, dashing, double-quick, electric, expeditious, express, fast, flashing, flat-out, fleet, flying, galloping, hasty, headlong, high-geared, high-velocity, hotted-up, hurrying, hurtling, hustling, hypersonic, immediate, instantaneous, jet-propelled, light-footed, meteoric, nifty, nimble, pelting, precipitate, prompt, quick, racing, rapid, rapid-fire, rattling, round, runaway, scorching, smart, snappy, souped-up, spanking, speedy, sudden, supersonic, tempestuous, ton-up, ultrasonic, volant, whirling, whizzing, winged, zippy

swill bilge, dishwater, ditchwater, drainage, hogwash, sewage, slops, slosh, slough, wallow, wash out

swimmer
may indicate a fish
See list at **fish**.

swirl eddy, flounder, grovel, gurge, mill around, mix, moil, roil, seethe, spin, stir, surge, tumble, twirl, wallow, welter, whirlpool
may indicate an anagram

sycophancy abjectness, arse-licking, backscratching, bootlicking, bowing-and-scraping, brown-nosing, crawling, cringing, fawning, grovelling, ingratiation, mealymouthing, obeisance, obsequiousness, parasitism, prostration, servility, soft-soaping, sponging, time-serving, toadyism, truckling

sycophant apple-polisher, arse-licker, bootlicker, brownie, brown-noser, cat's paw, crawler, creature, creep, doormat, dupe, groveller, instrument, kowtower, lackie, lapdog, lickspit, mealymouth, minion, poodle, puppet, slave, smoothie, stooge, suck, time-server, toady, Uriah Heep, yes-man

sycophantic apple-polishing, backscratching, beggarly, bootlicking, bowing, brown-nosing, cowering, crawling, creeping, creepy, cringing, fawning, flattering, footlicking, free-loading, grovelling, handshaking, hangdog, ingratiating, kowtowing, leechlike, mealy-mouthed, obeisant, obsequious, oily, parasitic, prostrate, scraping, servile, slimy, smarmy, sneaking, snivelling, soapy, soft-soaping, sponging, time-serving, toadyish, truckling, unctuous, whining

symbolism evocation, hint, iconography, implication, meaning, representation, ritualism, semiotics, signalling, significance

symmetrical balanced, chiastic, correspondent, counterbalanced, enantiomorphic, equal, equilateral, even, even-sided, harmonious, interacting, proportional, reciprocal, rhythmic, uniform, well-proportioned

symmetrize balance, coordinate, correlate, counterbalance, equalize, equilibrate, even, harmonize, match, proportion, regularize

symmetry balance, chiasmus, congruence, coordinateness, correlation, correspondence, counterbalance, equality, equilibrium, equipose, harmony, interrelation, parallelism, proportion, reciprocity, rhyme, uniformity

synchronism coincidence, concurrence, contemporaneity, isochronism, lip-sync, simultaneity, sync

synchronized in step, in time, isochronal, phased, timed

synthetic artificial, bogus, counterfeit, dummy, ersatz, fake, false, imitation, man-made, mock, phony, plastic, pretend, pseudo, put-on, quasi, sham, simulated, so-called, specious, spurious

syrupy cloying, honeyed, soppy, treacly, viscous

systematize catalogue, categorize, classify, codify, grade, group, index, methodize, pigeonhole, place, position, prioritize, rank, rationalize, sift, sort out, standardize, tabulate

·T·

ABBREVIATIONS

T	junction • model • shirt • te • Territorial • Testament • ton • tonne
TA	tantalum • Territorial Army • thanks
TB	trial balance • tuberculosis
TEL	telegram • telephone
TEMP	temperature • temporary
TESSA	Tax-Exempt Special Savings Account
TI	titanium
TINA	there is no alternative
TM	thulium • trademark • transcendental meditation
TP	third party
TT	abstainer • race • teetotal • Tourist Trophy

table board, bureau, chart, davenport, desk, diagram, drop-leaf, escritoire, gate-leg, lectern, list, pedestal, periodic, propose, put forward, reading desk, roll-top desk, secretaire, slant-top desk, submit, writing desk
See also list at **furniture.**

taciturn antisocial, diffident, mum, quiet, reserved, reticent, self-contained, shtoom, shy, sullen, tight-lipped, uncommunicative, unforthcoming, unsociable, withdrawn

taciturnity brevity, brusqueness, curtness, diffidence, evasiveness, gruffness, quietness, reserve, reticence, secrecy, shortness, shyness, sullenness, uncommunicativeness

tackle attempt, equipment, gear, rig, rigging, speculate, take on, undertake, venture

tactics advantage, brinkmanship, campaign, contrivance, cunning, deed, delay, diplomacy, gambit, game, governance, line, logistics, manoeuvres, move, opportunism, outflanking, plan, policy, politics, programme, shift, skill, statesmanship, stratagem, strategy, tactic, trick

tail butt, end, fag end, follow, rear, shadow, trail, train

tailor accoutre, costume, custom-make, design, fit out, rig out, style
may indicate an anagram

tailoring dressmaking, habilimentation, hosiery

take accept, acquire, annex, appropriate, capture, colonize, confiscate, conquer, earmark, get, grab, grasp, obtain, plagiarize, remove, requisition, seize, snatch, steal, subject, subjugate, usurp, win

take away abduct, amputate, apprehend, arrest, behead, blackmail, borrow, caponize, capture, castrate, circumcise, commandeer, confiscate, cop, curtail, cut, decapitate, deduct, delete, denude, despoil, dig, disencumber, displace, dispossess, divest, dock, doff, dupe, emasculate, embezzle, enslave, eradicate, erase, excise, extort, extract, fix, fleece, geld, grab, hijack, imitate, kidnap, kill, ladle, loot, lop, manhandle, manipulate, milk, mine, mug, nab, nick, outwit, peel, pilfer, pillage, pinch, plagiarize, pluck, plunder, prune, purloin, raid, relegate, relocate, remove, rob, sack, sequestrate, sever, shanghai, shift, shoplift, shorten, shovel, shunt, side, skin, skyjack, snatch, spay, steal, strip, subtract, swindle, tap, thieve, trap, uncover, unman

take back annex, confiscate, deprive, disinherit, dispossess, distrain, divest, evict, expropriate, foreclose, impound, levy, recapture, reclaim, recoup, recover, regain, repossess, retrieve, seize, sequester, tax

taken from
may indicate a hidden word

taken up
may indicate a backword

take off blast off, fly, gyre upward, kite, launch, lift off, plane, rocket, skyrocket, soar, spire, zoom

taking acquisition, annexation, appropriation, arrogation, assumption, avaricious, capture, clutching, colonization, commandeering, confiscation, conquering, deceptive, extortionate, getting, grabbing, grasping, greedy, manipulative, obtaining, plagiarism, plundered, possession, predatory, requisitionary, rip-off, seizure, snatching, takeover, thieving, winning

takings boodle, booty, catch, earnings, haul, levy, pickings, plunder, prize, proceeds, receipts, revenue, savings, spoils, swag, tax, turnover, winnings

talisman amber, amulet, ankh, bell, black cat, bloodstone, charm, crucifix, emblem, fairy ring, familiar spirit, fetish, four-leaf clover, garlic, horseshoe, juju, lodestone, magic carpet, magic circle, mandala, mascot, mojo, obi, periapt, phylactery, rabbit's foot, relic, scarab, shooting star, silver bullet, tiki, totem, wishbone, wishing well

talk babble, blab, blah, chat, chew the fat, chinwag, debate, discuss, gab, gabble, gas, gossip, guff, hot air, jabber, jaw, palaver, prating, prattle, rap, tittle-tattle, waffle, witter, yak

talkative babbling, chattering, communicative, eloquent, fluent, gabbling, gabby, garrulous, gassy, glib, jabbering, jibbering, long-winded, loquacious, multiloquent, prolix, verbose, voluble, wordy

talkativeness blah, blarney, chattiness, eloquence, fluency, gabbiness, garrulousness, gassiness, glibness, logomania, logorrhoea, long-windedness, loquacity, multiloquence, prolixity, spiel, verbal diarrhoea, verbiage, verbosity, volubility, wordiness

tall Amazonian, colossal, gangling, gangly, giant, gigantic, knee-high, lanky, leggy, long-legged, long-limbed, long-necked, monumental, Olympian, rangy, shoulder-high, statuesque

tangle jungle, labyrinth, maze, snarl, web
may indicate an anagram

tap bleed, brush, dab, drain, exploit, faucet, flick, flip, outlet, pat, peck, pick, rap, spigot, spout, stopcock, tip, touch, valve, whisk

tapered attenuated, cone-shaped, conical, convergent, fusiform, peaked, pointed, wedge-shaped

tar AB, bitumen, creosote, pitch, sailor, salt

tarnish deaden, dirty, dull, muddy, rust, sully, tone down

tartan check, checked, chequer, chequered, damascene, fasciate, harlequin, inlay, marquetry, mosaic, parquetry, patched, patchwork, piebald, pinto, plaid, skewbald, tessellation

task assignment, bout, business, calling, chore, commission, deed, engagement, errand, exercise, feat, function, job, mission, office, operation, place, profession, project, responsibility, service, shift, station, stint, stretch, trick, watch, work

taste aestheticism, appreciate, degust, deliciousness, diet, discrimination, drink, eat, enjoy, experience, lick, nibble, palatability, palate, peck at, pick at, refinement, relish, sample, sapidity, savour, smack, sniff at, style, test, try, unpalatability

tasteful artistic, charming, cultivated, discriminating, elegant, refined

tasteless banal, bland, boring, coarse, crude, diluted, dry, dull, feeble, flat, flavourless, insipid, mild, monotonous, nondescript, obscene, offensive, plain, sickening, stale, tame, thin, unsalted, unseasoned, vapid, vulgar, weak, wishy-washy

tastelessness adulteration, aridity, bad taste, banality, blandness, boredom, coarseness, crudity, dilution, dryness, dullness, feebleness, flatness, gaudiness, glitz, insipidity, lifelessness, mildness, monotony, offensiveness, plainness, showiness, staleness, tameness, thinness, triteness, unsavouriness, vapidness, vulgarity, wateriness, weakness, wishy-washiness

tastiness delectability, deliciousness, lusciousness, palatability

tasty ambrosial, appetizing, comestible, dainty, delectable, delicious, drinkable, edible, epicurean, esculent, flavourful, juicy, luscious, moreish, mouthwatering, palatable, potable, pungent, salty, sapid, savoury, scrumptious, sharp, sour, spicy, succulent, sweet, tart, tempting, toothsome, yummy

taunt banter, barb, barracking, boo, brickbat, call names, catcall, chaff, guy, heckle, hiss, hoot, jeer, jibe, laugh at, mock, rail at, raspberry, scoff, sneer, sniff, snort, teasing, twit

tawdriness shoddiness, tackiness

tax accuse, cess, community charge, criticize, customs, dues, duty, levy, Peter's pence, rates, supertax, tariff, tithe

tax-free duty-free, post-free, zero-rated

taxing difficult, levying, strenuous

taxon class, cultivar, division, family, form, genus, kingdom, order, phylum, race, section, series, species, subclass, subdivision, subfamily, subkingdom, suborder, subphylum, subspecies, subtribe, superclass, superfamily, tribe, variety

taxonomy cladistics, classification, systematics

team band, camp, cast, circle, company, complement, corps, coterie, crew, group, orchestra, outfit, side, squad, troupe, unite with

tease kid, mock, rag, rib, scoff, twit *may indicate an anagram*

teens baker's dozen, fifteen, fortnight, fourteen, hexadecimal, long dozen, quindecagon, quindecaplet, quindecennial, sixteen, teenager, thirteen

telecommunication cable, communications satellite, fibre-optic cable, geostationary satellite, network, telegraphy, telephony, transmission, transmission line

telephone answering machine, bell, blower, buzz, call, cardphone, cellular phone, hang up, intercom, payphone, phone, public telephone, radiophone, ring, ring off, tinkle, videophone

telescope antenna, array, astronomical telescope, grazing-incidence telescope, heliostat, infrared telescope, optical telescope, radio dish, radio interferometer, radio telescope, receiver, reflector, refractor, solar telescope, X-ray telescope

television black-and-white, box, cable television, colour, idiot box, monochrome, pay television, receiver, remote control, satellite television, screen, telly

temperature calorie, calorific value, calorimeter, Celsius scale, centigrade scale, Fahrenheit scale, joule, Réaumur scale, therm, thermograph, thermometer

tempo beat, downbeat, metre, metronome, polyrythm, pulse, rhythm, syncopation, time, timing, upbeat

temporal temporary, time-based, time-related

tempt allure, attract, coax, ensnare, entice, excite, facilitate, inveigle, motivate, pander to, seduce, stimulate, tantalize, tease, tempt, titillate, wheedle

ten commandments, decade, decagon, decagram, decahedron, Decalogue, decapod, decathlon, decennium, tenner, tenth, tithe

tenacious attached, bull-headed, clingy, committed, dedicated, determined, devoted, dogged, enduring, faithful, forceful, indefatigable, insistent, loyal, obstinate, persevering, persistent, pertinacious, pressing, serious, stubborn, thorough, tireless, wholehearted, zealous

tenacity adherence, attachment, bull-headedness, compulsion, determination, endurance, fidelity, hardness, headstrongness, holding on, implacability, inexorability, inflexibility, insistence, loyalty, obstinacy, perseverance, persistence, pertinacious, pitilessness, pressure, relentlessness, ruthlessness, steeliness, sternness, stubbornness, tenaciousness

tend affect, approach, be disposed, care for, contribute, cultivate, incline, influence, lead to, lean, look after, minister, nurse, point to, prepare, redound, turn to

tendency bearing, bent, cast, climate, contribution, course, current, drift, fashion, habitude, idiosyncrasy, influence, instinct, knack, leaning, mannerism, proclivity, propensity, stream, swing, taste, tenor, tone, trait, trend, trick, turn

tending to apt to, biased, conducive to, inclining, intending, leading, leaning, liable to, likely, partial, prejudiced, probable, tendentious

tentative experimental, inquiring, on appro, on approval, pilot, probationary, searching, testing, trial

tenth decagonal, decahedral, decennial, decimal, decuple, denary, tenfold

tergiversate back-pedal, equivocate, forsake, recant, repent, resign, reverse, withdraw

tergiversator apostate, deserter, equivocator, hypocrite, recusant, renegade, tergiversant, traitor

term aeon, century, cycle, day, decade, designate, epoch, era, expression, fortnight, hour, label, millennium, minute, month, olympiad, period, quarter, season, second, semester, spell, tag, time, week, word, year

terminus destination, journey's end

terrestrial earthly, grounded, worldly

territory area, bailiwick, colony, commonwealth, country, dependency, domain, dominion, empire, kingdom, mandate, nation, patch, possession, power, principality, protectorate, realm, republic, state, sultanate, superpower

terrorism assassination, bombing, car bombing, guerrilla attack, hostage taking, kidnapping, letter bombing, sniping, terror tactics

test examination, experiment, ordeal, trial, try

tested chanced, checked, determined, essayed, estimated, researched, risked, tried, ventured, verified

testify affirm, allege, assert, attest, aver, avow, declare, grass, inform, sing, squeal, state, swear, witness

textile alpaca, angora, broadcloth, cashmere, cheesecloth, chenille, chiffon, chintz, cloth, corduroy, cotton, denim, drill, fabric, flannel, homespun, jute, khaddar, lace, linen, madras, material, merino, mohair, moleskin, muslin, poplin, sackcloth, satin, seersucker, shantung, silk, staple, stuff, suiting, taffeta, tissue, towelling, tussore, tweed, twill, velvet, vicuna, voile, wool

texture consistency, constitution, feel, finish, sensation, structure, surface, touch

thank acknowledge, applaud, appreciate, attribute, give credit, pay tribute, praise, recognize, reward, show appreciation, tip

thanking acknowledging, blessing, cognizant of, crediting, praising

thankless fruitless, unprofitable, unrecognized, unrewarding, useless

thanks appreciation, benediction, blessing, grace, gratitude, hymn, paean, praise, prayer, thanksgiving

theatre amphitheatre, arena, auditorium, big top, booth, cinema, circus, concert hall, fleapit, hall, hippodrome, movie theatre, music hall, nightclub, odeon, opera house, pavilion, picture house, playhouse, showboat, stadium, toy theatre, venue
See list of theatrical terms.

theft appropriation, autotheft, break-in, burglary, filching, grab, hold-up, job, joyriding, lift, nabbing, nicking, pinch, robbery, shoplifting, snatch, steal, swiping, taking

theological canonical, divine, doctrinal, eschatological, hagiological, hierological, metaphysical, religious, scriptural, soteriological

theology Christology, divinity, hagiology, hierology, liberation theology, Mariology, metaphysics, patristics, RE, religious education, RI, religious studies, RS, scripture, soteriology

theoretical abstract, academic, assumed, conceptual, conjectural, estimated, fanciful, fictional, guesstimated, hypothetical, ideal, imaginary, indicative, made-up, make-believe, mythical, notional, perceptual, philosophical, presumed, propositional, putative, speculative, suggestive, suppositional, suspected

theorize assume, believe, conceptualize, conjecture, estimate, guess, guesstimate, hypothesize, opine, presume, reckon, suggest, suppose, suspect

theory clue, conjecture, fancy, feeling, guess, hint, hunch, hypothesis, idea, indication, intuition, speculation, suggestion, supposition, suspicion

therapeutic curative, medicinal, preventive, prophylactic, remedial

therapy aftercare, course, cure, first aid, medicine, nursing, regimen, remedy, therapeutics, treatment

thesis affirmation, assertion, attestation, case, claim, evidence, grounds, hypothesis, issue, opinion, point, position, postulate, premise, pretext, proposition, stance, statement, testimony, topic

they say
may indicate a homophone

thick ample, barrel-chested, bone-headed, broad, bulky, bull-necked, chunky, clabbered, clotted, coagulated, crowded, curdled, deep, dense, dim, dull, dumb, fat, heavy, idiotic, incrassate, lumpy, massive, obtuse, packed, padded, slow-witted, solid, stocky, stout, stupid, sturdy, substantial, swollen, thickened, thickset, wide

thicken cake, cement, churn, clabber, clot, coagulate, cohere, compress, condense, congeal, conglomerate, consolidate, constipate, crowd, crust, curdle, emulsify, gel, gelatinize, harden, incrassate, inspissate, intensify, jell, jellify, lopper, reduce, set, solidify, swarm

thickness body, breadth, bulk, bulkiness, chunkiness, density, depth, fatness, fullness, heaviness, mass, massiveness, solidity, stoutness, viscosity, width

thick-skinned callous, coarse, hard, insensitive

thieving body-snatching, brigandish, buccanneering, burglarious, foraging,

THEATRICAL TERMS

ABOVE
ACOUSTICS
ACT
ACTOR
ACTOR-MANAGER
ACTRESS
AD LIB
ADVERTISEMENT
  CURTAIN
AGENT
AMPHITHEATRE
ANTI-MASQUE
APRON
ARC
ARENA
ASIDE
ASM
ASPHALEIAN
  SYSTEM
AUDITION
AUDITORIUM
AULAEUM
AUTHOR'S NIGHT
AVANT-GARDE
BACKCLOTH
BACKING FLAT
BACKSTAGE
BALCONY
BARN DOOR
  SHUTTER
BARREL
BATTEN
BELOW
BENEFIT
BESPEAK
  PERFORMANCE
BLACKOUT
BLUE
BOARDS
BOAT TRUCK
BOOK
BOOK CEILING
BOOK FLAT
BOOK WING
BOOM
BORDER
BORDER LIGHT
BOX OFFICE
BOX SET
BRACE
BRIDGE
BRISTLE TRAP
BUILT STUFF
BUSKER
CALL BOARD
CALL BOY
CALL DOOR
CARBON ARC
CARPET CUT
CATWALK

CAULDRON TRAP
CEILING-CLOTH
CELLAR
CENTRE
CHAIRMAN
CHOREOGRAPHY
CIRCLE
CIRCUIT
CLOTH
CLOUD
COMPOSITE
  SETTING
CONCERT PARTY
CONTOUR CURTAIN
CORNER TRAP
CORSICAN TRAP
COSTUME DRAMA
COUNTERWEIGHT
  SYSTEM
COURTROOM
  DRAMA
CRITIC
CUP-AND-SAUCER
  DRAMA
CURTAIN
CURTAIN CALL
CURTAIN-MUSIC
CURTAIN SET
CUT-CLOTH
CYCLORAMA
DESIGNER
DETAIL SCENERY
DEUS EX MACHINA
DIMMER
DIORAMA
DIRECTOR
DOWNSTAGE
DRAG ARTIST
DRAMATIS
  PERSONAE
DRAPERY SETTING
DRAWING-ROOM
  DRAMA
DRESS CIRCLE
DRESS REHEARSAL
DROP
DUMB SHOW
ELEVATOR
EPILOGUE
EXIT
FALLING FLAP
FAN EFFECT
FAUTEUIL
FEMALE
  IMPERSONATOR
FLAT
FLEXIBLE STAGING
FLIES
FLIPPER
FLOAT

FLOODLIGHT
FLYING EFFECT
FOLLOW SPOT
FOOTLIGHT
FOOTLIGHTS TRAP
FORMAL STAGE
FOX WEDGE
FOYER
FRESNEL SPOT
FRONT OF HOUSE
GAFF
GALLERY
GAUZE
GEGGIE
GEL
GENERAL UTILITY
GHOST GLIDE
GLORY
GOBO
GODS
GRAVE TRAP
GREEN ROOM
GRID
GROOVE
GROUNDROW
HALL KEEPER
HALLS
HAM
HAND-PROPS
HOIST
HOUSE LIGHT
IMPRESARIO
IMPROVISATION
INCIDENTAL MUSIC
INNER STAGE
INSET
IRIS
JACKKNIFE STAGE
JORNADA
JUVENILE
KUPPELHORIZONT
LASHLINE
LATERNA MAGICA
LEG
LEKO
LIBRETTO
LIGHT BATTEN
LIGHT CONSOLE
LIGHTING
LIGHT PIPE
LIMELIGHT
LINSENSCHEIN-
  WERFER
LOBSTERSCOPE
LOFT BLOCK
LOW COMEDIAN
LYCOPODIUM
LYRIC
MAKE-UP
MANAGER

MANET
MARIONETTE
MASK
MASKING PIECE
MATINÉE
MAZARINE FLOOR
MEZZANINE FLOOR
NEUMES
NOISES OFF
ODEUM
OFF-BROADWAY
OFF-OFF-
  BROADWAY
OFF STAGE
OLD MAN
OLD WOMAN
OLIO
ON STAGE
OP
OPEN STAGE
ORCHESTRA
PAGEANT LANTERN
PANORAMA
PARADISO
PARALLEL
PASS DOOR
PENNY GAFF
PEPPER'S GHOST
PERCH
PERIAKTOI
PINSPOT
PIPE
PIPE BATTEN
PIT
PLATFORM (STAGE)
PLAYBILL
PORTAL OPENING
POSTER
PRODUCER
PROFILE BOARD
PROFILE SPOT
PROJECTOR
PROLOGUE
PROMENADE
PROMPTER
PROMPT SIDE
PROP
PROSCENIUM ARCH
PROSCENIUM
  BORDER
PROSCENIUM
  DOORS
PROVINCES
PUPPET
QUICK-CHANGE
  ROOM
RAIL
RAIN BOX
RAKE
REFLECTOR

THEATRICAL TERMS

REHEARSAL	SET	STAGE-DOOR	TOGGLE
REPERTORY	SET PIECE	KEEPER	TOP DROP
RETURN	SHOW PORTAL	STAGE-KEEPER	TORMENTOR
REVERBERATOR	SIGHT LINE	STAGE LIGHTING	TRANSPARENCY
REVOLVING STAGE	SILL IRON	STAGE MANAGER	TRAPS
RISE-AND-SINK	SIPARIUM	STAGE PROP	TRAVELLER
ROD-PUPPET	SKENE	STAGE RAKE	TRAVERSE CURTAIN
ROLL CEILING	SKY BORDER	STAGE SETTING	TREE BORDER
ROLL-OUT	SKY CLOTH	STALL	TRICKWORK
ROPE HOUSE	SKY DOME	STAR TRAP	TRILOGY
ROSTRUM	SLAPSTICK	STEREOPTICON	TRITAGONIST
ROYALTY	SLIPS	STICHOMYTHIA	TRUCK
RUN	SLIP STAGE	STILE	TUMBLER
RUNDHORIZONT	SLOTE	STOCK COMPANY	TWO-FOLD
RUNWAY	SM	STRIP LIGHT	TWOPENNY GAFF
SADDLE-IRON	SOCK	STROBE LIGHT	UNDERSTUDY
SAFETY CURTAIN	SOUBRETTE	SUPERNUMERARY	UPPER CIRCLE
SAND-CLOTH	SOUND EFFECTS	SWITCHBOARD	UPSTAGE
SCENARIO	SPECTATORY	TABLEAU	VALANCE
SCENE	SPIELTREPPE	TABS	VAMP TRAP
SCENE DOCK	SPOT BAR	TAIL	VISOR
SCENE RELIEF	SPOTLIGHT	TEASER	WAGGON STAGE
SCENERY	STAGE	TECHNICAL REHEARSAL	WALK-ON
SCIOPTICON	STAGE CLOTH	TELARI	WARDROBE
SCISSOR CROSS	STAGE CREW	THREE-FOLD	WATER ROWS
SCRIM	STAGE	THROWLINE	WIND MACHINE
SCRUTO	DIRECTION	THUNDER RUN	WING
SEA ROW	STAGE DOOR	THUNDERSHEET	WORD REHEARSAL

grave-robbing, kleptomaniac, larcenous, looting, marauding, pillaging, piratelike, plundering, plunderous, poaching, predatory, privateering, purloining, raiding, ravaging, sacking, skyjacking, spolitory, stealing, sticky-fingered despoiling, theft

thin adulterate, attenuate, bony, cut, dilute, etherealize, exhaust, gangling, gasify, gawky, gracile, lanky, lean, narrow-waisted, puny, rangy, rarefy, scarce, scattered, scraggy, scrawny, skinny, slender, slight, slim, small-framed, spare, svelte, sylphlike, tenuous, transparent, twiggy, underweight, vaporize, wasp-waisted, water down, weaken, weedy, willowy, wiry

thing being, body, entity, happening, item, monad, object, phenomenon, something, substance

think cerebrate, cogitate, cognize, conceptualize, consider, deduce, deliberate, ideate, imagine, induce, intuit, meditate, perceive, ponder, ratiocinate, rationalize, reason, ruminate, speculate

thinker academic, brainbox, dreamer, egghead, genius, highbrow, ideologist, intellectual, philosopher, professor, scholar, student

thinned attenuated, diluted, flattened, pressed, rarefied, runny, watered-down, watery, weak

thinness attenuation, boniness, fewness, gangliness, gawkiness, gracility, lankiness, leanness, meagreness, paucity, puniness, ranginess, rarefaction, runniness, scantiness, scragginess, scrawniness, skinniness, slenderness, slightness, slimness, spareness, sparseness, twigginess, wateriness, weakness, weediness, willowiness, wiriness

third third age, third degree, third eye, third party, third person, Third World, tierce

thirst dehydration, drought, dryness, xerostomia

thirsty dry, parched

thorn awn, barb, briar, bristle, burr, prickle, thistle

thoroughbred aristocratic, blue-blooded, classy, cultivated, pedigree, purebred, refined, well-bred

thought care, cerebration, cogitation, cognition, concern, deduction, idea, ratiocination, reasoning, rumination, suggestion, thinking

thoughtful attentive, caring, cerebral, circumspect, cogitative, cognitive, considerate, contemplative, deep, dreaming, intellectual, introspective, judicious, meditative, mental, pensive, philosophical, profound, reasonable, reasoning, reflective, ruminative, sapient, sensible, sound, speculative, thinking

thoughtfulness brown study, care, carefulness, circumspection, concentration, concern, consideration, contemplation, daydreaming, depth, introspection, judiciousness, meditation, musing, pensiveness, profundity, reflection, retrospection, reverie, speculation

thoughtless absent-minded, blank, carefree, devil-may-care, easygoing, empty-headed, fatuous, foolish, happy-go-lucky, ignorant, inane, inconsiderate, insensitive, mindless, oblivious, selfish, uncaring, unreflective, unthinking, vacant, vacuous

thoughtlessness blankness, disregard, ignorance, inconsideration, indifference, insensitivity, selfishness, stupidity

thousand grand, K, kilo, kilobyte, kilogram, kilometre, lakh, millenarian, millenary, millenial, millennium, milligram, millilitre, millimetre, millipede, myriad, thousandfold, thousandth

three cube, cubed, Musketeers, ternary, tertiary, third, threefold, threesome, treble, trebleness, trey, triad, triadic, triality, trifold, triform, trimor-phic, trimorphism, trinal, trinary, trine, trinity, trio, triple, tripleness, triplex, triplicate, triplicity, triune

three parts shamrock, three-decker, three-dimensional, three-hander, three-wheeler, trefoil, triangle, triangular, tricorn, tricycle, trident, tridentate, tridimensional, triennial, triennium, trifoliate, trigonal, trihebdomadary, trihedral, trilateral, trilingual, trilogy, trimaran, trimester, trimestrial, trimeter, trimetric, trinomial, tripedal, triplet, tripod, tripodic, triptych, tristich, trithedron, triumvirate, trivet, troika

thrift austerity, carefulness, cheeseparing, economy, frugality, prudence

thrifty austere, canny, careful, cheeseparing, conserving, economical, economizing, frugal, meagre, prudent, saving, scrimpy, sparing, spartan

thrive bloom, blossom, burgeon, flourish, improve, prosper, succeed

throng army, array, bevy, brood, bunch, cloud, clutter, colony, congregation, covey, crowd, crush, drove, fleet, flight, flock, hail, hive, horde, host, jam, legion, mass, mob, multitude, nest, pack, press, rout, ruck, shoal, swarm, troop

throw bowl, bung, cast, catapult, chuck, fire, fling, flip, heave, hurl, hurtle, launch, lob, pass, pelt, pitch, propel, shy, snowball, stone, swipe, toss, york
may indicate an anagram

throw away bin, defenestrate, discard, jettison, junk, precipitate, scrap

throwing casting, chucking, flinging, heaving, hurling, jaculation, lobbing, pelting, pitching, precipitation, projection, slinging, trajection

thud bump, clunk, electric storm, plonk, plop, plump, plunk, rainstorm, tempest, thump

thwart baffle, balk, bilk, confound, deny, foil, frustrate, hamper, hinder, refuse, stonewall

tick oscillate, pulse, swing, throb, undulate

tide current, ebb, equinoctial tide, flood, flow, neap tide, riptide

tidied cleared up, disentangled, neat, straightened out, tidy, unravelled, unsnarled, untangled

tidy clean, clear up, considerable, correct, debug, disentangle, groom, iron out, neaten, ordered, rearrange, smarten up, smooth, spruce up, straighten, substantial, unravel, unsnarl, untangle, worthwhile
may indicate an anagram

tied attached, bound, fastened, fixed, glued, hitched, immovable, interwoven, jammed, knotted, lashed, plaited, secure, secured, spliced, stitched, wedged, yoked

tightrope walker equilibrist, funambulist, high-wire artist, ropewalker

till cash register, cultivate, plough, until

tillage crop-spraying, cultivation, culture, dunging, ethering, fertilizing, flowering, fruition, harrowing, harvesting, hay-making, heathering, hedge-laying, hedging, irrigation, muck-spreading, planting, plashing, pleaching, ploughing, silaging, sowing, tilth, weeding

timber alburum, branchwood, brushwood, cork, duramen, firewood, heartwood, pulpwood, sapwood, trunkwood, wetwood

time aeon, age, century, chiliad, clock, count, day, decade, decennium, duration, epoch, era, fortnight, generation, hour, instant, judge, lifetime, microsecond, millenium, millisecond, minute, moment, monitor, month, nanosecond, period, quarter, quinquennium, record, schedule, second, set, slate, space-time, synchronize, timetable, week, year
See also list at **clock**.

timekeeping annalistic, calendar-making, calendrical, chronographic, chronologic, chronometric, dating, diaristic, horological, scheduling, temporal, timetabling, timing

timeless ageless, continuous, dateless, eternal, everlasting, immortal, lasting, perpetual, sempiternal, unceasing, undying

timelessness changelessness, eternity, neverness, sempiternity

timeliness appropriateness, aptness, auspiciousness, convenience, favourableness, fitness, maturity, opportuneness, propitiousness, providence, readiness, ripeness, suitability

timely appropriate, apropos, auspicious, befitting, convenient, favourable, felicitous, fortunate, happy, lucky, opportune, propitious, providential, seasonable, suitable, suited, welcome

timer chronograph, chronometer, clock, counter, horologe, timepiece, watch

timetable calendar, course, curriculum, diary, journal, list, programme, schedule

timid cowardly, faint-hearted, ineffectual, insipid, jittery, jumpy, nervy, panicky, pusillanimous, shy, spineless, squeamish, tremulous, weak, wet, wimpish, wishy-washy

timidity cowardice, faint-heartedness, jitteryness, jumpiness, nervousness, pusillanimity, spinelessness, squeamishness, tremulousness, weakness

tip advise, chaos, dump, end, gratuity, hint, incline, indicate, lean, list, mess, point, shambles, signal, slant, slope, spike, suggest, teeter

tipsy
may indicate an anagram

title deeds, entitle, ownership, rights, style, term

toast cheers, drink to, heat, pledge, salute, warm

toilet bedpan, bog, chamber pot,

closestool, commode, convenience, gazunder, grooming, jerry, latrine, lavatory, loo, po, potty, stool, throne, thunderbox, washing

tolerable adequate, average, fair, fifty-fifty, fresh, indifferent, mediocre, middling, OK, okey-doke, ordinary, passable, respectable, satisfactory, so-so, sound, standard, sufficient, unexceptionable

tolerate bear with, forbear

tomfoolery antics, buffoonery, burlesque, capers, clowning, drollery, farce, high jinks, horseplay, jape, practical joke, prank, scrape, shenanigans, silliness, skylarking, trick, whimsicality

tongue argot, idiom, jargon, parlance, patois, slang, speech, talk, vocalism, vulgate

tonic cordial, pick-me-up, refresher, restorative, reviver, roborant, stimulant

tool apparatus, appliance, contrivance, device, gadget, implement, instrument, machine, utensil
See list of tools.

toothed comblike, corniculate, cornute, craggy, cusped, denticulate, dentiform, emarginate, fanged, horned, jagged, muricate, notched, odontoid, pectinate, rough, serrated, snagged, tusked

toothless biteless, edentate, teethless

top apical, cap, capital, chief, climactic, climax, consummate, cover, crown, culminate, frosting, head, highest, icing, kill, lead, leading, maximum, meridian, overarch, paramount, peak, polar, roof, summital, superstratum, supreme, surface, surmount, tiptop, topping, topside, topsoil, ultimate, uppermost, upside, vertical, zenithal

topic angle, argument, basis, concern, contents, course, drift, essence, foundation, gist, idea, interest, keynote, leitmotiv, matter, meat, message, motif, pith, plot, point, programme, project, proposition, rubric, statement, subject, supposition, text, theme, theorem, thesis, tract, treatise

topical contemporary, current, happening, immediate, present, timely, up-to-date, up-to-the-minute

topography cartography, chorography, geodesy, geography, navigation, orienteering, surveying, triangulation

topsy-turvy
may indicate an anagram

torment abuse, attack, bash, beat, blackmail, bully, bullyrag, demand, frighten, harass, harm, harry, hound, hurt, injure, intimidate, maltreat, menace, molest, oppress, persecute, plague, rape, scare, spite, terrorize, threaten, thwart, torture, trouble, tyrannize, vex, victimize

torsion distortion, torque, twisting, warp

torture anguish, distress, iron boot, Iron Maiden, kneecap, martyr, mutilate, pain, persecute, pilliwinks, press, rack, Scavenger's Daughter, suffering, thumbscrew, torment, torture chamber, treadmill, triangle, wheel
may indicate an anagram

total aggregate, all, amount to, bill, come to, count, entirety, equal, factor, gross, make, net, nett, number, product, quantity, reckoning, result, score, sum, summation, tally, whole

touch abut, aesthesia, affect, brush, caress, concreteness, connect, consistency, contact, dab, feel, feeling, finger, fondle, fumble, goose, graze, grope, handle, hit, impress, impression, jab, join, kiss, knead, manipulate, manoeuvre, massage, maul, meet, move, nudge, nuzzle, palpability, palpate, pat, paw, poke, press, prod, reality, rub, sensation, sensitivity, shave, skim, solidity, stir, stroke, tactile, tactility, tangibility, tap, texture, vibration

touchable concrete, material, palpable, real, solid, substantial, tactile, tactual, tangible

TOOLS

ADZE
ANVIL
AUGER
AWL
AXE
BARKING
 IRONS
BARK MILL
BARROW
BAR SHEAR
BEAKIRON
BEELE
BELT
 ADJUSTER
BELT PUNCH
BENCH
BENCH
 HOOK
BENCH PEG
BENDER
BESOM
BETTY
BEVEL
BILL (HOOK)
BISTOURY
BIT
BLADE
BLOOMARY
BLOWER
BLOWING
 MACHINE
BLOWLAMP
BLOWPIPE
BOASTER
BOATHOOK
BODKIN
BOLT AUGER
BOOT CRIMP
BORCER
BORE
BORER
BOWDRILL
BOW-SAW
BRACE(-AND-
 BIT)
BRADAWL
BRANDING
 IRON
BRAYER
BREAST DRILL
BREASTPLOUGH
BROACH
BROG
BULL NOSE
BURIN
BURR
BURTON
BUSH
 HARROW
BUTTERIS

CALIPERS
CANKER BIT
CANNIPERS
CAN OPENER
CANTHOOK
CAPSTAN
CARDING
 MACHINE
CARPENTER'S
 BENCH
CART
CATLING
CAULKING
 TOOL
CAUTERY
CELT
CENTRE BIT
CHAFF
 CUTTER
CHAIN
 BLOCKS
CHAIN
 WRENCH
CHAMFER
CHASER
CHEESE PRESS
CHIP-AXE
CHISEL
CHOPPER
CHOPPING
 BLOCK
CHOPPING
 KNIFE
CHUCK
CHURN
CLAMP
CLAMS
CLASP
CLASPKNIFE
CLAW
 HAMMER
CLEAT
CLEAVER
COLD CHISEL
COLTER
COMPASSES
CORKSCREW
COTTON GIN
COULOIR
COULTER
COUNTER
 GAUGE
COUNTERSINK
CRAB
CRADEL
 SCYTHE
CRAMP
CREVET
CRIMPING
 IRON

CRISPER
CRISPING IRON
CRISPING PIN
CROOM
CROSSCUT
 SAW
CROWBAR
CROW MILL
CROZE
CRUCIBLE
CRUSET
CULTIVATOR
CUPEL
CURLING
 TONGS
CURRY COMB
CUTTER BAR
CUVETTE
CYLINDER
 PRESS
DERRICK
DIAMOND
DIBBER
DIBBLE
DIE
DIE STOCK
DOFFER
DOG-BFIT
DOG CLUTCH
DOLLY
DOWEL BIT
DRAINING
 ENGINE
DRAINING
 PLOUGH
DRAW KNIFE
DRAW-PLATE
DRAY PLOUGH
DREDGE
DREDGING
 MACHINE
DRIFT BOLTS
DRILL
DRILLING
 MACHINE
DRILL PLOUGH
DRILLPRESS
DRILLSTOCK
DRIVER
DRIVING SHAFT
DRIVING
 WHEEL
DRUDGER
EDGE TOOL
ELECTRIC DRILL
EMERY
 GRINDER
EMERY WHEEL
ENTRENCHING
 TOOL

EXCAVATOR
EYELETEER
FAN
FANNER
FANNING MILL
FAUCET
FERRET
FILATORY
FILE
FILLISTER
FINING POT
FISTUCA
FLAIL
FLAME GUN
FLANG
FLAX COMB
FLOUR DRESSER
FOLDER
FORCEPS
FORGE
FORK
FORK CHUCK
FRETSAW
FROW
FRUGGIN
GAD
GAGE
GAS PLIERS
GAUGE
GAVEL
GAVELOCK
GEE CRAMP
GIMLET
GIN
GLASS
 FURNACE
GOUGE
GRADINE
GRAINER
GRAPNEL
GRAPPLING-
 IRON
GRAVER
GRINDSTONE
GRUB AXE
GRUBBING
 HOE
HACKLE
HACKSAW
HAMMER
HAMMER AXE
HANDBRACE
HANDLOOM
HANDMILL
HANDSAW
HANDSCREW
HANDSPIKE
HAND VICE
HARROW
HATCHET

HAY FORK
HAY KNIFE
HELVEHAMMER
HINK
HOD
HOE
HOIST
HOLING AXE
HOOK
HORSE HOE
HUMMELLER
HYDRAULIC
 JACK
HYDRAULIC
 RAM
IMPLEMENT
INCUS
INSTRUMENT
JACK
JACKKNIFE
JACKPLANE
JACKS
JACKSCREW
JAGGER
JAGGING
 IRON
JEMMY
JIG
JIGGER
JIG SAW
JIMMY
JOINTER
KNIFE
LADDER
LAPSTONE
LAST
LATHE
LAWNMOWER
LEAD MILL
LEVEL
LEVER
LOOM
LOY
MACHINE
 TOOL
MALL
MALLET
MANDREL
MANDREL
 LATHE
MARLINE SPIKE
MASONRY BIT
MASTICATOR
MATTOCK
MAUL
MITRE BLOCK
MITRE BOX
MOLEGRIP
MONKEY
 BLOCK

TOOLS continued

MONKEY
WRENCH
MORTAR
MOTOR
MOWER
MOULD BOARD
MOWER
MUCK RAKE
MULE
MULLER
NAIL
NAIL PUNCH
NIPPERS
NUT HOOK
NUT WRENCH
OILSTONE
OLIVER
PACKING
NEEDLE
PAINTBRUSH
PAINT PAD
PAINT ROLLER
PALLET
PANEL SAW
PARER
PENCIL
PERFORATOR
PESTLE AND
MORTAR
PICK(AXE)
PICKLOCK
PIERCER
PIKE
PINCERS ·
PIPE WRENCH
PITCH FORK
PITSAW
PLANE (IRON)
PLANER
PLANISHER
PLIERS
PLOUGH-
(SHARE)
PLOW
PLUMB
PLUMB BOB
PLUMBLINE
PLUMBRULE
PLUMMET
PNEUMATIC
DRILL
POINTED
AWL
POLE AXE
POLISHER
PONTEE
POOLER
POUNDER
POWER SAW
PREEN

PRICKER
PRISE
PRONG
PRONG-HOE
PRUNING
HOOK
PRUNING
KNIFE
PULLEY BLOCKS
PUMP SCREW-
DRIVER
PUNCH
PUNCHEON
QUERN
QUOIN
RABBET
PLANE
RAKE
RAMMER
RASP
RASPER
RATCH
RAZOR
REAPER
REAPING
HOOK
REAPING
MACHINE
RIDDLE
RIPSAW
RUBBER
RULE
RUNNING
BLOCK
SALT-PAN
SANDER
SARSE
SAW
SAWING
STOOL
SAW-SET
SAW WREST
SCALPEL
SCAUPER
SCISSORS
SCRAPER
SCREEN
SCREW
SCREW-
DRIVER
SCREWER
SCREWJACK
SCREW
PRESS
SCRIBE AWL
SCRIBER
SCRIBING
BLOCK
SCRIBING
IRON

SCUFFLER
SCYTHE
SEED LOP
SEGGER
SEWING
MACHINE
SHEARLEGS
SHEARS
SHEEP HOOK
SHOVEL
SICKLE
SIFTER
SINGLE-
EDGED
SKEWER
SKIM
COULTER
SLATE AXE
SLEDGE
SLEDGE
HAMMER
SLEEK STONE
SLICER
SLIDING BEVEL
SMOOTHING
PLANE
SNATCH
BLOCK
SNOW-
PLOUGH
SOCK
SOCKET CHISEL
SOLDERING
BOLT
SOLDERING
IRON
SOWING
MACHINE
SPADDLE
SPADE
SPANNER
SPIKE
SPILE
SPILL
SPINNING
JENNY
SPINNING
WHEEL
SPIRIT LEVEL
SPITTLE
SPOKESHAVE
SPRAYER
SPUD
SQUARE
SQUARING
ROD
STEAM
HAMMER
STEAM PRESS
STEELYARD

STEPLADDER
STIDDY
STILETTO
STITHY
STONE
BREAKER
STONE
HAMMER
STRAIGHTEDGE
STRAW
CUTTER
STRICKLE
STRIKE
STRIKE BLOCK
STROCAL
STUBBLE RAKE
SUBSOIL
PLOUGH
SUGAR MILL
SWAGE
SWARD CUTTER
SWINGLE
KNIFE
SWINGLING
KNIFE
SWING-
PLOUGH
TACKLE
TAPEMEASURE
TEMSE
TENONER
TENON SAW
TENTER
TENTERHOOK
THIMBLE
TIIROSTLE
THRUSTING
SCREW
THUMBSCREW
THUMBSTALL
TILT HAMMER
TIN OPENER
TOMMY
TONGS
TOOTH KEY
TRENCH
PLOUGH
TREPAN
TRESTLE
TRIBLET
TRIP HAMMER
TROMP
TRONE
TROWEL
TRUG
TRY SQUARE
T-SQUARE
TUBBER
TURF CUTTER
TURFING IRON

TURFING SPADE
TURF SPADE
TURN BENCH
TURNBUCKLE
TURNING
LATHE
TURNSCREW
TURREL
TWEEZERS
TWIBILL
TWIST BIT
TWISTER
TWO-FOOT
RULE
TWO-HOLE
PLIERS
VICE
WARPING
HOOK
WARPING
POST
WATER
BELLOWS
WATERCAN
WATERCRANE
WATERGAUGE
WATERLEVEL
WATERMILL
WATER RAM
WEDGE
WEED HOOK
WEEDING
CHISEL
WEEDING
FORCEPS
WEEDING
FORK
WEEDING
HOOK
WEEDING
RHIM
WEEDING
TONGS
WEIGHING
MACHINE
WHEEL-
BARROW
WHEEL BRACE
WHIM
WHIP-SAW
WHITTLE
WIMBLE
WINCH
WINDLASS
WINDMILL
WOOLDER
WRENCH
ZAX

touchiness irascibility, irritability, oversensitivity, raw feelings, sore point

touching abutting, adjacent, adjoining, bordering, caressing, colliding, connecting, contiguous, crashing, emotional, fingering, fondling, glancing, goosing, groping, hand-in-glove, hand-in-hand, handling, holding, interfacing, intersecting, manipulating, massaging, meeting, moving, overlapping, palpating, petting, pitiful, rubbing, stroking

tough adamant, bombproof, boned, bulletproof, chip-proof, durable, fireproof, firm, fractureproof, hard-wearing, indestructible, indigestible, inelastic, inflexible, infrangible, lasting, muscle-bound, pokerlike, resistant, rigid, rugged, shatterproof, shockproof, solid, starchy, stark, stiff, strong, sturdy, taut, tense, tight, unbreakable, unrelaxed, unsprung, untearable

toughened annealed, case-hardened, hardened, strengthened, tanned, tempered, vulcanized

toughness chewiness, cohesiveness, durability, firmness, hardness, indigestibility, inedibility, infrangibility, lastingness, leatheriness, resistance, rigidness, rubberiness, ruggedness, solidness, stiffness, strength, stringiness, sturdiness, survivability, unbreakableness, viscidity

tow drag, draw, haul, pull, tug

town boom, borough, built-up area, burgh, city, county, downtown, market, megalopolis, metropolis, new, precinct, township, uptown, urban area

townsman burgess, burgher, citizen, city-dweller, commuter, metropolitan, oppidan, townee, townsfolk, urbanite

toxic deadly, germ-laden, lethal, mephitic, pestilent, poisoned, poisonous, polluted, septic, venomous

track branch line, course, follow, groove, hunt, lane, line, loop, main line, orbit, path, print, rail, road, route, row, siding, song, spur, trace, trail, trajectory

traction draught, drawing, drayage, haulage, heaving, pulling, retractiveness, towage, tugging

trade agiotage, arbitrage, barter, black market, brokerage, business, commerce, commercialize, deal, exchange, export, factorage, factorship, float, import, incorporate, intervene, market, merchandise, nationalize, peddle, privatize, profiteer, profiteering, profit-making, promote, prostitution, push, racketeer, racketeering, sell, share-pushing, smuggle, smuggling, stock-jobbing, swap, traffic, trafficking, transaction, truck

trader broker, businessman, dealer, distributor, exporter, fence, horse-trader, importer, jobber, merchant, profiteer, purchaser, racketeer, retailer, seller, smuggler, speculator, vendor, wholesaler

tradition consuetude, convention, custom, folklore, folksong, folk tale, habit, law, legend, lore, myth, praxis, precedent, prescription, rite, ritual, symbol, taboo

traditional conservative, conventional, customery, habitual, old-fashioned, usual

tragedy calamity, catastrophe, distaster, melodrama, misfortune

train bogie, coach, coupling, double header, drawbar, draw gear, express, freight train, goods train, instruct, king bolt, mail train, milk train, night mail, passenger train, practise, rake, slow train, stopping train, tail, teach, tutor, twin bill

traitor betrayer, double agent, double-crosser, double-dealer, informer, Judas, quisling, serpent, treasonist, turncoat

transcendent blessed, enlightened, perfect, sublime, supreme, transcendental

transfer barter, bequeathal, change-over, channel, conversion, decant, delivery, delocalization, deportation, displacement, exchange, expulsion, extradition, gift, handover, interchange, metathesis, metempsychosis, moving, relegation, relocation, removal, reversion, sale, shift, siphon, substitution, swap, trade, transfuse, transition, translocate, transmission, transmit, transplacement, transplant, transposal, transpose

transferring assigned, bequeathing, bestowable, consignable, conveyed, devisable, exchangeable, inheritable, made over, negotiable

transfiguration improvement, rebuilding, refurbishment, restoration, transformation

transform alchemize, deform, distort, make into, metabolize, metamorphose, modify, mould, mutate, re-educate, reform, rehabilitate, remodel, reorganize, reshape, restructure, shape, transfigure, translate, transmogrify, transmute, transubstantiate, turn into
may indicate an anagram

transformation conversion, metamorphosis, mutation, transfiguration, transmogrification, transmutation, transubstantiation

transformative convertive, metabolic, metamorphic, metamorphous, mutative, transmutative, transubstantial

transgress breach, deviate, encroach, entrench, err, fall, impinge, infringe, intrude, invade, lapse, sin, trespass, usurp, violate

transgression breach, crime, encroachment, incursion, infestation, infraction, infringement, intrusion, invasion, sin, taking liberties, trespass, usurpation, violation

transience brevity, ephemerality, evanescence, fugacity, impermanence, instability, momentariness, quickness, suddenness, transitoriness, volatility

transient brief, crumble away, decaying, disappearing, ephemeral, evanesce, evanescent, evaporate, fading, fleeting, flit, flying, fugitive, melt away, meteoric, momentary, passing, perishable, quick, rot, short, shortlived, sudden, transitory, unstable, vanish, volatile

translate adapt, amplify, cipher, copy, decipher, decode, encode, interpret, move, paraphrase, photocopy, plagiarize, read, redact, rehash, relocate, render, restate, reword, shift, simplify, transcribe, transfer, transliterate
may indicate an anagram

translated deciphered, decoded, paraphrased, restated, reworded, transliterated, word-for-word

translation adaptation, amplification, crib, decipherment, decoding, edition, exegesis, key, paraphrase, pony, redaction, rendering, restatement, rewording, simplification, transcription, transliteration, transumption, unscrambling, version

translucency diaphanousness, filminess, fineness, flimsiness, gauziness, insubstantiality, milkiness, mistiness, opalescence, pearliness, sheerness, smokiness, thinness, vaporousness

translucent diaphanous, filmy, fine, flimsy, gauzy, insubstantial, lucent, open-textured, revealing, see-through, sheer, thin, vaporous

transmission broadcast, communication, conduction, contact, convection, decantation, diffusion, dispersal, dispersion, dissemination, infection, perfusion, spread, transduction, transfusion, transpiration

transparency clarity, cleanness, clearness, cloudlessness, colourlessness, crystallinity, glassiness, limpidity, pellucidity, purity, vitreousness, wateriness

transparent clarified, clear, cloudless, colourless, crystalline, dioptric, glassy, hyaline, limpid, liquid, pellucid, pure, refractive, transpicuous, vitreous, watery

transport airlift, carry, cartage, commuting, consign, containerization, convey, conveyance, deliver, dispatch, distribute, distribution, expedite, export, ferry, forward, forwarding, freight, hand over, haul, haulage, heave, hump, lift, load, lug, manhandle, move, pack, palletization, portage, push, remit, remove, send, sending, ship, shipment, take, tote, transmit, transship, transshipment, truck , vehicle
See also list at **vehicle**.

transportable movable, portable

transportation airlift, asportation, bridge, carriage, carry, cartage, conveyance, delivery, dispatch, export, expressage, freightage, handover, haulage, humping, import, lighterage, passage, portage, posting, sending, shipment, transit, transshipment, truckage, vection, waft, waggonage

trap ambush, artifice, catch, catch-22, danger, deceive, deception, dupe, entrap, firetrap, gin, hazard, inveigle, minefield, net, obstacle, pit, pitfall, quagmire, ruse, snag, snare, springe, stratagem, subterfuge, surprise, trapdoor, trick

trapped ambushed, baited, caught, cornered, ginned, hijacked, hooked, kidnapped, meshed, mined, netted, snared, trawled, webbed
may indicate a split word

treacherous betraying, doubledealing, duplicitous, faithless, falsehearted, inconstant, perfidious, treasonous

treasurer accountant, almoner, banker, bookkeeper, bursar, cashier, financier, payer, purser, teller

treasury almonry, bank, building society, bursary, cash box, coffer, counting house, custom house, depository, exchequer, piggy bank, public purse, safe, strongbox, strongroom

treat advise, amputate, anaesthetize, antisepticize, attend, bandage, bind, bleed, bonus, cauterize, control, crown, cure, curette, deal with, delicacy, disinfect, doctor, dope, dose, draw, drench, dress, drug, entertain, extract, fill, foment, gift, good, goody, gratify, handle, hospitalize, immunize, inject, inoculate, luxury, manipulate, massage, medicate, minister, negotiate, nurse, operate, parley, pasteurize, perfuse, phlebotomize, physic, plaster, poultice, prescribe, process, pull, purge, purify, revive, sanitate, set, splendid, staunch, sterilize, stop, tend, transfuse, trepan, trephine, vaccinate

treatment actions, administration, aftercare, control, counselling, dealings, diplomacy, direction, handling, management, medication, nursing, orchestration, organization, regulation, rehabilitation, surgery, tact, therapy, transactions

tree bonsai, broadleaf, bush, Christmas tree, conifer, deciduous, evergreen, fruiter, hardwood, maiden, ornamental, palm, sapling, shade tree, shrub, softwood, standard, timber tree, tree fern, tropical hardwood

treelike arboraceous, arboreal, arborescent, branching, bushy, coniferous, dendriform, dendritic, dendroid, evergreen, gnarled, palmaceous, palmate, piny, resinous, shrubby, willowy

trendiness fad, fashion, futurism, modernism

trial appeal, assize, hearing, inquest, inquiry, inquisition, judgment, pleadings, retrial, sentence, sessions, sitting, verdict

tribunal bench, board, confessional, council, ecclesia, forum, judicatory, throne, wardmote

tribute congratulation, health, levy, praise, reward, tax, testimonial, toast

trick artifice, bamboozle, betray, blind, bluff, catch, cheat, chicane, circumvent, collude, con, connive, conspire, contrivance, contrive, deceive, defraud, design, device, diddle, diversion, divert, dodge, double-cross, dupe, feint, fetch, fool, fudge, gambit, gimmick, hoodwink, kid, machinate, manipulate, outmanoeuvre, outsmart, outwit, pass, ploy, rip-off, ruse, scheme, sham, shift, sleight, spoof, sting, stratagem, swindle, wile, wrinkle

tricking artifice, bamboozlement, chicanery, circumvention, collusion, connivance, conspiracy, diddling, dodgery, dupery, enmeshment, ensnarement, entanglement, entrapment, flimflam, hanky-panky, hoodwinking, jiggery-pokery, machination, manipulation, mockery, quackery, ridicule, sharp practice, shenanigan, skulduggery, sorcery, witchcraft

tricky
may indicate an anagram

trident missile, rocket, trefoil, triangle, tripod

trifle bagatelle, bauble, bric-a-brac, brummagem, cake, chaff, chickenfeed, curio, detail, diversion, doit, drop, fleabite, fraction, frippery, gaud, gewgaw, gimcrack, gossamer, inessential, iota, jest, joke, jot, jumble, junk, kickshaw, knickknack, minutiae, nothing, novelty, peanuts, peccadillo, pinprick, plaything, pudding, sideshow, tat, technicality, toy, trinket, trivia, triviality, whit, white elephant

trill chorus, quaver, tremolo, vibrato, warble

trinkets braid, feathers, flounce, frill, fringe, frippery, furbelow, gandery, gew-gaws, knick-knacks, ribbon, ruffle, spangles, sparklers

trip capsize, career, crash, expedition, fall, fall headlong, hallucinate, journey, lurch, overbalance, overturn, pitch, slip, sprawl, spreadeagle, stagger, stumble, topple, totter, tumble, voyage

triple cube, treble, triplicate

trisected three-part, trichotomous, trifid, trifurcated, tripartite

trivial cheap, childish, commonplace, featherbrained, foolish, footling, frivolous, inferior, insubstantial, lightweight, nit-picking, nominal, nugatory, parochial, pettifogging, petty, piddling, piffling, poor, puerile, rubbishy, second-rate, shallow, small, small-time, superficial, tiny, token, trifling, twopenny-halfpenny, worthless

triviality cheapness, flippancy, frivolousness, inferiority, inutility, mediocrity, pettiness, shallowness, smallness, superficiality, uselessness, worthlessness

trivialize belittle, degrade, demote, denigrate, disparage, humiliate, mock, relegate, scorn

trophy award, chaplet, citation, crown, cup, decoration, garland, garter, gong, honour, laurels, medal, medallion, palm, plate, pot, prize, reward, ribbon, spurs, statuette, wreath

trouble annoy, bother, disadvantage, discommode, disrupt, disturb, embarrass, handicap, hassle, hinder, irk, irritate, obstruct, penalize, pester, put out, upset, vex
may indicate an anagram

troubled annoyed, anxious, baffled, beset, bewildered, bothered, confused, deadlocked, distressed, embarrassed, harassed, inconvenienced, in difficulties, mystified, nonplussed, perplexed, perturbed, plagued, put out, puzzled, snookered, stuck, stumped, turbulent, vexed, violent, worried

troublemaker handful, imp, mischief-maker, nuisance, pest, rascal, scallywag, scamp

troublesome bloody-minded, censorious, contrary, critical, demanding, disapproving, discontented, disobedient, disruptive, fastidious, faultfinding, finicky, fussy, grudging, headstrong, intractable, moody, naughty, nit-picking, obdurate, obstinate, obstreperous, particular, pedantic, pernickety, perverse, refractory, stroppy, stubborn, unmanageable, wayward

trousers bags, bell-bottoms, Bermuda shorts, bloomers, bluejeans, breeches, breeks, britches, cords, denims, drainpipes, dungarees, flannels, flares, galligaskins, hipsters, hot pants, jeans, jodhpurs, knee breeches, knickerbockers, lederhosen, Levi's, long trousers, overalls, Oxford bags, pantaloons, pants, pedal pushers, pinstripes, plus fours, riding breeches, shorts, ski pants, slacks, trews

truant absentee, AWOL, cut, defected, deserted, flit, mitch, scat, scram, skedaddle, skive

truck artic, articulated vehicle, cart, communication, connection, dealings, juggernaut, lorry, tractor, trailer, transporter, van, wagon
See also list at **vehicle**.

true authentic, direct, factual, genuine, honest-to-God, honest-to-goodness, real, right, straight, total, unfictitious, unmistaken, utter, veracious, veritable

truism aphorism, axiom, cliché, dictum, maxim, platitude, precept, principle, proverb, saw

truth authenticity, fact, historicity, honesty, reality, rightness, unerroneousness, unmistakenness, unspeciousness, unspuriousness, veracity, verity

truthful artless, bald, blunt, candid, direct, downright, forthright, frank, guileless, honest, ingenuous, naive, objective, open, openhearted, outspoken, plain, realistic, simple, sincere, straightforward, unaffected, unassuming, unbiased, undisguised, unexaggerated, unflattering, unpretending, unpretentious, veracious, veridical

truthfulness artlessness, baldness, bluntness, candour, directness, downrightness, forthrightness, frankness, guilelessness, honesty, ingenuousness, naivety, objectivity, openness, outspokenness, plainness, probity, simpleness, sincerity, straightforwardness, unaffectedness, veracity

try attempt, beaver away, buckle down, concentrate, endeavour, examine, exert oneself, experiment, judge, labour, pass judgment, persevere, persist, put on trial, score, slave, strain, strive, struggle, sweat, take pains, test, toil, work

tumult brouhaha, bustle, commotion, confusion, din, disturbance, frenzy, furore, hubbub, hurly-burly, moil, racket, rout, rush, stir, turmoil
may indicate an anagram

tunnel bore, burrow, Chunnel, excavate, métro, mine, sap, subway, tube, underground, undermine, underpass

tunnelling boring, burrowing, caving, digging, excavation, mining, potholing, sapping, speleology

turbulence effervescence, ferment, fermentation, seethe, seething, turbidity

turbulent boiling, bouncy, bumpy, choppy, effervescent, fuming, pitching, rolling, rough, seething, stormy, tempestuous
may indicate an anagram

turning bowling, centrifugation, pirouetting, pivoting, reeling, rolling, spinning, spiral, swirling, swivel, torque, torsion, trolling, trundling, twirling, twisting, volutation, wheeling, whir, whirling
may indicate an anagram

tutelary custodial, guardian, guarding, protective, shepherdlike, surrogate, vigilant, watchful

tutorship chair, fellowship, instructorship, lectureship, professorship, readership, schoolmastery

twelfth duodecimal, duodenary

twelve dodecagon, dodecahedron, dozen, duodecimal, duodecimo, midnight, noon, Twelfth Day, twelfth man, Twelfth Night, twelvemonth

twenty forty, pony, quadragenarian, score, vicenary, vicennial, vigesimal

twin carbon-copy, clone, copy, counterpart, doppelgänger, double, duplicate, lookalike, match, pair

twist bend, crook, curve, distort, dogleg, hairpin, maniuplate, meander, pull, snake, spin, turn, twine, twirl, weave, whirl, wind, zigzag
may indicate an anagram

two bifold, binary, brace, couple, coupled, deuce, double, dual, duet, duo, duple, duplex, dyad, dyadic, matched, mated, pair, paired, second, secondary, square, squared, twain, twinned, twofold, twosome

two-sided ambidextrous, biannual, bicameral, biennial, bifocal, biform, bifurcate, bilateral, bilingual, binocular, bipartite, bipedal, bisexual, double-sided, dual-purpose, two-dimensional, two-ply, two-storey, two-way

type brand, cast, character, colour, complexion, domain, feather, font, form, frame, genre, genus, grain, hue, ilk, key, keyboard, kidney, kind, label, league, line, make, manner, mark, marque, mould, nature, persuasion, printing, realm, shape, sort, species, sphere, stamp, strain, stripe, style, typeface, variety, version
may indicate an anagram

typical characteristic, defining, definitive, distinctive, expected, generic, normal, ordinary, particular, peculiar, representative, special, specific, stereotypical

·U·

ABBREVIATIONS

U	boat • film • uncle • universal • upper • you
UC	upper case
UFO	unidentified flying object
UHF	ultrahigh frequency
UHT	milk (ultra-heat-treated)
UJ	Union Jack
UK	United Kingdom
ULT	in the last month (Latin: *ultimo*) • ultimate
UN	United Nations
UNCLE	United Network Command for Law Enforcement (TV)
US	ultrasound scanning • United States • useless
UV	ultraviolet

ugliness drabness, garishness, gaudiness, hideousness, loudness, plainness, shabbiness, tackiness, tawdriness, vulgarity

ugly awkward, coarse, contorted, defaced, deformed, dingy, disfigured, distasteful, distressing, drab, dreary, dull, foul, garish, gaudy, gory, graceless, grisly, gross, grotty, gruesome, hideous, homely, ill-favoured, inelegant, loud, meretricious, misbegotten, misshapen, monstrous, mutilated, plain, repulsive, tacky, tarty, tasteless, tawdry, unaesthetic, unattractive, unbecoming, uncouth, ungainly, unlovely, unprepossessing, unseemly, unshapely, unsightly, vulgar, wan
may indicate an anagram

ululant bellowing, deep-throated, full-throated, howling, wailful, wailing, yowling

unaccustomed green, inexperienced, innocent, new, nonobservant, rusty, uneducated, unfamiliar, unhabituated, unseasoned, unskilful, untaught, untrained, unused, unwonted

unadorned ascetic, austere, plain, prudish, puritanical, restrained, simple, spartan, strait-laced, uncoloured, undecorated, unembellished, ungarnished, unornamented, unpainted, untrimmed, unvarnished

unapproachable aloof, disdainful, distant, obstinate, prickly, stand-offish, stiff-necked, touchy

unbelievable amazing, bizarre, counterintuitive, doubtful, dubious, fabulous, fantastic, far-fetched, incredible, ineffable, miraculous, mysterious, mystical, questionable, suspicious, unlikely, weird, wonderful

unbowed fearless, proud, rampant, unafraid, unbeaten, undaunted

uncertainty agnosticism, conjecture, contestability, controvertibility, disputability, distrust, doubt, doubtfulness, dubiousness, enigma, guesswork, hesitation, indecision, misgiving, mistrust, Pyrrhonism, questionableness, scepticism, unsureness, wavering

uncertified unascertained, unauthenticated, unchecked, uncorroborated, undocumented, unofficial, unproved, unratified, unsigned, unverified

unchaste amoral, brazen, fallen, fast, flaunting, immodest, impure, light, loose, meretricious, naughty, nymphomaniac, philandering, promiscuous, prostituted, scarlet, seduced, sex-mad, shameless, tarty, unblushing, unvirtuous, wanton, whorish, womanizing

unclaimed derelict, remaining, unappropriated, unowned, unpossessed

unclean contaminated, corrupt, dirty, fetid, flyblown, foul, grotty, grubby, impure, insanitary, maggoty, manky, mucky, nasty, profane, septic, soiled, sordid, squalid, stained, tainted, unholy, unhygienic, unpurified, unrefined, unsterilized, unwashed, yucky

uncommunicative buttoned-up, cagey, clamlike, close, discreet, evasive, poker-faced, secretive, tight-lipped, uninformative, vague

unconditional anything goes, catch-as-catch-can, unlimited, unrestricted, without strings

unconscious asleep, catatonic, comatose, concussed, instinctive, involuntary, out cold, stunned, subconscious, subliminal

unconventional avant-garde, Bohemian, eccentric, experimental, freaky, freethinking, fringe, independent, individualistic, maverick, nonconformist, non-U, odd, original, strange, uncommon, unprecedented, untraditional, unusual
may indicate an anagram

uncooked bloody, cold, half-baked, half-cooked, pink, rare, raw, red, underdone, unprepared

uncooperative bloody-minded, contrary, disobedient, fractious, negative, obstinate, obstructive, oppugnant, perverse, reactionary, recalcitrant, refractory, resistant, stubborn, unhelpful, unwilling

uncover bare, discover, disrobe, divest, exhibit, expose, open, peel off, reveal, strip, tear off, undo, undress, unearth

unctuous greasy, oily, slimy, smarmy

uncut entire, faultless, flawless, intact, inviolate, perfect, pure, unabridged, unadulterated, unbroken, uncontaminated, undamaged, undiminished, undivided, unexpurgated, unharmed, unimpaired, unspoiled, untouched, virgin

undaunted bold, brave, game, heroic, indomitable, steadfast, unbeaten, unconquered, unfearing, unflinching, unhesitant, unshaken, unshrinking, unwavering

underestimate belittle, discount, disparage, minimize, miscalculate, misjudge, misprize, patronize, pooh-pooh, scorn, soft-pedal, underpraise, underprice, underrate, understate, undervalue

underestimation cynicism, defeatism, deprecation, depreciation, detraction, disesteem, dishonour, disregard, disrepute, minimization, miscalculation, misjudgment, modesty, neglect, pessimism, underrating, understatement, undervaluation

underfed anorexic, emaciated, famine-stricken, famished, fasting, hungry, lean, macerated, ravenous, scraggy, skinny, spare, starved, stunted, thin, undernourished, voracious, wasting

underground buried, clandestine, hypogeal, resistance movement, secret, subterranean, subway, tube, tunnel, undercover, underworld

underpass catacombs, secret passage, subway, tunnel

understaffed shorthanded, undermanned

understand comprehend, dig, empathize, fathom, follow, grasp, have insight, know, learn, master, penetrate, realize, rumble, savvy, seize, sympathize, take in, twig

understanding apprehension, comprehension, empathy, grasp, knowledge, learning, mastery, perception, realization, recognition, sympathy

understate minimize, underemphasize, underestimate, underplay, underrate, underreckon, undervalue

understatement conservativeness, underestimation, undervaluation, unobtrusiveness, unsubstantiality

undertake agree, assume, attempt, begin, challenge, commit, confront, contract, dare, devote oneself, direct, do, endeavour, engage, execute, initiate, launch, manage, pioneer, pledge, promise, pursue, set to, start, tackle, try, venture, volunteer, vow

undertaker elegist, embalmer, epitaphist, eulogist, funeral director, gravedigger, keener, monument mason, mourner, mute, necrologist, obituary writer, pallbearer, sexton, weeper

undertaking accord, action, adventure, affair, agreement, alliance, arrangement, assent, assignment, attempt, bargaining, bartering, business, campaign, case, cause, commitment, compact, contract, cooperation, covenant, deal, deed, design, effort, emprise, endeavour, engagement, enterprise, exercise, feat, gambling, ideal, inquiry, job, matter, mise, mission, negotiation, obligation, occupation, operation, pact, partnership, pilgrimage, plan, pledge, principle, programme, project, promise, purpose, quest, ratification, seal, search, security, settlement, signature, speculation, struggle, subject, task, topic, try, understanding, venture, work

undervalued belittled, denigrated, disparaged, disregarded, ignored, neglected, underestimated, underrated

underwater bathypelagic, benthic, deep-sea, deep-water, immersed, subaqua, submarine, submerged, suboceanic, sunk, undersea

underwear Balmoral, bloomers, body, body stocking, boxer shorts, bra, brassiere, briefs, camiknickers, camisole, chemise, combinations, corset, crinoline, crop top, drawers, foundation garment, French knickers, girdle, half-slip, knickers, lingerie, pantalets, panties, pants, panty girdle, petticoat, roll-on, scanties, shift, shorts, singlet, slip, smalls, stays, step-ins, supporter, suspender belt, teddy, trunks, underclothes, undergarments, underskirt, underthings, undies, unmentionables, vest, Y-fronts

undeviating direct, straight, unswerving

undirected random, unguided, unschooled, untaught

undiscriminating catholic, indelicate, indifferent, insensitive, omnivorous, promiscuous, tasteless, uncritical, undifferentiating, undiscerning, unselective

undress bare, change, denuding, disrobe, divestment, doff, drop, exhibitionism, flashing, gymnosophy, mooning, naturism, nudism, remove, skinny-dipping, streaking, strip, striptease, toplessness, unbutton, unclothe, uncover, undo, unhook, unlace, untie, unveil, unzip

undressed bare-bollock, bared, naked, nuddy, nude, starkers, stripped, unclad

undue excessive, gratuitous, immoderate, uncalled-for, undeserved, unearned, unexpected, unjustified, unlooked-for, unmerited, unnecessary, unwarranted

unearth discover, disentomb, disinter, drill, exhume, mine, quarry

unemphatic amorphous, boring, colourless, commonplace, dry, dull, feeble, flaccid, flat, inane, ineffective, insipid, lame, languid, limp, loose, meagre, monotonous, pointless, prosaic, prosy, schmaltzy, shapeless,

smooth, stale, tame, thin, unconvincing, undramatic, unexciting, unimpassioned, uninspired, unspirited, vapid, wan, weak, wersh, wishy-washy

unemployed disengaged, fallow, free, idle, jobless, laid off, redundant, resting, unengaged, unoccupied, unused

unemployment depression, discharge, dismissal, joblessness, lay-off, recession, redundancy, resignation, retirement, shutdown, slump

unenthusiastic apathetic, half-hearted, lukewarm, uncooperative, unhelpful

unequal asymmetrical, different, disparate, disproportionate, ill-matched, ill-sorted, incongruent, irregular, lopsided, mismatched, odd, top-heavy, unbalanced, unequable, unequalled, uneven, variable, variegated

uneven bitty, bumpy, choppy, dotted, jerky, jolty, patchy, rough, scrappy, snatchy, spotty, unbalanced, unequal

unexpected accidental, chance, fluky, fortuitous, freakish, rare, surprising, unanticipated, unforeseeable, unforeseen, unguessed, unpredictable, unpredicted

unexpectedness miracle, miraculousness, oddity, prodigy, rarity, surprise, the unforeseen, wonder

unexplained enigmatic, mysterious, uncertain, unresolved, unsolvable

unfairness bias, discrimination, favouritism, inequity, injustice, one-sidedness, unevenness, wrongness

unfaithful adulterous, cheating, deceitful, faithless, false, fickle, two-timing

unfamiliar mould-breaking, newfangled, nontraditional, novel, unheard of, unknown, unprecedented, untested, untried, unused
may indicate an anagram

unfeeling anaesthetized, blockish, clumsy, hardened, heedless, impassive, impervious, insensitive, insentient, nerveless, numb, oblivious, senseless, stolid, unaware, unemotional, unmindful, unresponsive

unfinished approximate, crude, cursory, incomplete, preliminary, raw, rough-and-ready, rudimentary, shapeless, sketchy, unpolished, unrefined, vague

unfit ill-adapted, inadmissible, inapplicable, inapposite, inappropriate, inapt, incompatible, ineligible, inexpedient, infelicitous, malapropos, out of shape, unbecoming, unhealthy, unqualified, unseemly, unsuitable, untimely, wrong

unforgivable inexcusable, objectionable, reprehensible, unjustifiable, unpardonable

ungrateful discourteous, inconsiderate, rude, selfish, unappreciative, ungracious, unthankful

unguent balm, chrismal, chrismatory, lotion, ointment

unhealthy anaemic, anorexic, bilious, carcinogenic, corrupt, debased, decrepit, delicate, dirty, emaciated, harmful, ill, infirm, invalid, jaundiced, malnourished, mangy, peaky, polluted, run down, sickly, tired, toxic, undernourished, unfit, unhygienic, unsound, valetudinarian, weak

unhurried deliberate, gentle, gradual, idle, indolent, inert, languid, languorous, lazy, leisurely, lethargic, listless, meticulous, moderate, patient, relaxed, slack, slothful, sluggardly, sluggish

unhygienic airless, baneful, dirty, filthy, flea-bitten, flyblown, fuggy, fusty, harmful, humid, indigestible, inedible, injurious, insalubrious, miasmal, mouldy, muggy, musty, noxious, poisonous, polluted, rat-infested, rotten, smoke-filled, sordid, squalid, stuffy, unclean, undrinkable, unhealthy, unsanitary, unventilated, unwholesome

unification articulation, assemblage, astriction, collection, composition, contraction, jointing, knitting, knotting, ligation, linking, oneness, organization, structure, tightening, togetherness, uniting, weaving, welding

uniform alike, blunt, consistent, constant, continuing, continuous, curved, equal, even, flat, harmonious, harrowed, homogeneous, horizontal, identical, immutable, inevitable, ironed, level, livery, military uniform, national dress, outfit, permanent, persistent, plane, regimentals, regular, rolled, rounded, routine, same, school uniform, smooth, stable, steadfast, steady, steamrolled, straight, symmetric, unbroken, unchanging, uncrumpled, undeviating, unerring, unruffled, unvarying, unwrinkled, waterworn

uniformity consistency, constancy, continuousness, evenness, habit, harmony, homogeneity, inevitability, levelness, permanence, persistence, regularity, repetition, routine, sameness, similarity, smoothness, stability, steadfastness, steadiness, straightness, symmetry, unchangeableness, unerringness

unimportance emptiness, immateriality, insignificance, nothingness, nullity, secondariness, vacancy

unimportant circumstantial, dispensable, expendable, forgettable, forgivable, immaterial, inappreciable, inconsequential, ineffectual, inessential, insignificant, insubstantial, irrelevant, little, negligible, nondescript, small, superficial, trifling, trivial, uninfluential, unnecessary, venial

unintelligence dimness, dimwittedness, folly, hebetude, incomprehension, obtuseness, stupidity

unintelligent blockheaded, childish, daft, dense, dim(-witted), doltish, dopey, dull, dumb, empty-headed, fatuous, foolish, ignorant, illogical, imitative, immature, inane, infantile, loony, nutty, oafish, obtuse, puerile, silly, soft, stolid, stupid, thick(headed), thoughtless, unimaginative, unperceptive, unthinking, unwise, witless

unintelligibility ambiguity, difficulty, equivocalness, illegibility, impenetrability, inaudibility, incommunicability, incomprehensibility, inconceivability, ineffability, inexplicability, inscrutability, meaninglessness, mystery, mystification, nonsense, obscurity, unaccountability, uncertainty, unreadability

unintelligible all Greek, arcane, cryptic, double Dutch, enigmatic, esoteric, garbled, gibbering, gnostic, hidden, illegible, impenetrable, inapprehensible, inarticulate, inaudible, incoherent, incommunicable, incomprehensible, inconceivable, ineffable, inexplicable, inexpressible, inscrutable, invisible, meaningless, mysterious, obscure, oracular, private, rambling, unaccountable, unclear, undecipherable, undiscernible, undiscoverable, unfathomable, unpronounceable, untranslatable, unutterable

uninterested aloof, apathetic, bored, complacent, cool, detached, disengaged, distant, heedless, impassive, inactive, indifferent, insensible, insouciant, nonchalant, non-partisan, objective, phlegmatic, unbiased, unconcerned, unenthusiastic, uninvolved, unmoved, unresponsive, unthinking

union agglutination, alliance, assembly, association, bond, coagulation, coalescence, coalition, cohesion, coitus, collection, combination, commerce, commonweal, commonwealth, communication, concatenation, concourse, concretion, concurrence, confederation, confluence, congress, connection, consolidation, convergence, crowd, exchange, federation, fusion, gathering, intercourse, involvement, joining, junction, liaison, link, meeting, merger, network, rendezvous, solidification, synthesis, trade

unit atom, brick, building block, cell, component, corps, entirety, entity, Gestalt, integer, item, module, molecule, particle, piece, singularity, totality
See also list at **measurement**.

unite adhere, assemble, associate, blend, bracket, clinch, coalesce, cohere, collect, combine, compact, compress, comprise, concentrate, condense, consolidate, constrict, converge, couple, embrace, engage, fuse, gather, grapple, grip, hyphenate, include, incorporate, integrate, interlock, join, liaise, link, marry, mass, match, meet, merge, mix, mobilize, narrow, pack, pair, tauten, truss, unify

universal comprehensive, cosmic, cosmopolitan, galactic, general, global, international, national, nationwide, planetary, unlimited, worldwide

universe cosmos, creation, outer space
See also lists at **astronomer**; **planet**.

university academy, alma mater, campus, college, community college, FE college, polytechnic, sixth-form college

unjust biased, chauvinistic, discriminatory, inequitable, intolerant, one-sided, partial, partisan, preconceived, predisposed, preferential, prejudged, prejudiced, prejudicial, sectarian, subjective, undemocratic, unfair

unknown anonymous, blank, closed book, dark horse, enigma, guesswork, ineffable, John Doe, Mr Nobody, mysterious, mystery, n, obscure, secret, strange, uncharted, undiscovered, unexplained, unexplored, unfamiliar, unidentified, unperceived, unrecognized, unseen, x

unload discharge, dump, unburden, unlade, unpack, unship

unlucky accident-prone, accursed, hapless, ill-fated, luckless, star-crossed, unfortunate, washed-up

unmelodious atonal, cracked, droning, flat, off, off-key, off-pitch, sharp, singsong, toneless, tuneless, unmusical, untuned

unmoved apathetic, blank, blasé, calm, cold-blooded, cold-hearted, collected, composed, cool, disinterested, dull, impassive, indifferent, insouciant, nonchalant, phlegmatic, sanguine, serene, spiritless, steadfast, still, tranquil, unadmiring, unaroused, unconcerned, unenthusiastic, unexcited, unimaginative, unimpressed, uninspired, unsurprised, unwavering, wonderless

unoccupied available, empty, unfilled, uninhabited, unlived-in, untenanted, vacant

unpalatability bile, bitterness, gall, sourness

unpalatable acid, acrid, bad, bitter, brackish, contaminated, corked, curdled, dank, disagreeable, disgusting, fermented, foul-tasting, harsh, high, inedible, mouldy, nasty, nauseating, off, poisonous, rancid, rotten, rough, sour, stale, toxic, turned, unappetizing, unattractive, undrinkable, uneatable, uninviting, unpleasant, unsavoury, unwholesome

unplanned accidental, coincidental, hasty, jerry-built, makeshift, rash, reckless, rushed, temporary, unpremeditated

unpleasant annoying, base, beastly, despicable, disagreeable, discomfiting, discordant, disgusting, disliked, displeasing, distasteful, hateful, horrible, horrid, hurtful, invidious, irksome, loathsome, lowly, nasty, nauseating, odious, offensive, painful, petty, rebarbative, repulsive, revolting, shabby, sickening, small-minded, sordid, spiteful, squalid, trying, unacceptable, uncomfortable, unharmonious, unkind, unpalatable, unsavoury, unwelcome

unpleasantness affront, baseness, beastliness, disagreeableness, discomfort, distastefulness, hurtfulness, lowliness, nastiness, offence, offensiveness, pain, pettiness, repulsiveness, shabbiness, spite, squalor, umbrage, unpalatability

unpredictability illogicality, inconsistency, inexplicability, irrationality, quirkiness, randomness, unaccountability, uncertainty

unprepared backward, behind, caught napping, disorganized, exposed, improvised, inexpectant, late, slow, spontaneous, surprised, unarranged, unguarded, unready, unrehearsed, vulnerable

unprofitable break-even, deficient, loss-making, non-profit-making, pointless, prodigal, unremunerative, wasteful

unprotected defenceless, exposed, ill-equipped, pregnable, unarmed, undefended, unfortified, unguarded, untenable, vulnerable

unreal artificial, bogus, counterfeit, elusive, ethereal, fake, false, fanciful, fantastical, fleeting, flimsy, forged, ghostly, illusory, imaginary, impalpable, inauthentic, incorporeal, indefinite, insubstantial, intangible, invented, make-believe, mythical, nebulous, non-existent, obscure, phantasmal, phoney, shadowy, sham, spectral, spurious, tenuous, undefined, vague

unrealistic abstract, fantastic, idealistic, impractical, romantic, surreal, utopian, visionary

unreality fantasy, imagination, make-believe, non-existence

unrecognizable altered, changed, distorted, hidden, incognizable, indefinite, indistinct, indistinguishable, undefined, unidentifiable, unknowable

unrelated alien, detached, disassociated, discrete, divorced, exotic, free, inapplicable, inapposite, inappropriate, inapt, independent, irrelevant, rootless, segregated, separate, singular, unaffiliated, unallied, unconnected, uninvolved

unreliability eccentricity, fallibility, hazard, inconsistency, instability, insubstantiality, irregularity, precariousness, risk, transience, treacherousness, unpredictability, unsoundness, unsteadiness, untrustworthiness

unreliable dangerous, dishonest, eccentric, erratic, fallible, hazardous, inconsistent, insecure, irregular, perfidious, perilous, precarious, risky, shaky, transient, treacherous, undependable, unpredictable, unsound, unstable, unsteady, untrustworthy

unrestrained exaggerated, excessive, extreme, fantastical, hyperbolic, immoderate, inordinate, magnified, ostentatious, outrageous, preposterous, profuse, showy, wild

unsafe critical, crumbling, dangerous, delicate, dicey, dicky, doubtful, frail, heart-stopping, insecure, last-minute, last-second, leaky, nerve-racking, precarious, rickety, risky, shaky, slippery, treacherous, unbalanced, unreliable, unsound, unstable, unsteady, untrustworthy, weak

unsaid half-spoken, hinted, implied, indicated, inferred, insinuated, intimated, meant, suggested, tacit, unarticulated, undeclared, understood, undivulged, unexpressed, unmentioned, unproclaimed, unprofessed, unpromoted, unpronounced, unpublished, unspoken, unsung, untold, unuttered, unvoiced, unwritten

unsatisfactory disappointing, disapproved of, dissatisfactory, inadequate, insufficient, rejected, substandard, unacceptable, unapproved, uncommendable, unpopular, unpraiseworthy

unselfish altruistic, benevolent, big-hearted, charitable, compassionate, considerate, generous, high-minded, honest, humble, idealistic, kind, modest, munificent, noble, open-handed, self-abnegating, self-denying, self-effacing, selfless, self-sacrificing, sympathetic

unsociability aloofness, apartness, detachment, discourtesy, incompatibility, indifference, inhospitality, remoteness, reticence, standoffishness, taciturnity, unapproachability, unclubbability, uncommunicativeness, uncongeniality, unfriendliness, ungregariousness, unreceptiveness

unsociable aloof, cool, detached, distant, forbidding, frigid, haughty, icy, impolite, inaccessible, private, reclusive, remote, removed, reticent, retiring, seclusive, self-contained, standoffish, uncommunicative, uncompanionable, unforthcoming, unfriendly, ungregarious, withdrawn

unsolved undiscovered, undivulged, unexplained, unguessed, unknown, unrevealed, unsuspected, untraced

unspecified indefinite, indeterminate, unmentioned, unnamed, vague

unsteady easy-going, flexible, good-natured, impressionable, pliant, suggestible, teetering, tottering, unreliable

unstick detach, free, knock off, loose, separate, shake off, undo, unfasten, unglue, unpin, unseat

unsuccessful abortive, addled, failed, useless, vain

untidiness carelessness, dirtiness, dishevelment, grubbiness, messiness, neglect, scruffiness, shabbiness, shoddiness, slatternliness, slipshodness, slobbishness, sloppiness, slovenliness, sluttishness, sordidness, squalidness, uncleanness, unkemptness

untidy bedraggled, careless, crumpled, dirty, dishevelled, filthy, grubby, messy, ragged, ruffled, scruffy, shabby, shambolic, shoddy, slatternly, slipshod, slobbish, slovenly, sluttish, squalid, tousled, unclean, unkempt, unsightly

untimely awkward, disrupting, disturbing, early, ill-starred, immature, inappropriate, inapt, inauspicious, inconvenient, inexpedient, inopportune, interrupting, intrusive, late, mistimed, ominous, out of sync, premature, unbefitting, unfavourable, unpropitious, unpunctual, unseasonable, unsuited

untrained apprentice, artless, ignorant, inexperienced, natural, simple, uncultivated, undrilled, unexercised, uninstructed, unpractised, unprocessed, unrefined, unskilled, unsophisticated, untaught, untutored, unworked

untrue concocted, distorted, dreamed-up, erroneous, exaggerated, fabricated, fallacious, false, fictionalized, imagined, inaccurate, libelous, misrepresented, nonsensical, perjurious, perverted, slanderous, understated

unusable impractical, ineffectual, unemployable, useless

unused deferred, fallow, idle, in abeyance, in hand, in reserve, pigeon-holed, preserved, reserved, suspended, unapplied, undisposed of, untried, wasted

unusual aberrant, abnormal, anomalous, bizarre, curious, eccentric, erratic, exceptional, exotic, far-out, freakish, freaky, funny, grotesque, idiosyncratic, incoherent, incongruous, individual, kooky, monstrous, nonconforming, odd, oddball, original, outlandish, peculiar, queer, rare, rum, singular, strange, uncommon, unconventional, unique, unorthodox, way-out, weird, whimsical
may indicate an anagram

unusualness aberrance, abnormality, anomalousness, bizarreness, curiosity, eccentricity, exceptionality, extraordinariness, freakishness, grotesqueness, incongruousness, individuality, monstrousness, moodiness, nonconformity, oddity, oddness, originality, outlandishness, peculiarity, queerness, quirkiness, rareness, rarity, singularity, strangeness, uncommonness, unconventionality, uniqueness, unorthodoxy, weirdness, whimsicality

unwarranted excessive, exorbitant, overreaching, surplus, uncalled-for, undue

unwilling averse, demurring, disinclined, indisposed, loath, reluctant

unwillingness demur, disagreement, disinclination, dislike, indisposition, loathness, objection, protest, reluctance

unworldliness dematerialization, disembodiment, disincarnation, ghostliness, immateriality, impalpability, imponderability, incorporeity, insubstantiality, intangibility, otherworldliness, religion, shadowiness, spirituality, unearthliness, unreality

unyielding adamant, case-hardened, chronic, determined, dogged, dour, firm, grim, hard-boiled, hard-nosed, immovable, implacable, incurable, inelastic, inexorable, inflexible, intransigent, irreversible, merciless, obdurate, persevering, persistent, pitiless, resolute, rigid, stiff, tenacious, unappeasable, unbending, uncompromising, uninfluenced, unmoved, unrelenting, wooden

upland heights, high country, highland, mesa, plateau, tableland, wold

uprise ascend, fight, mutiny, overthrow, rebel, revolt, secede, wake up

upset capsize, change, destabilize, dismay, disturb, fluctuate, heel, lean, lilt, list, mess up, miss, overcompensate, overturn, rock, sad, skew, sway, swing, tilt, traumatize, vary
may indicate an anagram

up-to-dateness currency, modernity, topicality, trendiness

upturn elevation, fountain, get better, gush, improve, increase, jet, slope up, spiral, spout, spurt, steepen, surge, trend upwards, updraught, upgrade, upgrowth, uplift, upsurge, upsweep, upswing, upthrow
may indicate an anagram

Ur old city

urban citified, civic, gentrified, interurban, metropolitan, municipal, oppidan, parochial, subtopian, suburban, suburbanized

urbanization gentrification, industrialization, suburbanization

urge desire, drive, exhort, goad, impulsion, insist, itch, push, spur, stampede, whip, yearning

urination bed-wetting, enuresis, leak, micturation, pee, piss, slash, wee

usability capacity, employability, function, good, merit, serviceability, value, virtue, workability, worth

usable advantageous, applicable, available, consumable, convertible, current, disposable, employable, exploitable, fit, functioning, profitable, recyclable, reusable, serviceable, useful, utilizable, valid, workable, working

use absorb, abuse, advantage, applicability, application, avail, benefit, brandish, carefulness, consume, consumption, control, conversion, convertibility, demand, deployment, disposal, drive, employment, enjoyment, exercise, exhaustion, expend, exploitation, fatigue, form, function, good, habit, handle, ill-treatment, management, misuse, mould, need, operate, ply, point, possession, power, practicality, practice, practise, profit, purpose, reclamation, recourse, recycling, resort, reuse, service, spend, squander, task, tax, treat, usefulness, usufruct, utility, utilization, waste, wield, wont, work

used beaten, cast-off, consumed, depleted, dilapidated, dog-eared, down-at-heel, drained, employed, exercised, exhausted, exploited, hackneyed, hand-me-down, instrumental, occupied, pre-owned, reclaimed, recycled, reused, second-hand, shabby, shopsoiled, spent, stale, subservient, threadbare, utilitarian, utilized, (well-)worn

useful adaptable, advisable, applicable, applied, available, commodious, convenient, disposable, expedient, functional, handy, helpful, multipurpose, operative, practical, pragmatic, sensible, suitable, throwaway, utilitarian, versatile

usefulness adaptability, aid, applicability, application, avail, availability, commodity, convenience, employment, expediency, functionalism, handiness, helpfulness, point, practicality, purpose, readiness, service, suitability, utility, versatility

useless abrogated, dud, effete, feckless, futile, impotent, impractical, inadequate, inapplicable, incompetent, inefficient, inept, inoperative, inutile, invalid, kaput, nonfunctional, null, obsolete, ornamental, outmoded, powerless, redundant, screwed-up, spent, superfluous, unable, unapt, unemployable, unfit, unhelpful, unsaleable, unserviceable, unsuitable, unusable, unworkable, valueless, void, worthless

uselessness dispensability, disposability, disservice, effeteness, expendability, fecklessness, futility, impotence, impracticality, inability, inadequacy, inapplicability, incompetence, inconvenience, inefficiency, ineptitude, inexpedience, inutility, powerlessness, redundancy, superfluousness, unaptness, unemployability, unfitness, unhelpfulness, unsaleability, unskilfulness, unsuitability, unworkability, worthlessness

usurp appropriate, arrogate, assume, encroach, infringe, invade, seize, squat, steal, trespass, violate

utterance address, aside, comment, crack, declaration, dictum, ejaculation, exclamation, expression, gasp, greeting, interjection, locution, murmur, mutter, phoneme, pronouncement, remark, response, say, speech, statement, vocalization, whisper

uttered
may indicate a homophone

·V·

ABBREVIATIONS

V	five • vein • velocity • verb • verse • versus • via • victory • violin
VA	Virginia • Vice-Admiral
VAC	vacancy • vacation • vacuum
VAD	Voluntary Aid Detachment
VAN	advantage
VAT	value-added tax
VC	Vice-Chairman • Vice-Chancellor • Victoria Cross
VCR	video-cassette recorder
VDU	visual display unit
VE	Victory in Europe
VET	veteran • veterinarian
VF	very fair • video frequency
VG	very good
VIP	very important person
VIR	Queen Victoria (Latin: *Victoria Imperatrix Regina*)
VIZ	namely (Latin: *videlicet*)
VJ	Victory over Japan
VO	very old • Victorian Order
VR	Queen Victoria (Latin: *Victoria Regina*) • virtual reality
VS	see above (Latin: *vide supra*) • versus
VSOP	very superior old pale

vacant absent, blank, daydreaming, devoid, empty, vacuous, void

vacillate change, coquet, dart, dither, drift, equivocate, fidget, flirt, flit, float, fluctuate, hesitate, hover, oscillate, palter, quibble, seesaw, shillyshally, shuffle, stall, sway, swing, tease, teeter, tergiversate, trifle with, vary, waver, wobble
may indicate an anagram

vacillation caprice, deviation, equivocation, inconsistency, irresolution, versatility, whim

vague desultory, indistinct, inexact, interchangeable, undefined, undifferentiated, undistinguished
may indicate an anagram

vain big-headed, conceited, immodest, insubstantial, megalomaniac, overproud, self-important, snooty, strutting, stuck-up, swaggering, swanky, swash-buckling

valediction fond farewell, goodbye, send-off

validate ascertain, assure, attest, authenticate, certify, check, clinch, collate, confirm, corroborate, demonstrate, document, endorse, ensure, establish, guarantee, prove, ratify, record, reinforce, second, sign, substantiate, support, sustain, uphold, validate, verify, vindicate, warrant

valley basin, canyon, chimney, chine, cirque, clough, coomb, corrie, couloir, crevasse, cwm, dale, dell, depression, dingle, dip, ditch, fjord, glen, gorge, gully, ravine, rift, vale

valuable blue-chip, costly, exclusive, expensive, gilt-edged, inestimable, infrequent, invaluable, irreplaceable, meaningful, precious, priceless, prized, rare, rich, scarce, significant, treasured, unique, valued, worthwhile

valuation assessment, bounty, premium, prize, reward

value appreciate, dearth, esteem, evaluate, invaluableness, moral, preciousness, price, pricelessness, principle, rarity, revere, scarcity, significance, treasure, valuableness, worth

values beliefs, morals, principles

vanish die, disappear, dissolve, end, evaporate, expire, fade, peter out

vanity big-headedness, conceit, ego(t)ism, immodesty, insubstantiality, megalomania, narcissism, overproudness, self-importance, vainness

vanquish capture, conquer, constrain, control, defeat, discipline, dominate, intimidate, master, oppress, overcome, overpower, repress, restrain, suppress, tyrannize

vantage point bridge, cockpit, crow's nest, observation post, watchtower

vaporization aeration, annihilation, atomization, distillation, etherealization, evaporation, exhalation, fumigation, gasification, killing, sublimation, volatilization

vaporize disembody, dispel, disperse, dissipate, liquidate, scatter

vaporizer aerosol, atomizer, spray

vapour cloud, fog, gas, mist, steam

variegate band, bar, blot, brindle, check, chequer, cloud, crack, craze, damascene, dapple, discolour, diversify, dot, dust, enamel, fox, freckle, grizzle, inlay, maculate, marble, mottle, patch, pattern, pepper, powder, spangle, speckle, spot, sprinkle, stain, stipple, streak, striate, stripe, stud, tessellate, vein

variegated chameleonic, colourful, embroidered, florid, kaleidoscopic, many-hued, motley, multicoloured, ornamental, pied, polychromatic, varicoloured

variegation dichroism, difference, diversification, iridescence, moiré, motley, opalescence, pearliness, polychromatism, variety

various certain, composite, divers, diverse, many-sided, multifaceted, multifarious, multiform, multilateral, multipurpose, polygonal, polymorphous, some, sundry, versatile

vary change, convert, deviate, distort, diversify, fluctuate, modify, waver
may indicate an anagram

vastness endlessness, hugeness, immenseness, infinity, space

vaulted arched, bowed, curved, fanned, jumped, leaped, ribbed

vegetarian frugivorous, fruitarian, graminivorous, herbivorous, lactovegetarian, vegan, veggie

vegetate bud, burgeon, dehisce, flourish, flower, gemmate, germinate, grow, leaf, lie dormant, overgrow, overrun, photosynthesize, root, shoot, sprout, stagnate, unfold

vegetating comatose, dormant, indolent, inert, slothful, stagnating, torpid

vehemence ardour, enthusiasm, feeling, fervour, fire, gusto, inspiration, passion, vigour, vim

vehicle conveyance, machine, means, medium
See list of vehicles.

veil camouflage, chador, cover, disguise, domino, front, hide, mask, purdah, shroud, yashmak

venial excusable, forgivable, slight, trifling

ventilated air-conditioned, air-cooled, cooled, fanned, fresh

ventilation aerage, aeration, air-conditioning, air cooling, airing, de-

VEHICLES

AMBULANCE
ARABA
AUTO
AUTOBUS
AUTOCAR
AUTOMOBILE
BAIL GHARRY
BAROUCHE
BEACHWAGON
BERLIN
BICYCLE
BIKE
BLACK MARIA
BMX
BOAT-TRAIN
BOB-SLED
BOB-SLEIGH
BONE-BREAKER
BRAKE
BRANCARD
BRITZKA
BROUGHAM
BROWSER
BUBBLECAR
BUCKBOARD
BUGGY
BULLOCK-CART
BUS
CAB
CABLE-CAR
CABRIOLET
CALÈCHE
CAPE-CART
CAR
CARAVAN
CAROCHE
CARRIAGE
CARRIOLE
CART
CHAISE
CHAR-À-BANC
CHARIOT
CLARENCE
CLASH
COACH (AND
  FOUR)
COASTER
CONVERTIBLE
COUPÉ
CRATE
CURRICLE
CYCLE(-RICKSHAW)
DANDY
DEAD-CART
DÉSOBLIGEANT
DIESEL (TRAIN)
DILIGENCE
DOG-CART
DOOLY
DORMEUSE

DOUBLE-DECKER
DRAG
DRAY
DROSHKY
EKKA
ELECTRIC TRAIN
ESTATE-CAR
EXPRESS TRAIN
FIACRE
FIRE-ENGINE
FLIVVER
FLY
FOUR-DOOR
FOUR-IN-HAND
FOUR-WHEELER
FREIGHT TRAIN
FUNICULAR
GIG
GO-CART
GOODS TRAIN
GOVERNESS-CART
GROWLER
GUN-CARRIAGE
HACK
HACKERY
HACKNEY-
  CARRIAGE
HANSOM
HARD-TOP
HEARSE
HORSE-AND-CART
HORSE-BUS
HORSE-CAB
HORSE-CARRIAGE
HORSE-CART
HORSELESS
  CARRIAGE
HORSE-VAN
HOTROD
HURDLE
ICE-YACHT
JALOPY
JAUNTING-CAR
JEEP
JINRICKSHA(W)
JITNEY
KIBITZKA
LANDAU(LETTE)
LIMBER
LIMOUSINE
LITTER
LOCAL TRAIN
LOCOMOTIVE
LORRY
LUGE
LUGGAGE TRAIN
MAGLEV
MAIL-COACH
MAIL-PHÆTON
METRO

MILKFLOAT
MILK TRAIN
MODEL-T
MONOCYCLE
MONORAIL
MOPED
MOTOR
MOTOR-BIKE
MOTOR-CAR
MOTOR-COACH
MOTOR-CYCLE
MOTORIZED
  BICYCLE
MOTOR-VAN
NIGHT TRAIN
OLD CROCK
OMNIBUS
OPEN-CAR
OUTSIDE CAR
PADDYWAGON
PALANKEEN
PALANQUIN
PALKI
PANTECHNICON
PASSENGER TRAIN
PEDAL-CYCLE
PENNYFARTHING
PHAETON
PONY-CART
PONY ENGINE
POST-CHAISE
PRAIRIE-SCHOONER
PUFFING BILLY
PULLMAN
PUSH-BIKE
QUADRICYCLE
QUADRIGA
RACING CAR
RACING CHARIOT
RAILWAY TRAIN
RATTLETRAP
RICKSHAW
RIDING-CARRIAGE
ROADSTER
ROCKET
RUNABOUT
SALOON
SCOOTER
SEDAN(-CHAIR)
SHANDRYDAN
SHAY
SHOOTING-BRAKE
SHUNTER
SIDE-CAR
SINCLAIR C5
SINGLE-DECKER
SIT-UP-AND-BEG
SLED(GE)
SLEIGH
SNOCAT

SNOWPLOUGH
SOCIABLE
SOUPED-UP CAR
SPORTS CAR
STAFF CAR
STAGE-COACH
STAGE-WAGON
STATE COACH
STATION-WAGON
STEAM-CAR
STEAM-ENGINE
STEAM-OMNIBUS
STEAM-ROLLER
STREET-CAR
STRETCHER
SULKY
SURREY
TALLY-HO
TANDEM
TANKER
TARANTASS
TAXI(-CAB)
THIKA-GHARRY
THROUGH TRAIN
TILBURY
TIN LIZZIE
TOBOGGAN
TONGA
TOURER
TRACTION ENGINE
TRACTOR
TRAILER
TRAIN
TRAM
TRAP
TRAVELLING
  CARRIAGE
TRICAR
TRICYCLE
TROLLEY(-BUS)
TROLLEY-CAR
TRUCK
TUBE
TUMBRIL
TWO-DOOR
TWO-SEATER
TWO-WHEELER
UNDERGROUND
  TRAIN
UNICORN
UNICYCLE
VAN
VELOCIPEDE
VICTORIA
VIS-À-VIS
WAGON(ETTE)
WAIN
WEASEL
WHISKEY
WHITECHAPEL

odorization, fanning, fumigation, oxygenation

venture adventure, aim, bid, business, crack, dare, effort, endeavour, enterprise, exercise, experiment, fling, gambit, go, goal, intention, objective, operation, propose, quest, risk, seeking, shot, speculation, stab, suggest, trial, try, undertaking, whack

verbal enunciated, lingual, linguistic, oral, pronounced, spoken, vocal, vocalized, voiced

verbiage babble, baloney, blah, blarney, blether, bunkum, claptrap, drivel, drool, eyewash, flannel, flapdoodle, flimflam, flummery, gabble, galimatias, gas, guff, hooey, humbug, jabber, jaw, junk, line, malarkey, moonshine, patter, poppycock, prate, prattle, psychobabble, spiel, trumpery, vapouring, wind, yackety-yak, yammer

verdant fresh, grassy, green, leafy, rural

verdict acquittal, adjudication, award, conclusion, condemnation, decision, decree, edict, finding, order, pronouncement, ruling, sentence

verifiable authentic, certifiable, documented, proved, recorded, seconded, witnessed

verification affirmation, ascertainment, assurance, attestation, authentication, averment, avouchment, avowal, certification, collation, confirmation, crosscheck, determination, documentation, double check, ratification, surety, validation

verified affirmed, assured, attested, authenticated, averred, avouched, avowed, certain, certified, checked, collated, confirmed, corroborated, documented, proved, ratified, sure, validated

verify ascertain, check, confirm, determine, prove, substantiate

verminous flea-bitten, grubby, infested, lousy, maggoty, moth-eaten, weevilly

vertical erect, plumb, plunging, precipitous, sheer, standing, straight, upended, upright

verticality drop, erectness, fall, perpendicularity, precipitousness, sheerness, squareness, steepness, straightness, uprightness

vessel amphora, barrel, boat, bucket, caddy, cask, cistern, coal scuttle, craft, drum, dustbin, ewer, firkin, hogshead, hopper, jar, jug, keg, pail, pipe, pitcher, puncheon, ship, silo, skull, SS, tank, tun, urn, vase, vat, watering can
See list of ships and boats.

vestige fingermark, footprint, mark, piste, relic, remains, scent, spoor, stain, tidemark, trace, track, trail, tyremark

veterinarian horseleech, vet, veterinary, veterinary surgeon

veto abolish, abrogation, annulment, ban, blackball, cancel, check, circumscribe, countermand, counterorder, crackdown, criminalize, curfew, debar, denial, deny, disallowance, embargo, exclude, exclusion, excommunicate, forbid, illicitness, impede, impediment, inhibit, injunction, interdict, obstacle, obstruct, ostracism, ostracize, outlaw, prevent, prohibition, rebuff, refusal, refuse, reject, repeal, repression, restraint, restriction, revoke, suppression, suspend, suspension, taboo, temperance, turn down, unpermissibility, withhold permission

vibrate agitate, beat, drum, flicker, flutter, heave, palpitate, pant, pulsate, quiver, rattle, resonate, shake, shiver, throb, tick, tremble

vibrating agitating, beating, flickering, palpitating, pulsating, quivering, resonant, rhythmic, shaking, shivering, staccato, throbbing

vibration agitation, arrhythmia, beat, drumming, flickering, flutter, heartbeat, palpitation, pitter-patter, pulsation, pulse, quivering, rataplan, rat-a-tat, resonance, rhythm, shaking, shivering, staccato, tempo, throb, throbbing, tremor, trill

vice amorality, carnality, debauchery, degeneracy, degradation, depravity, immorality, impurity, indecency, lust, perversion, profligacy, turpitude, unvirtuousness, vulgarity

victorious crushing, invincible, prizewinning, quelling, the best, triumphant, unbeaten, unbowed, undefeated, unvanquished, winning, world-beating

victory beating, conquest, hiding, knockout, KO, licking, overrunning, pushover, rout, success, thrashing, triumph, trouncing, walkover, whipping, win

view aspect, attitude, landscape, opinion, outlook, panorama, prospect, scene, show, sight, spectacle, vista

viewpoint amphitheatre, arena, aspect, belvedere, bias, bird's-eye view, bleachers, bridge, cinema, crow's nest, eyeshot, gazebo, grandstand, impres-

---

SHIPS AND BOATS

ARGO	DINGHY	LUGGER	SCULLER
ARK	DOGGER	MAIL-SHIP	SEALER
BANANA-BOAT	DORY	MAIL-STEAMER	SHELL
BARGE	DOUBLE-CANOE	MERCHANT SHIP	SHIP'S BOAT
BARK	DREDGER	MOTORBOAT	SHOWBOAT
BARQUE(NTINE)	DRIFTER	MOTORSHIP	SKIFF
BAWLEY	DROMOND	MUD-HOPPER	SLAVER
BILANDER	DUG-OUT	NOAH'S ARK	SLAVE-SHIP
BIREME	ESCORT VESSEL	NOBBY	SLOOP
BOAT	FELUCCA	OCEAN	SMACK
BRIG(ANTINE)	FERRY	GREYHOUND	SNOW
BUCENTAUR	FIRESHIP	OUTBOARD	SPEEDBOAT
BUDGEROW	FISHING-BOAT	OUTRIGGER	STEAMBOAT
BUMBOAT	FISHING SMACK	PACKET	STEAMER
BUSS	FLOATING PALACE	PADDLE-BOAT	STEAMSHIP
CABIN-CRUISER	FLY-BOAT	PASSENGER SHIP	STERN-WHEELER
CAIQUE	FOLDBOAT	PENTECONTER	STORESHIP
CANOE	FREIGHTER	PICKET BOAT	SUBMARINE
CARAVEL	FRIGATE	PILOT VESSEL	TANKER
CARGO-BOAT	FUNNY	PINNACE	TARTANE
CARRACK	GABBARD	PIRAGUA	TEA-CLIPPER
CARVEL	GALLEON	PIRATE-SHIP	TENDER
CATAMARAN	GALLEY	PLEASURE BOAT	THREE-MASTER
CHANNEL STEAMER	GALLIVAT	POLACCA	TOWBOAT
CHASSE-MARÉE	GONDOLA	POLACRE	TRAIN-FERRY
CLIPPER	GRAB	PRAHU	TRAMP
COASTER	HERRING-FISHER	PRISON-SHIP	TRANSPORT SHIP
COASTING VESSEL	HOOKER	PROA	TRAWLER
COBLE	HOPPER(-BARGE)	PUNT	TRIREME
COCKBOAT	HOSPITAL SHIP	QUADRIREME	TROW
COCKLE-SHELL	HOUSE BOAT	QUINQUEREME	TUG
COG	HOY	RAFT	U-BOAT
COLLIER	JANGADA	RANDAN	UMIAK
CORACLE	JOLLY-BOAT	RIVER-BOAT	VIKING-SHIP
CORSAIR	JUNK	ROTOR SHIP	WAR SHIP
CORVETTE	KAYAK	ROWBOAT	WHALER
CRIS-CRAFT	KETCH	ROWING BOAT	WIND-JAMMER
CRUMSTER	LAUNCH	SAIC	XEBEC
CURRACH	LIFEBOAT	SAILBOAT	YACHT
CUTTER	LIGHTSHIP	SAILING BARGE	YAWL
DAHABIYA	LINER	SAILING-SHIP	
DANDY	LONG-BOAT	SAMPAN	
DHOW	LORCHA	SCHOONER	

sion, mirador, observatory, perspective, premise, range, scope, slant, stadium, stand, standpoint, theatre, theory, view, watch tower

vigilant apprehensive, careful, prognostic, watchful

vilification attack, calumny, defamation, denunciation, execration, fulmination, libel, obloquy, onslaught, opprobrium, reproach, revilement, scurrility, slander, slanging match, threat, thundering, verbal abuse, vituperation

vilify abuse, accuse, asperse, attack, blackguard, call names, chide, condemn, debase, defame, defile, degrade, denunciate, disgrace, execrate, fulminate, gossip, insinuate, inveigh, libel, rail, rebuke, reproach, revile, round upon, scold, slander, slur, threaten, thunder, tongue-lash, vituperate, whisper

village hamlet, pueblo, rural village, thorp

vindicable admissible, allowable, arguable, condonable, defensible, dispensable, excusable, exemptible, explainable, forgivable, justifiable, pardonable, reasonable, refutable, remissible, venial, warrantable

vindicate absolve, acquit, clear, discharge, dismiss, exculpate, excuse, exonerate, free, liberate, pardon, purge, rehabilitate, reinstate, release, remit, restore

vindication absolution, acquittal, clearance, compurgation, discharge, dismissal, exculpation, exoneration, pardon, purging, rehabilitation, reinstatement, release, remission, restitution, restoration

vindicatory apologetic, corroborative, defensive, exculpatory, excusatory, exonerative, explanatory, extenuating, justifying, mitigative, palliative, qualifying, rebutting, refuting, rejoining, remissive, retorting, supportive

vindictive malevolent, malicious, punitive, requiting, retributive, spiteful, unforgiving, vengeful, venomous

violence aggression, barbarity, bestiality, bloodlust, bloodthirstiness, boisterousness, brute force, destructiveness, energy, excess, ferocity, fierceness, force, forcefulness, frenzy, fury, harshness, homicide, hooliganism, intensity, might, murder, murderousness, passion, power, rape, roughness, savagery, severity, slaughter, strength, strong-arm tactics, terrorism, thuggery, torture, vandalism, vehemence, violation, virulence, wildness

violent acute, aggressive, agitated, angry, ardent, barbarous, bellicose, berserk, bestial, bloodthirsty, boiling, brutal, bursting, cataclysmic, catastrophic, convulsive, cruel, devastating, ebullient, enraged, eruptive, excessive, explosive, extreme, ferocious, fervent, fierce, fiery, forceful, frantic, frenetic, frenzied, fuming, furious, harsh, headstrong, heavy-handed, hotheaded, hysterical, impassioned, intense, irrepressible, kicking, murderous, powerful, rabid, raging, rampant, ravening, riotous, roaring, rough, savage, severe, stormy, struggling, tempestuous, thrashing, threatening, tumultuous, turbulent, tyrannical, unmitigated, uproarious, vehement, vicious, virulent, warlike, wild
may indicate an anagram

virginal abstinent, chaste, continent, innocent, maidenly, new, pure

virginity abstinence, chastity, continence, freshness, maidenhood, purity, self-denial

virtual almost, artificial, imaginary, quasi

virtue advantage, altruism, asset, benefit, benevolence, character, charity, chastity, decency, disinterestedness, duty, faith, fine qualities, fortitude, generosity, godliness, goodness, good point, grace, holiness, honesty, honour, hope, innocence, integrity, justice, love, magnanimity, morality, nobleness, obedience, philanthropy, plus point, probity, prudence, purity, righteousness, saintliness, sanctity, self-control, skill, soberness, stainlessness, temperance, unselfishness, uprightness, virginity

virtuous altruistic, angelic, benevolent, blameless, chivalrous, decent, disinterested, generous, godly, good, guiltless, holy, honourable, idealistic, immaculate, impeccable, innocent, irreproachable, magnanimous, moral, noble, philanthropic, proper, righteous, saintly, sanctified, spiritual, spotless, stainless, uncorrupt, unselfish, upright

visceral abdominal, bodily, cardiovascular, gutsy, heartfelt, internal, intestinal, splanchnic, vital

viscosity adhesiveness, clamminess, colloidality, doughiness, gelatinousness, glueyness, glutinousness, gooeyness, gumminess, incrassation, inspissation, lentor, mucilaginousness, pastiness, ropiness, spissitude, stickiness, stringiness, syrupiness, tackiness, tenacity, thickening, toughness, treacliness, viscidity, viscousness

viscous adhesive, clammy, colloidal, emulsive, gaumy, gluey, glutinous, gumbo, gummy, heavy, incrassate, inspissate, mucilaginous, oily, ropy, slabby, sticky, stodgy, stringy, tacky, thick, tough, viscid, waxy

visibility conspicuousness, detectability, discernibility, distinctness, evidence, eyeshot, horizon, identifiability, observability, overtness, perceivability, perceptibility, presence, range, recognizability, revelation, skyline, tangibility

visible apparent, available, clear(-cut), concrete, conspicuous, detectable, discernible, discoverable, distinct, distinguishable, evident, exposed, external, eye-catching, eye-opening, identifiable, manifest, material, noticeable, observ-

able, obvious, open, outward, overt, palpable, patent, perceivable, perceptible, plain, present, public, recognizable, spectacular, superficial, surface, tangible, unconcealed, unmistakeable, viewable

vision dream, eyesight, fantasy, hallucination, ideal, manifestion, perception, plan, seeing, sight

visit frequent, haunt, relax, see, sojourn, stay, unbend, weekend

visual binocular, illusionary, imaginary, ocular, ophthalmic, optical, panoramic, scenic, visional

visual aid bifocals, binoculars, contacts, eyeglass, eyeshade, frames, glasses, goggles, lenses, lorgnette, loupe, magnifying glass, microreader, monocle, opera glasses, pince-nez, shades, specs, spyglass, sunglasses, telescope

visualization anticipation, awareness, consideration, contemplation, discernment, foresight, imagination, insight, perception, perspicacity, planning, prevision, understanding

visualize anticipate, consider, contemplate, discern, foresee, imagine, perceive, picture, plan

vitality animation, boldness, dash, drive, dynamism, energy, get-up-and-go, liveliness, panache, pep, raciness, spirit, spunk, verve, vigour, vivacity, vividness, zest, zip

vituperate curse, defame, execrate, revile, vilify

vituperative abusive, attacking, blasting, calumnious, defamatory, denunciatory, ignominious, libellous, opprobrious, reproachful, reviling, slanderous, threatening, vilifying, vitriolic

vivid bright, clear, graphic, life-like, poignant, realistic, strong

vocative calling, invocatory, salutatory, valedictory

vociferous bellowing, booming, clamorous, deafening, full-throated, loud, loudmouthed, noisy, obstreperous, roaring, screaming, shouting, stentorian, talkative, thundering, uproarious, vocal, yelling

voice assert, larynx, speak, utterance, vocal chords, voice box, vote

voiceless aphonic, dumb, dysphonic, infant, mute, silent, surd

voicelessness aphonia, dumbness, dysphonia, gesticulation, gesture, muteness, sign language, silence, whisper

void clean out, clear out, deplete, eliminate, emptiness, empty, evacuate, eviscerate, exhaust, infinity, invalid, nothingness, obsolete, pump out, purge, remove, siphon off, space, vacuum, vent

volatile changeable, evaporable, hot-tempered, mercurial, unstable, vaporescent, vapourable
may indicate an anagram

volatility evaporability, instability, irascibility, vapourability, variability

volcanic eruptive, explosive, laval, molten, pyroclastic, seismic

volcano aa, active volcano, ash, caldera, cone, crater, ejecta, eruption, Etna, fissure, fumurole, gas vent, geyser, inactive volcano, Krakatoa, lava, magma, melt, pahoehoe, pumice, shield volcano, Stromboli, tephra, vent, volcanism

voluntary altruistic, charity, humanitarian, offered, philanthropic, self-appointed, spontaneous, unbidden, unforced, unpaid, unprompted, volunteering

volunteer charity worker, furnish, give, lend, loan, missionary, offer, present, provide, sacrifice oneself

vomit be sick, bring up, chunder, gag, heave, puke, regurgitate, retch, spew, spit

vomiting egestion, emesis, gagging, heaving, nausea, puking, regurgitation, retching, seasick, sick, sickness, travelsick, vomitive

vortex charybdis, cyclone, eddy, gurge, maelstrom, surge, swirl, tornado, waterspout, whirl, whirlpool, whirlwind

vow adjure, affidavit, assurance, charge, commitment, deposition, guarantee, oath, pledge, promise, solemn word, statement, swear, sworn testimony, testify, vouch for, word

vowed assured, committed, depositional, guaranteed, on oath, pledged, promised, sworn, true, vouched

voyeurism Peeping Tom, sexploitation

vulgar barbaric, cheap, coarse, common, crude, fraction, gandy, garish, glitzy, gross, ill-bred, inelegant, infra-dig, loud, meretricious, non-U, ostentatious, parvenu, plebby, plebeian, primitive, rude, savage, showy, tawdry, uncultured, unfeminine, ungentlemanly, unladylike, wild

vulgarity bad taste, coarseness, commonness, crassness, crudeness, gaucheness, indecency, inelegance, insensitivity, obscenity, raciness, tackiness, tawdriness

vulgarize cheapen, coarsen, commercialize, popularize

vulnerability Achilles' heel, defect, defencelessness, easy target, exposure, failing, flaw, helplessness, imperfection, innocence, insecurity, instability, liability, naivety, nakedness, nonimmunity, openness, pregnability, susceptibility, tender spot, unsoundness, weakness

vulnerable defenceless, exposed, expugnable, helpless, isolated, liable, naive, open to, pregnable, stranded, susceptible, unarmed, unarmoured, unattended, unaware, undefended, unfortified, unguarded, unprepared, unprotected, unready, unshielded, unsupported

·W·

ABBREVIATIONS

W	watt • week • west • wicket • width • wife
WAAF	Women's Auxiliary Air Force
WASP	white Anglo-Saxon Protestant
WC	London district • water closet • without change
WE	week ending
WG	cricketer (W. G. Grace) • wire gauge
WI	West Indies • Women's Institute
WILCO	will comply
WIP	work in progress
WO	walkover • War Office • welfare officer • written off
WORM	write once read many times (computing)
WP	weather permitting • word processing
WR	King William (Latin: *Willelmus Rex*)
WRAC	Women's Royal Army Corps
WRAF	Women's Royal Air Force
WRNS	Women's Royal Naval Service
WRVS	Women's Royal Voluntary Service

wait await, dally, dawdle, delay, dilly-dally, hang fire, hold-up, linger, loiter, pause, stay, stop, tarry

walk amble, lane, lope, march, mince, occupation, path, patter, perambulate, potter, roam, saunter, shuffle, stagger, stride, stroll, strut, toddle, tour, tramp, waddle, walkway, wander

walking living, on foot, on the hoof, shanks's pony

wall abutment, barrier, bulwark, buttress, embankment, fence

wandering abstracted, circuitousness, circumbendibus, circumlocution, devious, digression, discursive, divagatory, drifting, errant, erratic, error, excursus, gypsy, homeless, inattentive, lapse, migrant, nomadic, pererration, peripatetic, rambling, roaming, stateless, straying, travelling, vagrancy, vagrant
may indicate an anagram

war Ares, Armageddon, arms, Athena, attrition, battles, Bellona, besieging, blitz, blitzkrieg, campaigning, civil, class, conflict, crusade, defence, Eris, Fea, fighting, germ warfare, guerrilla warfare, incursion, Indra, intervention, invasion, jihad, jungle warfare, Karttikeya, Mars, nuclear, Odin, sabre-rattling, Tyr, warpath, Wotan
See also list at **weapon**.

warlike aggressive, battle-hungry, bellicose, belligerent, bloodthirsty, combative, cruel, fierce, gung-ho, hawkish, militaristic, pugnacious, Ramboesque, tough, unpacific, war-fevered, war-loving, warmongering

warm affectionate, balmy, clement, close, damp, fair, friendly, heat up, humid, loving, mild, moderate, muggy, reheat, sticky, summery, temperate, welcoming

warm-hearted amiable, amicable, cordial, ebullient, friendly, generous, hospitable, kind

warmonger assail, assault, attack, besiege, combat, crusade, declare war, demagogue, make trouble, rabble-rouse, storm

warn admonish, advise, alert, apprise, augur, caution, counsel, forewarn, hint, inform, lour, menace, notify, predict, prepare, remind, reprove, threaten, tip, wink

warned advised, cautioned, cautious, counselled, forearmed, forewarned, prepared, wary

warning admonition, admonitory, advice, advisable, alarm, announcement, augury, boding, caution, caveat, counsel, danger, deterrent, dissuasive, example, exemplary, expostulation, foreboding, forewarning, frightening, hint, ill-omened, indication, information, instructive, intelligence, lesson, menace, minatory, monitory, news, notification, nudge, omen, ominous, pinch, portent, prediction, premonition, premonitory, presageful, prognostic, protesting, publication, reprimand, sign, signal, siren, symptomatic, threat, tip-off, ultimatum, wink

warrant authorize, certificate, document, expect, justify

warring aggressive, armed, arrayed, attacking, battling, bellicose, belligerent, called-up, campaigning, competing, conscripted, defending, embattled, engaged, fighting, militant, mobilized, opposed, uniformed
may indicate an anagram

washer boiler, copper, dishwasher, dolly, laundrette, ring, washboard, washing machine, washtub

waste abuse, atrophy, blow, blue, burn, crap, damage, decay, decline, deteriorate, devour, dissipation, drain, dregs, emaciate, extravagance, fritter away, fruitlessness, garbage, gut, impair, improvidence, kill, lavish, leak, leftover, loss, melt away, misapply, misspend, misuse, obsolescence, overproduction, overspending, pollute,

prodigality, refuse, remnants, rubbish, scraps, shrivel, slag, spillage, splurge, spree, squander, superfluity, superfluous, thriftlessness, throwaway, trash, unproductiveness, unused, unwanted, useless, wilt, wither, worthless

wasteful extravagant, improvident, lavish, prodigal, spendthrift, thriftless, uneconomic, unnecessary

waste product excrement, garbage, leftovers, litter, refuse, rubbish, scraps, toxic waste

watch digital watch, duty, fob, guard, half-hunter, hunter, invigilate, lookout, monitor, observe, oversee, pocket watch, repeater, shift, supervise, turnip, vigil, wristwatch
See also list at **clock**.

watchful alert, attentive, careful, circumspect, curious, heedful, observant, on guard, scrutinizing, sharp-eyed, surveying, vigilant, wary

watchfulness alertness, examination, finickiness, guarding, inspection, invigilation, lookout, observance, stakeout, surveillance, vigilance, wariness

water Adam's ale, Adam's wine, aqua, brine, deluge, douse, drench, drouk, drown, duck, dunk, eau, flood, flow on, fluid, fountain, H_2O, hydrate, hydrol, ice, imbrue, immerse, inundate, irrigate, leach, liquid, lixiviate, meltwater, mineral water, moisten, moisture, percolate, permeate, pour on, rain, rose water, saturate, sluice, soak, soda water, souse, spring, sprinkle, submerge, submerse, swamp, waterlog, well, wet

waterfall cascade, cataract, chute, force, linn, nappe, rapids, shoot

wateriness dampness, dewiness, moistness, raininess, runniness, sloppiness, weakness, wetness

watering affusion, aspergation, drenching, hosing, irrigation, soaking, spargefaction, splashing, spraying, sprinkling, squirting, wetting

waterproof dampproof, dry-shod, flood proof, rainproof, showerproof, snug, stormproof, watertight

waterway aqueduct, canal, cut, ferry crossing, lake, ocean track, river, seaway, steamer route

watery aquatic, aqueous, hydrated, hydraulic, hydrodynamic, hydrometric, hydrostatic, hydrous

wave beckon, billow, bore, brandish, breaker, choppy sea, crimp, eagre, flap, float, flourish, flutter, fly, foam, froth, gesture, heave, perm, ripple, roller, shake, spume, surf, surge, swell, tidal wave, tsunami, undercurrent, undulate, undulation, wag, wavelet, waviness, white horses, wield

waving beckoning, oscillating, shaking, sinusoidal, tremulous, undulating

way alley, approach, beaten track, behaviour, conduct, constitutional, fashion, form, groove, guise, lane, lifestyle, manner, means, method, mode, order, passage, path, practice, procedure, process, progress, road, round, route, routine, run, rut, skill, style, system, tack, tactics, technique, tone, tramlines, treadmill, wise
may indicate an anagram

way out avenue, bizarre, channel, door, egress, emergency exit, escape hatch, escape route, exit, fire escape, freakish, gate, loophole, path, port, weird

weak brittle, cowardly, creaky, defenceless, delicate, dithery, drooping, feeble, flaccid, floppy, fragile, gimcrack, helpless, impotent, indecisive, ineffectual, limp, powerless, puny, relaxed, rickety, sagging, seedy, shoddy, slack, soft, thin, untenable, watery, wobbly, wonky

weaken adulterate, break, consume, cripple, crumble, damage, debilitate, decimate, decline, deflate, demilitarize, denude, deplete, deprive, dilute, diminish, disable, disarm, dodder, drain, droop, dwindle, emaciate, enfeeble, exhaust, expose, extenuate, fade, fail, faint, fall, flag, flop, halt, harm, hurt, impair, impoverish, incapacitate, injure, invalidate, lame, languish, lessen, limp, maim, mar, muffle, mute, neutralize, reduce, rob, sag, sap, shake, sicken, slacken, soften, split, spoil, sprain, stagger, starve, strain, strip, teeter, thin, totter, tremble, undermine, unnerve, wear, wilt, wound, yield

weakened debilitated, dissipated, enervated, exhausted, failed, fatigued, impoverished, sapped, tired, wearied, weary

weakling baby, chicken, coward, doormat, drip, dupe, hypochondriac, infant, invalid, jellyfish, kitten, lightweight, milksop, namby-pamby, pansy, pushover, sissy, softy, victim, weed, wet, wimp

weakness Achilles' heel, cowardice, damage, defect, defencelessness, delicacy, delicateness, dilution, feebleness, flaccidity, flaw, floppiness, fragility, harmlessness, helplessness, impotence, indecision, innocence, instability, limpness, looseness, puniness, slackness, smallness, thinness, vulnerability, wateriness

weak-willed chicken, cowardly, dithering, effete, gutless, half-hearted, hesitant, indecisive, irresolute, lily-livered, mealy-mouthed, nervous, pusillanimous, scared, sheepish, spineless, timid, vacillating, wavering, yellow

wealth abundance, affluence, assets, bonanza, capital, estate, fortune, gain, income, investments, means, money, moneymaking, possessions, profit, profusion, property, prosperity, resources, richness, savings

wealthy affluent, comfortable, flush, loaded, moneyed, propertied, prosperous, rich, well-endowed, well-heeled, well-off, well-paid, well-situated, well-to-do

weapon
See list of weapons.

wear ablation, abrasion, attire oneself, attrition, clothe oneself, collision, corrosion, detrition, don, dress in, erasure, erosion, have on, obliteration, rubbing out, sandblasting

weather air density, air pressure, anticyclone, blackthorn winter, conditions, crumble, cyclone, depression, dewpoint, dog days, endure, erode, forecast, frontal system, general synopsis, Groundhog Day, halcyon days, humidity, hurricane, Indian summer, isobar, isotherm, mature, outlook, pattern, pressure system, ridge, rust, sunshine, survive, temperature, the elements, tornado, trough, warm sector, wear down, weather lore, wind-chill factor, wind speed

weave brush, felt, intertwine, knit, mat, nap, network, web, weftage
may indicate an anagram

weaving interweaving, knitting, knotting, lacing, list, plain weave, selvage, shoot, twill, twining, warp, webbing, weft

wedding betrothal, elopement, espousal, hymenal rites, joining, linking, marriage, merging, nuptials, spousal, uniting, vows, wedding ceremony

weep blub, blubber, cry, howl, run, sigh, snivel, sob, ululate, wail

WEAPONS

ASSEGAI	CUDGEL	KNOBKERRIE	SALTPETRE
A-BOMB	CUTLASS	KNUCKLE-DUSTER	SCIMITAR
ACOUSTIC MINE	DAGGER	KRIS	SCUD MISSILE
ARBALEST	DART	KUKRI	SEMTEX
ARROW	DEFENSIVE MISSILE	LANCE	SHELL
ATOM BOMB	DEPTH CHARGE	LANDMINE	SHILLELAGH
ATOMIC WARHEAD	DIRK	LATHI	SHORT
AXE	DOODLEBUG	LETTER BOMB	SHRAPNELL
BALLISTA	DYNAMITE	LIMPET MINE	SKEAN-DHU
BALLISTIC MISSILE	ÉPÉF,	LONGBOW	SLING
BATTERING RAM	EXOCET	LYDDITE	STAFF
BATTLE-AXE	FALCHION	MACE	STAR SHELL
BAYONET	FIREBOMB	MACHETE	STAVE
BAZOOKA	FIREWORKS	MAGNETIC MINE	STICK
BILBO	FLARE	MAILBOMB	STILETTO
BILL	FLÉCHETTE	MANGONEL	SURFACE-TO-AIR
BLADE	FLICK KNIFE	MATCHET	MISSILE
BLOWPIPE	FLYING BOMB	MELINITE	SWORD
BLUDGEON	FOIL	MINE	SWORDSTICK
BOLA	GAFF	MOLOTOV	THROWSTICK
BOMBSHELL	GAS SHELL	COCKTAIL	TIME BOMB
BOOMERANG	GELIGNITE	NAILBOMB	TIN FISH
BOW	GISARME	NAPALM BOMB	TNT
BOWIE KNIFE	GREEK FIRE	NITROGLYCERINE	TOLEDO
BRASS KNUCKLES	GRENADE	PANGA	TOMAHAWK
BROADSWORD	GUIDED MISSILE	PARANG	TORPEDO
BULLET	HALBERD	PARTISAN	TREBUCHET
CATAPULT	HAND GRENADE	PATRIOT	TRIDENT
CAVALRY SWORD	HANGER	PELLET	TRUNCHEON
CHOPPER	HARPOON	PIKE	V-1
CLAYMORE	HATCHET	POLARIS	V-2
CLUB	H-BOMB	POLEAXE	WARHAMMER
CORDITE	INCENDIARY	QUARTERSTAFF	WARHEAD
COSH	JAVELIN	RAPIER	WHIZ-BANG
CROSSBOW	JERID	ROCKET	WOOMERA
CRUISE MISSILE	KNIFE	SABRE	YATAGHAN

weigh consider, influence, measure, weigh in

weight burden, heaviness, importance, lead, plumb, plumb bob, plummet, sinker
See also list at **measurement**.

welcome accept, accommodate, back-slapping, call in, embrace, grant asylum, greet, handshake, hug, invite, kiss, naturalize, pleasant, protect, safeguard, shelter, warmth

welcoming greeting, hailing, hospitable, inviting

welfare happiness, health, safety, social services, social work, well-being

well-behaved biddable, bland, ceremonious, compliant, conventional, correct, courteous, cultivated, cultured, de rigueur, dignified, diplomatic, docile, dutiful, elegant, ethical, flattering, formal, genteel, gentlemanly, good, gracious, ladylike, law-abiding, obedient, polished, polite, refined, respectful, smooth, suave, sweet-talking, urbane, virtuous, well-bred, well-mannered, willing

well-known blatant, celebrated, famous, flagrant, glaring, infamous, manifest, notorious, popular, renowned, sensational

well-off affluent, flush, loaded, prosperous, rich, solvent, wealthy, well-heeled, well-to-do

wet awash, bathed, dipped, drenched, dripping, drowned, ducked, dunked, effete, feeble, flooded, soaked, sodden, soggy, sopping, soppy, soused, steeped, streaming, submerged, swamped, waterlogged, wringing

wetting damping, humectant, hydrotherapeutic, irrigational, irriguous, moistening, watering

wheel cartwheel, charka, cog, flywheel, gear, gearwheel, Ixion's wheel, pinwheel, rotate, roll, spinning jenny, trundle, turn

whim boutade, brainstorm, craze, crotchet, escapade, fad, fancy, fit, flip-flop, flirtation, freak, humour, idea, idiosyncrasy, impulse, kink, maggot, megrim, mood, notion, peculiarity, quirk, temperament, vagary, whimsy

whimsical capricious, fanciful, flattering, temperamental, timeserving

whisper breathe, crackle, croon, drone, hint, hum, moan, mumble, murmur, mutter, purr, rumour, rustle, sigh, susurrate, whine

whispering aside, hiss, mumble, murmur, mutter, sigh, surd, undertone

white alabaster, albescent, albinotic, argent, Caucasian, chalky, creamy, ecru, fair-skinned, greige, ivory, lactescent, lily-white, magnolia, marble, milky, off-white, pale, pallid, pearly, pure-white, silver, snow-white, unbleached, undyed, whitish
See also list at **colours**.

white-haired canescent, grizzled, hoary, pepper-and-salt

whiten blanch, blanco, bleach, blench, calcimine, clean, decolorize, etiolate, fade, frost, grizzle, pale, pipeclay, silver, wash, whitewash

whiteness achromatism, albescence, albinism, canescence, chalkiness, colourlessness, creaminess, etiolation, fairness, greyness, hoariness, lactescence, milkiness, paleness, pearliness, sallowness, silveriness, snowiness

whole across-the-board, all, all-embracing, all-inclusive, completeness, comprehensive, entire, every, fullness, general, generalization, global, gross, holism, holistic, inclusiveness, indissoluble, indivisibility, inseparable, integral, integrity, international, joined, one, oneness, single, solid, total, unanimous, undivided, unified, united, unity, universal, worldwide

wholesale all at once, all-embracing, all-inclusive, blanket, broad, bulk, carpet, catholic, comprehensive, general, global, universal, wide, wide-ranging, widespread, world-wide

wicked abominable, atrocious, bad, base, beastly, brutal, callous, conscienceless, corrupt, criminal, cruel, delinquent, despicable, deteriorating, disgraceful, dishonest, disobedient, disreputable, erring, evil, excellent, fallen, flagrant, foul, hard-hearted, heinous, hellish, improper, inexpiable, infamous, inhuman, iniquitous, irredeemable, irremissible, knavish, maleficent, malevolent, misbehaving, miscreant, naughty, nefarious, outrageous, rascally, recidivous, reprehensible, roguish, rotten, shameless, sinful, transgressing, trespassing, unatonable, unforgivable, unpardonable, unprincipled, unrighteous, unscrupulous, vicious, vile, villainous, worthless, wrong *may indicate an anagram*

wickedness abomination, atrocity, badness, baseness, brutality, corruption, criminality, cruelty, delinquency, dishonesty, disobedience, disrepute, enormity, evil, evildoing, flagitiousness, flagrancy, heinousness, hellishness, improbity, infamy, inhumanity, iniquity, knavery, malevolence, misbehaviour, naughtiness, obscenity, outrage, peccability, roguery, shamelessness, sin, sinfulness, transgression, trespass, unrighteousness, viciousness, vileness, villainy, vitiation, wrong, wrongdoing

wide-eyed agape, agog, breathless, dumbfounded, dumbstruck, inarticulate, open-mouthed, popeyed, round-eyed, silenced, speechless, transfixed, wordless

widespread endemic, epidemic, extensive, omnipresent, pandemic, pervasive, rampant, rife, ubiquitous

widowed bereaved, husbandless, wifeless

wield brandish, carry, handle, hold, use

wieldiness adaptability, convenience, feasibility, flexibility, handiness, manageability, manoeuvrability, pliability, pliancy, practicality, workability

wieldy adaptable, convenient, ductile, easy-flowing, easy-running, flexible, foolproof, handy, malleable, manageable, manoeuvrable, pliable, practical, smooth-running, tractable, untroublesome, well-oiled, yielding

wife better half, common-law wife, concubine, good lady, goodwife, goody, housewife, lady, matron, missis, old dutch, old lady, squaw

wig false hair, hairpiece, rug, toupé

wilderness bewilderment, desert, outback, waste

wilful bloody-minded, bullheaded, dogged, headstrong, intransigent, mulish, obdurate, obstinate, pigheaded, self-willed, stubborn, wayward

will bequest, choice, codicil, conation, constancy, desire, disposition, estate, fancy, firmness, inclination, inheritance, intent, intention, legacy, mind, option, pleasure, preference, purpose,

---

NOTABLE WINDS

AUSTRU	FÖHN	MISTRAL	SNOW EATER
BERG	G(H)IBLI	MONSOON	SOLANO
BISE	GREGALE	NOR'EASTER	SOUTHERLY BUSTER
BORA	EUROCLYDON	NOR'WESTER	TEHUANTEPEC
BRICKFIELDER	HABOOB	PAMPERO	TRAMONTANA
BURAN	HARMATTAN	PAPAGAYO	TRAMONTANE
CAPE DOCTOR	K(H)AMSIN	SANTA ANA	WET CHINOOK
CHINOOK	LEVANTER	SIMOOM	WILLIWAW
ETESIAN	LIBECC(H)IO	SANIEL	WILLY-WILLY
FOEHN	MELTEMI	SIROCCO	ZONDA

reliability, self-control, self-possession, self-restraint, stability, staunchness, steadfastness, steadiness, testament, volition, willing, wish

willed bequeathed, conative, deliberate, disposed, intended, intentional, volitional, willing

willing agreeable, assenting, bequeathing, consenting, content, disposed, game, inclined, prepared, prone, ready, receptive

willingness consent, gameness, readiness, receptiveness

willpower determination, resoluteness, self-control, single-mindedness, steadfastness, tenacity

wind Auster, baloney, blast, Boreas, breath, breeze, coil, crosscurrent, crosswind, downdraught, Eurus, flatulence, gale, gas, gust, head, hint, hurricane, information, knock the breath out of, meander, prevailing, reel, roll, scud, sea breeze, squall, storm, tail, tornado, twine, typhoon, updraught, wind storm, zephyr, zigzag
See list of notable winds.

windiness blast, blow, breeziness, flatulence, gust, gustiness, verbosity

windy anemological, biting, bitter, blowy, blustery, boreal, breezy, freezing, gale-force, gusty, icy, insubstantial, long-winded, loquacious, northerly, squally

winnings cut, draw, lottery, lucky dip, prize, raffle, rake-off

winter brumal, Christmas, hibernal, hibernation, hiemal, midwinter, the Season, wintertime, yule, yuletide

wisdom acumen, astuteness, comprehension, craftiness, cunning, discernment, discretion, discrimination, enlightenment, erudition, experience, farsightedness, foresight, forethought, insight, intuition, judgment, judiciousness, knowledge, learning, level-headedness, objectivity, penetration, perception, perspicacity, profundity,

prudence, reason, sagacity, sapience, shrewdness, tact, understanding

wise acute, astute, balanced, broad-minded, circumspect, deep, diplomatic, discerning, discreet, erudite, fair-minded, highbrow, impartial, intellectual, judicious, just, knowledgeable, learned, level-headed, objective, oracular, owl, perceptive, perspicacious, politic, profound, prudent, rational, reasoning, reflecting, sagacious, sapient, sensible, Solomon, statesmanlike, tactful, thinking, thoughtful, understanding, unprejudiced, well-advised

wish desire, hope, want, will

wit badinage, banter, brains, buffoonery, clowning, humorist, intelligence, irony, jesting, joking, joshing, kidding, quipping, repartee, sarcasm, teasing, wordplay

witch enchanter, enchantress, lamia, lorelei, mage, magician, magus, medicine man, Merlin, mermaid, necromancer, shaman, siren, sorcerer, sorceress, spellbinder, warlock, witch doctor, wizard

witchcraft bedevilment, black art, black magic, chaos magic, diablerie, enchantment, fetishism, gramyre, magianism, magic, natural magic, necromancy, sorcery, spellcraft, sympathetic magic, thaumaturgy, theurgy, totemism, vampirism, voodooism, white magic, Wicca, witchery, wizardry

witchlike alchemic, charming, demonic, diabolic, druidic, enchanting, entrancing, fascinating, fetishistic, hypnotic, incantational, magical, necromantic, shamanic, spellbinding, totemistic, voodooistic, wizardly

withdraw abandon, bow out, cease, check out, chuck, clock out, depart, die, ditch, dump, evacuate, exit, leave, pull out, quit, relinquish, resign, retire, retreat, secede, sign off, stand down, stop, submit, turn back, vacate, walk out

withstand bar, block, check, defy, disobey, endure, hinder, obstruct, refuse, resist

womenfolk distaff side, matronage, the girls, the sisterhood, womanhood

wonder admiration, amazement, astonishment, astoundment, awe, bafflement, bewilderment, consternation, dumbfoundment, fascination, fear, gape, gasp, gawk, gawp, goggle at, hero-worship, idolize, love, marvel, miracle, puzzlement, raptness, shock, spectacle, stare, stupefaction, surprise, uncertainty, whistle

wonderful A1, ace, admirable, amazing, astounding, aweful, bang-on, breathtaking, brill, classy, corking, cosmic, dandy, excellent, exceptional, exquisite, extraordinary, fab(ulous), fantastic, gorgeous, grand, groovy, hunky-dory, impressive, improbable, incredible, indescribable, inexpressible, jammy, magic, marvellous, miraculous, phenomenal, prodigious, remarkable, scrumptious, sensational, smashing, spiffing, strange, stunning, stupendous, superb, surprising, swell, top-notch, topping, unbelievable, unexpected, unprecedented, unusual, wizard

wondering admiring, aghast, amazed, astonished, astounded, awestruck, bewildered, blinded, dazed, dazzled, dumbfounded, fascinated, flabbergasted, gob-smacked, impressed, marvelling, puzzled, rapt, scandalized, shocked, spellbound, stupefied, surprised, thunderstruck

wonder-working deed, exploit, feat, magic, miracle-working, sorcery, spellbinding, teratology, thaumatology

wood blockboard, boarding, chipboard, copse, cordwood, deal, faggot, flitch, forest, hardboard, hardwood, heartwood, log, lumber, plank, plywood, pole, post, puncheon, sapwood, shake, slab, slat, softwood, spinney, splat, stand, stave, stick, timber

woodcrafted carved, engraved, pyrographic, sculpted, turned, whittled, wood-blocked, woodburned, woodcut, woodprinted, xylographic, xylopyrographic

wooded afforested, arboreous, forestal, forested, reafforested, sylvan, timbered, tree-covered, woodland

woodland arbour, bocage, bosket, bower, brake, brush, chaparral, coppice, copse, covert, holt, hurst, plantation, spinney, stand, thicket, wood, woods

woodwork cabinet-making, carpentry, engraving, joinery, lignography, pyrography, pyrogravure, timberwork, treen, whittling, wood-block printing, woodburning, woodcarving, woodcraft, woodcut, woodprint, wood sculpting, wood turning, xylography, xylopyrography

woody ashen, beechen, hard-grained, ligneous, ligniform, oaken, soft-grained, stiff, stilted, treen, wooden

word announcement, call, catchword, coinage, command, cry, define, hail, inscribe, invitation, logos, name, neologism, nonce word, phrase, pledge, proclamation, promise, publication, rephrase, rewrite, rumour, shibboleth, shout, slogan, story, summons, term, verbalize, verbum, views, watchword, write

worded glossarial, lexical, phrased, verbal, vocabular

wordy diffuse, loquacious, verbose, waffling

work assignment, beaver away, career, chores, creation, donkey-work, drudgery, duty, effort, fag, freelance, function, go, grind, grindstone, homework, housework, industry, job, knead, labour, legwork, manipulate, moil, moonlight, oeuvre, op, operate, opus, overwork, performance, piecework, production, slave, slavery, slog, spade-

work, strain, sweat, swink, taskwork, toil, travail, treadmill, vocation
See also list at **occupation**.

workable achievable, doable, manageable, manoeuvrable, negotiable, operable, possible, practicable, practical, useful, viable

worker ant, artisan, beaver, bee, breadwinner, charwoman, dogsbody, drudge, employee, executive, factotum, fag, flunky, freelance, hack, hand, handyman, labourer, menial, moiler, operative, participator, pieceworker, servant, slave, toiler, volunteer

workforce labour force, manpower, personnel, staff, workers

working active, busy, employed, exercising, functioning, industrious, labouring, operable, practising

work of art chef-d'oeuvre, magnum opus, masterpiece, old master

world cosmos, earth, globe, macrocosm, microcosm, planet, universe

wormlike cestoid, fluky, helminthic, helminthological, leechlike, vermicular

worried anxious, caring, concerned, fretting, harassed, haunted, plagued, solicitous, tormented, troubled

worry agonize over, angst, anxiety, care, concern, fear for, fretting, harass, haunt, plague, solicitude, torment, trouble, uneasiness
may indicate an anagram

worship acclaim, adoration, adulation, appeasement, applaud, atone, awe, celebrate, contemplate, dedication, devotion, dignify, esteem, exaltation, extolment, fast, genuflect, glorification, hallow, honour, humility, kneel, laud, magnify, meditate, obey, oblation, offering, piety, pilgrimage, praise, pray, propitiate, prostration, respect, reverence, sacrifice, veneration

worshipful adoring, anthropolatrous, devoted, devotional, hero-worshipping, honourable, honoured, humbled, majestic, penitent, praising, prayerful, prostrate, reverent(ial), supplicatory, venerational

worshipper celebrant, chapelgoer, churchgoer, communicant, congregation, fan, flock, fold, follower, parishioner, sheep, venerator

worth admiration, beneficence, brilliance, costliness, credit, desert, eminence, esteem, excellence, flawlessness, goodness, greatness, health, magnificence, merit, nobility, perfection, praiseworthiness, pricelessness, quality, quintessence, rarity, respect, skill, soundness, superiority, value, virtue, virtuosity

worthless futile, insignificant, paltry, pointless, unimportant, valueless

worthwhile advantageous, beneficial, favourable, good, helpful, kind, profitable, sound, useful

worthy admirable, admired, approved, braw, brilliant, commendable, creditable, dazzling, deserving, distinguished, eminent, esteemed, estimable, excellent, exemplary, glorious, good, great, just, justified, laudable, magnificent, marvellous, meritorious, noble, notable, respected, rightful, sensational, splendid, terrific, valued, virtuous, wonderful

woven brushed, coarse, felted, fine (-weave), intertwined, knitted, looped, meshed, napped, netted, open-weave, sheer, tangled, twill

wrap bandage, bind, box, circumscribe, cloak, contain, crate, dress, encase, enclose, encompass, enfold, envelop, frame, net, pack, package, shawl, sheath, sheathe, shroud, stole, surround, swathe

wrapping binding, box, envelope, involucre, jacket, packaging, sheath, shroud

wrinkle crease, crinkle, crow's-foot,

crumple, furrow, knit, laugh-line, line, pucker

wrinkly creased, crinkly, knitted, lined, puckered, rough, rugged, rugose, seamed

write characterize, compose, correspond, delineate, describe, document, dramatize, elegize, express, inform, pen, poetize, portray, prosify, record, report, represent, rhyme, versify

wrong abomination, abuse, biased, crime, defame, erroneous, error, evil, false, felony, harm, hurt, immorality, inaccurate, incorrect, infraction, infringement, injury, malign, maltreat, mischief, misdeed, misdemeanour, mistaken, offence, offend, oppress, out-of-line, prejudiced, sin, transgression, trespass, uneven, unfair, unjust, untrue, vice, wickedness
may indicate an anagram

·X, Y, Z·

ABBREVIATIONS

X	card • Christ • cross • error • film • kiss • place on a map • ten • unknown person or factor
XE	xenon
XL	extra large
XN	Christian
XO	cognac
Y	yard • year • yttrium
YB	year book
YC	Young Conservative
YD	yard
YO	yarn over • years old
YT	yacht
Z	zero • zone
ZI	zone of interior
ZIP	zone improvement plan
ZN	zinc

xenophobic chauvinistic, insular, isolationist, jingoistic, nationalistic, parochial, racist

xerox carbon, copy, duplicate, photostat

Xmas Christmas, Noel, yuletide

x-ray radiogram, Roentgen, screening, shadowgraph

xylophone marimba, vibraphone
See also list at **orchestra**.

yellow amber, aureate, beige, buff, champagne, chartreuse, chrome yellow, citrine, citron, Claude tint, creamy, fallow, gamboge, gilt, gold, honey-coloured, luteolin, massicot, mustard, old-gold, or, orpiment, primrose-yellow, tawny, weld, xanthophyll
See also list at **colours**.

yellowish flavescent, fulvous, jaundiced, luteous, sulphurous, xanthous

yelp bark, crow, growl, howl, snap, snarl, sob, squeak, wail, whine, yap

yes affirmative, amen, aye, certification, endorsement, OK, ratification, validation, yea, yeah

yield adapt, agree, appease, believe, bow to, buy, comply, concede, consent, crop, fall for, give, harvest, knuckle under, lose face, obey, output, proceeds, produce, production, relent, submit, succumb, surrender

yielding bending, bumper, fertile, fruitful, giving in, harvested, productive, prolific, relenting
may indicate an anagram

yoke anchor, bind, claw, collar, coupling, drawbar, grapple, halter, harness, hook, join, lasso, lead, leash, link, loop, noose, reins, ribbons, tether, traces, unite

young adolescent, babyish, boyish, brood, chick, childlike, children, clutch, daughters, embryonic, fingerling, fledgling, fresh, frogspawn, fry, girlish, hatch, immature, infantile, innocent, issue, junior, juvenile, kids, knee-high, litter, maidenly, minor, naive, nestling, new, offspring, poult, preschool, pubescent, pullet, sons, spawn, tadpole, teenage, underage, unfledged, virginal

youngster adolescent, junior, juvenile, kid, minor, teenager, teenybopper, young'un, youth

youth adolescence, apprenticeship, immaturity, maidenhood, minority, nonage, puberty, puerility, pupillage, salad days, schooldays, teens, wardship

youthfulness childishness, freshness, immaturity, juvenescence, maidenliness, sappiness, vigour, youngness

zany comic, idiotic, mad, wacky
may indicate an anagram

zero blob, duck, infinitesimal, love, nil, no, none, nothing, nought, O, squat, zilch

zone area, equator, horse latitudes, region, roaring forties, subtropics, tropics

zoo aquarium, aviary, menagerie, reserve, safari park

zoom focus on, hurry, rush, whizz

zoophilism animalism, animality, bestiality, zoophilia

zymurgy brewing, fermentation

·Appendix·

CONTENTS

ANAGRAM INDICATORS

Abandoned
Abound
Abomination
Abroad
Abstract
Aberrant
Abnormal
Abortion
Absurd
Accidental
Accommodated
Accommodation
Acrobatic
Actively
Adapt(ed)
Addled
Adjust(ed)
Adrift
Addled
Adulterated
Affect(ed)
Afflict(ed)
Afloat
Afresh
After a fashion
After injury
Aftermath of
Agony
Agitate(d)
Agitator
Alloy
All sorts
À la mode
Ailing
Alchemy
All over the
 place
All at sea
All wrong
All over
Alias
Alien
Altered

Alternative
Amalgam
Amalgamate
Amazing
Ambiguous
Amend
Amended
Amiss
Analysis
Anarchy
Anew
Anguish
Angry
Animated
Annoyed
Anomaly
Anomalous
Another
Anyhow
Anyway
Apart
Appallingly
Appear
Appointed
Arch
Arising from
Around
Arrange(d)
Arrangement
Artful
Artificial
As a result
Askew
Assemble(d)
Assembly
Astonishing
Assailed
Assaulted
Assorted
Astray
At fault
At liberty
At odds

Atomized
At sixes and
 sevens
Atrocious
At variance
Astray
Author of
All change
All round
Awful(ly)
Awkward
Awry
Bad(ly)
Barmy
Barney
Bash(ed)
Bastard
Bats
Battered
Beat
Beaten-up
Become
Bedevilled
Bedlam
Bedraggled
Befuddle(d)
Bemused
Belt
Bend
Bendy
Bent
Berserk
Bewildered
Bibulous
Biff
Bizarre
Blended
Blighted
Blitz
Blend
Bloomer
Bludgeon
Blunder

Blur
Botch(ed)
Bother
Bottled
Bouncing
Break
Breakdown
Breakup
Brew
Broach
Broadcast
Broke(n)
Bruise
Brutalize
Buck
Buckle(d)
Buckling
Bucks
Budge
Buffet
Build
Building
Bumble
Bump
Bungled
Burst
Bust
Butcher
By accident
By arrangement
By mistake
Calamitous(ly)
Camouflaged
Can be
Cancel
Caper
Capricious(ly)
Carelessly
Carnage
Cascade
Casserole
Cast
Cast off

Catastrophic
Causes
Cavort
Change(able)
Changed
Chaos
Chaotic
Chew
Chewed up
Chicanery
Chopped up
Chop suey
Churn
Clumsy
Clumsily
Cobbled
Corkscrew
Cocktail
Coin
Collapse
Collapsing
Collection
Combustible
Come to be
Come to grief
Commotion
Compact
Complicated
Components
Compose(d)
Composer
Composing
Composition
Compound
Comprise
Conceal(ing)
Concoction
Confound(ed)
Conjuring
Constituents
Constitution
Construct(ion)
Contorted
Contraption
Contrivance
Contrive(d)
Conversion

Converted
Convertible
Convert(s)
Convulsed
Cook(ed)
Corrected
Corrupt(ed)
Corruption
Could be
Crack(ed)
Crackers
Crafty
Crash
Crashes
Crazily
Crazy
Create(d)
Crooked
Criminal
Cross
Crude
Crumble
Crumbling
Crumpled
Cryptic
Cunning
Curdled
Cure
Curious(ly)
Curly
Curry
Cut
Daft
Damage(d)
Dancing
Dealt with
Debauched
Deceit
Deception
Deciphered
Decoded
Decomposed
Defective
Deficient
Deformed
Deformity
Delirious

Demented
Demolished
Demolition
Deplorably
Deploy(ed)
Deranged
Derivative of
Derivation
Derived from
Desecrated
Design
Despoil
Destroy(ed)
Deterioration
Devastate(d)
Devastation
Develop(er)
Development
Deviant
Deviation
Devilish
Devious
Devise
Dicky
Different(ly)
Difficult
Dilapidated
Directed to
Disarrange(d)
Disruption
Dissected
Dissipated
Dissolute
Dissolved
Dissonant
Distillation
Distort(ed)
Distortion
Distracted(ly)
Distraught
Distressed
Distribute(d)
Disturb(ed)
Disturbance
Dithering
Divergence
Divergent

Diversification
Diversified
Divert(ing)
Dizzy
Do
Doctor(ed)
Doddery
Dotty
Doubtful(ly)
Dozy
Drawn
Dreadful(ly)
Dress(ed)
Dressing
Drub
Drunk
Drunken(ly)
Dubious(ly)
Dud
Duff
Dynamite
Eccentric
Edit(ed)
Eerie
Effect(s)
Effervescent
Elbow
Elfin
Emanated
Embarrassed
Embody
Emend(ed)
Emendation
Emerge from
Employs
Engenders
Engendering
Engineer
Ensemble
Entangled
Entanglement
Errant
Erratic
Erring
Erroneous
Error
Erupting

Evil	For a change	Ground	In other words
Evolution	Forced	Hack	In revolt
Exceptional(ly)	Foreign	Hammer(ed)	In ruins
Excite(d)	Forge(d)	Hanky-panky	Insane
Exhibits	Form of	Haphazard	In shreds
Exotic	Forms	Hapless	Interfered with
Explode(d)	Formulating	Harassed	Intricate
Explosion	Foul	Harm	Invalid
Explosive	Found in	Hash(ed)	Invention
Extract of	Fractured	Hatches	Involved
Extraordinarily	Fragments	Hatching	Irregular(ity)
Extravagant	Frantic	Havoc	Irritated
Fabricated	Fraud	Haywire	Itinerant
Fabrication	Freak(ish)	Haze	Jar
Fabulous	Free(ly)	Helter-Skelter	Jazz
Failing	Frenzied	Hide	Jig
Failure	Frenzy	Hiding	Jittery
Fake	Fret	Higgledy	Jog
Fallacious	Frilly	Piggledy	Jolt
Falling	Frisky	Horrible	Jostled
False	Frolic	Hotch Potch	Juggle(d)
Falsified	Fuddle(d)	Hurt	Jumble(d)
Faltering	Fudge	Hybrid	Kind of
Fanciful	Fulminate	Idiotic	Kink(y)
Fancy	Function	Ill	Knead
Fantastic	Funny	Ill-composed	Knit
Far flung	Fuzzy	Ill-disposed	Labyrinthine
Fashion(ing)	Gambol	Ill-formed	Lawless
Faulty	Garbled	Ill-made	Leaping
Febrile	Garble	Ill-treated	Let loose
Ferment(ed)	Generates	Ill-used	Licked into
Feverish	Generating	Imbecile	shape
Fictional	Get-up	Impaired	Look silly
Fix	Ghastly	Imperfect	Loose(ly)
Flexible	Gibberish	Improper(ly)	Lousy
Flighty	Giddy	Inaccurate	Ludicrous
Fling	Give rise to	Inane	Lunatic
Flip	Gives	Included	Mad(ly)
Flounder	Gleaned from	Inconstant	Made from
Fluctuating	Going to	Induce	Made of
Fluctuation	Go off	Infamous	Made up
Fluid	Gone off	Infirm	Maim
Flurried	Go straight	Ingredients of	Make
Flustered	Go to pot	Inhabiting	Make-up
Foggy	Go to the dogs	Injured	Making
Foment	Go wrong	In order	Maladroit
Foolish(ly)	Grotesque	Inordinately	Malaise

Malformation
Malformed
Malfunction
Malleable
Maltreat(ed)
Maltreatment
Managed
Manager
Mangle(d)
Maniac
Manic
Manifest(ation)
Manipulate(d)
Manoeuvre
Marred
Marshal
Mash(ed)
Massage
Maul(ed)
Maybe
May become
Mayhem
Meandering
Medley
Mêlée
Mend(ed)
Mercurial
Mess
Messily
Metamorphosis
Migrant
Mince(d)
Misalliance
Miscontrued
Misdelivered
Misguided
Mishandled
Mishap
Misled
Mis-
   representation
Misrepresented
Misshapen
Mistake
Mistreated
Misused
Mix(ed)

Mixture
Mix-up
Mobile
Model(s)
Modification
Modified
Modify
Moither
Molest(ed)
Monkey with
Mould
Moved
Moving
Muck about
Muddle(d)
Mutable
Mutant
Mutant
Mutation
Mutative
Mutilate(d)
Mutilation
Mutinous
Mysterious(ly)
Nasty
Naturally
Naughty
Nauseous
Neatly
Neglected
Negligee
Negotiation
Negotiated
Nervously
New
New form of
Newly formed
Newly made
Nobbled
Nomadic
Not exactly
Not in order
Not properly
Not right
Not straight
Nova
Novel

Oblique
Obscure(d)
Obstreperous
Occasion
Odd
Of
Off
Off-colour
Open
Operate on
Order(ed)
Orderly
Orders
Organization
Organized
Originally
Otherwise
Out (of)
Outcome of
Outlandish
Outrageously
Over
Overturn
Peculiar
Perfidious
Perhaps
Perplexed
Perverse(ly)
Pervert(ed)
Phoney
Pie
Play
Playing tricks
Plying
Polluted
Poor
Posing as
Position
Possibly
Potential(ly)
Pound
Preparation
Prepare(d)
Print out
Problem
Problematic(al)
Process(ing)

Produces
Producing
Production
Properly
   organized
Properly
   presented
Pseudo
Pulverized
Pummelled
Put another way
Put out
Put right
Put straight
Puzzling
Quaking
Queasy
Queer (looking)
Questionable
Quirky
Quite different
Quivering
Rabid
Rage
Ragged
Rakish
Rambling
Random
Ransack
Ravaged
Ravish(ed)
Reactionary
Readjusted
Rearranged
Rearrangement
Reassembled
Reassembly
Rebel
Rebellious
Rebuilding
Rebuilt
Recalcitrant
Recast
Recipe
Reckless
Reconstructed
Rectification

Rectified
Redesigned
Rediscovered
Reeling
Reformation
Reformed
Refractory
Refurbished
Regulated
Regulation
Relay(ing)
Releasing
Remade
Remedy
Remodelled
Rendering
Rendition
Renovated
Renovation
Reorganization
Reorganized
Repair(ed)
Replaced
Replacement
Represent(ed)
Representation
Representing
Reproduce
Reproduction
Reshaped
Reshuffle
Resolution
Resolve(d)
Resort(ing)
Restless
Result
Resulting from
Review
Revised
Revolting
Revolution(ary)
Revolutionized
Revolver
Rewritten
Rickety
Ridiculous
Rigged

Riot
Rip
Rippling
Rock(y)
Rollicking
Rotary
Rotten
Roughly
Round
Roving
Rowdy
Rubbish
Rude
Ruffle(d)
Ruin(ed)
Ruinous
Rum
Rumpled
Running wild
Ruptured
Sabotage
Sack
Sadly
Salad
Salvaged from
Satanic
Saucy
Savage
Scatter(ed)
Scheme
Scramble(d)
Scratch(ed)
Scruffy
Scuffle
Sculpted
Send off/out
Senseless
Set
Setting
Settlement
Shake(n)
Shakedown
Shaky
Shambles
Shaped
Shatter(ed)
Shelled

Shift(ing)
Shilly-shally
Shimmering
Ship-shape
Shiver(ed)
Shocked
Should become
Showing
Shred
Shuffle(d)
Sick
Sifted
Silly
Skidding
Skipping
Skittish
Slap-happy
Slaughter
Sling
Slip
Slipping
Slipshod
Sloppy
Slovenly
Slyly
Smash(ed)
Smashing
Solution
Somehow
Somersault
Sorry state
Sort
Sorted out
Sort of
Soup
Sozzled
Spasmodic
Spattered
Spelt out
Spill
Spilt
Spin
Spinning
Splash
Splice(d)
Splinter
Split

Spoil
Spoilt
Sport(ing)
Sportive
Spray
Spread
Spurious
Squall
Squash
Squiffy
Squiggles
Stagger(ed)
Stampede
Start
State
Stew(ed)
Stir(red)
Storm(y)
Straight(en)
Strange
Stray(ing)
Strewn
Stricken
Struggle
Struggling
Stupid(ly)
Style
Submerged in
Superficial(ly)
Surgery
Surprising(ly)
Suspect
Swirl(ing)
Tailor(ed)
Tampered with
Tangle(d)
Tattered
Tatty
Tear
Tease
Tempestuously
Terrible
Tidied up
Tidy
Tilt
Tip
Tipsy

Appendix

Topsy turvy
To rights
Torment
Torn
Tortuous
Torture(d)
Toss
Touched
Train(ed)
Transferred
Transform(ed)
Transformation
Translate(d)
Translation
Transmutation
Transmute(d)
Transpose(d)
Transposition
Travesty
Treated
Trembling
Trick(y)
Trip
Trouble(d)
Troublesome
Tumble
Tumbledown
Tumbling
Tumult

Tumultuous
Turbulent
Turned
Twirl(ing)
Twist(ed)
Twister
Ugly
Uncertain
Uncommon
Unconventional
Undecided
Undisciplined
Undoing
Undone
Unduly
Uneasy
Unevenly
Unfamiliar
Unfortunately
Unfit
Unhappy
Unnatural(ly)
Unorthodox
Unravelled
Unreliable
Unrestrained
Unruly
Unsettled
Unsettling

Unsound
Unstable
Unsteady
Unstuck
Untidy
Unusual
Unwind
Upset
Vacillating
Vagabond
Vaguely
Vandalize(d)
Variable
Varied
Variety
Various(ly)
Vary
Version of
Vex
Via
Vigorously
Vile
Violate
Violent
Volatile
Wander(ing)
Warp(ed)
Warring
Wavering

Was
Wasted
Weave
Weird
Well-formed
Well-ordered
Well-organized
Well-varied
Whip
Whirl(ing)
Whisk
Wicked
Wild(ly)
Wind
Wobbly
Woolly
Work out
Worried
Worry
Woven
Wreck(ed)
Wrench
Wrested from
Wretched
Writhing
Wrong
Yields
Zany

HIDDEN WORD INDICATORS

A bit of
A little
About
Accommodating
Amid
A part of
A piece of
A portion of
Apparent
Around
Besiege
bit of
By no means all
Carried by
Content

Contributing to
Contained in
Content(s) of
Devour
Embraces
Embracing
Emerge from
Extracted from
Extremities
Found in
Fragment of
From
Gripped by
Held by
Held in

Herein
Hidden in
Holding
Imprison
In
Infer
Intrinsically
Not all
Nucleus
Nursing
Only some
Out of
Partially
Part of
Piece of

Portion of
Put into
Retirement
Secreted in
Section of
Seduce
Showing
Shown
Slice of
Some of
Split
Stuffing
Taken from
Wrapped up in

BACKWORD INDICATORS

Alternative way
Ascendant
Ascending
Back(ed)
Back-to-front
Backward
Brought back
Brought up
Capsized
Climbing
Come-back
Coming up
Contrariwise
Contrary
Elevated
Falling
Given back
Giving rise to
Giving up
Go back

Homing
In recession
In retreat
In retrospect
Inversion
Invert(ed)
Mounted
Mounting
Not written
  down
On reflection
Overturned
Raised
Recede
Recession
Reflective
Regress
Regression
Regressive
Retire

Retiring
Retreat
Retrocedent
Retrocessive
Retrograde
Retrogress
Retrogression
Retrogressive
Retrospective
Retroversion
Retrovert
Return(ed)
Reversal
Reverse(d)
Reverse word
Reversion
Revert
Rising
Sent back
Sent up

Set-back
Set up
Shown up
Swelling
Taken aback
Taken up
Turned back
Turned over
Turned up
Upbringing
Uplifted
Uplifting
Uppish
Uppity
Upset
Upside-down
Upward(s)
Write-up
Writing up
Written up

Appendix

SPLIT WORD INDICATORS

About
Absorbed in
Accepting
Accepted by
Accommodated
  by
Admitted by
Amid
Around
Assimilated by
Back(ing)
Beset by
Captured by
Carried by
Circumscribed
  by
Clutched by
Confined by/in
Contain
Content(s)
Cut by
Cutting
Dividing (by)
Embraced (by)
Embracing
Encircling
Encircled (by)
Enclosed (by)
Enclosed

Enclosure
Encompassed
  (by)
Encompassing
Engulfed (by)
Engulfing
Entering
Entrapped (by)
Entrapping
Entry
Enveloped (by)
Enveloping
Environment
Environs
Exterior
Filled by
Filling
Framed by/in
Framing
Get about
Go around
Go in
Grabbed by
Grabbing
Gripped by
Gripping
Harboured (by)
Hold
Holding captive

Holding
  prisoner
Housed (by)
Housing
Imbibed (by)
Impound
Impounded
  (by)
Imprisoned (by)
Imprisoning
Include
Included in
Incorporating
Interior
Interrupted (by)
Interrupting
Intervening in
In two words
Involved in
Involving
Keeping
Lining
Occupied by
Occupying
Outside
Parted by
Parting
Pocketed by
Pocketing

Received by
Received in
Receiving
Retained by
Retaining
Ringing
Separated by
Separating
Set about
Set in
Shelter
Sheltered by
Split by
Splitting
Stuffing
Surround
Surrounded by
Swallowed by
Swallow up
Take in
Taken in by
Trap
Trapped by/in
Tucked into
Upheaval
Within
Without
Wrapped in
Wrapping

PALINDROME INDICATORS

Backwards
Both ways
Cut back
Forwards and
  backwards
Gyrate

Preposterous
Rampant
Reactionary
Rebellious
Recess
Recidivist

Recurrent
Renegade
Retirement
Review
Revolutionary
Round

SHORTENING INDICATORS

Away (word or letter(s) to be omitted)

Bounds (may indicate outside letters)

Brief

Capless (delete first letter(s))

Centre (may indicate middle letters)

Compact

Decapitated (delete first letter)

Defaced (delete first letter)

Detailed (delete last letter)

Early stages of (may indicate first or second letters)

Empty (may indicate an 'o' in a word)

Endlessly (delete last letter)

Extreme (may indicate a first or last letter)

Foremost (may indicate the first letter(s) of word)

Foundations (may indicate the last letter(s) of a word)

Initially (may indicate the first letter(s) of a word)

In short

Minimum (may indicate the first letter)

Nonetheless (may indicate an 'o' to be omitted)

Top (may indicate the first letter of a word)

HOMOPHONE INDICATORS

Aurally

By the sound of it

Heard

Hear(say)

In speech

It's pronounced

It's rumoured

It's said

Listen to

Mutter(ed)

One hears

Orally

Phonetically

Pronounced

Reported

Rumoured

Said

Say

Sounds like

So to speak

Stated

They say

Utter

We hear